YANKEE AUTUMN IN ACADIANA

YANKEE AUTUMN IN ACADIANA

A Narrative of the
Great Texas Overland Expedition through Southwestern Louisiana
October–December 1863

David C. Edmonds

University of Louisiana at Lafayette Press
2024

ISBN 13 (paper): 978-1-959569-14-5

Originally printed in 1979 by the Acadiana Press
Library of Congress Catalog Card Number 79-67333
Reprinted in 2005 by the Center for Louisiana Studies
ISBN 1-887366-62-8

http://ulpress.org
University of Louisiana at Lafayette Press
P.O. Box 43558
Lafayette, LA 70504-3558

Printed in the United States

Library of Congress Cataloging-in-Publication Data

Names: Edmonds, David C., author.
Title: Yankee autumn in Acadiana : a narrative of the Great Texas Overland Expedition through southwestern Louisiana, October-December 1863 / David C. Edmonds.
Other titles: Narrative of the Great Texas Overland Expedition through southwestern Louisiana
Description: Lafayette, LA : University of Louisiana at Lafayette Press, 2024. | Reprint of: Yankee autumn in Acadiana / David C. Edmonds. Lafayette, La. : Acadiana Press, 1979. | Includes bibliographical references and index.
Identifiers: LCCN 2024030247 | ISBN 9781959569145 (paperback)
Subjects: LCSH: United States. Army. Department of the Gulf (1862-1865) | Louisiana--History--Civil War, 1861-1865. | United States--History--Civil War, 1861-1865--Regimental histories.
Classification: LCC E475.4 .E35 2024 | DDC 973.7/41--dc23/eng/20240809
LC record available at https://lccn.loc.gov/2024030247

TO THE MEMORY
OF
MY DEAR FATHER

FOREWORD

DURING A RECENT department meeting, a colleague casually stated, "History buffs can be rather fickle." He observed that their interest is frequently captured, and realigned, in accord with the release of a blockbuster film or attention-grabbing historical novel. The media frenzy surrounding films such as *Titanic* or *300*, as well as books like *Cold Mountain,* does suggest that public interest can be manipulated by skillful marketing. Some subjects nonetheless remain such a fixture in the public imagination that even when there is no new and epic film or book, popular fascination remains.

One of the most constant subjects commanding the attention of American history buffs is the national conflagration we know as the Civil War. Thousands of books and scores of films have appeared over the years detailing every imaginable angle of the conflict. Just when it seems that each issue and event connected with the war has been examined, analyzed, and reviewed to the utter limits of its relevance, a new project emerges that reignites popular interest. Perhaps equally important, new analysis often complexifies the contributions of existing studies, allowing for a more comprehensive assessment of the subject.

Depictions of the Civil War reveal both continuity and change. The celebration of the Union victory and the uncompromising certainty of the righteousness of the Federal cause found in the writings of James Ford Rhodes and Charles Francis Adams over time came to include the work of authors such as Shelby Foote and Charles Roland. The latter offered a more sympathetic appraisal of the Southern perspective while continuing to acknowledge the justice of the Union cause.

More recently, the rise of social justice movements has led to the removal of Confederate monuments, the renaming of streets, schools, and military bases, and a revision of the historical lexicon (changing "slave" to "enslaved person," as one example), all to reflect greater sympathy for those who fought against slavery and undo the so-called "Lost Cause" narrative that memorialized secession and those who fought for it.

In their zeal to correct what many perceive as the falsehoods of history, supporters of these actions have aroused concern that their efforts, at times, amount to an attempt to rewrite the facts. Critics contend that it is misguided and dangerous to apply the standards of the modern era to the thoughts and actions of actors and events that played out more than 150 years ago. Defenders respond that at no time in history was slavery regarded as a positive good by anyone, excepting the slaveholders. While few today dismiss such concerns, the passion surrounding this debate often compromises efforts to further analyze actions and actors of the war itself. And most scholars and history buffs alike agree that there remains a lot more to be learned about the Civil War.

It is in the certainty of such thinking and with awareness of the sustained hunger to learn more about issues and events connected to the war that the University of Louisiana at Lafayette Press determined to release a new edition of David C. Edmonds's *Yankee Autumn in Acadiana*. Edmonds's magnum opus on the ill-fated Great Texas Overland Expedition, which upended southwest Louisiana in the fall and winter of 1863, has served to delight enthusiasts and inform scholars for more than four decades.

The book is described as a narrative of the Great Texas Overland Expedition, and as such, it does not disappoint. Edmonds offers a moment-by-moment accounting of the campaign, providing meticulous detail from multiple points of view. The research supporting the narrative is diverse and simply exhaustive. The sheer volume of source material allows Edmonds to relate singular events from varied and often competing perspectives. Observations are not limited to Federal soldiers, Confederates, and the local population, instead they include deeply patriotic Federals as well as shirkers and criminals, vengeful determined Rebels alongside deserters and scoundrels, pro-Confederate residents alongside the "neutral" foreign-born, all amid a scattering of Unionists. Such attention to competing detail allows the reader to indulge in a comprehensive examination of events that extends to—quite literally—every day of the campaign.

The Great Texas Overland Expedition centered on three primary objectives. It would pacify southwestern Louisiana and remove the threat to Union-controlled New Orleans and the lower Mississippi delta, a feat that a brutally destructive campaign the preceding spring had failed to accomplish. More important, it would plant the Union flag west of the Sabine River, effectively taking Texas out of the war and denying the Confederacy the desperately needed men and matériel the Lone Star State offered. And, as an act of both political and military defiance, the campaign would culminate with a banks-of-the-Rio-Grande demonstration to Maximilian and his puppet French regime in Mexico, that the United States would tolerate no meddling in its own affairs and would soon be poised to enforce the Monroe Doctrine in the Americas.

Edmonds's description of the campaign reflects the continuity and change characterizing current Civil War historiography. His depiction of

Confederate soldiers ranges from fearless, fiery Texas cavalrymen, filthy to the bone but full of fight, to barely literate Cajun draftees who had little interest in the "American" war. The Yankees are broken into easterners and westerners, largely as a barometer of comparative analysis to determine who committed more depredations and looting. Edmonds depicts the soldiers from both armies as they appeared and behaved in their own eyes as well as those of their enemies and the local residents, ever with a nod to how their circumstances may be regarded today.

In an effort to bring the story to the reader as accurately as possible, he records direct quotes, diary entries, posted notices, etc., precisely as they would have been spoken or written at the time. Some readers may be offended by the inclusion of quotes detailing formerly enslaved people cheering on the "Linkum soders" or seeing a Confederate soldier's note to his wife written in the barely identifiable English of the hopelessly uneducated. Even as he strives for accuracy, Edmonds carefully reminds that the former, who never asked to be enslaved, was reflecting his contempt for his oppressors as he applauded the liberators, while the Rebel simply missed a wife he loved and sought to communicate with her in the best manner life afforded him.

Yankee Autumn in Acadiana also does some serious myth debunking. Residents of the affected region are often surprised to find that a celebrated family hero was actually part of a Confederate unit composed primarily of draft evaders and miscreants who often created as much trouble for their own side as that of the enemy. Similarly, many readers long accustomed to stories of Yankee gallantry and heroism will be surprised to find that little, if any, noble purpose accompanied the expedition. Despite faux orders to the contrary, Federal soldiers, officers, and enlisted men alike looted, plundered, and abused at virtually every house they encountered during the entire duration of the campaign. Perhaps exasperated by the failure of the expedition, in one of their last acts, a Federal column took aim and fired an enfilading volley of musketry into a crowd of citizens departing a church service in St. Martinsville, Louisiana (now St. Martinville).

Yankee Autumn above all reminds us that war brings suffering and misery that ripples far beyond the immediately affected people and places. But war also remains something that fascinates us. Few are disappointed with a work that is both accurate and compelling, and one that can weave acts of kindness and purpose into circumstances that often prove horrifying. In *Yankee Autumn in Acadiana*, David Edmonds has given us a study that entertains, educates, and reminds of the value that accompanies attention to detail. It is a study whose usefulness is only beginning!

Samuel C. Hyde Jr.

CONTENTS

PREFACE

ON THE NORTH bank of Bayou Carencro, near the crossing of the old Vermilionville-Opelousas stagecoach road, there stands an ancient cypress house with a wide front gallery, high-pitched roof, exposed ceiling beams and *bousillage* walls. Surrounded by giant pecan and oak trees and set on the edge of what was once called Buzzards' Prairie, this house is unique, not so much for its age and architectural lines as for the bloody events that are said to have occurred there during the Civil War.

According to oral tradition, a great battle was fought nearby, and, as the fighting ceased, the Yankees brought to the house their wounded, their dying and their dead. The mistress of the house, a young lady great with child and much abused by her unwelcome Yankee tenants, was said to have serenaded the dying troops, playing the piano and singing, while the surgeons went about their bloody work of amputating limbs and while soldiers thrashed upon her living room floor in the final throes of agony.

Today, more than a century later, the blood of those soldiers still stains darkly the old unpainted cypress floors. In the fields nearby, especially after a rainfall on freshly plowed earth, the rifled Minie balls of Civil War infantrymen, turned white by the elements, are readily visible. There is also an unmarked gravesite overlooking Bayou Carencro where green grass grows and cattle graze peacefully, oblivious to the secrets below.

Many of the older residents of Buzzards' Prairie are familiar with the stories passed down by their ancestors that the old house is yet occupied by restless spirits, angered and searching for the life that was so tragically ended in the flower of youth. Indeed, many are afraid to enter the house, except in broad daylight and in the company of others. There is even a tale that in late autumn, especially when the date coincides with the astrological conditions of the tragedy, one can hear the muffled cries of anguished men, cries that are soon silenced by the haunting refrain of a feminine voice singing softly to the beat of a piano.

Fascinated by these stories and by the physical evidence and consumed with a passion to learn the details, I commenced a research project more than seven years ago that ended with totally unexpected results. My initial intent was to satisfy my curiosity and perhaps write a short article on the mysteries of the old house.

As it turned out, however, the Civil War events on Bayou Carencro constituted only a brief portion of a much larger campaign—one that ranged in scope from New Orleans to Morgan City, up the Teche through Centerville, Franklin, New Iberia and St. Martinville, and across the prairies to Lafayette, Abbeville, Grand Coteau, Opelousas, Washington, Church Point, Leonville and Port Barre. In fact, it constituted the first American attempt ever to enforce the lofty but pretentious ideals of the Monroe Doctrine. Interestingly enough, this campaign was aimed not so much at Louisiana as Texas, and the objective was political rather than military.

Thus what started as a limited project to narrate the Civil War history of an old house has been expanded to a narration of the entire Great Texas Overland Expedition through southwestern Louisiana. Within these pages I have also endeavored to capture the flavor of the times by including incidents of camp life, the hardships of an army on the march, army discipline—or lack thereof—amusing anecdotes, and other items of local interest. For reasons of convenience I have chosen to arrange this narrative in chronological sequence—diary form—as opposed to a topical approach.

In the course of researching this book, I have visited and attempted to identify every location mentioned, frequently trampling over battle fields and ancient campsites, traversing snake-infested swamps, and cruising the myriad network of bayous and waterways of Louisiana. I have spoken to hundreds of individuals, visited several states and spent many hours in the dusty archives of countless libraries, courthouses, and churches.

When I first started this project, I was struck by the dearth of locally available sources. With only a few notable exceptions, the residents of southwestern Louisiana did not bother to record their experiences in diaries, personal correspondence or reminiscences. In fact, most of the locally available information survives only as legends.

Yet, there exists a veritable treasure of manuscripts, a majority of which are unpublished, about this tragic but unrecorded period of Louisiana history. For whatever reasons, a large portion of this primary material has gone unnoticed and ignored by historians, locked away in the archives of distant regions.

The most obvious source for any research project dealing with the Civil War in Louisiana is the much overused *War of the Rebellion, Official Records of the Union and Confederate Armies*, especially volume XXVI, which contains an entire chapter on the "Operations in the Teche Country." Most importantly, it lists those regiments, or military units, Union and Confederate, which participated in the autumn 1863 campaign in southwestern Louisiana.

With this information I began visiting or corresponding with libraries and individuals all over the country in an attempt to garner sources of information about those particular regiments for the period of September through December 1863. In the process I uncovered and examined thousands of pages of extant diaries, letters, personal reminiscences, newspaper reports, court-martial proceedings, service records, muster rolls and regimental histories written or recorded by soldiers and individuals, Confederate and Union alike, who actually participated in the autumn campaign. Among these treasures there are several accounts by Union surgeons describing in gory detail the events at the old house on Bayou Carencro.

By far the most important sources, and ones which to my knowledge have never before been employed in any significant work treating the period, are the voluminous legal claims growing out of the war. In Louisiana alone, and especially in the Acadiana region, more than two thousand individuals claiming to be either alien neutrals or loyal Unionists took their grievances to court. Depending on the circumstances, these claims were filed under the auspices of the French and American Claims Commission, the Mixed British and American Claims Commission, the U. S. Court of Claims or the Southern Claims Commission.

The transcripts and proceedings of individual cases—currently on file in the National Archives—are very lengthy, some of which run into the hundreds and even thousands of pages. Especially significant are the eyewitness depositions, sometimes quite dramatic, given by planters, merchants, slaves, "free people of color," Confederates, Yankees, clergymen, cotton factors, steamboat captains, politicians, speculators, physicians, housewives and many others. Though their reports were frequently exaggerated or flawed by biases and faulty memories, they nonetheless have preserved for posterity their own stories about life in wartime Louisiana.

These claims, when used in conjunction with traditional sources, add an entirely new and different perspective to the Civil War events which occurred so long ago in southwestern Louisiana. For example, a Yankee soldier might write home that he and his friends raided a certain plantation for provisions. A Confederate diary, recounting the same event, might add that his side managed to capture or kill a few of the plunderers. But when the plantation inhabitants tell their version in the reparation claims, it is a sad and dramatic tale of terror, abuse, dislocation, confiscation, destruction, privation and hunger.

Much of the information revealed in this book might prove disappointing to those individuals who heretofore had thought of their ancestors as being "good" Confederates of sterling character. Southwestern Louisiana, like other regions, had its share of unscrupulous speculators, jayhawkers, conscript evaders, deserters, Unionists, oath-takers, adulterers, rapists and miscegenetics. I have reluctantly acquiesed to several requests and deleted or tempered incidents—skeletons in family closets—which, I am told, might prove embarrassing if revealed. In other cases, also by request, I have omitted a name, or a portion thereof, for the same reason.

Aside from the sources mentioned, I have also relied on oral tradition to a small degree. Regretably, many of the stories related to me by countless individuals, though probably accurate, could simply not be supported by other materials or did not fit within the time period or subject covered in this work. On the other hand these oral sources frequently supplemented sketchy manuscript materials.

By comparing notes, I was also able to shed new light on an old work. Like other students of Civil War history in Louisiana I had long since dismissed Confederate Governor Henry W. Allen's *Official Report Relative to the Conduct of Federal Troops in Western Louisiana* as so much inflammatory Rebel propaganda. Incredibly, I was able to corroborate many of the outrageous incidents described in that tome from other sources, frequently Union ones, and in some cases the circumstances unravel as being even more deplorable than depicted by Allen's Confederate authors.

Most of the individuals and organizations assisting me in the research and preparation of this manuscript are duly acknowledged in the appropriate footnotes or bibliography. A few of these have requested anonymity because of possible family embarrassment and thus have not been noted. If there are omissions—and there are doubtless some—they result from a lapse of mind rather than of heart.

I am indebted to many members of the University of Southwestern Louisiana's Dupre Library, especially my good friends and colleagues Dennis Gibson, Carl Brasseaux and Anne Jane Marks, as well as Faye Backie, Jeff Baker and Anne Gianelloni. Also Nolan Sahuc, Timothy Reilly, J. P. McBride and Dean Thomas Arceneaux of the university community were most generous in the provision of their services and assistance. A small portion of my not inconsiderable financial outlay was defrayed by a grant from the USL Foundation for which I am grateful.

At Grand Coteau, Louisiana, I received kind and thoughtful assistance from Father James Carroll, S. J., of St. Charles College, Sister Odeide Mouton of the Academy of the Sacred Heart and Miss Catherine Carson of St. Charles Church.

At Sunset, Louisiana, Dennis and Lynette Chadeayne kindly permitted me, in the company of others, to trample across their property in the search for gravesites, artifacts and earthworks. Sylvan Davy spent many helpful hours with me on these snake, wasp and poison-ivy dodging occasions as did my good friends Senator Armand Brinkhaus of Sunset and Dr. Richard Saloom of Lafayette.

I am no less grateful to my former student, Bea Angelle of Cecilia, and her husband, Michael Usie, for guiding me through the endless swamps of the Grand Bois, Bayou Portage, Coteau Holmes and the back roads along the Teche.

Although I was ably assisted by numerous archivists and librarians all over the country, I wish especially to mention Dr. Josephine Harper of the State Historical Society of Wisconsin whose generous aid far exceeded the standard provision of time and services.

My dear friend and writing colleague, Morris Raphael of New Iberia, provided suggestions, sources and companionship, and helped inspire me with his own work, *The Battle in the Bayou Country*, relating to the spring 1863 "Teche Campaign."

Finally, I am deeply indebted to the Cher, not only for helping with the nitty-gritty work, but just for putting up with me through it all, never once complaining that she had become a Civil War widow.

David C. Edmonds
Bayou Carencro
Sunset, Louisiana

November 1979

CHAPTER ONE

FROM NEW ORLEANS TO BERWICK'S BAY

September 13 to October 2, 1863

IN THE DINGY working class village of Algiers, across the river from New Orleans, people were genuinely mystified. Even before dawn, restless sleepers were awakened and curious individuals peered out from behind shuttered windows. Only a few days before they had joined the residents of the Crescent City and had lined the levee for miles to watch the despised men in blue sail downstream. Flags had flown at high mast, bands had played patriotic tunes and weeping ladies had waved white handkerchiefs to the departing soldiers. The much rumored campaign to restore Texas to the Union had finally begun.[1] The Yankees were going to drive the Confederates from the Lone Star State, or so they bragged, while demonstrating to French Emperor Napoleon III and his puppet government in Mexico that Washington would not tolerate European encroachment in the Western Hemisphere. [2]

But now, even as the pleasant morning aroma of roasting coffee drifted over the river, the Army of the Gulf was on the move again. On the streets below, passing directly in front of the odoriferous iron works, were long formations of blue-coated infantry extending from the busy railroad terminal back to the Mississippi. At the landing, where silent workers normally huddled together in the dawn hours to await the ferry trip across to their jobs in the city, it appeared as though the entire Union fleet had dropped anchor. Steamer after steamer, ranging in size from small, flat-decked cattle carriers with over-sized paddle wheels to enormous multistoried, white columned luxury liners, discharged their military and human cargos along the muddy levee. Over on the New Orleans side, amid foreign warships and vessels of commerce from at least a dozen nations, the *North American*, *Meteor*, and *Emerald* took on cargo under the intimidating and suspicious gaze of crewmen aboard a British man-of-war and a French frigate.

On both banks it seemed as though the work was being done and order maintained by several regiments of blue-coated, French-speaking Louisiana blacks from the recently organized *Corps d' Afrique*. Massive barrels of salt-pork, square wooden boxes of crackers and hardtack, heavy ammunition crates and officers' trunks were loaded and unloaded under the watchful eyes and occasional curses of their white officers. At the same time cordons of black soldiers held back mobs of pushing and shoving peddlers trying to hawk their wares in half a dozen or more languages. For a small fee the departing Yankees could buy flowers, fruits, vegetables or pies from a ragged Irish or German immigrant, a Jewish, Lebanese or Syrian cart-pusher, a black-eyed "French" beauty, or a miscegenetic product of human bondage ranging in color from lily white to sable black

UNION FORCES marching Through New Orleans. ***(Harpers Weekly)***

Over on Canal Street a seemingly endless line of blue-coated and bearded soldiers plodded slowly toward the river wharves in the stifling early morning heat. In the procession were Zouave regiments, complete with Turkish fez and ostentatious pantaloons, as well as high-booted cavalrymen, sabers at their side, and red-hatted artillerymen leading spirited horses by the halter. Absent were the normally ubiquitous bell-ringing, horse-powered trolleys which regularly ran down the middle of the boulevard and up St. Charles Street as far as Union headquarters at the St. Charles Hotel. In their place were hundreds of white-topped mule-drawn wagons with the inscription U.S.A. on the side, as well as horses, mules, bronze artillery pieces, smooth-bore Napoleons, seige guns, rifled Parrotts, caissons and every piece of military hardware in existence at the time.

A Connecticut officer reflecting on the historical significance of the moment wondered how many times before and at how many different places had this same scene occurred. Add a few elephants, he thought, change the head gear, uniforms, language and artillery, and the Crescent City could just as well be ancient Carthage. Their destination—Texas—could even be the Roman Empire ruled over by a defiant and superior breed of military men. The Sabine might be the Rubicon, or perhaps even the Tiber.[3] And Hannibal? Well, Grant could play that role. But "Old Ulysses," as he was sometimes called, was recuperating in a New Orleans hospital, the victim of an alcohol-induced horse accident and could not accompany the expedition.[4] The star role for this, the second Texas expedition in less than two weeks, would instead be reserved for Major General Nathaniel Prentice Banks. And there the parallel ended, because Banks was not a Hannibal.

Neither was he a Grant, a Sheridan or a Sherman. In fact, he wasn't even a military man. Handsome, hazel-eyed, witty, charming and sophisticated, Banks' main qualifications for command of the Army of the Gulf were his political connections. Like Lincoln he had come up the hard way. A factory worker's son, he was nicknamed the "Bobbin Boy" because of his early employment in a Massachusetts factory, but Banks worked hard to overcome his proletariat background, eventually becoming proficient as a debator, attorney, editor, businessman and politician. From Speaker of the United States House of Representatives, he shifted with the political winds until he became Governor of the Commonwealth of Massachusetts. Finally, in 1861, over the vociferous complaints of disgruntled West Pointers and Radical Republicans, Banks, now as blue-blooded as any Bostonian Brahman, was appointed a Major General of volunteers by President Lincoln. His substandard military qualifications, Lincoln explained to critics, were more than offset by the morale, prestige, money and recruits he brought to the Union side.[5]

MAJOR GENERAL NATHANIEL P. BANKS
(Library of Congress)

Although an honest and forthright soldier, he proved consistently unsuccessful as a military tactician, though he buried himself in strategy books, including several on Napoleon. In his first battlefield encounter in the Shenandoah Valley in 1862, for example, Banks suffered a disastrous defeat at the hands of none other than Thomas J. "Stonewall" Jackson. In the subsequent retreat he left more than thirty percent of his forces, including the wounded, and most of his military supplies and equipage to the Confederates. When Jackson repeated the performance at Cedar Mountain, again taking large quantities of prisoners and Union supplies, the political general was derisively nicknamed the "Old Commissary General," a name he would continue to earn throughout the war.[6]

To be sure, it appeared as though Banks' military career would soon come to an unhappy end. Soldiers despised him and officers ridiculed his lofty mannerisms and tailored uniforms. Even Henry Wager Halleck, the general of generals and Lincoln's military advisor in Washington, frankly confessed in a letter to Sherman that "it seems little better than murder to give commands to such a man as Banks..." But Civil War politics prevailed. Banks had boundless political ambitions and fancied himself a serious presidential contender. If Lincoln suddenly dropped him it would probably be interpreted as a politically motivated action. Moreover, Banks might possibly seek a rapprochement with the Radical Republicans whom he had offended by his conservative actions on so many occasions, people like Benjamin Wade, Thaddeus Stevens, Henry Davis, and Zachariah Chandler. So in the infinite complicated political economy of the Civil War, it was better to keep him on as a major general than to inject him back into the Washington whirlwind. Where, then, could he be sent to cause the least harm?[7]

The Department of the Gulf, with headquarters in Union-occupied New Orleans, seemed an ideal choice for the well-polished general. After all, the city was more European than American and had more than its share of diplomatic missions, soirees and political intrigue. Besides, it was time to remove the current commander, Benjamin "Beast" Butler, another incompetent who heretofore had offended both Southerners and foreigners because of his obnoxious mannerisms, corruption and adherence to the principles of Radical Republicanism.[8]

Replacing Butler in late 1862, Banks wasted no time in formulating new military and civil ventures and in alienating the Radicals by relaxing military rule. In early 1863 he succeeded in chasing Confederate General Richard Taylor's tiny Army of Western Louisiana from Bayou Lafourche up to Alexandria. Turning his attention to Confederate-held Port Hudson in the summer, he met with several bloody repulses, capturing the place only after the fall of Vicksburg had rendered it untenable to the defenders. Nevertheless, he was subsequently awarded a Congressional citation of thanks "for the skill, courage, and endurance which compelled the surrender and thus removed the last obstruction to the free navigation of the Mississippi River."

By late 1863 Nathaniel Prentice Banks' political and military fortunes were on the ascendancy, except in Radical circles, and his name was almost as familiar in the victory-starved North as was "Stonewall" Jackson and "Jeb" Stuart in the South. Thinking to capitalize on his Port Hudson success and newly acquired fame, he proposed a movement on Mobile, which he believed could be easily taken, thereby adding another political feather to his hat. However, his superiors in Washington, especially Secretary of State William Seward, were more concerned for the moment about the Texas-Mexico-French connection.

There were disquieting rumors abroad that French Emperor Louis Napoleon, whose troops then held large portions of Mexico, was planning to annex not only Texas, but possibly Louisiana and Arizona as well. Worse still, the persistent "Conquer Texas" lobby was circulating rumors of an imminent French-Confederate rapprochement. Thus "Old Brains" Halleck instructed Banks as early as July to move on Texas "for reasons other than military." President Lincoln and Secretary Seward wished to demonstrate to the French usurpers that the Monroe Doctrine, which precluded European encroachment in the Western Hemisphere, was alive and well.[9]

Though Banks still preferred to move on Mobile, he nonetheless undertook his new assignments with characteristic enthusiasm. The Lone Star State, he rationalized, must be returned to the Union because "there are no more loyal men in the country than the Union men in Texas." He also believed that "rebellion in Louisiana was kept alive only by Texas." So confident was Banks of a quick success that he stated in mid-August that he would "plant the flag in Texas" inside of a week.

This he might have done had all gone according to plan. The Texans, he believed, would expect an assault at Galveston, where a previous attempt had failed. This time he would land a large expeditionary force at the ill-defended marshes of Sabine Pass on the border between Texas and Louisiana. As it turned out, however, his invasion force of several thousand men and a flotilla of gunboats were simply beaten off and badly bloodied by a rag-tag defensive force of only 43 Irish-Texas artillerymen under the command of a lowly lieutenant, Dick Dowling of County Galway. As if to mock Banks' earlier success at Port Hudson, the Confederate Congress subsequently awarded a citation of thanks to the Texas defenders.[10]

Yet, all was not lost. Perhaps, reasoned the Bay State general, he could still take Texas in a swift but bold overland invasion through southwestern Louisiana. After all, it should be relatively easy to ferry his men across the river to Algiers and take the railroad to Brashear (currently Morgan) City. From there he could march up the Atchafalaya and Teche as he had done the previous spring and eventually cross the open grassy prairies from New Iberia, Vermilionville or Opelousas to the Sabine River. If the attempt succeeded, not only would it salvage his tarnished military reputation, but it would considerably enhance his political fortunes after the war.

The Great Texas Overland Expedition, as the campaign was cynically dubbed by critics, began moving out of Algiers via the Brashear City railway on Sunday, September 13, 1863, less than a week after the Sabine fiasco. "Instead of Pullmans or even ordinary day coaches with seats or even box cars or stock cars," complained a soldier from Ohio, "we were piled upon a train of flat cars" some of which carried wagons, two to a car, while others were loaded with barrels and boxes. The unfortunate soldiers were thus forced to seek quarters "curled around the wheels, doubled up on the tongue, perched up on the driver's seat, or anywhere or anyplace a hand could be secured to keep from falling off."[11]

Though grumbling was inevitable, most of the troops were in high spirits and made the most of their predicament by joking and laughing or speculating aloud about the purpose of the expedition.

"I'll tell you what my opinion is about this movement," volunteered a New Yorker. "You see those musquitos (sic) up in Brashear City are mighty hungry, and may rebel against the government, so we are going to satiate their thirst for blood, and kind'er conciliate 'em, don't you see?"

Another New Yorker, recalling that his regiment had been in Brashear three or four times already, interjected: "Well, I just believe that Brashear City is the centre of gravity in this Department. If we get away from it a little ways, why the whole d----d concern would lose its balance."

"I say, Jim," said another, "they knew we were getting homesick, 'cause we hav'nt been in Brashear City for over a week."[12]

Still others talked about their pleasant rest and recuperation in New Orleans after the bloody engagements at Vicksburg and Port Hudson. The citizens of that lovely city were terribly hostile, recalled some of the ' 'Westerners" from Grants' XIII Army Corps. Perhaps so, but the veterans of the XIX Corps, who had been there much longer, could recall the bitterness of the residents surrounding old "Ben" Butler's infamous "Woman Order,"[13] the illegal hanging of William Mumford for tearing down the Stars and Stripes and the heinous murder of Susie Parker, a lady of the evening, who heaped abuse on Yankee soldiers and limited her favors to the Southern trade.

The memory of old New Orleans still conjured up visions of the happiest days of the war for most. Almost everyone had participated in a series of spine-tingling patriotic dress parades where the latest war

THE FRENCH MARKET in New Orleans during the Union occupation. *(Harper's Weekly)*

hero—U.S.Grant—was the center of attention. During "liberty" most had taken a public hack down the Canal, or shell road, to the crystal clear waters of Lake Pontchatrain. Others had visited Chalmette and the site of the Battle of New Orleans. Few would forget the Henry Clay monument or the St. Charles Hotel, or Jackson Park in the *Vieux Carre*, where "many of the boys cultivated an acquaintance with beautiful dark-eyed ladies as they lingered over their custard pie, milk, fruit and ice cream!" Susie Parker might have been unavailable, but there were plenty of others willing to share their affections for a Yankee dollar.[14]

All that was behind now and the reality of the moment was a "wheezy" old steam engine pulling the flat cars "over the line through swamps and bogs, lagoons and over bayous and through platoons of alligators lined up to watch." Screeching and lurching, the train seemed to stop every few minutes, either to load or to discharge passengers and cargo. Here was Jefferson, with its three houses and a small church. Nine miles distant was St. Charles station, devoid of even a solitary building. The train subsequently stopped at Boutte, Bayou des Allemands—where the station house lay in a pile of charred ruins—Raceland, and La Fourche near Union Camp Hubbard and Thibodaux.

No sooner had the train lurched to a screeching halt at Thibodaux than a number of sullen-looking "Louisiana" cavalrymen, who previously had served under the proud flag of Rhode Island, began leading and coaxing their horses into several empty cattle cars. Their commander, a tall ruggedly handsome colonel of cavalry, riding crop in hand, watched impatiently, occasionally pointing this way or that while shouting orders to his men.

Working rapidly, the grim-looking horsemen, some of whom were decked out in ill-fitting but obviously new regulation issue, completed their task and scrambled atop the already overcrowded cars. It was evident to any observer, even a raw recruit, that there was bad blood between Colonel Harai Robinson, commander of the 1st Louisiana Cavalry (Union) and his men.

Indeed, Colonel Robinson, a thirty-five-year-old native of New York City, was a remarkable figure—popular with some of his men and loathed by others. Known in New York social circles as Captain Robinson before the war, he was a well educated, multi-lingual businessman, merchant and shipowner. Sailing home from one of his subsidiary offices in Barranquilla, Colombia, early in 1861, he had donated a large shipment of arms through the mayor of New York to the Federal Army. Robinson wanted to be an active participant instead of a mere backer. Unable to raise and equip a regiment in his native state, he had instead moved to Union-occupied New Orleans where he was granted permission to recruit from among the Union sympathizers of that city. Yet, in spite of his best efforts, he was able to attract only a couple of dozen or so recruits, mainly Irish and German immigrants, some deserters from the Confederate side, conscript evaders and a few loyal Unionists.

Undaunted, Robinson soon appealed to headquarters of the Department of the Gulf, arguing persuasively that his proposed Union regiment—the 1st Louisiana Cavalry—would have tremendous propaganda value, even if most of its men were in fact Yankees. Convinced of this logic, General Nathaniel P. Banks, Commander of the Department of the Gulf, had instructed several regiments (nine from New York and one from Massachusetts) to turn over a dozen men each to Robinson's command. To further bolster the regiment, the entire 2nd Rhode Island Cavalry was ordered to join Robinson's "Louisiana" command.

Most of the Rhode Islanders were misfits and trouble makers who knew more about bar rooms and back alley brawls than how to saddle a horse. During the spring campaign in the Teche Country, for example, they were "notorious for lawlessness and want of discipline" and, according to General Banks, were "wholly worthless as soldiers." But they were also an independent lot and proud to serve under the Rhode Island flag. So when Special Order 209—the order transferring them to the 1st Louisiana—was read to them, they had immediately rebelled.

They had no intention of riding under the flag of a Rebel state in a sham Louisiana regiment. The entire group had then sat upon the ground.

Robinson, his authority challenged, "was certain that nothing but fear would prevent them from turning into a band of marauders." He had subsequently weaved his way through the seated men, picked out their two ringleaders, Privates Richard Murphy and Frederick Freeman, and personally dragged them out of the line.

"I chose severe and instantaneous measures," recalled Robinson. The two men were brought before the 1st Louisiana Cavalry where "their arms were tied behind them and a handkerchief was tied over their eyes." On Robinson's command both were then shot to death in front of their rebellious comrades.[15]

Colonel Robinson got his Rhode Islanders, but he also earned their everlasting enmity. Some of them vowed privately to desert or to kill him. In the meantime they would obey orders and await an opportunity.

Leaving LaFourche station amid a cloud of steam, the train soon reached Terrebonne and entered a dense swamp, alive with waterfowl, snakes and alligators. "It was fun for the boys to shoot the latter with harmless balls," noted a New Englander. Though many of the soldiers had passed here before, it was still an impressive sight:

> The long stretches of cypress swamps, thickets of Spanish bayonets, poisoned black waters overlaid with plants, rank and rampant vegetation, luxuriant foliage knit upon vines leaping from tree to tree, funereal with the ever present Spanish moss, furnished wonderfully new scenery to our Northern eyes.

Traveling at the phenomenal rate of 25 miles per hour, the train's engineer chose to ignore marker boards at four-mile intervals which boldly ordered: "Go Slow, 4 M.P.H." The motion of the cars "would make a dog sea-sick" complained an Iowa soldier. The "rickety" old track, he complained, had not been properly maintained or improved for years.[16]

It had not always been so. When the section between Algiers to Brashear City of The New Orleans, Opelousas and Great Western Railroad was completed in 1857, not only was it widely hailed as one of the great engineering feats of the 19th century, but it provided comfortable traveling accommodations for its customers. From Brashear City, eighty and one-fifth miles from Algiers station, steamboat service was available up the Atchafalaya to Grand Lake and beyond, or up the Teche and into western Louisiana, or downstream to the Gulf and on to Galveston. Thanks to the track, the lucrative markets of New Orleans were far more accessible than before.

So strategic was the railroad that the LaFourche and Terrebonne country, through which the track passed, was the scene of numerous bloody engagements in 1862 and mid-1863. Bridges had been burned, rails ripped up, box cars and engines destroyed, and control shifted from Confederate to Union and then back to Confederate again. In the fall of 1863 the railroad was once more in Union hands.[17]

Emerging from the swamp near Tigerville, the train made one final stop at Boeuf Station before it approached its destination "hooting and whistling." Once more the omnipresent Negro, bearing not "clout and hoe but clad in the uniform of the U.S.Army," made his appearance. Known as the Louisiana "Native Guards," they were stationed for miles alongside the track as railway guards. As the train passed slowly, some of the more impious Yankees called out: "Take off your hats!" or "Present Arms!" The responsive blacks, according to a New Hampshire soldier, would "show a wide battery of white teeth, throw up a gun with one hand and crack a thigh with the other, ejaculating with a roll of the eye, 'Bless the Lord Massa', 'Roll on Glory', 'going to the Kingdom".[18]

THE FIRST LOUISIANA NATIVE GUARDS, Corps d'Afrique, guarding The New Orleans, Opelousas and Great Western Railroad. ***(Harper's Weekly)***

Brashear (or Morgan) City was a "miserable dirty village of a dozen houses," which owed its very existence to the railroad. Whereas six years earlier there had been nothing save a few Indian mounds and cane fields, Dr. Walter Brashear's old plantation now possessed cattle pens to take care of livestock shipments from Texas, dormitories for train crews, a house for the station agent, sidetracks, and a turn table. There was also a hotel and coffee shop, a dry goods store, a bar and a few other business establishments alongside the tracks. "From its location," confided an Iowan to his diary, "it should become a flourishing city."[19]

The war had taken its toll, however, for like the track, the tiny village of three hundred or so inhabitants had changed hands a half dozen or more times. Lonely chimneys stood amid the charred remains of houses, business establishments and fortifications, as stark reminders of the strategic value placed on this location. Only three months earlier, while the bulk of Union forces were tied down at Port Hudson, it had been overwhelmed by a surprise Confederate attack. The Rebels were gone now, but not very far. Indeed, their semaphores, waving flags by day and lanterns at night, were plainly visible on an Indian mound a couple of miles northwest of the Union-held position. Spying on the troop movements, they would flash their intelligence to the rear where it would be picked up and relayed to the appropriate authorities.

BRASHEAR CITY during the Federal occupation. ***(Harper's Weekly)***

The concentration of Union forces at Brashear City had not taken the Confederates by surprise. In fact, as subsequent events would show, the Confederate commanders seemed about as well-informed of Banks' intention of moving on Texas via southwestern Louisiana as the Union generals. The Sabine Pass blunder had given away the secret, if ever there was one. So badly botched was that mission that Confederate General Kirby Smith, who commanded the entire Trans-Mississippi Confederacy from Shreveport, refused to believe the Sabine affair was a serious invasion attempt. Surely it had been a feint, he reasoned.

As a precautionary measure, Smith ordered the commander of the District of Texas, Major General J. Bankhead Magruder, to begin concentrating his forces on the Sabine near Niblett's Bluff. Meanwhile, the little Army of Western Louisiana, under Major General Richard Taylor, was directed to string out in a line from Vermilionville (Lafayette) in the south to Alexandria in the north. Not until the invaders committed themselves, agreed Smith, Magruder and Taylor, should they act. In the meantime the enemy would be closely watched by a small force of Texas and Louisiana cavalrymen who heretofore had been engaged as jayhawk exterminators and conscript enforcers.[20]

Only two mysteries remained for the Confederates to unravel—which route would the Yankees take and who would be the field commander? Confederate General Taylor, for one, was convinced that Grant would head the invasion. After all, it was his XIII Corps down in Brashear. In the days to come, however, they would discern that Banks had turned the reins over to Major General William B. Franklin, a mild-looking cigar smoking forty-year-old native of Pennsylvania.

MAJOR GENERAL WILLIAM B. FRANKLIN
(Harpers' Weekly)

For that they could all be thankful, because William Buel Franklin, who graduated first in the West Point Class (1843) in which U.S. Grant was twenty-first, was a disgraced exile from the Army of the Potomac. An engineer by profession, Franklin sported a heavy dark mustache and trim beard which, when combined with his somewhat roundish face and serious brooding eyes, suggested a man with a harmless, if not compassionate, disposition. Indeed, about the only thing Franklin had in common with Grant was his penchant for good cigars. From the War in Mexico to the First Manassas and the Peninsular Campaign, Franklin had shown great promise, frequently winning laudatory remarks from his superiors. But at Fredericksburg, General Ambrose Burnside, who commanded the dismal affair, placed the entire burden for the disaster on Franklin, subsequently demanding that he be cashiered. Transferred to the Gulf Department, where Washington's priorities were low, he was chosen by Banks to lead the Yankees into Texas. It was he who had led the expedition which had failed so miserably at Sabine Pass:

> General Franklin with ten thousand men
> Went out to sea, and then came back again.

Now it was he who would lead the Great Texas Overland Expedition through Louisiana. Indecisive and cautious, he nonetheless followed orders, was respectful of authority and always consulted with superiors before acting, and that lack of independence, apparently, was what Banks wanted in his field commanders.[21]

As for the route the invaders would choose, no one, not even Banks, had made a decision. Between Brasher City and Opelousas, there were at least a half dozen trails leading west toward Niblett's Bluff on the Sabine. Alternatively they could continue northward toward Alexandria and Shreveport and on into Texas. Confederate General Alfred Mouton, who commanded the observing forces, seemed to think that New Iberia would be the point of departure. "Should they do this," he wrote his superiors, "I hope it will produce a disaster; at any rate I can make them very unhappy."

In the meantime, Confederate General E. Kirby Smith, recalling how the good civilians of Virginia had hampered Union operations in the Old Dominion, decided to enlist the support of the local populace. Taking up the pen, he drafted a ringing Churchillian proclamation, which, when finished, bore a curious resemblance to a famous radio address of nearly eighty years later. Thousands of copies were published and distributed and soon appeared on trees, in Confederate post offices and just about every public place and newspaper in the threatened states:[22]

TO THE PEOPLE OF ARKANSAS, LOUISIANA, AND TEXAS

Your homes are now in peril. Vigorous efforts on your part can alone save portions of your States from invasion. You should contest the advance of the enemy at every thicket, gully, and stream; harass his rear and cut off his supplies. Thus will you prove important auxiliaries in my attempts to reach him in front and drive him routed from our soil. Determination and energy only can prevent his destruction of your homes. By a vigorous and united effort you preserve your property, you secure independence for yourselves and children—all that renders life desirable. Time is now our best friend. Endure awhile longer; victory and peace must crown our efforts.

E. Kirby Smith
Lieutenant General, Commanding

Back at Brashear City, the observing Confederate spies had plenty to report. Early every morning for more than three weeks, the long train pulled into the station loaded with troops and provisions, animals and munitions. New camps were springing up all over the open plain, until finally, as far as one could see, there was nothing but white tents and floating flags and blue forms. The warehouse and depot were rapidly filled with an immense store of war materiel while the railroad employees, civilian and military alike, were taxed to their utmost. Gunboats and transports once more plied the bay while the steamers *St. Charles* and *Thomas* ferried the troops across the Atchafalaya to the Berwick side.

On every hand the busy note of preparation was heard and seen. Day and night, ringing anvils told of wagons being repaired and the shoeing of horses and mules. "From every point," wrote a New Yorker, "was heard the clarion sounds of the bugle, the brazen music of bands, the shrill and inspiriting notes of the fife, and the rattling of drums." At the same time two Union fortresses, which had been overwhelmed and badly damaged by the Confederates in June, were being repaired and remounted.

In the meantime flocks and droves of contrabands seemed to gravitate toward the Union camp. Old men with canes, bare-headed and bare-footed children, women in short dresses "with bandanas wrapped over wooly pates" and carrying infants in their arms appeared; big and little, black and yellow, old and young, crippled and infirm, all with bundles and all kinds of trappings, came pouring in at every hour. Many secured employment in the camp as cooks, waiters, washer-women and teamsters. Still others were put to work on the fortifications or were loaded on the train and sent toward New Orleans.[23]

About a mile below Brashear, at the deserted home of a planter on "Cow-pen Island," the Yankees established their medical facilities. Hospital tents were added, and extensive preparations made to accommodate the wounded as well as the sick. There, among well-manicured grounds, shrubbery, flowers, and citrus trees, an alarming number of Northerners, sometimes eight or ten a day, succumbed to some mysterious fever or infirmity.[24]

Without a doubt, the area surrounding Brashear City was one of the most unhealthy in Louisiana. The undrained swamps, marshy

CONTRABANDS arriving in camp. ***(Harper's Weekly)***

campsites and infestations of mosquitos, when combined with the oppressive summer heat of southern Louisiana, made camp life almost unbearable. In order to protect the men as much as possible, some of the medical officers concocted a mixture of whiskey and quinine to be regularly rationed out. So universally used was this medicine that it soon became a subject of much amusement and many jests. At "Sick Call" in the morning, for example, hundreds of voices would simultaneously strike up, as an accompaniment to the fife and drum, the improvised words to the call:

> Dr. Jones says, Dr. Jones says:
> Come and get your quin, quin, quin, quinine,
> Come and get your quinine,
> Q-U-I-N-I-N-E!!!

On the west bank of the Atchafalaya, directly across from Brashear City, stood the tiny and badly damaged village of Berwick City. Like Brashear, Berwick was a "city in name only." Most of the houses and business establishments fronting the river had been deliberately burned by the Yankees as retaliation for harboring Rebel sharpshooters several months earlier. A large Indian mound, which one had been the most prominent feature of the village, was almost flattened to serve as a campsite, but even that was insufficient to serve the large numbers of troops concentrating in the tiny town.[25]

Indeed, the twin cities of Berwick and Brashear had never seen anything quite like it. Confederates had been in and out, but never more than a few thousand at a time. Even during the spring 1863 "Teche Campaign" when Union General Banks had concentrated his forces here for a march up through New Iberia, Opelousas and on to Alexandria, there had never been more than fifteen thousand troops at any one time. Now, most of the XIII Army Corps, Grant's "Westerners" from Vicksburg, were concentrating for the invasion, as well as the bulk of the XIX Army Corps. The Great Texas Overland Expedition comprised not less than fifty-one infantry regiments, fourteen regiments of cavalry, seventeen artillery batteries, and a half dozen engineer regiments or altogether about thirty thousand men.[26]

Just to feed, shelter and entertain a stationary army of that magnitude was a formidable task. To complicate matters the water was brackish and unwholesome, the late summer rains came down in torrents and, worse still, enormous mosquitos tormented the men day and night. As if that wasn't bad enough, very few of the troops had tents, and those that did frequently had to share them with "moccasin snakes of domestic tendencies."[27]

The soldiers of the 42nd Ohio Infantry, under the command of a political colonel named James A. Garfield, made the mistake of drinking the salty waters in spite of warnings to the contrary, with the result that most spent the first few days violently ill. The problem was partially solved by catching rain in open containers, including ponchos, and by robbing the nearby planters of their citrus crops. Shallow wells were dug, but even then the water was not entirely fresh.

In order to protect themselves against the ceaseless rains and subsequent flooding of the campsite, some of the more innovative soldiers built elevated bunks out of scrap lumber, supporting them on stakes driven into the ground. As they lay on these during the rain, they laughed at the curses and compaints of their less fortunate comrades who, in crude imitations of the steamboat leadsman frequently called out: "Two feet!, Two and a half!, Quarter less twain!, No Bottom!" Complained a poetic New Yorker:

> The rose is red, the grass is green,
> But mud like this, I've never seen.

When the afternoon rains failed and the heat became unbearable, Surgeon B. F. Stevenson of the 22nd Kentucky availed himself of a

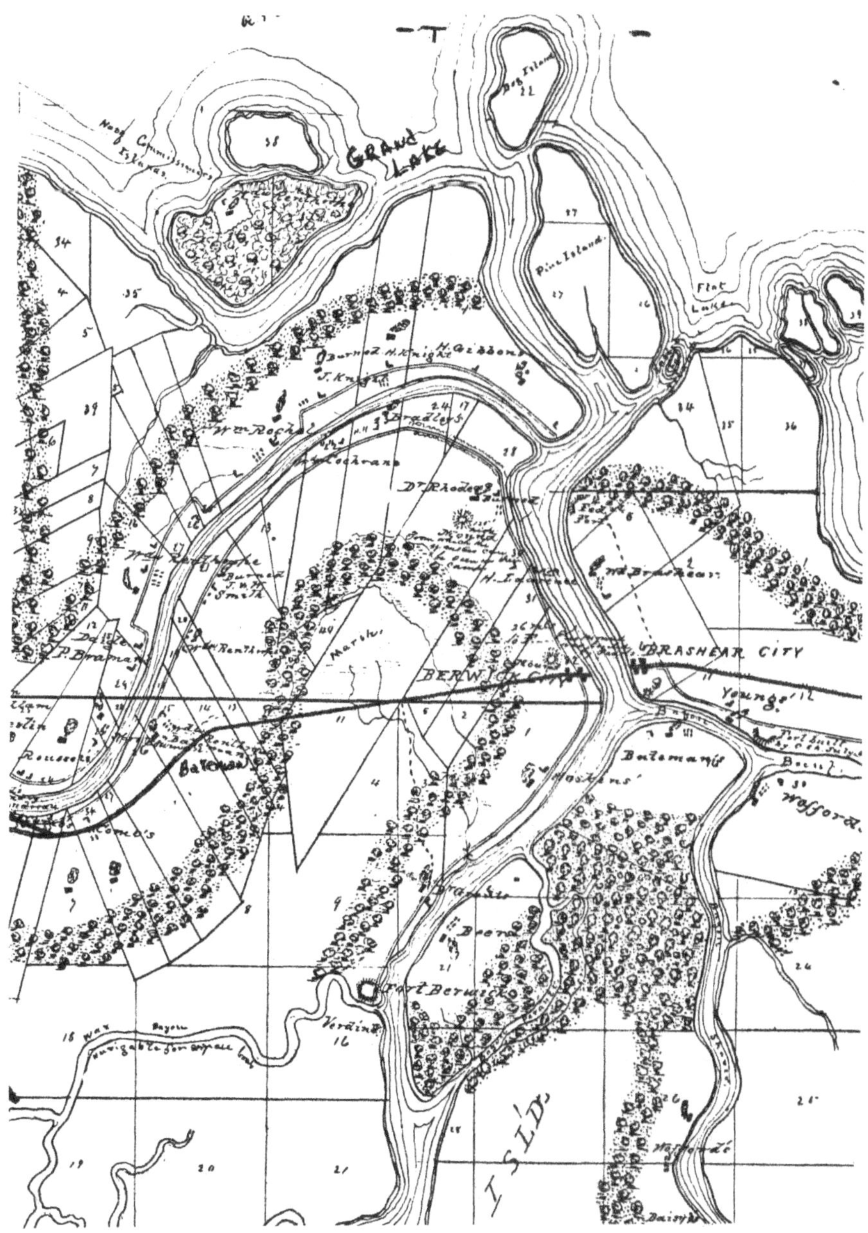

BRASHEAR (MORGAN) AND BERWICK CITIES from 1863 Confederate map of St. Mary Parish (National Archives)

plunge into the salty Atchafalaya. He was joined by the chief surgeon of the 1st Division, XIII Corps, B. B. Brashear (no relation to the local Brashears) as well as hundreds of other nude soldiers.[28]

One soldier who did not strip for the plunge was, in fact, a "very plain looking" female. A native of New Orleans, she had disguised herself as a male and enlisted in the 14th Maine Infantry with her lover, a former Confederate soldier. So small and slightly built was she that her company commander—who remained ignorant of her sex—excused her from heavy duty and assigned her instead to mending clothing and laundering.[29]

But even laundering was no easy matter in Brashear City. Corporal Rueben B. Scott of Bedford, Indiana, discovered that soap and salt water didn't mix very well. "When we tried to wash our face, clothing and hands," complained Scott, "it acted like grease, and the more we rubbed the greasier we got, until the air became blue with the unwritten language of irate soldiers." Worse still, recalled Scott "as night closed in, the great long-legged, blood-thirsty gallinippers made their appearance and we had to skirmish and fight to save our very heart's blood." In the distance, he wrote, "We could hear in the swamps near us the bellowing of alligators, like a herd of lost bulls."

During the daytime, weather permitting, the banks of the Atchafalaya were lined for miles with novice crab fishermen. "We just tie a piece of meat on a string," explained Corporal Isaac Jackson of the 83rd Ohio, "and throw in. They catch hold, and we haul him to the top of the water when we dip him out with a net fixed for the purpose."[30]

Perhaps the most marked feature of the Great Texas Overland Expedition was the dichotomy separating the "Easterners" of the XIX Army Corps from the "Westerners" of the XIII Corps. Set apart by customs, mannerisms, attitudes, accents and sometimes even religion, it was inevitable that they would constantly be at each other's throats. Grant's Westerners, the "heroes of Vicksburg" as they termed themselves, hailed mainly from Iowa, Illinois, Indiana, Wisconsin, Missouri and Ohio. According to Surgeon Harris Beecher of the 114th New York:

> The western men were strangers in this army, and attracted considerable attention from their peculiar habits and singular style of doing duty. They were, evidently, excellent fighting men, and were very proficient in drill; but they had a wonderful disregard of personal appearance, wearing all manner of dirty and outlandish costumes. They also took a special delight in destroying every species of rebel property that came within their reach, whether serviceable to them or not.

The Westerners were also "inveterate gamblers," recalled Beecher, and "arrant braggarts, continually dilating upon their wonderful achievements and forever depreciating the laudable efforts of others." They said they had come down from Vicksburg for the purpose of "showing these paper collar and white glove gents how to fight." They only wanted "the wooden nutmeg fellers" of the XIX Corps to keep out of the way and they would "finish rebellion in the Gulf Department in short order." On one point they both agreed: their commanding generals, from Banks right down to the brigadiers, were all second rate.

Unfortunately for all, such attitudes and subsequent ill feelings were not limited to good-natured bantering, but frequently took the forms of violence and bloodshed. From New Orleans to Algiers and Brashear and throughout the fall campaign, there would be many broken limbs, bloodied noses and blackened eyes—wounds which were occasionally quite critical. "I think either side would rather shoot at each other than at the Johnnies," confided a Wisconsin soldier to his diary.[31] So divisive and heated were the feelings, and so rebellious, unlawful and provoking were the Westerners, that the commanding generals were obliged to keep the two Army Corps a safe distance apart. Partly for this reason, the XIX Army Corps was ordered from Brashear to Camp Bisland, between Pattersonville and Centerville on the banks of Bayou Teche, on the 23rd of September, 1863.

In the meantime, the officers and men of the XIII Corps seemed bent on living up to their notorious reputation. On the evening of September 23rd, perhaps in celebration of the departure of the XIX Corps, every officer in camp, both of staff and of line, and "from lieutenant to general, got on a spree." The scene of the affair, the Brashear City Hotel, was enlivened by music, clinking of glasses and singing. Strangely enough, the attending officers wore their dress uniforms, their sabers neatly clinging to their belts, and even though they were to spend the evening dancing and frolicking, many of them wore spurs. From one end of camp to the other the restless men in the ranks, who went to no parties, listened to words sung by their drunken officers:

Go tell Aunt Nancy!
Go tell Aunt Nancy!
Her old gray goose is dead.
One she has been saving,
to make her feather bed.

Over in the camp of the 24th Indiana, where envy was running high, and their officers temporarily incapacitated, the Hoosier soldiers decided to have their own little spree. It didn't take long to learn that whiskey was kept in barrels beside pilings underneath the railroad warehouse. Procuring augurs, the soldiers enlisted the assistance of the guards and began boring holes into the containers. "The first trial was successful" recalled a soldier, "and one barrel was soon issued. Like a bee getting a taste of honey, the whole camp came rushing to divide."

Working hastily and in the dark, many of them slapped kettles or canteens beneath what they supposed to be commissary whiskey, but only to discover after the first taste that they had actually caught salty brine from barrels of salt beef, or "Red Horse."[32]

In the camp of the 46th Indiana, where another rowdy bunch of Hoosiers were quartered, resentment was running even higher. By orders of the provost marshal, the hotel where the officers caroused was strictly off limits to enlisted men, but what rankled the men even more was that the unidentified proprietress (possibly Maria Louisa Israel) seemed pleased with the orders. Perhaps a retaliatory visit would be in order.

Later that night after most of the activities had calmed down and when only the final tinkles of glasses, low chatter and isolated laughter could be heard, a large number of Hoosiers gathered in front of the hotel and commenced serenading the remaining occupants with war songs. While officers and their lady friends and citizens alike gathered on the balconies or listened from windows, another squad, under cover of darkness, silently entered the back rooms and began rolling out barrels of beer and whiskey, but the madame proprietress, ever alert, caught the culprits red-handed. Screaming and crying, she raised such a din that gallant officers rushed from the sides of their adoring ladies convinced that a murder was in progress. In fact, so disturbed was she that one of the regimental surgeons, another Indianian, took her in his charge. The good doctor subsequently gave the men a terrible tongue-lashing, severely reprimanding them for their unprincipled conduct. The serenaders listened attentively, and the young lady gave the doctor her "most profuse thanks for his gallant interference," but what neither doctor nor proprietress realized was that while one group was listening to the penetential lectures of the surgeon, another incorrigible squad of soldiers was back at work. Before long, they had "utterly sacked the premises." Unfortunately, the good doctor, who was quite innocent, was soon accused by the irrational proprietress of being a party to the conspiracy. Never again was he permitted to enter the Brashear City Hotel.[33]

The hotel owners were not, of course, the only civilians in Brashear and Berwick who suffered from the presence of the ill-disciplined XIII Corps. Mrs. Stephanie Trone (nee Menard) of Lyons, France, for example, had already been uprooted from her comfortable plantation near Thibodaux by the Yankees. Moving to Berwick, the forty-three-year-old widow opened a boarding house and took in sewing, but that house, too, was commandeered, and Madame Trone and her three minor daughters were turned out with nothing but a mattress and the clothing on their backs. Eventually, these refugees found shelter in an abandoned outbuilding. Reduced to penury, without any worldly possessions and no source of income, Madame Trone's health and eyesight failed, with the result that she was forced to beg sustenance of her conquerors.

Louis Laforest, a thirty-seven-year-old store owner from Bouches du Rhone, France, also lost his house, his store and its contents to the Yankees. Another Frenchman, Ambroise Narcisse Lucas, lost his house, furniture, and personal belongings, as well as his cooper's tools, lumber, molasses barrels and cotton. Similar circumstances befell Benjamin Leroy, Jean-Jean Dupre, Pierre Lahitte, Felicien and Valentine Aucoin, John Raggio, and many, many others.

The Yankees camped virtually in the yard of Pierre Loustaunau, a thirty-year-old baker from the Basse Pyrenees. Not only did they use his water well, but they also took his flour, lumber, cattle and hogs, board fence and everything else of value. Yet Loustaunau, despite his losses, was more fortunate than most, as the soldiers constructed a large brick oven behind his house and employed him to bake their bread.

Charles Forgues, a cross-eyed butcher and drayman, who lived at the home of Alexander Cardillac, was less fortunate. Known locally as "Mr. Charley," Forgues lost his two-wheeled, red-colored and zinc-topped cart as well as a herd of cattle. Two other butchers, John Burk and a Mr. Church, sought and obtained employment with the Yankees only after most of their own property had been destroyed or confiscated. The same happened to Charles Escudier, who later found employment as an interpretor and guide for the Federals.[34]

It was quite permissable to steal or destroy the property of these innocent Louisianians. After all, in the opinion of most of the invaders, they were Rebel sympathizers at best and possibly spies at worst. But an unwritten law, as an Iowan put it, was that: "Thou shalt not steal from a fellow soldier." One who did and who would pay dearly for his sins, was Private Richard Hughes of the lst Missouri Light Artillery Battery.

According to his court-martial transcript, Hughes, while his battery was at Vicksburg "did feloniously take, keep, and appropriate to his own use the sum of thirty dollars, being the contents of a pocket book belonging to Corporal Andrew J. Caldwell." For unknown reasons his court-martial was delayed until his unit reached Brashear City; he was found guilty and sentenced "to be dishonorably discharged from the service of the United States with the loss of all pay and that he have one half of his head shaved and that he then be drummed out of camp."

At the appointed hour of Hughes' dishonorable discharge, 5 o'clock P. M. September 24, 1863, the day after the big whiskey and hotel affair, the entire 3rd Division of the XIII Corps, numbering 3,679 men, was ordered to each side of the railroad track where they fell in facing each other. Private Hughes, disgraced and shorn, hat in hand and with buttons of his uniform neatly clipped off, was marched to the track. He betrayed no signs of remorse. To the contrary, noted a soldier from Wisconsin: "His eyes looked as though he would like to kill any man that looked at him." Starting at the railroad terminal, Hughes was forced to move on the double-quick down the entire mile-long stretch of hooting, jeering, cursing and kicking soldiers. He was prodded along the way by two soldiers on either side and by four on his rear, all of whom followed at "Charge Bayonets!" Behind this lively procession, two fifes and two snare drums piped out the music to "Rogue's March:"

> Poor old soldier, poor old soldier
> Tarrred and feathered, and sent to hell
> Because he wouldn't soldier well.

At the end of the line Private Richard Hughes disappeared down the railroad track and was never heard from again.[35]

CHAPTER TWO

UP THE TECHE

Headquarters XIII Corps
Berwick, La. October 2, 1863

The First and Third Divisions, Thirteenth Army Corps, with two days rations in haversacks, will take up their line of march, the First at 6 A.M., and the Third at 8 A.M. on the 3rd in column. . . The desertion of the column on the march, or straggling for purposes of pillage and plunder, is an offense punishable by death by the Articles of War, and will not be permitted. . .

By order of Maj. Gen. C.C. Washburn[1]

Saturday, October 3, 1863

THE GENERALS could not have chosen a more beautiful day to launch the invasion. For days the rain had come down in torrents. The campsites had been flooded, the roads and streets had turned into a quagmire and the men were wet and miserable, but today the wind was out of the north, the sun was shining and the weather was pleasantly cool. All things considered, it was a beautiful day in southern Louisiana.

In spite of the idle threats about capital punishment for straggling and foraging, the men were in high spirits. Out of Berwick City they filed, heading down the arrow straight railroad track toward the west. Laughing, joking and singing, they were on their way toward Texas.

Several miles west of the marching soldiers, at the point where the New Orleans, Opelousas and Great Western Railroad track came within a few yards of a bend in the lower Teche, the XIX Army Corps was also in motion. They had been camped at that junction for days, safely removed from their Western antagonists. Led by the cavalry regiments of Harai Robinson's 1st Louisiana (Union) and Edmund Davis' 1st Texas (Union), the long blue lines stretched for miles along the dirt road paralleling the east side of Bayou Teche.

Earlier in the day they, too, had been read stringent orders regarding the twin evils of straggling and foraging:[2]

During a march, the commanding officers of regiments will habitually march at the rear of their regiments, and will make it their particular duty to see that straggling is prevented, and that the men do not wander from the ranks into houses and fields near the line of march. They will inflict summary punishment upon men who do so straggle or wander, and in case of mutinous language, or disobedience of orders by stragglers, must use their power so far as to put the straggler to death.

The Major-General Commanding appeals to the officers and soldiers of the XIX Army Corps to assist him in enforcing these orders, begging them to remember that warring on an unarmed population is barbarous, and that robbing defenseless women and children, and insulting unarmed men, will only embitter the war, and make enemies where we should make friends.

Franklin had some very good reasons to be concerned. During the spring 1863 campaigns, when the XIX Army Corps chased the Confederates up the Atchafalaya and Teche, the behavior of the Easterners had been atrocious. They were equally as bad then as the Westerners were reputed to be now. Burning and pillaging, straggling and foraging, they had laid waste to the land from Brashear to Alexandria.[3]

All that was behind now, and their no-nonsense commander, General William Franklin, was determined that such outrages would not occur again. Even the most trifling offenses were dealt with severely.[4] As a result, the veterans of the XIX Corps, many of whom had already traversed this same road twice, had to content themselves with pointing out and discussing familiar sights. "Every house was familiar," wrote a New Yorker, "the men were acquainted with many of the citizens; they could tell the distance from place to place, and in fact knew as much of the Teche country as they did of their own townships."[5]

For the newcomers of the XIII Corps, however, it was new territory, and the boys were fascinated by the sights. The missing rails from the uncompleted track, they speculated, must have been used to cast Confederate armanents. In the distance, across fields where sugar cane had once flourished, stood the lonely chimneys and smokestacks of the burned out plantation homes of Dr. Joseph Rhodes, Henry Knight, widow Dorsino L. Renthrop and M. W. Bateman.[6]

The sight of so much destruction had a sobering effect on the men. Whereas only moments before they had been singing "When Johnnie Comes Marching Home" and "The Girl I Left Behind," thoughts now turned to more serious matters. Someone repeated a rumor, erroneous as usual, that Confederate General Mouton had been assassinated. Better yet, there was a story going around, gleaned from a newspaper article, that Texas General Bankhead Magruder had been killed by one of his subordinates "who caught the general in a criminal act with his wife."[7]

There were also some negative rumors which, unfortunately for the Yankees, turned out to be true. The tug *Leviathon*, it was said, had been captured in the Southwest Pass. Remembering the loss of two gunboats, the *Sachem* and *Clifton*, at Sabine Pass, a disgruntled Illinois infantryman snorted: "A few more such captures, and the Rebels will have our Navy." But the worst news was that the Texas and Louisiana Confederates had surprised and overwhelmed a detachment of the XIII Corps on Bayou Fordoche, near Morganza, only four days earlier. According to the early reports, which turned out to be accurate, more than five hundred Westerners had been killed, wounded or captured, thus destroying the highly-touted myth of the XIII Army Corps' invincibility.[8]

About five or six miles west of Berwick, just below Pattersonville on the lower Atchafalaya, the Westerners of the XIII Corps abandoned the more solid footing of the railroad track and headed up the wagon road on the west bank. Had the generals so chosen, the Corps could have continued along the track for seven or eight more miles until reaching the lower Teche; however, by taking the wagon route they were forced to march for miles out of their way. Complained George Crooke, adjutant for the 21st Iowa, "long-continued rains had reduced the roads to very bad condition, and the rich, loamy soil, thoroughly saturated, had, to use a nautical phrase, 'no bottom'." Another soldier noted that:[9]

> One who has never walked on Louisiana soil, when its surface has been moistened by rain, can form no adequate conception of its slippery, slimy, greasy character. It is easier to stand upright upon glaring ice, than in a Louisiana road at such times...Every few moments some luckless wight, in making a mis-step, was precipitated headlong in the mud, amid a great clatter of bayonets and canteens.

Once beyond Pattersonville—"a small but pretty village," according to a surgeon of the 60th Indiana—the troops soon reached the mouth of Bayou Teche.[10] For the next five or six miles they would witness scenes of unparalleled devastation. Earlier in the year, on two separate occasions, the lower Teche had been bloodily contested by the opposing forces. Gone were many of the opulent mansions where gentlemen of leisure had reaped a fortune from sugar cane and slavery. In their places were shell and sand covered driveways, shaded on both sides by massive live oaks, leading to lonesome chimneys standing amid the charred debris of dwelling houses, outbuildings and sugar mills. Immense groves of citrus trees, their golden fruit unharvested, lured the thirsty men from the column. Such was the sad state of affairs at the once substantial plantations of Ely Nash, Thomas Wilcoxen, A. A. Fusilier, Numa Cornay, P. C. Bethel and many others.

Approaching a bend in the Teche just below Judge William Palfrey's plantation, the men soon discovered why they had remained for two miserable weeks or longer around Brashear and Berwick. There, resting in the shallow waters of Bayou Teche, was the rusting hulk of the partially iron-clad Rebel gunboat, the *J. A. Cotton.* In January, during the so-called Battle of the *Cotton,* she had been scuttled after a desperate engagement that resulted in severe losses to the Union side. Her presence now, together with other Confederate obstructions, rendered it difficult for Union gunboats to enter the upper Teche. Complicating the situation was the fact that the bayou, in spite of the heavy rains, had not been so low for years. As a result, the entire Army of the Gulf—and the invasion of Texas—had been forced to wait around Brashear City for the arrival of light draught gunboats while demolition teams removed some of the obstructions.[11]

WRECK OF GUNBOAT COTTON IN Bayou Teche ***(Leslie's Illustrated Weekly)***

A short distance beyond the *Cotton,* near the point where the Teche turns sharply to the north, the long blue columns came across an old Confederate fortress (Fort Bisland) and a long barricaded ditch angling away from the bayou toward swampy marshes on both sides. It was here that the bloody Battle of Bisland had been fought back in April. "Marks of shot and shell were plainly visible on the adjoining trees and buildings," recalled a soldier in the 24th Indiana. Another soldier, a New Yorker, remarked that:

> The ground seemed not to have been trodden by human foot since the battle. Skeletons of horses lay where they had fallen, immense flocks of carrion birds hovered over the place, a luxuriant growth of weeds, ten feet high, covered the canefields—the whole scene was one of utter desolation.

Only a few days before, a Texas Confederate had reported seeing "here and there a part of Yankee uniforms and scattered about were legs and arms and heads which had escaped from their hastily dug graves. It was a ghastly sight indeed."[12]

A mile or so beyond these "grisly" scenes, past the burned out plantation home of Thomas Bisland, the troops came across what was once described as "the prettiest place up and down the bayou." Here lived Judge William Taylor Palfrey who had taken Sidney Ann Conrad as his bride many years before. She had long since passed away, but, as one of his ancient former slaves, Ellen Betts, recalled more than seventy years later, he had remarried a widow, Susan Cornelia Gates Barnard of Franklin, Louisiana (then residing in Mobile) who, in turn, bore him four sons:[13]

> Miss Cornelia was the finest woman in the world. Come Sunday morning she done put a bucket of dimes on the front gallery and stand there and throw dimes to the nigger children just like feeding chickens...Sometimes she done put the washtub of buttermilk on the back gallery, and us children bring up gourds and dip up that good old buttermilk till it git all drink up.

Judge Palfrey, or "Marse William," as he was called by Miss Ellen Betts, "am the greatest man what ever walk this earth." A native of Massachusetts, he was a veritable pillar of the community, having served as sheriff of St. Mary Parish, cashier of a bank he founded in Franklin, parish judge and state senator:

> ...when a whupping got to be done, old marse do it heself. He don't low no overseer to throw he gals down and pull up their dress and whup their bottoms like I hear some of 'em do...You couldn't find a yeller child on the place. He sure got no use for mixing black and white...When us niggers go down the road, folks say 'Them's (Palfrey's) niggers. Don't hit one of them niggers for God's sake, or (Palfrey) sure eat your jacket up'...was he still living I spect one part of he hands be with him today. I knows I would.

Like other planters along the lower Teche, Judge Palfrey had suffered a great deal because of the war. His young son, "Ned" (Edward) was killed fighting for the Confederacy. Another son, William, Jr., seemed intent on drinking himself into oblivion, and in the spring the Yankees had come with the result that the Battle of Bisland raged all around:

When the bullets starts raining down, Marse calls us and ship us way back into the woods...Us sure glad to 'scape from the Yankees...When us driv back to the plantation, such a sight I never seen. Law, the things I can tell. Them Yanks have kilt men and women. I seed babies pick up from the road with their brains bust right out. One old man am drawing water and a cannon ball shoots him right in the well. They draws him up with the fishing line. They's a old sugar boat on the bayou with blood and sugar running 'long the busted barrels. 'Lasses run in the bayou, and blood run in the ditches... Law, the time they have.[14]

Then, in mid-September the Yankees of the XIX Corps, "attracted by the shady trees and capacious cisterns of rain water" had made the Palfrey place their campsite once more. Judge Palfrey himself recalled the visit in a heart-rending, sometimes bitter, letter to his abolitionist brother John, then residing in Boston:

They used the lumber of my remaining buildings for fuel and building small shelters. The Federal troops burned, through mischievious wantoness, several of the venerable live-oak trees which adorned my front lawn, measuring 9 feet in diameter. (They) used my furniture for fuel and (left) my property in such a state of desolation as you cannot conceive...

Now, in October, the soldiers of the XIII Corps moved onto the plantation and, according to Miss Ellen Betts:

...they comes right in the house where Miss Cornelia eating her dinner. They march round the table, just scooping up meat and 'taters and grabbing cornpone right and left. Miss Cornelia don't say a word, just smile sweet as honey-cake. I reckon them soldiers mighta took the silver and such, only she charm 'em by being so quiet and ladylike. First thing you know, them soldiers curtsy to Missy and take themselves right out the door and don't come back.

In fact, the Yankees of the XIII Corps, on that particular evening in early October, were simply too tired and disheartened by the ravages of war they had just witnessed to bother about plundering the Palfrey Plantation. "We lay down in the field with the starry canopy of heaven for a cover," recalled a soldier in the 24th Indiana, "and slept soundly."[15]

Several miles north, at the camp of the XIX Army Corps, sleep was out of the question for a small group of New Yorkers. Despite General Franklin's efforts to keep these Easterners honest, they were bent on depredations that evening, expecially in and near the little village of Centerville. Among their victims were the proprietors of the Phoenix Saloon, several warehouse owners along the Teche, and a certain dry-goods merchant named T.D. Hine. At age thirty-nine, Hine, like Palfrey, was a transplanted Connecticut Yankee. Looted during the first invasion, the thrifty merchant had lost most of his inventory, including his steamboat, the *T.D. Hine*, but had managed to replenish his stock during the summer months. Now, the Yankees were back again, and this time they were accompanied by a colonel who bore the unlikely name of George M. Love.

A brigade commander in Godfrey Weitzel's infantry division and former colonel of the 116th New York, Love gained entrance to Hine's warehouse by breaking in the doors. The intrusion, said he, was occasioned by necessity; Rebels were believed to be in the vicinity. Love seemed more interested, however, in methodically sacking the store. In fact, so malicious were some of his men that they dumped most of the store's contents into the nearby Teche, including merchandise of dubious value.

One article which defied removal was a great iron safe. Citing some flimsy pretext about the safe harboring contraband evidence, Love instructed the angry merchant to open it, an order which Hine adamantly refused. His obstinacy, reasoned the intruders, was conclusive evidence that Hine was hiding something of value, either money or contraband. The Yankees, as persistent as Hine was obstinate, were determined to open that safe and toward that end labored faithfully throughout the night.

Working in shifts, and using bars of iron lashed together for a ramming rod, they finally caved in the side. But alas, the great iron safe contained nothing more than a little cash—Rebel money—some ledger books, and a few papers which bore no value except to the merchant. So infuriated were the Yankees over losing an entire night's sleep for naught that they proceeded to "annihilate the evidence of his credits." Turning his account books inside out, they trampled the leaves in the mud; papers were ripped asunder and scattered in the street or thrown into the Teche.[16]

Hine, in spite of his own severe losses, must surely have derived some perverse satisfaction from their disappointment.

Sunday, October 4, 1863

Taking up the line of march at daybreak, the boys from Iowa, Illinois, Indiana, Wisconsin and Ohio gazed curiously upon the magnificent sugar mansions along the lower Teche. One of these, the home of Mr. L. Tarlton, seemed to be a favorite of the Union generals. During the night Tarlton, an "ancient secesher" as he was called, had been the involuntary host of Major General Cadwalader C. Washburn, the temporary field commander of the XIII Corps.

Unlike many of the other planters who had long since lost their plantation slaves to the invaders, Tarlton seemed to enjoy the fidelity of his. One of these, the Fiddler, had come into the Union camp, violin in hand, and invited several officers to a genuine country musical. The performance was attended by C. E. H. Bonwill, special correspondent and artist for *Leslie's Illustrated Weekly* who subsequently depicted the "actual scene" for posterity:

> I found him under a tree, with some of his sable brethren around him listening to his performance on the violin, the younger dancing as though such music was too good to be lost, and of too salutory a nature to be enjoyed in quiet. But the most comical point of the whole was the presence of two mules, seen in the midst, looking on with an air of quiet drollery perfectly irresistible.

SCENE AT TARLTON'S PLANTATION on Bayou Teche. The steamer *A. G. Brown* is in the background. *(Leslie's Illustrated Weekly)*

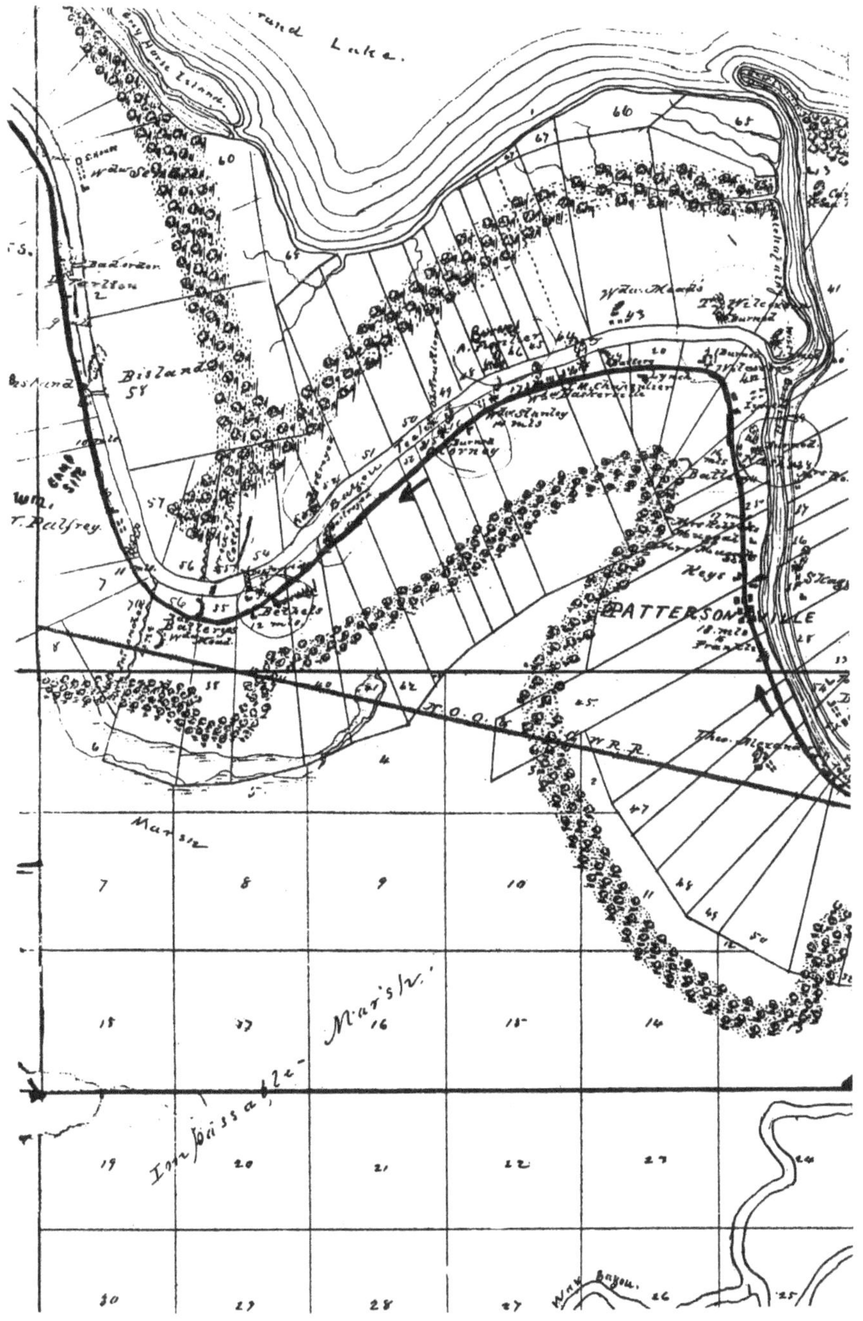

LOWER TECHE, from 1863 Confederate map of St. Mary Parish. (National Archives)

The night before the musical, and for almost two weeks prior to that time, the house had been employed by one of the Union's youngest generals, twenty-seven-year-old Godfrey Weitzel, a division commander in the XIX Corps. Weitzel, a West Point graduate, accomplished engineer and one of the best commanders in the Gulf Department, was by most accounts a crude-mannered, foul-tempered, arrogant, lascivious and flamboyant officer. Though he had lived in Louisiana for almost two years before the war, he consistently exhibited a low regard for the innocent civilians whom he considered as "bitter and uncompromising enemies of the United States." Indeed from Thibodaux to Brashear and from the lower Teche to Alexndria, Weitzel had commandeered the very finest plantation homes for his personal headquarters, frequently throwing the owners out, sacking the premises and, in many instances, leaving only ashes behind; nor was he sympathetic to the plight of blacks, as he occasionally railed at superiors for permitting military operations to be hampered by the large numbers of runaway slaves coming into Union lines.

At the Tarlton plantation, which he had converted to his own use while supervising the removal of obstructions from the Teche, he frequently horrified the household with behavior bordering on the perverse. "Generally intoxicated," as Tarlton subsequently complained, "he exhibited himself openly and shamelessly in fond dalliance with negro servant girls." Tarlton's daughters were so outdone by his "coarse manners and language, and by his indecent behavior" that they not only refused to entertain him or his staff at the piano but retreated in hiding "to their most secluded apartments." When the XIX Corps took up the line of march only the day before, the heavy-drinking young general had ridden into the yard and called out to his staff: "Come on boys; there are other rich plantations here to sack."[17]

"Rich" was an understatement, as there was nothing back home, save perhaps the public buildings in the courthouse square, to even remotely compare with these elegant dwellings. Instead of facing the road, along which the soldiers marched, the front of the mansions, with their broad galleries and large columns, were oriented toward a landing alongside the bayou. Most were square-built, two-story structures; some were built entirely of brick and stucco; and still others had a lower floor of brick and an upper one of wood.

A curious feature, and one worthy of comment by the invaders, was that each plantation had a "narrow" fronting of the highest best land called *terre de la premiere qualite* alongside the bayou. The grounds and surroundings were at once shaded by massive magnolias, moss draped live oaks, and were scented by gardens of jasmine, oleanders, altheas and roses. In the rear, facing the soldiers, were the carriage-houses, smoke houses, vegetable gardens, dovecotes, overseers' houses with their large plantation bells and row upon row of neat whitewashed slave quarters.

Perhaps the most universal feature was the large sugar house, or *sucrerie*, with its tall brick smokestack, steam powered grinding machinery, open kettles, cisterns and hogsheads. Virtually every plantation, large or small, possessed its own sugarhouse with the result that smokestacks were visible as far as the eye could see in all directions.

As in all parts of Louisiana, however, the war had left its mark. The slave quarters were practically deserted. There remained only the aged and decrepit, the handicapped and infirm and, in some instances, a few faithful *domestiques*. Most had deserted or had gone off with the "Linkum sojers" during the spring campaign. Those that returned or were subsequently recaptured had been removed to more secure locations in anticipation of the fall invasion. Like so many cattle, they had been herded over the open prairies toward Texas or placed in well guarded detention camps in the Atchafalaya wilderness.

Gone too were most of the white inhabitants. During the spring invasion they had remained at home only to be insulted, offended, and victimized. The soldiers of the XIX Army Corps, who now behaved like "perfect gentlemen," had left not a piece of furniture intact, not one window pane unbroken or anything of value behind. The shrubbery had been trampled; doors had been torn from their hinges; fences and outbuildings had been ripped down and consumed as firewood; livestock had been slaughtered and most of the produce had been confiscated. Even the once well manicured lawns were overgrown with rank weeds and vegetation. "Truly the South had paid (a) heavy penalty for the crime of secession," wrote a correspondent for the Lacon *Illinois Gazette*.

BRIGADIER GENERAL GODFREY WEITZEL
(Library of Congress)

In spite of these ugly scenes "the road looked more cheerful" than the burned-out buildings and debris of war they had seen the day before. Occasionally, wrote Captain William Titus Rigby of the 24th Iowa, "some of the houses we passed are inhabited, and at the doors and windows we could get glimpses of ladies, some old, some young."[18]

What most of the men did not know was that many of these "Rebel seceshers" as the planters were called, were neither Southern in origin nor were they all white. Large numbers of wealthy planters, perhaps a majority, hailed from such states as Massachusetts, New York, and Connecticut or had immigrated to Louisiana from France, England, Ireland or Spain. Many of these distinguished "Southern" families were without ancient lineage, but had gained position and influence by their own successful endeavors in the New World. Indeed, a small but not insignificant number were light-skinned "free men of color" who, years before, had been manumitted only to become wealthy slave-owners themselves.

Though many of these planters had originally cast their lot with the Confederacy by supplying money, produce, and sometimes their sons for the war effort, most had long since resigned themselves to the inevitability of Union domination. With few exceptions, they now claimed to be loyal Unionists and indicated their feelings by rushing to take the infamous Oath of Allegiance to the Union (see Appendix) and by exhibiting the Stars and Stripes over their mansions; others flew the Union Jack of England or the tricolor of France and begged for protection as alien neutrals.

Whereas "protection papers" had not been forthcoming during the spring invasion, they now appeared at practically every home or plantation of substantial size. The provost marshals of General Franklin's command seemed to be everywhere, posting papers to trees, the entrance to dwellings and to outbuildings. Very few things rankled the Westerners more than these protection papers. Complained an Iowan:[19]

> There were orange groves and sugar plantations innumerable, and warehouses filled with sugar too tempting to the XIII Army Corps to be resisted. For although the written safeguard of General Banks, posted over the main entrance of such warehouses, was generally respected, there were back and side doors where the voice of authority was silent. The oranges were ripe and delicious, hanging in clusters upon the trees, showing no certificates of loyalty, and not, therefore, by any sophistry, to be classed as forbidden fruit.

A few such minor violations of the spirit, if not the letter of the law, did not bring swift retribution upon the men, at least not those in the XIII Corps. No one was shot, as threatened, nor was anyone castigated or even lectured by their officers when straying off the road. Indeed no one seemed to care. Thus, by the time the head of the column reached Centerville, the men were flanking both sides of the road and straggling in the rear. Houses were entered, food and valuables were stolen and anything not useful frequently smashed.

Centerville, on Bayou Teche, "was a very nice little town," according to Sergeant Levi Hoag of the 24th Iowa. "The citizens," recalled Private Harry Watts of the 24th Indiana, "looked surprised to see us and were very inquisitive to know where we were going. But soldiers in the ranks are supposed to know nothing." A surgeon of the 60th Indiana, James B. Hunter, was surprised to see "peach trees in bloom." Had he inquired he would have been told that such temperate fruit trees as peaches, pears and apples sometimes blossom a second time during the long Louisiana summer, but probably will not produce the following year.[20]

A New Yorker, Lieutenant Lawrence Van Alstyne, then recruiting local blacks for a newly organized regiment of the *Corps d' Afrique*, was attracted to an orange tree in front of a house. "As I went into the yard," he recounted in his diary, "a young lady came out and, in a tone and with a look that almost froze me, asked what I was doing in her yard."

Van Alstyne was stunned by her hostile attitude and couldn't think what to say, but after regaining his composure, he replied: "I would like an orange."

Granting him his wish, the hostile young lady then pointed her finger toward the street and commanded: "Now that you have what you came after will you please go!"

The startled New Yorker, normally a gentlemanly sort, was so humiliated that he related the episode only to his diary. "That is a sort of southern hospitality I never read of in a book," he wrote that night. "Why I stood there like a chicken thief caught in the act, I don't know. If the Rebels were all like her I would resign and go home at once, for she did actually scare my wits all away from me." Van Alstyne eventually had to give the oranges away, "for I think they would have choked me."[21]

The unidentified lady with the orange tree was not, of course, the only civilian in Centerville visited by the marauding Yankees. William A. Riggs, a local attorney and former Confederate officer, watched with horror as the soldiers broke open every store and warehouse in town, including his own. Tobacco and sugar were taken from Mr. Louis Whitworth's warehouse and instantly distributed to the soldiers. The invaders also broke open stables and confiscated the horses of one Mr. Capron, William Cook (Senior and Junior) and George Vest, Riggs' brother-in-law.

One of the town's oldest practicing physicians, Dr. James Grout, just happened to be riding down the street while all the horse-seizing was going on. Several bluecoats grabbed the reins and ordered him to dismount, but the good doctor, an irascible old man, was not about to give in so easily. "If you take my horse," he stated defiantly, "you will also have to take me."

And so they did. For more than an hour the laughing soldiers, some of whom had been partaking of something more potent than tobacco, "led the horse around the streets with the doctor on him." Tiring of the affair, Dr. Grout finally dismounted and surrendered his horse, but not

CENTERVILLE, LOUISIANA, occupied by the 116th New York Infantry, Colonel Love's command. *(Leslie's Illustrated Weekly)*

before rendering a few gratuitous diagnostical opinions about the character of his tormentors.[22]

Leaving Centerville, the troops marched deeper into the Attakapas country, named for the reputedly cannibalistic Indians or "man-eaters" who had once inhabited the region. Without exception, every soldier who recorded his thoughts for the next few days commented on its beauty. It was, as many pointed out, "a veritable paradise," or "a garden of Eden," where Longfellow's Evangeline had once vainly searched for her beloved Gabriel:

> Beautiful is the land, with its prairies and forests of fruit trees. Under the feet a garden of flowers, and the bluest of heavens, bending above, and resting its dome on the walls of the forest. They who dwell there have named it the Eden of Louisiana.

It was also alligator country. Every hour or so the troops would fall out alongside the road and rest under the shade of massive cypress trees or moss draped live oaks. After a few minutes to catch their breaths, they would head to the banks of Bayou Teche, where the large scaley creatures were sunning themselves. "In this condition," wrote a war correspondent for the Wisconsin *State Journal*, "it often happens they are perturbed by some of Uncle Sams' Blue Coats, who cannot resist the temptation of a philosophical experiment—the visible effect of impinging lead upon a tough, horny hide." So many troops had already passed,

ENGAGEMENT WITH A REBEL ALLY on Bayou Teche was the caption on this sketch by an artist for *Harper's Weekly*.

complained a soldier bringing up the rear, that "We saw legions of dead alligators, but found few live ones for us to try our Enfield rifles upon."[23]

As the troops of the XIII Corps approached Franklin, some five miles upstream from Centerville, the advance guard came across the ruins of a large foundry, belonging to an Englishman named Charles Fleming, on the Bidell plantation. At one time the Fleming Foundry, as it was called, had been an important operation for the Confederate cause, especially in the manufacture of cannon and shot. During the spring campaign, however, the plant had been captured, the fixtures confiscated and much of the building destroyed by bombardment from the United States gunboat *Clifton*.

While the troops pondered the significance of the foundry, a war correspondent for the *Illinois Gazette* spotted a rather curious "deputation of citizens" wending their way down Bayou Teche toward the head of the column. A spokesman for the group, an elderly man who identified himself as the mayor of Franklin (presumably Alphene L. Tucker) requested a conference with the division commander, Brigadier General Stephen Gano Burbridge.

Burbridge, the grandson of a Revolutionary War veteran, farmer, lawyer and graduate of Kentucky Military Institute, received the group with a warm pleasant smile. Tall and commanding in appearance, the thirty-two-year-old general sported a shaggy Fu-Manchu beard and a wide-brimmed hat to cover the slicked-down hair on his prematurely balding head.

Would the general, asked the mayor, be so kind as to send a small force of guards into Franklin prior to the entry of Union troops? Earlier in the year, explained the spokesman, a group of Confederates, Colonel Valsin Fournet's Yellow Jacket Battalion, had ambushed a large Union wagon train passing through town. Though it was not the fault of the citizens, many of whom proclaimed Union sentiments, it was feared that some of the individual troops would now seek revenge by vandalizing private property. The Easterners of the XIX Corps, who had passed through during the morning and the day before, had posted such a guard and order was maintained.

General Burbridge had some very good reasons to sympathize with the plight of these helpless civilians. How well he knew the agony of being caught between the opposing forces for he was a social outcast in Kentucky where all his friends and relatives supported the Confederacy. Addressing himself to the group, he replied: "Gentlemen, the Thirteenth Army Corps are not thieves. Go back and tell the citizens of Franklin that my soldiers will not molest them if they do not insult them; and I would tell you gentlemen, the best protection you can have for your property is the American flag."

BRIGADIER GENERAL STEPHEN G. BURBRIDGE
(Library of Congress)

Lies, of course, all lies, but at least they were assuring words for the good citizens of Franklin and just to be sure, Kentuckian Burbridge sent forward the provost marshal with a guard detail.[24]

Franklin, Louisiana, situated just below Irish Bend (a large oxbow-shaped bend in Bayou Teche) was, and still is, the seat of justice in St. Mary Parish. Founded by a Pennsylvanian, Guinea Lewis, an admirer of Benjamin Franklin, it was the cultural, financial and agricultural hub of the region. A prosperous town, it possessed a weekly newspaper, the *Planter's Banner*, a bank, hotels, livery stables, three churches, a courthouse, jailhouse, billiard hall and other business establishments as well as a number of fine homes. Aside from New Orleans it was the biggest, cleanest, prettiest town the troops had seen in a long time; or as an Iowan put it: "Franklin is a lovely town surrounded by nature's fairest arts."

In the spring the Confederate gunboat *Diana* had been blown to pieces here, dynamited by the retreating Rebels. At the same time, the very bloody battle of Irish Bend had occurred nearby when General Banks had tried, and failed, to bag Confederate General Richard Taylor's little Louisiana army. It was here, back in June, that Union Colonel Thomas Chickering's eight-mile-long wagon train of plunder from St. Landry Parish had been ambushed from private houses alongside the Teche. So impassioned were the Yankees by this perfidious attack that a group was detailed to burn the entire village. Only the proximity of the pursuing Rebels had saved it from the torch.

So it was with a great deal of anxiety that the good citizens of Franklin crowded the sidewalks and watched for several days as thousands upon thousands of bluecoats paraded through the middle of their little town. Stores were padlocked and flags were displayed from every rooftop and window. Most prominent were the Stars and Stripes, but there was also a sprinkling of English, French, Spanish and Prussian flags as well as a number of white ones.

FRANKLIN, LOUISIANA, occupied by Federal troops in 1863.
(Leslie's Illustrated Weekly)

As each brigade entered town, the brigade band would strike up a marching tune, usually the "Star Spangled Banner," if not "Yankee Doodle" or "Rally Round the Flag." Soldiers and citizens alike seemed to enjoy the occasion. The only ugly note had occurred the day before when the troops of the 114th New York "made all manner of hateful remarks to the citizens who stood upon the sidewalks, gazing at another advent of the Yankee army." These same New Yorkers had accompanied Chickering's train back in June when it was ambushed and "they had not forgotten the cowardly and wanton attack that had been made upon them at this place."

Oran Perry, an officer from Richmond, Indiana, was struck by the mixing of the races that had apparently taken place in Franklin. "The few people that are left," he wrote home, "are French and negroes of every hue and complexion, the rainbow not excepted." Another Hoosier, Harry Watts of the 24th Indiana, was even more explicit. "While passing through this town," he recalled, "we saw a greater variety of females than we ever saw before. There were the white, yellows, the mulattos, the octoroons, the quadroons, and some baboons. They had all come out to see 'de Yankees'."[25]

A short distance northwest of town, out on the cut-off road leading across Irish Bend, the head of the column stopped to pitch camp near the property of Jesse T. Baldwin. The rear of the column, about three miles downstream from Franklin, rested near the opulent plantation home of a Confederate member of the Yellow Jacket Battalion, Captain Allen Hayes. The middle of the column, the XIII Corps, stopped for the night on or near the properties of J. H. Darnell, Judge John Moore, widow Bidell, Theodule and Euphrasy Carlin, James Murphy, S.L. Randall, W. Parkerson, Joseph Foster, Dr. James Smith and many others, rich and poor alike.[26]

The evening before they had gone to sleep hungry, fearful of punishment if caught foraging and depressed by their surroundings. But this evening the weather was beautiful, the officers were as nonchalant as ever and there were many wealthy plantations to plunder. There was also something new to the Northern eye. In the fields nearby were acres and acres of beautiful yellow sweet potatoes, or yams, as they are commonly called in Louisiana.

Before long foraging parties were straggling from camp in all directions. "We were not long in learning that yams stewed with chicken made the most delicious dish that many of us had eaten for two years," wrote Augustus Sinks of the 46th Indiana. An Iowan, Lieutenant Alfred A. Rigby, wrote: "Notwithstanding the strict orders against foraging, beef and sweet potatoes came into camp in abundance." A soldier from Wisconsin, Private Henry P. Whipple, felt that he had to rationalize his actions to his diary after filling his stomach with yams: "General Banks has issued written safeguards to (the planters) and says foraging on their

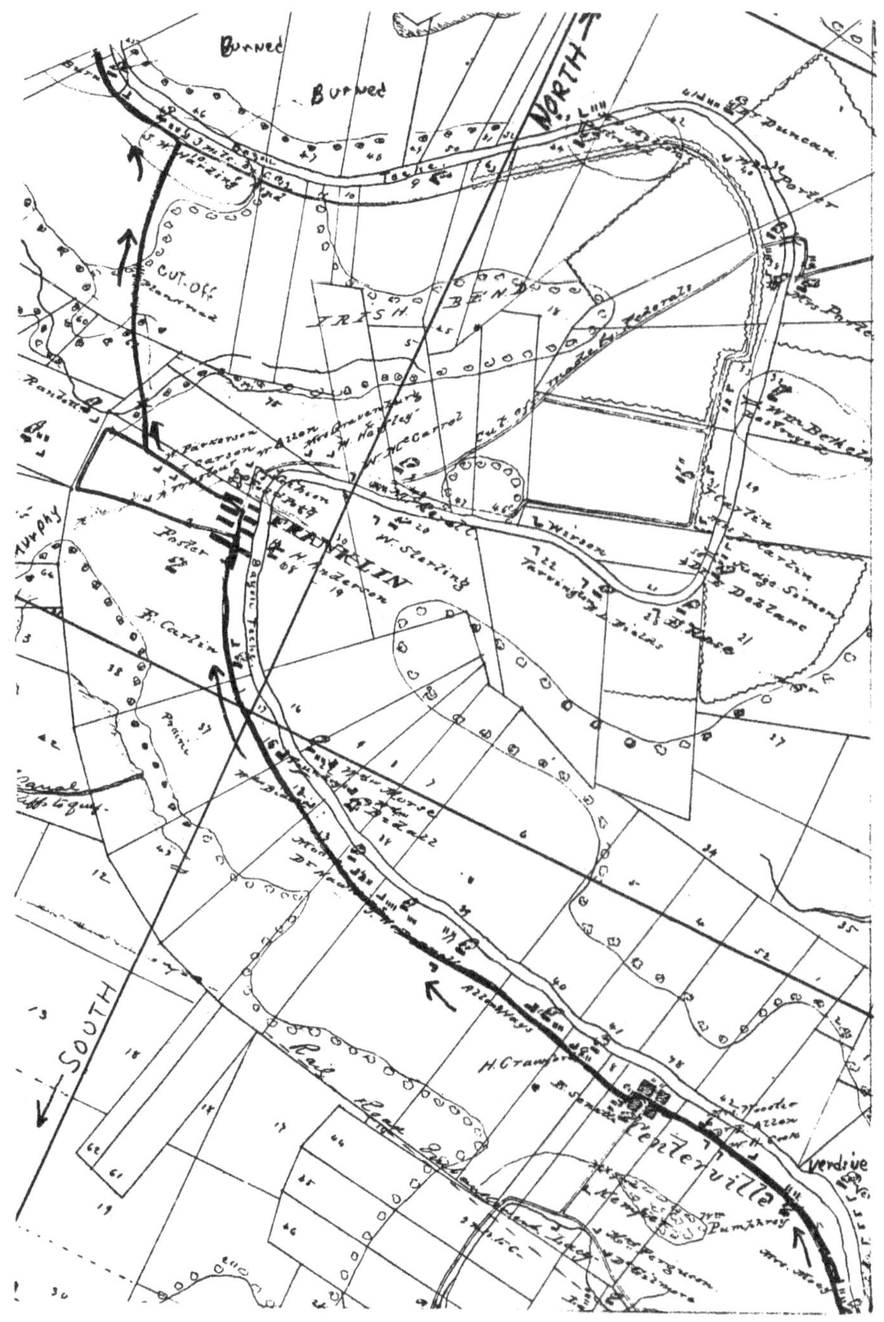

CENTERVILLE, FRANKLIN AND IRISH BEND from 1863 Confederate map of St. Mary Parish. (National Archives)

property by a Union soldier will be punished by death (but) these people are very wealthy and have been feeding the Rebel army for nothing."[27]

Among the generals in the XIII Corps, only one, Brigadier General Michael Kelly Lawler, seemed intent on enforcing Banks' orders. Loud of voice and large of frame, the forty-nine-year-old Irish-born Lawler was frequently likened to an ill-tempered grizzly, which he resembled with his black full beard and dark blue uniform. Discipline in his division was frequently enforced with his own powerful fists. To deal with drunks, he sometimes ordered his surgeons to feed them emetics in the guardhouse. Officers and men alike were frequently subjected to threats of violence and, on one occasion, he had summarily hanged a soldier for some trifling offense.

Standing before his tent near nightfall, "Big Mike" Lawler spotted a young Illinois soldier pulling boards from a planter's fence. There was nothing at all unusual about that. In the absence of tents and firewood, all the soldiers, even the Confederates, used such fences for cooking fuel and as sleeping boards to protect themselves from the moist Louisiana earth. Whether Lawler simply wanted to make an issue of the infraction or whether he was in a foul mood is uncertain. In any event he instructed his orderly to teach the young soldier a lesson by inflicting a few blows upon his body.

The startled soldier, completely ignorant of the cause of the assault, was not about to passively submit to the beating. Returning the blows, a general altercation ensued in which it appeared as though the culprit was gaining the upper hand. Lawler, who stood watching the affair from the entrance of his Sibley tent, must have concluded that the soldier's behavior was tantamount to mutiny, and mutiny would not be permitted in his division. Unsheathing his sword the big general charged like a mad bull, sword raised above his head while screaming at the top of his voice:"Kill the damned rascal! Kill him!"

And so he would have had not the frightened soldier been swift of foot. Fortunately for all, a contest was then going on between a group of magicians in the Chicago Mercantile Battery and the 56th Ohio Infantry. Eating fire, swallowing swords, cart-wheeling and performing all manner of acrobats, the entertainers had attracted a large number of onlookers with the result that Lawler's culprit soon disappeared among a sea of bluecoats. Red-faced and panting, the intemperate general soon returned to his tent. But the older brother of that Illinois soldier who had barely escaped with his life would not soon forget the event. Lawler, he vowed, would pay dearly.[28]

General Lawler would soon have more important matters demanding his attention. Even as his troops went about their business of preparing for the night, he was distracted by loud reports of artillery to the north. Like distant thunder, the low muffled sound reverberated over the treeless prairies, growing louder as it approached the concerned Yankees, until finally the ground seemed to rumble. Up near New Iberia Colonel Harai Robinson's sham Louisiana cavalry had finally met Colonel William Vincent's real Louisiana cavalry.

In Louisiana, Colonel William G. Vincent, a thirty-four-year-old native of New Orleans, was something of a legend. To many he was another John Mosby, a bigger-than-life guerilla whose heroic antics commanded the respect and admiration of all good Confederates. Schoolboys frequently ran away to join his 2nd Louisiana Cavalry. Horsemen from other regiments sometimes deserted their own to enlist in his. Youngsters adored and emulated him, frequently playing war games in which Vincent would ultimately drive away or kill all the bad guys.

BRIGADIER GENERAL MICHAEL K. LAWLER (Library of Congress)

He was also the scourge of jayhawkers and conscript evaders. Back in June, when jayhawking activities began picking up in Rapides, Calcasieu, St. Landry and Vermilion parishes, Brigadier General Alfred Mouton had issued a set of secret orders directing that "all disaffected persons, jayhawkers, etc., caught with arms, or proved to have been in arms against the Confederate authorities, should be shot without delay on the spot." Vincent's 2nd Louisiana, together with Fournet's Yellow Jacket Battalion and the 5th Texas Cavalry, had carried out these orders with a vengeance.

Led by Vincent's chief cavalry scout, the infamous Bailey Vincent of Vermilionville (Lafayette), the 2nd Louisiana Cavalry waged a war of terror and bloodshed against jayhawkers. Many were the unmarked graves, and many were the oak trees where one of Vincent's ropes had ended a life. On Bayou Mallet, a jayhawker stronghold in St. Landry Parish (near the present town of Lawtell), the very name Vincent struck fear into the hearts of disaffected citizens.

Vincent and his French-speaking cavalrymen, mainly residents of southwestern Louisiana, were also a scourge to the advancing Yankees. Dressed in Yankee blue—captured during the assault on Brashear City back in June—and accompanied by Colonel James P. Major's Texas cavalry brigade, they had never been entirely out of sight of Harai Robinson's advance guard of bogus Louisianians. Occasionally, a few shots would be exchanged, a fake charge would be made, or the Rebels would rush an isolated party and gather up prisoners. Until now, the Confederates had always given way before the Federal onslaught.

But no more. During his observations along the Teche, Mexican war hero Vincent, cunning as ever, found an opportunity too good to pass up. About two miles south of New Iberia, on the plantation of a wealthy New Orleans businessman and planter named S. O. Nelson, the roadway struck a deep hedge-lined drainage ditch (Nelson's Canal) which emptied the excess waters of the adjacent prairies into Bayou Teche. The only passage over the ditch was on a narrow brick culvert. A few yards upstream from that point, near the banks of the bayou, stood a thicket of cypress trees. What better place to conceal bushwackers, reasoned Vincent.

Though some details are missing, it appears that Robinson's "Louisiana" Yankees, together with Colonel Edmund Davis' 1st Texas Cavalry (Union) rode right into the trap. "Colonel Vincent ambuscaded them at Nelson's Bridge," wrote General Mouton that night, "leaving the road full of dead and wounded." Nonetheless it was but a short affair. Within moments the famed 2nd Massachusetts Battery of Light Artillery (Nims' Battery) joined the skirmish, driving off the Rebels with a barrage of screeching Schenkel shells.

So quickly did Vincent's two-hundred and fifty or so bluecoated cavalrymen depart that they left behind several wounded and a most curious piece of ordinance, a small breech-loading gun that threw a four-inch rifled shell. In an age of smooth-bore muzzle-loaders, this modern piece of weaponry, probably an English made Armstrong, attracted considerable attention among the Union soldiers, one of whom made the puzzled observation that "it was drawn by two little mules."[29]

CHAPTER THREE

FROM FRANKLIN TO NEW IBERIA

Monday, October 5th, 1863

FOR THE THIRD consecutive morning not a cloud appeared in the blue skies over southwestern Louisiana. The nights were pleasantly cool and the campsites much dryer. On the deeply rutted roadway, where mud and water had once made footing so treacherous, there were now several inches of finely pulverized dust. Worse still, by midmorning the weather had turned hot, with a blazing sun and no air stirred except that kicked up by the trampling of thousands of infantrymen, camp-followers, horses, mules, jackasses and some seven-hundred and fifty ammunition and supply wagons.

As the XIII Corps rolled over the prairie, taking the cut-off road from Franklin across Irish Bend, clouds of dust choked and blinded the men, turning their clothing, hair, eyebrows and faces into one dirty uniform color. For a moment there was some respite as the soldiers trampled across a corduroyed, or planked section, of a low-lying road near Bayou Yokely about midway out. Some even caught a glimpse of dead horses and a few grave markers at a point where the Rebel Texas and Louisiana cavalries had briefly tangled with their Union counterparts.

At the head of the long dirty blue column in the clear dust-free air rode Brigadier General Michael K. Lawler, the giant, irascible Irishman who headed the 1st Division. Surrounded by his headquarters staff he was, presumably, delighted to have his turn at the "right" or head of the column. Behind him, a color-bearer, distinguished by his cap, carried the 1st Division colors, a rectangular-shaped white banner with a red emblem at its center.

Lawler, in turn, was followed by another general and the headquarters staff of a brigade, their presence marked by a triangular flag. Behind these generals came a brigade of infantry, each regiment distinguished by its own colors, with a colonel in front and a heavily laden mule bringing up the rear. Then there was another brigade and still more regiments. Even the individual companies could be distinguished by the big fellows in front, tapering down to the little ones in the rear who seemed hard pressed to keep up the pace.

In the rear of each division, kicking up its own cloud of dust, were the artillery batteries. First came four enormous rifled Parrotts of the 2nd Illinois Artillery. Each cannon had once been well polished and would have sparkled brightly in the morning sunlight except for the dust-laden canvas coverings over the barrels. As it was, each piece was pulled along by teams of eight tugging horses which kicked up even more dust. Next in line was the 1st Indiana Battery with its two Rodman three-inchers, two twelve-pound brass Napoleons, and two twelve-pounder Howitzers. These were followed, in turn, by the 1st Wisconsin Battery, with four more heavy siege Parrotts under the command of a Lieutenant named Daniel Webster. Each battery was followed by the gunners; most of them rode on dark green iron-banded caissons and wore protective handkerchiefs over their mouths and nostrils.

There were also cavalry in the bristling swarm with a captain, major or colonel at the head and jingling troopers galloping behind, dashing in and out of the column to investigate some suspicious patch of woods or to look behind a farmhouse or outbuilding.

Several miles back, south of Franklin and behind dozens of other cavalry regiments, artillery batteries and thousands of infantrymen rolled the great white-topped wagons, many of them carrying such labels on the side as "Austin," "San Antonio," "Houston," and "Galveston." Driven by black teamsters and drawn by teams of long-earred mules, they were laden with rations, water, forage and reserve ammunition.

These mules were marvelous creatures. Awkward in appearance, noisy as a barnyard guinea, and endowed with a stubborn disposition, they seemed to thrive upon abuse. A certain soldier, almost asphyxiated by the dust and sweltering heat, and lying alongside the road to catch his breath, listened as the gruff teamsters coaxed their animals along with threats from long black lashes and an unrepeatable string of curses: "Yah moole!" shouted one, "I know you's tired an' weak, but there's no rest for man or beast."

Aside from the mules, perhaps no one suffered more on the march than the foot soldiers. Earlier in the day while the morning was cool and they were fresh from a good night's sleep, they had started up the road with a roll of drums and the crackling of bugles. Carrying their rifles at "Right Shoulder Shift" and with regimental flags flying, someone had struck up a song and all had joined in. Before long, however, the singing had died down to laughter and jokes and then to individual conversation and, finally, after a few miles in the heat and dust, there was nothing but the trampling of feet and an occasional outburst of groans, moans and curses. It was especially difficult for soldiers detailed as flankers, who had to "carry all that the others carry, but forsake the smooth and beaten path; climbing fences in a long line, pushing through brakes, wading through morasses, searching behind plantation buildings . . . to guard the line from rebs in ambush."

So hot and miserable was the march and so merciless the pace set by the insensitive and intemperate Lawler that it would be remembered for years. Who among them could soon forget the misery of blistered feet, the struggle to maintain one's place in the ranks, the running to catch up, the stumbling, the thirst for something to drink other than warm canteen water, the heat and the dust, knapsack straps cutting into one's shoulder, and the uniform desire to dispose of cartridge belts and clothing, canteens and packs and even rifles. Finally, when it seemed as though burning lungs could take no more, the order came to halt for ten minutes and everyone collapsed by the roadside.[1]

It was during one such break that a group of infantrymen, members of the 67th Indiana, discovered what for them was a God-send. There, in an abandoned stable along the road, was a broken down decrepit old mare. By a singular coincidence there was also a serviceable old cart, horse collar, trace chains, single tree, hame and other trappings. Although infantrymen were strictly forbidden to employ any kind of conveyance for hauling knapsacks or sore-footed soldiers, no one seemed to care and "Old Yellow," as she was called, was soon impressed into the Hoosier infantry, much to the delight of the footsore members of the 67th.[2]

The great army rolled on, complaining and cursing about Lawler, but functioning like a well oiled machine, snaking over the Irish Bend cutoff road until it once more struck the Teche near the burned out plantation home of S. W. Harding. About a half-mile further along, near another sharp bend in the Teche, there stood yet another lonely chimney, the remains of the R. H. Byrnes home. These two houses had been wantonly destroyed back during the spring invasion, because one had defiantly displayed the Confederate flag whereas the other had harbored a Rebel sharpshooter.[3]

Over the treeless prairies to the west, the marching soldiers commented on the badly ravaged plantation home of Captain F. O. Darby, which had been plundered by both Confederate and Union soldiers. In the spring, Darby, one of Vincent's cavalrymen, had barely escaped with his life when a group of Yankees, inebriated by the wines and liquors of his well-stocked cellar, had plundered and pillaged at gunpoint, taking livestock and carts, medicines, china, silver, bed and table linen, and the entire family wardrobe. As a parting gesture they had smashed all the furniture, broken the windows and "left the family standing on their bare floors."[4]

A short distance beyond Darby's, the marching soldiers came upon the home of Alexander Gabriel Fusilier de la Claire. There was no question about Fusilier's devotion to the lost cause. A thirty-four-year-old descendant of a French colonial settler and a member of one of the most distinguished families in the Attakapas, he, together with his father and brothers, owned a large tract of land along the Teche near Charenton and the Chitimacha Indian Settlement. Not far away from his house, at the point where the Fusilier property bordered the Des Lignes plantation (belonging to Martial Sorrel) there stood the remains of Confederate Camp Hunter, a once important camp of instruction. "A lovelier spot could not be found in the world," wrote a Union officer. "A hundred thousand men could be formed and marched here in turf as smooth as a billiard table."

Fusilier, as well as most of the local planters, had suffered a great deal because of that camp. First the Confederates had generously helped themselves to produce, livestock, lumber and fences, and, in general, were considered a nuisance.

Then, when the Yankees came in the spring of 1863, all the local inhabitants were looked upon as benefactors of the nearby camp and were treated accordingly. Among other things, they took Fusilier's steamer, the *Red Chief No. 2*, leaving him no means of livelihood. As a consequence he was forced to volunteer his services to the Confederacy. "I gave up the ship," he recalled many years later, "the negroes were knocking about doing hardly any work at all, and I was disgusted."[5]

COLONEL JAMES R. SLACK
(Courtesy Library of Congress)

His Negroes were not, however, entirely idle. No sooner did the long blue lines begin passing in front than an infantry brigade, Colonel James R. Slack's 2nd Brigade, 3rd Division, XIII Corps, dropped in for lunch. "Our stopping there brought out all the darkies, both old and young to see us," wrote Private Harry Watts of the 24th Indiana. "They told us the same old tale of 'Massa run, ha, ha, and Darkey stay, ho, ho'."

Colonel Slack, a forty-five-year-old lawyer, farmer, and school teacher from Huntington, Indiana, decided to avail himself of the opportunity for a little fun:

He ordered all the darkies, old and young to form in 'set' for a dance. He then had the martial band play and the darkies danced a genuine country 'hoe down' to a tune played on the fife and drum. The old ones seemed to enjoy the dance equally with the young. Their antics created considerable merriment amongst the boys who gave three cheers for Colonel Slack.

Slack probably needed the boost. A clean shaven man, a rarity in the Army of the Gulf, he was somewhat depressed because he had not yet been promoted to the rank of brigadier; nor was he entirely confident that he knew the goals of this expedition. Whereas practically everyone in Texas and Louisiana, Union and Confederate alike, seemed to know that the objective was Texas, Slack felt that he was being kept in the dark. And then there was his wife Anne back in Huntington. Perhaps, he hoped, she would be able to join him on the expedition. Only that morning, before leaving Franklin, he had posted a letter stating: "I have provided conveyance for you in the shape of a very fine ambulance. It is tight, water-proof, a good four-mule team and a careful driver, but you had better provide yourself with a good rubber *poncho*."[6]

Once beyond Fusilier's, the head of the column turned left at Camp Hunter and took another cutoff road across the Charenton Bend rather than follow the longer route along the bayou. About two miles along, they once more struck the Teche at Saule Plantation also owned by Martial Sorrel.

Here, a short distance off the road, lived Joseph Frere, a relative of the Fusiliers, who had not taken the precaution of secreting his household valuables during the previous spring. As a result, he had been conned, in the friendliest manner, to surrender virtually all his jewelry. Would he not, in return for protection, give up his watch, he had been courteously asked by a Yankee. But no sooner had the frightened planter extended the time piece than another bluecoat stepped forward. "Have you not something for me," he begged? Before long every bracelet, earring, wedding band, chain, brooch, and even a diamond stud on Frere's shirt had disappeared in a fruitless effort to gratify the petitioners' greed. The extortionists' then gave up all pretense of courtesy and proceeded to unceremoniously sack the premises.[7]

Not far away, also on the property of Martial Sorrel, stood the little store of Widow Pierre Stouff, a forty-five-year-old widow from Grandvillars, Department of Haut-Rhin. In the spring she, like Frere and everyone else, had been visited by the marauding Yankees. Now as the long blue columns passed by again, individual soldiers began darting in and out of her store, stealing merchandise off the shelf and chasing her *basse-cour* of chickens in the back yard. At one point an unidentified Union general entered the store. "I complained to him about his soldiers taking all I had," she recalled, "but I don't know what he answered, I did not speak English."[8]

About one mile north of widow Stouff's, between Bayou Teche and the roadway, there is a little rise of ground running up from the bayou and overlooking the flat extensive prairies to the west.

Here a wealthy Frenchman named Martial Sorrel had built a splendid two-story mansion with broad well-manicured lawns and tidy outbuildings and a grand view on all sides. In the front, along the tree enshrouded Teche, there was a little drawbridge operated by a hand crank and cables which led over onto the east bank where a narrow private road meandered through sugar cane fields, eventually terminating on Grand Lake beyond a section of the Great Cypress Swamp.

Late that afternoon, as the head of the XIII Corps approached the mansion, someone in the column spotted a small group of curious onlookers, white and black, leaning against the remains of a cypress rail fence, and shading their eyes from the late afternoon sun. Among the group was Paul Corner, the plantation manager, Gaspar Kobleur and Jean Deyris, the overseers, Dr. Annibal Maguire, the English-born plantation physician, and Septime Fortier, a refugee from his own burned out home in St. James Parish.

These same onlookers had played host to the relatively well-behaved Easterners of the XIX Corps only the night before, but the long blue columns now coming up the road surely meant trouble. Night was approaching and, without a doubt, the Westerners planned to camp here and plunder and destroy as the Easterners had done in the spring.

One of the mounted bluecoats near the front of the column, apparently a high-ranking officer by virtue of his wide-brim hat and "fine epaulets," spurred his horse ahead and drew to a halt in front of the onlookers. In heavily accented French the unidentified officer immediately revealed his poor command of the local language: "*Bon jour, Monsieur,*" he said, courteously tipping his hat.

Deeming it best not to antagonize this unwelcome Yankee by pointing out the hour of the day, Paul Corner returned the greeting: "*Bon jour, mon general,*" said he.

"Is this the Sorrel place?" asked the Yankee, again in atrocious French. "It is!" replied Corner, trying to supress his anxiety.

Corner, as well as the others, commenced breathing easier when the officer, just like an old neighbor, courteously inquired about the well-being of others who lived along the Teche, including Confederate Captain David Kerr, Theodore Fay, Augustine Labau, Gabriel Fusilier de La Claire, Carlos Grevenberg, and others. Though the officer's identity was never established (Corner seemed to think it was General Cuvier Grover) it was obvious that he had been here before, possibly during the spring invasion.[9]

Just as Corner was explaining that Sorrel, the plantation owner, was in France, and had been there for several years, he was utterly flabbergasted to find himself face to face with none other than Martial Sorrel himself, accompanied by his son-in-law Edouard A. Sillan, and riding at the side of General Cadwalader Washburn. Sorrel had heard about the depredations in the spring, when the Union soldiers had destroyed or had confiscated property valued at several hundred thousand dollars. Sailing from Paris to New Orleans, he arrived just in time to learn that another expedition was being fitted out and would soon be passing by his plantation. Apparently he won the friendship of the high command, including that of Banks himself, along with a promise of safeguard for his property and permission to accompany the army to his home.

Sorrel had adequate cause for concern. Each year he derived a princely revenue from the cultivation of sugar cane on his three plantations and, without a doubt, was one of the richest men in the Attakapas. Born at Chantesse, Department of Isere, France, in 1794, he had moved to Louisiana where he married the daughter and heiress of Frederic Pellerin, another wealthy planter in St. Mary Parish. With their plantations united, Sorrel grazed thousands of head of cattle and horses on his extensive pastures, which embraced over twenty-thousand acres of land, much of it fenced in. Everything that he purchased and used for cultivation of his large estates was of the best and costliest quality. He owned hundreds of slaves, but he never bought or sold a single one, leaving that unsavory task to his overseers. Of the vast herds of cattle that he raised, it was said that he rarely sold any, but kept them for the use of his family, his friends and his dependents.

Sorrel's life style as a gentlemen of leisure, absentee landlord, and man of wealth was severely disrupted by the war. He refused to support the Confederacy, although the Southerners, in turn, fought and died to uphold his source of wealth. When his son, Aruns Sorrel, was ordered to report to Camp Pratt to be conscripted into a Confederate regiment, the old man took him to France where they resided with his daughters, Emilie and Aimee, and his sons-in-law, Edouard and Emile Sillan. As a consequence of his actions the Confederates frequently levied upon his plantation for supplies and even established a large training camp—Camp Hunter—on the grounds bordering his plantation and that of the Fusiliers.

As if the Confederates weren't troublesome enough, General Banks' army, back in the spring, had swept through Sorrel's property with some fifteen thousand bluecoats, whose depots, garrisons, trains, detachments, transports and civil staff had lingered about until June. They had helped themselves freely to everything from barnyard chickens to sugar in the *sucrerie.* Fences had been destroyed, livestock taken, the grounds trampled and damaged and, worst of all for Sorrel, most of the slaves had followed the invaders. Now, the Yankees were back again, but they were forbidden to destroy or confiscate property by

General Franklin's express orders. If anything was taken, Sorrel had been assured by Franklin, he would be adequately compensated for his losses.

Many of the Union soldiers found such protection and guarantees ironic. These wealthy landowners, who derived their wealth from slavery, who fled to France or evaded the Confederate conscription laws for themselves and their sons by purchasing a substitute, or by claiming exemption as plantation managers, were now shielded by those who opposed human bondage. No such protection was accorded those who were less privileged and who fought to maintain such a lifestyle for these gentlemen. No wonder that old man Gabriel Fusilier de La Claire, a bona-fide Confederate who lived on a adjoining plantation, tugged on Sorrel's beard at every opportunity, thereby setting off a family feud that would last for years.[10]

Living just upstream from Sorrel was Theodore Fay, a native of Paris and another self-professed "Union man." Like Sorrel, Fay, age sixty-six, had suffered extensive financial losses by the presence of Union troops during the spring. Even his granddaughter's toys had been destroyed, but he had sheltered and apparently won the friendship of the Major General Commanding, Nathaniel P. Banks. Now, as the large army of Westerners went into camp on his plantation and that of the Sorrels and Grevenbergs, the invaders posted protection papers similar to the following over practically every doorway: "Mr. T. Fay has taken the Oath of Allegiance to the United States. He will not be molested in person or property."[11]

Virtually over the front door to the Fay home was posted another order:

> By authority of Maj. Gen. Franklin, a safeguard is hereby granted to Mr. Theodore Fay, his family and property. All officers and soldiers belonging to the army of the United States are therefore commanded to respect this safeguard, and to afford, if necessary, protection to the person, family and property of Mr. Theodore Fay, Parish of St. Mary's.
>
> Given at Headq's 19th Army Corps, the 4th day of October, 1863.

Indeed, everywhere the soldiers of the XIII Corps turned there was yet another protection paper. In addition, all the XIII Corps' division generals, including Burbridge, Lawler and George Francis McGinnis, had received a personal directive from General Franklin advising them to take the strictest precautions against illegal foraging, especially on the Fay, Sorrel and Grevenberg plantations.

If necessary, they were instructed, they should establish general quarters in the main dwelling houses. Lawler, of course, had his own peculiar methods for enforcing such instructions, but for General

George McGinnis, whose 3rd Division was camped nearest the Sorrel mansion, it was a different story. Not only were his troops the least disciplined in the XIII Corps, but they were also the most prolific foragers.

George F. McGinnis, a thirty-seven-year-old veteran of the Mexican War, had started his Civil War career in writer Lew Wallace's (of *Ben Hur* fame) 11th Indiana. A hat-maker by profession, he somehow took well to military life and rose rapidly in rank, especially after winning praise for his handling of troops at Shiloh, Corinth and Vicksburg. Perhaps for his lax discipline, he was also a favorite among the men who called him "Pap." Curiously enough he rode without a saddle, taking to it only in battle. "I can see him yet," wrote Lew Wallace in his autobiography, "a tall, ruddy, angular looking person, swinging forward loose-gaited at the head of the column, his sabre tucked foremost under his arm."[12]

McGinnis could also be excitable on occasion, especially when under pressure, and this was one of those occasions. Pitching his tent at the front doorsteps of Sorrel's mansion, he quickly called a conference with all his brigade and regimental commanders. Even before going into camp he had instructed them to lecture the men on the consequences of "burning of rails, killing of sheep or cattle, or the commission of the usual excesses." Now, he ordered them to post a guard around every single regiment for the evening.

To put it mildly, the men were furious. "This was considered a great invasion of their franchise," wrote a Hoosier. "We wonder which army Banks belongs to anyway," sneered a Wisconsin private. "A very unsensenable (sic) order in my opinion," wrote an Iowan in his diary. "A neutral French Creole?" scoffed Harry Watts. Why Sorrel was nothing but a Rebel and "such orders did not suit the minds of the boys for they did not believe in guarding rebel property."

If anyone knew how to circumvent such orders it was the boys of Colonel Thomas Bringhurst's 46th Indiana. It was they who had.pulled off the Brashear City Hotel caper and it was they who began plotting how to beat this one. Bringhurst, a Logansport (Indiana) attorney, was just as loath to enforce the order of posting a guard as were the men to receive it. Accordingly, he extracted a promise that none of the fence rails *on the regiment's front* would be disturbed if he ignored the order to post a guard. While the discussions were going on, however, and before any of the other regiments had posted their guards, the boys of the 46th were rapidly hauling in fences, chickens and other provisions. So fast did they work, in fact, that by the time the guards were out there was "not much to protect."

A short while later, just as the evening sun was sinking over the western horizon, General McGinnis noticed the missing fence rails and immediately sent out instructions for his regimental commanders to report to him at the mansion. As was customary on such occasions, a great deal of speculation was forthcoming as to why McGinnis had called the meeting. One of the Colonels, Daniel Macauley of the 11th Indiana, pointed to the brigade front and "suggested that the absence of fences on that line might have something to do with the business."

To be sure, "Pap" McGinnis was excited. "Pacing before his tent in an irate condition," he ignored the salutes of the worried colonels as they gathered before him. "He was as straight as a tent pole," recalled Colonel Bringhurst, "and held his head in the position of a very angry soldier."

BRIGADIER GENERAL GEORGE F. McGINNIS strikes a stiff Napoleonic pose (Library of Congress)

Stepping before the assembled officers, McGinnis asked acidly: "Gentlemen, did you happen to get an order requiring the posting of guards on the halt?"

"We did, sir," the colonels responded as in a chorus.

"How was the order obeyed? Look at the brigade front! The fences are all gone," shrieked the red-faced general.

Colonel Thomas Bringhurst, clearing his throat, summoned up the courage to refer the general to the fences, still standing, in front the 46th

Indiana. Doubting this, "Pap" McGinnis walked the short distance over toward the Hoosiers' campsite to see for himself. Shading his eyes from the evening sunlight, he finally replied: "Yes the Forty-sixth has obeyed the order. It is the only regiment that has done so. It has its fences intact."

That night, while the ever alert sentries walked their posts, the 46th Indiana—being the only one trusted by McGinnis—was called upon to guard a fat flock of sheep. It was, as a mutton-loving soldier might have wryly observed, like asking the big bad wolf himself to watch over the flock, especially since no one had bothered to take a head count.[13]

In spite of all the protection promises and guarantees of compensation for damages, Martial Sorrel did not trust his unwelcome guests. So extensive was his pastures, and so numerous his stables that the Westerners could take whatever they pleased and it would be days before he could get an accurate accounting. By then, they might be gone and no compensation would be forthcoming. With these thoughts in mind, the old Frenchman summoned his faithful servants, as well as his overseers and managers and assigned each to watch over some barn, stable, corral, chicken coop or other such minor treasures.

One of Sorrel's guards was Hyacinthe Balthazar, a twenty-one-year-old former slave who was charged with the stable mules. About 9 o'clock that night, just as Balthazar seemed to think all was going well, a large number of soldiers came rushing into the stables. The intruders immediately set about rounding up the mules and hitching them to buggies, wagons and carts, apparently in preparation for the following day's march. In the process fences were broken and doors were crashed in; mules kicked and brayed, and soldiers cursed the darkness. No one paid the slightest attention to Balthazar's protestations.

Well, perhaps they would listen to Martial Sorrel, reasoned Balthazar. Running the short distance to the mansion, he aroused the restless old man from his bed. Sorrel pulled on his boots, grabbed a shotgun and away he went stirring up pickets, generals and a large following as he neared the scene of the crime.

"He cried out to the soldiers who had the mules to halt," recalled the young guard, "and fired several shots," but without effect. Neither the mules, the culprits, nor Sorrel's temper was arrested.

A short distance down the road, another one of Sorrel's guards, Julien Etienne, was equally unsuccessful. "They took all the cows, the hogs and sheep and chickens—even mine," complained Etienne, "which they killed and ate." Another guard, Dorice Garrett, was forced to help the Yankees find mules at the point of a gun.

At widow Pierre Stouff's, the storekeeper, the Westerners took six milk cows, two beeves and about a half mile of cypress rail fencing. Over at Joseph and Adrian Frere's where the Assessor of St. Mary Parish, Sampson Pecautel, was temporarily quartered, they rounded up mules, chickens and still more fencing.[14]

Even Lawler's troops got into the act. As they did not dare trouble Sorrel, Fay or the Grevenbergs, they traveled up toward Jeanerette, where they proceeded to plunder the homes and barnyards of Annibal Maguire, Ursine Provost, Felix Guiberteau and Charles Auguste Esteve. Adam Nathan, a field hand at Guiberteau's, recalled: "I was on the gate; I told them not to take that stock, that it belonged to my old boss; they answered 'Go away, boy!' then opened the gate and drove the stock off."[15]

With so much booty coming into camp, it was inevitable that the soldiers of General McGinnis' command would feel deprived of their share. They were, after all, surrounded by guards and under orders to remain within the confines of their campsite. One of McGinnis' regiments, the 24th Indiana, had some experience in handling such matters. It was they who had looted a Brashear City warehouse, carting off commissary whiskey and saltpork brine even as their over-anxious guards looked on. Now it was they who cooked up a novel scheme, based on a few intestinal disorders, to distract the alert colonel's attention. Some of the troops, it seems, were quite uncomfortable, the result of matching tender Yankee stomachs with too many Louisiana sweet potatoes. They had dined on them the evening before and had nibbled on raw yams during the march. Now they were suffering the consequences. Stomachs rebelled, men groaned and complained, and there was an inordinate amount of traffic in the vicinity of the regimental latrine. With so much activity in and around camp, who would notice that the movement did not cease at the slit trenches? Private Harry Watts recalled:

> Colonel (William T. Spicely) got very little sleep that night as he was laying close to the guard line, and the sentinels kept hollering "Corporal of the Guard. Post Number one!" nearly all night which was a plan agreed upon by the guards. When the Colonel raised up from his blankets and wanted to know what in the devil there was so much hollering for, the guards answered that he wanted the corporal to relieve him as he was very much troubled with the diarrhea.

Colonel Spicely, himself troubled with a stomach bug, soon began to ignore the movement of soldiers running back and forth, some of them to slit trenches and others to chicken yards.[16]

And in the distance, the boom of cannon, somewhere north of New Iberia, rumbled off and on throughout the night. Apparently Robinson and Davis, heading the Union advance, was once more being harassed by Colonel William Vincent's Louisianians.

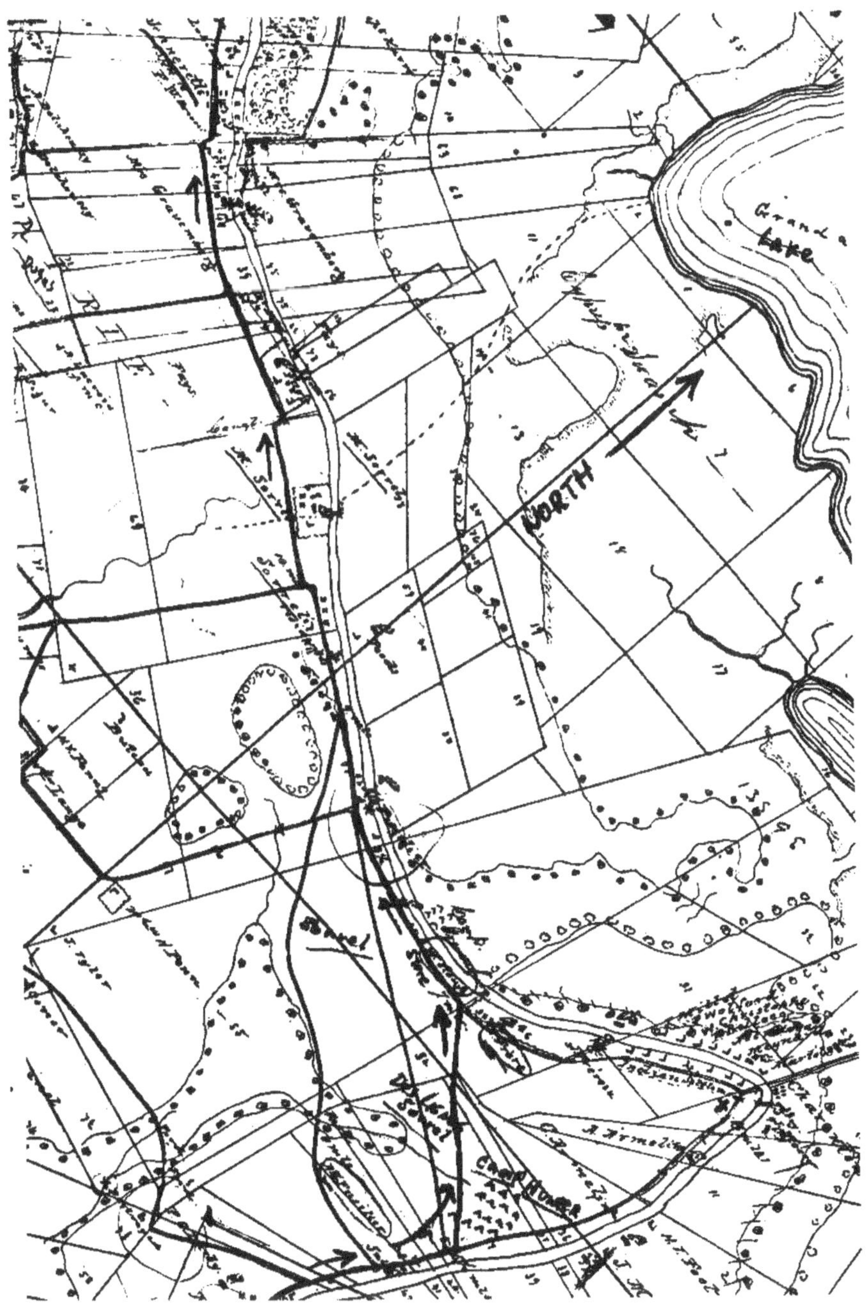

BAYOU TECHE BETWEEN FRANKLIN AND NEW IBERIA from 1863 Confederate map of St. Mary Parish (National Archives)

Tuesday, October 6, 1863

It was yet another beautiful fall day in the Attakapas. Birds were chirping happily, a gentle breeze flowed from the east, and it was pleasantly cool, but Martial Sorrel was furious. Accompanied by Major General Cadwalader Washburn and his staff and led by Hyacinthe Balthazar, the little group moved quickly from one area to another gloomily surveying the damage.

The troops had apparently enjoyed a Roman-style feast. Here were piles of malodorous offal, chicken feathers and wool, which together with the nearby carcasses of cattle and hogs attracted swarms of flies. Nearby, lying next to the charred remains of a cypress fence campfire were piles of cast-off bones. Indeed, from Jeanerette in the north, to Frere's plantation in the south, not a picket fence remained, save one small portion fronting the camp of the 46th Indiana.[17]

At the very least reasoned General Washburn, Sorrel, Fay and the others could reclaim those mules and horses which had been taken to ease the burden of the marching infantrymen on their overland trek toward Texas. Accordingly, orders went out for all such animals to be "turned over" to the quartermaster and, in turn, back to the owners.

The order was particularly distressing for some of the men in the 67th Indiana. It meant that "Old Yellow," who had rendered such notable services the previous day, would have to go. Furthermore, "Old Yellow" had been taken not from this "neutral" Frenchman but from some luckless Rebel planter alongside the road. Well, orders were orders but, if she had to go, why not have a little fun.

The harried quartermaster, trying to perform his duties before taking up the line of march, found "Old Yellow" lying on her side, "turned over" as ordered. Being a decrepit old mare, her ribs were showing beneath a skinny frame, and she was struggling to regain her feet, much as a horse might do in the final throes of death.

Turning on his heel, the quartermaster stalked off, muttering that he did not have the time or desire to bother with dying mares. Had he bothered to examine the suffering animal, however, he would have found not a dying mare but one struggling to get loose from all the ropes tied around her legs.

Three cheers went up in the camp of the 67th Indiana. What had started as a practical joke had ended with totally unexpected results. "Old Yellow" would soon be back in the Hoosier service.[18]

Before long the large army was on the march again, kicking up massive clouds of dust as it passed through the tiny village of Jeanerette and "viewing the same monotonous yet ever delightful scenery." The soldiers nonetheless passed burned out bridges, deserted plantations and a few curious onlookers along the road.

The experience of the past few days had accustomed the men to marching. By this time they had learned to keep their places and move more steadily, without so much lameness and fatigue as had previously been the case. Moreover, Lawler was not at the "right" and the older soldiers seemed to register their delight by their "peculiar, swinging, shambling gait." It was amusing, noted a soldier along the march, to hear the conversations carried on by the different parties as they trudged along:

> Sometimes they get into a loud discussions; now and then they break out in a patriotic song; again they will imitate all manner of domestic or wild animals, thereby calling forth shouts of laughter from their comrades. Occasionally they will ask all kinds of queer questions to such persons as they observe near the road.

One question frequently asked was: "Where have all the people gone?" During the first invasion, the roadside had been choked with liberated blacks, all fleeing the institution of slavery and all too anxious to follow the long blue columns to the promised land. The whites, too, had remained at home, innocently defiant and never dreaming that soldiers of the United States could in the presence of so much wealth turn into a large undisciplined mob more bent on rapine and plunder than on whipping the Rebels. So they had learned the hard way and were gone now, ironically having fled before an army of religious young midwestern farms boys who carried the Stars and Stripes. Most had gone to Texas or toward west and north Louisiana, carrying with them their few remaining slaves. "The refugees are clogging the road to Texas," wrote Judge John Moore, and "there is extortion in the pricing of all commodities." Another Louisianian, John F. Leigh, wrote Judge Moore from Houston informing him that Texas was "a hard road to travel." All the Negroes and most of the whites are ill, he wrote, victims of the "acclimating fever of refugees to this country."[19]

Not that the Westerners cared. Most did not fit the mold of the kind, gentle-hearted compassionate liberator rushing in to protect or care for these poor black refugees of war as depicted in many novels and dramatizations of Civil War events. No doubt there were some of these and possibly many, but the diaries, letters, legal claims, regimental histories and newspaper reports of the period tell a different story.

Blacks, it was generally felt, were useful as servants, bootblacks, cooks, and ditch diggers. Moreover, they were musicians who could entertain and who served as the butt for all manner of crude, sometimes cruel, practical jokes. Not a few soldiers hated them passionately, choosing to blame them for the misery of war and suffering. "How much white blood must be shed," asked one Yankee, "to save each black African hide?" Another, a Westerner who was wounded at Vicksburg, complained bitterly in a letter to his mother: "To think all this is caused by a nigger. I can hardly stand it."

Somewhere along the march that day one of these black-hating soldiers came across a small group of servants who, at the time, were sprawled beside a Cherokee rose hedge fence and heaping gratuitous praise upon the passing bluecoats. "Bress de lawd!" they shouted. "Bress you, Linkum sojers!"

Consumed by hate and fed up with such incessant lauding, the soldier in question fired back some very nasty remarks, including a few racial epithets which at the same time called into question the intelligence of blacks in general and these in particular. Such language, needless to say, did not go down well with the group. An old black mammy, "charcoal in color, wearing a red bandana about her head with a young child suckling at an exposed breast" quickly shot back: "Well if we'un's is so iggerant and you'uns is so smat," she asked, "then how come we'uns is sitting heah under a tree while you'uns is gwine off to get yo'self shot by a rebel?" And that was precisely why the antagonist was so sore.

Indeed, there was every reason for those blacks who remained to be less than enthusiastic about running off to help the Yankees. In the spring, the Union invasion had "turned the negroes crazy." Many of them turned on masters with a vengeance, plundering and burning, killing livestock, destroying produce and serving their liberators as though there was no tomorrow. After all, they claimed, these goods had "been acquired by their labor." By the tens of thousands they had run off, joining, in one case, Chickering's eight-mile long wagon train of booty heading down the Teche toward Brashear City. "How far ter de Jordan?" some had innocently asked.

As it turned out, the Atchafalaya was not the Jordon and neither was Berwick's Bay the elusive promised land. The young able-bodied males were quickly mustered into the military service—the *Corps d' Afrique* —while others were sent to Union-controlled plantations along the Mississippi. The elderly, the young, lame, and the sick were frequently left to fend for themselves. Taken away from the plantations' paternalistic environment, the only one they had ever known, many immediately succumbed to hunger, swamp fever, and exposure. A few had returned of their own volition; others were rounded up and taken back when the Confederates reoccupied the Teche and LaFourche country in the summer of 1863.

All of which is not to say that blacks were unhappy over this second invasion. On the contrary, those that remained stood alongside the road and cheered on the invaders; others, especially the young males and able-bodied females, tried to run away a second time. Before long, in fact, there was an army of camp followers in the rear of the Union column, but it was far smaller and much less enthusiastic than the one which nad clogged the roads in the spring. The road to Jordan, it must have seemed, was filled with toil, suffering and heartbreak.[20]

Not far upstream from Jeanerette, still on the west bank of Bayou Teche, the column passed a burned out bridge leading to the deserted mansion of Alfred Weeks. Here, next to a swamp of moss-covered cypress trees, water lillies and alligators, lived a beautiful young lady named Mary, who was enamored of Captain Oliver Semmes, the handsome former commander of the gunboat *Diana*, now in charge of the 2nd Confederate Artillery Battery (Semmes' Battery) and son of Confederate Admiral Raphael Semmes of *CSS Alabama* fame. It would not be long before Captain Semmes' blazing guns would be trained upon these very same Yankees.[21]

Above this point the soldiers found the Teche much more densely settled. Here was J. Dietlien's warehouse and there was Senetaire's store—all familiar sights to the Easterners, but entirely new sources of plunder for the Westerners. Across the Teche, inaccessible now because of the burned bridges, lived the Richardsons, the Vaughns, another Weeks family and the McCarthys. There was also a little schoolhouse, right next door to the Browns, followed by William Grevenberg, Dr. Duncan, Mrs. Thompson and Dubriel Olivier.

There was something unusual about the Dubriel Olivier mansion, at least to the soldiers of the XIX Army Corps. As they passed in front of the mansion the day before, it had been the subject of gesturing fingers, head-nodding, speculation and some spirited disagreements. The dwelling itself was just another mansion alongside the Teche. Olivier was wealthy, he was an extensive slaveowner, he had raised and equipped a company of soldiers for the Confederacy—or so it was argued—and, according to rumor, he was married to a Yankee woman who had come south to teach. So what was so unusual about that?

Back in the spring a large number of Yankee soldiers had gone crashing through the front doors, looting and smashing. Before long, however, they were confronted by a well-dressed, light skinned Negress, presumably the maid, who indignantly ordered them out. Laughing and jeering they had asked her: "Where is your master?" and at the same time they had rebuked her for not showing more respect for white folks.

Not that it made much difference to the intruders but, as it turned out, this lady was Aimee Gradenigo, the widow of Dubriel Olivier, who also happened to be black. She, like her former husband and many other *gens de coleur libre* —"free people of color"—in the Attakapas and Opelousas country, had shrewdly patterned her own life style after that of her wealthy white manumitters.[22]

Commenting on this curious phenomenon in a letter from New Iberia, an officer in the 12th Connecticut, John William Deforest, wrote:[23]

> You would be amazed to see the swarming mulattos and quadroons and octoroons who possess this region and call themselves Americans. Some of the richest planters, men of really great wealth, are of mixed descent. When we march through a town the people who gather to stare at us remind me of the Negro quarters of Philadelphia and New York. I understand that very few of them speak English and that they are nearly all extremely ignorant. These are not the former slaves, observe, but the former masters.

Only a short distance upstream from Olivier's, just beyond the St. Charles tannery, the soldiers of the XIII Corps finally caught up with their eastern comrades. The delay, they were told, was caused by some obstructions upstream in the Teche, and all would have to remain in camp here until further orders.

That was just fine with the boys from the XIII Corps, who immediately set about looking for boards and food. At the campsite of the 67th Indiana "Old Yellow" again rendered important service by hauling in loads of rails, "beneath which often lay a rebel hog." The 46th Indiana, Colonel Thomas Bringhurst's Hoosiers, wasted no time in "replenishing their haversacks," and the noisiest regiment of all, the diarrhea-suffering 24th Indiana, went on a "foraging spree" that lasted for days.

Among the foragers of the latter regiment was a certain "Fzs," a large blue-eyed, sandy-haired German, who, according to all accounts, was the funniest, most bungling character who ever shouldered a musket. His English, according to friends, was atrocious, and he possessed a brain which seemed to function as poorly. With his oversized shoes and awkward gait he never seemed to catch his elusive prey, whether it was fleeing chickens, a frightened porker or Rebel calf. But there was one golden treasure which never eluded him, possibly because it couldn't run away, and that was the prolific pumpkin which grew alongside the road in every ditch, weed-filled garden, or neglected field in southwestern Louisiana.

The foraging on that particular day had never been better and "most of the boys returned to camp laden with supplies." Recalled Private Harry Watts: "Any stranger to have passed through would imagine himself in a poultry yard to have seen the turkeys and chickens tied to every shebang." While waiting for "Fzs," who always seemed to get lost, the men cooked a "luxurious meal which no one ought to grumble at." The only complaint, again according to Private Watts, "was in the culinary arrangements, for we were very short of cooking utensils and had to cook our chickens on sticks in the ashes, or stew them in coffee pots."

Just as the sun was sinking over the western horizon and "Fzs" was about given up for lost, or possibly captured by the Rebels, a cheer went up from one of the campfires. Thundering over the prairie, came their lost hero with a broad grin upon his puffy red cheeks. Incredibly, he had "captured an old gray mare with a bridle on and came riding into camp as large as Lucifer—with his head up—and laden with a string of chickens, one pig, and an everlasting 'punkin'."[24]

For the plundered residents along the route the lowly pumpkin was a blessing in disguise, because after the XIII Corps had camped there for three days, there was not much left to eat. One planter, a butcher named Charles Clerc, watched the invaders take off all his tools, cart, horses and cattle. When he went into camp begging for some food for himself and family he was told he could have some only for payment. "They took my cow," Clerc recalled bitterly, "and I had to pay four cents a pound to get a piece of it."

Louis and Etienne Frilot, planters living on the site, complained fruitlessly as their cattle were driven away and their fences dismantled. At St. Charles tannery, owned by Jules Poirson and Francois Lanet, the damage was severe. Cattle were taken, as were hogs, chickens, horses, corn, a skiff and even the tannery tools. Many of the animals were slaughtered, cooked and eaten virtually in Poirson's yard.

"Everything was taken from the garden or destroyed," complained Mrs. Poirson. "The trees were uprooted and broken by the horses and mules; the pecan trees were cut down; the fence was burned; the potatoes were dug and the horses and mules of the soldiers ate the corn."

Poirson, a thirty-four-year-old Frenchman from Limcourt, Department of Vosges, France, added: "I never made any complaint to the officers—neither I or my partner—because I could not speak English and my partner, Francois Lanet (from Briancourt, Department of Haute-Marne) could speak but a little of it."

These scenes, differing only in minor details, repeated themselves at every house and outbuilding from the rear of the column downstream, and upstream as far as New Iberia. Eugene and Devezin Olivier, once wealthy and prestigious planters, were reduced to penury, as was S. O. Nelson, Dasincourt Borel, James H. Ford, Ellen Burke and Victor Boutte.[25] Thus, what to the Yankee was a few days of fun and feast, translated over as deprivation, humiliation, fright and, in some cases, starvation for these innocent civilian victims of war.

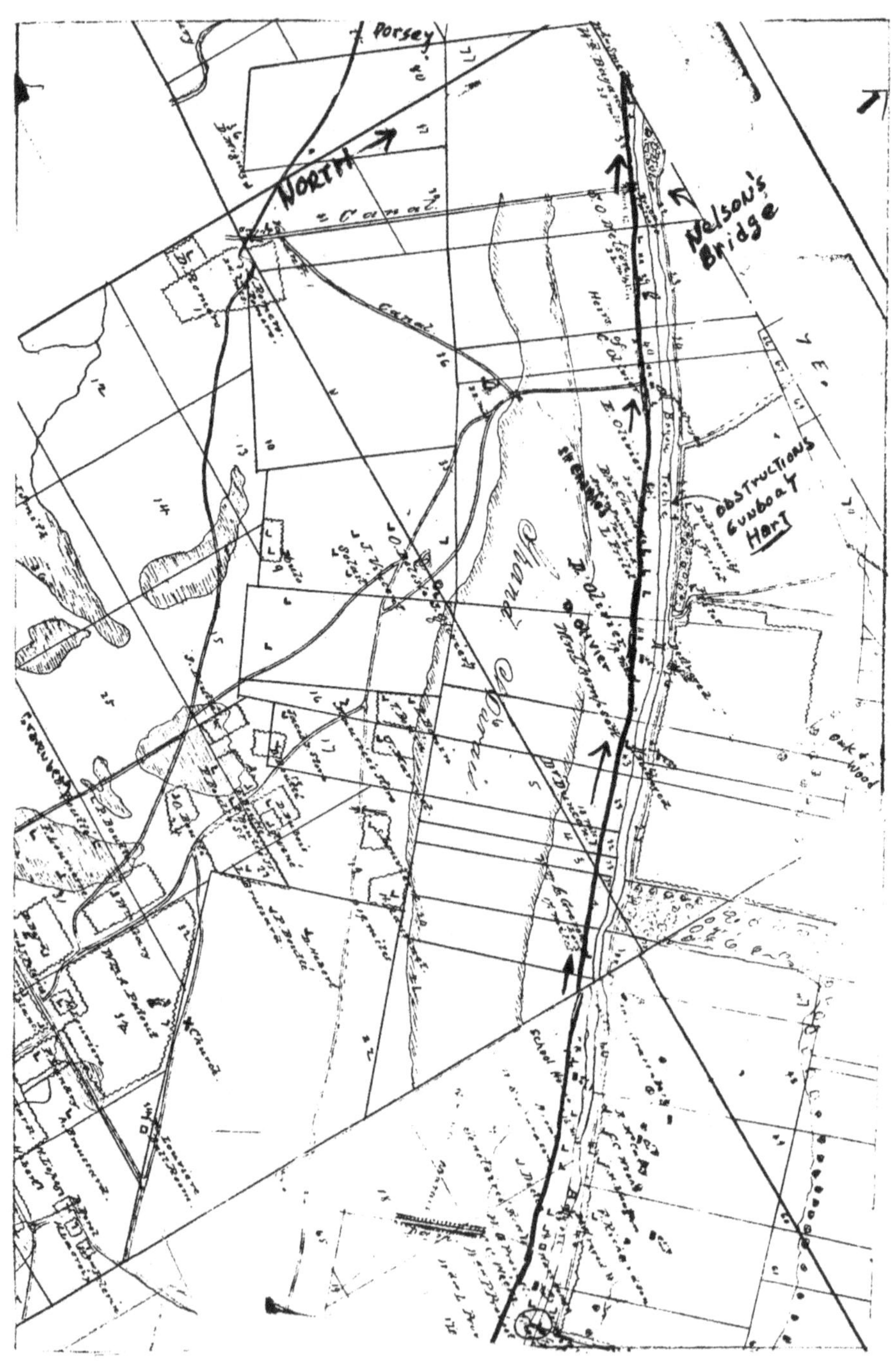

BELOW NEW IBERIA ON THE TECHE from 1863 map of St. Mary Parish (National Archives)

CHAPTER FOUR

AND OVER THE PRAIRIES

Wednesday, October 7, 1863

"BEAUTY," as Union General Lew Wallace once observed, "is altogether in the eye of the beholder." And so it was in New Iberia when, for three days in the fall of 1863, the long blue lines came marching through. A New Yorker remembered it as nothing more than "a collection of houses." Another New Yorker wrote that it was "commonly called by the inhabitants New Town." A soldier from Ohio made reference to its "surly citizens." A Hoosier, who had earlier passed through as a prisoner of the Confederates, wrote that it was "a little town with dirty streets, and a strong sheepy smell." Few apparently thought worse of it than an unidentified war correspondent for the *Wisconsin Home League*. "The inhabitants," he wrote, "are French and mongrel, ignorant, selfish and arrogant—fit subjects for a cursed rebellion."

New Iberia was also "beautiful," "pleasant," "large," "friendly," and "neat" with "several churches and some fine residences." Captain Charles A. Lucas—a former officer in the Belgian army, native French-speaker and member of the 24th Iowa Infantry observed that most of the inhabitants were friendly and "seemed to be for the Union."[1]

Indeed, in New Iberia, as in other areas of southwestern Louisiana, there were plenty of Union sympathizers. One of these was Dr. Alfred Duperier, a thirty-seven-year-old planter, physician, local politician and scion of one of the town's founding fathers. Standing on Main Street in a drizzling autumn rain, he and Mayor Alexis Derouen, Judge Theodore Fontelieu and several others officially surrendered the town to Union authorities.

Duperier told the Yankee generals that although New Iberia was a town of divided loyalties, the majority of its citizens remained faithful to the United States. He then implored them to avoid the atrocious behavior which had marred the spring invasion and occupation. At that time houses had been entered and their contents sacked or maliciously destroyed. Anything left behind had been carted off by Captain Alanson B. Long of the 52nd Massachusetts Infantry who had respected neither loyalty nor dark skins. Many of the blacks had been conscripted against their will while most of the local planters and businessmen, including Moses Adler, Charles Bouligny, Henry Taylor, J. D. Swayne, Phillip Rozier, Aime Hervien, James Fletcher Wyche, Bernard Subervielle and others, had been "cleaned out."[2]

NEW IBERIA, Louisiana, in 1863 ***(Leslie's Illustrated Weekly)***

In spite of Duperier's pleas for order the Yankee cavalrymen, led by Harai Robinson's bogus Louisianians, went charging through the streets and commenced bullying their way into shops, residences and churches. Under the pretext of looking for Rebel snipers, they knocked down doors, broke windows and threatened to shoot anyone who got in their way.

In the meantime, the Union provost marshals, the Signal Corps, the medical staff and the Union headquarters' staff began selecting facilities and supplies for their operations, as did the quartermasters, blacksmiths, farriers, regimental cooks, and even the men.

At the Planters' Hotel, owned by fifty-three-year-old Joseph Decourt of Bordeaux, France, the premises were converted into a hospital for the sick and wounded. Another medical station was established in the Episcopal church. Several grist mills around town were seized and put into operation, as was Jasper Gall's sawmill.

The U. S. Signal Corps moved their telegraph and communications equipment into Bernard LaPlene's billiard hall and barroom, and in the process literally booted LaPlene into the street. His barkeeper, Edward Marie, watched as they commenced drinking up all the liquor. "They cleaned the man out," recalled Marie, "clean up."

The Weeks' family mansion, known currently as The Shadows, was seized once again as a command post. "It was a quaint old house," recalled an earlier invader, "filled with rich, old furniture and costly china imported from France." Unfortunately for the owners, a half-dozen or so Rebels had used the premises to fire upon the advancing Yankees in the spring. After the defenders had been killed, one by one, their bodies were dragged into the front yard for public display. A Union officer, Captain John G. Mudge of Petersham, Massachusetts, explained what then occurred:

> ...in consideration of the well-known hostility of the owners to the Union and that the rebs had fired from this house upon our advance, the boys were allowed to go through it, sack, pillage and destroy every article within its walls...As I passed into the back court I saw Madam (presumably Mary Clara Conrad Weeks Moore) the lady of the house. She sat at the foot of a tree. Her long white hair hung loosely on her shoulders—a perfect picture of despair, hatred and rage with the ruin which surrounded her.

Major General Banks had subsequently used the house for his personal headquarters. And tonight, General William Franklin would rest his head here as would other generals in the days to come.

Even David Robert's blacksmith shop, over which flew the Union Jack, fell to the intruders. Unsatisfied with merely using the premises for their own smiths, they soon set about pulling down his fences, eating his chickens (including those of his next door neighbor, Dr. Henry Stubenger) and stealing his household valuables. Roberts, a native of Montreal, Canada, was quick to display his papers from the British Consulate. "During the past year," he acidly informed the intruders, "Eastern troops frequently came here, but without molesting me." The Westerners, however, only laughed at his pathetic protestations, or, as an Iowan put it: "Our men told him to go back to England if he did not like our ways."[3]

Thursday, October 8, 1863

The sun, absent for only one day, was shining again. There were a few mud holes from the previous day's rain but it had not cooled off. If anything, it was warmer.

And the Easterners of the XIX Army Corps were in motion again. Instead of turning to the right and following the road to St. Martinville, as some of them had done in the spring, they took the stagecoach road across the prairies toward Vermilionville. The two-day wait-over in New Iberia had been occasioned, not so much by the obstructions in Bayou Teche, which still remained, as by indecisiveness on the part of General Franklin and Banks. Which route should be taken, wondered field commander Franklin? Should they strike toward Texas across the prairies from New Iberia or should they advance toward Vermilionville, as they had done in the spring?

The latter option was finally decided upon by the Major General Commanding, Nathaniel P. Banks, then en route from Brashear via steamer. It would be too dangerous, he reasoned, to venture very far from their route of supplies—the Teche—with the possibility of Rebel cavalry hanging upon their rear. The route toward Vermilionville was off the Teche but it was a familiar one; it too connected with a road leading toward Texas and was easily accessible by wagon from the head of navigation below New Iberia on the Teche. In addition it left open another option. Opelousas was not far away and could easily be serviced by steamers and gunboats from Barre's Landing (Port Barre) on the Courtableau, which connected with Brashear City via the Atchafalaya.[4]

Moving forward, the troops passed the remains of Camp Pratt, a former Confederate camp of instruction on the banks of Spanish Lake and a now familiar sight to many of these soldiers. Named for militia General John G. Pratt, a resident of Opelousas and its first commander, it was thoroughly disliked by the reluctant Cajun conscripts who referred to it as "Camp Purgatory." A Yankee described it as nothing more than "a collection of plank wedge-tents with...small editions of the stars and bars flapping their greasy folds in the breeze."[5]

Beyond the Rebel camp the Yankees entered a new and different region—prairie country, broken only by an occasional tree line along some nameless coulee or by an "isle" of chinaberry trees, live oaks and magnolias surrounding the little cabin of a French-speaking planter or rancher.

This was also the heart of the Acadian, or Cajun country. Here, in the parishes of Lafayette, St. Martin and St. Landry the dispossessed inhabitants of *Nouvelle Acadie* had settled more than a century before. They had been exiled from their northern homeland by the British, then betrayed, as many felt, by Napoleon at the time of the Louisiana Purchase. Many had once lived along the lower Teche, but had forsaken their bayou holdings because of the contrasting lifestyles with the Anglo-Americans, Creoles, French and Spanish who seemed to believe that Cajuns, as they were called, were inately inferior. Out on the open prairies, however, they could pursue their own life style as *petit habitants*, not entirely without slaves, but in a setting where large families supplied most of their own labor.[6] Confederate General Richard Taylor, himself a Louisianian, could write compassionately of these people whom he knew and loved.[7]

> Isolated up to the time of the war, they spoke no language but their own patois; and, reading and writing not having come to them by nature, they were dependent for news on their *cures* and occasional peddlers, who tempted the women with chiffons and trinkets-...Their little *cabanas* dotted the broad prairie in all directions. Here, unchanged, was the French peasant of Fenelan and Bossuet...Tender and true were his traditions of *la belle France* and gentle was his nature.

Even the surnames were different. Before, along the lower Teche, the names had been mainly English, with a few French, Spanish and Irish ones thrown in. There now predominated such appelations as Boutte, Melancon, Bourque, Landry, Duhon, Guidry, Boudreaux, Babin, Broussard, Dugas, Trahan and Comeaux, their purity broken only by an occasional Lopez, Vincent, Hawkins, Miguez or Segura.

Occasionally the Yankees passed a house where someone had recently whitewashed a front gate and perhaps the chimney to indicate that a marriagable girl lived here. There was even a little French tune with appropriate lyrics:

> *C'est dans la maison la-bas*
> *qui a une cheminee blanche,*
> *La fille qui est dedans*
> *Est belle et bien plaisante*

To be sure French was the common language, and Catholicism the religion shared by all. And almost all the Acadians eked out a humble existence in a pastoral economy, grazing their branded herds of long-horned cattle *au large* on the endless prairies. But there the similarities ended, because there was no unanimity of opinion regarding the war. Like other things about them, their attitudes defied simple generalization. So wide in fact was the divergence of views and so mixed the emotions that fratricidal strife was inevitable.

Although they were French in every respect, they were also citizens of the Confederacy and as such, subject to the conscription laws of Louisiana. Many willingly served, volunteering early in the war, and had distinguished themselves on the faraway battlefields of Virginia and Tennessee, but others were strongly opposed to secession and wished either to remain loyal to the Union or to be left alone altogether by the "American" Confederates.

For the Acadians the bitterest pill of all was that the recently-arrived, more affluent Frenchmen managed to retain their French citizenship and were thus exempt from the conscription laws. Unlike the

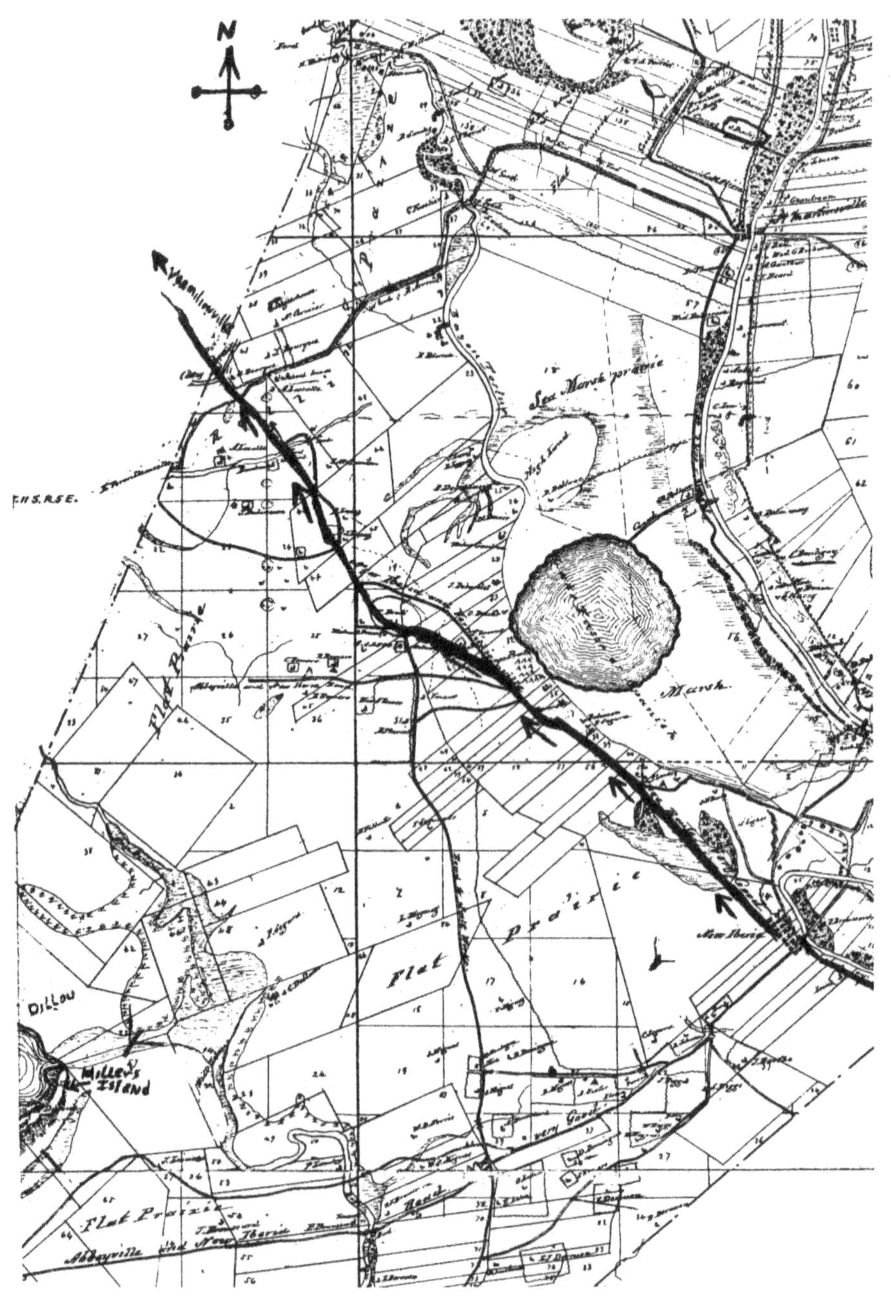

PRAIRIE COUNTRY between New Iberia and Vermilionville, from 1863 Confederate map of St. Martin Parish. (National Archives)

Acadians, who had come to Louisiana dispossessed and penniless, these new arrivals brought with them skills, education, money and household valuables. Many had become merchants, affluent planters, and even wartime speculators. When conscripted, as some were, they waged a successful legal battle against the state and remained civilian.[8] In the meantime the Acadians, who were no less French, were forced into uniform.

Although most had reluctantly submitted and fought for the Confederacy, others were taken at gunpoint. When such men were impressed they served poorly, frequently deserting and going home on the first occasion, or defecting to the enemy or, during a retreat, lagging behind to be deliberately captured.

The alternative was to flee to Texas, the Atchafalaya wilderness or to the lawless prairies of Vermilion or western St. Landry Parish. A few remained at home and devised all sort of ingenious hideaways. When the Confederate conscription teams came, as they inevitably did, the evaders took to holes in the ground, to attics, trees, underbrush, haylofts, piles of sheepskins or cowhides, and even to water troughs; and when the Union forces came through, some of the Acadians even joined a Yankee regiment, or served as scouts for the Union army while large numbers lined up to take the infamous Oath of Allegiance to the United States. (See Appendix).

As far as the loyal Confederates were concerned these people were traitors and, according to orders cut by Confederate General Alfred Mouton, himself of Acadian descent, the deserters and conscript evaders were to be treated as jayhawkers. Accordingly, they were relentlessly pursued by William Vincent's 2nd Louisiana Cavalry, Valsin Fournet's Yellow Jacket Battalion (which ironically had perhaps the highest desertion rate in the entire Confederacy) by H. A. McPhaill's despised "Texicans" of the 5th Texas Cavalry and by Opelousas militia General John G. Pratt, a transplanted Yankee. Many were hunted and tracked down with bloodhounds. Once caught they were either brutalized and sent back to their regiments or, in many cases, dispatched to eternity by a shotgun blast, firing squad or rope from a tree. Jayhawking for many became the only means of survival.

Indeed, Ozeme Carriere up in St. Landry Parish became something of spiritual inspiration to many Acadians. Throughout the early autumn, rumors began filtering in that he had survived yet another concerted effort to destroy his organization. Whether he was good or bad was beside the point. The fact is that he provided some modicum of security against the brutal enforcement of the conscription laws and thus, for many, was the only alternative to the executioners. No wonder that the Acadians were despised by the Texas and Louisiana Confederates. It also explains why the guards around "Camp Purgatory" (Camp Pratt) were not so much to keep outsiders out as to keep insiders in.[9]

CONSCRIPT EVADERS seek refuge in the Great Cypress Swamp *(Harper's Weekly)*

RELUCTANT REBELS fleeing from Confederate enrolling authorities *(Harper's Weekly)*

The Union invaders, like the Texas Confederates and conscript enforcers, also had a low regard for the poorer Cajuns of southwest Louisiana. Part of it might have been the heat during the march and the muggy humidity. Suffering from thirst they were frequently compelled to drink warm stagnant water from "sinkholes" or *marais* and ditches along the way. Then, too, the country bore the ravaging marks of Banks' earlier invasion. Fences had been torn down and burned, houses had been rifled, crops had been trampled down and the bones of butchered animals—some of them shot for no apparent purpose—were everywhere visible. At any rate the soldiers chose to accentuate the negative. "The country was inhabited with the most ignorant and wretched class of Creoles," wrote a New Yorker, "unable to speak the English language, or convey an intelligent idea in the national tongue." Wrote another:

> The inhabitants, nearly all French, have little or no labor to do, and invariably do as much less than little as the human system will bear. Ignorance, superstition and idleness are in the ascendant. They are, moreover, traitors and spies as far as their capacities go.

Equally nasty were the views of a war correspondent for *Harper's Weekly:*

> Without education, energy or ambition they are good representatives of the white trash. So little are they thought of that the niggers, when they want to express contempt for their own race, call him an Acadian nigger.

Such views, however contemptuous, seem to have been the rule rather than the exception. In all the dozens of extant letters, diaries, personal reminiscences and newspaper reports left behind by the invading Yankees, there are precious few kind words about these people. In fact, about the only person who saw anything positive about the Acadians was a surgeon of the 22nd Kentucky (Union), B. F. Stevenson, who wrote his wife Delia:

> With me the country has an added interest from the fact that here are found the descendants of the Acadians, the story of whose wrongs and wanderings Longfellow has so well embalmed in song. They lead pastoral lives, grazing their flocks and herds over the boundless prairies of this region. The present generation know only through tradition of the wrongs and sorrows of their progenitors.
>
> On the bleak shores of their northern island home, the Gallic blood of the tribe would have frozen out long before this, and the world would have lost Longfellow's song of tenderness and beauty. Here, however, under a genial sun, and in a fruitful happy clime, they have grown and expanded into stately stems, which, like the grand old oaks of this region, give support and protection to all the

> clinging tendrils that single them out for shelter. They are bland, courteous, and hospitable to excess.

Stevenson was the rare exception. The plain fact is that the Federals who invaded southwestern Louisiana in 1863 did not like the Acadians.[10]

Once in Lafayette Parish, the Yankees passed Boutte's half-way House where for generations, wayfarers had halted to rest and water their horses and to seek food and refreshments for themselves. It was a convenient location for the U. S. Signal Corps, who immediately commandeered the premises and outbuildings to post a semaphore team and telegraph operator.

Not far beyond, after crossing a treeless, rolling prairie and a few abandoned houses, they came upon the tiny community of Cote Gelee or, as it was subsequently called, Broussard. Here, amid beautifully rolling and undulating hills, were a post office, several stores and a few residents, mainly Broussards, Bernards, Melancons and Landrys.[11]

Cote Gelee, like dozens of other tiny communities in Louisiana, still retained the marks of the previous Union invasion. Houses had been plundered, a store had been burned and worst of all, a certain Mr. Fontenot, well advanced in years, had almost lost his life. A Yankee, it seems, had been quarreling over spoils with another and shot his comrade to death, and had left his prostrate body sprawled on the lawn before the frightened old fellow's house. With the passage of the next division, however, it was assumed that Fontenot had ended the unfortunate soldier's life. A firing squad was drawn up and the helpless old man, who frantically begged to converse with someone who understood French, was made to kneel before the corpse. Whether they would have shot him or not remains an open question. In any event a burial party soon arrived, sent back from the division in advance, and Fontenot, as he believed, was "rescued from the jaws of death."[12]

Now Fontenot, as well as most of the other residents, had fled in advance of the marching Union columns. And it was well that they had done so because the next day, a division of the XIII Corps would be passing through.

Just beyond Cote Gelee, the exact spot is uncertain, the division of Brigadier General Godfrey Weitzel went into camp for the night. Thirsty, tired and hungry, they were far too concerned about what they believed would be a severe battle at Vermilion Bayou four or five miles ahead to go out foraging for a decent meal. "It was universally known among rank and file," recalled a New Yorker, "that since the evacuation of this country in the spring, the enemy had concentrated a large force upon the northern bank, where he had constructed heavy earthworks." Accordingly, they lay down to sleep in the open prairie, "feasting in imagination upon fresh steaks and livers and choice bits," and trying hard not to worry about what the morrow might bring.[13]

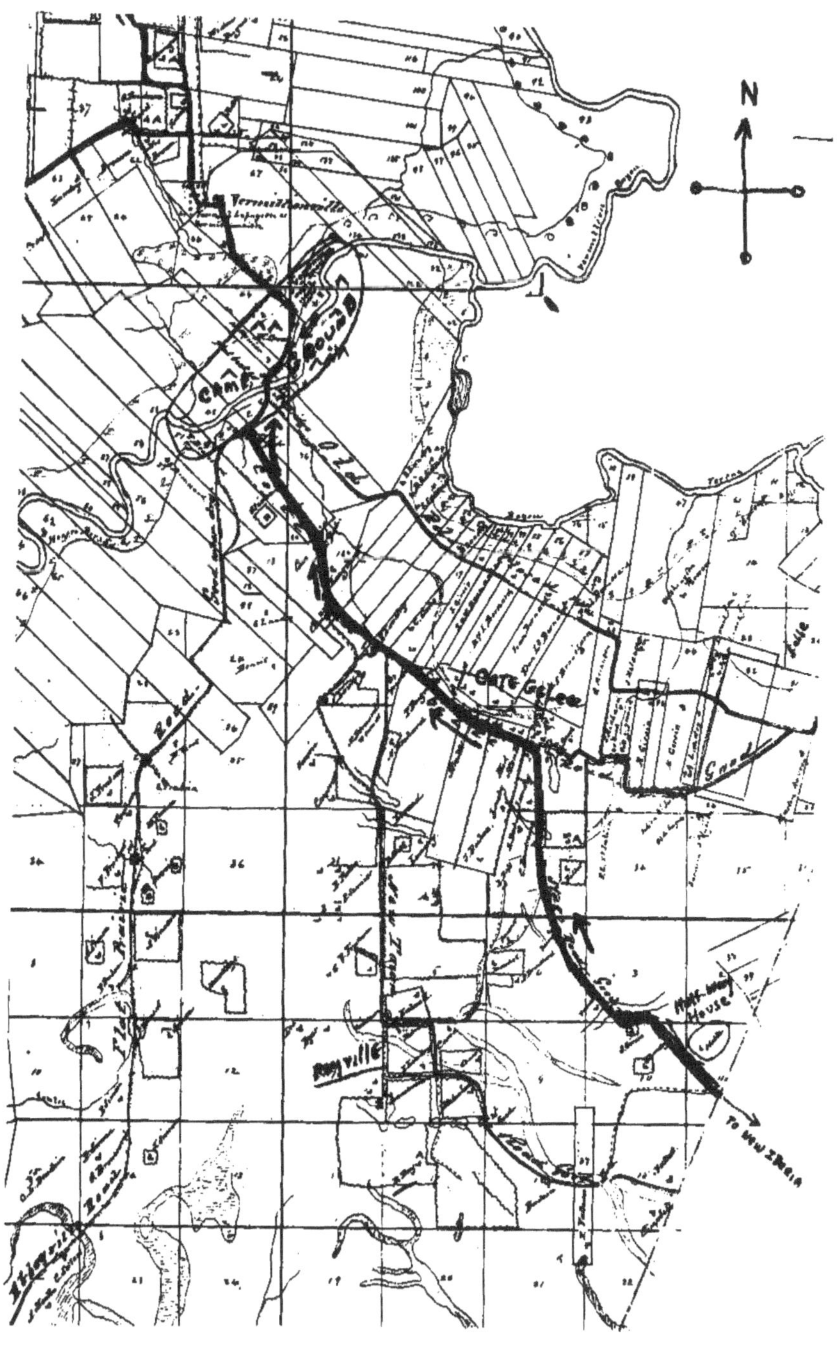

LAFAYETTE PARISH south of Vermilionville, from 1863 Confederate map (National Archives)

While the Easterners marched over the prairies toward the Vermilion, the little politician-turned-soldier, Major General Nathaniel P. Banks, was making his way up the Teche. Early that morning Banks, the architect of the Great Texas Overland Expedition, had boarded the steamer *A. G. Brown* at Brashear City in the company of staff, orderlies, newspaper correspondents and a few other VIP's. The security arrangements were extraordinary. Few people even knew of Banks' presence, and those who did were ignorant of his destination. No one, other than those who accompanied him, was permitted on board, and the general himself was quartered below decks as a precaution against snipers.

In spite of all the secrecy, the security measures and the preparations, the trip up the Atchafalaya and on into the Teche was anything but incident-free. The first problem occurred just below the site of the sunken Rebel gunboat, the *J. A. Cotton,* where the night before, the Union steamer *St. Charles* had run aground while trying to maneuver past the hazardous obstructions placed there by the Confederates.

What embarrassment, one wonders, if not panic, was experienced by the skipper of the striken vessel when he learned that General Banks himself, the Commander of the Department of the Gulf, in whose fate rested tens of thousands of men, was being held up because of his presence?

The efforts to free the *St. Charles* suddenly became frantic. Enlisting the assistance of Banks' steamer, the *A. G. Brown,* ropes and cables were fastened fore and aft, and all began working to tug her free.

On the deck of the *A. G. Brown,* watching with bemused interest, stood Major General E.O.C. Ord, the newly-appointed no-nonsense commander of the XIII Corps, en route to join his Westerners up near New Iberia. There was also Brigadier General Charles Stone, Banks' recently resurrected Chief of Staff, as well as Adjutant General J. Schuylar Crosby, Colonel Nathan A. M. Dudley (Banks' Assistant Chief of Staff) and several other high ranking officers. Indeed, double-breasted generals, colonels and majors were everywhere, with stars, eagles and leaves, as were slimmer and younger captains and lieutenants with single row buttons and highly-polished boots. There was even a political official from Iowa aboard, a certain Commissioner Daniels, as well as several newspaper correspondents, including one from the *New York Herald* and the *Wisconsin State Journal.*

Never before had these harassed skippers and crewmen been under such close scrutiny from so much brass. Desperately trying to succeed—and to please the onlooking crowd—the nervous pilot of the *A. G. Brown* failed to notice the overhanging boughs of a great live oak as the steamer tugged away, going backward. And when he did notice it was too late. With a scraping, breaking sound both smokestacks were soon sheared from their mooring plates and came crashing down upon the wheelhouse with a thundering noise. Amid the falling debris of tree limbs, smokestacks, and splinters, generals scurried for cover, colonels cried out in anguish, newspaper correspondents lost their notes and several crewmen, bodyguards and lieutenants went over the side.

Nonetheless the *St. Charles* and her red-faced skipper had been pulled free and now it was her turn to assist. Fortunately the damage to the *A. G. Brown* was not irreparable and , aside from a few bruises and broken bones, no one was seriously injured. After some unsightly improvisions, a lot of cursing and grumbling, and four more hours of delay, the *A. G. Brown* was pronounced seaworthy, if not exactly shipshape. Building up a head of steam, she once more proceeded up the Teche with her important human cargo.[14]

Bayou Teche, according to popular tradition, derived its name from the Attakapas word *Tenche*, meaning snake. Whether it came from the sheer abundance of these venomous reptiles along its banks, or the meandering, almost snake-like, course of its gentle southerly flow, or from the legendary presence of a mighty serpent in antiquity, no one really knows. At any rate it was navigable, depending on the time of year and size of vessel, from its mouth on the Atchafalaya almost as far north as its source on Bayou Courtableau near Barre's Landing.

Popularized in song and legend, especially in Longfellow's immortal *Evangeline*, it was one of the most beautiful streams in the south, even to the Yankees. A curious feature, and one which attracted the attention of all who traversed its course, was the solid green mat of water lotus (probably *nymphaea odorata)* anchored to the bottom by long tentacles. "It is as if you sailed into a green narrow meadow between walls of forest trees," noted Major H. A. Fenney, correspondent for the *Wisconsin State Journal*. "No water is visible. The wheels of the boat tear out great patches, which float about looking like islands, and speedily re-unite behind, hiding the channel from view." Another Yankee, Dr. B. F. Stevenson of the 22nd Kentucky, was reminded of Evangeline who, "in the long, long hours of almost hopeless solitude, paddled her canoe over the same lily-covered surface, enquiring of all chance comers for the whereabouts of Gabriel, the blacksmith's son."[15]

Standing on the deck, *New York Herald* correspondent Henry Thompson, marveled at its beauty:

> Nowhere in the south, before the war was there such a country of natural beauty and richness of soil as this 'paradise of the south'. While the palatial residence of the planters, rising as if out of the shrubbery which surrounds them, gives the whole scenery an air of unparalleled grandeur, thus gaining for it the appellation of 'the garden of Louisiana'.

Thompson, like the soldiers who preceded him on the road, noted the effects of war:

MAJOR GENERAL BANKS AND STAFF before departing New Orleans. Pictured with Banks from left are Major C. Von Herman, Lieutenant Charles S. Sargent, Colonel James G. Wilson, Colonel Horace B. Sargent, Colonel William S. Albert, Colonel E. G. Beckwith, General Charles P. Stone, Colonel John S. Clark, General N. P. Banks, Colonel S. B. Holabird, General Richard Arnold, Captain J. S. Crosby, General Alfred Lee, Captain William Roe, Colonel George Stipp, Major Norman Lieber, Major R. H. Alexander and Captain Charles Buckley. *(Harper's Weekly)*

STEAMER A. G. BROWN unloading supplies for General Weitzel at Tarleton's Plantation. *(Harper's Weekly)*

> These mansions are now silent and deserted. Plantations are desolate and overgrown with weeds and briars, while the cottages of the negroes are tenantless and fast falling to ruin. I noticed but two or three of these plantations under cultivation and the negroes at work on them in force.

One of these, so Thompson was told, was Mary Walton Porter's Oaklawn Manor, located just off the old Spanish Trail in Irish Bend. It was a palatial mansion which even by the standards of the Teche country was impressive for its size, beauty, landscaped grounds, works of art and other interior possessions. But like other opulent plantations along the Teche, Oaklawn owed much of its richness to the Southern institution of slavery.

Correspondent Thompson was also told that the Porter mansion had not been intruded upon, at least not during the fall campaign, because it was somewhat isolated and off the main line of march. More important, Madame Porter, like Sorrel, claimed to be a "loyal" citizen and thus was the subject of an extensive effort on the part of Union authorities to protect her from depredations. An entire company of bluecoats had been posted over the property "and marauding or even trespassing on the premises (was) severely punished."

It was also interesting to note that Madame Porter, a native of Newport, Rhode Island, was an exceptionally attractive middle-aged widow. Charming, intelligent and hospitable, she and her sister, Ana, a noted magazine writer, seemed to jump at every opportunity to wine, dine and otherwise entertain the Yankees, always declaring their undying loyalty to the Old Flag.

Her young son, by contrast, did not share these sentiments and so indicated by running off to join the Confederates, but only to be captured during the Battle of Irish Bend. This incident was a source of embarrassment as well as maternal grief. Nonetheless, the Madame, turning on her feminine charms, eventually secured his release. In short order the delinquent youth was sent off on a tour of Europe, far away from the pervasive conscription laws of Confederate Louisiana.

Most of the Yankee guests at Oaklawn Manor were struck, not so much by the hot-headed rashness of her young son, as by the defiantly charming and "intensely secesh" manner of a frequent visitor and neighbor, the beautiful Miss Lizzie McWilliams.

Lizzie, who was engaged to a Confederate major, had an unusually novel way of revealing her Southern sentiments. First she would listen courteously to all the boistering Union talk and would even participate in singing loyal tunes so long as someone else was at the piano, but inevitably the word would get around that she too was an accomplished pianist whereupon all would request that she grace their presence with some favorite tune. And her favorites were "Dixie" and the "Bonnie Blue Flag," which she was only too happy to render, much to the disgust and shock of the embarassed Union officers.[16]

OAKLAWN MANOR as it appeared in 1960 (Courtesy Lucile Barbour Holmes, Oaklawn Gardens)

Even as Henry Thompson, the enterprising young correspondent for the *Herald,* stood next to the saloon deck and listened to the endless speculation about how it was that Madame Porter was so privileged, the *A. G. Brown* encountered its second crisis. Without warning, gunfire erupted from the eastern bank and Rebel bullets began striking everywhere, breaking windows, splintering wood and perforating the already damaged smoke stacks. Rushing for cover through the open saloon door, Thompson felt a sharp sting as a Rebel Minie grazed his forehead, leaving a deep gash, considerable blood and severe pain.

Not that it did the wounded journalist much good, but he was then warned to stay off the deck for the remainder of the voyage. Since October 5th, he was told, when the Union advance had reached the vicinity of New Iberia, Rebel ambushers had been active along the upper bayou. Firing from trees and underbrush along the east bank, they rarely did much damage to the steamers, but occasionally ended some careless passenger's life. Thompson, who lived to tell his story, would never again stand around on the upper deck, daydreaming of Rebel mansions and *soirees* with beautiful secesh ladies.

About three miles below New Iberia the voyage ended. Actually the Teche was navigable much farther up, even during this season of low water, except that here was yet another obstruction, the Rebel gunboat *Hart*, a large iron-clad steamer which had been scuttled virtually in front of Eugene Olivier's mansion in order to keep her from falling into Union hands.

As the high-ranking officials disembarked at Olivier's Landing, they were greeted by Captain Charles S. Bulkley, a daredevil engineer, demolition expert and superintendent of the U. S. Military Telegraph Service for the Department of the Gulf. Shirtless and "soaking wet," Bulkley pointed out the work being done by an all-black outfit, members of the 3rd Engineers, *Corps d' Afrique*, who were engaged in an effort to remove the obstruction. Divers were going down with ropes, cables were being fastened to trees or hitched to teams of mules, and demolition teams were placing charges about the hulk. Should the general stop by tomorrow, Bulkley smartly informed Banks, he would witness some fireworks. Tonight, however, the normally meticulous but now slightly disheveled general was going to be the unwelcome house guest of the Olivier family.[17]

Madame Eugene Olivier must have experienced some mixed emotions about the famous man's presence. During the spring her home had been the scene of outrageous behavior. The Yankees had threatened to shoot her husband even as he held a young child in his arms. Only the interposition of the frantic lady had secured his release. Then a band of drunken dragoons (mounted infantry) had entered the house and proceeded to pillage and chase the female servants. The ladies of the house had been insulted, abused and threatened. Madame Olivier herself, somewhat advanced in years, had been accosted by a drunken soldier who, while thrusting a goblet of wine to her lips, rudely commanded: "Drink, you damned old rebel, drink to the Union!"

Surely she must have cursed her fate, if not the Confederate navy, for that sunken gunboat in her front yard. Now, the Yankees were there to stay, just as pervasive as before but far less offensive. A provost guard, under one Captain Ellis of the 174th New York, now guarded the property only because it was the head of navigation. He had taken possession of the outbuildings, food supplies and kitchen, as well as the servants' quarters. Under no circumstances, ordered Ellis, were the blacks to serve the family. Worse still, the Oliviers were denied access to their own household edibles. Whatever they desired, they were told by the Union captain, they must purchase from the servants whose labor had produced these goods.

That night, ironically, a large banquet was prepared for the visiting dignitaries. The food was abundant and the wine flowed freely. When the feast was over the servants were called in to consume what remained, even as the ladies of the house, including Madame Olivier, remained confined, and presumably hungry, in the upper apartments. Though cruel and thoughtless, it could have been worse. At the very least, Madame Olivier must have rationalized, the presence of Banks, the *Hart* and consequently, a provost guard, kept the drunken dragoons away.[18]

GUNBOAT HART, Confederate ironclad scuttled at Olivier's Landing near New Iberia. ***(Harper's Weekly)***

Friday, October 9, 1863

Great clouds of billowing smoke, rising high above the treeline of Vermilion Bayou, indicated that once more Pinhook Bridge was ablaze. The Pinhook, so called because it opened and closed like a pin to permit river traffic, had also been burned in the spring. Within a day, however, the advancing Yankees managed to construct a new one, using the lumber from Basil Crow's sugar house.[19] Now, that too was gone, burned for a second time by the Confederate defenders.

For a moment it seemed as though a great battle would be fought here. At least the Yankees thought so, and had been mentally preparing themselves for days. Indeed, everything pointed toward a monumental encounter. There, on a little knoll on the north bank, stood the ragged Rebels, some dressed in gray, others in "butternut" and not a few in muddy Yankee blue. Floating amid the group was a Texas flag, apparently some regiment from James P. Major's Brigade, and there sat

Colonel William Vincent, mounted on a spirited horse and backed by his jayhawk-exterminating Louisiana cavalrymen. Grouped closely together, their actual numbers obscured by the adjacent tree line, and with their officers riding to and fro beyond the burning bridge, it appeared as though the Rebels were going to stand and fight, all five hundred of them.[20]

But the Federals, who believed the enemy strength to be on the order of from two to three thousand, had come prepared. The road to Texas lay beyond the Vermilion and they were not going to be stopped here. In short order General William Franklin, the brilliant West Point engineer, began ordering his men into position for the assault.

The battle of Vermilion Bayou got underway at precisely 11 o'clock A.M. under a hot Louisiana sun. Leading the attack on the extreme right and focusing on a point roughly where Highway 182 now crosses the Vermilion, was thirty-six-year-old Edmund Jackson Davis, a feisty little Texas attorney, former judge and now colonel of cavalry. A handsome man with dark blue eyes, full beard and a mildly receding hairline, Davis, like the loyal Acadians, had been driven from his Texas home by the rabid secessionists. "Nothing could exceed the rancor with which the Confederate Texans spoke of these *renegados*," wrote a European observer. Now Davis, together with his all Texas cavalry of persecuted loyalists, many of them German, was striking a blow for Texas and the Union.[21]

To his immediate left, amid clouds of acrid smoke and incomprehensible bugle commands, were the rifled three-inch muzzle-loading Parrotts of Nims' 2nd Massachusetts Battery of Light Artillery. Just watching them operate was a spectacle to behold. First the full six-gun battery, followed by six ammunition-laden caissons, and pulled by seventy-two magnificent Vermont horses, went thundering over the prairie to the crackling of bugles blown by Captain Nims himself. Incredibly even the horses understood the commands. At the assigned location, the battery was halted and a long drawn out command was given on the bugle. ("Fire to the rear: Caissons, Pass your pieces, trot-march! In Battery!").

For a moment, with all the horses, men, polished guns and caissons flying in all directions, it seemed as though all were hopelessly confused. But as quickly as it started, the eight-hundred pound cannons, resting on their spoked carriages, were unlimbered in line, the cannoneers at their posts—ram-rods at the ready—and the piece limbers, caissons and horses stood at the prescribed distance to the rear.

The gunners were impressive, dressed as they were in dark blue uniforms with red trimmings, reinforced pants, russet leather leggins, cut away jackets with a loop, gray shirts, and red caps. Their commander, a forty-three-year-old Boston druggist named Ormand Nims, had drilled them, "damned and god-damned them"—officers and men alike—until they, together with Davis' Texans, were the best fighting unit in the Army of the Gulf. Merchants, gentlemen, educators and professionals all, this Boston battery would compare favorably even with the crack Washington Artillery of New Orleans (Confederate). Better yet they were the fighting equals of the famed Texas Valverde Battery with whom they would soon have to deal. Indeed, the presence of Nims and Davis, side by side, was a dead giveaway as to where the thrust would be heaviest.

CAPTAIN ORMAND F. NIMS
(Caroline Whitcomb, *History of The Second Massachusetts Battery*)

COLONEL EDMUND DAVIS
(Library of Congress)

At the command: "Commence firing !" shouted by Lieutenant William Marland, piece number one blazed away at the muzzle, jarring the carriage backward and scarring the ground beneath its trail. A group of Union skirmishers in front, stretched thinly for a mile or so along Vermilion Bayou, registered their approval with loud cheers as the first shell whistled over their heads, crashed through the trees and exploded somewhere over Crow Avenue (Pinhook Road).[22]

In the center, firing directly into and over Pinhook Bridge, were three Parrotts and three smooth-bore Napoleons of the lst United States (Regular) Artillery, Battery L, commanded by Captain Henry Closson. To the left of Closson, roughly facing the area known currently as Bendel Gardens, the six guns of the lst Indiana Artillery, Lieutenant

Lawrence Jacoby commanding, blazed away. The latter Battery, with its two Rodmans, two Parrotts and two bronze Napoleons were flanked by Harai Robinson's lst Louisiana (Union) Cavalry.

Another battery, presumably the 2nd Illinois, Battery A, commanded by Lieutenant Herman Borris, laid down a murderous barrage all up and down the bayou with its heavy twenty and thirty-pound shells. The "bull-dogs," as the Texans called the big guns, topped and felled trees, blasted great gashing craters into the opposite bank and soon enveloped both shores with a heavy acrid smoke. "For about an hour the firing was very warm" wrote an unidentified correspondent.[23]

The nastiest and most dangerous assignment fell to the store looting colonel with a tender name—George M. Love. For some reason Love had been demoted from his brigade command and sent back to his regiment, the 116th New York. Whether this had anything to do with his foraging propensities is uncertain. At any rate Love's regiment, together with Colonel William Kinsey's 161st New York, was ordered to fan out in a thin line and approach the bayou as skirmishers. "The ground over which we advanced was a level plain unobstructed by any trees," wrote a frightened soldier, "and our line was a sight worth seeing." Moving forward cautiously, fixed bayonets glistening from their pieces, the New Yorkers would rush a few yards and drop, occasionally firing their muskets, then rush again, all in a vain attempt to draw Rebel fire and reveal the enemy position.[24]

Rounding out the Union forces were two infantry divisions of the XIX Corps (Weitzel's and Grover's) and one brigade of the XIII Corps (Lionel Sheldon's 3rd Brigade, 1st Division). Marching by twos from the direction of Cote Gelee amid the rattling of musketry and boom of cannon, they quickly filed off the road and manuevered into assault formation. Each division consisted of two ranks and formed a shoulder to shoulder double line about a mile long. With Weitzel's division in the lead, followed by Cuvier Grover's and then Sheldon's brigade, the long blue lines moved forward, bayonets at the ready.

Never before, not even during the April assault on Pinhook, had there been such a spectacle on Vermilion Bayou. Thousands upon thousands of bluecoats, each regiment distinguished by its colors and peculiar uniforms, moved briskly over the fertile Louisiana soil. Their bayonets, thrust before them, glistened brightly in the noonday sun. The officers and sergeants competed with the roar of cannon and rattle of musketry by shouting a "move it on, lads!" here, and a "keep it straight!" there. The cadence of trampling feet was picked up and set down by dozens of little drummer boys, one of whom, John F. Robie of Manchester, New Hampshire, had just turned thirteen. An equal number of fifers of an equally tender age piped out the music, lending even more color and liveliness to the occasion.[25]

Regrettably, there are but few extant documents relating to the

Confederate participation in this affair. Nonetheless one can imagine the agonizing sense of helplessness experienced by the defending Texans and Louisianians as they gazed upon the scene before them. Overawed and intimidated by the numbers, choked by the smoke, and endangered by the exploding shells, they soon turned tail and ran, or, as a Texan put it: "We withdrew in brisk fashion."

Owing to the presence of so much smoke, dust and noise hanging over the area, however, the Union generals remained ignorant of the Confederate retreat. Accordingly the bombardment continued until the first wave of infantrymen—Weitzels' division—came even with the blazing artillery batteries. At that moment the firing ceased, and there fell such a profound silence over the area that only the most pessimistic believed the Rebels to be still lurking upon the opposite shore.

It was an especially difficult moment for the citizens of the tiny village of Vermilionville (Lafayette) about two miles north of the battle area. They had long since loaded their valuable household possessions and family heirlooms upon wagons, carts, family *caleches* and other means of conveyance. Many had already left, but others, still praying that by some miracle the Confederates could contain the invaders, remained behind. Earlier in the day, they had gathered upon the streets, balconies and even rooftops to catch a glimpse of the fighting. Some of the big rifled Parrotts had overshot their targets and had lobbed their deadly projectiles as far as the area currently occupied by the University of Southwestern Louisiana. The ground had rumbled, window panes had shattered, walls and houses had shaken on their foundations and the citizens hastened their departure, but the worst moment of all was when the big guns fell silent. After several anguished minutes of wondering and speculation, the cause soon became apparent. There, riding swiftly over the fields, were Vincent's and Major's ragged Confederate cavalrymen, headed in a northerly direction. The show was over, the Yankees were coming and it was time to get out of town.[26]

Back on the Vermilion neither Franklin nor his observers could discern with any degree of certainty that the defenders had in fact evacuated. Once more, Weitzel's infantry division moved forward, their orders being to close with the skirmishers—then lying concealed near the south bank—whereupon they were to direct two volleys into the opposite treeline and, if there was no reply, to send the skirmishers across.

The order to fire two volleys, though simple-sounding enough, was far more complicated than one might imagine. Their weapons consisted of caliber .58 Springfields and .577 English Enfields which fired a conical-shaped lead bullet. The latter, named Minie for its French inventor, was pronounced "minnie" by the soldiers and erroneously referred to as a ball. Unlike the rounded balls of an earlier age, the rifled Minie, in the hands of a trained infantryman, had a deadly accurate

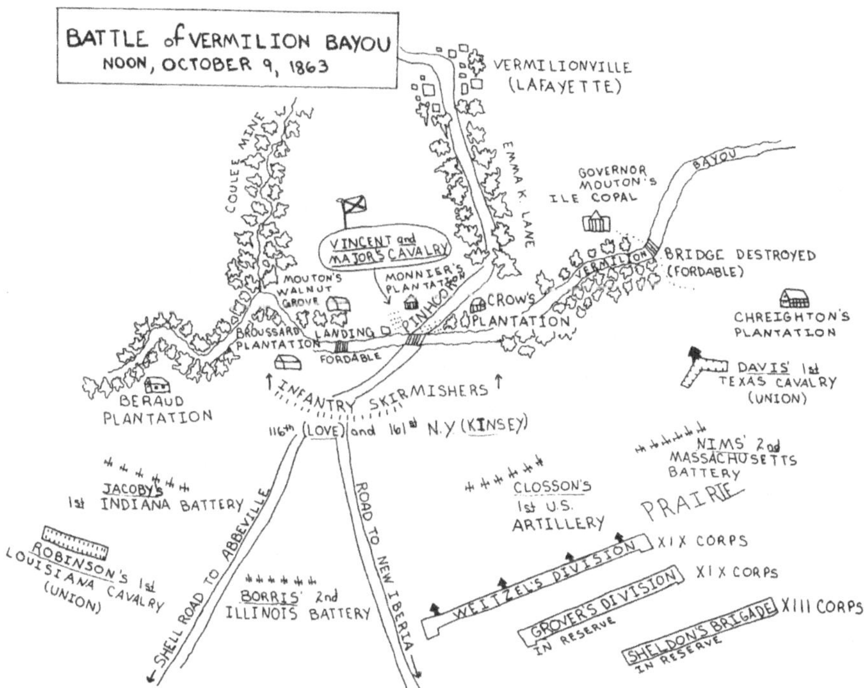

effective range of two hundred yards, and was lethal at twice or thrice that distance.

Its greatest shortcoming was the complicated procedure for reloading the weapon once it had been fired. In the unlikely event that there still remained concealed Rebels upon the opposite shore the exposed Yankees, unable to rapidly respond, would be at a severe disadvantage.

Approaching to within a few yards of the south bank without drawing fire, the front line of Weitzel's division dropped down on one knee and, on command, pulled the trigger, thereby igniting the charge with a percussion cap, and enfilading the opposite shore with a deadly volley.

All simple enough but now the reloading, a process involving nine separate and distinct operations. All up and down the mile-long line the command rang out: "Load! By the Numbers: Load!" Moving rapidly, each soldier placed his butt upon the ground and removed a paper cartridge from his heavy amunition belt. By this time the second line had moved ahead, knelt and fired.

If ever there was a time for praying this was it, the most vulnerable moment. Working furiously just as they had done so often during drill (the command then was "Load! In nine times; Load!") the paper end was bitten from the cartridge and the powder poured down the barrel. Then the lead "Minie ball," paper and all, was dropped in and rammed home, creating a distinct ringing sound. Finally, but not altogether in unison, the men raised their pieces, cocked the heavy clicking hammer with their thumbs and rushed ahead of their still loading comrades, ready to fire again. The entire process, from the moment of firing to reloading and back into kneeling position had taken a seemingly eternal thirty seconds or so.[27]

Fortunately for all, not a sound came from the opposite shore, save a limb, sheared from its support, which came belatedly crashing down, setting off a brief flurry of shots from a few nervous riflemen.

The battle of Vermilion Bayou, such as it was, ended in a bloodless victory for the Union. In spite of all the shooting, the massive artillery bombardment and the impressive display of strength, only five Yankees were wounded. One soldier, a gunner, suffered from a crushed foot, having inadvertantly placed it behind a carriage wheel during a discharge. Another had been wounded, though not seriously, by a gunshot from a careless comrade. There were only three bonafide casualties—a certain Major Cowen, and two privates. Fortunately, none were mortal and all had occurred when Davis' loyal Texas cavalrymen forded the bayou.[28]

Just as the smoke was clearing from Vermilion Bayou and the foot soldiers were breathing a welcome sigh of relief, the crackling of yet another bugle informed the men of the dramatic arrival of the Major General Commanding, Nathaniel P. Banks. Earlier in the day Banks, accompanied by an entourage of sycophants, including correspondents, generals and colonels and lesser politicians, had witnessed the successful explosion of charges placed under the wrecked gunboat *Hart* by the fearless Captain Charles S. Bulkley. Then, after issuing a few orders, including one to send a brigade of infantry back to the little town of Franklin (i.e. William Landram's 2nd Brigade, 4th Division, XIII Corps) he had departed for the front.

Now, stepping down from his flag-bedecked carriage, with its oak paneled and carpeted interior, Banks' appearance was more akin to that of royalty than to a fighting Union general. Neatly groomed and dressed in a tailored dark blue uniform, complete with sword and sash, highly-polished boots, clinking spurs and a bell-crowned hat, he seemed oddly out of place, especially when he was approached by his grimy and sweaty field commander, Major General William B. Franklin, who proceeded to brief him on the latest developments.

So optimistic was Banks over the state of affairs on the Vermilion that he immediately fired off a telegram to General-in-Chief H. W. Halleck back in Washington: "As soon as we cross the Vermilion," he wired, "I will inform you of my plans... No time will be lost in raising the flag (in Texas) as directed."[29]

CHAPTER FIVE

PAUSE ON THE VERMILION

Friday, October 9, 1863

NO SOONER had the 161st New York Infantry "forced the crossing" below the remains of Pinhook Bridge than a company of skirmishers, still soaking wet and covered with bayou mud, began swarming up the steep bank towards Walnut Grove plantation, the residence of Joseph Sosthene Mouton. Instead of Rebel sharpshooters, for whom they were looking, they found Henriette Odeide Mouton, the frightened and frail twenty-nine-year-old sister of Confederate General Alfred Mouton and her six young children.[1] Sensing no danger from such a helpless group, the soldiers proceeded to conduct themselves in a manner more characteristic of their skirmishing comrades from the 116th New York.

First came the search for household valuables, in the process of which furniture, mirrors and windows were smashed or broken. The next target was the outdoor kitchen where wines, preserves and other provisions were rapidly packed off. Anything that could not be immediately consumed was loaded aboard the family vehicles which, in turn, were hitched to Mouton's draft animals. Even the barnyard fowl were taken, their resistance to capture being registered by a noisy medley of cackles, caws and screeches. Once rested, and with a full stomach, the intruders departed as rapidly as they had come, leaving behind few objects of value.

Surrounded by the discarded and broken remains and without any means or the strength to care for her children, Odeide Mouton concluded that the best course of action lay in removing herself and the children to Ile Copal, her father's house (former Governor Alexandre Mouton) about a mile up the bayou, but even that was no easy matter. Two of the children were too young to walk and two others were too young to walk very far.

Searching through the wreckage, her ten-year-old son, Alexandre, solved the dilemma. In the barnyard was the chassis of an old surrey which, though "effaced by the weather," without leather or seats and almost devoid of spokes, was still serviceable. As luck would have it the Federals had left only one decrepit old horse, "Volan" by name.

Alexandre and his eight-year-old brother, "Bud" (Bordat) fashioned a harness by tearing burlap bags into straps. Three empty boxes were then placed on the frame as seats for Mrs. Mouton and the four youngest children. Finally, with Bud holding the wretched animal by one side of the makeshift reins and Alexandre by the other, the unlikely procession started their mile-long trek toward Governor Mouton's residence.

On reaching the hedge-lined road then known as Crow's Avenue (Pinhook Road) near the plantation homes of Jim Higginbotham and John Baumgartner, the group turned left and found themselves enveloped in a caravan of Union invaders who were then crossing an improvised bridge built on the remaining stringers of Pinhook Bridge. Creeping along amid the derisive shouts, hoots and crude efforts on the part of the Yankees to emulate what they erroneously perceived to be southern colloquialism, the refugees passed the elegant home of Henry Monnier, which still stands (as Judge Roy Bean's Saloon) and that of Basil Crow, where general headquarters would soon be established on the front lawn. "There were about three inches of dust on the highway," recalled young Alexandre, and "why we were not run over God only knows."[2]

Back at the Pinhook the Yankees were frantically trying to bridge the Vermilion. So far only three regiments, the 1st Texas Cavalry (Union) and the 116th and 161st New York Infantries had crossed over. Although it would not have been difficult to move all the infantry and cavalry forces across, there were some very good reasons for not doing so. In the first place, the flimsy temporary bridge would not support heavy artillery and wagons. More important was the possibility that once across a strong concentrated attack from the north could prove disastrous if there were no artillery support or avenues for retreat.

Most of the soldiers on the south bank had never before witnessed the construction of a temporary military bridge or pontoon. What they saw on the evening of October 9, 1863, was an impressive performance of precision and efficiency on the part of the *pontonniers* of the predominately black Engineer Corps. Unlike their counterparts in the Army of the Potomac, who used rigid wooden boats, the engineers of the Army of the Gulf were supplied with pneumatic pontoons made of India-rubber. When inflated by means of bellows designed specifically for that purpose, each pontoon would swell into three twenty-foot long cylindrical-shaped objects, all of which were joined together by rubber webbing.

With the north bank guarded by the 161st New York, two pontoon trains of four wagons each drew up and halted at the foot of the burned-out bridge. While one team of blacks from a "pioneer" regiment staked turpentine torches to illuminate the area, another proceeded to rapidly unload several crates of folded pontoons, anchors and cables.

Once inflated and dropped into the Vermilion, each rubber pontoon was straddled by four engineers who then propelled themselves out a short distance with a pulley and cable stretching from bank to bank. It was a tricky operation, especially when the current was swift, but the Vermilion had not been so low for years, so in short order the pontoon was arranged paralleling the bank and the anchor was dropped.

The next operation was performed by the balking crew who, with five heavy, long timbers or "balks," bridged the distance between the bank and the pontoon. One end was secured to the water-born craft with ropes or "lashes," and the other to a heavy horizontal abutment placed by yet another team on the south bank.

Working in rapid succession, the chess team then stepped forward and covered the balks with heavy plank flooring or "chesses" which had been taken from another wagon.

The final operation was performed by a side-rail team who lashed heavy timbers or "side-rails" to the outer edges of each side of the floor planks. Meanwhile the pontoon detail had launched another of their odd-looking vessels and the process was repeated until another section was completed.

By 9 o'clock P. M., after less than three hours of work, the *pontonniers* reached the opposite shore. It then remained for a detail of blacks to lay down a light covering of hay over the roadbed to improve traction. After some last minute adjustments, the two newly constructed bridges—one for infantry, the other for wagons, beasts and artillery—were pronounced fit for inspection.

The honors fell to Brigadier General Godfrey Weitzel, the handsome six-foot, twenty-eight-year-old commander of the First Division, XIX Army Corps. Always the colorful showoff, the swashbuckling former West Point engineer, himself a master builder, walked briskly to the center of the bridge where he joined the chief engineer, Major David C. Houston. With a prod here and a kick there, much as a prospective buyer would inspect a used wagon, Weitzel nodded his approval. After one final jump in the middle—which was lustily hurrahed by his men—the young general charged the opposite shore with drawn saber as though attacking some invisible Quixotic opponent. Joining Lieutenant Colonel William B. Kinsey, regimental commander of the 161st New York, Weitzel motioned to his brigade commander on the south bank, Colonel Charles J. Paine, to start the troops across.

On both banks, as well as in the middle, a team of engineers was posted to guard against unnecessary and possibly dangerous motion sometimes caused by the uniform cadence of marching soldiers. As each regiment struck the bridge a guard called out: "Rout Step!" "Rout Step!" Farther along, the order was needlessly repeated by another with the result that three thousand troops crossed over the Vermilion that night aping the command: "Rout Step!"[3]

Not everyone took the movement so good-naturedly. That very day a certain Major Alton, the New York paymaster, had arrived with General Banks' coterie. Learning that the major was there to pay off the New Yorkers, a group of zealots immediately set about seizing the doors, boxes and boards from the Chreighton plantation in order to fashion pay roll tables. Shortly before sundown, but about midway through the pay process, orders were passed to move out. One New Yorker, disappointed that payment would be deferred until the following day, pulled out his flattened pocketbook, extended it to paymaster Alton and complained that it already looked "as though an elephant had stomped on it."[4]

While Weitzel's foot soldiers crossed the infantry bridge, Captain Ormand F. Nims led his 2nd Massachusetts Battery of Light Artillery over the other. Once across, Nims moved up Pinhook road about one mile and began posting artillery pieces on the left side with the muzzles pointing toward Vermilionville. Meanwhile, Weitzel's Brigade continued on up Pinhook, past Colonel Edmund Davis and his 1st Texas Cavalry—then camped at the present location of Pinhook Road and University Avenue—and went into camp directly in front of Ile Copal, Governor Mouton's plantation.[5]

Located a short distance off the main road, between Pinhook and the Vermilion, Ile Copal exemplified southern opulence and luxury. A large and imposing two-storied brick colonial structure, the mansion was flanked by neat rows of brick slave houses which, though empty, were shaded by enormous pecan and live oak trees. In the garden were lemon and orange trees, some with fruit hanging from limbs, as well as a variety of vines and luxuriant shrubs ranging from roses to oleanders and sweet-scented jasmine. The interior, with its high plastered ceilings overlooking mosaic floors covered with Brussels carpets, was equally impressive. A wide frescoed hallway led into one of the largest and most extensive private library collections in Louisiana. Here were periodicals in various languages, sermons, poems, speeches, classics in Latin and a wide selection of books by contemporary writers. Somehow this magnificent home, with its solid mahogany furniture, expensive chinaware, large beveled mirrors, costly wainscot and elegant chimney ornaments of Parian and alabaster had escaped the ravages of the spring 1863 invasion of southwest Louisiana.[6]

Alexandre Mouton, former U. S. senator, and state governor of Louisiana, president of the state Secession Convention, and president of the *Comite de Vigilance de Vermilionville*, was not at home. He had learned the hard way, when the Yankees came through several months earlier, that men of power and influence were not treated kindly. At that time Mouton and his brother, Emile, along with another planter, Alexander Martin, had destroyed dozens of hogshead of sugar and molasses by rolling them into the Vermilion. He then defiantly remained at home

ILE COPAL, the Vermilion Bayou residence of Governor Alexandre Mouton ***(Leslie's Illustrated Weekly)***

ARMY OF THE GULF crossing Vermilion Bayou at Pinhook Bridge, October 10, 1863 ***(Leslie's Illustrated Weekly)***

while his son, Confederate General Alfred Mouton, led a retreating Louisiana brigade toward Alexandria. As the Yankees entered Vermilionville on that fateful April day in 1863 the old governor had been unceremoniously taken into custody and incarcerated for four long months in New Orleans.

Profiting by his experience with the Federal army, Mouton prudently fled toward Opelousas when it became inevitable that Vermilionville would fall again. He left at home several children, including his coquettish eighteen-year-old daughter by a second marriage, Ana Eliza (nicknamed "Pussy") another daughter, Cecilia, and his eldest and most attractive daughter, Mathilde.

Marie Celestine Mathilde Gardner (nee Mouton) or simply Mathilde, was also the wife of Confederate General Frank Gardner, then a Union prisoner. (It was he who had commanded the ill-fated Confederate garrison at Port Hudson.) At age thirty-two she was beautiful, vivacious and charming. Standing barely five feet tall this petite woman was an ardent, even vociferous, supporter of the Southern cause.

On that particular day, however, she was badly depressed. Not only were the hated Yankees back, but her younger sister Cecilia was ill with typhoid fever and had taken a turn for the worse. Only that morning Mathilde had sent a messenger to the village of Vermilionville to ask anyone going toward Opelousas to inform the governor that Cecilia was probably dying. As if that wasn't bad enough one of her own children, the youngest, had developed similiar symptoms. Then her other frail and sickly sister, Henriette Odeide, moved in with her six children and one of them was ill. Finally, Mathilde was concerned about her little half-sister "Pussy" who exhibited all the rebellious traits of most eighteen-year-olds. "Pussy" had been born and had lived in the city of Washington, D. C., when her father was a United States senator. Perhaps for this reason, and because her mother, Emma K. Gardner, was a New Yorker, "Pussy" did not seem to share the family animosity toward Northerners. Indeed she did not seem to mind at all the prospects of having so many men around, even Yankees.[7]

Saturday, October 10, 1863

At first light, even as the "captured" roosters crowed in the Union camp, one section of Nims' Battery, accompanied by Colonel Davis and his mounted Texas bluecoats, cautiously approached the small village of Vermilionville. Sighting a small picket outpost, possibly a company of Vincent's 2nd Louisiana Cavalry, the little "Yankee" Texan unsheathed his saber, raised it above his head and ordered a charge. He was ably assisted by two shells from Nims' guns which not only scattered the tiny Rebel force but jolted the remaining citizens of Vermilionville awake with a thundering roar.[8]

If Mathilde Mouton Gardner rushed to the window, as she undoubtedly did, she would have gazed out upon a sea of white tents extending in all directions away from Ile Copal. Downstairs, Mathilde noted, a squad of bluecoats was banging away at the front door. General Weitzel, or someone in his command, suspected that Confederate General Alfred Mouton might be hiding in the mansion and had ordered a party to search the premises. Young Alexandre, who witnessed the affair, recalled:

> These Union soldiers, without losing any time, proceeded up the stairs and headed for the room where my Aunt Cecilia was about to breathe her last. Mother (i.e. Odeide) got to the door first, barred it with her person and said 'my sister is about to meet her creator...I defy...you to enter this room.' They stood back and did not force their way in (but) expressed themselves that 'no better place a rebel would like to keep from being arrested.'

Although the intruders soon departed, the troubles in the Mouton household were far from over. Before noon of the same day, Brigadier General Cuvier Grover, accompanied by some three thousand officers and men of the Third Division of the XIX Army Corps also moved his command to Ile Copal. Meanwhile, another brigade of Weitzel's Division, also numbering about three thousand, moved in. They, in turn, were soon joined by Major General Franklin, the commander of the entire XIX Army Corps, who proceeded to establish his headquarters in a large white tent near the rear door of the Mouton mansion.

The kitchen, library and living room, as well as most of the household provisions, were occupied or seized for the use of the United States. A quartermaster established himself in the kitchen; pork, flour and clothing were distributed in the drawing room, amidst the unshattered elegance; the feet of sentinels treaded on marble pavements, and orderlies in rough uniforms brushed against rosewood. Even old Edith, the faithful family cook, was commandeered. Mathilde, Odeide and all the children meanwhile were confined to the upper apartments, but the worst blow of all was that the provost marshal denied them access to their own kitchen and stores of food.

The arrangement was especially irksome for young Alexandre Mouton who, though only ten, was mature enough to realize that his Aunt Mathilde could not possibly manage by herself. Alexandre's mother, Odeide, was much too frail and ill herself to be of any assistance and Cecilia was dying and had to be looked after constantly. And then there were a dozen or more little Moutons, most of whom were still in the blanket stage. Alexandre, the oldest of the lot, naively decided on a rash course of action. Perhaps, he reasoned, Major General Banks could be called upon for assistance.

Walking the short distance from Ile Copal to the home of Basil Crow, where the Major General Commanding was quartered, Alexandre confronted a sentry and demanded to see the famous general.

"But...who are you?" asked the astonished guard.

"A Rebel," boldly replied the boy in Cajun-accented English, "We are all Rebels here."

In the meantime General Banks, who was inside his big white headquarters tent, overheard the conversation. No doubt amused by what he heard and impressed by the youngster's perserverance, if not audacity, the graceful politician walked to the flap of his tent and shouted: "Let him in!"

Once inside, Alexandre was awed by the General's broad smile, ingratiating personality and "pleasing" appearance. Indeed Banks was decked out in full military regalia—double star on each shoulder; double row of shiny brass buttons in front; the sash of his office about his waist. The boy was also struck by the fact that Banks was a medium-sized man, much smaller than the towering figure he had pictured in his imagination. The iron-gray moustache over his mouth was shaped like a formidable archway, and somehow seemed out of place on a man with such a handsome face and pleasant voice.

YOUNG ALEXANDRE MOUTON, circa 1890 (Griffin Papers U.S.L. Archives)

"And what can I do for you?" asked the forty-seven-year-old former governor of Massachusetts.

Young Alexandre's rash boldness suddenly deserted him, and he began to tremble before the mighty man. Barefooted, dirty and dressed in a manner more akin to a street urchin than a wealthy planter's son, he somehow managed to relate the sad state of affairs at Ile Copal. More specifically he stressed the need for milk for the two infants, one of whom was ill at the time.

Whether Banks was impressed by the pleas of this innocent child or by sympathy for the family of an individual whose political career had paralleled his own is uncertain, but in any event he responded by sending two milk cows that very afternoon. At the very least the Mouton babies would not suffer.[9]

Sometime that morning, presumably after Alexandre returned from his successful mission, General Cuvier Grover entered Ile Copal through the large front doors. Grover, like Banks, had close political ties. (His brother, Lafayette Grover, was a U. S. senator and former Governor of Oregon). A graduate of West Point (finishing fourth in the class of 1844) he had once been a close friend and classmate of Mathilde Mouton Gardner's brother, Confederate General Alfred Mouton, and her husband, General Frank Gardner. Indeed, Gardner and Grover had served together in the old 10th United States Infantry, crossing the Rockies in the railroad operations of 1853 and fighting the Mormons on the Utah expedition just before the war. Thus the gentlemanly officer was elated when he inadvertantly came across his old friend's wife, Mathilde, conversing with some of the children in the hallway:

> It was his spurs in contact with the floor that had us turn around. He was a handsome officer, a long beard (and) that blue uniform with the brass button all going to make up a beautiful picture. All of a sudden he stepped toward (Mathilde) and said: 'How are you Mrs. Gardner?' with his right hand stretched out.

Startled by the intrusion, angry and frustrated at the family's fall from riches, and now confronted by an old friend, someone who could be called upon for assistance, Mathilde chose instead to insult this normally upright, courteous and incorruptible thirty-five-year-old general.

BRIGADIER GENERAL CUVIER GROVER (Library of Congress)

"Looking Grover straight in the eyes," as Alexandre subsequently related in his memoirs, "Mrs. Gardner replied in a very positive way and most audible language: 'How dare you!,' and turned her back."[10]

A short while later it became apparent why Grover was dressed in his military best. The Major General Commanding, back on Basil Crow's plantation, had called on all the corps, division and brigade commanders for an important strategy session. In all the thousands of pages of official correspondence surviving the war, not one word relates to the topic of that meeting. Indeed the meeting itself would have gone unrecorded for posterity except for an observant surgeon of the 22nd Kentucky Infantry

(Union) B. F. Stevenson, who posted another letter to his dear wife Delia that night:[11]

> We passed the Headquarters...whilst Banks, Franklin and their staffs were under the outspread branches of a great china tree. We were halted for a time just opposite their quarters, and I drew on them my field glass, and found a well supplied table with an ample spread of silver plate. The full, well-developed persons of the feeders...led me to question if this was making war in earnest. To me it looked, with their full faces, more like painted warriors on a painted canvas than real warfare.

Yet, unknown to Surgeon Stevenson, subsequent events make it clear that a major shift in strategy was decided upon (or at least related) at that meeting. Banks, it will be recalled, had been directed by his superiors to plant the Union flag in Texas "for reasons other than military." Following the disastrous and humiliating attempt to land an expeditionary force at Sabine Pass in early September, he had decided to move his Army of the Gulf up the Teche and over the prairies to the Sabine. Should this route prove difficult, the alternative was to march to Marshal, Texas, by way of Alexandria and Shreveport, Louisiana. Even as late as October 9, 1863, Banks seemed to be enthusiastically espousing one of these possibilities.

But the Great Texas Overland Expedition was bogging down. In the first place, reconnaissance details from Colonel Edmund J. Davis' cavalry were reporting that Taylor's Army of Western Louisiana, especially Green's cavalry, was awaiting just such a move. Yankees on foot and in the open were simply no match for the mounted cowboys and Cajuns. More importantly, Union spies and informers coming in from the west were reporting that a large army of mounted Texans under Confederate General Bankhead Magruder was concentrating for a repulsive action on the Sabine.

Several days after conferring with his generals in Vermilionville, Banks expressed his doubts about the invasion of Texas via southwestern Louisiana in a series of letters to "old Brains Halleck,"the General-in-Chief up in Washington:[12]

> To the Sabine we have a march from Opelousas and Vermilion of between one and two hundred miles without water, without supplies, and without other transportation than by wagon. At Niblett's Bluff, on the Sabine, we shall encounter all the possible force of the enemy in the State of Texas, and a powerful enemy hanging upon our rear throughout the whole march, which is now waiting for us between Alexandria and Opelousas.

With regard to the alternative route through Alexandria, Shreveport and Marshall, Banks noted that:

> We have a march (from Vermilionville) of from 350 to 400 miles without any communications than by wagon trains, and through a country utterly depleted of all its material resources. Either of these routes presents almost insuperable difficulties...While the army is preparing itself for one or the other of these movements, I propose to attempt a lodgement upon some point upon the coast (near) the Rio Grande.

Banks' decision, no doubt reached during his brief visit to Vermilionville, was one of the best kept secrets of the campaign. Not one diary, letter, official piece of correspondence or newspaper report from that day forward so much as hinted at a change in plans. Even some of the highest ranking officers were kept in the dark.[13]

Nonetheless, Banks did not entirely abandon the thought of using the Attakapas and Opelousas country as a base of operations. Before turning over his field command of the XIX and XIII Army Corps to Major General William Franklin, he ordered the latter to advance toward Opelousas, Barre's Landing and Washington. Meanwhile, some of the best regiments, including the crack 1st Texas Cavalry, were to be quietly withdrawn to prepare for an amphibious assault on the Rio Grande.[14]

During the night of October 10, 1863, even as Banks was mapping out his grand strategy for enforcing the Monroe Doctrine against the French in Mexico, the soldiers of the XIX Army Corps had their first genuine opportunity to supplement their diets with something other than official army rations. With the exceptions of the plundering which had occurred at Hine's store down in Centerville, and at Sosthene Mouton's Walnut Grove plantation on the Vermilion, the Easterners had behaved themselves, mainly because of Franklin's strict enforcement of orders against foraging.

The most likely target for foragers was the tiny village of Vermilionville, about two miles beyond the sprawling Union camp, but it was watched over by Weitzel's provost marshal. By contrast no one had thought to post guards along the Vermilion where many of the wealthier planters resided. Thus the Moutons, Crows, Chreightons, Dugas, Cafferys, Thibodeauxs, Martins, Berauds and others "lost immense quantities of what soldiers regard as the legitimate spoils of war, viz., pigs, chickens, potatoes and sugar." Captain John William Deforest, a noted journalist in the 12th Connecticut, penned a letter even as the goods were coming into camp:

> We forage like the locusts of Revelation. It is pitiful to see how quickly a herd of noble cattle will be slaughtered. Our Negro servants bring in pigs, sheep and fowls, whether we bid it or forbid it. Of course, after the creatures are dead and cooked, we eat them to save them, for wasting food is prejudicial to military discipline.

Dr. Harris Beecher, the assistant surgeon of the 114th New York, recalled that "wherever a pile of feathers, potato parings or offal could be discovered near a picket post in the morning, inquiries were made to find the perpetrator." These mysteries, according to Beecher, were never solved because "*mirabile dictu*, everyone clearly proved himself innocent."[15]

Sunday, October 11, 1863

Shortly before sunrise, a bugler of the XIX Army Corps, standing on the front steps of the Mouton mansion, blew out the notes to "The General." At this signal, several acres of white canvas tents and other sleeping accommodations, which before had been the prominent feature of the landscape, disappeared in a moment.

A few minutes later, General William B. Franklin, with the colors of XIX Corps headquarters borne at his heels, and followed by the members of his staff, rode smartly toward the front of the column then forming. Further along the line another bugler sounded the call to "Attention," following which the officers mounted their horses and the men took their place in column.

Just as the sun broke the horizon the lead bugler blew out the notes to "Forward." At this signal the commanding officers of each individual regiment, more than two dozen altogether, gave the orders which echoed all up and down the line: "Right Shoulder Shift!" and the march began amid groans and gripes and a half dozen or so tortured versions of "The Girl I Left Behind."

Heading toward Vermilionville via Emma K. Lane (now Jefferson Street), the Yankees were fascinated by the long avenue of live oak trees which has been planted many years before by Governor Mouton's slaves. So large and thick were these magnificent oaks that the tops had joined together over the roadway, shutting out light and giving the impression of passing through a long tunnel. One soldier, impressed with its beauty, called it "as fine an avenue of trees as I ever saw. It is over half a mile long and must have been planted 50 years ago."[16]

As the troops entered Vermilionville a brigade band struck up the stirring "but not welcome" strains of "The Red, White and Blue." From practically every rooftop in town there hung either a white towel, pillow case or handkerchief, Union Jack, tricolor or the Stars and Stripes. This was the second time that the Yankees had marched through Vermilionville and no one dared display the Confederate flag.

Most of the invaders were no more favorably impressed than they had been the first time. A New Yorker remembered it as "a town of some three hundred inhabitants, with two churches and a convent as its principal buildings." The inhabitants, he wrote, "usually called it La Fayette." Another soldier wrote his brother that although it was "about the size of other villages we have passed, it is not near so tastily built."

Commented another that "although these Creole French claimed to be neutral, it was plain to be seen that they did not appreciate our visit."

Looking for ways to liven the march, a Vermont Yankee spotted the tricolor flying from a house, possibly the home of Dr. B. J. Salles, and began chanting to the cadence of the marching soldiers "French flag, French flag," which was picked up and repeated by the others. Passing the home of Michael Garry and Richard Chargois, who flew the Union Jack, the chant changed to "British flag, British flag, British flag," then to "white flag, white flag, white flag," and so on.[17]

If there were any attractive girls in and about Vermilionville in the fall of 1863 they apparently remained behind closed doors. In the days before the wolf whistle, the custom among men in general, and soldiers, in particular, on spotting a pretty face was to emit a loud but fake throat-clearing sound which would then be picked up and repeated by others. There were no such throat-clearing incidents as the Yankees passed through Vermilionville. Quite the contrary, a regimental newspaper published several days later complained that:[18]

> There is certainly the d..dst ugliest class of ladies down here that the world can produce. They go promenading the streets with a dirty snuff-swab stick in their mouths, which looks for all the world like the smokestack of a gunboat, and there is scarcely one of them but that chews tobacco and smokes cigars.

Not that it mattered in Richmond or Washington but that subject seemed to be the only one regarding Vermilionville about which both Yankees and Rebels were in complete agreement.[19]

As the seemingly endless procession of footsoldiers, cavalry, artillery batteries, supply trains and camp followers dwindled to a trickle, both the citizens of Vermilionville and the newly arrived soldiers of the XIII Corps were treated to some very odd military spectacles. Before leaving Brashear City, a company of the black Louisiana Pioneer Corps, under the direction of Captain William F. Patterson of Kentucky, had rigged shafts and rims to the ends of hogshead-sized barrels. When fitted with wagon wheels and hitched to a single mule led by a black "muleskinner," these enormous barrels became water wagons which turned over and over as the train progressed. Several dozen of these odd-shaped contraptions, also marked with such names as "Galveston" and "Houston," now followed in the wake of the army, presumably for use should the Yankees decide to take the prairie route into Texas.

On the heels of this unlikely train came a less questionable spectacle. A crew of engineers, some of whom were riding in mule drawn wagons bearing the inscription "U. S. Signal Corps" on the side, were busily engaged laying down a six or seven-foot high telegraph line. Unknown to most of the soldiers, who heretofore had been in advance of the crew, the temporary line stretched back to Berwick's Bay, which was on a permanent link to New Orleans. So long as the line could be maintained, the generals in the field enjoyed almost instantaneous communications with Gulf Headquarters in New Orleans.

One curious onlooker, First Sergeant T. B. Marshall of the 83rd Ohio Regiment, decided to tag along for awhile. That night he recorded in his diary that the Signal Corps engineers could lay down an incredible four miles of line in one hour:[20]

> A wagon went along as fast as the horses could walk, and a small wire covered with rubber was reeled off. This was followed by a wagon (loaded with) long slim poles, one end of which was pointed (and driven into the ground) and to the other end the wire was fastened.

The observing Confederates were also baffled, not so much by the odd-looking water train as by the direction the Yankees were taking. Everyone in southwestern Louisiana, from plantation master down to the most humble slave, seemed to know that Texas was the ultimate objective of the expedition. Even the Confederate high command was convinced that *the* road to Texas was the Landry road (currently Eraste Landry Road) leading from Vermilionville across the open prairie to Niblett's Bluff on the Sabine.

For weeks Lieutenant General Kirby Smith, head of the Trans-Mississippi Department of the Confederacy (which included Texas, West Louisiana, Missouri, Arkansas and the Indian Country) had made his plans accordingly. He had alerted the commanding general of the District of Texas, J. Bankhead Magruder, to concentrate his eight thousand or so cowboys for a quick movement on Niblett's Bluff. Major General Richard Taylor, meanwhile, was ordered to concentrate his Army of Western Louisiana, consisting of Alfred Mouton's Louisiana infantry division, John G. Walker's Texas infantry division and Thomas Green's Texas cavalry division in and around Opelousas. The domain of Kirby-Smithdom, as the European-sized Trans-Mississippi Confederacy was called, was not going to capitulate without a fight. Thus at the very moment Franklin's Army Corps left Ile Copal, a Confederate courier, belonging to one of the Texas regiments, was dispatched to alert the main body of General Green's troops on Bayou Carencro. A second courier, carrying the same message, was sent to General Taylor's headquarters in Opelousas.[21]

Without a doubt the defending Confederates were relishing the thought of catching the entire XIX Army Corps out on the barren prairies, but it was not to be. No sooner had the marching, singing Yankees passed the junction leading toward Texas than a second pair of couriers was dispatched with new intelligence. Incredibly the invaders were moving toward the Carencro along the same route they had taken during the spring campaign. For the Confederates it was the first hint of a change in plans.

THE ARMY TELEGRAPH ***(Harper's Weekly)***

If the Rebels were disturbed, one can well imagine how the luckless planters of north Lafayette Parish must have felt, especially those living along the road between Vermilionville and Grand Coteau. During the spring campaign, when the sons of New York, Rhode Island, Connecticut, Vermont, New Hampshire, Massachusetts and Maine had taken the same route:[22]

> ...the road was filled with an indiscriminate mass of armed men, on horseback and on foot. Carts, wagons, cannon and caissons rolled along in most tumultous disorder, while to the right and to the left...were hundreds going empty-handed and returning laden. Disregarding the lanes and pathways, they broke through fields and enclosures...Country carts, horses, mules and oxen, followed by negro men, women and even children, laden with every conceivable object were mingling in the mass from every side.

The great majority of Franklin's men had been along at the time and had participated in the depredations which characterized the march, but now, thanks to the rigidly-enforced orders against such actions, the planters were temporarily spared the thoughtless plunder. The ranks had to content themselves with merely pointing out familiar landmarks and recalling some incident which to them was amusing, but which to the planters had been a nightmare.

Unlike the Teche region, where the elegant and classic lines of the sugar mansions had so impressed the invaders, Carencro Prairie was dotted with the small, low walled Acadian cottages of cypress timbers with high pitched roofs, mud and stick chimneys, outside stairways and mud and moss-filled *(bousillage)* walls. On the gallery of each house near the front door was a small *lavado* with a pail of water on top and a polished dipping gourd beside it. A lone chair placed directly before the entrance meant that no one was home. Many of these houses had been constructed *tout fait* over on the Mermentou River where there existed several *vapeur*-powered saw mills. They were then loaded aboard enormous wagons pulled by a dozen yoke of oxen and hauled (the occasion was called a *halerie* or *trainage)* to their permanent prairie locations. An oddity was that most were constructed in such a way that the depth was greater than the length (the length being from gable to gable). "Their houses are generally wretched-looking affairs," wrote one unimpressed Yankee, "without a window glass or mark of neatness or taste about them—mere blemishes upon the landscape."[23]

One of the reasons for the generally unfavorable impressions was the desolate appearance surrounding these modest homes. Why, wondered those who bothered to record their thoughts, were the fields uncultivated, the houses untended, and, in most cases, the inhabitants absent?

The answer was no great mystery to anyone who lived in Louisiana in 1863. The cypress rail fences, or *pieux*, which normally would keep out livestock, had been wantonly destroyed in the interminable search for firewood or sleeping boards, not only by marching Yankees but Confederates as well. Moreover, the few able-bodied slaves had long since deserted, and most of the men were away in the army. Besides, because of Confederate price rigging and the ever-present threat of invasion and confiscation (from both sides) it simply was not worth the effort to attempt a cash crop.

Had the Yankees been able to immediately move several miles north toward Opleousas, they would have found most of the citizens whose absence was so puzzling. When the retreating Confederates had passed the word of the Union advance, many of the residents quickly loaded the household valuables aboard wagons or the family *caleche* and fled. These refugees of war, many of whom were accompanied by faithful servants, now clogged the roads toward Opelousas.

Continuing along without resistance from the Confederates, the Yankees passed at least a few elegant plantation houses, including those of Antoine Emile Mouton (Governor Mouton's brother) and Confederate General Alfred Mouton (the Governor's son). Another old and proud family name frequently encountered along the route was that of Arceneaux. Almost a century before, Pierre Arceneaux (presumably Longfellow's Gabriel) the lost lover of Emmeline Labiche (Evangeline) had settled in nearby Beaubassin.[24] The descendants of Gabriel were now almost as numerous as the ubiquitous Moutons.

RESIDENCE OF ANTOINE MOUTON, recently destroyed by fire. (Griffin Papers, U.S.L. Archives)

The natural beauty of Carencro Prairie was, in the opinion of the invaders, unsurpassed. The gentle rolling terrain, the tree-lined coulees, and the green open prairies where cattle and horses grazed *au large* in the distance was the topic of many letters and diaries that night. But those who lived along the route, including the Dugas, Domingues, Latiolais, Benoits and Broussards, would not have appreciated the gratuitious remark made by one: "O for a thousand Yankee settlers to enter," he wrote, "and make a paradise of this magnificent region."[25]

Once beyond a small community called Carencro (usually spelled Carancro) by its French-speaking inhabitants, the Yankees halted. According to the intelligence reports brought in by scouts from the 1st Texas (Union) Cavalry, a brigade or more of Confederates were lying in ambush near the Bayou Carencro *pavure* (re-enforced ford).

The honor of "forcing the bayou" once more fell to Brigadier General Godfrey Weitzel who, by now, must have considered such an affair quite routine. Opening the assault on the Confederate position were the red-hatted artillerymen of the 1st United States Artillery, Battery L who, in rapid succession, lobbed four twenty-pound and four thirty-pound shells into the heavily wooded area near the Carencro crossing. When the expected response failed to materialize, Weitzel's New York skirmishers (the 116th and 161st infantry regiment) removed their knapsacks for quick maneuvering and moved cautiously forward with fixed bayonets. Although most expected some Rebel trick, such as the ambush that had occurred at Nelson's Bridge near New Iberia, they found to their great relief that Confederate Camp Carrion Crow had been entirely abandoned.

"The rebel General Green," complained a New York skirmisher, "was very much like the Irishman's flea: put your finger on him and he ain't there."[26]

In Opelousas, Louisiana, about twelve miles north of Carencro, the sound of the big guns brought "dread" to "both citizens and soldiers," Within moments a lone Confederate rider, dressed in a tattered "butternut" colored uniform, went dashing through the pot-holed streets bearing an ominous message: "*Les Federaux sont sur le Carencro!*" he shouted, "*Les Federaux sont sur le Carencro!*" ("The Yankees are on the Carencro").

Few places had suffered more from invasion, occupation and confiscation than Opelousas, St. Landry Parish's seat of government. Only a few months before, General Banks' military governor, Colonel Thomas E. Chickering of the 41st Massachusetts Infantry, had spent almost two months in Opelousas "collecting the valuable products of the country." Every house, farm and store in the parish, from Plaquemine Brulee to Barre's Landing, had been practically denuded by Chickering's efficient foraging teams. It had mattered little whether the residents were foreigners, Confederates, loyal Unionists, white or free men of color. The exigencies of war prevailed. Virtually everything had been taken, including cotton, sugar, fodder, corn, livestock, implements, wagons, slaves and anything else of value .

Thus the unwelcome news that the hated Yankees were once more approaching Opelousas created momentary pandemonium. As citizens and soldiers alike scrambled in all directions, the harried merchants, among whom were Jules Perrodin, Joseph Bloch, David Roos, Christian Morningveg, Antoine Christman and Gustof Donnatto f.m.c. (free man of color), responded by padlocking their shops and hiding their valu-

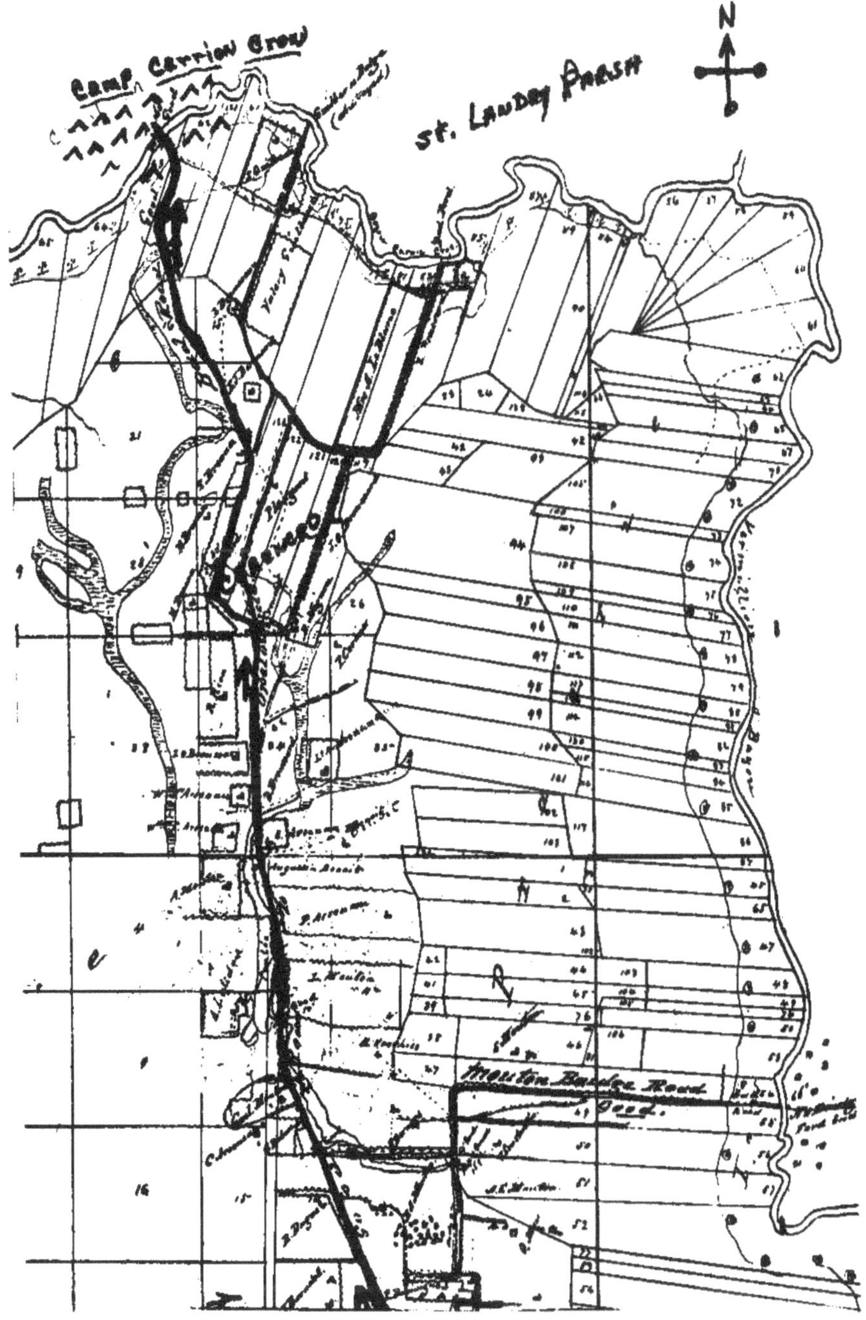

LAFAYETTE PARISH north of Vermilionville, from 1863 Confederate map (National Archives)

ables. Joel Sandoz, editor of the Opelousas *Courier*, hastily printed a last issue and closed down. An Opelousas barber, possibly G. W. Wallis of Ohio, took down the English-language sign which stated in bold block letters: "Free shaves tomorrow." A large number of prosperous planters, including George and Collin Adams, Theodore and Yorick Valade, Evariste Debaillion, Christoval and Francois Dupre, Oscar Alphen, and Omer Poiret, began herding their slaves and cattle toward the safety of the western open prairies. But few people were more concerned than a newcomer, Reverend James Earl Bradley, Pastor of the Episcopal Methodist Church. His "dear heart Annie" down in New Orleans would soon be arriving for their wedding. What would happen now, wondered Bradley, with the Yankees so near?[27]

Even the Confederate camps in and around Opelousas were in a turmoil. Sunday services were temporarily suspended; men hastily returned to their stations, and horses, wagons and soldiers alike scurried in all directions. Later that afternoon, when religious services were resumed, an assistant surgeon of the 16th Texas Dismounted Cavalry, David M. Ray, was astonished at the large numbers who turned out: "They had previous cared but little for preaching," he wrote, but now, with the Yankees so near, "many soldiers are being baptized." Another Texan, W. B. Hunter, wrote his sister that the "Feds are coming on us (but) I believe we can whip any number anywhere. All the bad ages (eggs?) have desirted (sic) and what men we have now are the true grit."

Over in the Louisiana camp, Colonel Henry Gray, commander of the 28th Louisiana Infantry, inadvertently overheard a conversation between two privates. "Banks never found but one army he could whip," complained the private in reference to the Army of Western Louisiana, "and he is everlasting pelting away at that one out of spite."[28]

Back on Bayou Carencro, Major General William Franklin, indecisive, cautious and unimaginative as ever, had no intention of marching on Opelousas that day. For more than a week his troops had been on the march without rest. Moreover there was a possibility that Texas could be reached from this location without the necessity of going on to Opelousas. And besides, the north side of the Carencro, with its gently rolling prairies, shaded banks and pastoral inhabitants, looked defensible, comfortable, and forageable. The Confederates had camped here off and on for years, so why not the Yankees?

CHAPTER SIX

YANKEES ON THE CARRION CROW

Sunday, October 11, 1863

BAYOU CARENCRO, a narrow "nasty, little stream," begins as runoff water from the innumberable prairie ravines or "coulees" in the area once known as Coulee Croche. Too narrow and shallow for navigation, it flows in a predominately easterly direction eventually forming a confluence with Bayou Fusilier where it becomes Bayou Vermilion. Like all the other coulees and bayous of southwestern Louisiana, it was at that time covered with a heavy growth of virgin timber, including moss-draped live oaks, sweetgums, black willows, hackberries and thorny water-locusts. The tree line, ranging from one to two hundred yards in width, ended abruptly on the prairie's edge. Perhaps its greatest significance then, as now, was that it served as the dividing line between St. Landry Parish to the north and Lafayette Parish to the south.

In the spring campaign, General Banks, together with his other generals (Grover, Weitzel, Dwight and Emory) had forded the rain-swollen Carencro during a torrential downpour. So heavy were the rains that the stream had overflowed its banks for a hundred yards or more on each side, forcing the men to wade over in waist deep water. In autumn, however, the bayou reaches a low stage, and the thirsty and footsore soldiers who crossed it on their overland trek toward Texas found "a dirty little brook, dignified by the name of bayou, and prefixed with the appropriate name of Carrion Crow." Every time it rained, complained a soldier from New Hampshire, it "filled six feet deep, but like the witch Gruel in *Macbeth*, it was 'thick and slab' with mud."

Although the French-speaking residents of the area called the stream "Carencro" (with considerable spelling variations) both the Yankees and the Texans knew it as the "Carrion Crow" and it frequently appeared as such on maps, official correspondence, and personal papers. Many soldiers were so intrigued by the unusual appelation that the name itself became a topic of conversation. "It struck me as an odd name to give a stream," recalled Adjutant-General Wickham Hoffman of General Franklin's staff. Hoffman "made inquiries and found that a Frenchman had settled upon its banks, named Carron Cro." A scribe from Wisconsin, by contrast, claimed that "the bayou gets its name from the great number of (Carrion Crow) buzzards that stay in the timber along its banks (and) when sitting on the dry limb of a tree, look nearly as large as a turkey."[1]

On the north bank at the very edge of what the Yankees called Buzzards' Prairie, there stood the relatively large Acadian style plantation home of Thelismar and Constance Guidry. Ile Carencro (or L'isle de Caron Cro), as it was called at the time, had been built for David Guidry and his wife, Modeste (nee Borda), about the turn of the century. Modeste was a foster sister to the legendary Emmeline Labiche (Evangeline) and was the aunt of Governor Alexandre Mouton. When she died in 1856 the family property including the cypress frame house with its *bousillage* walls, steep roof and large gallery passed on to her two grandchildren, Thelismar Guidry and his wife, Constance nee Guidry (a first cousin).[2]

ILE CARENCRO, home of Thelismar and Constance Guidry (Contemporary Photograph)

Like everyone else along the route, the Guidry family suffered from the earlier invasion. During the preceding April, for example, a group of drunks from a sham Louisiana Union regiment had wreaked havoc in the barnyard, wantonly shooting chickens, turkeys, geese and cattle. So incensed was Constance at the time that she had fallen upon her knees with outstretched arms and implored divine providence to reign "death, destruction and ruin" on the entire Federal army.[3] Now, with the Yankees back again Constance would curse fate for having placed her home and property along the main road. So convenient was the location that it had once served as a stagecoach stop and a favorite meeting place for the pre-war *comites de vigilance*. To make matters even worse, she was heavy with child.

At age thirty-two and pregnant Constance Guidry was still beautiful. A graduate of the Academy of Sacred Heart in Grand Coteau she nonetheless pursued a lifestyle contrary to the teachings of that institution. It was not so much her girlish couquettishness that offended the religious, or her penchant for drink and smelly cigars which she shared with many ladies of the day, as her behavior during her infrequent trips *au ville*. At least once a year she would whimsically pack her bags and head toward Barre's Landing (or New Iberia depending on the season) and book passage, all alone, via steamer for the sinful city of New Orleans. No one was sure of what she did on these trips, or why she would leave Thelismar, but the gossip mill had it that she and a friend, Felicite Neda Chretien (the former mistress of Chretien Point who then resided in the *Vieux Carre)* would spend their time shopping, gambling and cavorting.[4]

The war had changed all that. Husband Thelismar, a large landholder and slaveowner, was captivated by war fever and the righteousness of the Southern cause. It was his blood uncle, former Governor Alexandre Mouton, who had signed the declaration of secession from the Union, and he, Thelismar, felt obligated, along with all the other Moutons and Guidrys, to fight for Southern independence. Although he was an educated man and well-heeled financially, Thelismar nonetheless volunteered his services as a private soldier in the predominately Cajun, all volunteer 18th Louisiana Infantry which was then commanded by his friend, former classmate and first cousin, Colonel Alfred Mouton. As was the case with other "gentlemen" volunteers of the day, thirty-three-year-old Thelismar was permitted to bring along a sidearm, a mount and his own personal Negro servant, Jean Pierre Rubin.

Private Guidry's short military career had ended in the tragedy that was Shiloh. Dressed in dark blue uniforms, the 18th Louisiana was badly cut up by small arms and cannon fire from the Confederate side when they were mistaken for the enemy. In spite of this Mouton subsequently ordered a charge on a Union battery which resulted in more than 200 casualties for the 18th, among whom were Thelismar Guidry and Alfred Mouton. Colonel Mouton recovered from his wounds, but Thelismar, whose health was permanently impaired, returned to Constance at Ile Carencro.[5]

Only that morning Thelismar and Constance had taken breakfast in their home with Alfred Mouton, now a brigadier general, as well as General Green and Colonel James Major. No sooner had word come of the Union advance however, than all the men, including Thelismar, departed in the direction of Opelousas, leaving Constance and a twenty-two-year-old neice, Amelia, along with two recently adopted nephews, Onezime John and William O. Campbell (ages six and seven)[6] to face the invaders alone. According to oral tradition Constance, as well as Amelia and the two boys then stood on the long front gallery and watched helplessly while "thousands upon thousands" of soldiers and camp followers turned the surrounding fields "Yankee blue and tent white" as far as the eye could see.[7]

At 11 o'clock A.M. Major General William Franklin, accompanied by Brigadier General Cuvier Grover, approached the house on horseback. "Good morning," said Franklin in schoolboy French, "we will need your house for a few days." Shortly thereafter Franklin filed his first signal dispatch from Camp Carrion Crow:[8]

> I encamp the command beyond the bayou. The stream is wooded, but the water is only in pools...I anticipate no danger here.

Before nightfall of the same day, the Signal Corps team, atop the Guidry home, received instructions from General Banks at Basil Crow's plantation in Vermilionville:[9]

> The Major-General commanding has no special instructions for you beyond what will occur to you, viz, to hold your position in that quarter, and ascertain as much concerning the country in your front and on your flanks as possible...

Life for the Guidry family of Ile Carencro, like the Moutons of Ile Copal,would be nothing less than a nightmare for the next ten days. Constance, Amelia and the two boys, along with a "confidential" house servant, Augustin Domingue, were restricted to the upstairs portion of the house. Food was passed up in a basket. Franklin, and later other generals, occupied the living room while Grover pitched his tent near the dining room steps; the *pieux* (cypress panel) fence, a common feature on most plantations, was pulled down and consumed as firewood or sleeping boards; the corn crop and ox-driven *moulin a gru* (corn mill) was destroyed; and the livestock were slaughtered. Nonetheless Constance could—though she did not—consider herself relatively fortunate. With so many generals camped in and around her house and outbuildings, the stragglers stayed away. As a result her furniture was left intact, her valuables and person safe, and food was plentiful. Indeed she probably never knew of the distinction between the Easterners of the XIX Corps and the Westerners of the XIII Corps.

Monday, October 12, 1863

Early on the second day of the Federal presence, even before the dawn broke over a cloudless Louisiana sky, a Union picket out on Buzzards' Prairie spotted a lone figure approaching his position on foot. Louis Sibille, age twelve, had departed the house of his parents, Joseph and Penelope (nee Burleigh) Sibille, in the Coulee Croche area (currently Bristol) long before daylight. Though he was a regular boarding student at St. Charles College in Grand Coteau, he spent the weekends at home and returned before classes each Monday morning.

Surely he must have known, and his "neutral" parents must have been concerned, about the presence of *Federaux* along the Carencro. As it turned out, luck was on his side. The Yankee picket who had fixed Sibille in his gunsights was barely able to discern in the early morning light that it was only a boy. Thus, instead of being fired upon, the frightened lad was arrested, questioned and sent on his way with the stern warning to never again approach Union lines except in broad daylight and with a white flag.[10]

Louis Sibille was not the only one to come into Union lines that day. When Louisiana severed its ties with the Union, many of the residents of St. Landry Parish had gone off to war just as enthusiastically as anyone from South Carolina, Georgia or Mississippi, but the fall of New Orleans had been a crushing blow to morale. Now, after the devastating spring 1863 campaign, the fall of Vicksburg and Port Hudson, the ceaseless jayhawking and with the Yankees marching again, civilian resistance seemed to crumble. Not only had these earlier events underscored the inevitability of defeat, but the inhabitants were improverished and sick of war. As a result a steady trickle of Confederates and civilian prisoners, Rebel deserters, conscript evaders, parolees from Vicksburg and Port Hudson, runaway slaves, and citizens desiring to take the Oath of Allegiance came in. The latter group included not only those professing strong Union sentiments, but also foreign neutrals and planters in the quest of "protection papers" for themselves, their families and households. (See Appendix).

Among the deserters were Euclide Bernard, Valgran Verret, Ami Sandoz, Levy Stansbury, Demas Mallet, a certain McBride of Plaquemine Brulee,[11] and several Guidrys, Landrys, Guilbeaus and Breauxs. One of the conscript evaders, Caesar Miller, an innovating scoundrel from Plaquemine Brulee (present day Church Point), was said to be a member of Ozeme Carriere's notorious jayhawk band. Whenever Confederate authorities came looking for him at home he would merely lift specially arranged floorboards and slip into a hole under his house.

A more conscientious resistor was Deogene Savoie, who lived in a small *cabana* with his wife, Emilia Prejean, and his poor widowed mother virtually within the encampment on the Carencro. An eighteen-month-old baby, Onesime, had died during the spring invasion and occupation. Now, thoroughly sick of war, and too disheartened over his loss to become involved, Deogene spent most of his time dodging Confederate enrolling authorities. At times, especially when the Rebels were camped nearby, he would hide for days in the thick woods of the bordering bayou. His loyal wife would always save him food from the table, proclaiming to anyone who inquired that it was food for a "pet dog" that lived in the forest.[12]

Such treasonous behavior was not only a source of considerable embarrassment to the Confederate government, but elicited strong responses from the Texans. The latter, whose homes hadnot been disturbed and whose families resided safely beyond the Sabine, rarely missed an opportunity to heap verbal abuse upon the deserters, conscript evaders and oath-taking citizens of southwestern Louisiana. So intense was the criticism that at times it was adopted and echoed for propaganda purposes by the Yankees. For example, *New York Herald's* correspondent in the field, William Gatchell, filed the following dispatch from Camp Carrion Crow:[13]

> Our forces captured some prisoners. Many deserters and refugees came within our lines. The prisoners report the Texans in good spirits and determined to fight to the last. The rebel deserters are principally French Creoles, or Arcadians, (sic) whom the people of Texas and Louisiana despise for their cowardice and treachery.

The Texans and Louisianians also despised the Yankees and planned to make life as miserable as possible for these intruders. Typical was the attitude of Private John R. Cox, a Texas infantryman in the Gould Battalion (Arizona Brigade):[14]

> I had rather dy (sic) forty times than for them to run over our country like they have this but I think they will have a warm time of it before they do it. When they get into Texas, I want to see every lady turn out and fight them—big, little, old and young. I don't know whether I will live to get to Texas or not but if I do I intend to try and kil (sic) all of them I can before they get there.

Of all the possible scenarios perceived by the invaders in their overland trek toward Texas, none seemed more dangerous to the Yankees than a pitched battle with these Texans out on the open defenseless prairies. Time and again one heard the words that "Yankees on foot and in the open are simply no match for Texans on horseback."

On the other hand if the Yankees too were mounted their superior numbers would partially offset the superior horsemanship of the Rebels. After all the 1st Texas Cavalry (Union) and to a lesser extent the 1st

Louisiana (Union) "had shown such high efficiency" that the Union generals "considered the only factor necessary to success was more cavalry." And since they did not have more cavalry and would not be getting any, then "why not mount the infantry?"[15]

Thus on the morning of October 12, 1863, General Franklin's command received a telegraph message from Major General Banks:[16]

> The chief quartermasters of the XIII and XIX Army Corps will immediately adopt measures, under the direction of the Corps commanders, for seizing all the available horses suitable for cavalry or mounted infantry within the safe reach of the forces in the field. The seizures must be made by officers...and receipts for same will be issued to the owners thereof.

Among those infantry regiments getting the long awaited go-ahead were the 87th and 118th Illinois, the 16th Indiana, the 2nd Louisiana and the 160th and 75th New York.

Nowhere was the news received with more jubilation than in the 75th New York Infantry. No sooner had they received the authorization than parties were detailed to scour the countryside. The safest and most promising area was the Carencro settlement, just south of the Union encampment where the soldiers had witnessed so much beauty two days before. In short order the unwelcome visitors began calling on the Guilbeaus, the Brasseauxs, the LeBlancs, the Bernards and Breauxs.

Private James Hall of the 75th New York, who frequently accompanied such expeditions, recalled that although the able-bodied men were off in the Rebel army, the soldiers frequently encountered what they dreaded more than a fight:[17]

> Namely, the scoldings of old women and tears of the young and fair. The ladies would often come to their doors, and beg most piteously not to be deprived of their favorite family horse, or the old Dobbin...but the orders were to take all.

At the Carencro home of Dr. Romain Joseph Francez, a recent emigre from the Haute Pyrenees, France and surgeon for the Lafayette Parish Vigilante Committee, the New Yorkers came across a young slave, Julian Francis, then foddering the doctor's buggy mare. In the caste system of plantation life both Julian and the mare occupied a position of prestige. Julian was the doctor's *petit negre pour drive*. Not only did he usually chauffeur the doctor on his rounds but it was his job to extoll his master's virtues in the hope that this would somehow mitigate the widespread *gris gris* practices and the seeking out of some quack *traiter*. Julian was at home that day only because the doctor's wife, Athanais (nee Bernard) was expecting another child at any moment and he might be needed to find the doctor.

Dr. Francez's buggy horses, in fact any doctor's horse, was considered a cut or two above other buggy horses (which in turn was above a work horse, and so on). So beautiful and well manicured were they that the words "as beautiful as a doctor's horse" were frequently heard in relation to some fine object or animal. Thus when the Yankees approached the stalls, it was only natural that young Julian should assume a protective role. The officer in charge, a certain Captain Smith, inquired for Dr. Francez in perfect French.

"He is *en tournee*" (making sick calls) replied Julian.

"Well, we have come for horses," said Smith, who then ordered his soldiers into the barnyard where they proceeded to lead off seventeen Creole horses, five American horses, a mule, and several bridles, harnesses and saddles.

Julian, though loudly protesting the intrusion, was then ordered to saddle up the doctor's main buggy horse, "a beautiful American mare," which he did only under threats of violence. Once ready to leave, Smith turned and addressed the servant: "*Garcon*," said the officer, "you will tell the doctor that we were in absolute need of these animals and that vouchers will be given if he comes to our headquarters.

Hardly had the officer finished the sentence, however, than Doctor Francez himself drove up in his buggy. Breathing heavily and with a scowl of anger on his face the forty-six-year-old doctor rushed up to the offenders.

"I thought," said Dr. Francez, "that your general would have written an explanation about your visit to me. But to send you here like highwaymen I will not forgive."

The good doctor then stalked into the house to join his pregnant wife and, according to Julian, "was so exasperated that he shutted (sic) the door upon them, refusing to accept the vouchers." As if to add insult to injury, most of Dr. Francez's field hands, including young Julian Francis, Hypolite Francez, Adelard Bernard and Joseph Francez, went off with the Yankees to enlist in the 98th Regiment, United States Colored Infantry.[18]

DR. ROMAIN FRANCEZ, Circa 1840 (Courtesy Mrs. Eric Guilbeau, Carencro)

A short distance away, also on Dr. Francez's property, was the bakery of Simon Mathieu, a twenty-five-year-old immigrant who had come to Carencro from Haute Garonne, France, only a few years before. Mathieu, like Francez, had met with some success in the new world. By 1863 he was baking for and delivering to customers all over the northern portion of Lafayette Parish. Mathieu's delivery horses—seven medium-sized Creoles—were penned in a small enclosure behind the bakery where they were cared for by Joseph Dupre, a slave on the Francez plantation. Spotting the Creoles, the New Yorkers sped toward the enclosure, apparently in a footrace for the equine prizes. "In a very short time," recalled Dupre, "they had rendered themselves masters of the pen."[19]

While the 75th New York was engaged at one end of Carencro, a company of the 160th New York, under the command of First Lieutenant D. H. Winans, was on the other. At the same time, Joseph Baque, a thirty-three-year-old farmer from the Department of Haute Pyrenees, France, was feverishly trying to harvest his patch of sweet potatoes so that the produce could be moved to a place of safety. He had already dug out the adjacent field and, as was customary, was grazing his horses—one American stallion and two Creoles—in the recently harvested yam patch. Two black helpers, Noel Guidry and Etienne Mouton, looked up and spotted the New Yorkers. Recalled Mouton:

> They came along slowly, sometimes stopping at this store, sometimes at that one. There were at that time five stores at 'Carencro Settlement.' At their passage along Mr. Baque's field...a certain Lieutenant ordered me in French—and he spoke it very well—to crash down the fence, in order that he and his men may come over, which I did, and then the cavaliers entered the close and commenced right off to run after the horses.
>
> The Lieutenant, who remained near us addressed Mr. Baque in French, and told him his duty was to gather all the horses he could get; that he was sorry at being compelled to take his horses. Mr. Baque took the thing kindly of him, and then the officer handed over to him a receipt, and all went away.[20]

At the Carencro plantation home of Jacques Crouchet, things were much worse. The thirty-one-year-old Crouchet, from Haute Garonne, France, was at home with his wife, Euphraisie (nee Breaux) two young children, Henri and Lea, and a brother-in-law, Jean Breaux, when the front door was burst open by a detachment of soldiers. Unlike the other intruders, who had carried out seizures in strict obedience to regulations, this particular group of Easterners decided to avail themselves of tableware and kitchen utensils, a hundred or so chickens, a hogshead of sugar, sheets, blankets and quilts, a game pouch, and three head of cattle. Almost as an afterthought, several soldiers sprinted toward the barnyard where they found, and took, two pairs of dun-colored work horses.[21]

About four miles north of Carencro, on a ridge overlooking what some geologists have identified as the ancient Mississippi River Bed, stood the tiny village of Grand Coteau, one of the oldest permanent settlements in southwestern Louisiana. Depending on one's point of view the little town was a "village of considerable beauty" or there was "not much to see." On the outskirts lived such prominent citizens as Virginia McPherson, Alice and Ellen Duffy, William Burleigh and J. H. Wilberding. The latter, a Prussian, floated the tricolor of France over his plantation home, while the McPhersons, Duffys and Burleighs flew the British Union Jack. Such outward manifestations of neutrality had not deterred the invaders during their long march up the Teche and it would not deter the New Yorkers who marched in that day. In short order all the livestock disappeared, as did bridles, saddles, harnesses, wagons and many other objects of value.

Continuing on into town the Federals passed some very "handsome" Acadian-style homes which remain to this day. The town's general store, owned by French-born Eugene Petetin was an attractive target as was Henry Dunbar's drug store, Herman Brinkhaus' shoe shop, and the St. Charles Hotel across the street. The latter, owned by Nicolas Grimmer, "was a haven for travelers of the region." His piano playing daughter, Miss Maria Grimmer, was widely known as the "Belle" of Grand Coteau and had even captivated Confederate General Richard Taylor with her charms.[22]

Just beyond and to the north of these two establishments was one of the loveliest sights in all Louisiana, the St. Charles Jesuit College. A Confederate visitor, Pierre Felix Poche, had only recently described the college in his diary:[23]

> The buildings are spacious, neat and elegant, and all the outhouses are of the most orderly—handsome and commodious. A remarkable cleanliness pervades the whole establishment. The refectory, dormitories and class rooms all bespeak a laudable degree of care and attention. And the cisterns and other water commodities are unsurpassed. The institution raises some very superior stock of horses, and their stables, cow-stables, slaughter pens all display a systematic splendour.

Established in 1836 by eight French members of the Society of Jesus, St. Charles College, together with its sister institution, the Sacred Heart Academy, was among the most prestigious educational institutions in the South. Though it was not intended as an exclusive haven for the rich, the cream of Louisiana society was nonetheless well represented among the student body. Moreover, students from other states, and even other countries came to receive a classical education in the European Catholic tradition. Classes in the humanities, the sciences, languages, and, of course, theology, were conducted in French. There was scarcely a Louisiana regiment anywhere which could not count St. Charles alumni among its members.[24] General Alfred Mouton was a graduate of the College, as was Thelismar Guidry of Ile Carencro and other well-to-do local planters.

FACULTY AND STAFF at St. Charles College, Grand Coteau, circa 1860 (Courtesy Mrs. Fernand Gouaux, Lafayette).

Now, in the autumn of 1863, St. Charles could barely muster enough students, staff or assistants to justify its existence. When Louisiana seceded from the Union the oldest students deserted en masse to fight for Southern independence. War fever attacked even the priesthood, and several, making no pretense of ecclesiastical neutrality, left to become Confederate army chaplains.[25] Perhaps the greatest blow, however, came in April of 1863, when General Banks' XIX Army Corps had made an overnight stop on the nearby Carencro and Bourbeux. At that time an indeterminate number of slaves—a prominent feature of both the College and Convent—went off with the invaders.

In spite of hard times, most of the bluecoats were awed by the gracious wooded groves, the lovely walks, the beautiful gardens and orchards and the verdant pastures where beeves, milk cows, and, most importantly, "magnificent horses" grazed. The sight of so many beautiful animals was of course a temptation which the to-be-mounted Yankees could not resist. Wittin minutes dozens of soldiers went swarming through gates, over fences and across the carefully manicured lawns toward the stables and outbuildings.

SHADED WALK AT ST. CHARLES COLLEGE was planted by slaves in 1837
(The Borromean, Grand Coteau, December 1913)

The forty-five-year-old rector of the college, Father Felix Benausse of Marseilles, France, was horrified at the sight. Collaring a Union officer and speaking perfect English, though with a heavy accent, Father Benausse reminded the New Yorker that General Banks himself had protected the College and Convent in April and had provided "safe conduct" for faculty, staff and students. Although Benausse had not yet consulted with the commanding general on the Carencro, he said that he expected no less protection this time.[26]

The unidentified officer, apparently convinced by such logic, ordered the soldiers to withdraw. The officer would, he promised, consult with General Franklin before taking further action. Had the good fathers known, they could have offered thanks to the Almighty that the intruders were not the destructive Westerners of the XIII Corps. As it was, disaster was barely averted.

OLD COLLEGE BUILDING destroyed by fire in 1910 (St. Charles College Archives)

"THE WHITE HOUSE," cottage home of members of the Society of Jesus, St. Charles College, in 1863 (St. Charles College Archives)

The mission to Grand Coteau did not, however, return empty-handed. By some fortuitous stroke, the invaders came across none other than militia General John G. Pratt of Opelousas, then riding calmly through the streets of Grand Coteau in a *caleche*. The fifty-year-old Pratt, a native of Hartford, Connecticut, looked more like a fugitive moonshiner than the well-educated gentleman planter he professed to be. Though he sported a gray beard it

> looked more like porcupine quills than anything human, and to finish the beauty of his face, it was sprinkled miscellaneously from the chin to his eye brows with tobacco juice. His military apparel consists of a drab colored coat, with broad cape, pants of one piece, but very greasy; a dirty shirt, which had once been red, a rough pair of boots, and a broad brim straw hat. His pants were worn without suspenders, and very short in the waist, the flaps of the pockets hanging down like the ears of some old dilapidated dog.

Indeed Pratt, who was accompanied by his nephew, Captain James Pratt, then serving as his assistant adjutant-general, was a real prize. At one time Pratt had commanded a brigade of Louisiana volunteers but had resigned, so he claimed, on account of poor health. He was now engaged in enforcing the Confederate conscription laws in St. Landry Parish, an unsavory practice which, like slave trading, earned him a reputation as one of the most despicable men anywhere in Louisiana, especially among the persecuted Acadian Unionists.

Despite all this Pratt loudly protested his apprehension, claiming to be just another citizen in pursuit of "ordinary avocations," but his captors, who no doubt learned of his presence through the assistance of Unionists, were unconvinced. In reference to his arrest Pratt later sneered that "the citizens of every town and neighborhood were subject to arrest, confinement and release, under the Yankee system of *lettres-de-cachet*.[27] Pratt was no exception and, in view of his activities, was fortunate that he was not hung.

Tuesday, October 13, 1863

The morning began routinely enough. The "Assembly of Buglers" sounded at 5:30 A. M. signalling the men on Camp Carrion Crow to get out of their blankets and prepare for morning roll call. As was usual the first sounds to come from the masses of humanity sprawled upon the open ground included curses, groans, yawns and threats on the buglers' lives.

At precisely 5:45 A. M. the "Assembly" sounded, calling the men to fall in for roll call. Most emerged and lined up in various states of readiness. Here one pulled on trousers; and here was another with one boot on and the other in hand; others buttoned their blouse or scratched their heads and rubbed their eyes.

ARRESTING CITIZENS in Southwestern Louisiana

"Roll Call," once terminated, was a powerful cathartic for the majority and most headed at once to the slit trenches or "sinks" on the edge of camp. A few minutes later "Stable Call" sent the artillerymen and cavalrymen to the corrals where they were to groom and feed their horses:

> Come to the stable and work while you're able
> And give your poor horses some hay, oats and corn.

This was followed by "Breakfast Call" after which the duties of the day began in earnest. The 75th New York, for their part, sent parties out in three separate directions in the continuing search for horses.

Out on Buzzards' Prairie, not more than a mile north of Camp Carrion Crow, there lived a septuagenarian by the name of Robert Smith. The old fellow, dressed in his indigo blue *cottonnade* trousers, had just finished his breakfast of *cafe noir* and *couche-couche* and was saddling his only horse for a ride to Grand Coteau when his eye caught a glitter of early morning sunlight on something in the distance. Straining to see and no doubt concerned, he soon made out a column of men on foot numbering perhaps twenty-five. As he later related the story, it would have made no difference whether they had been Yankees, jayhawkers or Rebels. To him they were all enemies.

"Good morning," said a New Yorker as he approached the old man with the gray hair. "How do you like your horse?"

Smith, backing away defensively, understood and spoke enough English to reply "I like my horse just fine."

"Good," said the bluecoat, "I like him too," whereupon the latter took the reins from the old gentleman, mounted up and left. In the meantime the others entered Smith's modest dwelling and helped themselves to a meal of *gros gru,* bacon and eggs.[28]

At Grand Coteau, a few miles east of the Smith place, Dr. Edward Millard, a practicing physician of the town, rode through the front gates of St. Charles College. Accompanied by a delegation of officers belonging to the staff of Major General Franklin, Millard called on the rector to whom he presented a set of official "protection papers" and a promise of what Father Benausse called *salvum conductum:*

> A safeguard is hereby granted to the Roman Catholic College, its inmates and property. All officers and soldiers belonging to the United States are therefore commanded to respect this safeguard, and to afford, if necessary, protection to the inmates, their persons and property of the said college, situated in St. Landry Parish, La., situated at Grand Coteau.

So grateful was Father Benausse for the safeguard that he quickly drafted a message of thanks to the Union commander:

> Sir: As Resident of the Roman Catholic College at Grand Coteau and in the name of all the inmates of that institution, I return you thanks for the safeguard you have sent us...
> You will please accept the expression of our sincere feelings of gratitude. We pray that God himself may requite your kindness.

In the meantime the officiating paster, Father Franciscus Lespes, age forty-three of Pau, France, proceeded to note in his diary that the Yankees also furnished "*un picquet de quelques hommes pour nous proteger*" ("a picket of their men to protect us").[29]

Back on the Carencro, a bugler was blowing "Sick Call" when sharp firing broke out along the picket line, killing one Yankee and wounding several others. Frightened for their lives, several parties of foragers, including those of the 75th New York at Robert Smith's house, beat a quick retreat to the safety of camp.

Within moments a group of mounted Texans, numbering perhaps one thousand, began streaming south over the prairie from the bridge just behind the Chretien Point plantation home of Hypolite Chretien. "Boots and Saddles" called the artillerymen to their duty stations while the muffled beat of the long roll summoned the infantry to arms.

There then followed a dreary, energy-sapping excercise which continued for hours. First the Rebels would line up in battle formation from left to right fronting the Union position. A few rounds of ineffectual artillery would then be lobbed into the camp from some concealed position near Bayou Bourbeux, two miles north of the campsite. No sooner did the short barrage let up than the Texans would charge, or at least they pretended to charge. The long lines of bluecoated infantrymen, numbering perhaps five, six or seven times that of the opponent would then march a short distance forward where the advance line would drop down on one knee, level their Springfields and Enfields and await the slaughter that would surely follow if the Texans came close enough. At the last possible moment the Rebels would halt, backtrack, wait an hour or more and then "charge" again.

The fake Rebel charges, followed by the Union response, was as recurrent as the intermittent rain which continued throughout the day. Finally, about mid-afternoon, the Rebels seemed to tire of the cat and mouse game and withdrew to the north side of Bayou Bourbeux. A bugler on the Carencro blew "Fatigue Call" and camp life, such as it was, returned to normal.[30]

CHAPTER SEVEN

WESTERNERS IN VERMILIONVILLE

Sunday, October 11, 1863

AT ILE COPAL, some twelve miles to the rear of Union Camp Carrion Crow, Brigadier General Michael K. Lawler decided to plug a leak in his tent during a torrential downpour. Clad in black oilskins and muddy boots, he worked all alone, ignoring the lightning and drowning rain that had long since caused more sensible people to seek shelter. A big bear of a man, Irish-born Lawler could one moment be an intemperate thoughtless beast and the next a man of deep compassion. On a routine march he was noted for relentlessly driving his men as though their very lives depended on speed. It was he who in a violent outburst of temper near Franklin came very close to decapitating a young Illinois forager with his sword.

Unknown to Lawler, the older brother of that soldier, who was roaring drunk on "red eye," had sworn vengeance for his little brother's humiliation and had boasted openly that given half a chance he would kill the big man; and what better opportunity than now. There stood Lawler without his fast-fisted aid, apparently oblivious to the passions he could generate by his very presence.

Staggering up to Lawler's tent, the drunken soldier thrust a .58 caliber Enfield in the big general's face. "You are the man who wanted to kill my brother at Franklin," he shouted above the roar of distant thunder. "Now goddamn you, I'll kill you." Taking aim, the deranged man pulled the trigger and exploded the percussion cap but, incredibly, the wet charge failed to ignite. Though badly shaken, Lawler nonetheless recovered his wits and quickly moved to the attack, battering his would-be assassin to the muddy ground.

Had Lawler so chosen, he could have administered summary justice on the spot as he had done once before, or he could have had the drunk court-martialed and sent before a firing squad. However, for reasons known only to the vacillating general, he instead sentenced the soldier to a short term in the guard house and a stiff dose of laxatives. "Under a rough exterior and with crude manners," commented a bystander, "Lawler carries in his breast the heart of a hero."[1]

In the Mouton household, only a few feet away from where Lawler continued to work on his tent, things were not going well. Early that morning Dr. Francis Sterling Mudd, the family physician, had made the trek on foot from Vermilionville to Ile Copal. On the road he had encountered the marching XIX Corps, and then on arrival he was searched and harassed by soldiers of the XIII Corps. Still, Dr. Mudd worked desperately to save the life of the sick Mouton girl. All his efforts, unfortunately, were in vain and Marie Cecilia Acadi Mouton, age twenty-seven, quietly died around noontime on Sunday, October 11, 1863.

What then followed was more akin to a nightmare than reality. In normal times a death was attended to by a prescribed set of ancient Acadian practices. The honey bee hives were supposed to be covered by a piece of black cloth to "put the bees in mourning;" all mirrors were to be covered with cloths; the clocks were to be stopped to indicate that they need no longer mark the hours for the deceased; and all water containers were to be emptied in the belief that the departed might otherwise drown. Moreover, the body was supposed to be shrouded by two people unrelated to the family; and the deathbed linen and mattress was to be destroyed by fire. Finally, the body of the deceased was to be encircled by burning candles.[2]

But the honey bees were gone, their hives robbed and then destroyed by the *Federaux*. The mirrors were broken or taken for the use of the officers quartered below, as were the clocks and most of the candles. The water containers, already overtaxed in supplying the Federal army and attendant animals, could not be emptied; nor was the family allowed to receive visitors who might shroud the body and discard the filthy linen.

Although tragic, Cecilia's death was anything but unexpected. For days her sisters—Mathilde, Odeide and "Pussy"—and an ancient house servant called "Sib" had been keeping a large wooden "Star" candle box to be used as a makeshift coffin. The box was located downstairs in Yankee territory, but had so far remained undisturbed by the Union officers who were presumably aware of its purpose. However, on her way to make the arrangements Odeide Mouton, young Alexandre's frail and sick mother, was horrified to see a big Indiana soldier heading out the door with the candle box over his shoulder.

Summoning her remaining strength Odeide rushed up to the culprit and angrily exclaimed: "Please put this box of candles down! I am sure had you known its history you would never have laid eyes on it; it is to be used for the funeral of my sister."

The startled Yankee stopped for a moment and even acted apologetic for taking the box, but then he turned on his heels and walked away, ignoring the sick woman's pleas. At that point Odeide became quite irrational and lunged toward the thief. Screaming, scratching and kicking she succeeded in knocking the stolen item to the ground whereupon she sat on it and dared the soldier to touch it again. Fortunately for all, the altercation that was about to ensue was prevented by the approach of an unidentified high-ranking officer, a true gentleman in this case, who commanded the heartless offender to convey the heavy box back inside and up a steep flight of stairs to the room where the lifeless girl lay.

There then remained the problem of what to do about poor Cecilia's remains. With several thousand Yankees surrounding the grounds and all means of conveyance gone, how were the Mouton ladies to transport their departed sister's corpse a distance of approximately two miles to the family burial plot behind St. John's Catholic Church? Odeide was now too ill to assist, having exhausted her strength in the struggle for the pathetic coffin and was confined to bed. To ask these despicable Yankees for assistance—who no doubt were held responsible for the loss—would be unconscionable.

While the Mouton sisters were sadly pondering their options, old "Sib" entered the room with a note sent by one of the Union officers. The message was innocent enough. Several officers extended their sympathy and offered to assist. They also requested that they be given permission to come by and pay their final respects to Miss Cecilia.

Odeide Mouton was infuriated by the request. Lifting herself from the bed she grabbed a pen and quill and drafted a venomous reposte: "Your wishes are respectfully refused," she wrote, "and the sympathy you proffer, for no reason than to advance your morbid curiosity, please keep for yourself!"

Just as it seemed the ladies of Ile Copal would have to swallow their pride and turn to the Yankees anyway, there appeared a *deus ex machina* in the person of an old English brickmaker, Sebastian Chargois. Mr. "Bastian," as he was fondly known, had come to Vermilionville from London many years before and, with brothers Richard and Hubert, had become one of the leading businessmen of the town. Although his home had been plundered along with almost everyone else's, he managed to secure four serviceable wagon wheels attached to two separate axles. These wheels, the remains of an old hack, were joined together by several boards which he said could be used as a floor on which to place the wooden casket. Though crude, it was better than asking the Yankees for assistance, and the survivors of that unhappy Yankee autumn would recall many years later that it was as if divine providence had intervened on their behalf.

Monday, October 12, 1863

The funeral procession set off toward St. John's Church on a clear cool morning. There were none of the customary flowers or periwinkle leaves attached to the blanket-draped coffin; nor was there a beautiful black horse to assist the tearful relatives in conveying their burden. In fact there wasn't even a skinny jackass. Nonetheless, the Mouton family, assisted by friends and relatives from all over Vermilionville, managed to move the clumsy vehicle by manpower. Benjamin Steward, a blacksmith and one of the few faithful *domestiques* at Ile Copal was there to help, as were the Chreightons, Mudds, Crows, Monniers and many others. As they alternately pushed and pulled their burden, they were hampered by mud, deep ruts and incredulous Yankees who, every few yards it seemed, demanded to inspect the contents of the wooden box.

Once at their destination on land donated by and named for Cecilia's grandfather, Jean Mouton, the family found even more Yankees. Soldiers of the U. S. Signal Corps, under the command of Captain William A. Pigman, were not only camped in and around the church entrance, but a group of semaphore officers, standing on the steeple balcony—the highest point in town—were entertaining a number of onlookers with their curious "talking flags."

Inside the church, Father Etienne Jules Foltier, though old and ailing, delivered an elegant eulogy to the tearful audience. Cecilia Mouton was then interred at the foot of her mother's tomb in the Mouton family plot near the rear of St. John's Church. Her father, former Governor Alexandre Mouton, did not yet know of the tragedy.[3]

ST. JOHN'S CATHOLIC CHURCH occupied by a Union Signal Corps team in the fall of 1863. *(Leslie's Illustrated Weekly)*

Monday, October 12, 1863, was also an unusually busy day for the generals, colonels and provost marshals of the XIII Corps. They all agreed that something would soon have to be done about the lawless foraging which was exceeding all bounds of civilized behavior. At the same time precautionary measures needed to be adopted against the possibility of guerilla activities.

Responsibility for the latter fell to Cadwalader Colder Washburn, a forty-five-year-old Major General with clear blue eyes, a light complexion and a neatly cropped chin beard. Washburn was a former Republican congressman, lawyer and businessman from Wisconsin. As in the case of Banks, and possibly even Grover, his main qualification for command seemed to be his high political connections, if not his great wealth. The grandson of a Revolutionary War officer, he was a brother of Israel Washburn (Governor of Maine) and Elihu Washburn (a close intimate of President Lincoln and principal sponsor of U. S. Grant). Unlike Banks, whose polished eastern education, good looks and charming personality served to disarm critics, Washburn was dour, poorly educated, unimpressive in appearance and possessed of a fierce independence that bordered on arrogance. In spite of these shortcomings, however, Washburn was said to be brave, steady, respectable and, according to Charles Dana, Lincoln's Assistant Secretary of War, he exercised good judgement. All these qualities would be severely tested on the civilian population of Vermilionville during the next few days.[4]

Although there are few extant records of just what Washburn did, or why, it appears that the citizens of Vermilionville, under Washburn's instructions, were to be viewed as belonging to one of three separate groups, viz., those who openly sided with the United States (e.g., blacks and loyal Unionists); those who claimed to be neutral (e.g., foreigners, especially French and British) and; finally, those who openly sided with the Confederacy.

After setting up a receiving station on the courthouse square, the XIII Corps adjutant, under instructions from General Washburn, asked the citizens of Vermilionville and environs—whether loyalists, neutrals or Confederates—to come in and take the Oath of Allegiance to the Old Flag.

Not a few came by. Indeed at times there were so many, "especially among the poorer class of citizens," that the oral portion was frequently administered in groups rather than individually. Foremost among those taking the vows were the Cajun conscript evaders. "They are coming into our lines by the hundreds," wrote a soldier to the *Richmond Paladium*. "Many of them say they have not been home or inside of a house for eighteen months, but have been hiding in the swamps to avoid conscriptions."

The oath-taking ceremony, conducted by an officer and scribe with notarial powers, consisted of raising the right hand and repeating a litany of confusing pledges. There was no way to measure the sincerity of those who took, and then signed, the oath (usually with an "X"). Many, if not most, of the residents of Vermilionville were not only illiterate in their own tongue, but could neither speak, read nor write the English language and, even if they could, probably did not comprehend the oath's meaning.

Some, no doubt, were loyal Unionists. Many considered themselves neutral and wanted no part in the war, especially the conscript evaders; others, perhaps a majority, felt that the oath would protect themselves, their families and property from the senseless destruction and plunder then taking place. Among Vermilionville's leading citizens taking the oath were Honore Beraud, Joseph Boudreaux, Zephraim Doucet, W. H. Hawkins, M. Eloi Girard and Sheriff Richard Chargois. (See Appendix). Many of these citizens had once served as members of the pre-war *Comites de Vigilance* and most had relatives fighting for the Confederacy.

MAJOR GENERAL C. C. WASHBURN
(Harper's Weekly)

Neither the oath-givers nor the oath-takers were without their critics. To some it was analogous to striking a dark Faustian bargain—a pact with the devil. Confederate General John Pratt sneered that while the law-abiding citizens of southwestern Louisiana were "forced to take obligations of citizenship" they were not accorded the protection of that citizenship.

Confederate Colonel Gustave A. Breaux, himself a resident of Vermilionville, sounded a more vindictive note:

> A large number of men without principles (and) guided by cringing interests, have rushed to take the infamous Yankee oath of allegiance—while wishing no one harm, we are not sorry to see that such degrading acts do not relieve the actors from being plundered and ruined by those to whom they cringe, anymore than other citizens.

Office Provost Marshal General,

DEPARTMENT OF THE GULF,

New Iberia
New Orleans, Nov 19th 1863.

I do hereby solemnly and sincerely swear, in the presence of Almighty God, that I will support, protect and defend the Constitution and Government of the United States against all enemies, whether domestic or foreign, and that I will bear true and faithful allegiance and loyalty to the same, any Ordinance, Resolution or Law of any State, Convention or Legislature to the contrary notwithstanding; and further, that I take this oath, and assume all its responsibilities, legal and moral, of my own free will, and with a full determination, pledge and purpose to observe and fulfill it, and without any mental reservation or evasion whatsoever; and further, that I will well and faithfully perform all the duties that may be required of me by law, as a true and loyal citizen of the United States. And may God help me so to do!

Massell X Buteaux

Sworn to and subscribed before me, this 19th day of November 1863.

OATH OF ALLEGIANCE as administered to Massell Buteaux, November 19, 1863 in New Iberia (National Archives)

Perhaps more ominous than the relatively innocuous oath-taking ceremony were the interrogations that sometimes followed. In order to isolate those citizens considered as dangerous to the United States the "genuine" loyalists were asked to inform on their neighbors. In particular the Union authorities wished to identify—and confine—anyone who might be a spy, Confederate soldier, rabble-rouser, partisan supporter of the Confederacy, or anyone else known to speak out against the Union. Since just about everybody in Vermilionville was guilty of one or the other of these offenses—especially the last—it was inevitable that a number of citizens would be detained, sometimes quite arbitrarily, as in the case of Dr. Francis Sterling Mudd, Cecilia Mouton's physician.

Dr. Mudd's arrest, made "at the instigation of a Union man, a worthless fellow, who had been under the ban of the law for crimes not political," was a mystery to all. Mudd was a close friend of Governor Mouton and he was severely shaken by the death of young Cecilia. It is quite possible that he echoed the Mouton family's sentiments that the Yankees were partially responsible for Cecilia's death. At any rate, on the evening of October 12, 1863, while he was quietly sitting with his wife on the gallery of their (Sterling Avenue) home, the dwelling was surrounded by a squad of soldiers under the command of a certain Captain Martin. A warrant signed by Major General C. C. Washburn, then quartered at Henri Monnier's residence, was cited as the only authority for the apprehension.

According to a deposition filed with Confederate General Pratt the following year, Dr. Mudd begged to remain at home that night as his wife would be alone, and the next morning he would deliver himself up to the Union provost marshal, Captain J. B. Gorsuch. But the request was denied and Mudd was conducted the two miles or so to Basil Crow's cooper shop where he joined, or was soon joined by, paroled prisoners of war from the Vicksburg campaign as well as a number of prominent Louisiana residents, including General John G. Pratt of Opelousas; Supreme Court Justice Albert Voorhies of St. Martinville; Captain Theodore Devalcourt of Grand Coteau; John Republican Chreighton, Louis Couret, Romulus McBride and a Reverand Rand of Vermilionville; Valsin Broussard and Jules Guidry of Cote Gelee; and Colonel Daniel O'Bryan of Abbeville.

The apprehension of Militia General John G. Pratt, captured by Franklin's advance near Grand Coteau, was a source of considerable rejoicing among the conscript evaders. Wrote a correspondent for the *Richmond Paladium:*

> The Union men were glad to get him prisoner. They danced and jabbered around like so many Indians, and were much surprised that our Generals did not order him hung without ceremony. He has been a terror to all the loyal men of the country, hunting them down with dogs, like slaves, and those that escaped his savage cruelty, did so by fleeing to the swamps and cane brakes for safety. And now they are coming forth like the leaves of the forest, eager to be armed and swear eternal vengeance against their persecutors.

Pratt, not one to be outdone by inflammatory rhetoric, had a few choice words himself to describe his confinement by the Yankees on Basil Crow's plantation:[5]

> Here, among deserters, criminals of the army and negroes, besides suffering from the discomforts of (our) situation and the nauseous filth of fellow prisoners, (we) were subject(ed) constantly to the vulgar abuse of the guard, and of those whom curiosity attracted to the place.

As the Union dragnet swept through Vermilionville and environs, a curious case came to the attention of Provost Marshal Gorsuch. Colonel Daniel O'Bryan of Abbeville, the head of a militia regiment for Vermilion Parish, had arrived in Vermilionville for reasons that are unclear. His military organization had been formed by Louisiana state law as an instrument to maintain "peace and order" during the absence of most of the white male citizens and had questionable affliliation with the Confederate armed forces. Nonetheless, O'Bryan was considered to be a dangerous agent because he had served as a member of the state Secession Convention. At any rate he was spotted by a Union informer who was quick to notify Gorsuch of his presence. An "arrest squad," led by a Captain Lang of the 11th Wisconsin Infantry, cornered O'Bryan in Antoine Parker's shoeshop only after a spirited footrace through the streets of Vermilionville. "I no keep Secesh soldier here!" protested Parker in broken English even as O'Brian hid under a table in a back room. For this indiscretion Parker, too, was thrown in jail where he was accused of aiding an "enemy of the United States."[6]

Two other unpleasant, though necessary, duties fell to the Federal invaders. In the first place the large army had to be supplied with food and other provisions. For days the soldiers had been issued the standard marching rations of hardtack, salt pork and coffee, but because Lafayette Parish was so richly endowed by nature, fresh provisions were now available. Accordingly, each brigade regularly dispatched an official foraging party over the broad prairies to round up livestock, dairy products, vegetables and other goods. The foraging parties, all of which were accompanied by an officer, usually issued a receipt for the confiscated goods along with a promise to pay the unfortunate planter at some future date.

Among the most unfortunate were Chevalier and Elise Thibodeaux, who lived a short distance southeast of Pinhook Bridge. With the Federal lines stretching downstream to Jefferson Caffery's and upstream to John Chreighton's, the Thibodeaux plantation, located roughly at the midway point, was ideally suited as a forage receiving and distribution station. Surely the Thibodeauxs must have felt cursed. In the dark pre-war days of banditry and vigilante committees, they had regularly been victimized by cattle rustlers. Likewise, during the spring invasion of 1863 a Union regiment, the 114th New York, had confiscated what few cattle the "Texicans" had left. Now, in that tragic autumn they had nothing to give but their land, but even that was converted to the use of the Federal army. Especially appalling was the Federal practice of using Thibodeaux's barnyard as a slaughter pen. Not only did the butchers' bullets sometimes penetrate the walls of the feeble old man's house, but "the atmosphere around was infested by the stench of offal and putrified carcasses."

The second unpleasant task, closely related to the first, was the long standing order to confiscate the staple products of the rebellious states. During the spring invasion of 1863, large portions of southwestern Louisiana had been denuded by a well conceived and thoroughly executed operation, especially St. Landry and St. Martin Parishes. Though the Union invaders did not attempt to enforce the Confiscation

Act on the same scale during the fall campaign to Texas, they did take what came their way.

One unfortunate Frenchman who crossed their path was Jean Pierre Gueydan, a thirty-four-year-old merchant, cattle driver and, lately, opportunist, who resided in Abbeville. In his classic work on the history of the Vigilante Committees, Alexandre Barde referred to Gueydan as a "clean, honest, active merchant, acting and working always like the Wandering Jew of the legend. He brought with him the old traditions of French honor: self-respect, dignity and intelligence." Doubtless, Gueydan was, or had been, all these things, because of the war he was on the run from Confederate authorities for conscript evasion and, like so many others of the times, managed to carry on a lucrative speculation practice that few would have considered honorable. Many of the overtaxed Louisiana planters and ranchers, faced with possible destruction or seizure of their produce from both Confederates and Yankees were all too eager to sell to speculators, such as Gueydan, for a price far lower than what the New Orleans market would otherwise command.

As the Yankees moved into Lafayette Parish, Gueydan reasoned that the time had come to move out some of the cotton he had previously purchased from John Republican Chreighton of Vermilionville, as well as from Eloi Guidry and Norbert Landry in Cote Gelee. Claiming to be an avid Union supporter, Gueydan secured a safe conduct permit from the Union provost marshal in New Iberia and then arranged for twenty-four-year-old Jacques Bonnemaison, a Royville (present day Youngsville) merchant, to haul the cotton to Madame Eugene Olivier's on the Teche.

No sooner had Bonnemaison, together with forty-two-year-old Edouard Fabre, loaded the eleven bales of cotton at Chreighton's shed onto wagons than they were surrounded and then arrested by the invaders. Characteristically, the Yankees proceeded to seize not only Gueydan's cotton but also the remaining fifty bales on the Chreighton place despite the loud protest of Madame Euphemie Chreighton (nee Mouton) and her fifteen-year-old son Emile. With cotton then selling at the unprecedented price of .68 cents per pound (average factor prices in New Orleans) Chreighton and Gueydan's combined loss that day exceeded eighteen thousand dollars (i.e. 61 bales at 450 pounds per bale) or about $94,000 in terms of 1978 currency.[7]

Back in camp, the soldiers of the XIII Corps were grateful for the opportunity to rest, wash and replenish their supplies after the long march up the Teche. Moreover, the weather was generally warm and pleasant, the water in the Vermilion was sparkling clear, clean and plentiful, and the foraging was unsurpassed for variety and abundance. But a problem which had followed the Yankees up the Teche—indeed one which had plagued armies from time immemorial—was the ceaseless, unfounded rumors which circulated from regiment to regiment and camp to camp. Most of the rumors in Camp Vermilion centered around some spectacular defeat or victory, the death or capture of some prominent general, an impending battle or the objective of the autumn 1863 campaign.

That Texas was the ultimate destination of General Banks' invasion of southwestern Louisiana must have been the worst kept secret of the war. Whether they would have to fight the "Texicans," the Mexicans or the French was a never ending topic. Thus it came as no great surprise when it was announced that the French Emperor, Napoleon III, had invited Archduke Maximilian of Austria to help govern Mexico. Especially intriguing was a "grape vine dispatch" that France had recognized the Confederacy, an act that would constitute a *casus belli.* "Should such be the case," wrote Captain William Barney of the 29th Wisconsin Infantry "we away out here have come to the conclusion that we and the Mexicans—who will cooperate with us—can whip both Secesh and Frog-eaters."[8]

Although the common soldier did not fully comprehend the complexities of the Texas-Mexico-French connection (or the Monroe Doctrine for that matter), he did perceive that the French were the villains. That was at least partially the cause of the negative attitudes toward, and the ill-treatment of, the French-speaking residents of Louisiana. Thus, while eleven thousand or more ill-disciplined soldiers of the XIII Corps lay in camp along the Vermilion, the good citizens of Vermilionville suffered. Typical was the attitude of an Iowan who recalled:

> A great many of the people in this section were French, or claimed to be, and when we were marching through, claimed French protection by hanging out French flags. All good enough in their estimation, but a fat rooster or a sheep from a plantation over which a flag of France floated was just the same to us as from one carrying the rebel colors.

If a prize had been awarded the state whose soldiers plundered the most, Iowa and Indiana would surely have taken top honors. The 24th and 46th Indiana were especially active, having robbed and pillaged practically every merchant and planter from Berwick to Vermilionville. Almost as bad were the boys of the 24th Iowa. Known as the "temperance regiment" because its first colonel had been a Methodist minister, the Iowans were mainly farmers, predominantely protestant and deeply patriotic. But neither their religion, which they professed to take seriously, nor their crotchedly old eccentric colonel, John Q. Wilds, prevented them from despoiling the landscape. Even before reaching Ile Copal they had broken ranks in a frenzied rush to secure firewood and sleeping boards from what remained of Governor Mouton's sugar house. Hour after hour they straggled into camp, sometimes individually and sometimes in groups, carrying every object imaginable. Some pushed carts in which were stowed household objects such as clothing, china, trunks, furniture, jewelry and even stoves. Others carried chickens, geese, turkeys, hogs or sweet potatoes, while still others were driving or leading milk cows, bleating sheep or beeves.

REMAINS OF GOVERNOR MOUTON'S SUGARHOUSE
(Leslie's Illustrated Weekly)

Although Colonel Wilds had no stomach for such actions, he seemed pitifully helpless in his efforts to restrain them from "having a jolly good time." At first he tried harsh language, loudly "pitching into" the officers who, according to Wilds, "were just as bad as the men." When Captain William Titus Rigby was caught red-handed burning down a house (possibly Walnut Grove), Wilds lost his temper again. Grumbled Rigby: "He is the most unreasonable man to talk to when he is out of humor."

Having failed with words, the normally popular colonel placed sentinels, fifty in number, in a circle around the 24th Iowa campsite with orders to arrest anyone "going or coming." When the makeshift prison began to overflow with offenders—some sources stated as many as one-half the entire regiment—the old gray-haired colonel merely threw his arms up in disgust and gave up.

Colonel Wilds seemed to be an exception. Most officers from general down to lieutenant simply ignored the illegal foraging. Brigadier

General George McGinnis, who commanded the Third Division, collared a young soldier of the 28th Iowa "sneaking into camp with a good load of fat chickens," eight in number. "How many men must you share those chickens with?" asked the nervous general.

"Four, sir!" replied the frightened private.

"All right," commanded McGinnis, "there are four of us. You take four; leave me four, and don't get caught again!"

The very next day, the same general caught another group of Iowans *in flagrante delicto* in a yam patch. Riding his horse up to the culprits as they were "prying out the great big yellow fellows" with a bayonet McGinnis demanded to know what they were doing.

"Getting yams, sir!" replied a soldier.

"All right," commanded the general "but don't dig more than you can carry!"

Following closely on the heels of the Iowans and Hoosiers in terms of foraging talents were the boys from Wisconsin. Robert Steele, a thirty-one-year-old first lieutenant of the 23rd Wisconsin likened his troops to the "locust of Egypt," While one group was "cleaning out" the plantation home of Jefferson Caffery, another, among whom was Henry Whipple of the 29th Wisconsin, paid a call on Izidor Broussard.

Broussard, an ornery old planter living on the southeastern bank of Bayou Vermilion, would just as soon "shout and cuss" at a piece of machinery as a family servant. After the young soldiers had helped themselves to "seven ducks, six chickens and a hog," Broussard came up and loudly demanded compensation in Confederate currency. Incredibly; the Wisconsin youths paid up and left.

Even General C. C. Washburn, also of Wisconsin, seemed insensitive to the plunder. Several days after the XIII Corps' arrival in Vermilionville he reminded the 29th Wisconsin of General Banks' orders against illegal foraging. Said Washburn: "(You) must take nothing from a Union man!" In the next breath he reminded his captive audience "that there was not a Union resident within 300 miles."[9]

Not everyone suffered as a result of the Union pause on the Vermilion. In fact some individuals and establishments profited immensely, especially those engaged in plying the more sensual arts. Foremost among these was a *femme de coleur libre*, who owned and operated a popular bordello on the outskirts of Vermilionville. Among her sable beauties, who ranged in color from charcoal black to almost white, was a certain "*reine-Africaine*," a green-eyed, light-complexioned quadroon whose services were always in high demand, especially among the elite white clientele. With such choice merchandise available it was only natural that the more lascivious bluecoats of the XIII Army Corps would regularly frequent the establishment. So wealthy did the hardworking proprietress become that, according to tradition, she eventually retired to a life of leisure and opulence.

Another source of illicit pleasure, especially for men in the ranks, was the large number of camp followers. These "Abe's delights," as the runaway slaves were sometimes called, were camped about one mile south of Pinhook Bridge on the road leading to New Iberia. According to one source, there was a veritable "army" of young females operating out of crudely fashioned burlap tents, or just about any other convenient location—not all of which were private—who regularly dispensed their favors to the "Linkum sojers" for pecuniary gain, usually a Yankee dollar. Thus the religious farm boys from Iowa, Wisconsin, Illinois, Indiana and Ohio, many of whom had lost their virginity in the sin dens of New Orleans, now risked their health and their conscious for a frolic on the banks of the Vermilion.[10]

With so much debauching and foraging and with order having broken down to an alarming extent, several of Vermilionville's leading citizens, including Honore Beraud, Richard Chargois and Joseph Boudreaux, demanded an audience with Major General E. O. C. Ord, the recently arrived commander of the XIII Army Corps.

MAJOR GENERAL E. O. C. ORD
(Library of Congress)

Edward Otho Cresap Ord, age forty-five of Maryland, was a rarity among the Union generals of the Army of the Gulf. Without political connections, he was neither wealthy nor had he been exiled to the Gulf Department because of incompetence on the fields of Virginia as was the case with Banks, Franklin and Grover. On the contrary, he had demonstrated his proficiencies as a mathematician, Indian fighter, battlefield commander (at Corinth and Vicksburg) and had even participated in the pre-war expedition with Colonel Robert E. Lee in suppressing John Brown's raid on Harper's Ferry.

Ruggedly handsome with a heavy mane of premature gray hair, dark brooding eyes and a Stalin-type brush mustache, West Pointer Ord was strictly a no-nonsense commander. Though still recovering from a severe wound at Corinth and debilitated by the mysterious swamp fevers of southern Louisiana, Ord nonetheless had convinced Banks that he was fit for a field command and had accompanied the Major General Commanding up the Teche. Had he, in fact, been fit it is quite possible that together with Franklin, he could have suppressed the illegal foraging and outrageous behavior of the XIII Corps' Westerners, but as it turned out, Ord's poor health would soon preclude his further participation in the Great Texas Overland Expedition.[11]

Ord did not depart, however, before leaving his mark. Unlike Washburn, who seemed unconcerned with the complaints of local residents, Ord lent a sympathetic ear to the complaining citizens of Vermilionville. Sheriff Chargois, the principal spokesman for the complaining citizens, convinced the general that the good people of Vermilionville and surroundings were either loyal Unionists or neutral foreigners. The citizens, said Chargois, were "heartily tired of Texas rule"and would make "armed resistance to the Confederates." On the other hand, the appalling behavior of the Federals, as well as the lawlessness of the runaway slaves, served to push their sympathies back toward the Confederate fold.

Whether convinced by these arguments or just plain sick of the Corps' embarrassing behavior (or both), Ord concluded that the time had come for firm action. His first measure, cynically dubbed "Ord's Order," rivaled the infamous "Woman Decree" of Benjamin Butler for sheer audacity. Assembling the troops for a dress parade before Governor Mouton's mansion, General Ord, though seriously ill, rode his horse up and down the line while searching for the right words. Finally, after passing back and forth several times, he stopped before one brigade. "Red-faced and shouting" Ord recalled the words of General Sherman who earlier reported that the XIII Army Corps had "disgraced itself" by its pillaging in Mississippi. "The honor of a soldier is too sacred to be lost in this way!" shouted Ord between coughs.

There would be no more pillaging, violence or debauching and, just to be sure, Ord would hold each offending soldier's immediate superior officer personally responsible. Repeating the same lecture to each brigade, he then passed out written copies of his infamous order which not only was to be read to each individual regiment but was to be posted in conspicuous locations throughout Vermilionville:

> N0. 94
>
> Vermilionville Bayou, La., October 12, 1863
>
> IV. The citizens of Vermilionville, La. are authorized to organize themselves into a patrol, for the protection of themselves, their families, and personal property against marauders and thieves, white or black.
>
> By order of Maj. Gen. E. O. C. Ord

Ord delivered an even greater shock to the First Brigade of the First Division commanded by Colonel David Shunk, age forty, of Indianapolis, Indiana. Drawing his horse to a halt before that particular brigade, which Ord considered to be among the worst, the general instructed General Cadwalader C. Washburn to read a separate set of orders to the assembled troops:

> No. 42
>
> Camp on Vermilion Bayou, October 12, 1863
>
> Colonel Shunk is hereby relieved from the command of his brigade for failing to perform his duty and prevent marauding in his command. He will proceed to New Orleans, La., and report to the senior officer there, in arrest. Division commanders will cause this order to be read in each regiment at their parade today.
>
> By order of Maj. Gen. E. O. C. Ord

Each individual regiment responded to Ord's decrees by adopting rigid preventive measures against marauding, including "catch-calls" (surprise roll calls) endless drills, inspections and dress parades. In addition, extra guards were placed around camp and a special detail of civilian "patrol guards" of Louisiana residents stood armed watch over the tiny village of Vermilionville and surrounding area.

Many of the patrol guards were former members or leaders of the controversial pre-war *Comites de Vigilance aux Atakapas* who had once come very close to precipitating class warfare by their brutal tactics and circumvention of the judicial process. Theynow commanded the respect and gratitude of all law-abiding citizens in Lafayette Parish, whether black, white, loyas, "secesh" or neutral because all viewed the bluecoats, stragglers and camp followers as the greater threat.

On the other hand the invaders, who had intimidated, plundered and destroyed at will, were now subjected to the ludicrous and humiliating spectacle of armed Louisiana civilians hauling in Yankee soldiers and lawless blacks, some of whom were gagged and bound and treated as common criminals. Those unfortunate enough to be arrested were not only confined to all the humiliating, sometimes cruel punitive devices common to the times, but, if a soldier, were sentenced to one-month's suspension of pay.

Ord could not have created a greater furor if he had invited "Jeff" Davis to lunch. The decree permitting Louisiana residents to arm themselves "will make guerillas out of all the citizens," complained an Ohio soldier. Before long, rumors began circulating in the camp of the 29th Wisconsin that a "hungry" soldier had been "ruthlessly" gunned down by citzens for no greater sin than to help himself to a few sweet potatoes. Although the rumor proved false, a strong guard was placed around the various Wisconsin camps to prevent them from avenging the death of their comrade. "If the rumor had been true," wrote an Ohio soldier, "woe be to the unlucky citizen." An Iowan reacted by writing his father that "when the men are very hungry they must have something to eat; that order is older than anything the generals can bublish (sic)." Not everyone took the order so seriously. On the lighter side a Wisconsin soldier wrote in his diary: "The general seems afraid that the 'western devils,' as he calls us, are not strictly honest, but we never take anything unless we can carry it, or eat it where we find it."

In "Camp Indiana" Private Harry Watts wrote that "the orders came too late for we had already laid in a supply of fresh hog and sweet potatoes and 'Fzs' had brought in a pumpkin."

A few days later, General Ord, his physical condition worsening, voluntarily relinquished command of the XIII Corps in favor of Major General C. C. Washburn. As might be expected in such an emotionally charged atmosphere, the change in command set off another spate of rumors, mainly to the effect that Ord himself had been imprisoned by General Banks for the decree.[12]

While Vermilionville did not exactly return to normalcy, at least much of the illegal foraging had come to a halt.

Tuesday, October 13, 1863

At Ile Copal, the question of provisions for the living had to be dealt with. Although the Westerners of the XIII Corps were growing fat off the plunder of neighboring plantations, the Mouton family faced the very real threat of starvation. To be sure their hunger was not so much an evil plot on the part of the intruders, as it was the thoughtless nature of their occupation. The invaders were far too preoccupied with their own problems to worry about the welfare of a few women and children. To complicate matters for the Moutons, no one could even leave the main dwelling house without securing a written permit from the provost marshal. Worse still the persistent aromas from some savory dish being concocted in the family kitchen—which was strictly off limits to the occupants—must have been a source of considerable agony. Lesser families would have long since resorted to begging—and receiving—from their conquerors.

And so it was that early on the morning of October 13, 1863, one day after the funeral of Cecilia Mouton, Mathilde Mouton Gardner made a crucial decision. With the burden of caring for a sick sister and so many young children, she could no longer let pride take precedence over welfare.

Securing a pass from Provost Marshal Gorsuch, Mathilde headed down Pinhook road toward the disaster area that once was Basil Crow's plantation. Dressed in mourning apparel, which included a dark veil over her face, she presented herself in the headquarters tent inquiring for General Banks. She found instead Colonel Nathan A. M. Dudley of Massachusetts, the acting Chief of Staff who politely explained that the Major General Commmanding had already left but that he would be happy to assist.

"Whom have I the honor of addressing?" asked Mathilde in her unique Louisiana accent.

"Colonel Dudley, Madam."

Startled, Mathilde raised her veil for a closer look, thinking perhaps this was the same Dudley she had known in happier times. "Is this Lieutenant Dudley of the Tenth (United States) Infantry?" she asked.

Now recognizing Mathilde, the Colonel replied: "The same, Madam."

Before the war Colonel Dudley has been a lieutenant in the regular army under Captain Frank Gardner, Mathilde's New Yorker husband. When Louisiana seceded from the Union, Gardner espoused the Southern cause and "deserted" his regiment, then at some isolated western outpost in Utah and accepted a commission as lieutenant colonel in the Confederacy. So hasty was his departure that Mathilde and the children were left for a while under the care of Lieutenant Dudley and the United States flag.

NATHAN A. M. DUDLEY

FRANKLIN GARDNER
(Lafayette Museum)

> The information that her husband had been made colonel (and later general) was a source of great delight to Mrs. Gardner, and, in spite of (Dudley's)earnest protestations, she persisted in expressing the most disloyal sentiments, and sought, in every way, to insult the cause which he represented, and the flag which he loved and served.

Remembering all this now, Mathilde was deeply and bitterly humiliated. Under similar circumstances she had insulted and no doubt badly hurt General Grover, but the situation was different now. The children were hungry.

"Oh! Lieutenant," she cried, "I have come to beg some food for my starving children!" She then "hid her face in her hands and commenced to sob bitterly."

Later that day a large wagon, laden with provisions for the Mouton family, was unloaded at Ile Copal.[13]

While Mrs. Gardner was thus occupied, a different kind of confrontation was shaping up along the Vermilion, especially among the soldiers of Ohio and Iowa. For days, the major topic of conversation, aside from "Ord's Order" and foraging, had been the gubernatorial elections back home.

In Iowa, as in Ohio, the contest was between the Democratic "Copperheads," who stood for opposition to Lincoln's war policy, and the Republican "Unionists," who pledged their loyalty to the Lincoln administration. Although Iowa had long been characterized as a state divided by sectional strife, vigilante committees, lynchings and riots, few people could recall a more bitter election.

But the real contest was in Ohio where Clement Laird Vallandigham, a rabid anti-war candidate, had achieved martyrdom and national fame in the spring of 1863, when he had been arrested by the military authorities, tried before a military tribunal on trumped up charges and sentenced to banishment. His speeches were not only printed all over the South but the very name Vallandigham became a rallying cry for anti-war Democrats, North and South. Not surprisingly, the tall and handsome forty-three-year-old politician was the overwhelming favorite to represent the Democrats against the Republican's "war" candidate, *Cincinnati Enquirer* editor, John Brough.[14]

With so much factional strife in Ohio and Iowa it was only natural that some of it should spill over onto the banks of the Vermilion. By election day, October 13, 1863, what had once been good-natured squabbling between the Copperheads and those supporting the Union ticket now took on an uglier form. Pep rallies were frequently interrupted by hecklers; political posters favoring Vallandigham were pulled down and destroyed; and fisticuffs erupted throughout the camp. Nonetheless each regiment managed to elect three judges and two clerks to assist the official commissioners who had come down from each state to manage the election.

CLEMENT VALLANDIGHAM
(Harper's Weekly)

In the 83rd Ohio, the judges and clerks sat on the damp ground for the occasion, using only a small box for a desk. The 24th Iowa was more fortunate. Several interior doors which had once separated the rooms in some luckless planter's home were stretched across chairs. With a lonely sentinel maintaining order around each table, the soldiers lined up and filled out their ballots in a drizzling rain. Most of the men were voting for the first time in their lives and had eagerly awaited this moment; but no sooner did the balloting begin than the peal of artillery from Camp Carrion Crow, sounding like distant thunder, cast a gloomy spell over the entire camp by reminding them that a very real war was still on. Nonetheless, the results of the election, printed below in tabular form, seemed to provide some measure of satisfaction for both sides.

OHIO ELECTION TABULATION

	Brough	Vallandigham
48th Ohio Regiment	241	28
56th Ohio Regiment	167	57
83rd Ohio Regiment	149	20
96th Ohio Regiment	230	5
Total Votes Cast	787	110

IOWA ELECTION TABULATION

	Stone (Rep.)	Tuttle (Demo.)
21st Iowa Regiment	166	37
22nd Iowa Regiment	257	36
23rd Iowa Regiment	101	37
24th Iowa Regiment	271	10
28th Iowa Regiment	264	67
Total Votes Cast	1059	187

Although the Republicans carried the day by a wide margin, it came as something of a shock that the Copperhead minority—many of whom openly expressed sentiments for the Southern cause—was several times larger than suspected. As in the case of "Ord's Order," the election results gave rise to considerable grumbling among the faithful. That night, even as the booming of cannon erupted nearby, an Iowan noted in his diary that "President Lincoln should dismiss every commissioned officer who casts a vote for the arch-traitors and send them beyond our lines. In principal, they are as vile as their leaders." Less vindictive was the attitude of Sergeant T. B. Marshall, of Sidney, Ohio. "I am sorry to see any Val. votes at all," he wrote in his diary, "but political opinions must be respected."[15]

Wednesday, October 14, 1863

On the south bank of Bayou Vermilion, not far from the rubber pontoon bridge, there was camped a small regiment of black soldiers, members of the recently created *Corps d'Afrique*. Wearing bright red caps and Yankee uniforms, these singing, swaggering, French-speaking black Louisianians were part of a unique experiment. Since the fall of New Orleans in early 1862, large numbers of runaway slaves or "contrabands" as they were called, flocked to the Union lines. At first they were welcome. Not only would the movement deprive the rebellious areas of their labor force, but the spectacle of such multitudes fleeing before the institution of involuntary servitude could be exploited for propaganda purposes.

By the summer of 1862, however, the numbers had swelled to unmanageable proportions. Unable to care for themselves and unwilling to return to Confederate controlled regions, they soon choked the government bureacracy, overburdened the public purse, and clogged military operations all over the state. Major General Butler, Banks' predecessor in the Department of the Gulf, soon hit upon a novel idea. Many of the able-bodied women and children, as well as older males, could be relocated to Treasury-operated plantations along the Mississippi. Meanwhile, the able-bodied men could be mustered into such special military organizations as the Louisiana "Native Guards," the Louisiana "Pioneers" or the Louisiana "Engineers," all of which eventually was to be consolidated under the appealing and appropriate name *Corps d'Afrique*.

Initally the black regiments were expected to perform all the grubby duties eschewed by the white soldiers, namely guard duty, trenching, and construction of fortifications. Once their value as foot soldiers was realized, however, a number of United States Colored Infantry (USCI) regiments was created, notwithstanding loud Confederate protests. So indispensible did these regiments become, especially after the Port Hudson campaign of mid-1863, that Union authorities began actively recruiting blacks along the line of march. Besides, it was a convenient way to siphon off the legions of runaway slaves who otherwise would hamper military operations. "We use uneducated horses and mules taken from the enemy," General Banks was heard to remark. "Why not negroes?"[16]

Thus on Wednesday, October 14th, 1863, a team of twenty-five white recruiters, among whom was Lieutenant Lawrence Van Alstyne of Albany County, New York, arrived in Vermilionville. Less than three weeks earlier Van Alstyne and fellow travelers had mustered out of the 128th New York Infantry as men of the ranks to accept commissions in a to-be-created black regiment, the 90th U.S.C.I.

Nothing seemed to go right for Van Alstyne. On the train between Algiers and Brashear, for example, his food had been stolen. Down in Centerville, even as his fellow soldiers plundered at will, he had been thoroughly "pitched into" by a young "secesh" lady who caught him in her orange grove. Below New Iberia, where the engineers were attempting to remove the wrecked *Hart* from the Teche, he had tried to help when two blacks fell overboard, but they drowned in spite of his best efforts to save them. Now, it was he who rode a borrowed horse toward Vermilion Bayou because only he among the officers had been unable to secure a mount in spite of the fact that dozens of horses grazed *au large* on the prairies.

Perhaps today he would be more fortunate. Nearing the bayou he spotted several riderless horses hitched to a tree, one of which possessed an ordinary saddle and bridle, the other with military trappings. Obviously, reasoned the unlucky New Yorker, the one without the military gear had been stolen, and since it was "no crime to steal from a thief" then why not commandeer the horse.

The deed done, Van Alstyne crossed the pontoon bridge over the Vermilion and headed up Pinhook road. Yet he was deeply troubled by his conscious and not a little worried about getting caught. Before long, however, he came across an old "colored gentleman," who, it was readily apparent, was also having horse trouble. Though the rider was coaxing, kicking, cursing and whipping, he could not convince the animal, a beautiful black mare, to go anywhere except backwards and in a circle.

Seeing his opportunity, Van Alstyne quickly struck up a swap arrangement. The stranger, no doubt thinking himself fortunate and the Yankee a fool, switched the trappings, mounted up and rode happily toward the bayou where someone was probably searching for a horse. Van Alstyne congratulated himself on being a shrewd horse trader, and could scarcely disguise his glee, but when he attempted to mount up he was made all too aware of why the old black man had seemed so delighted over the swap:

> whether she had a grudge against me I don't know, but as she swung around she suddenly wheeled and with both her hind feet hit me squarely in the breast. My canteen had swung around in just the right position to receive the blow and that probably saved my life. As it was, the canteen was smashed...and I was knocked flat on the ground.

His pride shattered, but otherwise uninjured, Van Alstyne and his two dozen or more laughing, jibing companions moved through and beyond Vermilionville and went into camp between the plantation homes of Antoine Emile Mouton, the governor's brother, and General Alfred Mouton, the governor's son.

Unlike other plantations, where the slaves had long since run off to join the Federals or had been driven into Texas, the two Mouton plantations had "hundreds upon hundreds" of blacks who rushed out to greet them. Some were singing what sounded like "Glory to God" while others chanted "Abe Linkum" too.

After a lengthy feast that included a fat pig shot virtually under General Mouton's house, the Yankee visitors got down to the serious business of recruitment. Incredibly, not one of the officers spoke French, but after explaining their mission through several of the "English-speaking darkies," the blacks became "wild with joy" and rushed forward to sign up, even the women and children. "They were more anxious to enlist than we were to have them," confided Van Alstyne to his diary.

As darkness fell, both the soldiers and their hosts made common cause around an enormous bonfire. While fiddlers fiddled and drummers beat out the "bamboula" on a piece of cowhide stretched over a hollow stump, the others danced joyously around. There were some very good fiddlers, recalled Van Alstyne, and others "not so good." At any rate the noisy festival went on all night, progressing from dancing to singing to prayers with the only words understood by the visitors being "Massa Linkum" and "Linkum sojers."[17]

On Bayou Carencro some ten miles north of Van Alstyne's party, a night artillery duel broke out among the opposing forces. "We can her canins on the rite," wrote Robert Phelps, a barely literate Yankee on Bayou Vermilion, "but i dont think it is to mutch effect. i think it is the 19 army corps a sheling of the woods." Though the thundering roar shook houses and rattled windows in Vermilionville, it is doubtful that anyone at Van Alstyne's enlistment party could hear the noise. Nonetheless if anyone dancing around that bonfire had troubled to look in the direction of St. John's steeple, he would have seen an impressive, albeit ominous, display of torch communications.

Thursday, October 15, 1863

Daylight on the Vermilion found acres and acres of abandoned campsites. One division of the XIII *Corps d'Armee* had already departed toward the Carencro; others would follow shortly. The signal communications of the night before had meant exactly what everyone feared most. "Ther is a fite sure a nuf," wrote Robert Phelps to his wife.[18] In fact long before the sun broke the horizon on the morning of October 15, 1863, the "Battle of Buzzards' Prairie" was underway.

CHAPTER EIGHT

THE RESISTANCE STIFFENS

Tuesday, October 13, 1863

SEVERAL miles north of Union Camp Carrion Crow, near the point where the tiny Bayou Tesson (or Callaghan) crossed the Opelousas-to-Vermilionville stagecoach road, General Thomas Green sat down for an evening meal of pork and yams with his senior cavalry commanders, Colonels Arthur P. Bagby and James P. Major. Both Major and Bagby were West Point graduates and had served as frontier Indian fighters in the regular United States Army before joining Green's highly mobile and seemingly ubiquitous "horse" division.[1] Their task now, as it had been for more than two weeks, was not only to determine which route the advancing Federals planned to take in their overland trek toward Texas, but also how best to use their own limited resources to stop them.

Though rarely numbering more than three thousand, or about one-third the entire Confederate force in Louisiana, Green's division was made up of seasoned veterans and Indian fighters who had distinguished themselves in combat from Valverde to Irish Bend. Moreover, the defenders could be counted on for two very special reasons: the Louisianians were fighting on home soil against invaders who had once before confiscated, plundered and burned their way through southwestern Louisiana, while the Texans were well aware that the real objective of the enemy was not Louisiana, but the Lone Star State.

Nonetheless, Green's cavalry division was without a doubt one of the most ragtag, ill-disciplined and undersupplied military units to take the field since Spartacus and his slaves rose against Ceasar's legions. Commenting on the discipline of these troops, which was "shining by its utter absence," General Richard Taylor wrote:

> Their experience in war was limited to hunting down Comanches and, as in all new societies, distinctions of rank were unknown. Officers and men addressed each other as Tom, Dick or Harry, and had no more conception of military gradations than of the celestial hierarchy of the poets.

Initially these sons of Texas and Louisiana had ridden off to war in respectable homespun civilian clothing or, in some instances, in Confederate gray. As the war wore on, however, cotton and wool cloth became as scarce in beleaguered Louisiana as hard currency. Trousers, shirts, coats and blankets became tattered and torn, eventually scattering to the wind in rags or dissolving under dust, mud and pelting rain, and tents were practically unknown. More than a few of Green's bronzed and grimy horsemen hid their clothing deficiencies under flour-sack aprons or Mexican blankets wrapped around their waists. A Union prisoner described them as

> ...the most ragged, dirty-looking set of rascals I ever seen. There was plenty of pluck and spirit among them, but a great want of order and discipline. The only thing uniform about them was dirt—shirt, pants, and skin being all of a fine mud color. They all carried pistols and dirks, but while the greater number had Enfields, the rest were armed with Carbines and buckshot guns. The officers had little or nothing to distinguish them from the privates, though sometimes a suit of gray made its appearance.

COLONEL J. P. MAJOR
(Clement Evans, *Confederate Military History*)

COLONEL ARTHUR BAGBY
(Clement Evans, *Confederate Military History*)

Indeed barefooted cavalrymen, or Texans and Louisianians with feet bound in rags or rawhide, were about as common that autumn evening as colt six-shooters, Bowie knives and "chawing tobac."

The latter seemed an obsession with the Texans. There were few, if any, who did not constantly maintain an enormous wad of tobacco between their cheeks and gums; sometimes even as they slept. A European observer complained that it was next to impossible to put his head out the window of a coach without being subjected to "showers of tobacco juice from the mouths of Southern chivalry" atop the wagon. Nonetheless, observed the visitor, "they all had a bon-hommie honesty and straight forwardness, a natural courtesy and extreme good nature."

Oddly enough, the most important source of clothing and military supplies were the Federals. Many of Green's soldiers were dressed entirely in ill fitting Yankee blue, a result of the Confederate raid on Brashear City back in June. In fact, the temporary Confederate camp on Bayou Tesson could well have been mistaken for that of the enemy. A large portion of the camp provisions and military supplies, including scarce Sibley tents, blankets, stoves and utensils, boxes of hardtack, wagons, artillery pieces, rifles and even mules and horses bore the imprint USA. Only the ragged appearance and occasional occurrence of the letters CSA identified the real inhabitants.[2]

Aside from the innovative manner of securing provisions, the most striking feature of General Green's cavalry division was the wide chasm separating the Texans from the Louisianians. Unlike the Eastern versus Western regional rivalries which characterized General Banks' Army of the Gulf, the Army of Western Louisiana, including Green's cavalry division, was set apart by customs, culture, language, religion and, in some instances, loyalties.

As a general rule, the predominately Protestant Texans held the French-speaking Catholic Confederates of southwestern Louisiana in "profound contempt." Nothing rankled the cowboys more than the heavy desertion rate and apparent willingness on the part of the "kajuns" or "lazy, cowardly Creoles" to take the infamous loyalty oath in Union-controlled areas. Perhaps the only Louisiana unit which earned the respect, if not exactly the love, of the horsemen from beyond the Sabine was William Vincent's jayhawk-hunting 2nd Louisiana Cavalry, but even they viewed the "Texicans" as "crude clods" and called them "Commanches and thieves" who would steal, "even from their own officers" and "brag beyond all the bounds of truth." In many instances the Texans were considered by the people of southwest Louisiana as only slightly preferable to Yankees or jayhawkers.[3]

Yet these colorful and unpolished products of frontier America could generate charismatic leadership in men like Walter P. Lane, "Gotch" Hardeman, Oran Roberts, "Ed" Waller and "Tom" Green. General Thomas Green seemed to embody the most noble qualities.

Originally from Virginia, the forty-nine-year-old cavalry commander had moved west and joined the Texas army at an early age, defending the Lone Star State against Indian uprisings and Mexican invasions. After serving under General Zachary Taylor in the Mexican War, he became Clerk of the Texas Supreme Court until relations were severed with the Union. Green then rose rapidly from Colonel of the 5th Texas Mounted Rifles to brigade commander and eventually division commander.

Although well-educated, soft spoken and middle-aged, Green chewed tobacco, downed liquor and endured hardships as well as any rough-edged frontiersman, but he was not without faults. In combat he was noted for firing his men up on Louisiana rum and then leading charges with reckless abandon (or as Green called it, to "feel at the enemy") needlessly sacrificing life and limbs. "Danger seemed to be his element," recalled General Richard Taylor somewhat enviously, but "his men adored him and would follow wherever he led." A cavalryman of the 5th Texas probably represented the majority opinion when he wrote: "A braver soldier never shouldered a musket, a finer officer never wore epaulets..."[4]

Green's cavalry, sometimes aided by portions of Brigadier General Mouton's infantry command, had harassed and eluded the invaders from Brashear City to Vermilionville, always avoiding any encounter when odds favored the opponent. Picket duty, scouting and courier missions for the Federals was a nightmare with so many Indian fighters and jayhawk-hunters hovering nearby, waiting and watching for a mistake that could prove fatal. Dozens of Union prisoners were pulled out of the lines, especially stragglers, foragers and careless guards, and were taken to Opelousas for interrogation at General Richard Taylor's headquarters. The information derived from these prisoners, as well as that from occasional deserters, seemed to confirm the Confederate suspicion of a march on Texas from somewhere along the Teche.[5]

BRIGADIER GENERAL THOMAS GREEN (Clement Evans, *Confederate Military History*

The unpredictable Yankees had defied logic, however, and continued their northward advance to Vermilionville and then on to the Carencro, mystifying and discrediting the observing Rebel intelligence network. What were they up to, demanded an angry General Taylor of his cavalry commanders? Would they now strike west across the prairies from the Carencro or would they first occupy Opelousas to the north? The only way to find out, Taylor apparently told Green, was to capture someone in a position to know, for example a high-ranking officer or a member of a Signal Corps team.

Heeding Taylor's advice, a portion of Green's command (the 5th Texas, 2nd Louisiana and Semmes' Battery) led by Colonel Henry C. McNeill, left the Confederate camp at nightfall and struck a wagon trail leading in a southeasterly direction toward Grand Coteau. The Texans planned to scatter or capture any strays near the Jesuit College, while the Louisianians would reconnoiter the prairie between the Union encampments on the Carencro and the Vermilion.

About the time that the Texas cavalry was crossing the Bourbeux near the mouth of Bayou Bellevue, the faculty, staff and students of St. Charles College were preparing for the evening meal. Though sympathetic to the Confederate cause, they were now placed in the unenviable position of serving as hosts to uninvited guests from both sides. It seemed that just before each meal a number of Union officers, either from Camp Carrion Crow or those on picket duty in Grand Coteau, would put in an uninvited appearance. The priests made the most of these occasions, frequently proffering "spiritual nourishment," as well as a tour of the grounds and a warm meal.

On that particular evening, however, the Yankees were not to break bread with the Jesuits. In fact, hardly had the traditional recitation of the Blessing begun than the loud sounds of musketry erupted along the *picquet* lines. Without a word the Yankees grabbed their hats and rifles and rushed from the refectory. Several minutes later, but before anyone had succeeded in determining the nature of the disturbance, a number of ragged and grimy Texans appeared and proceeded to take their places in the hastily evacuated dining chairs. Unlike the Yankees, who had scrupulously respected the sanctity of the institution, "the friendly Confederates" departed only after consuming what remained of the evening meal and helping themselves to an ample supply of "requisitioned" goods. Such unexpected visits from both sides, according to Father Benausse, brought considerable *turban et confusionem* to St. Charles College.[6]

Even as the good fathers went about their business of restoring order to the college, Colonel William Vincent's command, consisting of the 2nd Louisiana and a section of Semmes' 2nd Regular Confederate Battery, headed toward their destination south of Grand Coteau. Not only did both these units contain Louisiana Cajuns whose linguistic talents might be needed, but some of the men had lived on this very same prairie since birth. Approaching a point near the junction of Pont des Mouton road and the Vermilion-Opelousas road, Vincent sighted his objective. There, atop an unidentified planter's home, stood a torchman of the U. S. Signal Corps who was then busily engaged in relaying a fiery signal communication with a brightly illuminated turpentine torch. Inside the house was a telegraph officer and a Signal Corps team, just what the Confederate commanding general had ordered.

The responsibility for guarding this vital communications link, and the northern portion of Union Camp Vermilion, was on forty-three-year-old Colonel John G. Mudd of St. Charles County, Missouri. It would not be unfair to say that Mudd was encountering considerable difficulties with his task. Indeed, for weeks he had been hiding the truth from everyone. An old nemesis, three separate bullet wounds, had returned to ravage his system. Physically and psychologically he was unfit to command but he refused to give in and return to New Orleans. For Mudd, the road to Texas had been filled with heartbreak and dogged determination to conquer his affliction. He had spent months in hospitals while resting, reading and waiting for the surgeon's certificate of good health. Now, in the middle of the campaign, he had no intention of relinquishing his command.

Nonetheless the illness was preying on him, frequently affecting his good judgement. The first problem arose when he mistakenly ordered Colonel Thomas J. Lucas, the commander of the 16th Indiana Mounted Infantry, to accompany General Franklin's XIX Army Corps on its march toward the Carencro. Thus, unknown to the generals on Camp Vermilion, their flank had remained uncovered for a critical one and one-half days. It was this error which had prompted the frantic flag-waving spectacle on the steeple of St. John's Church on the day of Cecilia Mouton's funeral.

Relying mainly on the 16th Indiana and the 2nd Illinois Cavalry, Mudd's brigade of cavalry (the 2nd Brigade of General Albert Lee's cavalry division) formed a chain-vidette system completely encircling the Signal Corps team. Hampered by large corn and cotton fields which "from neglect were overgrown with rank weeds from seven to ten feet in height," the men were stationed about twenty rods apart. Like Pavlov's dogs they had been conditioned to move, all at once, in the same general direction to the end of their respective beats and then to return. To their rear was a first, second and third reserve, all of which formed an elastic combination which could be moved for speedy concentration at any threatened point.

As darkness fell on the night of October 13th, the cavalry pickets were somewhat complacent; after all, they had been here for several days and not one Rebel had shown his face. Nonetheless, they took the usual precautionary measure of changing their positions before the Signal Corps station in order to confuse any possible enemy observers. Although the wisdom of this step was frequently demonstrated, the

Yankees discovered on that particular night that "the term 'southern hospitality' was capable of varied applications."[7]

The raid commenced with a shell barrage from Semmes' guns and was followed by a concentrated charge from the 2nd Louisiana. So quickly and without warning did Vincent strike that the communications station was taken without resistance. Even as the panic-stricken guards fled for their lives a party of Louisianians rushed into the house and captured signal officer J. L. Hallett, as well as a telegraph operator, two other members of the Signal Corps team, and three guards. Another group of raiders set about gathering up and smashing the equipment. As a final insult the Louisianians tied a section of telegraph wire to a saddle horn and rode away, destroying a mile or more of line.

Lieutenant Hallett of the U. S. Signal Corps team was beside himself with rage. The raid had succeeded, he later argued, only because of lax security on the part of the guards. For this Colonel Mudd, who was now guilty of a second blunder, would soon be demoted from brigade to regimental commander; but the worst part was that Hallett had been unable to destroy or even to hide his signal book and the little leather pouch marked U. S. Signal Corps which contained a number of secret dispatches.

On the other hand Confederate General Richard Taylor would be delighted. For days his intelligence officers could only speculate—usually erroneously—as to the enemy's choice of a route toward Texas. Taylor now knew that Opelousas and Barre's Landing was the next stop along the way, which was more than most of the Union generals knew.[8]

At Bayou Carencro, about two miles upstream from the Union encampment, an elderly Acadian farmer named Oge Guilbeau was almost as distressed as Lieutenant Hallett. His little *bousillage*-walled house with its steep roof and wide gallery was located on the Lafayette Parish side of the bayou, but in an area so remote that he felt relatively secure from the lawless foragers and horse thieves he had heard about in the Union camp. Guilbeau had heard all the shooting in Grand Coteau, and his little windowless house had shaken on its not-so-firm foundation when Semmes' Battery opened fire at the Signal Corps station. What aroused his curiosity the most, however, were the strange muffled sounds emanating from his barnyard.

Grabbing an ancient flintlock, he crept out to investigate, but only to find himself confronted by a half dozen or so "Americans," one of whom quickly disarmed him and threw the rusty relic into the darkness. Guilbeau had never been more frightened in his life. Not only was he shaking all over but his very knees felt as though they would give way at any moment; nor did it help when one of the soldiers thrust the muzzle of a rifle against his throat.

"Listen, *vieillard*," said the Yankee in tortured French, "there is no one here. You saw nothing. You heard nothing. Go back inside and you won't get hurt!"

Needless to say, the frightened old man beat a hasty retreat into the relative safety of his house. For hours he sat in the darkness and listened to the strange sounds in the barnyard. What were they doing, he wondered? He could not have known that their presence was all the more puzzling because of the rigidly enforced orders in the XIX Corps against illegal activities; and with so many Texans abroad it was quite dangerous to be outside camp perimeters.

The scene which greeted Guilbeau on the following morning was downright bizarre. In the barnyard, lying on their sides, or with hooves in the air, were more than a dozen of his best cattle. Aside from the fact that they were quite dead the carcasses seemed inviolate. Not one was carved up or mutilated; nor was there a drop of blood. The crime bore all the features of a ritual killing performed by practioners of the occult, a not unknown phenomenon in southwest Louisiana. Surely Guilbeau must have recalled the refrain of an old Acadian song about a cow named Caillette who died behind Uncle Joe's house:

> Caillette est crevee derriere chez l'oncle Joe,
> Les quartre pattes en l'air,
> la tete escrasee! Caillette, Caillette!

Examining them closely, Guilbeau soon unraveled the mystery. A neat incision had been made in the back of each animal's head and their brains were gone. Oge Guilbeau, as he later related the story, had lost his cattle that night to a band of "cerebral connisseurs."[9]

Wednesday, October 14, 1863

The morning dawned clear and pleasant. The rain, which had fallen off and on during the night, filled the kettles and other water receptacles in the opposing camps while forming "innumerable lagoons on the camp ground, temporarily diversifying the scenery."' At Grand Coteau and Carencro several parties of soldiers were "breaking-in" wild ponies from the previous day's catch. Out on Buzzards' Prairie, along a cypress rail fence in front of Chretien's plantation, sat two companies of Lancers belonging to the 5th Texas Cavalry. Armed with colt revolvers and what appeared to be twelve-inch blades mounted on nine foot shafts—

each of which was decorated with red pennants—these Merlin's cowboys presented a ludicrous early morning sight to the observing Yankees. Like so many equestrian statues out of a medieval age they sat in their saddles, watching and waiting.[10]

In the Bellevue community, south of Opelousas on the Opelousas-Vermilionville stagecoach road, two musket shots rang out loud and clear, causing the frightened citizenry to rush to their windows and doors. In happier days those two shots—an ancient Acadian custom—would have registered the news of a newborn son *(deux bals pour un garcon; un bal pour une fille)* but with the opposing armies so near it could mean anything. Within moments, however, Hypolite Miller, a poor local farmer, began making house calls with the happy news that his wife, Marie Anne Lamy, had just brought a healthy son, Emile, into the troubled world.[11]

At Camp Carrion Crow many of the Union soldiers began wondering aloud about the moribund Great Texas Overland Expedition. "It seemed as though the Texas campaign had become very infirm," wrote a New Yorker, "creeping along for a little time, with slow and tottering pace, it had nearly reached the end of its existence." Such doubts even gave rise to a camp riddle: "If the army moved thirty-five miles in two weeks, how long will it take to march to Nibletts' Bluff?"[12]

Unlike the Confederates, who could move from one point to another with a minimum of delay, the Federals were hampered by so many bureaucratic and logistical obstacles that the entire expedition became a source of derision to the Texans. The ever-cautious Franklin could not, or would not, advance on Opelousas—the next step on the route—before the arrival of his supply train, now enroute from Berwick's Bay. Moreover, although Franklin's XIX Corps alone outnumbered the entire Confederate army in Louisiana by about two to one, he refused to act without the "heroes of Vicksburg," the XIII Corps at his side. The latter, in turn, was delayed at Vermilionville, some twelve miles to the rear, by the illness of the Corps commander, Major General E.O.C. Ord.

Finally, and perhaps more important, Franklin's every move had to be cleared with the Major General Commanding, N.P. Banks, now back in New Orleans. Little wonder that Confederates and Yankees alike began deriding old "Commissary" Banks as " *Don Quixote de la Luisiana,*" while Franklin was his "Sancho Panza."[13]

Making the most of the delay, the 75th New York regiment, soon to be mounted infantry or dragoons, continued their horse seizures throughout the countryside. Everything from unbroken creoles to spare ribbed, limping broken down hacks of thirty years were taken. These commandeered mounts also included sturdy, slow paced draught animals and fleet, spirited mustangs as well as magnificent thoroughbreds. The very best were kept for mounting the regiment, while the less suitable were turned over to the quartermaster's department for transportation purposes.

Many of the captured animals had never known a saddle and resented every effort to place one upon their backs. "The work of breaking them in, with the attendant kicking, shying, prancing, throwing of riders and runaways, was amusing and adventurous in the extreme." Each time a Yankee "bit the dust," sometimes with fractured bones, a Louisiana black would take over and "with considerable skill," succeed, where the "Linkum sojer" had failed.

The job of making the infantry into horsemen was assigned to a number of skilled riders from the 1st Texas Cavalry (Union), but it was a difficult task. Some of the city boys seemed "unable to distinguish one end from the other," while the farm boys, whose equine experience was limited to walking behind a plow, seemed incapable of foregoing the traditional "Giddup!," "Whoa!," "Gee!" and "Haw!" for the more formal military commands.

During one of these exercises, the "boy" General, Godfrey Weitzel, happened to be riding past. Stopping to observe, he soon "burst into a fit of laughter over the sight." Not only did the horses range from every size, color, age, breed and sex, but the civilian saddles and bridles were of every color and style imaginable. The ludicrous appearance "awakened considerable mirth and elicited many derisive epithets from observing comrades." If the Rebels of horse-conscious Texas could have witnessed such scenes, noted a soldier, "the war would soon be over because they would all kill themselves laughing."

Nonetheless, the boys of the 75th New York dragoons were far too pleased with the privilege and pleasure of riding to concern themselves with the "sour grape" comments of their walking brethren. Besides, they were far too busy cooling and soaking their inflamed rear ends in the bayou if not depleting the surgeon's tent of vaseline.[14]

At precisely 4 o'clock P. M., just as the novice horsemen were wrapping up another exercise, Green's horse division of Texas and Louisiana Rebels seemed bent on visiting the Union camp. Like a late afternoon thundercloud, the entire division, numbering perhaps three thousand, roared over the horizon and drew up in front of Camp Carrion Crow.

For almost two hours "a desperate engagement ensued, and the tide of battle waxed warm." The initial assault was so rapid and unexpected that a dozen or more Union pickets fell at their post. As usual, the 161st New York regiments, in skirmish formation, marched boldly toward the center of the Texas line. The 5th Texas Cavalry, in turn, cut down the New York skirmishers with a withering hail of Minie balls.

On the extreme left of the Union lines was a large corn field belonging to Benjamin Guidry (a brother of Constance Guidry), "among the thick and tall stalks of which Rebel bushwhackers had concealed themselves." The 114th New York formed a line of battle on the edge, and moved forward, each man pushing over the corn stalks with his feet. "Like an immense mowing machine, it moved backward and forward, until the large crop of corn was lying flat on the ground."

Once the heavy artillery of a half dozen or so Union batteries began to find their range, Green's division withdrew to the treeline of Bayou Bourbeux about two miles north of the Carencro. From this vantage point, behind and beside the Chretien mansion, they continued the feint "until the sable wings of night came to close the bloody affair."[15]

No sooner had the shooting stopped than a different kind of confrontation began taking shape in the Union camp. It all started when Privates Michael "Big Mike" Fox and Charlie Annis, the regimental bullies of Company C in the 8th New Hampshire Infantry, then camped near the Carencro crossing, uncorked a bottle of "red eye" which they proceeded to spike with a touch of gunpowder. Fox was a big strapping fellow, well over six-feet in height, and a notorious troublemaker. Though only twenty-three-years-old and two years in the military, his service record was replete with notations of arrests and court-martials stemming from fights, stolen or damaged property and insubordination. According to unsubstantiated camp rumors, Fox had moved from an Irish shantytown in Boston to Manchester, New Hampshire, one step ahead of a hangman's noose.

Private Charlie Annis, another oversized troublemaker, spent most of his time defending the family name from mispronounciation. The one characteristic shared by both Fox and Annis was that neither could hold their liquor.

A short distance away from the tent where Fox and Annis were inebriating themselves was Prison Compound Number One where, under the spreading limbs of a large live oak, a half dozen or so ragged Texas cavalrymen from Waller's Battalion were incarcerated inside a rope corral. Now it was common knowledge in camp that these Texans claimed it took five Yankees to whip one Rebel or ten to whip a Texan. The claim was given some credence by the appearance and intimidating manner of the prisoners. Though dressed in rags the Texans were "a very fine looking lot of men." Long and lean, bronzed and bearded they seized upon every opportunity to torment their captors. Passersby were insulted, laughed at, called "midgets," splattered with accurate aims of tobacco juice, and told they would be "gobbled up" on the prairie. Each time a mounted Yankee would ride past, the prisoners would hoot, laugh, whistle, shout "Whoa!" or "Git-up!" or otherwise direct derogatory comments regarding the qualities of the creature if not the abilities of the rider.[16]

The conversation in the tent on "C" street eventually turned to the outrageous and provacative behavior of these Texans. Well fortified with rum, Fox stated that he could whip a Texas Rebel all by himself "with one hand tied behind." Several other drinking companions (who dared not disagree) egged him on. Finally, the drunken group filed out of the tent and headed down toward Prison Compound Number One.

Captain John R. Stokes, thirty-three-years-old, of Manchester, New Hampshire, had the misfortune of being Officer of the Day on that particular afternoon. Just as he was entering the headquarters tent for the evening meal, a din of shouts and curses erupted in the distance. Above the roar was a high-pitched voice yelling: "Corporal of the Guard, Compound Number One," which, in military jargon, meant trouble. Rushing to the scene, Stokes discovered that Fox and Annis, instead of fighting the Texans as they had boasted, were fighting each other.

Big Mike Fox, it seems, had swung at the sentinel guarding the prisoners. Recognizing the severity of this action, Charlie Annis tried to hold Fox back whereupon the latter called his drinking buddy by the name he so despised. In defense of his good family name, Annis began swinging wildly and a general conflagration began among the drunken group.

Captain Stokes, a humorless disciplinarian, calmly removed his pistol from its holster, put his free hand over one ear, and fired a shot into the air, an action which quickly ended the melee.

"If you do not break up and leave at once," announced Stokes, "I will have this entire group arrested."

The redoubtable Mike Fox, with a bleeding lip and clouded mind, stepped forward in a move that was to drastically alter his life from that day forward.

"The things that are happening here," retorted the drunk, "are none of your god-damn business, so leave us alone, officer!"

It wasn't so much Fox's behavior that angered Stokes, or even his choice of words. What irritated Stokes most was Fox's identity and the contemptuous manner with which he called him "officer." Many of the men in the ranks of the 8th New Hampshire, including Fox, were Irish Catholics only a few years removed from the peat bogs and potato beds; from famine, fairies and tyrannical priests; from Orangemen, British despotism and *gomcheen;* and from the persistent cycle of poverty which broke up close families by driving the young men to seek a better life in the New World. In America the old attitudes and hatreds broke down slowly. Even in the 8th New Hampshire there persisted the ancient conflicts which pitted Catholics against Protestants and Englishmen against Irishmen. The Irish who succeeded and became officers were not soon permitted to forget their humble origins; on the other hand the officers of Anglo origin were held in profound contempt by the Irishmen (and vice-versa).

Thus whether officer Stokes was Anglo-Protestant or Irish-Catholic was beside the point. As far as he was concerned his authority had been challenged and his dignity injured by someone whose socio-economic status was only slightly above that of an African slave. Taking out a pencil and memorandum book Stokes proceeded to jot down Fox's words, but the presence of the notebook made Big Mike even more belligerent. Cursing and swinging his arms wildly, Fox then lunged at Captain Stokes and knocked the memo pad to the ground.

Several of Fox's friends, possibly recognizing that he had committed, or was about to commit, a serious infraction, attempted to drag the cursing Irishman away, but Fox persisted. Acting like a wild man he broke free from his captors and once more charged toward the Officer of the Day.

Whether Fox actually struck Stokes or not was a matter of some debate. At any rate, Fox was eventually handcuffed and taken into custody, but even this did not stop him from heaping verbal abuse upon his arresting officer.

Fed up with these incessant insults and no doubt feeling the tide of vindictiveness rising in his chest, Stokes ordered the prisoner to be gagged and tied to a tree next to the Confederate prison compound. There Private Michael Fox was to spend the entire night in sight of the Texans whom he had well entertained.[17]

Yet there was something uncanny about the way trouble could spread when Mike Fox was around. A totally innocent victim of the altercation was First Lieutenant William J. Gannon, another twenty-three-year-old Irishman from Manchester and the commander of Fox's C Company. Gannon was suffering from an intestinal disorder at the time and was resting in his tent when Ezra B. Bell, the acting adjutant for that day, decided to use the occasion to further inflame the persistent grudges in the 8th New Hampshire.

Rushing into the tent, Bell grabbed Gannon's foot, shook it violently, and dragged him off his moss mattress. "Get up, god-damn you," shouted Bell, "your company is fighting and raising hell."

Jumping up, the groggy Gannon rushed into the street only to find that all was now tranquil. Fox was tied to a tree out of sight and everyone in Company C was carrying on as usual. "Well I guess it ain't my company that's fighting," he replied, "they're perfectly quiet." Bell persisted, rudely accusing Gannon not only of neglecting his duties, but also having his tent illegally pitched in front of the color line.

Bristling from this verbal abuse Gannon lost his temper and shouted: "Dry up, damn you, I don't want to hear another word out of your mouth!"

Acting Adjutant Bell, like Stokes before him, could not permit this challenge to his authority. "Well, in that case," declared Bell, "you're under arrest, so turn over your sword."

The stunned offender, though debilitated by his bout with diarrhea and still not completely awake, became so "exasperated" by Bell's "overbearing" manner that, "in conduct unbecoming an officer and a gentleman," he bodily threw the obnoxious adjutant out of his tent. With that, Bell picked himself up from a mudhole and headed toward the colonel's tent across the street, where he subsequently preferred charges of insubordination.[18]

The following morning Lieutenant William Gannon was relieved of his sword, a symbolic action tantamount to house arrest. Private Michael Fox, by conrast, was untied and led away to the prison compound. Though Fox must have been suffering the effects of the previous evening, he spotted Stokes whereupon he became as defiant as ever. He once again vowed to "get even" with Captain Stokes for tying him to the tree all night—even during an artillery bombardment—and "kill him" the first opportunity. As a final insult Stokes ordered that Fox be manacled with a ball and chain and placed under armed guard until a court-martial could be convened for these two upstart Irishmen. The saga of Michael Fox was far from over.

Thursday, October 15, 1863

It had been a nerve-wracking, sleepless and terror-filled night for the soldiers in Union Camp Carrion Crow. In the first place Confederate General Green, a master at psychological warfare, had moved his entire command to the west bank of the nearby Bourbeux. His campfires, stretching for almost two miles up the Chretien plantation road toward Opelousas (currently Blue Springs Road) gave the impression of an army numbering two or three times its actual size.[19] Even Franklin's spies and eyes, Edmund Davis' "Yankee" Texans, could not be certain that the balance of the Army of Western Louisiana, then resting near Opelousas, had not joined Green's horse division.

Worse still, as soon as the bugler sounded "Taps" in the Union Camp a series of loud explosions, preceded by the screeching, terrifying and unmistakable sound of incoming Parrotts, sent the sleepy Federals scurrying for their arms. Although the men thought it to be a prelude to a night attack, it turned out to be nothing more than another of Green's psychological weapons in the form of the long-ranged rifled Parrotts of the Texas Valverde Battery.

The six-piece Valverde Battery, captured from Union General E.R.S. Canby and the legendary Christopher "Kit" Carson at the Battle of Valverde, New Mexico, in early 1862, was to the Confederates what Nims' Battery was to the Yankees.[20] Under the able leadership of Captain (and later Governor of Texas) Joseph Sayers, one section of the Valverde Battery, numbering three pieces, had been quietly conveyed to a location out on Buzzards' Prairie. Making use of a stout rope, or prolonge, which attached the lunette of the carriages to the pintle hooks of the limbers, Sayers would fire one or two rounds "without limber" then move off to another location and fire again. Although the intermittent fire caused very little in the way of physical damage in the Union camp, it went on all night long and kept the Yankees awake.

With the approach of dawn Green concealed the main body of his cavalry forces, the 4th, 5th and 7th Texas, behind the remains of a long cypress fence fronting the Hypolite Chretien premises. On the extreme right, also in a concealed position, he placed the six field pieces of the Valverde Battery. The left, meanwhile, was held by Captain Olivier J. Semmes' 2nd Regular Confederate Battery.

Interestingly enough, before the day was out the Federals would have almost as many artillery batteries on the field as the presumptuous Rebels had pieces. But the Confederate disadvantage was offset to some extent by their greater experience in war. Almost all the Texas officers, and many of the men in the ranks, had spent a lifetime fighting Indians, Mexicans, and now Yankees. One of these, a forty-seven-year-old Mexican War hero named William Polk "Gotch" Hardeman, was almost as popular among the men as Green. "A better officer to his men is not in the service" wrote a cavalryman of the 4th Texas, "or a more gallant one does not walk Southern soil." Perhaps for this gallantry, Hardeman, a tall, slim Tennesseean-turned-Texan, was chosen as the bait to draw the Yankees into Green's elaborately prepared trap. Moving out with a company from each of the cavalry regiments, Hardeman began "to feel at" Union Camp Carrion Crow at first light.

By comparison with other Civil War engagements, the upcoming affair would be a relatively insignificant encounter. For the Confederates it constituted mainly an effort to determine the actual strength—and weakness—of the enemy. For West Pointer Franklin, however, it was more important, for the cautious Union General, once a promising young warrior, had been disgraced in combat from the fields of Virginia to Sabine Pass and was a subject of ridicule and scorn among the soldiers of the XIII Corps. Even the "nutmegs" and "fancy boys" of his own XIX Corps were saying that "he won't fight." But he would fight, and today he would show his true colors.

In short order Franklin ordered out Weitzel's division, a double line of Yankee blue stretching a mile or more from left to right. By the thousands they advanced across Buzzards' Prairie—Nims' and Davis on the right; Robinson and Clossen on the left; Love and Kinsey out front as skirmishers. In the rear was Grover's division, another mile-long double line of infantrymen, artillery batteries and cavalrymen. Drums were beating, flags were flying, fifes piped out the music and the fearless skirmishers led the way. The small, ragged band of Texans paled into insignificance by comparison and began backing cautiously toward Chretien's fence.

COLONEL W.P. HARDEMAN
(Evans, *Confederate Military History*)

Among the advancing New Yorkers was William Gatchell, a young and enterprising war correspondent for the *New York Herald.* That evening he would write that "Carrion Crow Bayou had a narrow escape from becoming historic, and standing side by side with Bull Run's classic ground." C.E.H. Bonwill, an artist and special correspondent with *Leslie's Illustrated Weekly*, also advanced with the long blue lines. He subsequently depicted the event in a pen and ink drawing, and it was forever preserved for posterity.

When it appeared as though the day was won, the heretofore concealed Confederate batteries opened with a murderous barrage, and the Battle of Buzzards' Prairie or, as the Texans called it, the Battle of Little Carrion Crow Bayou, was underway.

The high point of the battle came when "Sibley's Old Brigade," the 4th, 5th and 7th Texas, galloped out from behind the fence. Supported by a section of Semmes' Battery (three guns) and Waller's Battalion, and well fortified with green Louisiana rum, they made a classic cavalry dash on the Union right. With sabers glittering and a "hellish" Rebel

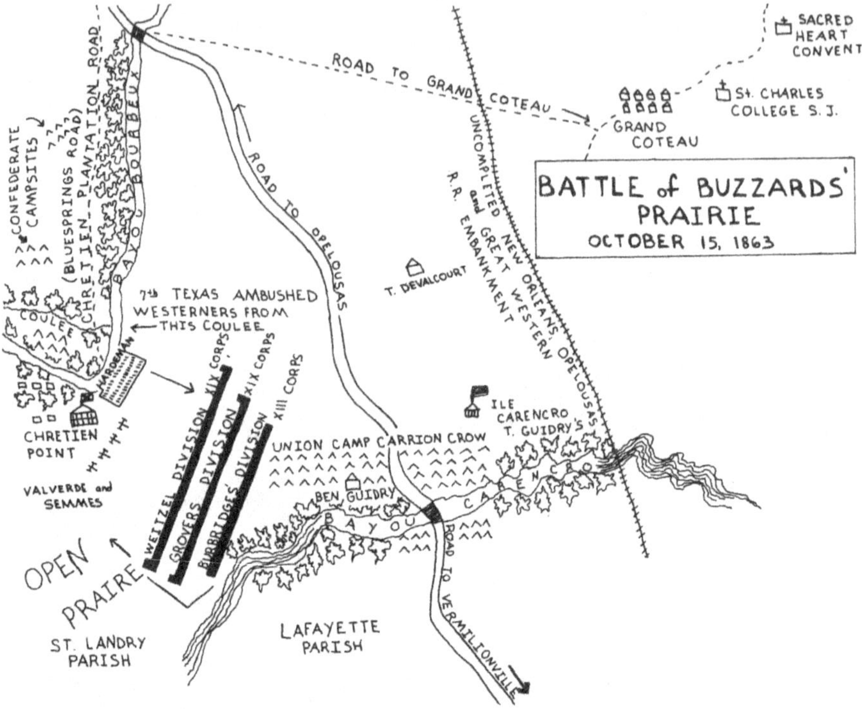

BATTLE OF BUZZARDS' PRAIRIE, October 15, 1863, near Chretien's Plantation *(Leslie's Illustrated Weekly)*

yell they momentarily turned Weitzel's 1st Brigade of Massachusetts and New York soldiers, some of whom began to flee the field in terror.

No sooner had the Texans closed on the panic-stricken infantrymen, however, running them down with their horses and swinging sabers left and right in the confusion, than Colonel Edmund Davis' "Yankee" Texans galloped up and launched a fierce counterattack. In the meantime a section of Nims' Battery, commanded by Captain Nims himself, moved into position and began pouring a deadly accurate fire of grape and cannister into the Rebel lines, driving them back toward the safety of Chretien's fence. Another section of Nims' Battery, commanded by Lieutenant William Marland, got the range on one of Semmes' guns and exploded the ammunition chest. One Rebel gunner was decapitated, another blown into eternity and two horses were killed. "Deadly business," noted a Massachusetts gunner that night in his diary.

It was not the first time that the roaring guns of Semmes and Nims had been trained on each other. Each had earned the other's respect on a bloody misty morning in Baton Rouge more than a year before. In the Battle of Buzzards' Prairie, however, it was the guns of Nims which gained the upper hand. "Their bombs bursted in our ranks, making frightful gaps," wrote a Texan to the Houston *Tri-Weekly Telegraph*. Company G of the 4th Texas, an all-German Company, lost seven men from one explosion. Finding themselves outnumbered, outgunned and taking heavy casualties, "Gotch" Hardeman now ordered the Texans to withdraw. "We found too stubborn a resistance and gave up the field," noted a Texas cavalryman. Neither side had accomplished a thing, but the field was strewn with the wounded, the dying and the dead from Texas, Louisiana, New York and Massachusetts.[21]

About two miles southwest of the battle zone, in the area called Coulee Croche (currently Bristol) Joseph Sibille's curiosity almost cost him his life. The blond-headed, blue-eyed Frenchman, father of the young Louis Sibille (who had carelessly crossed the Union lines on his way to St. Charles College the previous Monday) imprudently climbed atop his plantation bell for a better look. As if that wasn't suspicious-looking enough, he then ordered his English wife Penelope (nee Burleigh) to bring his Napoleon telescope which he had brought over from his home in the ancient province of Normandy.

Perched atop the bell, spyglass to his eye, tobacco planter Sibille looked for all the world like another of those tree climbing, housetop Confederate artillery officers directing fire toward the Union position. Within moments, however, he found himself looking into the muzzle of a dozen or more Yankee Enfields.

"What are you doing up there?" growled a no-nonsense officer. While Sibille did not understand English, he did understand the severity of the offense, and, through his wife Penelope (whose French was about as poor as Sibille's English) tried to explain away his actions.

But the Union officer was unsatisfied with the little Frenchman's explanation and demanded to know why Sibille was not out fighting with his Louisiana brethren in the Confederacy.

Sibille argued that he was a subject of the Emperor of France, and, as a neutral alien, was not subject to the conscript laws of Louisiana. As if to underline his point, Sibille raised his expensive looking-glass, which had been in the family for generations, and smashed it against the cypress wooden post supporting the plantation bell. Satisfied now, the Yankees rode away. The wonder of it all is that they had bothered to ask anything.[22]

The Battle of Buzzards' Prairie continued, off and on, for hours. The Confederates would withdraw to the relative safety of Chretien's fence and the shooting would momentarily cease. Then, like a Louisiana thunderstorm on a late summer afternoon, it would "make up" and another cavalry charge would be put into motion.

Both Rebels and Yankees kept wondering aloud why the ever-cautious Franklin with his overwhelming superiority in men and firepower did not take the offensive. Finally, at 10 o'clock A. M., the answer came. At that time bugles commenced blowing, drums began to beat, colorful regimental flags were hoisted and bayonets glistened in the morning sunlight as Brigadier General Stephen Gano Burbridge and his "heroes of Vicksburg," the Westerners from Illinois, Indiana, Wisconsin, Iowa and Ohio, came pouring across Buzzards' Prairie fresh from Vermilionville. Under any other circumstances the battle-weary Easterners of the XIX Corps would have dreaded the sight of so many Westerners, but now they cheered them on like fighting brothers.

JOSEPH SIBILLE
(Courtesy Mrs. Norwood Richard nee Sibille)

It was an event the Easterners would not soon be permitted to forget. In the last letter of his life, Private Gilbert Alonzo Jack, a nineteen-year-old farmer from Madison, Wisconsin, wrote that the XIX Corps "thought they had bushed a grizzley and daresent fotch him so they sent for the western boys." Ignoring the cheers of their exhausted

Eastern comrades, they were going to show these incompetent "nutmegs" how to make the Rebs "skedaddle."

And skedaddle they did, for "when battery after battery came up and went to hurling shot and shell and when line after line of bluecoats were formed across the prairie, and still more coming, the astonished Johnnies beat a precipitate retreat."[23] But not without one final blow at the advancing Yankees.

When it became apparent that these relentless but careless Westerners were going to pursue even beyond the Bourbeux, old Indian-fighter Hardeman displayed some of the skills that would eventually get himself promoted to brigadier. Dashing from regiment to regiment, Hardeman, tall and slim and sporting a fat mustache, ordered the 7th Texas Cavalry to dismount and conceal themselves in one of the many coulees crossing the Chretien plantation road. Meanwhile, the 4th and 5th Texas were to continue the rear guard skirmish, drawing the enemy across the Bourbeux and into the ambush.

Never suspecting a trap the Westerners boldly crossed the crude log bridges over the Bourbeux at a point behind the Chretien mansion and foolhardedly marched "right up to them" whereupon the Texans opened fire. What then followed was a scene reminiscent of the bloody ambush at Nelson's Bridge, where the road had been strewn with dead and wounded. Private W. R. Howell, a jayhawk-hunting cavalryman who participated in the carnage with the 5th Texas, noted that night in his diary that the ambush "stopped the gents for that day."[24]

Just as the fight seemed to be coming to a close, a messenger from the picket guard in Grand Coteau sprinted up to Franklin with some ominous news. A portion of the Rebel cavalry, he said, had skirted around from the north and was deploying near Sacred Heart Academy, apparently for a flank movement on the Yankees. Responding immediately, the Union commander ordered out Major Wickham Hoffman, his assistant adjutant-general, with a strong reconnaissance force.

Among the Yankees, no one knew the convent better than Hoffman. During the spring 1863 campaign he had personally delivered General Banks' promise of a safeguard to shield the institution "from the stragglers in the rear." It was he who had visited both St. Charles College and Sacred Heart Academy with Dr. Millard only two days before carrying the most recent set of "protection papers." Now it was he who might bring war to the secluded convent where some one-hundred and thirty young girls, mainly the cream of Louisiana society, were absorbing the spiritual and academic excellence which had prevailed there since 1821.

From the beginning of the war the Academy of Sacred Heart, "a dovecot in the woods, evoked the nuns' hopes that its remoteness would shelter it from army maneuvers." Such was not of course to be the case and the good mothers had long since resigned themselves to the inevitability of occupation and emancipation. Accordingly, they taught their pupils to do

> ...all the work formerly left to the slaves...they learned all kinds of manual and household work, taking turns in the care of the domitories, the refectory, the kitchen, at the dishwashing and the ironing. Some even asked to milk the cows.

It is a tribute to their thoughtfulness and compassion, that the Mother Superior could later write that "*La plus grande partie de nous domestiques noirs est restee fidele, malgre les tentationes de tout-genre*" (Most of our servants remained faithful, in spite of temptations from everyone).

SACRED HEART ACADEMY, Grand Coteau, Louisiana (Courtesy Archives of The Sacred Heart Academy)

Now the Lady Superior, Mother Aloysia Jouve, along with the other religious of the Academy, stood on the long iron-railed upper gallery and watched the skirmish which "erupted on the road leading to the convent." Although the woods resounded with the roar of cannon, the observers continued to "follow every move of the fighting."[25]

Fortunately, it was but a small affair and the Confederates were soon driven off. Major Hoffman came up, saluted the apprehensive ladies on the gallery and then galloped off in the direction of Buzzards' Prairie while still looking for Rebels.

Someone in the expedition remembered that during the spring campaign they had camped for the night in a certain house belonging to a Rebel captain about midway out on Buzzards' Prairie. Perhaps he would be at home. Indeed he was. Confederate Captain Theodore F. Devalcourt, age thirty-five, the enrolling officer for St. Landry Parish, was literally dragged from his home even as his wife Zoe (a sister of Constance Guidry) cried frantically. Just for good measure the Yankees thoroughly sacked his house, "taking three splendid double-barrelled shotguns and a case with two large pistols." William Gatchell's dispatch to the *New York Herald* that day characterized Devalcourt's misfortune as an "important capture."[26]

THEODORE DEVALCOURT, Circa 1890 (Courtesy Mrs. Carl Bourg, Port Arthur, Texas)

On the north and west bank of Bayou Bourbeux, where the victorious Yankees were engaged in the grisly work of gathering up their dead and wounded, someone spotted a lone hospital ambulance approaching from the direction of the Confederate lines. Had it not been for the white flag fluttering from the top, several thousand Westerners would gladly have opened fire. Even Captain Ormand Nims was obliged to suppress the desires of his sharpshooting gunners who were still bristling from the perfidious Rebel ambush against their careless Western comrades. As the wagon drew near, the Yankees could see that it was only a harmless white-headed old man accompanied by his black driver.

The old gentleman was none other than former Governor Alexandre Mouton who displayed his "safe conduct" pass from Confederate General Richard Taylor and asked to be escorted to General Franklin's headquarters. Only that morning he had learned of the mortal illness of his daughter Cecilia and had borrowed an ambulance so that she might be conveyed from Vermilionville to a place of safety.

Whatever else might be said of Union General Franklin, he was at least a gentleman, and a compassionate one at that. He very courteously received the sixty-year-old former governor and one-time United States senator with a military salute. Alexandre Mouton was then sent on his way with a small escort and a safe conduct pass. He apparently did not know that Cecilia had passed away several days before, and General Franklin did not have the heart to tell him.[27]

CHAPTER NINE

WESTERNERS ON THE BOURBEUX

Thursday, October 15, 1863

CHRETIEN POINT, the manorial home of Hypolite III and Celestine Chretien, stood at the head of a shaded oak alley near a horseshoe type bend in Bayou Bourbeux. A blend of French-Caribbean-Colonial and Greek Revival architecture it seemed oddly out of place in the prairie country, surrounded as it was by the more humble cottages of the rural Acadian planters and ranchers. Built between 1831 and 1835 for Hypolite II and Felicite (nee Neda) it had cost but seven thousand dollars for the labor (or about $43,000 in terms of 1978 currency). Yet, with its imposing two-story exterior, stuccoed brick circular columns, arched windows, carved mouldings and marbled fireplaces, it was as impressive as any of the splendid sugar mansions along the Teche.

Jean Lafitte was rumored to have been a regular visitor there after his disappearance from New Orleans, and widow Felicite was said to have shot a highwayman to death on the spiraling staircase during the dark days of banditry, cattle rustling and the vigilante committees. Shortly before the war the old cigar-chomping "Missus" (Felicite), who was hopelessly addicted to gambling, moved to New Orleans and left the mansion and extensive plantation to the care of her partially paralyzed forty-year-old son, Hypolite Chretien, and his wife, Celestine.

Hypolite III now stood on the damaged upper gallery of his home and watched apprehensively as a large body of mounted Federals rode cautiously up the oak-shaded lane. Would they burn the mansion, he wondered? Under similar circumstances in the spring, his "affable and charming" wife, thirty-seven-year-old Celestine Cantrelle of St. James Parish, had prepared an enormous feast which she spread under the giant live oaks to greet the advancing Yankees. General Banks was said to have been so charmed by her claims of Union loyalty and her "engaging talent for conversation and dazzling beauty" that he had posted guards around the home to keep out intruders.

Yet, in spite of Celestine's and mother-in-law Felicite's somewhat dubious claims to loyalty, one of her sons, Jules, ran away from St.

Charles College to join Vincent's 2nd Louisiana Cavalry. During the spring invasion even Celestine's most confidential *domestique* was quick to betray the fact that she had secreted most of her household jewelry in the well at the end of a long rope submerged just below the waterline. Most of the slaves, numbering about a hundred, had then followed their liberators off to Opelousas. Finally, in May 1863, Chretien Point had been visited by the efficient foraging teams of Colonel Thomas E. Chickering who proceeded to confiscate all the cotton, sugar, corn, mules, horses, hay, cattle, oxen, sheep, fowl, hogs, wagons and most everything else of value. Without slaves or money and with the frail Hypolite unable to work, the Chretiens were reduced to indigence and were forced into the humiliating circumstances of seeking out loans from the speculative moneylenders who thrived on other people's misery.

Still, reasoned Hypolite, the Federals might burn the place. After all Green's Texans had for days roamed the Chretien property at will. The largely empty slave quarters had been used by the Confederates as sleeping quarters; the cypress panel fence, located about one hundred yards in front, had served the Texans well as a defensive barrier. During the Buzzards' Prairie battle, as well as in countless other encounters, Rebel sharpshooters, observers, artillery and signal officers had perched in trees, atop cabins, and even where Hypolite now stood on the upper gallery. As a result some of the outbuildings had been reduced to rubble by Union artillery fire; the stuccoed brick and wood surface had been badly pitted and scarred by impacting bullets; the panes in the gracefully arched windows had been shattered; and a portion of the roof and upper gallery had been blown away by cannon fire.

As they drew nearer, Hypolite—sick, frail, and badly frightened—removed a handkerchief from his pocket and, according to oral tradition, waved the Masonic distress signal. In the distance a certain Union officer, also a Mason, was said to have recognized and acknowledged Chretien's signal. This incident, Hypolite later related, saved the mansion from the Yankee torch.

The story, while romantic enough, is somewhat misleading. The approaching "Yankees" were, without a doubt, a portion of Colonel Edmund Davis' loyal Texans. Their immediate mission was neither to burn nor to loot but to ascertain if the dwelling and outbuildings contained Rebel snipers. But Chretien, frightened as he was, could not have known this and the result was that he probably went through life believing that the house was spared by virtue of his membership in the secret brotherhood of Masons.

After thoroughly searching the premises, the Yankees proceeded to convert the grounds, outbuildings and lower floor of the house to the use of the Federal army. Slave cabins were employed as temporary hospital quarters where the wounded and sick were brought in, treated and sheltered. Even Hypolite Chretien was cared for by Union doctors, and provided with badly needed medicine. Meanwhile, the dead of both sides were interred on the north bank of the Bourbeux, not far behind the dwelling house.

Before long the once beautiful and well-manicured grounds of Chretien Point took on the same appearance as had Ile Copal, Ile Carencro, The Shadows and dozens of other homes between Brashear City and Opelousas. Sibley tents, fly tents and lean-to shelters sprang up by the hundreds, surrounding the house. The cypress fence rails, fifty-thousand altogether, disappeared one by one, victims of the ceaseless demands for firewood and sleeping boards.

CELESTINE CHRETIEN
(Courtesy Mrs. Jeanne Cornay)

Someone jokingly reminded the soldiers of the official order that they were to remove only the "top" rail. These orders were, of course, strictly obeyed until the supply of "top" rails was exhausted right down to the ground.

The intruders then set about taking whatever had been overlooked during, or accumulated since, the spring campaign, including five hundred bushels of corn, two large wagons and five sugar cane carts. As if that wasn't enough, they soon turned their attention to the house where General Burbridge had posted a guard for "protection" of the occupants.

Such precautions were a joke to the XIII Corps. While a lonely sentinel stood watch under the front gallery, dozens of soldiers simply used the back entrance and stripped the house right down to and including the large kitchen stove. "They took everything," subsequently complained Celestine. "They left only the land."[1]

Friday, October 16, 1863

In Opelousas, Louisiana, about nine miles north of the Union camp, an unidentified Confederate rode through the streets shouting an ominous message: *Les Federaux son sur le Bourbeux!*" he yelled, "*Les Federaux son sur le Bourbeux!*" (The Yankees are on the Bourbeux).

The bad news was offset to some extent by the groundless rumors circulating in town and in the nearby Confederate camps that Rebel General Bragg had surrounded Rosecrans' Army of the Cumberland at Chickamauga and "forced him to an unconditional surrender." A happier rumor was that Napoleon and Maximilian were organizing a force in Matamoras, Mexico, and would soon join ranks with the South. Finally, and most ridiculous, it was said that Ozeme Carriere, the notorious jayhawker, had been pardoned by Taylor and was organizing his cutthroat band to resist the Federal invasion.

Aside from the Union advance, the biggest news in Opelousas was the impending execution of J. J. Bowman, a private of the 28th Texas Cavalry. Bowman had deserted his command a few days earlier and was captured at night while attempting to enter the Union lines near Grand Coteau. Thinking his Confederate captors to be Federals, the intoxicated deserter had "made known everything" and as a result, he was convicted both of treason and desertion. When asked why he had deserted, Bowman replied: "Because I am tired of the service." To that Colonel J. P. Major was said to have remarked that he "would soon be discharged."

And so he was. At precisely 12 o'clock noon, October 16, 1863, about a mile north of the St. Landry Catholic Church, Private J. J. Bowman went before a twelve-man firing squad.[2]

Back along the Bourbeux the Westerners of the XIII Corps were crowing and taunting, "echoing at all hours the mistaken idea that no army raised east of the Alleghanies can be supposed to do fighting." For five long days, they were quick to point out, Franklin's huge sprawling army of Easterners had remained immobile along the Carencro, unable or unwilling to advance toward Opelousas. Then, on the very first day of the Westerners' arrival, Buzzards' Prairie had been conquered and the Union lines extended to Chretien Point on the Bourbeux and several miles beyond. If Grant and McClernand had led the expedition instead of Banks and Franklin, they scoffed, Texas would now be in Union hands, and possibly even Mexico.

With so much breastbeating among the narcissistic Westerners, General William Franklin very prudently decided to keep his Easterners of the XIX Corps along the Carencro, some two miles to the rear of Union Camp Bourbeux. Even there they were forced to endure the insults and unkind remarks made by a division of Westerners (McGinnis') marching through on their way from Vermilionville to the front. So obnoxious were many of the jeering soldiers and so heated were the exchanges that at one point during the morning a guard had to be posted on both sides of the road to keep the two army corps apart.[3]

Among the Westerners passing through Camp Carrion Crow that morning was a cavalry regiment, the 118th Illinois Mounted Infantry, commanded by Colonel John G. Fonda of Warsaw, Illinois. Fonda's regiment was the first of the newly-mounted infantry units to take the field and, though untested in the saddle, was to assume the duties previously performed by Edmund Davis' hard riding 1st Texas which was then preparing to join Banks in New Orleans. It would be a tough act to follow.

Just behind the Illinois horseman was another cavalry regiment, the 1st Louisiana (Union), commanded by none other than the wealthy merchant and shipowner, Harai Robinson of New York City. There was not a Westerner among them and precious few Louisianians. Most were from New York, Massachusetts and Rhode Island. It was the Rhode Islanders of that unit who had rebelled when forced to join the sham Louisiana regiment at Thibodaux. Now, less than two months after Robinson had ordered the summary execution of their ringleaders, they still despised him. And they were not alone in their hatred of the thirty-five-year-old commander. Over the weeks the Rhode Islanders had enlisted the support of others in the regiment, including several immigrants and a few native Louisianians, mainly Confederate deserters or conscript evaders, who now served as guides, scouts, couriers and spies. Several conspired to shoot Robinson at the first opportunity; others vowed to desert. In the meantime they would bide their time.

Surely General Franklin must have wondered if his men didn't hate one another more than the Rebels. At that time, however, he was more concerned about the real enemy, the Texans, who had simply disappeared after the Battle of Buzzards' Prairie. Where were they and what were they up to? With these thoughts in mind he ordered the newly-arrived cavalry brigade, consisting of the 118th Illinois, the 1st Louisiana, the 16th Missouri and the 14th New York, to pass up the marching soldiers and ride north toward Opelousas.

Fonda's horse, as the brigade was subsequently called, would not have to ride very far because at that very moment the Rebels of the 5th Texas Cavalry, along with Waller's Battalion and a section of the Valverde Battery were leaving the camp on Bayou Tesson. The Texans, under the command of Colonel Henry C. McNeill, had been ordered out to see what the Yankees were up to. Riding south on the Opelousas road, they "ran up on" Fonda's reconnaissance force about a mile north of the area currently known as Shuteston, virtually in front of John P. Hudson's plantation.

It was no contest at all. No sooner had the inexperienced Illinois horsemen spotted the bronzed Texans than they turned tail and fled. The New York, Missouri and Louisiana regiments, though somewhat more experienced, found themselves with no alternative but to follow suit. Down the muddy Opelousas road and across the grassy green prairies they galloped, past the home of Charles and Lezin Lavergne, Alexandre Richard, and Lewis Webb. In the rear, shooting and yelling like wild men and waving heir glittering sabers in the air, came the fearless cowboys.

Back on Bayou Bourbeux the soldiers of the newly-arrived division of Brigadier General George McGinnis stood at the edge of the camp and commenced "shouting words of encouragement" to the oncoming blue tide. Not since Vicksburg had they seen so much action. Recalled Private Harry Watts of the 24th Indiana:

> We had hardly got our 'shebangs' put up before an alarm was raised by a party running toward camp like the devil was after them. Cavalry riding for their lives, men on foot, running mules snorting, drivers whipping and cursing, all coming down the prairie, pell mell, towards our camp with a few mounted rebs in their rear, helping them along with an occasional shot. Such a scene we never before witnessed.

The correspondent for the *New York Herald*, William Gatchell, watched as both McGinnis and Burbridge ordered their respective brigades into battle formation. Colonel Edmund Davis, thoroughly disgusted by the performance of his replacement, quickly ordered the 1st Texas (Union) to cast aside their bags and gear they had just loaded for the trip to New Orleans and mount up for the rescue. Then with sabers raised above their heads, the hard riding loyal Texans charged directly toward the oncoming panic-stricken cavalrymen of Fonda's brigade. It appeared for all the world as though Davis planned to do battle with the fleeing Yankees unless they turned around to face their adversaries.

Captain Charles Rice, who had previously arranged his ten-pounder Parrotts of the 17th Ohio Battery for just such an event, was the first to open fire. When shells began dropping all around, wrote a Hoosier, "the approaching Texans concluded that discretion was the better part of valor and broke and fled." Julian Wood, a soldier in the 96th Ohio wrote his parents that the Rebels got "out of dat mud hole like you neber did see and away they went as if trying to outrun the wind."

The Texas Confederates were not, however, finished. Their arrival at the Union camp had been so rapid and unexpected that they had overtaken a forage train of produce and confiscated cattle out near the plantation home of Urbaine Lavergne. Now, even as the helpless Yankee infantry looked on, the retreating Texans "who are all mounted and can run around us most any time" began rounding up cattle.

The scene was just too much for a certain gunner in the 25th New York Battery. Determined to show these Westerners that Easterners too could fight, he raced his piece across the prairie at "breakneck" speed. Drawing up within range of "the venturesome dogs," he adjusted the range, opened fire and dropped a shell "in their midst" even as Isaac Jackson, a young corporal in the 83rd Ohio, looked on:

> As the smoke cleared away we could see it had divided the party in about two equal parts. They collected themselves together and hurried to the protection of the trees when he landed another shell in the trees. I stood immediately behind the gun when it was fired and my eye caught sight of the shell and followed it through its entire journey. I have heard this could be done but never witnessed it until today.

Although the gunner "received many compliments for his fine markmanship," the short barrage had killed only one horse, five cows and wounded one Texan.

By this time Colonel Davis, cursing, shouting and threatening to unleash his loyalists Texans against the Yankees, had managed to regroup the scattered and disorderly Union cavalry brigade. The skirmish, which had started with the Yankees fleeing south and the Texans in hot pursuit, now found the Texans racing north and the Yankees in hot pursuit. Up the Opelousas road they went, past Lewis Webb's and Alexandre Richard's where a few barking dogs joined in the chase. The residents, if they were home, most certainly were baffled by it all.

A few miles north of all the shooting, at the point of the advance Rebel pickets, Colonel William "Gotch" Hardeman decided to try his luck with another ambush. On the south border of Lezin Lavergne's plantation was the barbed wire of the times, a thorny, impenetrable *bois d'arc* (osage orange) hedge. There he ordered several companies of Texans to dismount and conceal themselves, while the others were supposed to "get badly frightened all at once and run, seemingly for life." Had Hardeman known that the Yankees too were led by Texans he wouldn't have wasted his time. As it turned out lawyer Davis, himself an Indian fighter, was far too crafty to be fooled, or as a Texan put it, "the Yankees smelt a mice" and gave up the chase before reaching the impromptu ambush. The Rebels did, however, capture three "Yankee" Texans who ventured too far.[4]

In the meantime Union General Burbridge, back on the Bourbeux, set about looking for ways to protect against such bold frontal assaults. The road north from Chretien's Point—a horseshoe bend in the Bourbeux behind the Chretien mansion—paralleled the heavily wooded bayou for some five miles in the direction of Opelousas. The west, or left side of the road, was gentle rolling terrain—the Opelousas Prairie—whereas the bayou was on the right. Along the route were numerous small coulees, or ravines, crossing the road from right to left and terminating in the open prairie. It was in one of these that "Gotch" Hardeman had laid his ambush the day before. It was also in these that the Rebels posted their pickets. Well, if they served the Texans, reasoned Burbridge, they could also serve the Yankees. Accordingly, he posted an elastic combination of troops in each of the ravines. If they were hit in front, they could fall back to the one behind, and so on.

The most dangerous picket position, the advance or forward outpost, was assigned to a detachment of soldiers from an Indiana regiment. It was located near the point where the Chretien plantation road struck the main Opelousas to Vermilionville stagecoach road, and was about a hundred yards south of the Confederate pickets. Occasionally, when the opposing forces were in such close proximity, a kind of *modus vivendi* would be worked out whereby neither side would fire on the other. But the Texans were uncooperative and planned to make life as unbearable as possible for the Westerners. They had heard of the notorious reputation of the XIII Corps and, besides, these same Yankees planned to invade the Lone Star State and plunder there as they had plundered in Louisiana. Thus hardly had the Union pickets settled in than the Texans opened fire, slightly wounding one of the guards. Infuriated that the Rebels refused to respect the unwritten agreement, one of the Hoosiers began shouting and cursing. Each insult, which was usually greeted by the discharge of a weapon, was returned in kind. After several hours of such rancorous exchange one of the Texans yelled a challenge across the field: "Hello you skulking blue-belly! Why don't you come out like a man and give me a fair crack at you?"

Rising to the challenge, one of the Hoosiers "leaned his gun against the tree, stepped into the open and with folded arms awaited the bullet of the butternut." Within seconds a Minie ball "went whizzing by a couple of feet off target."

Apparently pleased that he had tempted fate and survived, the daredevil bluecoat then picked up his rifle and yelled: "Now Johnnie, it's your turn. Face front, fair and stand still!" When no one appeared in the opposite field, the impatient Indiana soldier, Springfield at the ready, yelled across once more: "Well come on out, Johnny! What are you waiting for!"

"What!" shouted back the concealed Texan, "Do you think I'm a goddamn fool like you!"[5]

Saturday, October 17, 1863

The day dawned beautifully clear and cool. Perhaps for this reason the Texans, who could also appreciate such a "beautiful fall day," failed to make their usual morning demonstration. Even the picket lines, where Texans and Hoosiers had been waging their own private war, seemed unusually quiet. Down in Vermilionville General Franklin's long supply train finally arrived, and on the Carencro horse racing was the order of the day for the Easterners.

All was not well on Buzzards' Prairie. In fact, for Louis Francois Desire Arnaud it was a miserable day. Arnaud, a forty-six-year-old planter and rancher from Jansin Canton, Department of the Basse Alps, France, watched helplessly as a detachment of the 96th Ohio harvested his yam patch "for military purposes." Like the Guidrys, Chretiens, Moutons, Oliviers, Sorrels and Palfreys, Arnaud's misfortune stemmed from the fact that his house and property straddled the main roadway. Arnaud and his once-widowed English wife, Sarah (nee Burleigh—a sister-in-law of Joseph Sibille), had acquired this two-hundred-arpent tract of land just to the north of the opulent Chretien plantation in 1848. By 1861, when Louisiana seceded from the Union, the couple was prospering. In addition to a medium-sized Acadian-style home with a separate kitchen, the Arnauds possessed a large barn, a cotton and corn house, several slave cottages, an unspecified number of livestock and about twelve adult slaves.

The buildings and a fifty-arpent tract of heavily wooded land on the east bank of Bayou Bourbeux were enclosed with a lengthy cypress panel *(pieux)* fence. Within this enclosure Arnaud raised oxen, beef cattle, mules, horses, hogs and chickens. The remaining land was devoted to the cultivation of cotton, corn and yams, depending on relative prices. The little plantation was bordered in its entirety by a deep drainage ditch and a three-foot-high sod fence, a not uncommon sight in pre-barbed wire Louisiana.

As the war dragged on, however, the Arnaud's fortune declined. In the first place, Sarah's eyesight began to fail; in fact, by 1863 she was totally sightless. Moreover, the revenues from farming began to dwindle under Confederate price rigging, stifling regulations and "soft" currençy. As if that wasn't bad enough, the Bayous Carencro and Bourbeux became popular camping sites for the omnipresent Texas and Louisiana Confederates. Finally, good Southern citizens—including French ones—were levied upon to support the cause.

Then the Yankees came. During the first invasion in the spring of 1863 an endless column of muddy foot soldiers, artillery pieces, mule-drawn supply wagons and cavalry forces had plodded slowly past the Arnaud residence. The Easterners of the XIX Corps had flocked by the hundreds to the water well drawing and drinking, pouring and soaking. Most, refreshed by the cool water had marched off singing:

> Oh! We'll hang Jeff Davis
> From a tall palmetto tree

Behind the military columns had come the civilian wagons and ox carts loaded with *impedimenta* taken from houses along the way. Then came legions of stragglers, runaway slaves and camp followers from the very young to the very old, driving before them a veritable "Noah's Ark" of Louisiana farm animals.

Arnaud, along with other French residents, had tried desperately to protect his property by displaying the French tricolor and protesting vehemently in his native tongue, but it had been all to no avail. The old blind lady recalled how they had raced through the house taking capotes, pantaloons, silk vests, earrings, a gold cross, Confederate money, cravats, towels, and her husband's French double-barreled shotgun. In addition, her gold wedding ring had been brutally torn from her finger. Even Arnaud's old black hat, which he rarely removed, had been pulled from his head. The marauders had also smashed the furniture, broke the china, carried away all the preserved food and, in the most contemptible act of all, stuffed portions of dead farm animals and offal down the water well.

ARMY OF THE GULF halts for water in southwestern Louisiana *(Harper's Weekly)*

The badly depressed little Frenchman, unlike many others in southwest Louisiana, had made a gallant effort to repair the damage. His neighbors and relatives, in the best traditions of the Acadian spirit, had pitched in with a *coup de main*, offering to help with labor, fowl, food, livestock and draft animals. Eventually Arnaud had purchased a new black hat, shooed away the Carrion Crow vultures on the edge of the water well, and with a handkerchief tied about his face, had lowered himself into the odoriferous well where he proceeded to remove the offensive matter. By mid-summer 1863, after a great deal of hard work, the little plantation on the Bourbeux appeared to be headed toward a bumper fall harvest of yams and maize.

It was not to be because now, on that beautiful Saturday morning in October, the Federals were back again and this time they were more destructive than ever. For some incomprehensible reason, Arnaud went into the Union camp early that morning and took the Oath of Allegiance, possibly thinking that this would safeguard his property against foragers. It did not. No sooner did he return home, now dedicated to the preservation of the Union, than he found yet another unit of soldiers, under Lieutenant Silas Baldwin, harvesting his corn crop.

Feeling that he could no longer tolerate their confiscatory actions, Arnaud became quite belligerent, and began to loudly denounce the Union foragers as well as the flag he had just sworn to uphold. All of course to no avail. Within moments he found himself bound and gagged and on the way to a primitive stockade in Camp Carrion Crow. There he found many of his friends and neighbors also under arrest, including Joseph Boudreaux, Urbaine Lavergne, Don Louis Savoie and Joseph Miller. An Illinois soldier writing from Camp Bourbeux that very day must surely have had Arnaud in mind when he noted that

> ...from New Iberia to Carrion Crow bayou the country is settled mostly by French. One half of them are yet French citizens, although they have lived here some 20 years. I must confess that I detest the man who has enjoyed all the privileges of an American citizen for 20 years and yet not think enough of his country to take out naturalization papers. . . . They hoist the French flag and ask for protection. Let them be for us or against us. I ignore all neutrality.

So apparently did the others of the XIII Corps. With Arnaud incarcerated, and his helpless wife unable to prevent marauding—or even to see it—the lawless foragers quickly helped themselves to what remained of Arnaud's property. In short order the cotton house, cornhouse, barn and slave buildings were emptied of contents and dismantled, board by board, or stripped of siding and flooring. The railing from the cypress panel fence disappeared, one by one, as did all the family livestock. As a final insult even the posts were pulled from the ground and consumed as firewood. What had once been a prosperous, neat little plantation now took on the appearance of a disaster zone.[6]

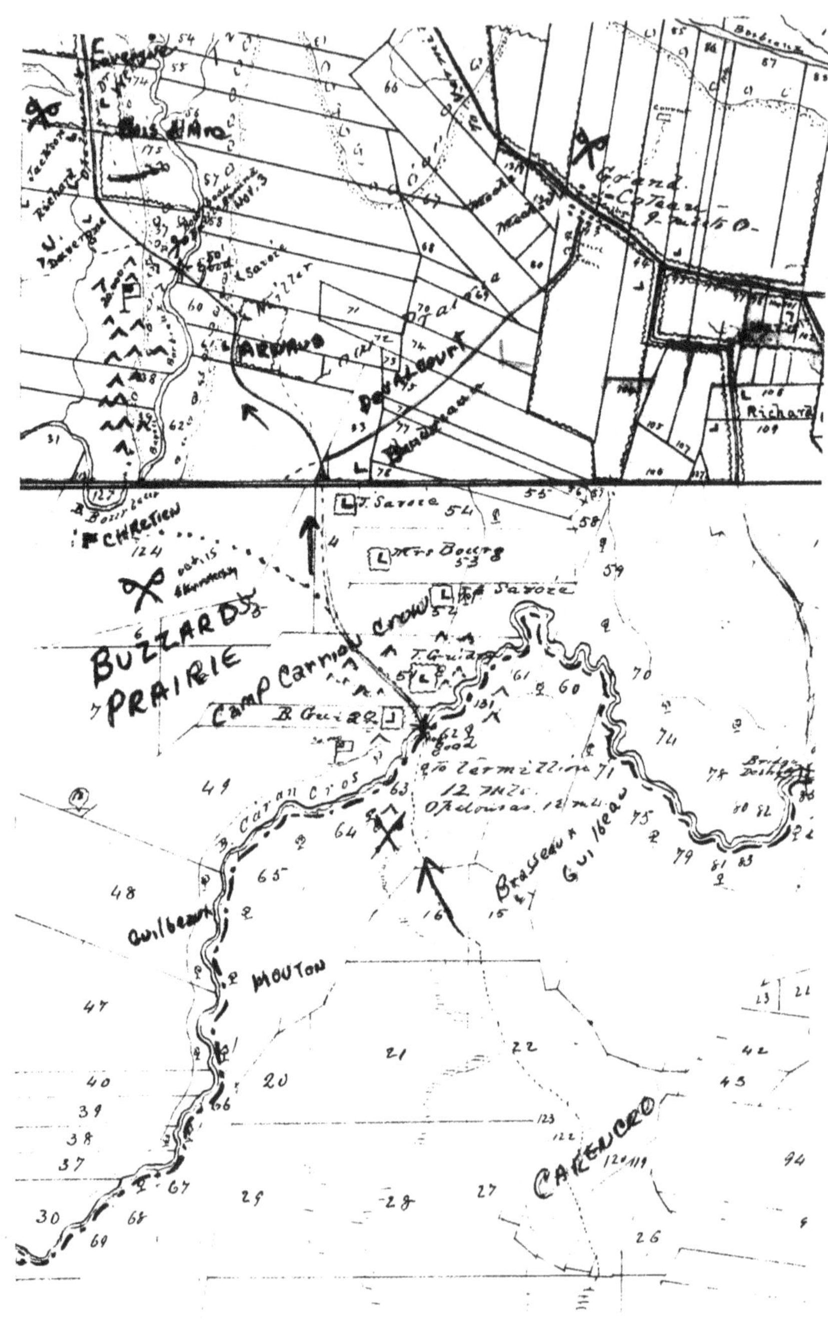

CAMP CARRION CROW, GRAND COTEAU AND BUZZARDS' PRAIRIE from 1863 Confederate map of St. Landry Parish (National Archives)

In the meantime the Easterners at Camp Carrion Crow were growing restless. The Rebels were no longer a threat now that the Westerners had moved to the advance on Bayou Bourbeux. As a result, depredations in the surrounding countryside became more frequent as did the complaints and inquiries "as to what had become of our advance into Texas."

In order to relieve the tedium, a member of General Franklin's staff—perhaps Franklin himself—hit upon the novel idea of arranging horse races for the men. The weather "was delightful" that Saturday morning and there were some exceptionally fine confiscated horses in camp, especially those belonging to the regimental commanders and general staff officers. Accordingly, the rules were established, the fields staked off, and the entire Union camp became absorbed in the ancient sport. The contagion even "spread to the Negro servants, and many a young African showed his speed to crowds of idle soldiers."[7]

While his troops were thus whiling away the hours General Franklin pondered his situation. He was genuinely concerned about the delay of the Texas expedition, and he had heard nothing from Banks for days. He did not yet know that his supply train was on the way, nor did he know what his next move should be. His last instructions had been merely to hold this position and to ascertain the strength of the enemy. Should he ask for additional instructions? Finally, his mind made up, the restless general fired off a telegram to the Chief of Staff in New Orleans:

> The order of the commanding general, issued just before he left for New Orleans seemed to be based upon the feasibility of opening water communication with Barre's Landing. Is it his intention that we shall move before that is determined?

Within hours Franklin had his answer:[8]

> It is the desire of the Major-General Commanding that an advance should be made sufficiently to cover the Courtableau and insure the safety of Barre's Landing.

So that was it. Banks expected him to move his command to Opelousas and Barre's Landing. From Franklin's position on the Carencro, there were two possible routes to Barre's Landing. The first, and most feasible, was to follow the main road to Opelousas, then turn east to Barre's Landing seven miles beyond; the other was through Grand Coteau to Juncion (Arnaudville) on the Teche. From the latter place, his troops could turn north and follow the Teche on either side to its origin on the Courtableau.

To get there was easier said than done. The enemy, Franklin noted, was "very pertinacious and annoying." As a result, the cautious general concluded to do nothing until both routes had been thoroughly reconnoitered.

Getting the nod for the dangerous mission was Colonel John G. Fonda, the newly appointed forty-year-old commander of the inexperienced cavalry brigade on Bayou Bourbeux. This was the same brigade which had been so disgracefully driven from the Opelousas road the day before. Today Colonel Edmund Davis and his loyal Texans, now enroute to Berwick's Bay, would not be around to save them. But no matter, the road to Opelousas was heavily wooded for five miles or more along the right side, thereby affording excellent cover for infantry. Fonda would just have to take along an infantry brigade.

At precisely 2 o'clock P.M., Fonda's cavalry brigade, accompanied by Colonel Richard Owen's brigade of infantry (the 60th and 67th Indiana, 83rd and 96th Ohio, and the 23rd Wisconsin) and sections of several batteries, started up the road toward Opelousas. The astonished Confederate pickets thought the long delayed advance to Opelousas had commenced and mounted up and ran.

Running was the last thing on the minds of Sebastian Dupre and Marguerite Miller, who, at that very moment, were beginning the slow walk down the aisle toward the marriage altar in the St. Landry Catholic Church in nearby Opelousas. The happy occasion was soon interupted, however, by the bass boom of cannon in the distance. Windows rattled, the ground rumbled and the old church edifice seemed to be shaking off its very foundation, but the wedding went on. Unknown to the marriage party, Fonda's reconnaissance force had run up on the entire Rebel cavalry division, led by General Green himself, down at Charles Lavergne's plantation near present day Shuteston.

At the point of contact, Surgeon James Hunter of the 60th Indiana Infantry looked out on the treeless Opelousas prairie and commented that "it was a grand site for a pitched battle." Hunter failed to notice the presence of a little Cajun house situated about midway between the two opposing forces complete with chinaberry trees, picket fence, barn and outbuildings. The little "island" belonged to either a Lavergne, Miller or Richard family and seemed to be the focus of a concentrated artillery barrage from both sides. The Yankees lined their infantry up behind the same *bois d'arc* hedge that the Texans had unsuccessfully employed the day before. Then the cavalry played the Texans' game. A group would charge toward the little island and bring down the screeching Parrotts and Napoleons of the Valverde and Semmes' Batteries.

The Union cavalry would then pretend to "get scared" and rush back to the hedge, attempting to draw the Confederates within range of the infantry. But Green's horse had fought in too many battles in too many places to be outwitted by this inexperienced bunch. His Texans would pursue only a short distance and pull up short of the house, whereupon they would bring down the rifled Parrotts and heavy guns of Nims' and the 17th Ohio Batteries.[9]

Not that anyone seemed to care but the house was not vacant. Inside were four frightened little boys, ranging in age from four to twelve, who huddled together with their panic-stricken mother while the artillery duel raged over their very heads. Their father, like countless other innocent civilians, was off on the western prairies standing guard over the family livestock. At one point during the cannonading the frightened inhabitants rushed from the house and headed toward what they believed to be the relative safety of the open fields. Neither side apparently noticed, or cared if they did notice.

Finally, during one of Fonda's fake charges, the innocent refugees were discovered. The little boys were frantically trying to conceal themselves in the furrow of a sweet potato patch. Beside them was their dead mother lying in a pool of her own blood. Grief-stricken, dirty, crying, and clad in white cotton dresses—the customary attire of young males—the little French-speaking boys were picked up and taken to the Union camp. There they were treated for minor wounds, clothed and fed. Just who they were, or whatever happened to them, remains a mystery.[10]

Interestingly enough, not one person on the Confederate or Union side was so much as scratched. The reconnaissance mission, if it could be called that, had accomplished nothing.

Sunday, October 18, 1863

Aside from religious services and an occasional horse race, virtually nothing of importance occurred near Buzzards' Prairie. On the other hand, Lieutenant Lawrence Van Alstyne, over in the Great Cypress Swamp east of Vermilionville, was engaged in a harrowing experience. In his search for black recruits, the jinxed New Yorker and his party had been led to the Great Cypress Swamp near the Pont des Breaux (Breaux Bridge) only the day before. At that time they had encountered several blacks "wild with joy, and eager to become Linkum Sojers."

One of these was a certain French-speaking quadroon who, together with his wife (or mistress), farmed a small peanut patch. He also owned "the most perfect picture of a horse" that Van Alstyne had "ever looked at." Both the black and his horse had been recruited and taken back to Vermilionville where the animal attracted the attention of all. So intrigued was the regimental commander, Colonel George Parker of Poughkeepsie, New York, that he immediately struck up a bargain and bought the animal. As part of the arrangement the new recruit was to return home that night on the horse, and, after bidding his spouse and children farewell, would report for duty early Sunday morning.

By noontime Sunday, with neither the horse nor the recruit in sight, it became apparent that the gullible Parker had been outwitted. "The Colonel was mad clear through," noted Van Alstyne, and roared that "he was going to find that horse, or else find a dead nigger." Saddling up, Colonel Parker and Van Alstyne started once more toward the Great Cypress Swamp.

Riding east toward Pont des Breaux, the unlucky New Yorkers came to a point where the flat treeless prairie—Prairie Maronne—stopped abruptly at the edge of an almost impenetrable forest. Not that it meant anything to Van Alstyne or Parker, but they had just entered the mysterious and one-time dangerous domain of "Abdel-el-Coco."

Coco was a handsome and brilliant free mulatto who, more than a half century before, had taken two white girls as mistresses and peopled the edge of the dark forest with his progeny. Here, in a little clearing surrounded by luxuriant growth, this "African Don Juan" had build a modest clay house with a straw roof which once served as a sanctuary for runaway slaves, bandits and fugitives from justice. It had also been a house of prostitution, a veritable den of iniquity, with such a sinister reputation that it was spoken of only in whispers. Demonology was practiced in Coco's domain, or so it was said, with wild orgies, rituals and sacrifice; and exasperated mothers all over the Attakapas frequently corrected disorderly children by threatening to "give them to Coco." Very few honest people dared venture into the area, not even armed parties of deer hunters who believed that both the house and its inhabitants were of supernatural origin.

Coco was gone now, exiled along with his women and children by the pre-war *comites de vigilance*. Most of them had gone to New Orleans where, it was rumored, Coco had passed away. With the advent of Civil War, however, some of the exiles had made their way back to their place of birth. Without a doubt Van Alstyne and the colonel had been outwitted by a son of "Abdel-el-Coco."

Entering a trail in the dense swamp behind this house of myths, the New Yorkers spotted the culprit running across a little clearing. Only after a spirited chase was he brought to bay. "He said his horse had got away and he was trying to find him, and had been looking for him all morning," recalled Van Alstyne. Disbelieving, the colonel drew his revolver, pointed it in the face of the frightened black man and ordered him to march toward the limb of a massive oak tree. Van Alstyne was told to get his picket rope ready for a hanging:

> The nig...began to beg but the Colonel told me to throw the line over a limb, for he was going to keep his word. Whether he did really intend to hang him or not I don't know, but I proceeded to get the rope in position for a real hanging.

Before the foul deed could be carried out, however, "the rascal owned up." The horse, said he, was hidden in the swamp some distance away, and if the Colonel would spare his life, he would take him there. The entire group then proceeded down a beaten path for a mile or more, going deeper and deeper into the dark forest. Suspecting an ambush, the Colonel dropped Van Alstyne off all alone at a bend and went on, revolver in hand.

Never in his life had Van Alstyne been left alone in such forbidding surroundings. The swamp was at once beautiful and frightening; it was also green, lush and barely touched by civilization. Enormous bell-bottom, moss-draped cypress trees, their "gnarled knees" protruding six feet or more above the hyacinth-covered water line, looked for all the world like giant forest monsters. High above him, hidden from view in the dense, verdant foliage was an ornothological paradise. Ivory-billed woodpeckers hammered away at soft and decaying bark; mystical bald-headed blackbirds flitted from tree to tree; and Carolina parakeets and carrier pigeons sang their respective tunes.

The admiration was fleeting. Beneath the swamp's loveliness was a mass of slops and stinks and pestilence; it was an area inhabited with giant alligators, and "bears, wolves, wildcats and venomous reptiles as big as any in Barnum's menagerie." By night, mosquitos came in clouds, bringing painful bites, and the mysterious swamp diseases of southern Louisiana. Moreover the swamps were hot and humid in spite of the pleasant weather, steaming in the odor of its own decay.

It was getting darker, observed the jinxed soldier, and then he remembered the tales he had heard about the people of the forest. It was said that these swamps were the homes of outlaws, black and white; that they could live here "undisturbed by the laws that govern other people;" that runaway slaves found homes here, where they raised families and would kill one another just as soon as they would an outsider.

And there were stories of the supernatural and the occult. These people, he had heard, were practitioners of the black arts. On the one hand a faith-healing *traiteur* could remove a wart simply by making a cross and saying a few secret words while a *gris-gris* shaman could dispatch an enemy with a curse so devastating that the body would decompose within hours after death.

With his mind thus occupied, Van Alstyne discerned a movement in the shadows. Only fifteen minutes had transpired since he was left alone in the mysterious wilderness. The approaching footsteps and voices soon revealed the Colonel, the "black rascal" and one beautiful horse. It was with a great deal of relief that Van Alstyne and party mounted up and "made tracks for camp."[11]

SCENE FROM A LOUISIANA SWAMP ***(Harper's Weekly)***

Monday, October 19, 1863

At the Ile Carencro plantation home of Thelismar and Constance Guidry, halfway between Opelousas and Vermilionville, General William Franklin, the forty-year-old commander of the XIX Army Corps, was as confused as ever. Only two days before he had been instructed by Banks to secure Barre's Landing on the Courtableau. This was confirmed by a courier dispatch from Vermilionville with the message that the *Red Chief*, a small supply steamer (captured near Port Hudson during the summer) was already en route to Barre's Landing from Brashear City.

Then on Sunday, the day before, Franklin had received a message which seemed to countermand the original orders. Could this be accurate? Franklin fired off another dispatch:

> As I understand the wishes of the commanding general, New Iberia is to be held, and Barre's Landing...is to be let go...If, however, the steamer has started for Barre's Landing, she ought to be sent back.

The telegraph reply came back within hours:[12]

> The steamer *Red Chief* has gone to the Courtableau, and cannot be stopped. My dispatch of yesterday cannot have got to you correctly, if you understand it that Barre's Landing is to be let go. It is exactly the wish of the commanding general that Barre's Landing shall be occupied...or the steamer *Red Chief* will certainly be captured.

Interestingly enough, Confederate General Richard Taylor, back in Opelousas, was not confused. Thanks to the recent capture of a Union Signal Corps team, complete with secret code books, the shrewd son of a former U. S. President found himself with the means of intercepting signal messages. Toward this end Confederate guerillas were ordered to sabotage the telegraph wires at every opportunity, forcing the Yankees to rely on signal communication. The garbled communique received by Franklin had, in fact, been relayed part of the way by signals. That the Confederates had intercepted and correctly interpreted that same message suggests that Taylor's forces might have been doing more than just reading Federal communications.

Once the snafu was cleared, Franklin returned his reconnaissance teams to the field, but here was yet another weak link in the Union command. Heretofore, his spies and eyes, as well as the spearhead of his movement, had been the hard-riding loyal Texas *renegados* of Colonel Edmund Davis. Riding far in advance they had cleared the way, frequently sending the Rebels running, and had brought back reliable intelligence reports.

Now, that duty fell to Colonel John G. Fonda, a forty-year-old chronic sufferer of rheumatism from Illinois. Unlike many of the other Union cavalrymen (or mounted infantrymen), Fonda was a skilled horseman and had even brought his personal mount, saddle and trappings to Louisiana. Fonda had previously served as commander of a prisoner of war camp in Illinois where he was remembered by Alabama prisoners as a kind-hearted jailer who adhered to a rigid code of honor not unlike that of Southern gentlemen of the day. Rising rapidly from a lieutenant under Lew Wallace, he became major of the 12th Illinois Cavalry, then Colonel of the 118th Illinois Mounted Infantry and, finally, commander of his very own brigade.

Fonda was not a Davis, nor were his mounted Illinois infantrymen as skilled in the saddle as the Texans they replaced (or the ones they confronted). Twice Fonda's horse had gone out and twice they had failed. This time General Franklin suggested to the goateed cavalry commander that he take along the shrewd and calculating brigadier general from Kentucky, Stephen Gano Burbridge, as well as Ormand Nims and his crack 2nd Massachusetts Battery.

At about 2 o'clock P. M., the reconnaissance force left the Union Camp on Bayou Bourbeux. Though it was only about one-half the size of the last mission, it still numbered more than one thousand. Up the Opelousas road they went, past Charles Lavergne's and Lewis Webb's, driving in the pickets of the 4th Texas Cavalry. On reaching the well-known *bois d'arc* hedge, Fonda, on the advice of Burbridge, deployed his men in battle formation. The 23rd Wisconsin, Colonel Joshua Guppey commanding, and the 34th Indiana Infantry regiments were placed on each side of the road while the 118th Illinois Mounted Infantry, flanked by Harai Robinson's 1st Louisiana Cavalry, took the advance; the rear was brought up by the 17th Ohio and 2nd Massachusetts Batteries, along with portions of the 6th Missouri and 14th New York Cavalry regiments.

Incredibly, the Rebels were nowhere in sight. Continuing their advance the Yankees passed the plantation homes of John P. Hudson and Benjamin Rogers until they reached the old brick factory directly in front of Rebel General John G. Pratt's home. At this point a small tree lined coulee (a portion of Bayou Sylvan) crossed the road. According to several Negroes, who rushed out to warn the invaders, there was a Confederate force of some four thousand men camped just beyond the coulee on a ridge (currently Bellevue Cemetery) where they had prepared an ambush.

Among those waiting in the tree-lined coulee was Captain Julius Giesecke of New Braunfels, Texas. The Teutonic Texan and his all German company (Co. G) had been on picket with the 4th Texas when it appeared as though "the whole Yankee army began to move up on us." As the Yankees approached the tree line, Giesecke's regiment opened fire, an act which drove the Federal skirmishers back to the main body. At the same time the 5th Texas Cavalry, which heretofore had remained concealed behind the trees, made an appearance on the Union left.

Perhaps it was fortunate for all that the remainder of Green's command was not at home, as the blacks had erroneously reported. Fonda did not of course know this and, under the circumstances, decided to withdraw. But no sooner had his troops commenced the retrograde movement than a messenger arrived from General Franklin. The commanding general apparently wanted Fonda to taste blood, or perhaps he entertained the hopes of moving the entire command several miles closer to Opelousas. At any rate he ordered the Illinois Colonel to "hold the positions."

And Fonda did just that. After consulting with General Burbridge he "drew in his forces" directly on the road. Several other pieces of artillery were sent up from the Carrion Crow and Bourbeux camps and a heavy artillery bombardment began. For several hours the guns of Nims' Battery and the 17th Ohio lobbed shells from one end of the treeline to the other. Trees fell, craters were dug, fires were set and the Texans kept their distance.[13]

Only five miles away, in Opelousas, there was "naught but excitement." James Earl Bradley, the Methodist minister whose wedding was delayed by the Federal advance, wrote in his diary that "the town is like a small sea, swept by a storm." Although they had been expecting the invaders to occupy the town for several days, many had waited for the last moments to take the necessary measures. Now, with the enemy on the outskirts, the exodus accelerated. A veritable caravan of mules, cattle, horses, wagons, masters and slaves was soon on the western roads heading toward Texas. They had at least left with some good news. Bragg, it was confirmed, had decisively defeated Rosecrans. Better yet it was rumored that Napoleon's fleet was sinking U. S. warships downriver from New Orleans.[14]

COLONEL JOHN G. FONDA
(Library of Congress)

The Yankees did not, however, move on Opelousas that day. In fact, a short while after sunset, Franklin sent out another messenger with instructions for the force to withdraw. It was well that they did so because General Taylor, accompanied by the remainder of Green's command, soon arrived on the scene.

For all the noise and destruction, only three Texans had been killed and three wounded. Fonda, who lost an equal number, then filed an apologetic report. "I regret that the reconnaissance was not more extended," he wrote to Franklin, "but am satisfied it would have been imprudent to go farther with so small a force."[15] He was right.

Even as Colonel Fonda was out skirmishing with the Texans, at least two open-air general court-martials were taking place in Union Camp Carrion Crow. One was that of Surgeon A. C. Livingston of the 110th New York Infantry who was charged with straggling down near Pattersonville. The other was the military trial of Lieutenant William Gannon of the 8th New Hampshire Infantry. Gannon, it will be recalled, was charged with striking and insulting a superior officer, and with disobeying orders by refusing to help quell a disturbance in his company.

While there was never much question about Gannon's guilt, the defense nonetheless attempted to show that his actions were provoked by the offensive behavior of the acting regimental adjutant, Ezra Bell. Despite this fact—which was sustained by virtually every witness—Gannon was no less guilty and, as a result, was sentenced to be "cashiered." All this, according to one observer, "because of Mike Fox" who was still in chains and awaiting his own court-martial.[16]

CHAPTER TEN

THE ROAD TO OPELOUSAS

Tuesday, October 20, 1863

WHEN HANNIBAL of ancient Carthage invaded the Italian Peninsula in 217 B. C., the Roman defenders were ill-prepared for war. As a result the Carthagenian elephants-and-horse cavalry trounced legion after legion of Roman soldiers on the field. With the very survival of Rome at stake, the famous general, censor and consul of Rome, Quintus Fabius Maximus, developed and employed some unusual military tactics. Rather than engage Hannibal and his superior forces out on the open plains, Fabius pursued, harassed and eluded the invaders in the confines of terrain favorable to Rome. Those successful tactics earned for Fabius the surname *cunctator* "the delayer," and gained for Rome the necessary time to prepare for war.

In Shreveport, Louisiana, two hundred miles or more north of the Union advance, Lieutenant General Edmund Kirby Smith likened his situation as commander of the Trans-Mississippi Confederacy to that of Fabius. At age thirty-nine the Florida born general was responsible for an area as large and almost as diverse as western Europe; not that he wasn't eminently qualified. An 1841 graduate of West Point, he had served with distinction in the Mexican War and was a mathematics professor at West Point before going to the frontier as an Indian-fighter and eventually botanist on the Mexican Boundary Commission. During the early war years he was noted for his accomplishments at Bull Run, where he was severely wounded, and his participation in the invasion of Kentucky. For the latter he was awarded the incipient nation's highest distinction, the Confederate Thanks of Congress, and command of the Trans-Mississippi Department.[1]

It would not be unfair to say that Smith had reconciled himself to the inevitable. The fall of New Orleans had shattered the myth of invincibility in his Department, and then the Yankees had run rampant during the spring Teche Campaign. Looting, burning and confiscating they had moved from New Orleans to Alexandria practically unopposed, further reducing civilian morale and the will to resist; neither could the disasters at Port Hudson and Vicksburg be written off as mere aberrations. Clearly the Confederates were out-gunned and outmanned and there was no way that the incongruous little Army of Western Louisiana, numbering between five and eight thousand, could possibly hold back the blue tide in pitched battle. Another defeat and morale would completely collapse. Thus, the only way to avoid shedding more Southern blood than necessary was to adopt guerilla tactics and avoid combat when odds favored the opponent.

Confederate General Richard Taylor, by contrast, favored a much bolder approach. He was, after all, the son of "old Rough and Ready" and, as field commander of the Army of Western Louisiana, believed himself to be better qualified to make combat decisions than the desk general up in Shreveport. Educated at Harvard, Yale, Edinburgh and in France he possessed superb literary talents and was a close personal friend and brother-in-law of President Jefferson Davis. Among his friends and associates before the war were Ulysses S. Grant, William Tecumseh Sherman and Andrew Johnson.

LIEUTENANT GENERAL EDMUND KIRBY SMITH
(Library of Congress)

MAJOR GENERAL RICHARD TAYLOR
(Library of Congress)

Zach Taylor's thirty-seven-year-old son also possessed some of his father's fighting qualities. It was he who had commanded the Stonewall Division at Cedar Mountain which so thoroughly trounced and disgraced Nathaniel P. Banks. At the Second Bull Run, he again led the division to victory, and at Fredericksburg he watched another current adversary, William B. Franklin, go down in disgrace. During the spring Teche Campaign he had fought and then led his ragged army out of what seemed certain entrapment at Irish Bend, and, in the summer, he conceived the plan which led to the capture of Brashear City. With such a long string of success and surrounded as he was by ambition (Mouton) and recklessness (Green), Taylor was spoiling for a fight.

Characteristically, Taylor's bold approach, as well as his occasional arrogance and abrasive, almost contemptible, attitude toward superiors conflicted with the more cautious policies of Kirby Smith. Rarely did a day pass that Taylor did not write a message (or messages) to Smith describing just how he, Taylor, planned to handle the Yankees. Worse still were his not infrequent suggestions as to how Smith should run the Trans-Mississippi Confederacy. During the summer, for example, he had asked Smith to join him in the field and assume personal responsibility for the relief of Vicksburg. Smith's subsequent refusal, claiming that he was too busy at Shreveport to take to the field, so antagonized Taylor that, in his memoirs, he barely refrained from accusing his superior of cowardice.

Now, with the Federals approaching Opelousas, Taylor began to importune Smith's headquarters for permission to drive them back to Berwick's Bay. Only Smith's repeated assurances that reinforcements from Arkansas and Texas would soon be available kept Taylor in check and prevented him from offering battle at some point below Opelousas. Taylor persisted, protesting that between Washington, Louisiana, and the Red River, there were no good defensive positions.The invaders should be dispersed now, he contended, before they occupied the whole of lower Louisiana.[2]

Smith's temper, like Taylor's, had been simmering just below a boil ever since the unsolicited advice on Vicksburg; now it seemed to boil over. Fed up with his brash younger general's gratuitous contentions and apparent recklessness, Smith decided to introduce Taylor to Quintus Fabius Maximus.[3]

> ...Difficult as you may find it, you must exercise great caution in your operations. You must restrain your own impulses as well as the desires of your men. The Fabian policy is now our true policy. In the present state of the public mind, a defeat to your little army would be ruinous in its effects. When you strike, you must do so only with strong hopes of success.

The message, though judicious in nature and diplomatic in tone, infuriated Taylor. It was the last straw, he raged. For weeks each of Taylor's suggestions to Smith had met with a cool reception and was usually acknowledged with a reminder that Smith, as commander of the Trans-Mississippi, was responsible for affairs in Texas, the Indian territory, Arkansas and Missouri as well as in western Louisiana. At the moment, Smith reminded Taylor, the District of Texas was also in danger, and the commander, J. Bankhead Magruder, was making demands for men and material which could not possibly be supplied. But Taylor would hear nothing of this. He was being patronized by a general "too occupied with picnic, blackberry and crawfish parties, and his young wife" to concern himself with the war. Smith, believed Taylor, was guilty of cowardice, if not incompetence, an opinion he seemed only too happy to share with anyone who would listen. As a result there soon arose among Taylor's friends "a disposition to criticize, misrepresent, and condemn everything done by or connected with General Smith."[4]

While Taylor fumed in Opelousas, Union General Franklin, still on the Carencro, received the welcome news that his supply train of several hundred wagons was ready to leave Vermilionville for the front. Better yet, another brigade from the XIII Corps had just moved from Vermilionville to the Bourbeux (Colonel Henry Washburn's) and, together with a newly arrived artillery battery (Jacoby's 1st Indiana) was ready for action.

Accordingly, he wired General Banks in New Orleans of his plans:[5]

> Tomorrow I shall march the whole force now at Carrion Crow (and Bourbeux) Bayou to Barre's Landing, if possible. This course I consider necessary on account of the departure of the *Red Chief* and consequent reconnaissance. The enemy is in force about two and one half miles this side of Opelousas.

Although the men in the two Union camps would not be officially notified of Franklin's plan until nightfall, they were nonetheless ordered at noontime to prepare two days cooked rations, a dead giveaway; and they could not have been happier. For ten days the Easterners had remained idle on the Carencro whereas the Westerners on the Bourbeux had not had a moment's rest for five days. Now, the moribund Texas expedition was about to get underway once more. Captain William Barney of the 29th Wisconsin decided to write a letter just in case it might be his last. Though he could scarcely disguise his glee, he was clearly concerned about the Texas "mounted infantry" waiting up the road. "We are prepared to give old secesh a good drubbing," he wrote, but "they will be so good as to help us go as short a distance as possible."

Corporal Isaac Jackson of the 83rd Ohio was also delighted, believing as he did that the Texans could not possibly be worse than the camp, the food and the water on Bayou Bourbeux. "Here we are without tents," he wrote to his sister, "and the nights are getting cold. Our crackers are full of little black bugs and worms but that is all the bread we have. We have good beef but the way it is cooked would sicken you." About the only good news was that the people along the Bourbeux "are loyal to a great degree because they are taking the oath to the old flag."

These "loyalists," however, would probably not have approved of Jackson's next remark that "many of the soldiers say after the war is over they are coming down here to settle down and live."

Even as Jackson complained of army life in Louisiana, a portion of Franklin's wagon trains began rolling into camp. Almost immediately, regimental quartermasters from the Carencro to the Bourbeux set about passing out blankets, new clothing, shelter tents and wormless rations. As if to underline their happiness, Lew Wallace's old regiment, the 11th Indiana, put on their new uniforms and entertained the troops by parading across the rolling prairies while regimental bands from both camps provided the marching music.[6]

Farther south, down near New Iberia, Lieutenant Lawrence Van Alstyne was anything but happy. Only the day before he and his all white non-French-speaking recruiting detail, three in number, had left Bayou Vermilion for Brashear City with approximately 200 Louisiana blacks. Most of the white officers were about as young, inexperienced and incompetent as Van Alstyne and had so indicated by permitting the recruits' wives, girl friends and children to visit them in camp. There they had remained drinking, singing, dancing, frolicking and consuming all the rations allotted them until the hour came to move out.

BLACK RECRUITS bidding farewell. ***(Harper's Weekly)***

The trek to New Iberia had been sheer agony. One old mule-drawn cart was loaded with exhausted black bodies, as were the officers' horses. Before long the cart had broken down, and the small Creole horses were unable to carry their burden. By some miracle they had eventually reached their destination and took up quarters in a vacant schoolhouse. The exhausted white officers immediately collapsed in a corner to get some rest, but "before we were asleep," Van Alstyne noted in his diary

> ...we heard a fiddle tuning up and in a little while a dance was started and was in full blast. How long it lasted I don't know, but when I awoke about sunrise the inmates of the schoolhouse were sleeping like the dead.

Van Alstyne's troubles were far from over. Early that morning they had set out for a point about two miles below New Iberia where they were to catch the *A. G. Brown* to Brashear City. But no sooner had they moved into an old sugar house for shelter than a heated quarrel erupted among the black recruits. Though the cause remained a mystery to the three nervous New Yorkers, the "jabbering" seemed to center around a lovely young mulattress named Margaret.

Margaret, as Van Alstyne subsequently learned, was the daughter of a certain white judge. Her master had gone off to fight for the Confederates, and her husband, the head black on the plantation, was subsequently hanged during the spring when he attempted to run off with Chickering's train.

At any rate the angry recruits soon divided into two opposing groups with the leader of each vying for Margaret's attention. Even as the frightened white officers walked among them trying to restore order, the two forces proceeded to fortify their positions by rolling empty sugar hogsheads into two parallel rows facing each other. Stationing themselves behind the barrels the "generals" in command began to "jaw at each other across the field." No one paid the slightest attention to the efforts of the protesting whites:

> The men each had a hogshead stave for a weapon. For flags they used bandanna handkerchiefs, and for drums a piece of board upon which one man pounded while another held it up.
>
> One of the generals made a speech which made the other side fighting mad, and they all jumped over the breastworks and met in the space between, batting each other over the head with their weapons, and yelling with all the power of their lungs. We thought sure they would kill each other, for the blows they struck broke some of the staves into splinters. Just as we were going to try and interfere one side surrendered and were marched off, prisoners.

Against her wishes, Margaret was quickly dragged to the center of the field by the victorious "general." He then demanded his reward in the form of a kiss, but Margaret, taking one look at the puckered lips, instead drew back her arm and rewarded him with a resounding slap across the face. "I could not tell whether she blushed or not," wrote Van Alstyne, "but suppose of course she did." Unfortunately her hasty action did not end the affair as both sides began quarreling again. Within moments, however, the general whose *machismo* was much imperiled then swallowed his pride, dropped upon his knees and implored the "dusky maiden" to give him his due if, for no other reason, to restore peace.

Margaret ultimately relented and stuck out her hand for him to kiss—an act which led to many cheers and a full surrender. The battle was over, peace declared and Van Alstyne was much relieved. "There had been some blood shed," noted the New Yorker, "and the wonder is that no heads were broken."[7]

Back on Camp Bourbeux, rumors of an impending battle began to circulate. The most immediate cause of the speculation was a lengthy staff meeting called by General Franklin at lunch time. According to the most persistent scenario, Opelousas was to be assaulted before daybreak the following morning. The rumors persisted, grew and spilled over from company to company, regiment to regiment and from the Bourbeux camp to the Carencro. By late afternoon discussion centered on the frightening rumor that Kirby Smith had ordered Taylor's army to hold Opelousas "at all hazards" whereas Banks had instructed Franklin to take Opelousas "at any cost."

LIEUTENANT LAWRENCE VAN ALSTYNE, circa 1890 (Van Alstyne, *Diary of an Enlisted Man*)

As officers began straggling back from the various staff meetings the worst suspicions were confirmed. Orders were passed to prepare for breaking camp at an early hour. Although the destination was not identified, the "battle of Opelousas" was rapidly escalating to the level of a Vicksburg, Chickamagua or Shiloh.

In order to avoid arousing the suspicions of Green's Texans, the usual number of pickets were to be posted that night. Orders were passed to avoid contact and possible capture lest the enemy learn of the proposed movements. Nonetheless picket duty fell in part that night to a slapstick Indiana outfit, members of the 24th Infantry, who were more concerned with barter, foraging and fun than with the exigencies of war.

Once on the picket line, the Hoosiers carefully reconnoittered the area in front where the Confederate pickets were posted. Most had been assigned to this duty too many times to be frightened. Both they and their Confederate counterparts viewed picket assignments as an unpleasant duty which deprived them of badly needed rest. Fortunately both sides were now observing the unwritten agreement, cemented over the years and at hundreds of meeting places, that war in its usual form was sufficiently dangerous without the necessity for individual hostilities.

As the last rays of light faded from the distant horizon, an Indiana soldier noted what he later described as the "unmistakable odor of tobacco" drifting across from the area in front. "Hey Reb! You there?" he yelled.

Though the subsequent dialogue amounted to nothing more than an attempt to swap tobacco for coffee, anyone listening would have been completely baffled by the coded language. The precise words were not recorded, but a Texan, recalling many such incidents in southwestern Louisiana, gave an illustrative account:

> "From whence do you come?" yelled a Texan.
>
> "From a camp of horse thieves on the Rio Grande," answered the pleased Hoosiers.
>
> "What came you here to do?"
>
> "To learn how to improve myself in horse thieving."
>
> "Then you are a horse thief, I presume?"
>
> "I am so taken," answered the Yankee, "and accepted by all the 'craft' on the Rio Grande."
>
> "Horse thief!" shouted the Texan, "can you advance and give the proper sign and hailing words?"
>
> "Can you respond?" shot back the Hoosier.
>
> "Yes."
>
> "Give you (the sign)!" commanded the Yankee.
>
> "Coffee!" answered the Texan.
>
> "Tobacco!" responded the Hoosier.

After several more minutes of cautious dialogue to assure that both parties were in earnest, several ragged, bewiskered and dirty Texans materialized. A Mexican blanket was spread before the bluecoats and the bartering began. Several pounds of Yankee coffee was soon swapped for a few plugs of Rebel tobacco. Whiskey, sugar, hardtack, newspapers, and medicine also changed hands, as did a few other items. Indeed it must have seemed as though a genuine sense of camaraderie was emerging, but the unnatural interlocution was quickly terminated when a Texan rushed up with the unwelcome news that the Officer of the Day, making his normal inspection rounds, was approaching.[8]

About three miles south of the bartering soldiers, on a little hill near the Ile Carencro headquarters of General William Franklin, there was camped another fun-loving, ill-disciplined Hoosier regiment, Colonel Thomas Bringhurst's 46th Indiana. Though Bringhurst and regiment belonged to the XIII Corps, he had for some inexplicable reason been ordered to provide a guard for the commanding general's headquarters, virtually in the middle of the XIX Corps' Carrion Crow camp.

Among the soldiers of the 46th Indiana was a certain Charles Baum, the regimental eccentric. Baum, who spent most of his time combing his rabbinical beard, reading, and quoting from the scriptures, was charged with the company's powder and ammunition supplies. On this particular evening he decided to fortify himself and friends for the following day's march by boiling a piece of beef in the mess kettle over an open fire.

But alas, southwestern Louisiana was without rocks on which to prop up kettles, and there were no bricks nearby. Scouting around, Baum came across something even better: an oblong-shaped unexploded, Schenkle shell, obviously a dud. Sticking the pointed end into the ground in the middle of his campfire and his kettle on the flat upper surface, Baum pulled up a crate of Minie balls for a chair and was soon in business. His horrified mess mates, by contrast, took one look at the improvised mess kettle and scurried off for cover.

Now "Taps" had already been sounded and not a soul could be seen "except an occasional darkey stirring up the fire under his mess-kettle." At nearby Ile Carencro, General William Franklin was genuinely concerned about the march on Opelousas and had summoned his generals for one final conference. Constance Guidry, in a bedroom upstairs, was eavesdropping, and her English was sufficient to understand that the Yankees were finally leaving. Elated, she had just turned to relay the happy news to the others when suddenly, and without warning, "the solemn stillness of night was broken by a blinding flash of light and the loud report of a bursting shell whose pieces flew hissing and singing in all directions."

Within a moment the camp was in an uproar. From one side to the other men went rushing from their tents cursing Rebels for another night attack; officers were shouting orders and "dashing about in search of the cause of the alarm"; and over on the hill where the shell exploded they were also looking for Charles Baum and a mess kettle, but in neither case was the search successful. In fact a shallow crater marked the spot where the careless Hoosier had last been seen "on his knees blowing the coals." Several tents had been swept away, including Baum's, but no one else was hurt. Incredibly the powder in Baum's tent had not ignited but the case of Minie balls which had served as his chair had been thrown into the air and its contents scattered over a wide area. Not until midnight did the camp of the 46th Indiana manage to settle down for the night, less one piece of beef, one mess kettle, several tents, a crate of Minie balls and one very foolish soldier.[9]

Wednesday, October 21, 1863

At first light, or about 5:12 A. M., the Army of the Gulf was on the march. The XIII Army Corps, under Burbridge, McGinnis and Cameron, and the cavalry, under Colonel John Fonda, marched up the west bank of Bayou Bourbeux on the Chretien plantation road. Meanwhile, the XIX Corps with General William Franklin at the head, moved up the main road from the Carencro, joining the Westerners near the picket spot where the contraband goods had traded hands the night before. They halted only long enough to line up in battle formation.

At the head of the large assault force rode John Fonda and his horse brigade. He was followed by two infantry brigades of the XIII Corps (McGinnis and Burbridge), one of the XIX Corps (Weitzel) and a half dozen or more artillery batteries. The balance of the two corps, along with the long supply trains, would bring up the rear.

Though they knew the road to Opelousas was fraught with danger, the men were in high spirits. Flanking both sides of the road, they laughed and joked about "going to Texas." As soon as the bugle sounded someone struck up a tune and the Army of the Gulf headed toward Opelousas singing "The Girl I Left Behind."

Picket duty for the Confederates that particular day fell to Colonel Henry C. McNeill's 5th Texas Calvary. It had been unusually quiet the day and night before and most of the Texans were expecting a leisurely day. But now, on the advance post, a dozen or more groggy Rebels must have strained their incredulous eyes in the early morning light as thousands and thousands of singing, swaggering bluecoats came over the horizon. Mounting up, the Texans immediately headed toward Bayou Tesson where for the third time they would report that the entire Federal army was on the march.

As the Texans rode off, Colonel John G. Fonda, perhaps remembering the times he had been pursued and humilated by these very same horsemen, ordered the 118th Illinois to charge. "Away we went full speed," wrote Samuel Gordon of Springfield, Illinois, "over fences, across ditches, through old corn fields where the weeds were as high as our heads on horseback, yelling as we went like so many Indians."

Approaching the well known *bois d'arc* hedge, the oncoming Yankees came within sight of the plantation home of Charles and

Celestine (nee Bourque) Lavergne where, at that very moment a number of calvary officers of the 5th Texas had just sat down for breakfast. The Lavergne family, with their house just off the main road, was a convenient foraging target for both sides. During the spring campaign they had been victimized not only by the main Union column and the stragglers in the rear but also by Colonel Chickering's confiscatory practices. Although they did not care for the "Texicans" anymore than anyone else in Louisiana, the mounted horsemen were at least paying guests, thus making them far more preferable than the destructive Yankee "Americans."

Possibly in anticipation that the *Federaux* would soon clean them out again, the breakfast menu that morning was extraordinary. Roast beef, turkey, goose and chicken were on the table, along with sweet potatoes, biscuits, cornbread, bacon and other delicacies "too numerous to mention." No sooner had the hungry Texans sat down, however, than "the storm burst upon them."

"They were a very prudent set of fellows," wrote Samuel Gordon to his wife. "Seeing our column advancing so rapidly upon them they forgot all about breakfast, mounted their horses and took for the woods." Gordon, along with his mounted infantry comrades, "had the satisfaction of helping to eat" the elaborate meal.[10]

In the rear of the advancing Yankees, just north of the point where the Vermilionville-to-Opelousas road crosses over Bayou Bourbeux, Dr. Harris Beecher, regimental surgeon for the 114th New York Infantry, observed a most curious sight. There, at a halt, was the *impedimenta*-laden wagon train of the XIII Corps:

> The wagons were loaded to the bows with everything one could mention, from a coffee mill to a darkey baby. Their livestock was equally varied. Dogs, cows, goats, Shetland ponies, roosters and a tame bear embraced a part of the collection. It almost equalled the sight Noah must have produced when he opened the doors of his ark.

In that "wonderful procession," also attracting a great deal of attention, was an immense iron oven, no doubt Chretien's, in a wagon pulled by two horses. The driver, a young Ohio teamster, was continually asked, "What is that masheen for?" According to Beecher, he had a new answer for each interrogator:

> To one, he said it was a magazine; to another, a cell for prisoners; to another still, a portable steam gun. But he exceeded the range of credibility when he avowed the concern to be a bullet mould, or a piece of stove pipe.

As the XIX Corps moved on, a great deal of "humorous badinage" passed between the Easterners and the Westerners. A New Yorker, observing a goose enclosed in a cage suspended behind a wagon, asked, "Where did that goose come from?"

"Deserted from the Nineteenth Corps" replied the Westerner.

Quick and pointed came the retort: "Birds of a feather flock together."

Farther on, several Westerners standing near the smelly carcass of a dead mule called out: "Here you Eastern chaps, come and fill your haversacks with fresh meat."

"No," said a New Yorker, hitching his gun to his shoulder, "We ain't selfish; we'll wait till you have finished your meal."

"Say," said another Easterner, "you have most every kind of calamity in your wagon."

"No," answered the Westerner, "I haven't got any of the Nineteenth Corps along with me."[11]

While all this friendly bantering was going on the 75th New York Infantry was engaged in their favorite avocation of horse collecting. Apparently a large number of officers and men had acquired "contraband" mounts while on the Carencro in spite of orders to the contrary. But Franklin, who was determined that the infantry should walk to Texas, had posted the 75th New York alongside the line of march with orders to confiscate horses from anyone who was not entitled to one by rank or position. In a very short time, the 75th had collected enough animals to mount yet another company.[12]

Several miles north of the wagon caravan, at the same spot where Fonda's reconnaissance mission had been faced down by the 4th Texas two days earlier, the long awaited "battle" of Opelousas seemed to be taking shape. There, behind the damaged trees and stumps along Bayou Sylvain, stood a long line of dismounted Texans with rifles at the ready. The Yankees could not have known that it was only Colonel Henry McNeill and a few hundred horsemen of the 5th Texas Cavalry. The small Confederate force planned to delay the advance only long enough for Green's horse division, camped in the area known as Bellevue, to make their getaway.

The Union assault on the fragile Confederate position was such an impressive and colorful spectacle that it became a source of considerable pride for all who participated. Certainly nothing like it had ever occurred before—or since—on the Opelousas Prairie. Not less than 12,000 bluecoats marching in four separate double-line formations, each of which stretched a mile or more across the grassy prairie, took part in the noisy parade.

Opening the assault on the Confederate position were the fast guns of Nims' 2nd Massachusetts Battery. Almost instantly Privates J. J. Whitesides and V. A. Lallier fell dead from their saddles; a half dozen or more Texans were severely wounded. As soon as the short barrage lifted, but before the heavy acrid smoke cleared away, Colonel John G. Fonda started the long blue lines toward the treeline.

Captain William Barney of the 29th Wisconsin had "never felt so much like fighting as then. Everything was in such good shape for a fuss," he wrote in an exaggerated letter to his brother:

> Ours was the first line (actually the second) and composed of five regiments marching by the front. With fixed bayonets and colors flying, the whole presented a sight well worth the seeing. When our skirmishers, of which each regiment sent out two companies deployed about six feet apart, commenced firing, our brigade sent up one of those cheers such as Westerners only can give and it was took up by the next line, then by the next of the XIX Corps who cheered as loud as Eastern men can cheer—which is not very loud.

On the extreme right of the third line was the Louisiana (colored) Pioneer Corps, about three hundred strong. Wearing bright red caps, these "red-heads," as they were called, "marched with perfect alignment into the weeds" clearing away obstructions while singing the original "Battle Hymn of the Republic:"

> John Brown's body lies a-mouldering in the grave!
> His soul goes marching on.
> He's gone to be a soldier in the army of the Lord!
> His soul goes marching on.
> They will hang Jeff Davis to a sour apple tree!
> As they march along.

Inspired by the singing, each of the brigade brass bands struck up "Yankee Doodle;" and the artillery batteries, drummers and fifers joined in with their share of the noise. "The rebs at that moment advanced in splendid style—by the rear rank!" wrote Captain William Barney. "Such a skedaddling no person can imagine who never saw Secesh run when hard pressed by the Yankee barbarians."

Once beyond the treeline the Yankees found to their delight that the Texans had evacuated their campsite so quickly "that they did not have time to eat their breakfast." Large quantities of freshly prepared cornbread, coffee and sweet potatoes, "still roasting in the ashes," were devoured by the hungry newcomers.

Just north of Bayou Tesson, on a little hill where the New Orleans, Opelousas and Great Western railroad right of way crossed the Opelousas road, the rear guard 5th Texas put up one last desperate stand, momentarily halting the large army. Once more the Yankees

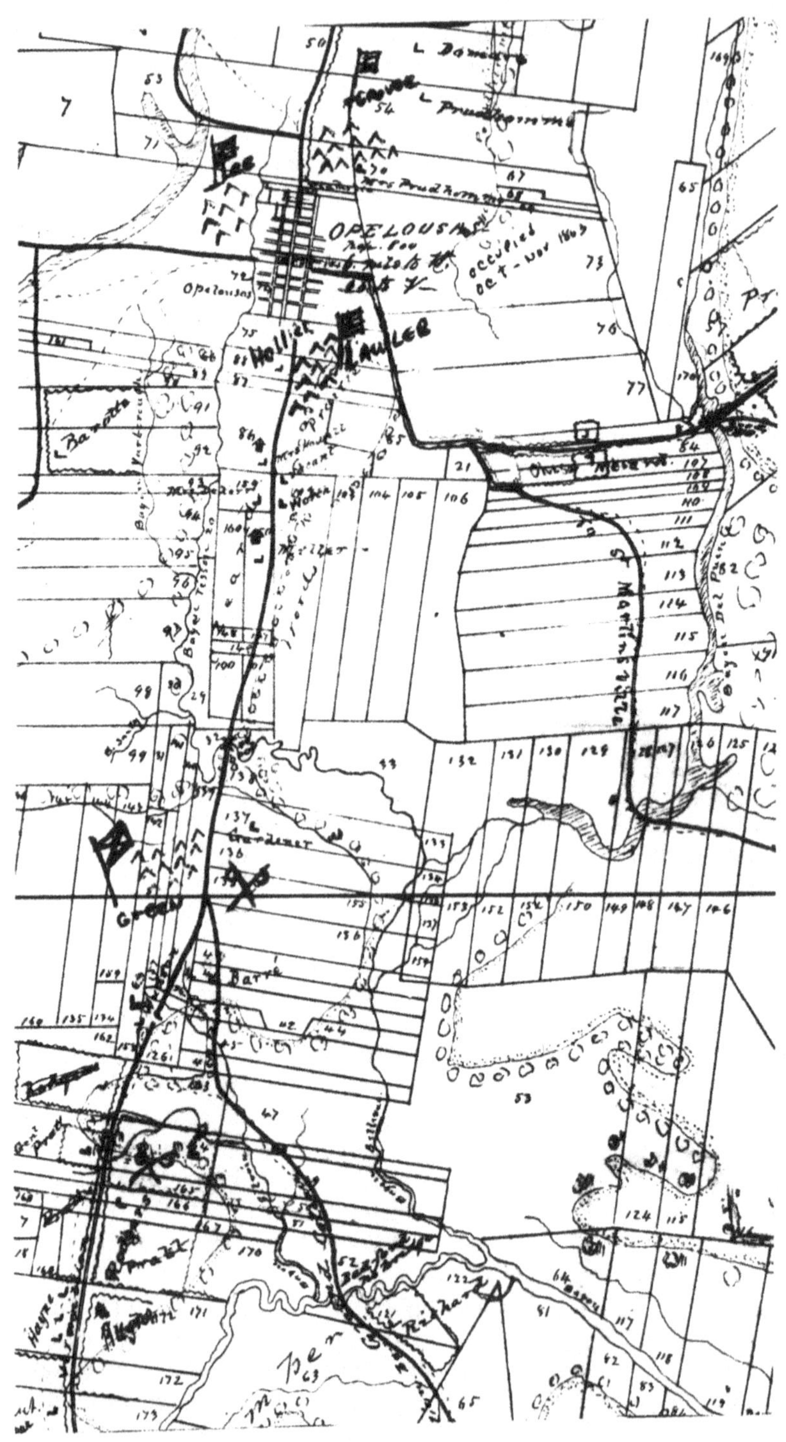
OPELOUSAS
occupied
Oct - Nov 1863
Opelousas
Bayou Teche
St Martinsville

advanced with fixed bayonets, colors flying and drums beating, but "the fun was finally brought to a close by sending a few messengers amongst them in the shape of shells" followed by a charge from Fonda's horse brigade.

From their new position north of Bayou Tesson the Yankees halted one last time to appraise the situation. The "dust was six inches deep in the road" and they could plainly see a cloud being raised by the retreating Rebels. Once Fonda's horse had determined that the retreat was in earnest the Army of the Gulf switched from battle formation into marching columns. Laughing, joking and singing they started once more up the road toward Opelousas.[13]

And back along the Carencro, Desire Arnaud was a free man. Nonetheless, one can imagine the agony experienced by the black-hatted little Frenchman as he walked the short distance from the primitive stockade to his once happy home. What he found surpassed even his worst expectations. Between the 17th of October, when he was first arrested, and October 21st, when the Yankees left for Opelousas, soldiers of the 83rd Ohio had converted a portion of his yard and gallery into a slaughter pen; cattle, swine and other livestock had been driven into an area enclosed with a five-foot high picket fence where they were butchered and stripped of only the most edible portions. The carcasses and offal were left for the carrion crow vultures which had already decended on the place by the thousands.

As if that wasn't enough, the corn and most of the yam patch was gone; only the frames of the outbuildings stood. The ubiquitous carrion crow buzzards were roosting on his rooftop, and the stench was intolerable; but at least his poor blind wife was alive and unharmed, and the despicable blue-uniformed "Americans" were finally gone, or so Desire Arnaud prayed.[14]

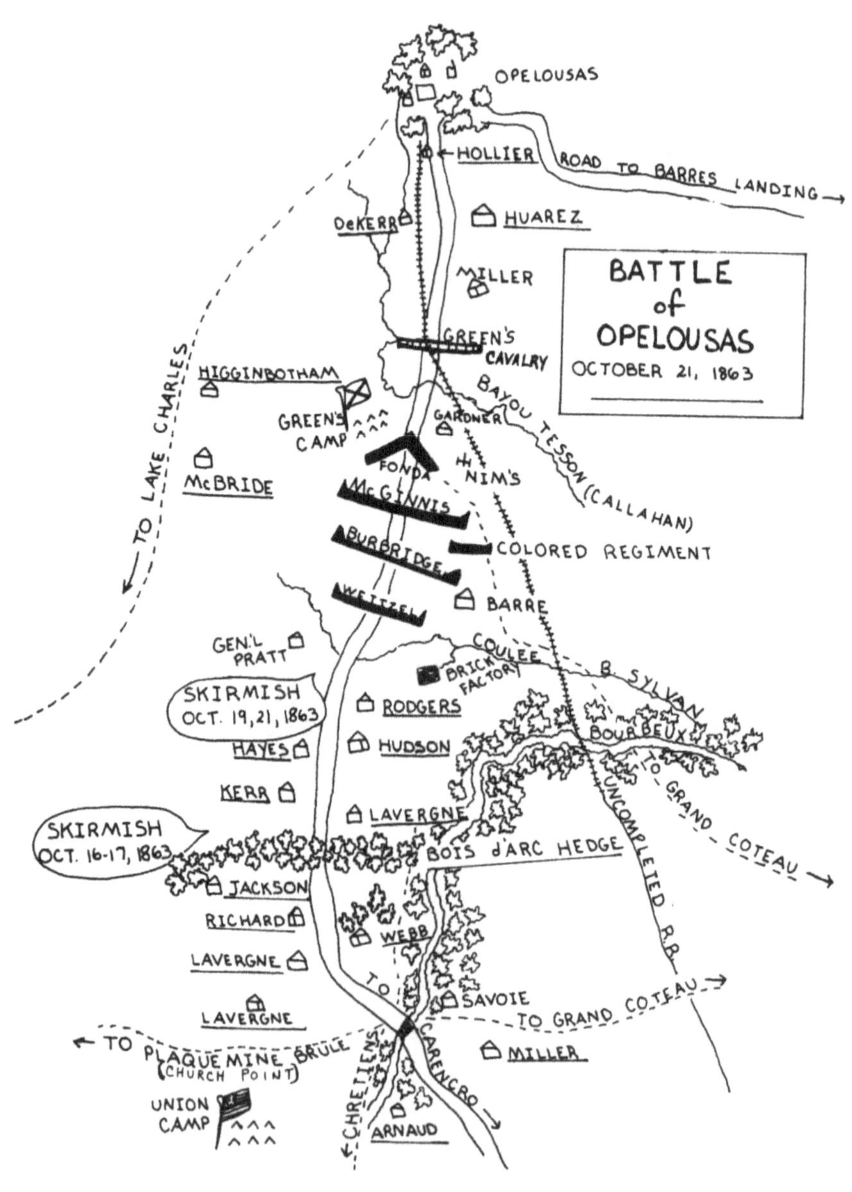

ROAD TO OPELOUSAS from 1863 Confederate map of St. Landry Parish (National Archives)

CHAPTER ELEVEN

FROM OPELOUSAS TO BARRE'S LANDING

Friday, October 21, 1863

TO AN OBSERVER there seemed no order to the Confederate retreat. Mule-drawn supply wagons, driven by cursing, whiplashing teamsters, intermingled with cavalry, caissons, artillery pieces and men on foot in a headlong rush to safety. The wounded, some in wagons, some perilously mounted on horseback and still others on foot, made their way through the crowded streets of Opelousas as best they could.

The evacuation was especially difficult for the Army of Western Louisiana's medical authorities. So denuded was the parish after the spring occupation that it had been considered safe enough to establish semi-permanent medical facilities. Hundreds of sick and wounded as well as tons of medical supplies were quartered in private homes in and around Opelousas. Presumably they had not been evacuated because General Taylor had planned to bring on a general engagement outside the city. But that was before the Fabian Policy directive. Now, the infirm, the wounded and the medical stores, merely added to the confusion.[1]

As if the retreat wasn't noisy enough, Fathers Gilbert and Francois Raymond, parish priests since 1854 and Confederate spies, began tolling the church bells in a manner universally recognized as an alarm. Like the Mexican revolutionary hero, Father Miguel de Hidalgo y Costilla, who had opened his country's drive for independence on the village church bells of tiny Dolores, the brothers Raymond pulled and tugged for hours, notifying the startled residents for miles around that the Yankees were finally coming.[2]

A short distance northwest of town in the direction of Ville Platte (called Flat Town by the Yankees), Minister James Earl Bradley listened to the "battle now raging just below. The rattle of small arms and the roar of larger guns is continuous," he noted. Reverend Bradley must have wondered if he would ever be united in matrimony with his dear Ann who was then in New Orleans. Her arrival had already been postponed by the Texas expedition and he had received no news for days. Now, even as the cannon boomed, he began praying[3]

> Oh Lord God of our fathers, have mercy upon us, and save us. O give the victory to our suffering, bleeding arms. Save us O God, from the chains of our enemies...

Not far away, at the Ville Platte home of Jacques and Euphemie (nee Fusilier) Guillory, there was even more cause for concern. Madame Guillory, caught up in the noise and excitement and concerned that she and the children would have to evacuate at any moment, went into labor. Thus, while a noisy caravan of wagons and caissons and fleeing civilians passed on the road in front, little Homere Guillory was born, apparently without assistance—or complication.[4]

At the Confederate camp near Moundville, just north of Washington, Captain A. W. Hyatt of the New Orleans Crescent Regiment was also listening to "the artillery firing below." When word came to stand by, he hastily jotted in his diary:

> Everything in commotion; tents struck, and we await the order to move. Everything moves quickly, and with life; horsemen go in a gallop, here and there, and even the mules in the teams go by in a trot. A fight or a foot race? I don't know yet.

The Texans were equally puzzled by the movements. Captain George O'Brian of Speight's Infantry Battalion was ordered "to have everything in readiness to load on wagons at a moment's notice." When orders finally came, "all were on the *qui vive* to know whether it was a fight or a retreat."

The suspense did not last for long. Within a short period of time, a portion of Green's division, the old Sibley Brigade, appeared on the road leading up the Bayou Boeuf toward Holmesville. The Louisiana and Texas Confederates fell in behind, leaving "wars and rumors of war and devastation behind."

The presence of the crack Sibley Brigade on a retreat suggested that Dick Taylor was reluctantly taking Quintus Fabius Maximus seriously. Angered and frustrated by what he believed to be the stupidity of his superior and by the persistent rumors circulating among his men that Opelousas was in flames, he rode up and down the retreating columns cursing and swearing at mules, men and even wagons. Captain Arthur Hyatt, who obviously did not know Taylor very well, noted that normally he "is a quiet unassuming (sic) little fellow."[5]

Contrary to rumors, Opelousas was not in flames. In fact when Colonels John Fonda and Harai Robinson rode into town at 11 o'clock P. M., the streets were unusually quiet and orderly. Not a gray uniform was in sight. The Stars and Stripes had miraculously appeared all over the town and, together with all the tricolors, Union Jacks and white flags which seemed to flutter above every rooftop and from every window, lent a festive air to the occasion.

According to Samuel Gordon, who rode alongside Colonel Fonda, the streets, galleries and balconies were crowded with curious onlookers:

> The street in which we passed through was lined on both sides with the inhabitants, young and old, rich and poor, black and white, all mixed up together. It was very easy to tell by their looks how each one felt. Some looked sour enough to make sour kraut. Others look desidely (sic) pleased, particularly the darkies. They represented the very picture of good nature with a broad grin upon their faces. They implored a God's blessing upon us as we passed.

Miss Fanny Borden, a teenage beauty who stood watching the procession from near the Dietlien home, implored no blessing. Although she was the subject of interest for a young Union soldier, who very gallantly removed his hat and bowed, Miss Fanny blushingly turned her back. As she related the story many years later she then lifted her long skirts to her ankles, raised her pretty nose in the air and stalked away.

As Fonda and Robinson cautiously approached the courthouse square, they were greeted by a now familiar sight. There, standing in the street before the courthouse and holding a fluttering white flag of truce were the town fathers. The spokesman, presumably F. A. King, President of the Board of Police, announced that Opelousas was formally surrendering and would submit to bluecoat rule without resistance. But Fonda was unconvinced of their sincerity. After all, Opelousas was a Rebel stronghold and these men could not possibly have held office without the blessing of Confederate authorities. Dispensing with formalities, he very quickly had the group marched into the courthouse and placed under arrest.[6]

Depending on one's view point, the town of Opelousas was either "dreary," "dilapidated," "rusty," "mean," "dirty," and "ugly," or it was "pleasant," "beautiful," "neat," "nice," and "friendly." A departing Texan claimed it was "nearly as large as Houston," whereas an incoming New Yorker found it "small and insignificant."

For more than a hundred years before the Yankees came, Opelousas had been the commercial, judicial and cultural center of a thriving agricultural area. The tree-shaded little town of some 1500 inhabitants could count more than its share of doctors, lawyers, politicians, merchants, coffeehouse keepers, tanners; coopers, barbers and prostitutes. It could also boast of some very splendid mansions, a *fais-do-do* dance hall, several churches and schools, a fine courthouse, a convent and several newspapers. Finally, it shared the distinction of having once served as the Confederate capitol of Louisiana.

The most intriguing fact about Opelousas, at least for the invaders, seemed to be the newly planted fall vegetable gardens, a novelty for

Northern eyes. "The people here sow and plant the year round," wrote an Illinois cavalryman. An Ohio soldier noted in his diary that, "I saw some onions growing and some cabbage plants. Rather an advance in gardening to what we have been used to." Still another Ohio soldier wrote his mother about the "flowers and peas, and yards arround (sic) the houses full of roses and poses of all description."

Most of the marching Yankees were not to enjoy the sights for very long. Fonda's cavalry brigade turned left onto the Bayou Mallet road (currently U. S. Highway 190 West) and went into camp on the west side of Bayou Tesson in the outskirts of Opelousas. Meanwhile, Brigadier General Cuvier Grover and his 3rd Division of the XIX Corps passed on through Opelousas and went into camp on Widow Michael Prudhomme's Ringrose Plantation near St. Landry Catholic Church. Finally, the two divisions of the XIII Corps (McGinnis and Burbridge) as well as Weitzel's division of the XIX Corps turned toward the east, away from Texas, and marched past Confederate Camp Hamilton the road toward the Mississippi. "What this was done for I cannot devine," complained a puzzled soldier from Ohio.

The answer was not long in coming. When the two divisions of the XIII Corps reached Barre's Landing (Port Barre) they found Colonel Henry D. Washburn with yet another infantry brigade, together with Brigadier General Albert Lee and Mudd's cavalry brigade. The latter forces, numbering perhaps five thousand, had left Vermilionville early that morning and, with only minor resistance, took a more direct route through Grand Coteau, Leonville, Notleyville and up the Bayou Teche to its source on the Courtableau.[7]

Thursday, October 22, 1863

It had been a miserably wet night, and was still raining as several thousand men at Barre's Landing "crawled out from under their blankets like so many drowned rats." A number of regiments had not yet received tents while still others were without shelter because of a delay in the supply trains. The sight of Barre's Landing, such as it was, did not help matters. Corporal Isaac Jackson, who had complained loud and long about Camp Bourbeux, now found his situation even worse. "Our camp here is not near as nice as it was," he wrote, "nor is the country as pleasant. It is kind of a dreary looking wilderness."[8]

Barre's Landing was not a town, nor was it a settlement or village. In fact, for a hundred years or more before the Yankees came, it had served as a sort of crossroads for the early settlers who came up the Courtableau from the Mississippi and Atchafalaya to the Opelousas country.[9]

The little steamboat landing and trading post had been the scene of two very recent and tragic disasters even before the Union occupation of October 1863. The first disaster occurred on February 28, 1863, when a powerful tornado swept across the landscape taking houses, warehouses, stores and lives, including Honore DeJean, his wife, Carmelite (nee Verret), his son Emile, daughter Matilde, the warehouse keeper, Eugene Riquet, and a neighbor, Mrs. Thelesphore Zeringue.[10] Three months later, in May 1863, Colonel Thomas Chickering's forces had occupied and used the area as a depot and shipping center for the products confiscated by his troops throughout St. Landry Parish. Commenting on the place at the time, Colonel Samuel Holabird, Chief Quartermaster of the Department of the Gulf wrote:[11]

> There was no house, shed or shelter, decent water, or decent people about there...Negroes, pigs and soldiers lounged, rolled, ate and slept on and in (the confiscated) cotton.

Now, only one day after the most recent occupation, the Yankees arrested Honore DeJean's only surviving son, Octave DeJean, as well as a neighboring planter, Charles Close. By noontime, when the Courtableau was bridged by Major David C. Houston's black engineers, the invaders also arrested storekeeper J. P. Saizan, a "Captain of Patrols" and his neighbor, Joseph R. Melancon.

HEADWATERS OF THE TECHE at Barre's Landing on Bayou Courtableau as it appeared to a Union artist in 1863. ***(Leslie's Illustrated Weekly)***

Then it was Raimondi Deshotel's turn. At age twenty-eight, Deshotel, like so many other pioneer settlers of the region, was known as a heavy-drinker, and a mean one at that. According to oral tradition, he had sent a number of men to their graves as a result of personal feuds. His most heinous deed, and one which he was said to boast of, was the wanton personal slaying of several slaves who had attempted to run away and join Chickering's wagon exodus during the spring invasion.

However, he was no match for the Westerners, who after shivering and suffering without shelter throughout the night, were more concerned with the lumber siding on Deshotel's cotton gin than his unsavory reputation. The large edifice simply disappeared, board by board, even as the angry planter heaped verbal abuse and idle threats upon them from the nearby prison compound. Once into the floor boards, they found an extra bonus. There, beneath the cotton gin and protected from the elements, Deshotel had cleverly concealed several thousand recently tanned cow hides belonging to Dominique Lalanne of Washington, Louisiana. For the first time since leaving Berwick's Bay, many of the soldiers had material for tents. "These were all right and afforded us a good shelter and even kept the rain away," wrote a soldier from Ohio, "but when water soaked, our olfactories were compelled to do extra duty. We dubbed this 'cow skin' camp."[12]

Julius Wood, a soldier in the 96th Ohio, came up with an equally ingenious shelter. While other soldiers were raiding Deshotel's pecan trees or gathering "persimmons in the woods," if not admiring the exotic palmetto plants, Wood came into possession of a large sugar hogshead. Rolling the clumsy contraption back into camp, Wood and "bedfellows" put some boards about the middle and covered it with Spanish moss. With their blankets on top, it was both dry and soft. "They laugh at us about our doghouse," he wrote his mother, "but 'comfort before looks' is the soldier's motto."[13]

A short distance south of Barre's Landing, near the point where the tiny Marie Croquant (or "little Teche") flows into the Teche, there was yet another sprawling Union Camp. Major General William Franklin, still concerned about the Eastern vs. Western regional conflict, had prudently stationed General Weitzel's division of the XIX Corps on the properties of Captain Eliakim Littel and Adolphe Arnault, a safe two miles or so away from the offensive Westerners.

Interestingly enough, the commanding general, who established his field headquarters with Weitzel's division, committed a minor error which was to baffle civil war scholars for generations. On all the Union maps, the letter "M" in Maria Croquant was so blurred as to render interpretation all but impossible. Franklin read it as a "B," possibly thinking of Barre, and all Union correspondence thereafter refers to the bayou as the Barri-Croquant.[14] Commenting on the jawbreaker, Surgeon Harris Beecher of the 114th New York borrowed a phrase from Lord Byron:

> ...Phoebus what a name,
> To fill the speaking trump of future fame.

Although the Marie Croquant was quite "beautiful," Surgeon Beecher and others complained that the continual rains "conspired with the low and marshy soil to make this camp the muddiest and most intolerable spot the boys had ever before experienced." Even the rations seemed to be "scanty and unwholesome," usually containing an "extra quantity of live meat." Sweet potatoes, which before had been "so abundant and so luscious" were nowhere available.[15]

The reason, Beecher well knew, was that all the local planters had once before felt the heavy hand of Union occupation. One of these, Adolphe Arnault, had already lost seventeen bales of cotton and an undetermined amount of other goods when Chickering's efficient foragers came through during the spring. Now, with these same Easterners back again, he and his son, Pierre, and wife, Jean Moral, were quick to take the Oath of Allegiance (see Appendix) in hopes that somehow their property would be protected, but it was all to no avail. Like Desire Arnaud of Buzzards' Prairie, no sooner had the Arnaults returned home from the oath-taking ceremony than a party of armed foragers came up and proceeded to help themselves to the remaining livestock, produce and buildings.

Similar scenes occurred at the homes of Onezime and Simon Marks, Francois Coullon Devilliers, Joseph Rayon, Francois Vautrot, Francois Castille, Ludger Lastrapes and dozens of other settlers along the upper Teche.[16]

At least part of the plunder was due to the interminable search for horses on the part of the 75th New York Infantry, soon to be mounted dragoons. On the second day of their occupation the New Yorkers impressed several guides, including Evarist Wright, (a forty-eight-year-old slave on the F. C. Devilliers plantation) and Geraud Donatte (a forty-two-year-old white carpenter) and headed across Prairie Laurent to Gros Chevreuil (currently Leonville) where they found a recently arrived, but poorly educated, Frenchman named Joseph Camy.

Camy, like Deshotel, had an interesting if not unusual background. Born in Accors, Department of the Lower Pyrenees, the thirty-two-year-old Frenchman had immigrated to Leonville in 1856. At first he had worked as a common laborer for Jules Mistric and his wife Michel (nee Vabre), later becoming a clerk in their small general merchandise store on the north bank of Bayou Teche. Before long, however, Joseph Camy and Mrs. Mistric were involved in a great deal more than just working together in the store. In fact, said an observant neighbor, Camy "ran Jules right off and took possession of his store and wife; poor Jules came back, but they put him out again."

Now, that neighbor, forty-two-year-old Joseph Roy, together with Jules' twelve-year-old son, Leon Mistric, watched from across the road to see if the foul-tempered little Frenchman would put the New Yorkers out of the store. He did not. Indeed, on their exit all but the officers were loaded down with "boots, shoes and some other stuff" which Camy later claimed was valued at $500.00. A few even entered Camy's (or Mistric's) house and helped themselves to some badly needed bedcovers and blankets. To complete their day, they rounded up three American horses and a cart and headed back toward Camp Barri-Croquant.[17]

On their return, the New Yorkers noticed yet another little store out on Prairie Laurent about halfway between present-day Leonville and Notleyville. As in the case of Joseph Camy, the brothers Emile Eugene and Edmond Pascal Hauguel had come to Louisiana from Limpiville, Department of the Seine Infereure, in 1856. Also like Camy, they had been conscripted for a short period of time into a Louisiana infantry regiment. And, finally, like Camy, their store was a target for the 75th New York dragoon-aspirants. Thirty-four-year-old Emile Eugene Hauguel and his brother-in-law, Jean Baptiste Hebert, watched helplessly as the intruders

> ...came to our premises and broke open our store door, and were about to break into a large box inside our store which contained goods and merchandise...Seeing resistance useless, I delivered them the keys of the box.
> We protested against the breaking into of our store and the taking of our merchandise. We claimed our French nationality (and) showed them a small French flag, or tri-color, in our store. They tore down the same, threw it on the road and stomped on it, saying 'Damn the French flag!'

Inside the box, according to Hauguel, were woolen goods, notions, ribbons, laces and bracelets. They also took all the hardware and crockery, and everything else in the store. Protested Hauguel: "I came to this country to make money and not to mix in politics." As a parting insult, his heretofore faithful slave, twenty-four-year-old Manuel Anderson, marched off with the Yankees to enlist in the invaders' army.[18]

On the same day that southwestern Louisiana's upper Teche residents were reeling under the confiscatory practices of the second Union invasion, a very different sort of drama was unraveling in Opelousas. The parish courthouse, normally the habitat of Confederate enrolling officers, judges and other parish and municipal officials, was now the

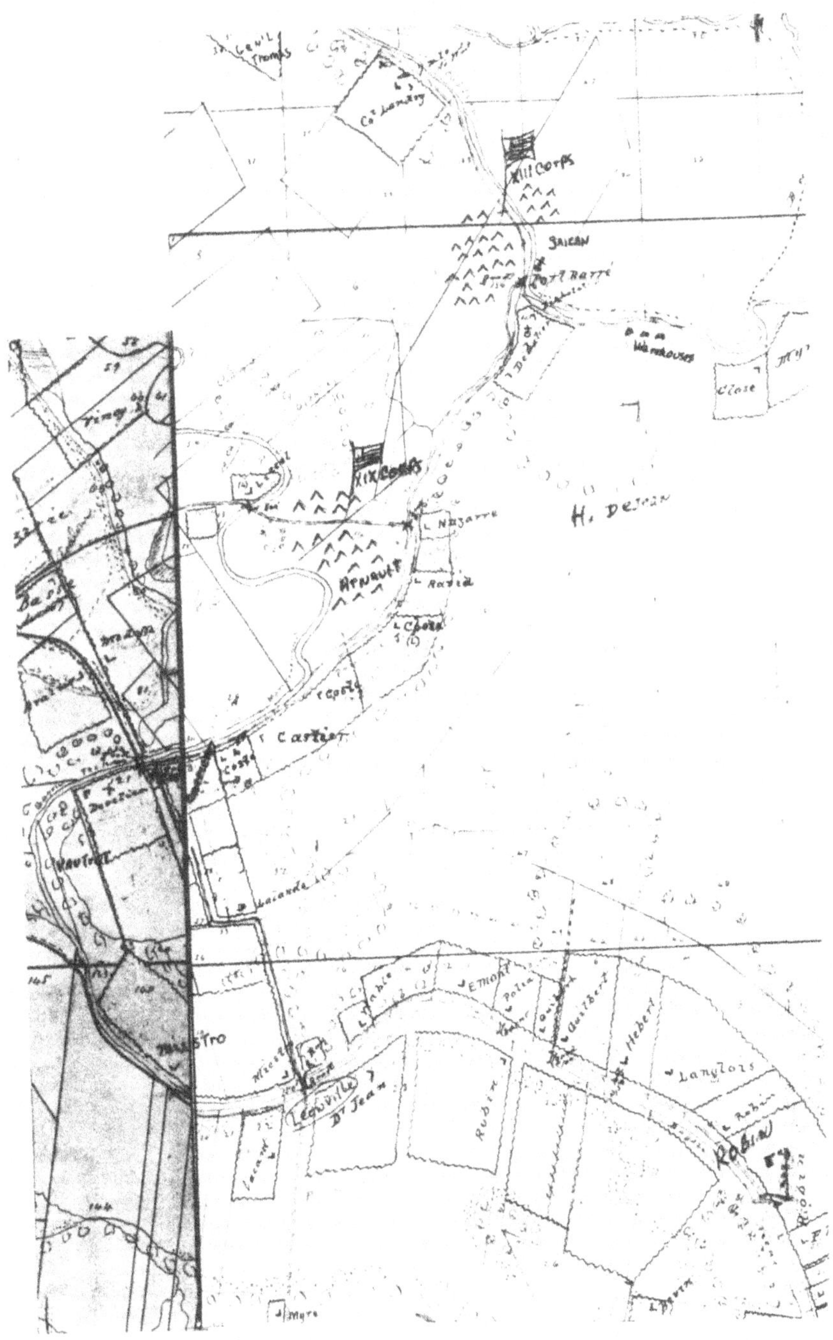

PORT BARRE and vicinity from 1863 Confederate map of St. Landry Parish. (National Archives)

receiving center for "loyal" Unionists desiring to reaffirm their allegiance to the Old Flag. As was the case in Franklin, New Iberia, Vermilionville, and on the Carencro and Bourbeux they came in by the dozens, many of whom were paroled Confederates from their Vicksburg capture.

Atop the courthouse, standing on a platform outside the dome were several flag-waving officers of the U.S. Signal Corps. Here, raised far above the trees and houses of the town, was an uninterrupted view of the surrounding prairie as far as the eye could reach in any direction. The signal officers, with their indecipherable motions, were in constant and almost instantaneous communication with Barre's Landing and Vermilionville.[19]

And inside the courthouse, in the large trial room where the accused had faced their accusers for generations, Private Michael "Big Mike" Fox was about to be brought before a general court-martial. This court, convened under the provisions of the Articles of War, bore little resemblance to a civilian court of law. In the first place, a number of Union officers—who constituted the judge and jury—were to be seated

OPELOUSAS COURTHOUSE circa 1863 was used as a prison and Signal Corps station by Union forces. ***(Leslie's Illustrated Weekly)***

at a long rectangular table facing the defendant. The president of the court, Lieutenant Colonel William M. Green of the 173rd New York, would be positioned at the center. He would be flanked by three officers, positioned according to rank on both sides.

The only officer present with a legal background was the judge advocate, the prosecutor in this case, Captain B. W. Frost of the 26th Massachusetts. Unlike the others, Frost would sit at a separate table to the right and front of the president and was free to move around.

The accused, Private Michael Fox of the 8th New Hampshire, sat all alone at a table to the left and front of the president's table. Even though he was handcuffed and dressed in a faded uniform he was imposing because of his size and past record of defiance. Two armed guards stood behind the intemperate private just in case he should get out of hand.

"All rise!"

President Green, dressed in his military best, swept in with his entourage and seated himself at the head table. He then opened the proceeding by reading Special Order No. 80, establishing the legitimacy of the proceedings.

"Private Michael Fox! You are hereby arraigned before this court." The charges, as read by Green, consisted of calling Stokes a "damned son of a bitch," disobeying orders and striking Stokes, and threatening to "murder Stokes at the first opportunity," all of which, according to Green, was in violation of The Ninth Article of War and "prejudicial to good order and military discipline." Looking at the accused, President Green then asked: "Private Fox, how do you plead...?

"Not guilty, sir!" replied Fox as each charge was read.

Once more the charges were read and Fox repeated his plea of not guilty to all except the charge of threatening Stokes' life, which he readily admitted. All the witnesses were then directed to withdraw from the courtroom except Captain Joseph J. Ladd, of Fox's 8th New Hampshire regiment.

"Do you swear to tell the truth, the whole truth, and nothing but the truth, so help you God?" the Captain was asked by Green.

Ladd, his left hand resting on a bible, replied: "I do."

"What was the nature of the words (passing between Fox and Stokes)?"asked Judge Advocate Frost.

"The accused," answered Ladd, "asked the Officer of the Day (Stokes) what he was having him tied up for. Captain Stokes replied that "since you have struck me, I am having you tied." Private Fox denied this but afterwards indirectly admitted this, stating that he would strike him again. I think the precise language he—the accused—used, was that he would 'mash his jaw'."

Private Fox, unsteeped in legal training, sat quietly listening. Unlike the current Uniform Code of Military Justice, the prisoner was not represented by counsel. He could, however, cross-examine the captain himself if he so desired but declined the opportunity when offered.

The second witness for the prosecution was none other than Captain Stokes himself.

"What was the nature of the conversation (passing between you and Fox during the disturbance)?" asked Judge Advocate Frost.

"I asked him to stop fighting and quarreling," answered Stokes, "but he replied by telling me to go to hell."

"Did he use any violence toward you at that time?"

He did; by striking me and striking at me."

"Did he use other insulting language than what you have stated?"

"He did, sir. He told me to go to hell and kiss his arse; and called me a damned scoundrel, damned coward, crooked-legged, black-whiskered pirate and many other unbecoming names."

The questioning continued and again non-lawyer Fox declined to cross-examine the witness.

The third witness for the prosecution, Lieutenant James H. Sanders, also of the 8th New Hampshire, was sworn in and questioned by Judge Advocate Frost:

"Did anything occur directly between Captain Stokes and the Accused?"

"The first I saw," replied Sanders, "was Captain Stokes take out a memorandum book to take down the names of those fighting, when the accused came up and struck him, and made the remark, 'Captain Stokes, you think you are a hell of a feller'. He—the accused—then struck at him, while Stokes was warding off the blows, and knocked the book and pencil out of his hand."

"Did you hear the accused use any insulting language towards Captain Stokes?"

"I did. He called him a 'god-damned son of a bitch' and repeated that 'you are a hell of a feller' several times, and called him a 'god-damned coward' and various other expressions."

Once more Fox declined to cross-examine the witness whereupon a fourth witness, Lieutenant George E. Messer of the 8th New Hampshire, was sworn in and questioned by the prosecution.

"Did you hear the accused use any insulting language toward Captain Stokes?"

"He did, sir. He called him a coward, said he would pay him for tying him up to a tree, and told (Stokes) if he ever got out of it, he would shoot him."

Private Fox was then called upon to present testimony in his own defense. Throughout the prosecution's case he had sat unusually subdued, apparently intimitated and overwhelmed by the evidence and by the stark stares of the well-dressed officers who sat facing him, not to mention the crowd of curious onlookers, civilian and military alike, who had jammed the courtroom to witness this exercise in military justice. Clearly he was out of his element. His language was that of the gutter, of bar rooms and of Irish immigrants in a Boston shantytown and not of the finer points in military law. The only justice he had ever known was that which could be enforced by his own two fists, and now he was called upon to answer for just that.

Fox stood, his leg chains rattling, and nervously called upon Sergeant John Harrington of the 8th New Hampshire. Totally incompetent as an attorney, Fox then proceeded, inadvertently, to inculpate himself by the very nature of his questions.

"Was you there when I was fighting with Annis?"

"Yes sir," replied the equally nervous sergeant.

The second witness, Private Michael Griffin, also of the 8th New Hampshire, was asked the same incriminating question. Non-lawyer Fox then proceeded to tighten the noose about his own neck.

"Was you present at the disturbance which I was involved in?" asked the prisoner.

"Yes Sir," said Griffin.

"Was there not a crowd trying to carry me to my tent?"

"Yes Sir."

Aside from these damaging observations, Fox's witnesses saw nothing, heard nothing, knew nothing. Judge Advocate Frost, obviously pleased with such a clumsy defense, stood up and commented: "The Judge Advocate submits this case to the court without further remark."

The court, which began at 8 A. M. now cleared for deliberation. It was not yet 11 o'clock of the same morning.

At 5 P. M. the blue-uniformed gentlemen of the court filed back into the courtroom.

"The accused will rise!"

"This court," continued President Green, "having maturely weighed and considered the evidence adduced, find the Accused, Private Michael Fox, Co. C, 8th Regiment, New Hampshire Volunteers, as follows: of the first specification, first charge—guilty."

And so it went. The word "guilty" following each charge and each specification.

President Green then dropped a bombshell: "This court does therefore sentence him, Private Michael Fox, Co. C, 8th Regiment, New Hampshire Volunteers, to be shot to death with musketry at such time and place as the Commanding General may direct."

The severity of the sentence jolted the entire courtroom. Within minutes the word spread from regiment to regiment and camp to camp and on to Barre's Landing and Camp Barri-Croquant that Fox, "the soldier who dared stand up to officers," was to be shot. The death sentence was normally reserved for such serious offenses as murder, rape, desertion, treason, sleeping on a dangerous post, or defection to the enemy; but assaults, threats, insubordination and abusive insults against officers were so common, especially under the influence of liquor, that they were usually disposed of by sentencing the offender to the guard house under ball and chain and loss of pay for some designated period. A capital punishment for such a trifling offense was bound to create resentment, especially in an atmosphere already poisoned with contempt for officers who seemed unable to get the army to Texas.

Even providence seemed displeased with the verdict. On that particular day, October 22, 1863, the weather was relatively wet and warm with southerly breezes blowing inland from the gulf. About midnight, however, the winds shifted abruptly from south to northwest which, to a Louisiana planter, meant trouble. Most of the local inhabitants very quickly began the ancient Acadian practice of covering mirrors with cloth in the belief that this would protect them from bad weather.

The heavens then put on a celestial display which so impressed the invaders that virtually every military dispatch, diary notation or letter written within the next few days made reference to the storm. The lightning and roar of thunder was incessant for hours. Rain, and occasionally hail, pelted down in torrents. Worst of all was the wind which uprooted trees, blew Yankee tents to shreds and destroyed or severely damaged homes. Several soldiers, Union and Confederate, were killed and others badly injured by falling limbs or other debris hurtling through the air. Without a doubt Opelousas was hit by a tornado that night.

While the storm was at its worst a New Hampshire soldier commented that "Fox must have broken loose and got hold of Stokes." Another remarked that the "gods were angry because of the gross injustice done to Fox."

At a time when superstition, rather than science, provided a simple answer to the incomprehensible, one wonders how many frightened souls that night saw some relationship between the storm and the court decision. Surely some of those who sat on the court had a restless night.[20]

Friday, October 23, 1863

At Camp Barri-Croquant, five miles east of Opelousas, the cold front and torrential rains which started the night before seemed more intense than ever. While some troops huddled around half-drowned fires trying to keep warm under rubber ponchos, others cowered inside the protection of their makeshift shelters. Very few cared about the Texas expedition anymore and fewer still wondered why they were camped at this miserable place. Just to be dry and warm, and with a full stomach was far more important than Texas, Rebels, or the interminable search for horses.

The gloomy atmosphere was pervasive. Even General Franklin was affected. What, he wondered was he supposed to do now? In spite of the rains, the waters on the Courtableau failed to rise, and it would be impossible under the prevailing low water conditions for the *Red Chief* to reach Barre's Landing. Was it possible that the streams of western Louisiana rose and fell only with the Mississippi? And what about the possibility of a Rebel ambush farther downstream should the *Red Chief* attempt to enter? This, at least, he could look into. Already he had dispatched two of his most daring cavalry officers and scouts downstream in a flatboat.[21]

The most immediate problem for Franklin was the question of supplies for his men and animals. Barre's Landing and vicinity was a miserable spot for foraging because Colonel Chickering's forces had so stripped the area of fodder and grains, sugar and cotton, and livestock of all kinds, that there was hardly anything left for the impoverished inhabitants, much less enough to support a large army.[22] Even the grazing was poor. Fields where crops once grew or herds had prospered were covered with rank weeds fit for nothing except to conceal bushwhackers.

There was one other possibility. Franklin's supply train of five hundred or more wagons, now en route from Vermilionville, was loaded with provisions for the long trek to Texas, but that would be needed once they struck the prairies. Should he give the orders to begin consuming it now, or should he try to live off the land for the time being? The Major General Commanding, Nathaniel Banks, was still in New Orleans and was not very helpful. His latest dispatch merely directed Franklin to hold his position for the time being. Perhaps a dispatch to Banks would be in order:[23]

> General: My troops hold Opelousas and Barre's Landing. On account of a violent storm now raging, movements must be delayed some time, and I shall act according to my best judgement...Shall be very glad to get definite instructions. Forage is very scarce here...There seems to be no chance of the boat's arrival. The trains could not possibly move today.

Franklin was mistaken about one thing. Even as he was writing, his supply train, under the command of Brigadier General Michael K. Lawler, the big indiscreet Irishman, was in motion in spite of the weather. They had left Vermilionville early on the morning of the 22nd in the company of three infantry brigades of the XIII Corps and had spent a stormy night on the north bank of Bayou Bourbeux.

"Big Mike" Lawler, who was considered by Lincoln's Assistant Secretary of War, Charles A. Dana, to be "as brave as a lion and had abut as much brain" seemed intent on living up to his unsavory reputation. If they were going to get wet, reasoned Lawler, they may as well do so on the road to Opelousas. Accordingly, at 6 A. M., he started the long train up the muddy road directly into a strong north wind.

Unfortunately it was not underway very fast. Somehow orders had gone awry and there was an infernal traffic tie-up, and the division moved at a crawl. The road led up an ill-defined section of high ground which had recently been turned into a quagmire by the churning and beating of infantry, guns, horses and supply wagons. The infantry column was supposed to march to the front but for reasons known only to Lawler found itself behind miles of slow-moving or bogged-down wagons, ambulances, caissons, battery forges and other lumbering vehicles.

Some of the footsoldiers attempted to leave the road and pass this tangle, but they found themselves tripping and slipping and sloshing along through ankle-deep mud, soggy field furrows and water-filled ditches. Especially burdensome was the build-up of Louisiana "gumbo" on the bottom of boots, growing heavier and heavier until at some point the entire clump would suddenly release and cause many of the men to believe that they had stepped right out of their shoes.

Had it not been so cold the situation would have been funny. It was an occasion that B. F. Stevenson, the surgeon of the 22nd Kentucky would never forget:

> In less than half an hour after getting underway the clothes of all were saturated, the driving sluice penetrating almost instantly. The men could barely keep comfortable when in motion, but in the first four hours it was safe to say they were standing at halt half the time. We had in advance of the column five hundred wagons and ambulances, and the arrest of one arrested all in the rear...It was the most miserable day of my life.

Perhaps no regiment suffered more during the cold rainy march than the 24th Iowa. Captain Charles Williams' son, a frail and sickly eighteen-year-old, Private Charlie, Jr., was so "feverish and indisposed" that he had to be transported in an ambulance. Captain William Titus Rigby, who commanded a company of the 24th Iowa, was almost as bad off. A few days before, the regimental surgeon had clumsily removed a badly decayed tooth, and he was still suffering the after effects. During the night Rigby had been awakened by the storm only to find himself soaked and suffering from chills. Now, during Lawler's senseless drive to reach Opelousas the "rain came down in torrents" and the north wind blew directly in his face:

> You can guess that our situation just then was anything but comfortable. I had my rubber blanket over my shoulder which kept the upper part of my body dry, but all the water that fell on it ran by the shortest route down my pants, directly into my boots...The chill began to come on me again, though I had taken quinine, by 9 o'clock I was shaking all over. By the time we got to Opelousas I was as thoroughly uncomfortable as I ever remember to have been in my life.

Colonel James R. Slack, agc fifty-two, of Huntington, Indiana, was also among the wet soldiers. Although Slack was mounted he was no less miserable, but at least he could occupy his mind with personal matters. For weeks he had been carrying on a running feud with his wife, Ann, back in Huntington. First he had implored her to come along on the Texas expedition; she agreed, but kept finding excuses to delay her departure. With each new letter he had become more irascible. Why didn't she send more news about the elections, and the children, and affairs at home? "You are always so vague and unsatisfactory," he had written that very day. Then he would lecture her on how to spell "corps" (not "core" or "corpse") and tell her to be more "reciprocal" and "pay more attention to the study of human nature."

There was also the matter of promotion. Slack had commanded an entire infantry brigade for over a year, a position usually reserved for a brigadier general, but he was still a "bird" colonel. At least part of it had to do with his "poor education" and complete lack of military training. Still, he had proven himself capable on more than one occasion. The extremely sensitive and sometimes intemperate colonel would probably have been quite upset had he known that Lincoln's Assistant Secretary of War considered him to be "a solid, steady man, brave, thorough and sensible, but (one who would) never set the river afire."

Just now Slack was cold, wet and miserable, and he was far more concerned with reaching Opelousas than setting rivers afire. Spurring his horse ahead he soon reached the outskirts and halted to confer with Lawler and the other brigade commanders. And there they tarried for more than an hour while aids scurried back and forth in search of a reasonably high campsite.

Incredibly, the only sites rendered suitable for occupancy were situated south of Opelousas, along the road which the troops had just traversed. The long train was put into reverse motion and several thousand, cursing, swearing, complaining Westerners headed back south on the Opelousas road.

Colonel Slack and his brigade were fortunate. They moved back only a half mile or so and went into camp on the plantation property of some nameless planter near the current site of the Cresswell Shopping Center. Slack himself commandeered a nearby frame house for his headquarters. "It is an old dilapadated building with sides filled with brick," *(briquerre-entre-poteaux)* he wrote, "but it is dry and more comfortable than a tent." About a mile farther south, near the site of the old Jim Bowie residence, the 2nd Brigade of Lawler's 1st Division set up housekeeping. But, the wagon trains, along with Colonel Lionel Sheldon's 3rd Brigade, was forced to move back almost five miles to the site of the old Confederate camp near George W. Gardiner's home. It had been a miserably botched operation.[24]

In Opelousas, on the extreme southern outskirts, there lived a poor Cajun named Joseph Hollier. A painter by occupation, he brought in extra income by hanging wall paper, repairing old furniture and putting glass into windows (glazier). He and his wife, Asoline Gonor, and their two little girls, aged ten and eleven, had every reason to despise Northerners. During the spring 1863 occupation, they had suffered at the hands of stragglers, runaway slaves, soldiers and officers alike. Though their worldly possessions consisted of only a small frame house, a couple of outbuildings and a few arpents of land, they had not been overlooked by the infamous piano-maker from Massachusetts, Colonel Thomas E. Chickering.[25]Virtually everything of value had been taken or rendered useless by the thoughtless intruders.

So when the inevitable knock on their door came at 11 o'clock that rainy Friday morning, the thirty-three-year-old Hollier must have expected the worst. What he found, however, was anything but threatening. There, standing in the rain and thoroughly drenched, were two sandy-haired and blue-eyed boys from Iowa, one of whom appeared to be quite ill. Indeed, Captain William Titus Rigby, quaking with the chills, had neither the energy nor the courage to backtrack with his brigade. He had instead been assisted to Hollier's house by his cousin and friend, Lieutenant Alfred A. Rigby.

Rushing the Rigby cousins inside, Hollier threw some more logs on the fire and ordered his petite thirty-year-old wife to prepare an old family nostrum guaranteed to relieve chills, fever, dyspepsia and just about anything else. Within a short period of time, Captain William Titus Rigby and cousin Alfred were in warm dry clothing for the first time in two days. Hardly had the sick captain been directed to a sofa and covered with blankets than he fell into a deep, badly-needed sleep. That night Alfred Rigby confided his emotions to his diary:[26]

> The blazing fire and agreeable manner of our host made me feel perfectly at home and completely banished the ill feelings toward rebs in general which had been heightened by the pelting storm of the forenoon.

Back in camp the Rigby boys' companions were not so lucky. Most of the troops were furious at the blundering generals, especially Lawler, for bringing on such misery. A lumber yard was found nearby and a certain gin house was dismantled for shelter, sleeping boards and firewood, but still they were wet and cold.

So it surprised no one when Private Henry Hefflefinger, a thirty-nine-year-old wagon maker from Muscatine, Iowa, decided to vent his rage on General Lawler. "Old Heff," as he was called, was roaring drunk on Louisiana "lightning" and, like so many of the others, had vowed to kill the Irishman if ever he saw him again. Now, he had his chance. There stood Lawler, in the rain as usual, consulting with Colonel Slack. Grabbing his Enfield, Hefflefinger began shooting in all directions and making "quite a noise in camp" before he was pinned down and dragged away. Fortunately no one was hurt, not even Lawler, who soon rode off, apparently unaware that he had narrowly escaped yet another attempt on his life.[27]

Saturday, October 24, 1863

Captain William Titus Rigby slept much later than usual. He and cousin Alfred had bedded down in a soft goose-down mattress after consuming a lavish supper. The chills were gone, and, except for a minor headache, he felt fine. Looking out the window, Rigby was startled to see the ground as white as an Iowa winter. No longer would the "roses and poses" and flowers be blooming. Southwestern Louisiana had been hit by an unusually early and very severe cold snap.

On the other hand the sun was shining and Madame Hollier had prepared a delicious breakfast of roast chicken, grits and corn cakes. During the meal the boys also noticed for the first time just how profusely decorated was a rural Acadian home. On the interior walls were large and brightly colored prints, among which were the family's patron saints, the Wedding of the Blessed Mary, the Consolatrix of All Afflictions and the Good Shepherd. On the mantlepiece, near a rosary and holy water font, was a small statue of the Virgin, perhaps our Lady of the Lourdes. Surrounding this was a panorama of pictures, clippings, labels, stamps, tobacco packages and perfume bottles.

After commenting on the homey atmosphere and "spending a few hours in pleasant conversation, we took our departure," wrote cousin Alfred. "Our most urgent requests could not induce our worthy hosts to accept of any recompense for their kindness."

From that day forward, the Rigbys, who had maligned Louisianians from Berwick's bay to the Carencro, would have nothing but kind remarks for Louisiana's innocent civilians. And as long as they were in Opelousas, no other Yankees would be permitted to enter the Hollier home except them.[28]

In the wagon train camp on George Gardiner's plantation south of Opelousas, a company of soldiers from Colonel James A. Garfield's 42nd Ohio was ordered out on a foraging expedition. Striking across the prairie in a westerly direction without their politician-commander, they soon reached the Opelousas-Lake Charles road in the region then known as Plaquemine Brule. It was not the first time that bluecoats had visited that region. During the spring occupation, Colonel Chickering's forces had swept the road on both sides from the tiny settlement of Plaquemine Brule (now Church Point) north to Opelousas. Hypolite A. Guidry had lost goods to the Yankees—as had Eugenie Giraud, William Fisher, William Percy Breaux, Walter Mcbride, Charles Smith, Theodule Daigle, Onezime L. Guidry and dozens of others.

On this beautiful, but cold, Saturday morning a dozen or so of the boys from Ohio decided to stop for lunch at the plantation home of widow Giles Higginbotham. The old lady seemed harmless enough. Her son, Joseph Jenison, was off in the Rebel army, and she was alone except for two daughters and several faithful black *domestiques*. Stacking their arms near the front door as was their custom, the Yankees were soon enjoying a meal of yams, *cochon de lait* and gumbo.

It must have been a delicious meal, for they paid but little heed to the long column of bluecoated cavalrymen approaching from the south. Someone guessed that it was probably a portion of Fonda's cavalry out on a reconnaissance mission, but why, they wondered, were they "surrounding the house" and taking "possession of the muskets" still stacked in the yard? They found out soon enough. The "bluecoats" were, in fact, Rebels, one of whom entered the dining room and announced in a heavy Cajun accent that they were all under arrest.

Colonel William Vincent's 2nd Louisiana Cavalry had struck again, and before the day was over they would round up still more Yankee strays.[29]

In the meantime, Confederate General Richard Taylor, then camped with his command north of Opelousas near Moundville, was having the same troubles as his Union counterpart. Until now, the forage problem had been but a minor difficulty. He had simply spread his army in a long thin line from Alexandria to Berwick's Bay, purchasing (or confiscating) supplies at Confederate-imposed low prices. But the Federal advance had forced him to concentrate his forces at the same time as planters and ranchers were moving their livestock and produce toward the safety of the open western prairies.

The forage problem was at least partially ameliorated by Smith's "Fabian policy" directive. If Taylor could not attack, then why concentrate? Accordingly, when the Yankees took Opelousas, he had scattered his small army along both sides of Bayou Boeuf from Moundville to Holmesville and along the Big Cane Road from Big Cane Village to

Cheneyville. Meanwhile, the Confederate pickets extended south as far as the north bank of the Courtableau in Washington, six miles above Union-occupied Opelousas.

Aside from the foraging question, Taylor's main problem continued to be the heavy desertion rate. Some of the Texans were quite bitter over being forced to fight in Louisiana when it appeared as though the Louisianians themselves had lost all interest (Vincent's cavalry excepted). But desertion was punishable by death in the Texas camps, and the frequent executions—at least one a week—kept the cowboys east of the Sabine.[30]

Not so in Alfred Mouton's Louisiana brigade. The Acadians were among the most dispirited and depressed in the Trans-Mississippi Confederacy, especially the conscripts. For the second time they sat helplessly by while the northern "Americans" went plundering and burning their way through southwest Louisiana. Their homes had been damaged or destroyed, their crops confiscated; and their women and children left helpless. It was an American war and many wanted no part of it.

It had not always been so. Many had openly sided with the Confederacy and had enthusiastically enlisted when Louisiana seceded from the Union, and they had fought bravely from Shiloh to Berwick, Bisland and Irish Bend. In happier times they had sat around their campfires playing *boure*, eating *boudin* and singing war songs. One of them, Lieutenant Philibert Rogay, was so outdone by the words of a Yankee marching song:

> Oh! We'll hang Jeff Davis
> From a tall crabapple tree

that he had composed his very own *Louisianne Marsellaise:*

> *Lincoln, Lincoln*
> *On te pendre, Lincoln*

The Louisiana Frenchmen, like their Texas counterparts, were also occasionally evaluated by Yankee prisoners, one of whom, Lieutenant George C. Harding of the 21st Indiana Infantry, wrote an interesting characterization:

> I will try and tell what a Cajun is. He is a half-savage creature, of mixed French and Indian blood, lives in swamps and subsists by hunting and fishing and cultivating small patches of corn and sweet potatoes. They are sallow, dried up, and mummy-like in appearance, and stolid and stupid in expression. The wants of the Cajun are few, and his habits are simple. With a bit of cornbread, a potato, and a clove of garlic, with an occasional indulgence in stewed

> crawfish, he gets along quite comfortably, and for luxuries, smokes husk cigarettes and drinks rum—when he can get it.
>
> The Cajun has great powers of endurance, but not much stomach for a fight...desertions were quite frequent, sometimes as many as thirty or forty stampeding in a single night. But they would be caught, brought back, (and) made to wear a barrell for a week or two.
>
> I can not say that we were abused by the Cajuns. They did not insult, but exasperated us dreadfully. In the cool of the evening, they would gather about our quarters, and stand, or sit squatted on their haunches, for hours, not saying a word to us, or to each other, but regarding us with a grim, stupid stare, reminding me strongly of the lower class of Choctaws, who in the Indian country, sit and gaze at a circus bull.

An equally erroneous characterization was written by Theophilus Noel, a Texan and sometimes correspondent for the *New Orleans Picayune:*

> You must not use the word 'Cagin', implying thereby that there is any nigger blood in the party to whom you are talking anymore than you must not speak in any way disrespectful of the Roman Catholic church, unless you want to fill an unmarked grave by the stilletto route.

By late October, Mouton's command, which numbered more than three thousand on the muster rolls, was down to fewer than eight hundred. Some of his regiments, including the 18th Louisiana, Fournet's Yellow Jacket Battalion, the New Orleans Crescent Regiment and Beard's 11th Battalion, were little more than skeleton organizations. For this reason, General Kirby Smith promulgated his controversial General Orders No. 54, calling for a consolidation of these regiments. Though well-intended it threw officers and men "into a dreadful state of excitement" and merely accelerated the desertion rate. "This brigade is decidedly stung with a bug," wrote Captain Arthur Hyatt of the Crescent regiment:[31]

> The men are very much dissatisfied and disertions (sic) are numerous and daily. The causes assigned for this very unfortunate state of affairs are: First, because they are afraid of being taken to Texas; second, they object to a consolidation of the troops, and; third, they desert because *they can do so with impunity*, no notice being taken of it.
>
> Had (Mouton) punished desertion as it deserved, at the start, he would today have had a large brigade, and few deserters. But he rather encouraged it than otherwise, by the little notice he took of it. It is said that he feared to shoot a conscript, lest it should make him unpopular in his state, and affect his chances for the gubernational (sic) chair.

Jean Jacques Alfred Alexandre Mouton, the son of former Governor and U. S. Senator Alexandre Mouton, probably did have political ambitions. A graduate of St. Charles College in Grand Coteau and later the United States Military Academy, the bilingual general was handsome, able, daring and innovative. Himself of Acadian descent, he was loved by the loyal Confederates in his command and respected by his peers, but his short military career had earned him a record of mixed results. At West Point, he graduated near the bottom of his class in 1850 (thirty-eighth out of forty-four). During the battle of Shiloh, where he commanded the 18th Louisiana Infantry as a colonel, his handsome face had been so badly scarred that he soon covered it with a full beard. Once recovered—but with impaired vision—he took to the field again as a brigadier but only to be driven from the Lafourche country in 1862. In early 1863 he, nonetheless, earned high marks for his gallant and imaginative defensive tactics during the Battle of Bisland. At age thirty-four he was at the prime of his military career and almost everyone believed that a bright political future awaited him.

But the contention that he was soft on deserters and conscript evaders would have drawn a laugh from Ozeme Carriere. In fact Mouton was one of the commanders of the pre-war vigilante committees which so unceremoniously had driven the bandits from the soil of St. Martin, Vermilion, St. Landry, and Lafayette Parishes. Moreover, unknown to his potential constituency, it was he who had directed Colonels Vincent and Fournet, as well as General Pratt, to undertake brutal repressive measures against the disenchanted citizens of southwest Louisiana. Like Banks, Mouton must have reasoned that military discipline was prejudicial to his political ambition. Perhaps for this reason his vigorous, even ruthless, campaign against "disaffected persons" was waged in secret. One of his "secret orders" inadvertently fell into Union hands and was subsequently published in the Union-controlled New Orleans *Era*. The following excerpt speaks for itself:

BRIGADIER GENERAL ALFRED MOUTON (Clement Evans, *Confederate Military History*)

Headquarters, Forces South of Red
River, Vermilionville, June 12, 1863

Information has been received that there are bands of outlaws, deserters, conscripts and stragglers from a point above Hineston...in the parish of Rapides, down to the lower parishes extending into Calcasieu, through to the Bayou Teche, which are committing depredations, robberies and incendiarism, and who are openly violating the Confederate laws...Such men can only be considered as outlaws, highwaymen and traitors.

In consequence:

You will proceed...to scour the whole country...in search of these bands (which) beyond the pale of society, must be exterminated, especially the leaders; and every man found with arms for the purpose of resisting Confederate laws, or against whom satisfactory evidence may be given, must be executed on the spot.

No prisoners should be taken...(except) conscripts (who should be) ordered to report to Camp Pratt forthwith, with the injunction that if you overtake them again they will be executed on the spot.

By order of
Brigadier General Alfred Mouton

These instructions are to be kept secret, and no one is allowed to know the object of your movements.

CAJUN CONSCRIPT on picket duty was chained to a tree and watched over by others according to this satirical sketch by a Union artist in *Leslie's Illustrated Weekly*.

Even while the troops were brushing off the early morning frost, Captain Hyatt noted that nine more conscripts in Mouton's brigade had disappeared overnight. Despised by their Texas allies, brutalized and persecuted by Confederate enforcement authorities and their homes vandalized by the bluecoats, they were reluctant Rebels at best. Largely for this reason Mouton's troops were stationed just outside Holmesville near the Milburn plantation. If they were going to desert, or seek sanctuary with Ozeme Carriere's jayhawkers, they would have to pass through the odious Texans on their way south.[32]

CHAPTER TWELVE

IN OPELOUSAS COUNTRY

Saturday, October 24, 1863

EAST OF OPELOUSAS at Camp Barri-Croquant, General William Franklin seemed unable to decide how to proceed or what to do next. Instead of massing his army for a decisive push toward some specific objective, he had scattered his twenty-seven thousand man force into a half-dozen or more piecemeal camps in and around Opelousas. At the moment he didn't even know where the Rebels were located or what they were up to. Aside from a few mounted observers hovering nearby, they had simply evaporated when Opelousas fell to the Federals. Though he desperately needed to send out a reconnaissance detail to establish their whereabouts, the weather until now had been so unfavorable that no one, save Lawler, was foolish enough to venture out into it.

Shortly after daybreak, however, the rain let up and the skies began to clear. It even appeared as though the sun might put in a welcome appearance. Summoning his senior cavalry commander, General Albert Lee, Franklin immediately ordered him up the road toward Washington with instructions to find the Rebels.

Accompanied by brigade commanders Fonda and Mudd, Lee's division went first to Opelousas and then headed up Donatto's Lane into a cold biting north wind. In spite of the cold and the ever-present threat of mounted Texans, Lee noted that Yankee foragers were out in force. At the plantation home of Juste Bertinot, a forty-seven-year-old French-born planter, a group of Irishmen from Michael Fox's 8th New Hampshire regiment was loading their haversacks with sugar. Farther along was the home of Auguste Donatto and a certain Mr. Lemelle, wealthy free men of color whose race had prevented neither plunder from Yankees nor fidelity on the part of their many slaves. In fact all the planters along the road to Washington, including widow William Prudhomme, Clement Hollier, Elishu Andrus, Louis Henri Lastrapes, George Bullard, Damoville Dejean, Soloman Harman and many others had already been, or would soon be, visited by the unwelcome invaders.

Just beyond the tiny Bayou Carron, about six miles north of Opelousas, Lee's cavalry entered Washington, Louisiana, or as they called it "Niggertown." It was said to have taken this name from a wealthy family of industrious free men of color, Antoine, Francois and

Dennis Lemelle, who owned large tracts of land and large numbers of slaves. Though the community had been settled as long, or longer, than Opelousas, it was not until 1830 that it was incorporated under the name of Washington. Dr. Harris Beecher, fascinated as he was with names, wondered

> ...why they gave it such a name of old renown,
> this dreary, dingy, muddy, melancholy town.

With a population of about one thousand, Washington was the most important town in St. Landry Parish next to Opelousas. The little town owed its existence to Bayou Courtableau which, depending on the season, was navigable to that point. As a result it became a large shipping center for sugar, cotton, livestock and other products of the parish. Like Opelousas it contained a number of churches, warehouses, inns, factories, and some very fine homes.

Also, like Opelousas, it had been occupied in the spring and stripped of its valuable products. The bridge had been burned, private homes had been commandeered for army use, and the town was the scene of wanton destruction, depredations and atrocities. Among those who had suffered the most were Abraham Millspaugh, Francois Vinsonneau, Charles Gauthier, Gustave Skelhiemer, R. S. Wilkins, Willis Eves, L. M. Melancon, Francois Troinon, Orahmel Hinkley, Jacob Eberhard, Pierre Casse and Dominique Lalanne.

The Yankees who entered Washington that cold Saturday morning were not interested in plunder. Fanning out in all directions they began entering houses, bars, warehouses, and other establishments in search of "Johnnies" or civilians who could provide information on the whereabouts of Green's elusive Texans and Louisianians. By sheer good fortune they managed to capture yet another Confederate militia commander, General James Trudeau, as well as a Texan from Waller's Battalion, Lieutenant R. R. Bolling (who subsequently took the Oath of Allegiance).

Incredibly they found the bridge over the wide but low waters of Bayou Courtableau intact. During the spring it had been burned by the citizens of Washington to hinder the Union advance. General Banks, then quartered at Gerand Carriere's house, subsequently summoned the town officials and acidly informed them "that if he ever came to Washington again, he should expect to find a new bridge at this point, otherwise he should lay the town in ashes."[1]

Crossing over onto Confederate Captain Lewis D. Prescott's property, they soon found themselves confronted by a few mounted "partisan rangers" from Colonel J. P. Major's cavalry brigade. The Texans were up to their old tricks. A small group would charge, halt, discharge their pieces and withdraw. Some of Fonda's hotheads wanted to return

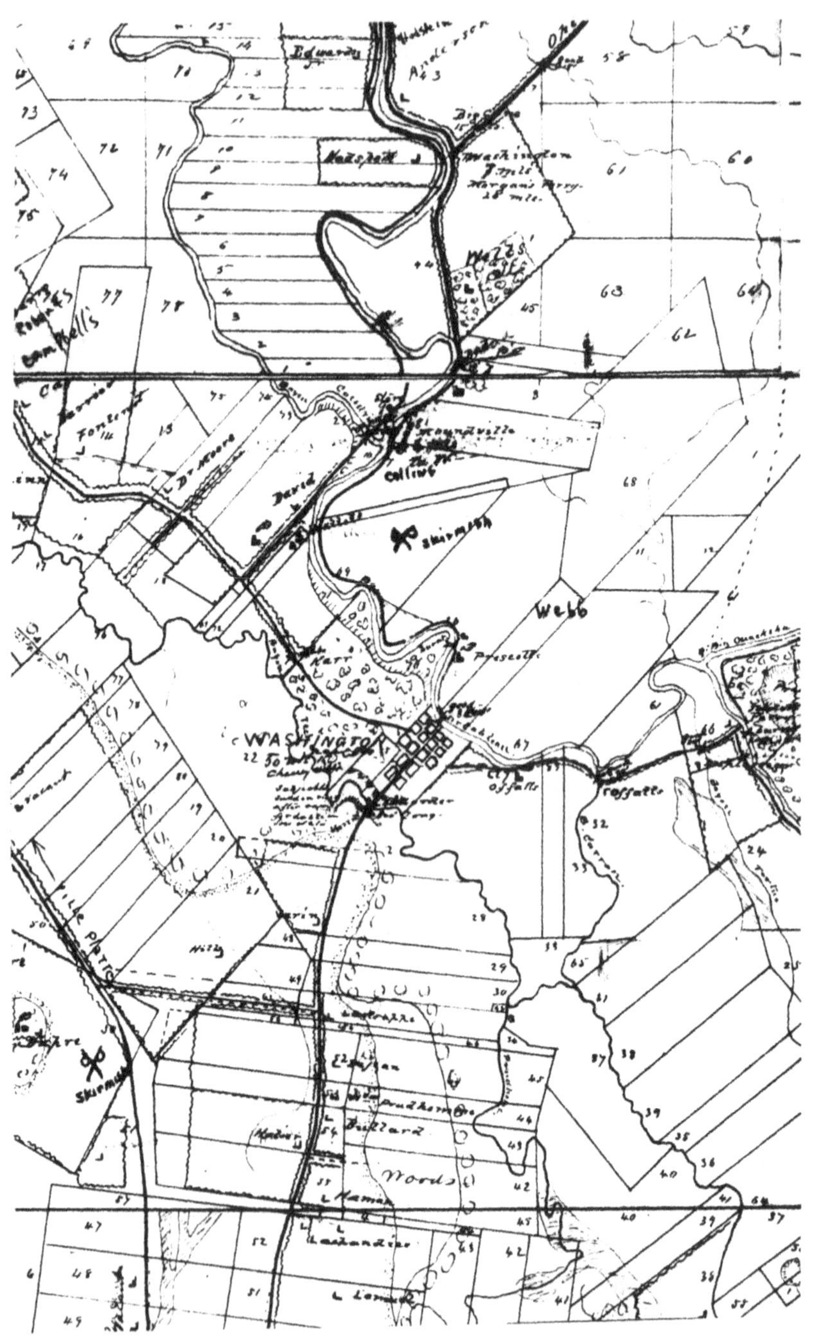

WASHINGTON AND VICINITY from 1863 Confederate Map (National Archives)

the charge, but the more experienced division commander, twenty-nine-year-old Brigadier General Albert Lee, would permit nothing of the sort.

Albert Lindley Lee, an attorney by profession and former supreme court justice of Kansas (formerly of New York) had at least one very good reason for his reluctance. Back during the Vicksburg siege, when he momentarily exposed himself to the defenders, he was struck down by a Rebel bullet. He had recovered but still walked with a slight limp. With dark piercing eyes, thick black hair and an apron-style beard that looked more fake than real, he bore little resemblance to his famous namesake in the Army of Virginia. Nonetheless, he was imaginative, innovative and, like Fonda, as much at home in the saddle as were the Texans.

Very cautiously and in battle formation, Lee's large cavalry force plodded past the Woodland plantation of Dr. Louis Archibald Webb, turned left near Home Place, and rode on toward Moundville. Somewhere up ahead, suspected Judge Lee, was a Rebel trap.

Indeed, about three miles north of Washington, near the confluence of Bayous Cocodrie and Boeuf (the headwaters of Bayou Courtableau) General Richard Taylor had prepared one of the most elaborate ambushes of the campaign. General John G. Walker's entire Texas infantry division was there, fresh from Arkansas, as was Major's brigade of mounted partisan rangers and almost every artillery battery in the Army of Louisiana (viz. the Valverde, Semmes', Edgar's, Daniel's, Mesh's, Haldeman's and Cornay's). All were drawn up just north of Moundville (so called because of Indian mounds in the area) not far from Peter Collin's store. One of the infantrymen, Samuel Farrow, "thought we were really going to get into it." Another Texan, J. P. Blessington, described the occasion in his diary:

> General Taylor formed his line of battle in a position to sweep the road that they would be most likely to advance on; parks of artillery were planted, ready to belch forth at a moments notice; the infantry was sheltered by a ditch in their front. Every minute seemed like an hour to us, till the ball should be opened.

Among those waiting in the ditch was Texas Colonel Oran M. Roberts, who, like the advancing Lee, was a former supreme court justice. Moreover, like his Union counterpart, Roberts had moved west at an early age to become one of the most influential men in his state. He had presided over the Texas Secession Convention and, because of his political connections, had incurred the wrath of the ailing loyalist, Sam Houston. Now, Roberts too was ailing, the victim of overexposure, hardship and too many Louisiana swamps. With his heavy white beard, drawn face and skinny frame he was scarcely able to take to the saddle, much less command an infantry brigade. But he was also possessed of a fighting spirit and political ambitions which, like the "Creole general," Alfred Mouton, would keep him near the scene of action.

BRIGADIER GENERAL ALBERT L. LEE (Library of Congress)

COLONEL ORAN M. ROBERTS (Evans, *Confederate Military History*)

As Judge Lee drew near, Judge Roberts' brigade opened fire, killing and wounding a number of the advance skirmishers. The medical report of Dr. Madison Reece, Surgeon of the 118th Illinois, described what happened to some of the Illinois cavalrymen:

> Henry Chandler, Private, was shot through the right breast (and killed). He was carried off the field out of the enemy's fire on a horse, lying before the rider, on the horse's neck and from there on a blanket to the ambulance.
>
> Fredrick Spear, Private, received a simple contused wound of the right great toe. He is of the opinion that this wound was caused by the bullet that passed through the body of Private Chandler, as he was in his rear....

There then occurred a most curious incident which, when described by an old Confederate veteran some fifty years later, must have seemed more like a distant dream than reality. From a nearby plantation house (possibly Woodland) there appeared a "well-dressed matronly looking lady" who came galloping across the field on a spirited horse. Positioning herself in front of the astonished Texans, she commenced a series of "frantic gestures" while shouting, "Come on and let us whip the darned Yankees!" So stirred were the Confederates, recalled the old vet, that "we charged with a tremendous yell, she being in the lead."

General Taylor's report of the affair indicated only that the Federals "declined" an engagement. He failed to mention that Colonel Roberts, supported by the Texas Rangers (and one mysterious lady) chased Lee right back into Washington, capturing two dozen Yankees.[2]

Sunday, October 25, 1863

It was a clear and cold Sunday morning in the Opelousas country. The mudholes were frozen over and frost covered the ground, but it was not as cold as the preceding day. At Barre's Landing, as well as at the camps in and around Opelousas, each regiment was preparing for an open-air religious ceremony. In Opelousas, where the bluecoats outnumbered the citizens by a ratio of about ten to one, virtually every church flew the Stars and Stripes, and each was to be the scene of a Union sermon.

Perhaps the most solemn meeting was the one held just outside the Opelousas Methodist Episcopal Church. There, in a tiny graveyard which was so "tastefully fenced and adorned with shrubbery and flowers," Private Henry Chandler of the 118th Illinois was interred, as was Private Clarence Powers of the same regiment who had died that very morning when he was thrown from a confiscated horse.[3]

At Barre's Landing east of Opelousas, the troops of the XIII Corps were getting tired of army rations. The weather had been much too disagreeable for foraging and, even had it not, where were foot soldiers to go in such a desolate location? Now, with the weather so beautiful, many of the regiments passed orders to prepare for an "official" foraging expedition anyway.

Fanning out in all directions, the hungry foot soldiers headed down bayous, up trails, across prairies and into swamps. "Everything that seemed likely to be fit to eat was chased down with the desperation of a foe," wrote a soldier from Wisconsin, "and sweet potatoes had to suffer likewise."

In happier times the citizens of the upper Teche would have been preparing to celebrate the *fete de la roulaison*, or grinding festival, when the last cane crop was harvested. It had always been a joyful occasion, attended by whites and blacks, masters and slaves, old and young. All would have danced, eaten, drunk, courted and otherwise have had a good time. But the crop of 1863 had been an unusually poor one. Many farmers had not even bothered to plant after the disruptive spring invasion, occupation, destruction and widespread seizures; and what little there was would be harvested, not by the hard-working *habitants*, but by the foraging invaders. There would be no *roulaisson* in 1863.

In the Gros Chevreuil vicinity the foragers called on Jean and Victoria Prevot, Michael Emonet, Jacob Hirsch, Cyprien Lalonde and a settlement of relatively wealthy *gens de couleur libre*.

The latter were not so anomalous in ante-bellum Louisiana as one might imagine. According to the 1858 report of the assessor's office, the free colored population of St. Landry Parish was listed at 1,596, while whites numbered 11,969 and the slave population 12,236. Some had descended from light-skinned Haitian refugees who fled to French Louisiana from the tyranny of Toussaint L'Ouverture. Others, perhaps the majority, were the miscegenetic products of some illicit union between whites and mulattos and were called quadroons. In the laissez-faire environment of the parish many had become *petits habitants* and pursued a lifestyle not unlike that of the Acadians. A few, adopting the vices as well as the virtues of their white manumitters, had acquired large tracts of land and numerous slaves. Spurned and even persecuted by the whites (especially by the over-zealous members of the pre-war *comites de vigilance)* and disdainful of darker skin, they sought the company of each other, thereby creating a unique caste of light-skinned "blacks" which has survived, at least in Louisiana, to the present.

Neither the color of their skin nor their special status mattered to the Yankees. The cattle, horses and sugar of Alphonse and A. D. Meuillon, Alexandre Lemelle, Jules Frilot, Sosthene Auzenne and Zenon Rideau, all free men of color, were taken and consumed just as readily as the goods seized from the nearby home of Andre Robin whose father, Napoleon Robin, had served the little Corsican as a general in the French *Grande Armee*.

Back in Camp Barri-Croquant, a correspondent for the Hartford *Wisconsin Home League*, identified only as "Random," sat on a wooden bucket and wrote his dispatch as the mule-drawn forage wagons came rolling back in:[4]

> Our boys continue to forage and come into camp loaded down with poultry, pigs, hogs, sugar and honey. A chap stands now within my range of vision who was out on such an expedition. The fates made him unlucky, and at the same time the sweetest young man in our midst. He was in a sugar house and while leaning over a molasses hogshead went in head first, and was rescued by a comrade who discovered his boots on the surface...

FORAGING IN LOUISIANA exceeded all bounds of civilized behavior according to eyewitnesses *(Harper's Weekly)*

While the boys from the XIII Corps were thus supplementing their diets with Cajun *sirop de batterie* and engaging in taffy-pulling, the dragoons of the 75th New York were still looking for horses, bridles and saddles. They too were concentrating on the densely-settled prairies in the vicinity of Leonville. Among those visited were Andre and Hypolite Mallet, Francois Guillory, Adelaid Lanclos and Romain Dupre. Some of these settlers had practiced considerable "ingenuity" in secreting their property. Bridles and saddles were found up chimneys, in attics, under beds, in closets and even buried in the ground. "Much was the merriment in camp over tales of these discoveries," wrote one soldier.

Less humorous was the experience of a detachment which crossed over the Courtableau and headed north toward Bayou Wauksha. After paying calls on James Bihm, Elbert Gantt and a certain Dr. Thomas, they became lost in a tract of woods. Someone spotted a herd of swine and, supposing that the animals might lead toward human habitation, commenced driving them slowly. Following the pigs for some distance, the party came unexpectedly upon what was erroneously described as "a huge rock in the forest, under an overhanging shelf of which they found sheltered five magnificent horses."

The New Yorkers did not get very far with their prize, however, before their attention was diverted to "an old man mounted on a most cadaverous and ancient looking beast." The old man, whoever he was, rode up and explained how he had succeeded until now in keeping his horses hidden from both Texas Rangers and Federal troops. He then begged, "in the most piteous tones and with tears trickling down his wrinkled yellow cheeks" to at least let him keep one of the horses, a certain black pony, "which was the favorite saddle horse of his only daughter, and who would be almost killed at the loss." But the heartless dragoons informed him that their orders were to take all, and he was finally convinced that his "appeals and expostulations were in vain." Still, he followed them back to Camp Barri-Croquant and even took the Oath of Allegiance in the hopes that he might somehow recover his property. After finding his efforts fruitless, he came once more to the men who had taken his daughter's pony, and begged them, if the pony was ever injured or disabled, to send him word, so that he might come and take it.

Scenes such as this were frequent in the Union camp, and even the troops of the 75th New York admitted that "the hearts of the men were often deeply touched."[5]

Monday, Tuesday, and Wednesday, October 26-28, 1863

The early days of the week were unusually quiet. The cold front, which had brought such misery to all, had passed through and brought warmer weather, but cloudy skies to the Opelousas country. In the absence of General Ord, who was suffering in New Orleans with typhoid fever, the illegal foraging once more began to get out of hand. "Catch roll-calls," arrests, and fines slowed, but did not stop, the destructive Westerners of the XIII Corps. A few reconnaissance missions were sent out, mainly on the road to Flat Town, and runaway slaves were coming in by the hundreds. Once more the restless troops began inquiring about Texas.

And General William Franklin was as indecisive as ever. His superior, Major General Banks, chose to ignore his oft-repeated "request for definite instructions." The *Red Chief* would not be coming; the Courtableau did in fact rise and fall with the Mississippi; and the supply problem was becoming severe. It appeared as though Franklin would have to make a critical decision all by himself, and he signalled Banks to that effect:

> ...I think I shall hold my advance in the vicinity of Carrion Crow Bayou, as by taking that position, I can get forage more easily, and the supply of provisions can be kept up.

Franklin was also preoccupied with Banks' instructions to contact Ozeme Carriere, one of the most notorious jayhawkers in Louisiana. Ozeme Carriere and fellow travelers belonged to the western prairies of St. Landry (present-day Acadia) and Vermilion parishes in the sparsely settled areas beyond the Bayous Plaquemine Brulet and Mallet. For more than a half century this country was the refuge of the "idle and the depraved, who avoided the haunts of civilizations." Indeed, they subsisted on the industry of others, and among their numbers were those who had been dispersed by the pre-war *comites de vigilance*. Like Newt Knight in Mississippi, Carriere had surrounded himself with disenchanted conscript evaders, deserters from both armies, runaway slaves and even "free men of color." Looting and burning, raping and killing, they had spread a reign of terror throughout St. Landry and surrounding parishes. Not surprisingly, the Carriere brothers, Ozeme, Hilaire and Ursin, and a sister, Carmelite, and the Saunier brothers were among the most wanted fugitives in Confederate Louisiana.

In spite of rumors to the contrary, Carriere was alive and well and living in the wooded area of Bayou Mallet west of Opelousas. He even boasted that he had "witnessed his own execution" back in August when the Confederates shot his brother, Hilaire. Now, he was making life as miserable as possible for the Rebels. Not only did he actively encourage desertion, harbor conscript evaders, stragglers and deserters, but he waged his own private war against the Confederates by ambushing, sniping, intimidating, and raiding isolated outposts. He and his small band of hardcore followers also left a trail of death, destruction, plunder and ravished women in their wake.

Thus, on the one hand Carriere was a bloodthirsty depraved criminal, especially to the law-abiding, Confederate-supporting citizens of St. Landry Parish, while, on the other, he was held in high esteem by the sanctuary-seeking disenchanted conscript evaders, deserters and their families who elevated him to folk hero status—the Robin Hood of Mallet Woods.

One of his admirers was Major General Nathaniel P. Banks, who employed the jayhawkers' services in the spring and considered Carriere and his men to be "loyal Unionists." Banks failed to make the distinction between such outlaws as Carriere and the genuinely loyal and law-abiding citizens (e.g., Boudreaux, Beraud, Doucet, Girard and Chargois in Vermilionville) or even the Cajun conscript evaders and deserters who wanted no part of the war on either side. To Banks, apparently, anyone opposed to the Confederates was a "loyal" Union man.

It is quite possible that General Franklin, who by all accounts was an honest, decent and compassionate man, had no more respect for Carriere's kind than did his Confederate counterparts; but Banks, in three separate telegrams as well as in private conversation, instructed

UNION SCOUTS, mainly Louisianians, described as a most "desperate" set of men. *(Harper's Weekly)*

his field commander to raise a regiment of these men and commission their leaders as officers under the flag of the United States. Franklin did try, or at least he said he tried, but his efforts netted him only one small group of free men of color, the Independent Bayou Mallet Scouts under the command of Captain Martin Guillory. The discipline of army life, especially under Franklin, was not Carriere's element.[6]

As if Franklin did not have enough troubles with military matters, the runaway blacks began flocking to camp in ever increasing numbers. So long as the army was on the move only a trickle joined in, but now even Dr. Harris Beecher, normally complacent and tolerant, was complaining:

> ...It seemed as though the resources of the country, in this respect, were inexhaustible. They were omnipresent. By day they were stalking through the company streets, with pans of molasses candy for sale. The nights were made hideous by their dances and prayer meetings, disturbing the sleep of the men.

More than two weeks before, at Camp Carrion Crow, Franklin had asked Banks for permission to employ these runaways:

> The short-handedness of some of the field batteries in this corps can be corrected in some degree by the substitution of Negro drivers of battery wagons and forges and afterward caissons. I therefore respectfully request authority to make these changes....

Banks had concurred, but still Franklin was unable to bring order into the chaotic situation. Many of the able-bodied males were mustered into the *Corps d'Afrique* and sent down to Brashear City for training. Some of the females, meanwhile, were transported on to New Orleans for further transfer to government managed plantations along the Mississippi. Still they came and posed health problems, hampered military operations and further taxed the citizens of the upper Teche as well as the military authorities with their need for provisions.

So depressing was the mood in camp that General Weitzel attempted to lift the spirits of the troops (and take their minds off Texas) by throwing a big party, ostensibly to celebrate the anniversary of the battle of Labadieville—his first engagement. A great deal of confiscated food was consumed, speeches were made in front of a giant bonfire and a "couple of brass bands added to the eclat of the occasion." Surgeon Harris Beecher, who attended the gala event, noted that certain "bibulous fluids were also circulated and a few did not their spiriting gently." This little affair, recalled the New Yorker "was a bright and refreshing oasis in the midst of a barren desert of monotonous and arduous life."[7]

At Quartier-Plaissance, west of Opelousas, James Earl Bradley saw his first Yankee. The young Methodist minister, who lived with Collin George Adams near the plantation of former Louisiana Governor Jean-Jaques Dupre, thought he saw Federals each day, but each time it turned out to be some of Vincent's bluecoated Louisiana cavalrymen. But on Monday morning, one genuine bluecoat, no doubt a straggler from Fonda's reconnaissance mission to Flat Town, came riding up the lane toward the Adam's home. "He asked for some bread and milk," wrote Bradley, "and we gave him some, but he was as restless as a beast in a cage."

A short time afterwards, however, the Federals "made up for the time past." An entire cavalry regiment, Harai Robinson's 1st Louisiana (Union) came riding up the lane, some of them breaking down fences and riding across the fields. Bradley was at home with Mrs. Adams (nee Francina Brown) and her two daughters, twenty-year-old Amanda and little Susan, age nine. The master of the house, fifty-year-old Collin

Adams, was a wealthy planter from Shelby County, Tennessee, but was not at home as he had long since driven his slaves and livestock to the relative safety of Pine Prairie:

> I went outside and was saluted by the colonel, who interrogated me about 'the rebels', their camps, etc.... While we were conversing, one of his men seized 'old Jackson', an old horse in the stable; the colonel said he shouldn't take him but the fellow seemed to be the superior of his commanding officer, for he went off with him.

Bradley, it should be noted, was a Chauvinist in the true sense of the word, blindly devoted to the Confederate cause, and divulged nothing of value to his Union interrogaters. He also tried very hard to suppress his sentiments, as well as his anger at being forced to postpone his wedding, even to the extent of feigning loyalty. Nonetheless, wrote Bradley

> ...they entered the house, searched every room and found the only (saddle) on the place. It belonged to Miss Amanda's deceased brother, but they took it. They examined the cabins, robbed us of our dinner (and robbed) the Negroes too. It was such fun to see a big darkie in the cabins daring white soldiers to search him. But God held them in restraint, for they never offered us any words of insult.

Minister Bradley and the Adams family were not so fortunate on the next visit. Early on the morning of Tuesday, October 27, 1863, a group of mounted Federals, also members of Harai Robinson's 1st Louisiana, rode up to the front door and proceeded to start an argument among themselves, apparently over whether or not to sack the house. A small altercation then ensued and one group rushed into the house "as though hellish devils." Some of their companions soon caught them, however, and "in a moment they were scattered about the floor."

Bradley beseeched them to go at once, but to no avail. He even raised his arms toward heaven and commenced praying. Still they did not desist. Finally he began lecturing them on the sinfulness of their ways and invoked the Commandment that Thou Shalt Not Steal, but his futile efforts served merely to antagonize the trespassers who pushed him aside with the rejoinder that God was on the side of the Union. Some of the men in the regiment then displayed the type of conduct which got them transferred to Harai Robinson's command in the first place:

> They began a pillage that the Devil himself would blush at. Everything fell before them in the shape of poultry, hogs, corn, hay, etc. They loaded 10 wagons, and any number of horses, Though we treated them very kindly...they got so low as to cut up and break my buggy. I had rather be united in death then linked with such devils.

Frustrated and angered by these incessant visitations on the part of Robinson's cavalrymen, Bradley decided on a rash course of action. Major General William Franklin, he had heard, was a strict disciplinarian who frowned on such behavior. Bradley sat down and drafted a strongly worded letter relating the "depredations" committed by the Union cavalry. Before leaving the house he wrote a silent prayer in his diary:

> O give me calmness and courage for this day. If I go to prison, be with me, and protect the dear family with whom I live. Amen.

Stuffing his pocket with what he described as a small bottle of homemade gold coins, Minister Bradley started down the road toward Opelousas. The money might be needed to induce a guard to deliver his complaint to the Yankee general. Besides, Bradley had another mission to perform. A few days earlier a neighbor, Theodore Valade, had returned from New Orleans with a packet of letters from Reverend Charles Evans addressed to Father Gilbert Raymond in Opelousas. Would Bradley, asked Valade, be so kind as to deliver the letters to the good Father? Now, walking toward Opelousas, Bradley was troubled with the knowledge that the letters would have to pass through Yankee censors before they could be delivered. Perhaps it was well that he had brought a little bribery money.

At Ringrose plantation, the home of Widow Michel William Prudhomme (nee Anna Young) not far from the St. Landry Catholic Church, Bradley came upon Union headquarters, but instead of General William Franklin, for whom he was looking, he was told that the forces in Opelousas were commanded by Brigadier General Cuvier Grover. Well, Grover would be just fine, Bradley told the cooperative guard who took the proffered protest note, the letters, and the money and disappeared into the imposing two-story home where General Grover was quartered.

Within an hour, a messenger exited with a set of "protection papers" from the thirty-five-year-old West Point general. There was also an oral promise to "inquire into the depredations" and to deliver the letters to Father Raymond. Feeling quite pleased with himself, Bradley uttered a silent prayer of relief and walked on home.

No sooner did he reach the Adams house, however, than a detachment of the 118th Illinois, under Captain Arthur W. Marsh, came riding up the lane to the front door.

"Is this Mr. Adams plantation?" asked the twenty-five-year-old officer from Hamilton, Illinois.

"It is!" replied Bradley.

After commenting on the beauty of the place and establishing Bradley's identification, Marsh then addressed the minister.

"You sent a communication to General Grover today. Well, the general desires to see you, and we are here to conduct you to him."

In Opelousas once more, Bradley was ushered in to see none other than a very angry colonel named John Fonda whom he had implicated in his letter of protest. Fonda directed some "sharply worded questions" toward Bradley regarding the conduct of his troops. Apparently unsatisfied with the answers, the Union colonel then took the minister by the arm as though he were a prisoner and ushered him into General Grover's office.

The commanding general, seated in the presence of staff and orderlies, was at the time penning his signature to some document. Finishing, he looked up and said: "Mr. Bradley, I arrest you as a suspicious and dangerous character!"

"Two of those letters," continued Grover, "contained contraband intelligence, and give me grounds to infer that you are a secret agent here for such business!"

One of Grover's orderlies, an "upstart officer," in Bradley's words, added: "We can't allow our flag to be insulted," whereupon guards were called in to unceremoniously conduct the startled minister several blocks away to the courthouse jail. His silent prayer had proven prophetic.[8]

CHAPTER THIRTEEN

YANKEE JUSTICE IN ST. LANDRY PARISH

Thursday and Friday, October 29-30, 1863

THE END of the week was shaping up as miserably as the day Lawler's division marched to Opelousas. Another cold front, a slow-moving one, began dropping its chilly waters on Opelousas and Barre's Landing turning roads and camps alike into a quagmire.

The mood in camp was as depressing as the weather. Franklin was concerned that he would be unable to move his big thirty-pounder Parrotts because of the mud. Each regiment was reporting large numbers of deserters—though it is not clear where they could go from Barre's Landing—and the Easterners and the Westerners were at each others throats again. Hardly did a day pass that some altercation did not occur, usually among foragers seeking the same prey. For one fleeting moment, Franklin thought he had found a solution to the friction and he wired Banks of his plan:

> Having now been for some time in command of this department in the field, I have considered some changes of details which, in my opinion, should be made.
> ...The Thirteenth and Nineteenth Army Corps, so long as they serve together, should be embodied into one corps.
> ...I have seen great want of discipline, and a tendency to disobedience...caused by the fact that the two corps are from different sections..., do not know each other, and are consequently jealous of each other. I think that the combination will, in a great degree, correct this, and that the experiment is worth while.

The Major General Commanding, Nathaniel P. Banks, was far too preoccupied at the time to concern himself with Franklin's problems. Unknown to the latter, the commander of the Department of the Gulf had already "sailed for the Rio Grande" setting in motion yet a third attempt to "plant the flag in Texas" in less than two months. Somehow, hoped Banks, he might yet salvage his reputation as a general and enhance his political fortunes.[1]

On his own now and without guidance or instructions from New Orleans, Franklin decided to act. A brigade of troops under General Robert A. Cameron was ordered from Barre's Landing to the campsites south of Opelousas near the supply train which Lawler had abandoned. No sooner had they gone into camp than "Fzs," the pumpkin-eater of the 24th Indiana, "went after a sack of potatoes." Frustrated in his efforts to find any—Lawler's division having made a clean sweep of the area—the mysterious teutonic soldier "finally made his appearance with a-a-a-Punkin."

Meanwhile, Lawler's division—three brigades of infantry numbering about five thousand—was ordered back toward New Iberia. They went as they had come, marching fast and in the rain. "It was a very hard march," complained a soldier in the 21st Iowa, "and all suffered severely." Lawler, who led the column, "kept it moving as fast as his horse could walk, giving no thought, apparently, to the men behind him, who, with blistered feet, many of them barefoot and carrying their shoes, lugged at a quickstep their heavy load." That night, as darkness fell and the order was given to halt and make camp, a loud shout of approval went up when someone facetiously announced: "Lawler's horse has given out."[2]

In spite of the mud, rain and miserably cold weather, Colonels John Fonda and Harai Robinson were still trying to supply the army with forage. On Thursday, October 29, 1863, the day after Minister Bradley's arrest, they set out once more on the road to Flat Town (Ville Platte). Just north of the Adams house near Quartier Plaissance, they plundered the small plantation of Sabastian, Baptiste, Adolphe and George Malveaux, all *gens de couleur libre.* Not far away they called upon Jaochim Pitre, Theodore and Yorick Valade (whose letters were responsible for Bradley's incarceration), A. H. Gradeniyo, Oscar Halphen, Francois Poiret, Christoval Dupre, Laurent Dupre, Cyprien Dupre, Dr. James Thompson, Cassimir Rougeau, f.m.c., and an eccentric old Frenchman named Bleze Motte.[3]

The next morning, Friday the 30th, Fonda and Robinson once more started up the road toward Flat Town with a long train of empty supply wagons. Along the way they stopped at the homes of Dr. Lewis Debaillon, Yves and Antoine Vidrine, Marceline Lafleur, Nicholas Lahaye, Ozeme Fontenot (a member of Vincent's 2nd Louisiana), Antoine and Theophile Fontenot and Louis Balthazar, f.m.c. All seemed peaceful enough. After all, they had been out on this road a dozen times or more and had never encountered anything more harmful than a few old men, women and children and one uppety Methodist minister.

This day would be different. One of the planters along the way, evidently as weary of foragers as Minister Bradley, had informed the "real" Louisiana cavalry, Colonel William Vincent's 2nd Louisiana, of their regular visits. The bluecoated Louisianians, as inconspicuous as the day they had captured Colonel Garfield's foragers, were waiting in ambush. They very quietly rode up to and captured several squads of Robinson's Louisiana cavalry before the others caught on. Within moments, however, the alarm was sounded and a genuine stampede was set in motion toward Opelousas. Down the muddy road and across the marshy prairies they went in a thundering yelling gallop, Vincent's Louisianians in hot pursuit, some of them rising in their stirrups with gleaming sabers extended toward the fleeing terror-stricken foragers. At the Adam's plantation young Amanda and Susanne rushed outside and began applauding even as the Yankees streaked by "fleeing like frightened hogs." It was Vincent's finest hour.

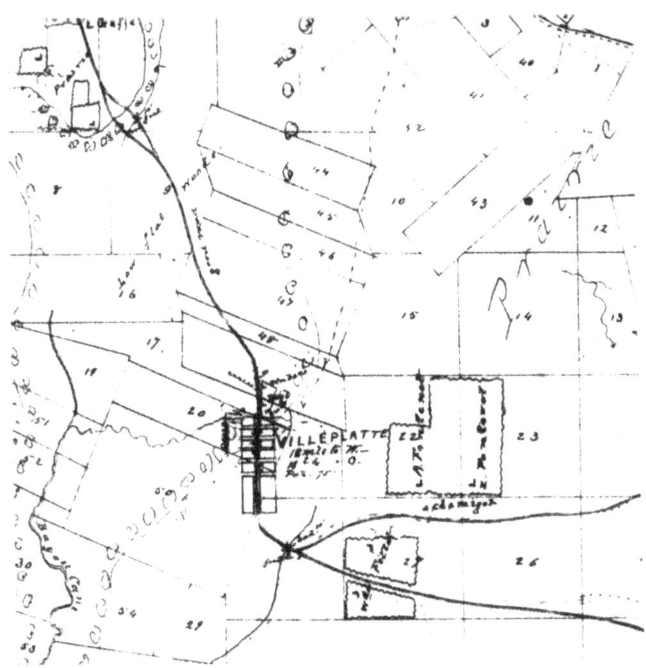

VILLE PLATE AND VICINITY from 1863 Confederate map of St. Landry Parish (National Archives)

Hearing the commotion from his Ringrose plantation headquarters, General Cuvier Grover quickly ordered Colonel James R. Slack's Westerners, together with a brigade of the XIX Corps, to move "on the double quick" toward the north and west of Opelousas. Many of the Westerners were reminded of their very first day on Bayou Bourbeux, when Fonda's horse had come galloping into camp with the Texans on their tails. Just as they had done before, the infantrymen drew up in battle formation, permitted their fleeing comrades to rush past, and then fired a few ineffectual rounds at the Rebels who drew up short of range. In the meantime, complained a disgruntled Illinois cavalryman, "the rain came down in torrents, deluging (sic) the whole country and giving all of us a thorough soaking."

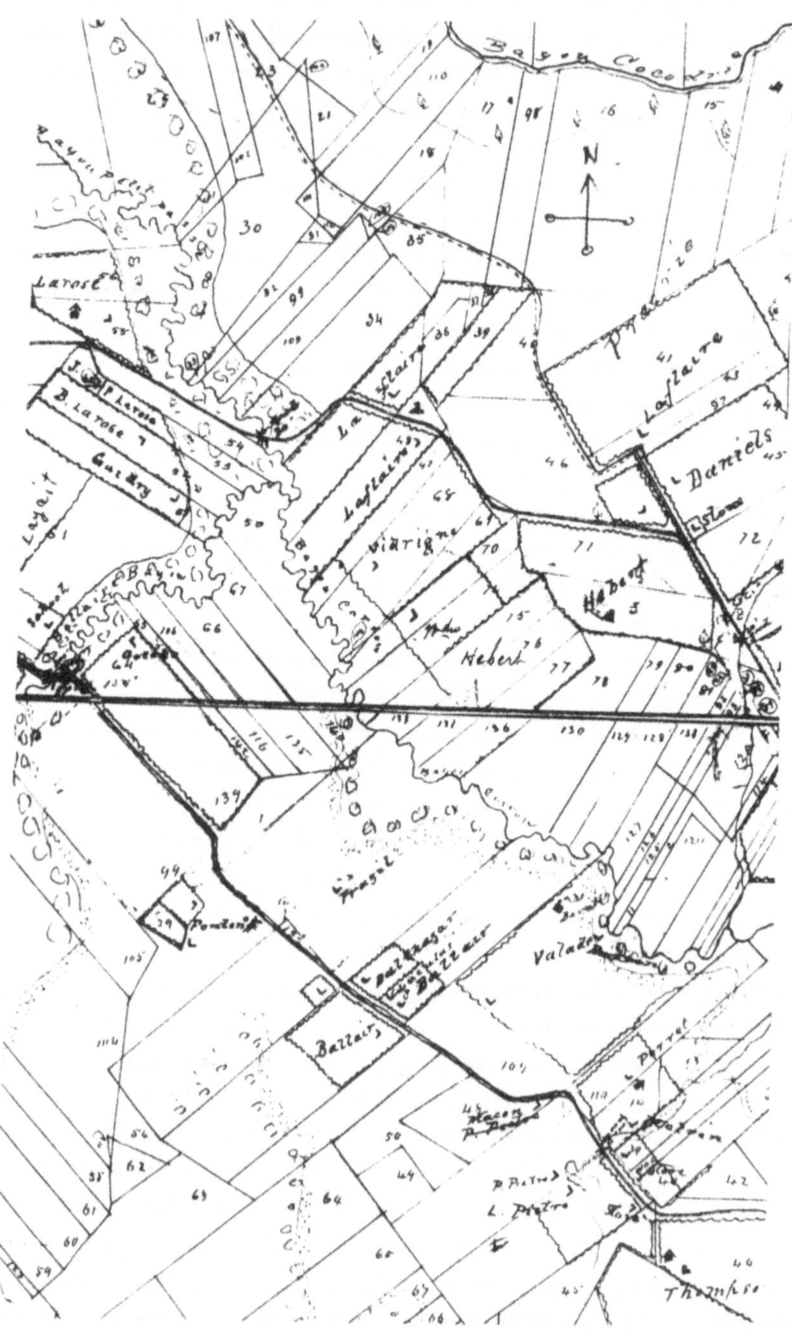

AREA BETWEEN OPELOUSAS AND VILLE PLATTE from 1863 Confederate map. (National Archives)

When the rains finally ceased, the two infantry brigades, supported by some badly embarrassed cavalrymen "scouted around the rest of the day, but could not find any rebs." Samuel Gordon, an officer of the 118th Illinois wrote his wife that "the scamps smelt the rat and crawled into their hiding places. We returned to camp about sunset, tired, wet, cold and hungry." And, he might have added, without a couple dozen cavalrymen of the 1st Louisiana (Union).[4]

Down at the Opelousas jail, James Earl Bradley found himself among some very distinguished company. Private Michael Fox, the condemned prisoner from the 8th New Hampshire was there, as were "negroes of both sides" and a few common criminals. For sheer good company he found the entire Opelousas Board of Police, including F. A. King, E. C. Dupre, Omer Poiret, Joel Sandoz, his nineteen-year-old son, Leonce, and Carville Julien Gonor.

The elder Sandoz, a forty-five-year-old native of Switzerland, was the founder and publisher of the weekly democratic mouthpiece, the *Opelousas Courier*. An avid supporter of the Confederacy, Sandoz even printed the anti-war speeches of Ohio's maverick politician, Clement Vallandigham. During the spring campaign his presses had been silenced only when the Yankees dumped the entire works into Bayou Tesson. This time, however, he had crated his new machinery and hauled it to a place of safekeeping in anticipation of the Union occupation. To his everlasting credit the *Courier's* presses continued to roll throughout the war—much of the time using colorful wall paper—preserving for posterity the war-torn history of St. Landry Parish.

FATHER GILBERT RAYMOND
(*Daily World*, Opelousas, Louisiana)

Conspicuous by his absence from jail was Father Gilbert Raymond. After all it had been Father Raymond's correspondence which caused Bradley his uncomfortable and embarrassing predicament. Just before and during the Union advance, Raymond had spent several weeks in New Orleans, as well as in the LaFourche country and at Berwick's Bay. Raymond had befriended some of the Federal high command and even brought back a reasonably accurate report of their strength. Perhaps it was this friendship which prevented his arrest now, in spite of the allegedly incriminating letters, or perhaps the Yankees had merely used the letters as a subterfuge to arrest Bradley's big mouth and obvious Confederate sympathies. At any rate Father Raymond's movements were closely watched by the Federals occupying the church and rectory.

Still, Bradley must have been troubled by these thoughts when he sent a note to the good priest by a "kind and sympathetic" jailer, a certain Lieutenant Hoyt:

> I'm under arrest for certain letters. Please go to Gen. Grover and get his permission to come and see me.
>
> Yours in distress.

Raymond came, as did Dr. George Hill, Miss Maggie White and a certain sister Levy bringing blankets, food and words of sympathy, but he was not released. Finally, and in desperation, Bradley wrote to General Grover:

> ...my overconfidence in my friend (either Raymond, Valade or Evans?) was my only crime, if crime it be...Please release me and let me return to that helpless (Adams) family.

Bradley's only consolation was that Father Raymond finally spoke to Grover about the matter. The general, according to Raymond's report of the interview, said he was holding the minister for other charges. "He is bearing communications to the rebels," claimed Grover, and is "aiding both sides."

When this was communicated to Bradley, the normally passive man of God lost his bearing for a moment, exclaiming that it was "a lie and vile slander! May God curse them as an army and nation!" In the meantime he would cool his heels in the Opelousas jail along with Michael Fox and the other good citizens of St. Landry Parish.[5]

Predictably the case of Michael Fox was becoming something of a *cause celebre*. Ever since the night of the storm, resentment had festered, grown and spilled over from regiment to regiment until it seemed to envelop the entire XIX Army Corps command. Officers, it was argued, could pillage, forage and get drunk or disorderly without incurring the wrath of higher authorities. They could even strike or insult superiors—as in the case of Lieutenant Gannon—and get off lightly. Moreover, officers could verbally or physically abuse private soldiers who had no recourse except to "bow in meek submission." Finally, officers could deprive a soldier of his very life. Not one enlisted man had sat on that court which sentenced Fox to death.

Not a few officers were in accord with the resentment. The assistant adjutant general of the 3rd Division, Major Duncan S. Walker, pleaded with Generals Franklin and Grover to rescind, or at least delay, the execution. According to Walker, who was an attorney in private life, a field commander did not have the legal authority to execute a death sentence. Even Franklin's own adjutant, Major Wickham Hoffman, pleaded for a reprieve.

Nonetheless Grover and Franklin, no strangers to military executions, had strong convictions about the necessity for discipline and harsh punishment. Feeling the pressures building, the generals decided to dispose of the matter as quickly as possible. Thus, on the morning of October 30, 1863, General Franklin, still camped with his command on Bayou Marie Croquant, sent General Order No. 21 to Grover in which he approved the execution for the following day. In an effort to mollify the enlisted men, Franklin directed that the following words be read at the execution:

> The Commanding General states for the information of this command, that all *officers* and enlisted men, who may be convicted of violations of discipline as gross as that of which Private Michael Fox, 8th New Hampshire Volunteers, has been convicted, will have the full measure of punishment awarded to them, whenever the courts will find them guilty.

Ironically, Franklin's orders directing the execution was then stamped with the official seal of the XIX Army Corps: LIBERTY AND JUSTICE.

Characteristically, no one bothered to inform prisoner Fox of his impending execution until well after nightfall. Nonetheless the condemned man had long since resigned himself to his fate and, when informed, answered that he would "stand it like a brick."

The adjutant of the 8th New Hampshire, Major Thomas Connelly, along with Lieutenant William Gannon, stopped by to pay their last respects. They were soon joined by Father Gilbert Raymond and the regimental chaplain of the New Hampshire regiment, Reverend Daniel P. Cilley.

While Fox was laying bare his soul to these men of the cloth, who should stop by but Fox's nemesis, the former officer of the day, Captain John R. Stokes. Searching for words to express his feelings, Stokes finally murmured something to the effect that he felt very sorry for the condemned man.

Perhaps it was the sight of Stokes, or perhaps it was Stokes' choice of words. At any rate Fox underwent a sudden transmogrification. Whereas moments before he was meekly confessing his sins, he now became big bad Mike Fox again.

"Well you need not feel sorry for me, you cowardly son-of-a-bitch," snorted Fox. "I am going to die tomorrow, and if ever there was a man come back to this world, I'll haunt you night and day."

To be sure Stokes slipped away as quickly as he had come. The confused clergymen, on the other hand, were doubtless left with mouths agape at such a violent and vindictive outburst on the part of a man about to meet his maker.

As the evening wore on it occurred to someone that a grave had to be dug. The duty fell to Sergeant John Farley, age twenty-four, who, together with Corporal Dan Hartnett and an unidentified private, checked out two spades and a lantern from regimental quartermaster Charles Bowen and headed toward the graveyard in a drizzling cold rain. The New Hampshire private, who did most of the digging, growled long and hard about having to dig a hole in the darkness and in such miserable weather. When the site was about three-feet deep, someone observed that "Fox was not your average-sized soldier," with the result that more dirt and more growls came out of the wet hole.

In the distance the gravediggers could hear the soft notes of "Pleyel's Hymn." It was one of the brigade bands practicing the Death March:[6]

> We are traveling home to God
> In the way the Fathers trod
> They are happy now and we,
> Soon their happiness shall see.

Saturday, October 31, 1863

The dawn found Major Thomas Connelly, the thirty-three-year-old adjutant of Fox's 8th New Hampshire, riding alone on the road between Opelousas and Barre's Landing. Irish-born Connelly was incensed over the decision to shoot Fox and had departed Opelousas an hour or more before sunrise hoping to convince General Franklin to commute the death sentence. Braving the cold morning air and the ever-present threat of capture, this good Samaritan experienced some hair-raising encounters along the route.

To be sure Connelly was an educated man, but he was also an Irishman and keenly aware that the date, October 31, was Allhallows' eve, the last day of *Samhain*, the ancient Celtic and Anglo-Saxon summer. It was a day for association with the dead, for fire rites, for the practice of divination and for expiatory sacrifice. Laws and pledges must be renewed not only by the ancient Druids but by the common man as well. Perhaps, reasoned Connelly, it was a propitious time to consult the general.

Connelly was also aware that Allhallows' eve took on a mischevious, sometimes even sinister, significance, with ghosts, hobgoblins, fairies, demons and apparitions of all kinds roaming abroad. Shuttering at the thought, Connelly rounded a sharp bend in a wooded section of the trail and pulled up sharply. There, before his disbelieving eyes, was the most spine-tingling, frightening scene he had ever before witnessed. Someone had strung a number of putrid human corpses, or remains thereof, from moss-draped trees at intervals along the way. While blinking his eyes and no doubt hoping they were only apparitions which could be chased away by starting a fire, no matter how small, the Union Major discerned that the morbid scene was all too real. Though the significance was unclear, any old Cajun knew that there could be no more unfortunate gris gris than to meet a corpse on the road. Whether this was the grisly work of Ozeme Carriere and his depraved band of jayhawkers or Vincent's ruthless counter-jayhawkers is uncertain, but for Connelly it was a traumatic experience.

Once beyond Lastie Nezat's plantation, just as the good Major was beginning to settle down, he rounded another bend and found himself face to face with a second apparition, a mounted Confederàte headed directly toward him.

"Good morning, Yank," said the equally startled Texan with a salute.

"And a find good morning to you, Johnnie," answered the horrified Connelly in a shaky Irish-laced voice.

Eyeing each other cautiously the two riders came even, passed, and, at the same time, spurred their horses into a sprint. The war was bad enough without these two frightened souls engaging in individual combat in the middle of a Louisiana swamp. Besides, the Texan was in for another jolt up the trail.

To his everlasting relief, Connelly soon reached the Yankee pickets at Madame Arnault's plantation and entered the sprawling Union camp as the sun was rising. The chilling rain which preceded the cold front of the night before had long since passed leaving the morning uncomfortably cold but clear.

On confronting Major General Franklin, Connelly complained that "it was an outrage to shoot (Fox) for so small a crime." Franklin, however, was unmoved by these irate protestations. Mounting his horse and with a cavalry escort from General Lee, the commanding general started off toward Opelousas. He was going to witness the execution.[7]

By 11:15 A.M. Brigadier General Grover's command was drawn up in the crisp cold air fronting the St. Landry Catholic Church. Considering the large number of troops ordered to witness this morbid affair the preparations were no small matter. Several cavalry regiments and two artillery commands formed the interior double rank of a military formation known as a three-sided square. Eight regiments of infantry, along with a section of the crack 2nd Massachusetts Battery ("Nims' Battery") were formed in double ranks on the exterior line of the square. At precisely 11:30 A. M. Generals Franklin and Grover, accompanied by a number of high-ranking staff officers, walked into the center. They were greeted with the silent but contemptuous gaze of several thousand men of the ranks.

According to military convention, the execution procession was to file through the long double lines of Grover's command and terminate its "death march" on the open side of the square. The entire procession would be led by the provost marshal mounted on his steed. This military "sheriff" would be followed by the band playing the sad notes of "Pleyel's Hymn." Next would come four men bearing a coffin; after which the condemned prisoner, accompanied by Chaplin Cilley and two armed guards, would follow; behind this sad group would be the execution detail—twelve privates, one officer and two "noncoms" from the 8th New Hampshire.

An equal number of privates and officers would follow as a reserve guard should the first detail become fainthearted. All the muskets, save two, would be loaded with ball cartridges. The others would be loaded with blanks, but none of the executioners would know who had the blanks or the lethal balls.

Once in the square Fox was to be blindfolded and read General Orders No. 21 directing his execution. Finally, the prisoner was to be permitted a few moments with Chaplin Cilley before meeting his appointment with destiny.

While the troops were lined up awaiting the procession, a certain private in Fox's 8th New Hampshire, "who had seen men blown apart and dismembered on the field of battle," now blanched at the thought of termination by musketry. In an effort to rationalize the scene he was about to witness, the nervous soldier directed a whispered inquiry to a bewhiskered sergeant in Fox's company.

"Do you think Fox was lying about striking Stokes?" he asked.

The question, while innocent enough, evoked a rash of nervous giggles from the assembled group.

"Fox," answered the sergeant, "lies so much that nobody believes him."

According to the sergeant, Fox had once stumbled upon a large number of cured hams while foraging near Port Hudson. Hurrying back to his regiment, the now condemned soldier related an exaggerated version of his find and asked for assistance in hauling in the load. But knowing him as a story teller, if not outright liar, not a soul came forward.

Thinking to convince his doubters, Fox, according to the sergeant, admitted he was lying about the number of hams he had uncovered.

"The problem was," continued the sergeant, "no one believed he was telling the truth even when he admitted he was lying."

What had once been nervous giggles in the formation now broke into open laughter. Several soldiers inched nearer or inclined their heads in an effort to catch the conversation. According to the sergeant, Fox was near the point of tears over his failure to secure help in bringing in the forage. Finally, several members of his company agreed to go out even at the risk of being arrested or captured, but when the group arrived at the place where Fox had found the hams, "someone else had already stolen the bacon."

The nervous little soldier was unable to contain himself and doubled over with laughter, an act which attracted the attention of his company commander who rushed up and demanded to know "what in hell is so amusing about an execution?" The officer then proceeded to launch a blistering verbal barrage against the innocent soldier.

"Your behavior," he shouted, "is so disgraceful to this regiment that I am dismissing you from the formation with orders to report to me this afternoon for a work detail."

The unidentified soldier, no doubt delighted over his good fortune in not having to witness the execution, "moved out on the double quick." Someone commented on how Fox "can cause so much trouble even when he's not here."

The troubles caused by Private Fox were far from over. According to General Orders No. 21—the execution order—the condemned man was to arrive at the open side of the square by 11:45 A. M. The distance between the Opelousas courthouse, where Fox was incarcerated, and the church, where the square was formed, was just under three-quarters of a mile. In order to arrive on schedule, the detail would have to depart the courthouse some fifteen minutes in advance.

The appointed moment approached, then passed, but still the procession was nowhere in sight.

Lieutenant Dana W. King, assistant to the assistant adjutant-general in the 8th New Hampshire was dispatched by one of the impatient generals to see about the delay.

Once down at the courthouse, King learned that the provost marshal had been patiently waiting outside with the band, coffin carriers, guards and execution detail, when at precisely 11:30 he had entered the courthouse and walked downstairs to the prisoner's quarters. But Fox was not there. In his place, locked up behind bars, was a badly embarrassed guard. Fox, together with at least a half dozen others, "had flown the coop." It was as though some knight errant had stolen the poor fellow away in the night.

Back in the square some red-faced generals pondered their next move. The assembled men did not yet know of the daring breakout and neither Generals Franklin nor Grover were about to inform them. Instead General Franklin announced to the men that he had decided to delay the execution and would defer the whole matter to Major General Banks, commander of the Department of the Gulf.

ST. LANDRY CATHOLIC CHURCH occupied by Union forces, October 1863. ***(Leslie's Illustrated Weekly)***

An embarrassing roar of approval followed Franklin's words. The Don from La Mancha could not have botched it better, but at least he and Grover, along with their staffs, could walk off the field with heads held high.

No one bothered to record for posterity just how Big Mike escaped. According to one unlikely account written many years later, he slipped away during the Rebel attack on Fonda's foragers. While there is no evidence to support this contention, Fox's escape was almost certainly engineered by some of his irate companions. Indeed, the regimental rolls for Company C of the 8th New Hampshire indicates a number of unexplained absences during the months of October and November 1863.

And where did Fox go after his breakout? According to the most romantic account he was harbored by a sympathetic Opelousas family where he became attached to a certain young Cajun girl. The night after the escape, again according to hearsay, Fox visited his gravesite in the biting cold near the St. Landry Church. Feeling a nervous urge in his stomach and no doubt aware that it was Allhallows' eve, when Irishmen everywhere could indulge in a little nonsense, he unbuckled his pants, squatted on the edge, and proceeded to empty his bowels and bladder into the hole which he had cheated out a corpse. Then, in a defiant move reminiscent of graffiti from another war, Big Mike picked up a stick and scrawled some unprintable words which, in effect, stated that Mike Fox relieved himself here.[8]

Sunday, November 1, 1863

At long last General William Franklin began to exercise his limited authority as field commander. The Courtableau, with only one foot of water at Barre's Landing, was not going to rise; nor was the forage situation improving. It was also clear that any further movements toward the north would result in a fight with General Taylor's elusive little army. Under normal circumstances a fight would be fine, but a battle at this juncture would merely delay, if not halt, the movement toward Texas. On the other hand a retrograde movement toward a more secure base of supplies, say, on the Carencro or in Vermilionville, or even New Iberia, would not preclude a march toward the Sabine.

Thus the Great Texas Overland Expedition was put into reverse motion. Generals Weitzel, Grover and Lee, with their two divisions of the XIX Corps and one cavalry brigade (Mudd's) fell back toward the Vermilion. McGinnis and Burbridge, with their two divisions of the XIII Corps and Fonda's cavalry brigade, started down the road toward the old familiar camping grounds on Buzzards' Prairie.

Inadvertantly, Franklin's decision to move anticipated correctly the desires of his superior, Major General Nathaniel P. Banks, enroute to Texas with an amphibious assault force. As soon as Franklin arrived at the Carencro, he received a dispatch from Banks' Chief of Staff, Brigadier General Charles P. Stone in New Orleans:

> The Major-General Commanding sailed from the Southwest Pass...Should he be successful in effecting a lodgement (on the Texas Coast) as he desires, he will immediately dispatch steamers to Berwick Bay, to receive troops as re-enforcements...He desires that the troops should therefore, be so disposed as to enable the prompt shipment of as many as the available steamers can transport...

On the other hand Banks' did not write off the overland expedition through Louisiana:

> ...it is desirable that the enemy should still regard the movement in your direction as the real one, and as much show as possible should be made of an intended push westward toward the Sabine, or northwesterly toward Alexandria. Again, it may become necessary to make the movement in one of those directions...

Clearly the campaign to restore Texas to the Union, whether by land or by sea, was not going well. For more than a month the cumbersome overland expedition had made a false start or two, crept ahead a few miles, and then ground to a halt as soon as another gray will-o-the-wisp flickered into view. Now the expedition was "advancing in the wrong direction."

Whereas Banks' grand strategy—if it could be dignified by that term—made imminent sense to Franklin, it served to confuse others, Confederate as well as Union, thereby reinforcing the widely held view that the Army of the Gulf was led by a group of bungling, indecisive, ineffectual and incompetent generals—which it was. The "Old Commissary-General," never very popular among the men in the Gulf Department, was now referred to as General "Napoleon" P. Banks or, even more scornfully, "Mr. Banks," the civilian general. William Gatchell, special correspondent for the *New York Herald*, began heaping literary abuse upon the commanders even before the retrograde movement commenced:

> For some time past it has seemed as if the War Department had created this department into a sort of Botany Bay. . .The department has been inflicted with the refuse and debris of other armies in the shape of politico-civil-military impracticables, in the garb of generals...

Harry Watts, a private in the 24th Indiana, had thought all along that the delay at Opelousas and Barre's Landing was for a fresh supply of commissaries:[9]

> ...but when we started, we turned our faces south and it was plainly to be seen that the bubble had burst and the Great Texas Overland Expedition was a failure owing to too much strategy by General Banks.

While the Yankees were expressing sentiments of dismay, if not outright contempt for their generals, the citizens of Opelousas and Barre's Landing were both delighted and embittered. Most of the political prisoners, including James Earl Bradley, Joel and Leonce Sandoz, Raimondi Deshotels, Octave Dejean and Charles Close were set free. On the other hand the hostilities and divisiveness which had characterized the Opelousas country since the first invasion grew even more intense. Whites who had taken the loyalty oath were besmirched with the appelation "jayhawker" and insulted, abused and snubbed as were those who had fraternized with or shown any sympathy for the Yankees. Old friends sometimes became violent enemies as was the case when Octave Dejean, the only surviving son of Honore Dejean (the tornado victim) was gunned down in an Opelousas bar by his neighbor, Charles Close. Likewise Captain Bailey Vincent, a scout and notorious troublemaker in William Vincent's cavalry, shot and killed a man in another bar fight. Minister Bradley's one remaining buggy horse, a skinny old mare, was stolen by a jayhawker and he too was viewed with suspicion.[10]

One of the greatest social tragedies of the occupation was that the industrious light-skinned free men of color, including the Meullions, Donatos, Malveauxs, Auzennes, Frilots, Rideaus, Balthazars and Lemelles, who had enjoyed a position of esteem and respect, would soon be just plain "niggers" in the eyes of whites. It would be generations before the wounds healed.

CHAPTER FOURTEEN

DOUBLE TRAGEDY ON BUZZARDS' PRAIRIE

Sunday, November 1, 1863

NO SOONER had the most religion-conscious regiment of the XIII Army Corps—the 24th Iowa—gone into camp on Bayou Carencro than eighteen-year-old Charlie Williams, the son of Captain Charles P. Williams of the same regiment, took a turn for the worse. Private Williams, it will be recalled, had fallen ill during Lawler's cold, wet, windy and senseless march to Opelousas on October 23rd. On reaching the Yankee-occupied town, his sickness had been diagnosed as the ague, a malarial fever characterized by successive cold, hot and sweaty fits. To complicate matters, the frail and sick Iowan contracted a case of chronic diarrhea, causing his condition to deteriorate with each succeeding day.

Possibly because he was Captain Williams' son, Charlie Jr. received very special care. Not only were drum drills and other noisy activities banned from camp during his illness, but the chief medical officer of the 24th Iowa, Surgeon John Witherwax, provided the sick soldier with around-the-clock attention. During the retrograde movement to the Carencro, for example, young Williams rode in a two-wheeled field ambulance under the watchful eye of Assistant Surgeon Sylvannus Cook. But the bumpy movement over wet, boggy and deeply rutted trails proved to be more than the critically ill Williams could bear. Shortly after reaching the Carencro on the warm rainy Sunday evening of November 1st, 1863, he passed away. Clearly, the storm of October 23rd had claimed yet another victim, and Lawler, the big thoughtless general, had earned more enemies.[1]

Even as young Charlie Williams was drawing his last breath, the bells of St. Charles College in nearby Grand Coteau commenced pealing loudly, baffling Confederate and Union pickets alike. By sheer coincidence the residents of the tiny Jesuit-dominated village were celebrating an ancient Roman Catholic ritual, the *clocketeur des trepasses*, or bellman of the dead. Earlier in the day, in accordance wih the practice of All Saints' Day, they had prayed for those deceased members believed to be in Heaven. That night, however, on the eve of All Souls' Day, the living faithful were ringing bells and praying aloud for those departed souls of less sterling characters who were believed to be suffering in purgatory. So, in spite of war, occupation, destruction and suffering, the residents of Grand Coteau, clad in black vestments, rushed about the village streets ringing little hand bells and chanting loudly:[2]

Reveillez! Reveillez!
Entre vous gens qui dormez,
Pensez a l'eternite!
Priez Dieu pour les fidele trepasses,
Requiescat in Pace!

Charlie Williams was not the only soul who might have appreciated the ceremonies that day. Only the day before, on Allhallows' eve, the seventeen-month-old daughter of Francois and Eleonore (nee Stelly) Robin, little Emilie, had passed away near Leonville. She would be joined in death, even before the night ended, by many others who had suffered in the path of the Union army, including thirteen-year-old Onesia Prejean of Grand Coteau and one-month-old Joseph Sidney Johnson of Opelousas. Truly the war was beginning to reap its grim harvest in the civilian populace, especially among the young.[3]

While the village bells tolled for the dead, Colonel James Slack, back in Camp Carrion Crow, penned yet another letter to his dear wife Ann. He had just learned that she would not, after all, be joining him in Louisiana. Though clearly disappointed, he nonetheless seemed relieved. Something had gone awry with the Great Texas Overland Expedition anyway. Thus, with the warm rain beating softly against his brand new "white as wool" tent, Slack's thoughts turned to more romantic notions:[4]

> Could have taken you along just as well as not. Have a very nice rug to lay down alongside my cot, a nice candle stand and every comfort of camp life. The bed is rather narrow for two, but guess we could have both got into it, and had a very comfortable time—Don't you think so?

Over in the camp of the 24th Indiana, near the Carencro bridge, the Hoosiers from Company F were up to their usual nonsense. At the center of attention was a pile of "monster sweet potatoes" which had been "captured" that day. One in particular was said to weigh "nearly five pounds and was near fifteen-inches in circumference and about a foot in length."

The pudgy company glutton, a nineteen-year-old private named Joe Bowers of Evansville, Indiana, cast one hungry look at the oversized yam and wagered a Yankee dollar that he could consume the whole thing for breakfast. Rising to the occasion, Bill Brannan bet a dollar that Bowers claim was bigger than his inflated stomach. Thus challenged, the money was put up and the "gormanderizing" event set for daybreak.

Monday, November 2, 1863

Early Monday morning, while a thick fog hung over Buzzards' Prairie, the disputed yam was boiled and pronounced fit for consumption. Most of Company F was present for the occasion, including the enterprising Harry Watts, whose foraging talents were nothing short of ingenious, and "Fzs"the famous pumpkin eater. With the appearance of Joe Bowers, who had gone to bed on an empty stomach, bets were freely offered and taken. Not wanting to disappoint his audience—or to lose his dollar—Bowers took a deep breath and began eating, all the while being cheered on even by those who bet against him. The only thing lacking was an Acadian string and wind band playing *Lache Pas La Patate:*

> Joe progressed very well until about half done when he began to gasp and call for water which was given him, when he began again and stuck to it manfully and kept crowding it down, very often nearly choking. When he had the last piece in his mouth and was about to crowd it down—his commissary already too full—he gave a heave, and threw out the whole of it, making Joe too sick for duty for several days.

Nonetheless the bet was decided in favor of Bowers who "took his dollar and went to bed cursing his luck and big potatoes."[5]

The 24th Iowa, unlike the 24th Indiana, was concerned with more serious matters. It appeared as though the entire regiment planned to turn out for the funeral of Charlie Williams. Even the grave-digging detail, which normally would be assigned to slackers and disciplinary cases, was made up of real volunteers.

For some reason Colonel John Q. Wilds decided that the regiment should be provided an abundant meal after the funeral. It may be that the crotchety old commander felt this to be the opportune moment to make up for his parsimonious behavior back in Vermilionville when he so zealously enforced General Ord's decree against foraging. At any rate Wilds ordered Company C, under the command of Jeremiah C. Gue, out onto Buzzards' Prairie with instructions to bring back a wagon load of sweet potatoes.

Jeremiah Gue, a popular and dark eyed twenty-four-year-old Captain from Tipton, Iowa, left Camp Carrion Crow with his sweet potato detail shortly before 1 o'clock p. m. An artist before the war, the short and swarthy officer now commandered two mule wagons—empty except for several spades—and a company of perhaps sixty armed foot-soldiers. The foraging detail crossed a tiny coulee and marched past the spot where the gravediggers were occupied with their grim task. On the left was an ancient watering hole which had served prairie Indians and early settlers alike for centuries. Dozens of blue-uniformed soldiers were standing in line awaiting their turn to fill empty canteens or company water barrels. Perhaps in reference to the gravesite of Charlie Williams, Captain Gue shared his feelings with one of the crude wagon drivers. "Oh how I wish this cruel war were over and I could go home to Iowa," he said.

About three miles north of the potato detail, near the point where tiny Bayou Sylvain empties into Bayou Bourbeux, a company of Confederate cavalrymen, perhaps forty in all, entered Buzzards' Prairie. Dressed in Yankee blue which had been captured several months earlier at Berwicks' Bay, Captain Kelly's company of the 2nd Louisiana Cavalry (Vincent's regiment) was on a reconnaissance mission. Superior in horsemanship to anything the Yankees could field, they rode boldly toward Camp Carrion Crow.

In the meantime, Jeremiah Gue continued past the guarded plantation home of Thelismar and Constance Guidry, where the 3rd Division colors indicated that it was occupied by Brigadier General George F. McGinnis who, at the time, was suffering with ague. Not more than two hundred yards northwest of McGinnis' headquarters, Captain Gue spotted the blue-coated Louisianians drawn up in front of the remains of an old cypress rail fence. Gue then made a fatal error. Supposing them to be Union cavalrymen, he spurred his horse forward and rode alone toward the curious Rebels.

On reaching a spot somewhere between 50 and 100 yards from the horsemen, Gue, according to a Union mule-driver, raised his arm in a salute when, without warning, the lead Louisianian, "Pete" Aleman, a private from Abbeville, Louisiana, leveled his "carbine" and fired. Another eyewitness stated that the "ragged appearance" of the Rebels gave them away, causing the suspicious captain to attempt a last ditch effort to wheel his horse about, but it was too late. The Confederate ball entered Gue's breast at a point exactly between the shoulders and killed him instantly. Whatever other virtues Aleman may have possessed, his aim was deadly accurate.

Unsatisfied with merely killing a Yankee, Aleman spurred his horse over the fence and dismounted next to the dead Iowan. He then proceeded to relieve his victim of all personal effects, including watch, pistol, sword, boots and clothing leaving Gue stripped down to his drawers.[6]

The entire episode, which lasted at most one minute, was witnessed not only by the stunned potato detail, but by several hundred other Yankees at the edge of Camp Carrion Crow. Not until the Louisianians began to depart, however, did it dawn on anyone that they were, in fact,

Rebels, at which time a few ineffectual shots expedited their departure.[7]

Hardly had Gue's body cooled off than Buzzards' Prairie was aswarm with cavalry and infantry in a fruitless search for the assassins. The idea that Rebel "guerillas" could operate unimpeded and in broad daylight between two large Union camps was unnerving.

Frustrated and vindictive, the search parties soon turned their attention to the helpless and suffering planters. Practically every adult male on the prairie, including Desire Arnaud, Joseph Boudreaux, and Don Louis Miller, was arrested and brought into camp for interrogation. Just for good measure the roving parties helped themselves to the remaining unharvested patches of sweet potatoes which they brought back to camp by the wagon loads.

The unsupervised foraging was finally brought to a halt, not by the efforts of Union officers, but by the loud report of artillery in the distance. Although it was nothing more than a minor demonstration put on by some of Green's Texans in front of the Bourbeux camp, the nervous Yankees in Camp Carrion Crow interpreted it as a prelude to attack. Accordingly everything was dropped for the time being—including Charlie Williams' funeral—while the troops prepared to move to the support of the Bourbeux defenders. Once it became apparent that the Rebels were not going to attack—at least not at that moment—General Washburn gave the orders to break up and stand by in camp.[8]

For the 24th Iowa the first order of business was the funeral of young Charlie Williams. Stunned by this double tragedy and sobered by the frightening illustration of how close is the living to the dead, the entire regiment, most of whom had been close friends in Iowa even before the war, turned out for the affair. Starting at the Carencro crossing, where the regimental musicians commenced playing the solemn notes of the "Dead March," the large procession followed close on the rear of the wagon bearing the body. The funeral of a private in any other regiment would have been disposed of with as little fuss as possible, but this was the close-knit 24th Iowa where everyone was special. Thus the procession was organized according to military convention, with privates in the front, corporals and sergeants behind and followed in order by lieutenants, captains, majors and finally, by the old gray-headed colonel who brought up the rear.

The "wail" of the fifes and the painful throb of the muffled drum commanded the attention of the entire camp. Soldiers in other regiments momentarily ceased their activities and silently watched; cavalrymen and teamsters respectfully moved to the side of the road, many of them removing their hats or rendering a smart military salute in the mistaken belief that the departed was a high-ranking officer.

On reaching the gravesite the entire regiment drew up in a hollow square. The officiating chaplain, Captain Elias Skinner, walked silently into the center of the somber gathering, bible to his breast, and commenced the eulogy in a low shaky voice.

"We meet today under the most painful of circumstances," he intoned. "God's way may seem strange to mortal beings."

A short moment later came the grand hymn, "Mourn not that his Kin are Far," rendered by a quartet of soldiers. The notes rose and swelled, their voices choked, and they had to wipe away tears to see the words:

> Sleeping soft, the youth shall lie
> Calmly here beneath the sod,
> Where, a living sacrifice
> He his body gave to God.

The words and the music were not new. Many of those present had heard the same words dozens of times before and in dozens of places. Yet there was something sincerely moving about this solemn occasion. A father's son—an only son—was being buried and, unlike previous occasions, both father and son were part of this regiment. Chaplain Skinner continued:

> Man that is born of a woman hath but a short time to live, and is full of misery. In the midst of life we are in death. Suffer us not, at our last hour, for any pains of death to fall from thee. We therefore commit young Charles Williams' body to the ground; earth to earth, ashes to ashes, dust to dust; in sure and certain hope of the Resurrection to eternal life.

Unable to contain his emotions, Captain Charles P. Williams, who heretofore had stood ramrod erect, dropped to his knees and, with hands to face, sobbed quietly. In the meantime a young lieutenant, tears streaking his drawn face, shouted "Fire," whereupon the honor guard rendered one final salute with a volley of musketry.

While the damp Louisiana soil was being shoveled onto the crude wooden coffin, one observer noted that there was not "a dry face among those who attended." But the ordeal was not yet over. Hardly had the shaken group started back to camp than several soldiers picked up the same spades used to bury Charlie Williams and commenced digging again, this time for Jeremiah Gue.[9]

> Now let martial music sound!
> Beat the dead-march for the brave!
> Lower him gently in the ground!
> Fire a volley o'er his grave!

CHAPTER FIFTEEN

DISASTER ON THE BOURBEUX

Monday, November 2, 1863

ON THE WEST bank of Bayou Bourbeux, near the crossing of the Vermilionville-Opelousas stagecoach road, Brigadier General Stephen Gano Burbridge was anything but comfortable. For some inexplicable reason he was expected to hold this rearguard position with only one infantry brigade (Richard Owen's) and one cavalry brigade (Fonda's), altogether about 1700 strong. Even Green's Confederate horse was stronger, and Burbridge was all too aware that they had already moved up to the old Rebel campsite at Bellevue near Bayou Tesson.

At the very least Burbridge thought he held a defensible position. His right and left flanks (north and south) were protected by heavily wooded coulees through which the enemy's cavalry could not move. The same was true of his rear where Bayou Bourbeux offered a natural barrier to an attack from the east. Moreover, Union Camp Carrion Crow was just a short distance across Buzzards' Prairie. There, Washburn and McGinnis were encamped with a much larger force.

The only way Green could attack, reasoned Burbridge, was across the open Opelousas Prairie to the west. That approach, however, narrowed to a three-hundred yard bottleneck in front of the camp, an easily defensible position. There he posted the mobile Parrotts of Nims' 2nd Massachusetts and the 17th Ohio Batteries.

Still, the position seemed precarious, especially in view of the incessant Confederate demonstrations. At 4 A.M., for example, even as a heavy fog hung over the area, shooting erupted along the picket line, and the long roll called the men to their places in battle formation. Once it was determined that the disturbance was only a picket skirmish, the men returned to camp and proceeded to eat breakfast. About 10 o'clock the long roll beat again and the men fell in for another hour or so of skirmishing. Meanwhile, the camp "darkies" loaded the equipage and supplies and stood by their teams in preparation for a possible hasty evacuation.

Burbridge could not determine Green's strategy. Would the Texas general be content merely to harass the pickets, or was he planning to bring on a general engagement? Perhaps a demonstration of his own would be in order. With this thought in mind, Burbridge dispatched his entire force, both the cavalry and infantry brigade, up the Opelousas road.

Sticking close to the treeline, the little horse advanced cautiously toward the Rebel positions. On reaching the familiar *bois d'arc* hedge on the southern end of Charles Lavergne's plantation, the Union batteries opened fire on several hundred mounted Texans out on the Opelousas Prairie. With that, an artillery duel commenced, lasting almost all day. The high point of the skirmish came when a shell, fired from one of the big Parrotts of the 17th Ohio, burst upon a small cabin killing six Rebel snipers. Shortly thereafter the Texans began withdrawing toward Bayou Tesson, and Burbridge's force returned to their rearguard position on the Bourbeux.[1]

As the last rays of sunlight faded over the distant horizon and darkness settled on the gloomy Union camp, a series of erroneous rumors further dampened the frightened men's spirits. Washburn, it was said, had moved his force from the Carencro to Vermilionville and the Rebels had moved around to the rear, surrounding Camp Bourbeux. Green's forces, it was further rumored, had done the unthinkable and displayed the black flag during the day, meaning that no quarter would be asked nor would any be given. In other words the upcoming battle would be a struggle to the last man.

Why Burbridge had chosen to reveal his strength during the day—or weakness in this case—was a genuine mystery and was another whispered topic of conversation around every campfire. Perhaps the thirty-two-year-old general was living up to his reputation as "a mediocre officer, brave, rather pretentious, a good fellow, but not destined for greatness." In any event hardly a soul slept along the Bourbeux that night, and the incessant firing along the dark picket lines suggested that a night attack was imminent. Few could recall being in more frightening circumstances.

Several times during the night Burbridge sent a courier the three miles distance across Buzzards' Prairie asking his superior, General Washburn, for permission to withdraw to Camp Carrion Crow. At first Washburn merely reminded Burbridge that it was Franklin, then in Vermilionville, who desired that both positions be held. But when Burbridge persisted, arguing that it was only a matter of time before the Rebels attacked, Washburn replied with "laconic sarcasm," suggesting that "apprehensions of danger arose from nothing but a scare." According to Dr. J. T. Woods, regimental surgeon of the 96th Ohio, "no alternative was left but to calmly await the onset and die like Romans."[2]

As if the situation wasn't already bad enough, an ominous event soon occurred along the picket lines. Six soldiers of Harai Robinson's 1st Louisiana Cavalry (Union) deserted. One of these, Private Theodore Hauser of New Orleans, had been awaiting this opportunity for months. Originally a Confederate infantryman, he had been detained in New

Orleans by the occupation and had joined the Union regiment as a means to support himself and family. Now, Hauser, together with at least five Robinson-hating Rhode Islanders, went into the Rebel lines where they proceeded to tell everything they knew about the positions, strengths, and weaknesses of the isolated Union outpost.

While Robinson was left to ponder the consequences of his rash actions near Thibodaux several months earlier, when he had incurred the wrath of the Rhode Islanders for executing their mutinous ringleaders, another Union Colonel, Joshua J. Guppey of the 23rd Wisconsin, attempted to repair the damage. No sooner did he learn of the defections than he instructed his officer of the day, Captain James M. Bull, to change the countersign.[3]

Confederate General Thomas Green was not planning to bring on a night action, so changing the countersign was for naught. He was, instead, thinking of how Burbridge had insulated himself against a cavalry attack. Accordingly, he dispatched a night courier to Colonel Oran Roberts, then camped with his infantry brigade of Texans on the north side of the Washington bridge:[4]

> The Gen'l Comdg. directs that you report at his headquarters (the Catholic Church) with your *whole* command *by daylight tomorrow morning.*.

Tuesday, November 3, 1863

A pall of early morning fog, not so dense as that of the preceding day, hung over Buzzards' Prairie, preserving the unique airs of camp life. The familiar smell of a thousand or more dying wood fires mixed pleasantly with the aromas from just as many coffee pots. There was also the pungent smell of horse manure, and one restless soldier even claimed he could detect a faint aroma of tobacco juice drifting over the area, a sure sign that Texans were nearby.

Elsewhere, the Union newspapers of November 3rd contained nothing unusual. Dr. Henry Ward Beecher, the lascivious brother of Harriet Beecher Stowe, was in London lecturing on the evils of slavery and the merits of female suffrage; someone had invented and the War Department was looking into the use of an "infernal machine"; there was a severe train accident on the New Orleans, Opelousas and Great Western Railroad near Thibodaux; another heineous gangland-type slaying involving two Sicilians had occurred in New Orleans; and for the Wisconsin soldiers in the field it was election day.

Nowhere could one find more support for Lincoln and the Union ticket, represented by J. T. Lewis, than in Wisconsin. Though it was a state of immigrants, mainly German and Scandinavian, more than thirteen percent of its 700,000 inhabitants were under arms. Regiments in the field, like the state, reflected its foreign-born content. Colonel Guppey's 23rd Wisconsin, for example, was more than one-half German. Much of the remainder spoke either Cymraeg (Welsh) or some Scandinavian language.

Thus it was with a great deal of enthusiasm that the Bourbeux camp received Major H. A. Fenney, Wisconsin paymaster and election commissioner. Fenney would have been very easy for a Louisianian to dislike. During his long trek up the Teche from Berwick's Bay he had written one derogatory comment after another about the people. Now, on election day, he and Guppey had requested of General Burbridge lighter duty for the Wisconsin soldiers so that he might both pay them and record their votes.

Unfortunately for the voters, the Confederates were in a most uncooperative mood. No sooner did "Reveille" sound than the muffled beat of the long roll summoned the men to battle formation for more than an hour. After breakfast the long roll beat again, further frustrating Fenney's efforts. The paymaster did not seem to appreciate the severity of the situation. "We all supposed it to be a mere guerilla annoyance," he wrote, "and felt quite as safe as if in the streets of Madison." His assistant, a certain Major Brigdon, was struck by the unusual voting facilities:

> ...they use, generally, cartridge boxes for ballot boxes. How suggestive the picture! The cartridge box emptied of its load of death-dealing missiles, to receive a gentler ballot. War putting aside the sword, to take up a mightier weapon.

When the boys of the 23rd Wisconsin finally fell into line to vote, it was to the tune of Captain Charles S. Rice's 17th Ohio Battery lobbing shells into isolated groups of Texans riding nearby. Some of the voters "jocosely suggested" that the Rebels were "trying to get into camp to vote for Palmer," the "Copperhead" candidate. Others wondered out loud if "the butternuts knew what the statute penalty was for disturbing an election."[5]

Even as the soldiers of Wisconsin continued to exercise their constitutional privilege, Sarah Burleigh Arnaud, the blind wife of Desire Arnaud who lived just across the bayou from the Union camp, was receiving an unidentified caller. The visitor, either a neighbor or relative, found her ill, hungry and alone except for two very ancient and faithful former slaves and a small black girl named Rachael. Her husband Desire was gone, having been arrested by the invaders in connection with the death of Captain Gue, and all the household provisions had been taken by the thoughtless foragers.

The visitor went for help. Shortly thereafter two other old slave women and a small white girl, identified only as Modeste, arrived. They brought with them several baskets of provisions, including *pain maize*, buttermilk, pumpkins and a concoction of some old secret family nostrum designed to ameliorate Madame Arnaud's malaise.

Throughout the morning, the ladies heard the ominous cannonading on the north and west side of Bayou Bourbeux. In addition, small numbers of mounted Yankees kept going past the house, first one way, then the other. Clearly something was going on. Finally, just a few minutes past twelve noon, all hell broke loose. The noise from across the Bourbeux became one steady deafening roar, rendering individual explosions indiscernable.[6]

Farther south on Bayou Carencro, General Washburn's troops had been enjoying a meal of pork and yams recently "appropriated" from neighboring planters. Hardly had the feast commenced than the report of artillery called them to arms. The response was automatic: mule teams were frantically hitched to wagons by cursing drivers; the artillery pieces were limbered up to the strains of "Boots and Saddles" and foot soldiers were herded up the road under a storm of shouts and insults.[7]

At the St. Landry Catholic Church in Opelousas, Father Gilbert Raymond had just donned his sacred vestments for yet another wedding ceremony. The last time he had officiated at a wedding, on October 19th, the church had been very nearly shaken off its foundation by heavy artillery fire. The Yankees were gone now and Joseph Bourque and Francoise Aureline Stelley, accompanied by family and friends and weeping mothers, were ready to walk the aisle. Twice they had postponed this wedding because of the Union presence, but today, no matter what, they were determined to unite in matrimony.

No sooner had Father Raymond commenced the ceremony, however, than the boom of cannon forced him into a speedy recitation of the marriage vows. Occasionally, while he was attempting to shout above the din, the artillery would suddenly die down and he would be embarrassed to hear his loud voice reverberating throughout the church. Finally, once the vows were exchanged, a lady friend of the bride came forward to sing a melancholy tune for the young couple. In it, which no one could hear for all the noise, she bemoaned the loss of sweet liberty and the impending forfeiture of her young friend's virginity:[8]

> Adieu, fleur de jeunesse!
> Il faut enfin t'abandonner
> La noble qualite de fille
> Me faut aujourd'hui la quitter

In the meantime the Bourbeux defenders seemed more than equal to the task at hand. What they did not know, however, was that even as Nims' guns and the heavy Parrotts of the 17th Ohio kept the roaming Texans at bay, a group of Texas infantrymen, numbering about a thousand, were quietly approaching their position through the unguarded woods.

Early that morning, long before the Wisconsin soldiers had commenced voting, Colonel Oran Roberts, the Texas secessionist-turned-soldier, had taken breakfast with General Thomas Green in Opelousas. Roberts was instructed to march down the Opelousas road toward Bellevue, past the Confederate camp near Bayou Tesson, and move on toward Benjamin Rogers' and Lezin Lavergne's plantations. From the latter place he was to turn left and approach the Union position through the thick woods between the road and bayou. Their plans thus established, Roberts had marched his anomalous brigade of Texas foot soldiers ("Walker's web-footed cavalry") through Opelousas singing a parody to the strains of "Dixie":[9]

Oh there was a Yankee by the name of Banks,
but he couldn't climb a Stonewall fence.
Just giveaway, giveaway, giveaway commissaries.

They had marched not less than twenty miles from a point north of Washington and were about to go into battle without rest. On reaching the famous *bois d'arc* hedge at the southern end of Lezin Lavergne's plantation, Colonel Roberts, "though very pale and feeble" and recovering from a severe illness, gave the command: "Left, half wheel!," placing the 11th Texas on the extreme left, the 18th in the center and the 15th on the right. With the gallant old saber-waving Colonel leading the way, the Texans encountered "deep gullies, logs, brush, branches and curves of the bayou." The 11th Texas "crossed and recrossed the bayou, sinking in mud and water to their waists."[10]

Still, Union General Burbridge remained completely ignorant of Roberts' approach through the woods. As far as he knew, the only Rebels in the vicinity were General Green's mounted Texans, and it was common knowledge that they would not stray very far from their beloved horses. For that reason, he and his brigade commander, Colonel Richard Owen, simply ordered the 17th Ohio Battery out onto the open prairie near the north side of Urbaine Lavergne's house, where they could more easily shell Green's mounted Texans. The field battery was accompanied by the 67th Indiana Infantry, about two hundred strong, and the 6th Missouri Cavalry. The remaining infantry regiments—the 23rd Wisconsin, 96th Ohio and 60th Indiana—were drawn up from left to right, respectively, facing west toward the open prairie, rather than north toward the real danger.

Dr. James B. Hunter, assistant surgeon of the 60th Indiana, was among the first to spot Roberts and his advancing infantrymen. Thinking their skirmishers to be merely a small body of dismounted cavalry sent to harass the rear he nonetheless dispatched a rider to inform General Burbridge of their presence. Within moments, however, a loud Rebel yell rent the air as wave after wave of gray-coated Texans, bayonets thrust before them, charged the exposed right flank of the 60th

Indiana. "Balls whistled and popped around us until we were obliged to retreat precipitately, recalled Surgeon Hunter.[11]

Racing away from the Texas infantrymen and their "hidious yells" which "were by no means pleasant," the 60th Indiana fled directly through the ranks of the 96th Ohio which, in turn, joined the rout. General Burbridge, attempting to forestall disaster, galloped to and fro before the fleeing Westerners as though attempting to turn a herd of stampeding cattle. Waving his hat, shouting, cursing and making threats upon the officers' lives, he managed, at least temporarily, to slow them to a walk. He then rushed back to the 23rd Wisconsin, still stationed near the front of the camp, and shouted to Colonel Guppey: "For God's sake, go in 23rd and stop them! You will find it hotter than hell."[12]

As paymaster Fenney and Brigdon looked on, the 23rd Wisconsin broke into a double-quick, moved toward the timbers and disappeared from sight while smoke drifted down upon them. Guppey seemed to be everywhere. Shouting and cursing he was up and down the field in a fury, his face dripping perspiration, his black horse all flecked with foam. Dashing through the underbrush with drawn saber, he somehow managed to head off the retreating Ohio and Indiana soldiers and rally them in a small coulee, or ravine, on the north side of camp. From that point they poured volley after volley of deadly accurate fire into Roberts' Texans.

Private J. F. Greer of the 18th Texas fell mortally wounded as a Minie struck his thigh. His brother, M. G. Greer, was hit on the thorax. Corporal E. Willingham of the same regiment had a portion of his face laid open by a piece of shrapnel. Over in the 15th Texas, casualties were equally heavy. Private W. F. Pribble was instantly killed as a ball entered his head. Before the day was over, his brother, James Pribble, would be captured. Private H. Story was struck in the scrotum. Dropping his hand to the wounded area, his hand, too, was shattered by a Yankee bullet. At almost the same moment Private P. Alonzo felt a bullet glance off his Enfield. Looking down he was horrified to note that his right index finger—his trigger finger—had disappeared from his hand.[13]

With the Texans slowed down in the woods, General Burbridge then directed his attention to the activities on the western prairies, where hordes of Confederate horsemen were forming near the north side of the exposed 67th Indiana Infantry and 17th Ohio Battery. The 17th Ohio fired off several salvos, limbered up to the waiting teams of frightened horses and very prudently retreated back to a point near camp. The 6th Missouri Cavalry quickly followed suit.

The engagement—called the Battle of Carrion Crow Bayou by the Texans—was quickly turning into a rout, and was to give new words to an old Confederate tune, "Here's Your Mule":[14]

When Green he got to Carrion Crow,
On his mule, on his mule,
Said he, "I'll fight with half a show";
On his mule, on his mule.
The cavalry commenced attack,
And soon they drove the Yankees back.
Green's lips with joy began to smack,
On his mule, on his mule!

Yet, in spite of overwhelming Confederate superiority on the prairie, the 67th Indiana, numbering about two hundred, were not being driven back. On the contrary, they appeared to be maneuvering to engage Green's cavalry even though they were outnumbered by more than ten to one.

General Burbridge reasoned that the men of 67th, under their Prussian-born commander, Colonel Theodore E. Buehler, would be far more effective if they would fall back to a position just south of the coulee. There they could better defend themselves while preventing the Texans from attacking the rear of the forces engaged there.

Burbridge then dispatched an aide, Captain George W. Friedley, with instructions for the endangered 67th Indiana to fall back. The 67th, at that time, was positioned about a half mile west of the battle then raging in the woods and about two-thirds of a mile from the nearest other treeline. But Buehler, in recognition of the impossibility of marching his men that distance over the open prairie while almost surrounded by the saber-waving Texans, instead ordered the regiment to form into a hollow square—a standard military manuever for infantry confronted by cavalry. Observing this manuever through his field glasses, Burbridge supposed that Friedley did not get through and sent out a second aide with instructions to fall back.

If Buehler's situation was precarious, one can well imagine the emotions experienced in the nearby house of Urbaine Lavergne. Since the middle of October when the Federals had marched back into their lives, the little plantation had been the scene of daily skirmishes, foraging or some other outrage. The barn and outbuildings, already stripped of produce by the plundering Westerners, had been reduced to little more than rubble by artillery bombardments from both sides; several neighbors, and possibly close relatives, had been killed or badly injured during such engagements; then Urbaine Lavergne, age fifty-six, had been arrested as yet another dangerous suspect following the death of Captain Gue. That left at home Mrs. Lavergne (nee Aureline Richard) and seven children, mainly girls, ranging in age from five to twenty.

Now, as the biggest battle yet raged over their heads, the terrified inhabitants sought cover under tables, in armoires or inside the fireplace. In the meantime cannon fire toppled chinaberry trees, blasted craters in the yard and blew open windows and doors. During a slack point in the exchange, little Charles Nicholas Lavergne, a battle-hardened veteran at age eight, rushed out of his hiding place and quickly slammed the damaged front door shut. No sooner did he return to his sanctuary, however, than it was blown open again, knocking the latch-pin off the door and filling the house with dust, splinters and smoke. Once more little Charles slammed the door and replaced the pin, but only to see it blown open again. Frustrated in his efforts he marched back to the door, closed it and once more inserted the latch-pin, this time resolving to hold the pin in place as the dangerous artillery barrage rocked the house back and forth.

Even as the courageous youngster stood by the door with his hand over the latch-pin, an enormous explosion rent the air, blasting the door from its very hinges and sending its splintered remains careening across the cypress wood floor. Incredibly Charles Nicolas Lavergne was not killed, nor was he even injured, but he nonetheless very prudently scurried back to a place of relative safety. Only later did it occur to him that by some strange quirk of fate he still held the latch-pin in his hand.[15]

In the meantime Buehler's 67th Indiana found its situation deteriorating badly. Not only were some of the mounted Texans making their way to the left and rear of the embattled regiment but a rapidly advancing dismounted force, the 4th and 5th Texas (referred to by the men as the 1st and 2nd Texas) was approaching through the high weeds and cornstalks from the north. To further compound matters, the famed Valverde and Daniels' Batteries were within easy range and could, at any moment, annihilate the Hoosiers—and the Lavergne family—with grape and cannister:

> The First and Second did dismount
> Off their mules, off their mules;
> No time was there their force to count,
> Nor their mules, nor their mules;
> But boldly pushing thro' the weeds,
> Spent not their time with words, but deeds;
> Caused many a Yank to count their beads,
> On their mules, on their mules!

Burbridge could not from his position see the approach of the dismounted cavalry, the artillery batteries, or the large numbers of mounted Texans filing down and around the left flank of the 67th Indiana. Seeing no response to his instructions, he angrily dispatched yet a third messenger with more strongly worded instructions. By this time, however, the infantry regiment was almost surrounded by Madison's, Lane's and Stone's Partisan Texas Rangers, and even General Burbridge recognized the impossibility of salvation. Accordingly, the entire 67th Indiana Infantry, for the second time in its short inglorious history, struck the regimental colors and fell into Confederate hands intact. Clearly two hundred Yankees on foot and in the open were no match for several thousand Texans on horseback:[16]

> Two regiments further on the right,
> On their mules, on their mules
> Caused many a Yank the dust to bite,
> Off their mules, off their mules.
> Their names was Madison's and Lane's;
> They gave the Yanks the fits and pains,
> While some they held on by the manes,
> Of their mules, of their mules.

The entire spectacle was witnessed by Dr. J. T. Woods, regimental surgeon of the 96th Ohio, who was tending the wounded near the tree line. "The fierce cavalry sweep like a whirlwind among them with gleaming sabres," he wrote. "The swift riders enfold them and, almost without resistance, march them away captive before our eyes."

Writing forty years after the event, Corporal Rueben B. Scott of the captured 67th Indiana made an attempt to glorify his regiment's disgrace for posterity. Scott wrote that the Hoosier regiment was under orders to "hold the place at all hazards." Presumably for that reason Buehler refused the orders to fall back:

> When Burbrage (sic) again sends orders to fall back to the woods...it is now too late, as Green's masses were upon us...and entirely surrounding us...and they pour a storm of minie into our ranks; and by this time the cavalry was charging us, upon flank and rear...while at this juncture both forces become all mixed, and a pandemonium of sticking with bayonets, clubbing of muskets and shooting with revolvers. Meanwhile a storm of grape and cannister was pouring into this fighting mass from front and rear, while a cloud of smoke is spread over the scene.

After a great deal more smoke, blood, cannister, grape and wind, Scott, writing in the present-tense, noted that "Green's men overpowers our troops and are marching us off as prisoners." He failed to explain how it was that for all the clubbing, stabbing and cannon fire, only ten men in the 67th were wounded and all these from gunfire.[17] The only damage they inflicted upon the attacking Texans fell entirely on James Holt of the 5th Texas Cavalry, who had his ring finger severed from his hand.

Back in the coulee, where Roberts' Texas infantrymen had caught the Federals off guard, both sides were engaged in "a desperate and prolonged struggle." With fixed bayonets the long gray lines of Texas infantry "steadily advanced in quick-time to the base booming of cannon and the tenor rattling of minie." By the dozens they continued to

CAPTURE OF THE 67TH INDIANA according to Corporal Rueben Scott in his *History of the 67th Regiment.*

CAPTURE OF THE 67TH INDIANA as depicted by C.E.H. Bonwill, special artist for *Leslie's Illustrated Weekly.*

fall. Captain J.L.H. Stillwell of the 11th Texas was struck in both buttocks as he turned to urge on his men. Private L. Wimberly of the same regiment fell with a Minie ball through his throat. A friend, Private W. A. Thompson, stooped to help, but was shot through the head and instantly killed.

Private Tyre Hancock of Dallas, Texas, one of the advance skirmishers, "saw a fine large tree which I was determined to get to." So determined was he that on reaching his destination he looked back to see that he had run far ahead of his comrades. From that point of relative safety he looked on in horror as his good friend, Green Duncan, was shot dead while trying to reach the tree. "This little battle has never figured much in history," wrote Hancock some fifty years later, "but it was quite an event with us that took part in it."

Even Colonel Roberts, the salty old judge had a close call. As he approached the ravine a Yankee took aim and fired, but hit his horse instead. Colonel Roberts stumbled up and; waving his saber aloft, shouted "Charge 'em boys!"

Up to that point, about eighty yards distance from the ravine, the Confederates had fired but little. But now, according to a Texas correspondent identified only as Exum "our boys poured a murderous fire on them along the whole line."[18]

The volley was indeed murderous. In Joshua Guppey's 23rd Wisconsin more than three dozen fell wounded or were killed under the withering barrage. Guppey himself was struck near the left knee. "He sank upon the ground," according to one of his men, "telling the boys to 'rally on them, boys! Rally on them! Never give up'!" His Sergeant-Major, John L. Jolley, was hit in the abdomen and right arm. Private Alonzo Gilbert Jack, a nineteen-year-old farmboy from Madison, Wisconsin, was struck in the face and instantly killed. He had written his last letter from this same location only two weeks before.[19]

The casualties in the 60th Indiana were equally frightening. Corporal Charles McGarvey stood to take aim and was hit by three balls. Sergeant Henry Endicott fell pierced with a ball in his left eye; others fell by the dozens, many of them killed instantly or mortally wounded.[20]

Hardest hit was the 96th Ohio. Not less than a dozen died fighting in the ravine while some three dozen more fell wounded, many of them severely. Among the latter was Private Julius V. Wood, who had constructed the hogshead shelter back in Barre's Landing. His right arm, in fact his writing arm, was so badly shattered that it would soon have to be removed. Dr. J. T. Woods looked on with horror as the color-bearer fell, while "a sweet-faced young boy," Charley Stanfield, dropped as "a bullet whistles through his breast." Rushing to the latter, Woods heard him whisper the word "mother" before expiring. William McDonald, a sixteen-year-old private in the 96th, managed to slip away unscathed. He would live to fight one more great battle, but with George Armstrong Custer at Little Big Horn.[21]

Unable to withstand the punishment, the coulee defenders broke and ran and were pursued by "a shout such as only Texans can give." On emerging from the woods, however, the terror-striken "heroes of Vicksburg" found not safety, but Green's cavalry "with open arms to receive them."

Witnessing the disaster from the road in front of the Union camp was the Wisconsin paymaster and commissioner, Major H. A. Fenney. On seeing his regiment fleeing the woods in front and the Texas horsemen coming on "with the velocity of the wind," he quickly "bundled his greenbacks promiscuously" into a black iron box, commandeered a mule-drawn ambulance and disappeared under a cloud of gunsmoke near the bridge. Assistant paymaster Brigdon was last seen hanging out the rear firing at a "squad of greedy Rebel cavalry at his very heels."[22]

By contrast, the war correspondent for the *New York Herald* stood his ground. For weeks he had written one scathing report after another regarding the competency—or lack thereof—of the generalship in the Army of the Gulf. Now, in the highest traditions of journalism, William Gatchell intended to verify his contention. Wearing a wide-brimmed white hat and with his civilian trousers tucked neatly into polished boots, Gatchell planted a white flag beside himself, drew up a barrel, sat down and began taking notes. There he sat with bullets whizzing all around until it became clear that Judge Roberts and his Texas infantrymen had little respect for the northeastern press. Mounting his horse, he finally bolted for the rear, but only to have the animal shot from under him. Though unharmed, William Gatchell would spend the next two months in a Rebel prison.[23]

At the bayou bridge the soldiers of the 83rd Ohio seemed to be moving in the wrong direction, creating a traffic problem. An hour or so before, they had started toward Grand Coteau on a foraging expedition, but on hearing the report of artillery and musketry they had rushed back and began crossing over just in time to see their frightened comrades rushing from the woods. Finding themselves moving one direction and their retreating comrades another, the 83rd was about to join the rout until the omnipresent Burbridge galloped up and gestured frantically toward a stranded section of the 17th Ohio. "For God's sake, boys, save the battery!" he shouted. "You have never run yet, and I know you will not run now. Will you save the battery?"

Needing no further coaxing, the 83rd Ohio, three hundred strong, formed into a hollow square and marched boldly toward the big gun, temporarily driving back the startled Texans. On reaching the desperate artillerymen, some of whom were fighting Texans with their rammers, the 83rd found the lead team dead and all the other horses wounded. Working rapidly, they cut loose the traces, limbered the gun up to some badly wounded horse flesh and started it toward the bridge.

On their retreat, Sergeant Datus Meyers, the color-bearer, spotted his counterpart in the 23rd Wisconsin, Sergeant Henry Morton, struggling with his regiment's colors. Though badly wounded, (his leg would have to be amputated) Morton was still trying to hold the Wisconsin colors aloft. Meyers rushed over and, with the assistance of another Ohioan, Private George Sweeney, managed to carry the colors to a place of safety.

Another Ohio soldier, Corporal Isaac Jackson, stumbled and fell even as the Rebel cavalry was coming down on their rear, "swearing and cursing" and striking the battery horses with their sabers. Jumping up, Jackson ran alongside one of the caissons he had just helped to save. The officer in charge, wrote Jackson, "was frantically urging the drivers on with language very forcible and full of meaning." The frightened corporal managed to grab hold of the fifth, or spare, wheel mounted on back and was dragged to a place of safety across the bayou.[24]

The commander of the 96th Ohio, Colonel Albert H. Brown, would have posterity believe that he too was saved by a freakish bit of luck. A veteran of the Mexican War, having served as a private under Zachary Taylor, he was attempting to lead his troops to safety across the bayou. "Brave boys," he called out over the din of battle, "to stay is death; fall back as best as you can to the other side of the woods. We will rally there."

Brown then proceeded to "empty his revolver into the advancing Rebel cavalry." The return fire, according to Brown, inflicted a slight wound on his horse and "in a mad frenzy the animal dashed away," conveniently toward the bayou, and "with one desperate leap clears the ravine":[25]

Our cannoneers did play,
On their mules, on their mules,
Off crowds of Yankees in their way,
On their mules, on their mules.
Our infantry did then advance,
And bid the Yanks St. Vitus dance;
Here some escaped—must been for chance,
On their mules, on their mules.

There then occurred a spectacle which must have been one of the most unusual of the entire campaign. The Texas Confederates, clothed in rags, armed with their own muskets, Bowie knives, squirrel rifles or double-barreled shotguns, and riding their own steeds, were in desperate need of provisions. The Union camp, being rapidly abandoned by its previous inhabitants, provided a far more attractive target than the hundreds of fleeing, panic-stricken Yankees. Consequently, the victors proceeded to sack the camp, taking clothing, money, tents, blankets, small arms and ammunition, horses, mules, wagons and anything else of value. "Their proclivities to steal," wrote a correspondent for the

COLONEL JOSHUA J. GUPPEY
(Library of Congress)

COLONEL A. H. BROWN
(Woods, Services of the 96th Ohio)

ATTACK ON THE 60TH INDIANA through the wooded approach to Union Camp Bourbeux *(Leslie's Illustrated Weekly)*

Lacon *Illinois Gazette*, "checked the progress of the enemy, or else we might have fared worse."

Standing amid the debris were dozens of black cooks, assistants and camp followers, many of whom were waving white flags to indicate their status as non-combatants. Some of the Texans managed to mobilize this frightened group and ordered them to pile up the undesirable booty and put it to the torch. Consumed in the fire were muster-rolls, company records, private letters and diaries, and, most importantly, Major Fenney's completed election ballots.[26]

While the sacking was going on, hundreds of Union soldiers were still trying to make their way to the rear, many of whom were totally ignored by their conquerors. Indeed, supply wagons, artillery pieces, foot soldiers and cavalrymen were clogging the narrow log bridge. Others, panicked by the marauding Texans, simply jumped into the water or directed their mule teams across without benefit of bridge. As a result wagons were mired, caissons and artillery overturned, and numerous animals—including at least two soldiers—were drowned in the murky waters.

According to one scribe, Burbridge himself was among the last across. Falling in unnoticed among the 96th Ohio, the Kentucky general seized the battle flag of the regiment and "in full defiant tones begins to sing that grand old battle hymn"

> Rally round the flag, boys
> Rally once again,
> Shouting the battle-cry of freedom

A soldier of the 17th Ohio, a "stolid German artilleryman," was sighted by a Texan as he was "stoically marching to the rear, carrying his swab-stick on his shoulder." Galloping up and pointing a revolver in his face, the Confederate commanded him to surrender, but the artilleryman had just seen the Texan empty his revolver and instead "hit his horse over the head with such a blow that it knocked him down," sending the "reb off and away in no time." A second Texan rushed up brandishing a not-empty revolver and shouted "Halt! Halt! you Yankee vagabound":

> The insulted and indignant gunner turned quickly on his heel, at the same instant replying, 'you go to hell', and furiously swinging his swab-stick, smashed the head of his would-be captor into jelly. Instantly 'shouldering arms' he marched on, unconcerned as ever, toward the Carrion Crow.

Another group of retreating Germans, members of the 23rd Wisconsin, directed some obscene remarks in their own language toward the plundering Texans. A flood of equally profane German was hurled back by a group of teutonic Texans, who were busily engaged disassembling tents.[27]

Private John Griffin Jones, a Welshman in Guppey's 23rd Wisconsin, was collared by a big Texan while making his way to the "biough." Writing in Cymraeg, the strange, consonant-laden Celtic tongue of Wales, he explained the incident to his parents as translated below:[28]

> I was forced to lay down my arms and 'run on the double-quick to the rear, you son of a bitch'. I went as ordered until I found that there was no one guarding me, so I threw myself on the ground and pretended to be dead. They passed me by the hundred...and did not waste time to look at me.

Perhaps the only bona fide hero of the fiasco was twenty-three-year-old William Marland, a gunnery lieutenant in the 2nd Massachusetts. Marland was trying to maneuver his big Parrott gun off the field when several Texans came up and ordered him to the rear. His captors were distracted, however, by the possibility of the more lucrative personal booty in the unoccupied tents and, as in the case of Jones, left him even before he had turned around. Seeing his opportunity and with the strains of "Boots and Saddles" stirring his blood, Marland made a courageous decision to rush the bayou with his eight-horse team, notwithstanding the fact that the bridge was then under the control of Major Nathaniel Caraway's skirmishers from the 11th Texas Infantry.

Marland's lone charge across the bridge caused several astonished Texans to jump, or be dumped, into the muddy waters. The bringing off of this section of Nims' Battery deservedly earned for Marland his nation's highest honor, a Congressional Medal of Honor and, in Washburn's words, "extorted (sic) the admiration of every beholder," even the Texans.[29]

The first phase of the battle ended with almost total victory for the attacking Confederates. The west bank was now cleared of the Union presence except for hundreds of prisoners, the abandoned dead and wounded, and the accoutrements of war scattered over the field.

Yet, the real prize was on the east bank. There, amid the remnants of the decimated infantry brigade, was a long supply train then guarded by Fonda's horse. Thinking to cut them off, Green ordered across "Ed" Waller's Battalion and Colonel P.T. Herbert's 7th Texas Cavalry (frequently referred to as the 3rd Texas):

> The Yankees their distance did enlarge,
> On their mules, on their mules,
> When Herbert led the Third to charge
> On their mules, on their mules.
> He charged the troops of Wisconsin;'
> For shot nor shell cared he a pin,

But cried, my boys, go in and win,
On your mules, on your mules!

If Sarah Burleigh Arnaud had not been blind and if she had dared look, she would have witnessed that portion of the Battle of Bayou Bourbeux which took place on the east bank. Even without looking, the terrified lady knew the fighting was drawing near. Indeed, Confederate artillery shells, aimed at the retreating soldiers, were exploding all around. The two little girls, Rachael and Modeste, were ordered into the fireplace by an old slave woman. There, the terrified girls were told, they would be safe from the explosions and the bullets now impacting against the house.[30]

Buzzards' Prairie was alive with noise and the spectacle of animals, men, wagons and artillery pieces going in all directions. On the road in front of the Arnaud house, a train of mule-drawn supply wagons, not less than two miles long and driven by black teamsters, rushed "over the prairie in a flat stampede," heading "pell-mell," toward the Carencro. From the woods in back came what remained of the "heroes of Vicksburg" most of whom had discarded their muskets and, as Harry Watts related it, were "double quick running for dear life. The mules snorting, the drivers whipping and a cursing, men riding, others on foot, 'helter skelter', with the rebel cavalry in their rear a coming at a full charge."[31]

At the same time reinforcements from Camp Carrion Crow were headed in the opposite direction. Colonel James R. Slack, whose brigade was moving to the rescue, saw "wagons filled with great healthy men with their guns in their hands, teams in a full run, negroes eyes nearly all white, looking back over their shoulders." Slack wrote his wife that "I abused the cowardly pups as much as I had time and ability to do, and our boys jeered them a great deal, but they took no offense at it. It was a novel sight indeed."

Colonel Thomas Bringhurst, whose 46th Indiana Infantry was in the lead, was stunned to see so many "men, wagon trains, and artillery dashing out of the woods. Rebel cavalrymen were...striking teamsters and artillerymen with their sabers. Many of them were overtaken and the men killed." Thinking to head off the Rebels, he ordered his men to conceal themselves in the south ditch bordering Arnaud's property.

Among the terror-stricken and fleeing Yankees were paymasters Fenney and Brigdon of Wisconsin. Their mule-drawn ambulance was driven by Jonathan Pratt, a recently recruited black teamster. Pratt, who had once belonged to General John Pratt of Opelousas, feared for his very life if captured and was furiously urging on his mules to greater speed.

As the ambulance approached Desire Arnaud's property, Pratt decided to take a short cut rather than follow the meandering of the

NEW YORK HERALD CORRESPONDENTS in the field (National Archives)

LIEUTENANT WILLIAM MARLAND, 2nd Massachusetts Battery, earned the Congressional Medal of Honor for his heroic dash across the Bourbeux.

road. But, alas, Arnaud's sod fence and ditch forced the group to parallel the obstacle until they could turn south in front of the Frenchman's house. The pursuing Texans, by contrast, simply jumped the ditch, crossed to the rear, and were rapidly approaching the train from the side. "It appeared as though our chances for going to Dixie were of the first class" wrote Fenney.

Just behind Fenney was another terror-stricken Yankee, George W. Friedley, General Burbridge's aid, who was riding his horse "at a rate that would be a credit to a trained racer." On both sides and to his rear were six or eight Texans "screaming and yelling, hair flying, flourishing revolvers and sabres in the air calling on him to surrender":

> When Burbridge heard of Green's Brigade,
> On their mules, on their mules,
> Thus to his aid-de-camps he said:
> 'On your mules, on your mules!
> I see that Green is at his old pranks,
> He's no respect for us poor Yanks;
> I'm off to join my old friend Banks;
> Where's my mule! Where's my mule!

Just as it appeared that Fenney, Friedley and the train would be cut off by the flanking Texans, Thomas Bringhurt's 46th Indiana, who heretofore had distinguished themselves only by their foraging propensities, sprang from the southern ditch of Arnaud's property and began firing rapidly, dropping several Texans on the spot. At almost the same moment a section of Nims' Battery galloped up and began pouring shot and shell into the Confederates without even unlimbering from their prolonges. Friedley, finding himself out of immediate danger, rode up to Bringhurst saluting and exclaiming, "My God Colonel," he cried, "I never was so glad to see you in my life."[32]

One of the Texans, Private A. L. Clark of Waller's Battalion, spurred his horse to the rear in an attempt to excape the ambuscade but only to crash head-on into an oncoming wagon. The unfortunate Confederate was propelled forward by his momentum, glanced off the side of the wagon, and landed in a heap beside the road. The black teamsters, unable to free the tangle of dead and broken animals, abandoned their burden and moved off afoot. Several other Texans came up, examined their wounded companion and, finding that his right leg was shattered, carefully removed him to Arnaud's front gallery. There Clark remained for hours crying out in pain.[33]

For some reason, one of the Texans rode his horse up onto the porch and then through the large front door of Arnaud's house. On his exit an officer inquired if anyone was inside.

"Just a sick lady and some old darkies," he answered.

"Well, get them the hell out before they all get killed!" commanded the superior.

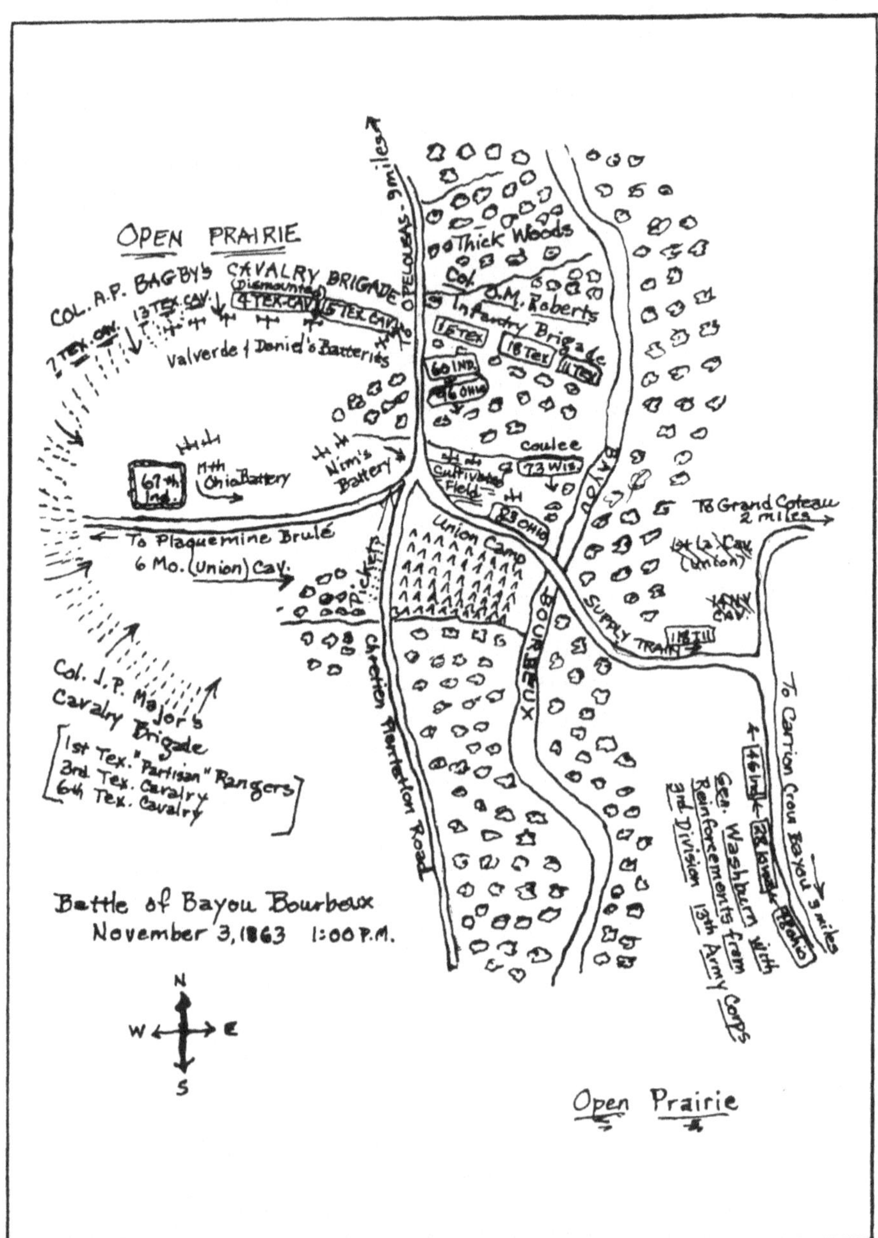

OPEN PRAIRIE
COL. A.P. BAGBY'S CAVALRY BRIGADE
(Dismounted)
7 TEX. CAV.
13 TEX. CAV.
4 TEX. CAV.
5 TEX. CAV.
Valverde & Daniel's Batteries
To OPELOUSAS - 9 miles
Thick Woods
Col. O.M. Roberts Infantry Brigade
15 TEX
18 TEX
11 TEX
60 IND.
96 OHIO
17th Ohio Battery
67th Ind.
Nim's Battery
Coulee
73 WIS.
Cultivated Field
23 OHIO
To Grand Coteau 2 miles
To Plaquemine Brulé
6 Mo. (Union) Cav.
Pickets
Union Camp
1st (La.) Cav. (Union)
14 N.Y. CAV.
SUPPLY TRAIN
118 ILL.
BAYOU BOURBEUX
Chretien Plantation Road
Col. J.P. Major's Cavalry Brigade
1st Tex. "Partisan" Rangers
3rd Tex. Cavalry
6th Tex. Cavalry
To Carrion Crow Bayou 3 miles
46 Ind.
Gen. Washburn with Reinforcements from 3rd Division 13th Army Corps
Battle of Bayou Bourbeux
November 3, 1863 1:00 P.M.
N
W
E
S
Open Prairie

According to oral history, the stranded females, including two very frightened little girls names Rachel and Modeste, were placed on horses and hastily moved several hundred yards away to a point (present day Sunset) where a group of citizens had come out to delight in the Yankee rout.

William Burleigh, Sarah's brother, would never forget that day. At the time he lived in the Burleigh family home currently on Burleigh Lane near the village of Grand Coteau. Frightened by the possibility that the battle would spill over to Grand Coteau, he had sent his wife and children to a relative's home. Then, like dozens of other Grand Coteau residents, he had climbed onto his roof to get a glimpse of the fighting. Even while the battle raged Sarah was brought to his house "by two or three negroes in a half-naked condition." She was bleeding from scratches, hysterical and too sick to comprehend what was happening. It would be days before she could even speak.[34]

Sarah Burleigh was not the only female casualty of the conflict. A short distance away, also in Grand Coteau, Marie Coralie Breaux, the pregnant wife of Valsin Breaux, was so terrified of the battle then raging that she, like so many others in the paths of the opposing armies, soon gave birth to Jean Baptiste Breaux.[35]

Back at Camp Carrion Crow, Captain William Titus Rigby, now fully recovered from his bout with the ague, had watched apprehensively as the 3rd Division of the XIII Corps marched to the support of the Bourbeux defenders. Rigby's regiment, the 24th Iowa, along with the 24th Indiana, the 29th Wisconsin and a small portion of the 56th Ohio had been left behind to guard the sprawling camp. That day was also Rigby's birthday and he could never remember a more unhappy one. Two days ago Charlie Williams had died. The day before his friend, Captain Gue, was assassinated and he, as officer of the day for the 24th Iowa, was in charge of the funeral detail. Now, much to his disgust, the sad affair would have to be postponed because of the activity on the Bourbeux. And if that wasn't bad enough, sharp firing soon broke out along the front of the camp.

Rushing toward the firing, Rigby and his cousin, Alfred, met "a large squad of negroes of both sexes running for dear life from the sharp crack of musketry and roar of cannon." Apparently Colonel George W. Baylor's 1st Texas Mounted Rifles (sometimes called the 2nd Regiment Arizona Brigade) had swept around the left flank of the besieged Bourbeux defenders, crossed the bayou behind the Chretien plantation, and commenced an assault on Camp Carrion Crow.

At the scene of the shooting were two companies of the 56th Ohio who were then guarding an unspecified number of artillery pieces. Captain Thomas W. Kinney, age twenty-two and one of the officers of the day, eventually managed to rally his small forces even as he frantically attempted to locate the other officers of the guard.

The absent officers, Lieutenants Henry M. Goldsmith and Joseph S. Patterson, were much too occupied at the time to concern themselves with the war. In fact, during all the confusion, they had ransacked the quartermaster's tent, in the process of which they consumed an entire month's supply of Hostetter's Celebrated Stomach Bitters:

> Against the vapors foul prepare:'
> That fever taint the heavy air;
> Drink not unmixed the waters found;
> in prairies, woods, or marshy ground.

When Captain Kinney found them, he entered their tent exclaiming and cursing about their not being at their stations, but was stopped short by the ludicrous scene of several rows of empty bottles lined up as though soldiers in dress formation. Goldsmith was staggering about the tent gesturing toward the bottles and lecturing Patterson on the finer points of company drill. Taking notice of Kinney, Goldsmith simply "waved him off, telling him to go on with the d--- war, that they were in no way interested."

Fortunately for all, the attack on Camp Carrion Crow was but a small affair and the Texans were driven off after losing two or three men. The only casualty on the Union side was Captain Gue's funeral. During the excitement four of his men very quickly scooped out a shallow hole on the south bank and unceremoniously dumped his blanket-draped body into it.[36]

In the meantime the reinforcements from Camp Carrion Crow, their numbers bolstered by Fonda's horse and the few who had managed to escape, commenced a counterattack against the Rebels out on Buzzards' Prairie. With drums beating and flags flying, the Yankees advanced over the tortured ground of Desire Arnaud's little plantation. The right flank, supported by an artillery barrage from Nims' Battery, moved forward slowly over the field where corn once flourished. The center of the Union line crossed Arnaud's ditch, dodged craters made by exploding shells and advanced through the yam patch and past the damaged house where a young Texan lay dying on the porch.

On reaching the Bourbeux crossing—which was soon to be dubbed "Marland's bridge"—Colonel Harai Robinson and his 1st Louisiana charged across, scattering the Texans, cutting their lines in two and temporarily taking almost a hundred prisoners. Private Tyre Hancock of the 11th Texas recalled that five or six of Robinson's daredevil cavalrymen galloped straight into the Rebel lines with pistols blazing even after the Texans had surrendered. One of these, Private John Rodgers, allegedly shot not less than six Texans to death before he was himself dropped by a Confederate bullet. Hancock claimed to have escaped certain death at the hands of these vindictive cavalrymen by falling to the ground "like I was killed."

Surprised by the suddenness of the counterattack, Colonel Oran Roberts, then helping to plunder the Union camp, gave the command "Right-about Face; Forward March!." Firing rapidly, the Texans dropped a number of "Louisiana" cavalrymen from their saddles.[37]

Seeing the commotion from the opposite, or east bank, Colonel John Fonda and the remaining forces of his cavalry brigade also charged across, but the now organized Confederates poured a withering fire into these newcomers, driving them back. In the process Fonda's horse (i.e. the one he was riding) was shot from under him, forcing the Illinois colonel to retreat by foot. He was quickly followed by Robinson's 1st Louisiana (Union) who was able to bring off only about one-half of his Texas prisoners.[38]

An unidentified soldier in the 29th Wisconsin, who had just reached the battlefield, was quite stunned to look upon Robinson's prisoners. "They were the hardest looking chaps I have ever seen before," he wrote. "Swarthy, tall and gaunt, ragged and unshorn, my idea of southern chivalry sunk still deeper."

One of the camp blacks, probably a cook, crossed over to safety on a "beautiful" captured horse while leading some luckless Texas Ranger at the point of a revolver in front. He and he alone, he bragged, had taken the Rebel:[39]

> When asked why he didn't let his prisoner ride and he go afoot, he grinningly replied, rolling his eyes and showing a quantity of ivory that would honor an elephant, 'He wouldn't let me ride when I was picking cotton, so he'll walk now, sho!'

While the Confederate prisoners were being marched toward Camp Carrion Crow, Confederate General Green, back on the west bank, galloped up to the bridge to discuss his next move with Roberts. Green's command was now equal to if not superior in size to the counterattacking Yankees. But the Texans had already won the day and nothing further could be accomplished by standing their ground against the heavier Union artillery. Besides, Green was well aware of the Fabian policy. "Deeming it imprudent to fight this large additional force," reported the Texan, "I withdrew slowly and without loss."[40]

CHAPTER SIXTEEN

HOSPITALS AND PRISON CAMPS

Tuesday, November 3, 1863

UNION GENERAL BURBRIDGE, standing near the west side of "Marland's Bridge," looked out upon a sea of utter destruction. On his left, where the First Brigade's neatly pitched white tents had once graced the rolling landscape, there was nothing save a few piles of rejected and smoldering booty. On the ground nearby, not far away from the overturned *New York Herald* wagon, were the broken ballot boxes of the Wisconsin regiments, their valuable contents scattering in the wind. Not only had the plundering Texans taken all the tents, clothing, money, blankets and other personal belongings, but they had even eaten the freshly cooked dinner and then departed with the messpots.

On the right, amid more smoking debris as far as the eye could see, lay the dead, the dying and the badly wounded, Union and Confederate alike. Dr. J. T. Woods, surgeon of the 96th Ohio, wept openly as he recalled a poetic refrain describing the emotions of the men:

> Strange horror seizes them
> And pangs unfelt before

Some of the dead rested in "ghastly pools of blood" or mixed in with the charred remains of wagons, dead horses and mules or fallen trees. A gunner of the 17th Ohio Battery, his face blackened by smoke and gunpowder, walked aimlessly among the dead humming the music to "Rally Round the Flag."[1]

Though small by comparison with many Civil War affairs, it had been a devastating engagement for the forces involved. Union losses in killed, wounded and captured were reported at 716, or more than one-half the entire First Brigade of Burbridge's infantry division. Other Union losses included 36 dead horses, an unspecified number of artillery pieces and most of the camp equipage.[2] Confederate casualties were reported at only 180 killed, wounded or captured, but, as it turned out, their losses in the killed and wounded category actually exceeded those of the Union side.

Yet, there was a happy note. As the Yankees began the grim task of sorting through the ruins and looking for wounded, a "dead" soldier struggled out of a mud hole to embrace his saviors. He was none other than Private John Griffin Jones, the Welshman of the 23rd Wisconsin. Though dirty, hungry and unsure of what had happened, he was nonetheless alive and unscathed but hopping mad. "It will be a sorry day when we get at them again," he scowled.[3]

The Confederate dead were loaded into wagons like so much cordwood and then hauled by the all-black Pioneer Corps to a location north of Urbaigne Lavergne's house. There, near the point of Buehler's last stand, they were unceremoniously buried in a shallow grave along with unexploded missiles, broken guns and other discarded weaponry.[4] The dead bluecoats fared somewhat better. Though there were no blankets to enshroud the corpses they were at least interred individually in shallow graves near the edge of camp. Wooden markers were then placed on the site for future identification. After a brief burial ceremony, punctuated by wailing fifes and muffled drums, the survivors took one "look at the little yellow mounds" and fell back to the Carencro.[5]

Even as the dispirited and decimated brigade of defeated Westerners entered Camp Carrion Crow from the north, another Westerner, Corporal Frank McGregor of the 83rd Ohio, was entering the sprawling Union camp from the south. Badly wounded at Vicksburg, McGregor had been convalescing for months at various hospitals in Memphis and New Orleans, awaiting the surgeons' certificate of good health. He was well enough to travel now and he planned to go home and marry his childhood sweetheart, Susie, as soon as he could get away from this dreadful war. For the time being, however, he was "in splendid spirits" and was looking forward to this reunion with the boys of the 83rd.

Rushing into camp just as the sun was disappearing over the horizon, McGregor was stunned to hear from the pickets that most of his brigade had fallen in battle that very day. "Thinking they were only trying to make a game or, as is so often the case in telling of a battle, making it a great deal worse than it was," McGregor went on with his inquiries until he came upon a group of ragged, "bloodthirsty" Texas prisoners. "That brigade was all cut to pieces," shouted a defiant Rebel, "they was all gobbled up on the Prairie."

Disbelieving, but "fearing the worst," McGregor spotted the yellow hospital flag near the front entrance of the L'ile Carrion Crow plantation home of Thelismar and Constance Guidry. Ambulances were pouring in. "I immediately went over there in a state of doubt, fear and excitement," wrote McGregor to Susie:[6]

> On looking among the wounded and those lying outside who had died on their journey from the battlefield, many of them lying on the ground in their last throes of agony, with no one paying any atten-

> tion, I could not recognize any of them. The surgeons were going on, busy with their dreadful work of amputation. The bloody work, the groans of the wounded, the dead lying so still covered with blood. Oh Susie, 'twas a dreadful sight, and this, thought I, is the meeting with the boys I had thought of so often.

The work was indeed dreadful. Even while the battle raged, Dr. James Bradbridge Hunter, a twenty-five-year-old surgeon of the 60th Indiana, began the grisly task of hauling the wounded from the field. Selecting the Guidry plantation as a regimental—and subsequently brigade—hospital, the Evansville, Indiana, doctor divided his medical team, numbering about twenty-five, into work details.

One group, the regular medical team, was detailed as stretcher-bearers and drivers for the two and four-wheeled ambulances, making several trips to and from the field of battle. Another group, comprising mainly musicians from the regimental band, began piling up cotton in the house, barn and other outbuildings to accommodate the wounded. They were ably assisted by the Guidrys' house slave, Augustin Domingue. The hospital steward opened the medical chests and laid out the surgical supplies, including saws, opiates, chloroform and bottles of whiskey. In the meantime, a group normally detailed as cooks heated water, prepared tea or coffee and soup, and put sponges to soak.

As the wounded began pouring in, Hunter was soon joined by the Surgeon-in-Chief of the 4th Division, Dr. John S. McGrew, and the regimental surgeons and assistant surgeons of each regiment. One of these, a Dr. Slaughter, was anathema to the wounded, not so much for his reputation, as for his unlikely name.

The gory business of amputations, dressing wounds and caring for the wounded was conducted in a setting so medically primitive that even Walt Whitman would find it difficult to describe similar scenes in poetic verse. Operating tables were hastily improvised by removing several large cypress doors from their hinges and placing them across chairs in the Guidrys' living room. There, under the dim light of sperm-oil candles and turpentine-fueled army lanterns, the Union surgeons continued their work throughout the night. Working unscrubbed and with sleeves rolled up to their elbows, their bare arms and linen aprons smeared with blood and their surgical knives frequently held between clenched teeth, they violated every canon of modern asepsis. Orderlies used the same blood-soaked sponge to cleanse wound after wound, after which the surgeons would hastily examine each and resolve whether or not to cut off an injured or maimed limb with a bloodied surgical saw.

Lying on a pile of soiled cotton on the porch and awaiting the unwelcome, even dreaded cry of "Next!," was Private Julius V. Wood of the 96th Ohio Infantry. Wood was an articulate, obviously well-educated soldier who had participated in plunder and pillage with his Western companions from Berwick's Bay to Barre's Landing and had gleefully described his unlawful activities in dozens of letters, written in beautiful script, to his family and friends. It was he who had described the "roses and poses" of Opelousas; had referred to the Rebs as "venturesome dogs" and had built sleeping quarters in one of Raimondi Deshotel's confiscated hogshead sugar barrels at Barre's Landing. Now, barely alive from the loss of blood and with his writing arm shattered and hopelessly maimed, he underwent a "deathbed conversion," seeking salvation in the belief that he would never survive the amputation that was about to follow.

As the work progressed, the surgeons who subsequently removed Wood's right arm—and saved his life—were no doubt sensitive to the vociferous criticism, mainly in the Northern press, that limbs were uselessly sacrificed by incompetent Civil War doctors; that many of the surgeons were drunkards who could not find employment in civilian life; that surgeons were especially fond of amputating, and just as likely to amputate for a flesh wound as for a badly fractured bone.

But there was a very good reason for such excesses—if it could be accurately called that. The vast majority of wounds during the Bourbeux affair, as in other Civil War engagements, was inflicted by gunfire. In fact, less than a half dozen wounds were due to some other misfortune, such as cannon fire or bayonet-sticking (at least among the survivors). Traveling at low velocity, the conodial-shaped lead Minie "ball" readily flattened on impact. It frequently lodged in tissues, usually carrying with it particles of clothing and skin and, if it struck a bone, would shatter two or three inches of it. On exit the bullet left a violently lacerated appearance all out of proportion to its already large caliber (ranging from ,58 to .71). When combined with the universal disregard for sanitation, the wound invariably became infected and, according to a popular saying, "If the bullet didn't get you, the infection would."

Surgeon Hunter, who frequently wrote his medical notes and diary in an almost indecipherable Pitman system of shorthand, commented that "it is sad indeed to see men with whom we are so familiar stricken down in a moment, or mutilated and rendered wretched by a single ounce of lead." The dead, wrote Hunter, were stacked in neat rows under a tree at a corner of the house while the amputated limbs were thrown onto a "dreadful" pile near the front gallery. "It looks strange," wrote a Massachusetts soldier, "to see a leg with its stocking lying on the grass."

For Constance Guidry, her niece Amelia and the young children, it was a nightmare. Virtually every room, save their own in the upper portion, was filled with wounded and dying soldiers. The soldiers' anguished cries, together with the overpowering smell of chloroform, blood, and the musky odor of unginned cotton made sleep impossible.

Unlike other houses, which had been looted by lawless blacks or straggling Yankees, Madame Guidry's home had remained relatively inviolate. It was a convenient site for the generals to employ as headquarters—or hospitals—and the stragglers had stayed away. For this reason her beautiful and expensive piano, ironically a Chickering brand, was still intact and undamaged. Moving to the keyboard, Constance remembered how she had played and sang for her dear wounded Thelismar after he had returned from Shiloh. Now, to the delight of all, she began playing a soft lullaby and singing the words in French.[7]

DIARY FACSIMILE OF Surgeon James B. Hunter, 60th Indiana Infantry. Hunter frequently made his notes in Pitman shorthand. (Courtesy Lilly Library, Indiana University, Bloomington)

Several miles north of the Union hospital, at the Bellevue plantation home of Benjamin Rogers on the Opelousas road, there was occurring an almost identical scene. Perhaps the only difference were the accents, the color of the uniforms and the absence of a sympathetic pianist. The Confederate doctors, including chief Surgeon George Cupples, Dr. John Bronough of the 5th Texas Cavalry, Dr. Samuel B. Meaney of the 4th, and Dr. T. B. Greenwood of the 7th, worked furiously to save the lives of the wounded, both Union and Confederate.

The Yankees would not likely attack them here. After all General Green's cavalry was camped on Bayou Tesson, just a short distance away. Vincent's horse was stationed both in the front and rear and, for extra protection, the six brass guns of the Saint Mary's Cannoneers, commanded by Captain Florian Cornay, stood in position.

Though the medical teams of both sides employed similar, and equally primitive, surgical techniques, the Confederates were sometimes more successful in saving lives than their Union counterparts. The reason for this was that they had rediscovered, quite by accident, a surgical practice employed by French doctors during the Napoleonic wars. When a wound was left exposed it would soon become covered with flies and, subsequently, maggots. Whereas the Union surgeons brushed away the maggots—and usually covered the wound with an unsterile dressing—the Rebels chose to ignore them with the result that the unsightly little creatures would eat away the infected portions and frequently save a life.

Unlike the Yankees—who were forced to rely on their own resources—the Confederates were ably assisted by dozens of citizens. Although the Louisianians "had never seemed to care before," groaned a wounded Texan, the citizens of the Opelousas country were so genuinely delighted that their tormentors had been trounced that they came from miles around, clogging the roads with private wagons and buggies, and crowding the streets of Opelousas on both sides to cheer on the victorious Confederates. "God bless the Texans!" they shouted, "We are safe when you stand between us and the Federals." Recalled a Texan:

> They handed us trays filled with cake and lemonade and sandwiches and other good things and we were compelled to fill our pockets. We gave three cheers for the women of Opelousas and felt—every one of us—that we could fight for, and, if necessary, die for such heroic women. Many men shed tears over the demonstration, and it is no wonder they did.

Each wounded soldier was treated like a hero, receiving very special and individual care. The less severe cases were immediately conveyed to the Opelousas Courthouse where yet another hospital, staffed with volunteer women and local doctors, was established. It was "a scene that melted into tears the most obdurate," wrote a Texan:

> The ladies of Opelousas and its vicinity, young and old, Catholic and Protestant, came crowding in, and waited upon our men just as if they had been their husbands and brothers. Long will be remembered with heartfelt gratitude, by the Texas soldiers, the appreciative kindness and sympathy of the Louisiana ladies.

The tender care did not, however, ameliorate the pathetic scene at the Rogers' home. The Confederates had initiated the attack and, in spite of Green's report to the contrary, had lost more in wounded and killed than the enemy. In fact not less than thirty Texans expired on or shortly after reaching the temporary hospital and were interred in the yard on the north side of the house. In addition, the Confederate surgeons were burdened with dozens of wounded Union prisoners, many of them quite severe.

Even Reverend James Earl Bradley, Yankee-hater that he was, was moved to tears by the condition of a wounded Federal. Once the bluecoats had released him, he had returned to the Adams home to find the family safe, but two small Negro boys severely ill. Their deaths the next day had served only to intensify his hatred for the Northerners. But now, as he gazed upon an amputation being performed on a young Union soldier, barely old enough to shave, Bradley experienced different emotions. As he was the only Protestant minister around, he tried to comfort the boy even as he "was on the eve of expiring." In "his last moments" the afflicted soldier whispered his name and address and asked the good minister to write his family. Bradley's hate, such as it was, drained from him even as the boy passed into eternity.[8]

ROGERS' HOME, used as a Confederate hospital following the Battle of Bayou Bourbeux, was razed for its valuable lumber even as this book was going to press. (Contemporary photograph)

In the meantime, Dr. Harris Beecher, back in Vermilionville, was wondering aloud about the Great Texas Overland Expedition. Three weeks earlier, he complained, their overland advance toward Texas had halted here on the grassy lawns of Governor Mouton's residence. Little had he imagined that "in so short a time, they would be doing duty again upon this identical spot. Such events impress a soldier with the idea that it is folly for him to predict the future," wrote the poetic New Yorker:

> There's a divinity that shapes our ends,
> Rough-hew them how we will.

Like so many of the others in the XIX Corps, Beecher was concerned about the noise in the direction of Camp Carrion Crow. Not since Port Hudson had he heard so much cannonading. Even the ground seemed to rumble. When darkness fell, Beecher "could not help but observe and remark upon the wonderful activity of the signal lights, which were flashing to and fro upon the Catholic church in the village." Almost everyone agreed that there was "something in the wind."

And indeed there was. Washburn, McGinnis, Burbridge and the others, back on the Carencro, were certain that another attack was inevitable. Thus, at midnight on the evening of November 3rd, 1863, General Godfrey Weitzel and his 1st Division—two brigades of infantry—accompanied by Mudd's (or Lee's) Cavalry brigade, marched from Vermilionville back to Camp Carrion Crow.[9]

Wednesday, November 4, 1863

Arriving at daybreak, the XIX Corps found that all was quiet on the Carencro. The only excitement of the day occurred about noon when two Texans—Colonel G. J. Hampton and Lieutenant G. B. Crain—entered the camp bearing a flag of truce. Would the Yankees exchange the Confederate wounded for their own? they asked. Officers would not be included in the deal. The agreement struck, some three dozen bluecoats, most of them badly injured, were hauled into camp in ambulances bearing the imprint C. S. A. on the side. In the presence of hundreds of curious onlooker, many of whom were muttering contemptuously under their breath, the Texans loaded up their own and with a final salute climbed aboard and drove away.[10]

Surgeon Beecher, thinking to help with the new arrivals, strolled over to the hospital where he found Hunter, McGrew, Slaughter and the others still "busy at their bloody work." A short distance away "rows of dead bodies were laid out upon the grass" where they were being buried "as fast as graves could be dug."[11]

Aside from the hospital and burial ceremonies, the biggest attraction along the Carencro was the Texas prisoners, then corraled under a group of large live oak trees near the bridge. Group after group of soldiers passed by to see for themselves what kind of men could inflict so much damage. They were not disappointed. The big Texans, like so many wild caged animals, heaped intimidating threats, tobacco juice and verbal abuse on any and all who drew near.

One of the visitors, Lieutenant Robert Steele of Joshua Guppey's 23rd Wisconsin, came into possession of a personal letter from one of the prisoners. So amused was he over its contents that he sent it to his wife, Rhoda, along with a few self-righteous comments. "You will see," wrote Steele, "what the people of Texas do and what they wright (sic) about as well as a speciman (sic) of penmanship."

Though the Confederate's letter did not survive the war, Steele probably had in mind the type of letter written by Private James Carr, a young Texan then camped north of Opelousas:[12]

> I have bin down a looken at the feds that Ginerl Green has taken prisners in a fite down below here...he taken a bout six hundred prisners and kiled about five hundred ded on the ground...(never) herd how menney wagons he took. I seen the prisners. That mutch I no...Tha aire a stil fiten yet...

Apparently, the Yankee prisoners in Opelousas were drawing just as many visitors as were the Texans on the Carencro. On the first day of their capture the entire group, more than five hundred in number, was marched to the square fronting the St. Landry Catholic Church. From that point the wounded had been taken to the courthouse where they were treated and, with the exception of officers, subsequently exchanged.

On the second day of their captivity, on November 4, 1863, the cold and miserable group started out on a seemingly interminable march toward north Louisiana. A few miles north of Washington, on the road toward Cheneyville, they were overtaken by Confederate General Richard Taylor, then en route to Alexandria in his favorite vehicle, a converted ambulance. When Taylor ordered his faithful black driver, "Old Tom," to pull out onto the prairie to pass the large blue column, he noticed Colonel Joshua Guppey limping along with his leg bandaged:

> Surprised at this, I stopped to inquire the reason, and was told that the Colonel refused to separate from his men. Descending from the ambulance, I approached him, and, as gently as possible, remonstrated against the folly of walking on a wounded leg...His regiment was from Wisconsin, recruited among his neighbors and friends, and he was unwilling to leave it. I insisted on his riding with me, for a time at least...With much reluctance he got into the ambulance and we drove on.

According to Corporal Reuben Scott, who gave to posterity the unlikely blood and smoke account of the 67th Indiana's capture, the hungry and tired group of prisoners soon reached Cheneyville. Unknown to Scott, who seemed to think his group was the first Yankees ever to visit the tiny village, Cheneyville had suffered badly at the hands of the invading XIX Corps in the spring:

> On arriving there, we found all the porches and platforms crowded ...assembled to see the great free show...But upon their countenances seemed to be a look of disappointment...What it was we were unable to learn until some of the more bold said to us: "Why we'uns thought you'uns had horns, but you'uns look like we'uns."

So much for Corporal Scott's credibility.[13]

Even as the vanquished continued their northerly trek, the victors, back on Bayou Bourbeux, were marking the gravesites of their lost comrades and paying tribute to their heroes. Especially noteworthy were the accolades showered upon Colonel Oran Roberts, the Texas judge-turned-warrior. The ceremony was capped by the presentation of a Union Kettle drum. George McKnight, an officer in Waller's Texas Battalion, read from notes he had jotted on the back of an official Union document picked up on the field:[14]

> Colonel Roberts:
>
> I am requested by the men of Waller's Battalion, Texas Cavalry, to deliver to your charge a drum captured on the battlefield yesterday by Henry Beasely, a soldier of our command. We tender it as a slight token of our high appreciation of the gallantry and general good conduct displayed by yourself and the infantry under your command.
>
> On that field your men compared favorably with the veterans of Green and Major's where achievements upon other fields had already won high renown...It furnishes gratifying evidence that the Texan is from habit a horseman and prefers the cavalry sword. Yet the sons of the Lone Star State can accommodate themselves to any arm which the necessities of our country may require...The valor of your men reflects additional lustre upon the Lone Star escutcheon. This battle, fought by Texans alone, is another warning as to what (the enemy) may expect to suffer should he ever meet the sons of Texas upon their own soil...We present the drum without injunction in full confidence that when it shall beat for action, your brave men will not be slow to respond to the call.

At Camp Carrion Crow, about three miles south, Madame Guidry was waging a verbal war with the Yankees. Several months earlier she and husband Thelismar had sold their cotton, some eighteen thousand pounds, to Jules Perrodin, a French merchant in Opelousas. As was the custom of the day, Perrodin had left the unginned cotton, valued at $12,000 (about $73,500 in 1978 currency) in Guidry's *cotonerie* until it could be transported to market in New Orleans. It was this same cotton which had been used as bedding for the wounded soldiers.

LIEUTENANT H. M. POLLARD directed the confiscation of cotton at the Guidry plantation. (Carpenter, *History of the 8th Vermont Volunteers*)

Considering the circumstances, Constance had not complained at the time. After all they had used only a small portion of it, and besides, it was there at Perrodin's risk, not hers. But now, one day after the battle, she looked outside to see the 8th Vermont Infantry loading the cotton onto wagons. Rushing out, she collared Lieutenant Henry M. Pollard, who was standing on the front gallery shouting instructions to the confiscation teams.

"I told the Federal officer," recalled Mrs. Guidry, "that the cotton belonged to a French citizen living in the town of Opelousas." Pollard very courteously replied that "This French citizen would be better satisfied to know that his cotton was in (our) hands than in those of the rebels." Continuing his unpleasant task, Pollard, along with Perrodin's cotton soon disappeared over the bayou in the direction of Vermilionville.[15]

As darkness fell on the night of November 4, 1863, Constance Guidry could never recall being in more miserable circumstances. The fun and good life of ante-bellum New Orleans must have appeared as only a remote dream. Perrodin's cotton was gone, as was the other produce at the Carencro, and she knew not whether Thelismar was alive or dead. In the meantime wounded soldiers, blood and soiled cotton still covered her floors, and the men were still suffering and dying.

At one point during the night, even as Constance was playing the piano and singing, a delirious soldier "plunged his pocket knife into his neck." Surgeon Hunter, by then finished with the grisly operations, simply took out his diary and made the clinical observation in Pitman shorthand that the unfortunate soldier "severed the vertebral artery and lacerated the thyroid plexus." Hunter closed his entry with the obvious by adding that "He, of course, died."[16]

Thursday, November 5th, 1863

At daybreak on the Carencro, during a cold drizzling rain, the entire Union force gathered up their wounded and fell back to the Vermilion. The Confederates, who must have had advance notice of their departure, almost immediately set up housekeeping on the evacuated campsite.

Constance Guidry opened her door that happy morning and found Private Thelismar Guidry alive and unharmed. The last she had seen or heard of him was October 11th, more than three weeks before, when he had fled the house with cousin Alfred Mouton.

Across Buzzards' Prairie at Chretien Point, Madame Celestine Cantrelle Chretien was preparing for a long overdue trip to Opelousas. She and her husband, Hypolite, and the children were in desperate need of food, medicine and other provisions. They had survived the long occupation, the daily skirmishes and the battle, but were practically reduced to "indigence." It could have been worse. Hypolite, claiming to be a loyal Unionist, had taken the Oath of Allegiance and was subsequently befriended by several unidentified officers. "They came to him in the house," recalled Celestine, "and brought him quinine and whiskey, and sat down in the room and talked with him." Perhaps for this reason they had successfully managed to sequester certain household valuables, livestock and provisions, wagons and conveyance vehicles.

Now, with the Yankees gone and the Confederates back on their usual camping grounds, Celestine stepped up on her *caleche* and started up the road toward Opelousas. Passing the site where the battle occurred only two days before, she was without a doubt horrified by the devastation. There, in a drizzling rain, were thousands of Carrion Crow vultures feasting upon the remains of rotting and unburied horses and mules even as a team of Confederates, under the supervision of Lieutenant O. M. Airhuit of the 11th Texas Infantry, was busily engaged in raising a large mound of earth over their dead breathren. So offensive was the smell that many of them had placed protective handkerchiefs over their mouths and nostrils.

Farther along at a very narrow and muddy point in the road, Madame Chretien encountered a certain hostile citizen identified only by the name of Leger. The latter had suffered a great deal and, like many of the poorer residents of Louisiana, blamed his misfortunes on the wealthy planters. They—the wealthy—had started this war, or so the reasoning went, but their sons could purchase a substitute for military service, or could claim exemption because of their connections or by virtue of their status as large planters.

With the innocent and sensitive Celestine before him, he saw an opportunity to vent his anger. Had he followed the custom of the day, he would have, because of his lower social standing, moved off the road and into the mud to permit this beautiful and wealthy lady to pass. This time, however, he remained in his place and directed a barrage of curses and insults at the stunned lady, concluding, finally, by ordering her to give way for him to pass.

Celestine, it should be noted, was the very opposite of her coarse and cigar chomping mother-in-law, Felicite Neda Chretien, who, no doubt, would have handled this "upstart peasant" with a sharp tongue-lashing. She instead silently moved to the side in lady-like dignity and waited for this hate-filled man to pass. Her reward was a liberal splashing of mud from the wagon wheels.[17]

For Desire Arnaud, the situation that rainy Thursday morning was even less happy. Released by the Yankees, the sad little man who had come to America with such high hopes walked once more from the Carencro to his damaged home out on Buzzards' Prairie. What he found was a hopelessly irreparable mess:

> There was no corn, no stock, no chickens (and) nothing to eat. There was no fencing and a terrible stench about the place owning to the Federals having butchered stock there...The houses were broken open and nothing but a skeleton remained.

Arnaud went into the empty remains of his once happy home, sat down on the floor, or what remained of it, and burst into tears.[18]

CHAPTER SEVENTEEN

RECRIMINATIONS AND RETREAT

Thursday, November 5, 1863

RARELY had the soldiers of the XIII Corps been so depressed. Humiliated in battle and likened to common criminals because of their foraging propensities, they felt betrayed, especially by their Eastern leaders. Now, instead of marching west toward their ultimate destination in Texas, they were heading back toward the village of Vermilionville where, according to rumor, they would rest and recuperate a few days before resuming the advance.

Before departing Camp Carrion Crow some of the generals, perhaps in an effort to boost the men's morale, had referred to the Bourbeux disaster as a "victory" because the Westerners had in the end driven the Texans from the field. "A few more such victories," sneered Sylvester Bishop of the 11th Indiana, "would not leave us many men." Neither was Harry Watts deceived. Why the fall back to Vermilionville, he complained, was nothing more than[1]

> a masterly advance on the rear, with the rebs advancing in the same direction...If we had a general with as much spunk as a mouse, we would have turned about and whipt them soundly. This was the first time the 13th Army Corps ever turned its back...

As they marched through Carencro and on toward Vermilionville someone started a rumor, erroneous as usual, that "protection papers" had been found in the pockets of many of the Confederate dead. The whole idea was absurd because none of the dead Texans held property in Louisiana and, even if they had, would not have been entitled to protection papers owing to their military status. Nonetheless, the rumor took hold and passed from company to company and from regiment to regiment. Some ingenious soul even managed to compose a marching song to that effect:[2]

> Twas on the morn of November third,
> The rebels thought they'd cage the bird.
> With protection papers in their pockets
> They pounced upon us like a rocket.

The general verdict was then that "protection papers had played out." If they couldn't whip the Texans, they could at least vent their rage on the innocent civilians between the Carencro and Vermilionville. As a result they began stopping at homes along the way, including those of Charles Brown, Hypolite and Louis Arseneaux, Jean Baptiste Clement and two Spaniards, Antonio Ynojosa (or Hinojosa) and Ramon Riu (variously spelled Reu, Rhiu, and Rue). Farther along they also plundered the homes of Gabriel Duhon, Rosemand Dugas, Coquelin Latiolais and Cyprien Arceneaux.

At the Arceneaux place there lived Benoit Cazaudebat, a thirty-five-year-old "peddling merchant" from the Haute Pyrenees. Cazaudebat, who was wed to Azelie, one of Arceneaux's sisters, had recently purchased an expensive sewing machine, a Wheeler and Wilson Brand, for his then pregnant wife. As it turned out the machine itself became a subject of dispute for two of the intruders. One, recalled Cazaudebat, "contended that it was silver and the other saying it was not." To decide the controversy "one of the soldiers broke the machine, while the other scratched the metallic part with his sword." In addition they broke an armoire and other furniture, stole all the household edibles and took with them Cazaudebat's wedding suit and shoes, his wife's jewelry and just about everything else of value.[3]

Once in Vermilionville the plunder continued, but sometimes for more noble purposes. The wounded, for example, still had to be cared for, a fact which occasioned a visit to the little store of Michael "Monsieur Lemas" Joseph, a thirty-year-old "French Israelite" from Hellimere, the Department of Moselle. Joseph and his wife Caroline Bloch were speculators who made their living as buyers of sugar, hides, cotton, rum and other produce which they stored in a "shanty" behind their residence on the courthouse square.

About noontime on November 5, 1863, during a heavy rain, several army wagons pulled up to the shanty and began loading cotton even as Joseph's brother-in-law, Jacob Bloch, and a friend, Abraham Haas, looked on. The cotton, said a Federal officer, was needed as mattresses for the wounded, then quartered at the nearby courthouse, but just for good measure they also took several hogsheads of sugar, two hundred hides and three barrels of green Louisiana rum.

Caroline Joseph stood watching the affair through her kitchen window. She had never been so frightened in her life, mainly because she and her three little boys, Lemas, Lazard and Julius, were harboring a bedridden Confederate soldier, Gottschalk Feitel. The latter, a "German Israelite," was recuperating from an illness which had almost cost him his life. Only weeks before he had been told by the Confederate surgeons that his case was terminal. Well, if he was going to die, he told the surgeons, he desired to do so among others of the Jewish faith. Granting him this "last wish," he was taken to the Joseph residence where, instead of dying, he was slowly regaining his health.

There then occurred what seemed a second miracle. To the everlasting relief of all, the Yankees finished loading their booty, mounted up and, without so much as a glance at the house, drove out of sight.[4]

Friday, November 6, 1863

Rumors of "an enormous Confederate victory" began appearing in Northern newspapers. An article in the *Chicago Tribune*, surrounded as it was by advertisements for Dr. Sweet's Liniment, Roback's Bitters, and Helmbold's Extract Buchu, erroneously printed the news that Banks and his entire staff had been captured during the "Carrion Crow" engagement.

The papers would soon receive more accurate news because on that sunny Friday morning, for the first time since the battle, the survivors had a few spare moments to write letters and make reports. Most of the correspondence written from Vermilion Bayou was highly critical, and some of it would subsequently appear in Northern newspapers, of necessity from an anonymous source. A Wisconsin "Ink," for example, referred to the Bourbeux affair as a "disgrace" and a "grand back out." Another Wisconsin soldier, "Random," wrote that "Dick Taylor knew the imbecile qualities of the powers that rule this Texas expedition."

Most of the critics agreed that Burbridge, the tall Kentucky general, had handled the situation admirably, and he was cited for numerous instances of personal gallantry. "Pap" McGinnis, being ill at the time, also escaped criticism. General Washburn, in turn, was both damned—because he refused to unite the two forces—and praised—because he responded so rapidly with reinforcements. Franklin and Banks, by contrast, were subjected to a heavy barrage of vilification from all sides. "We think the blame of this disaster is entirely on General Franklin's shoulders," wrote Isaac Jackson, a soldier in the 83rd Ohio. Another critic, a war correspondent for the *Milwaukee Daily Sentinel*, complained "that the officer who so culpably and disastrously failed to succor Pope's half starved army in Virginia has not been changed in his disposition by the gulf breezes."

Even the Confederates joined in. The *Louisiana Democrat*, *Shreveport News* and *Opelousas Courier* crowed "Bully for Tom Green" (or "long live Tom Green") while the Houston *Tri-Weekly Telegraph* called the Federal army the "laughing stock" of the Trans-Mississippi:

> If a crazy set of fools had broken loose from Bedlam...they could not have acted in a more ridiculous manner, or more like natural-born fools, than has the 'Franklin Invaders'...This Yankee Sancho Panza Franklin ought to be presented with a leather medal or wooden spoon...Like his great namesake, he may yet take to kite-flying.
>
> Adoo Yankee General, Adoo, and next time you come, bring along your knitting.

In Abbeville, Louisiana, the defeat of General Banks' army gave rise to a new rash of "Banks' Jokes," one of which was recounted by Judge Joshua Baker, a refugee from the Teche country who had recently returned from the battlefields of Virginia where Banks earned his sobriquet "Old Commissary." It seemed that a Rebel sympathizer, according to Baker, was arrested by a Union general in Virginia who was concerned about fraternization and contraband trade between the opposing armies.

"I have some questions for you and I wish you to tell the truth," said the general to his prisoner.

"I will."

"Well, sir, do you know of anyone who has passed out of the rebel lines and come into ours, then went back to the rebels?"

"Yes, sir, I do."

"Who was it, you damned scoundrel?"

"General (J. E. B.) Stuart, Sir."

At this the general grew furious, cursed his prisoner and threatened his life if he did not respond truthfully.

"Now, you damned rascal," continued the general, "do you know of anyone in the Federal lines who furnish the rebels with provisions?"

"I do, Sir."

"Well, who is it, you damned scoundrel?"

"General Banks, Sir."[5]

With so many "disparaging remarks having appeared in a large part of the public newspapers" it was inevitable that recriminations and scapegoatism would soon set in, even at the highest levels. So why not lay the blame on someone other than Franklin, Washburn and Banks. Colonel Joshua Guppey had fought gallantly before falling prisoner so he was not a very good candidate for scapegoating; so had the commanders of the 60th Indiana and the 83rd and 96th Ohio. Colonels Fonda and Robinson had joined the battle late, but had followed orders and were even cited for acts of courage. Colonel Richard Owen, the brigade commander, had also acted reasonably well.

But, alas, Colonel Theodore Buehler, the Prussian-born commander of the 67th Indiana, had not followed orders and, as a result lost an entire infantry regiment, at least according to the generals. No one apparently was troubled by the thought that Buehler, with two hundred infantrymen, was out on the open prairie under specific orders from Burbridge and had done the only sensible thing to do when surrounded by three thousand mounted Texas Rangers: surrender.The alternative, as Buehler himself would bluntly argue, "was death." Nonetheless, General Burbridge and Washburn pressed the matter with the regular commander of the XIII Corps, Major General E. O. C. Ord, and subsequently with Banks, the Major General Commanding. Thus, a Court of Inquiry would soon find Buehler guilty and he would be "discharged the service for misbehavior in front of the enemy."[6]

Another participant in the Bourbeux affair, Colonel Thomas Bringhurst, a former attorney from Logansport, Indiana, must have considered himself even less fortunate than the disgraced Prussian. Bringhurst, a hero of the November 3rd engagement, had been assigned the very dangerous task of bringing up the rear of the retreating Union forces from the Carrion Crow with his 46th Indiana Infantry. All the other troops had moved on through Vermilionville and gone into camp on the bayou two miles east of town. Bringhurst, however, had been ordered to a point west of town on Pierre Bemal's property near the current location of West University Avenue at St. John's cemetery. For some reason, a large portion of medical and commissary stores, together with the wounded from the Bourbeux affair, was still quartered in the old courthouse directly across the street from Homer Bailey's home. Owing to the vulnerability of this position, Bringhurst's regiment was ordered to stave off thousands of advancing Rebels with his three-hundred man force until the town could be evacuated, hopefully that night. "General Franklin," wrote one soldier, "baited the trap with the 46th Regiment."

From his lookout atop the steeple platform at St. John's Catholic Church, Bringhurst had "a fine view of the surrounding country." Virtually every movement of the Rebels for a distance of five miles or more "could be distinctly seen" and reported by semaphore to the rear or to any of several other isolated outposts.

About noontime the forty-three-year-old colonel noted that the enemy, then located at a point between the property of Emile Antoine Mouton (near present-day I-10) and the current location of Four Corners, seemed to be manuevering into battle formation. The Chief Signal Officer, Captain William A. Pigman, immediately ordered a subordinate to flash this information back to Franklin's headquarters on Basil Crow's plantation.

While the beat of the long roll summoned the men to arms back on the Vermilion, Bringhurst spotted yet another curious development. Handing his field glasses to Lieutenant Thomas Howes, the twenty-one-year-old quartermaster of the 46th, Bringhurst asked for an opinion. Adjusting the glass, Howe reported that he could see "four wagons, loaded with cotton, coming directly from the direction of the Rebel army."

The cotton, as it turned out, belonged to three Carencro planters—Dr. Romain J. Francez, Francois Abadie, and widow Ozeme Comeaux—who had been badly misinformed. According to their information the Yankees were falling back rapidly to Berwick's Bay and had long since evacuated Vermilionville. Like many other planters, rich and poor, they had successfully concealed a portion of their cotton during the Union occupation and now wanted to get it off their hands. So when Zenon Broussard, an allegedly unsavory opportunist, offered to haul their cotton to Olivier's Landing, below New Iberia, they had jumped at the opportunity.

Broussard, alias "*six-doigts*," was known by some as a "greedy shylocks," the money lender of Carencro, who would perform almost any service for a fee. So unsavory was his reputation that he was said to have fathered children by his own illegitimate mulattress daughter. He was forever dreaming up some Machiavellian scheme to make—or save—money. During the first Union advance, for example, Broussard had placed his gold in earthenware crocks and with the help of an old slave named Josie had buried it near the house. In return for the slave's silence he had even promised to buy him a new linen suit after the danger was passed. Josie had honored the agreement but Broussard had not.[7]

Now, two of Broussard's semi-literate white teamsters, Felix Malapart and Simon Mathieu, together with two blacks—former slaves of Dr. Francez—entered the Union lines carrying thirty-two bales of very expensive cotton. For Colonel Thomas Bringhurst and his beleagured forces it was like a godsend. Thirty-two bales of cotton rolled against that picket fence would make a formidable obstacle, at least giving them some protection from Rebel bullets. "It was precautionary and a measure of defense absolutely necessary," recalled Bringhurst.

The adjutant, James M. Watts of Delphi, Indiana, and Captain Frank Swigart, another Logansport attorney, ordered the surprised teamsters to immediately unload their burden. Instead of following orders, however, the four teamsters huddled together for a conference, "jabbering" away in French just as though they had some choice in the matter. Finally, one of the black teamsters, Antoine Guchereau, came over and addressed the Union officers in broken English. They would, he said, "acquiese" provided they were given a receipt for the cotton and it would be returned as soon as the Yankees evacuated the area. Colonel Bringhurst, whether taken in by their audacity or too concerned about the Rebels to think twice, quickly agreed and wrote out a most extraordinary receipt:

> This is to certify that I have this day taken thirty-two (32) bales of cotton, marked R.J.F. and F. Abadie, for the purpose of making a breastwork on the outside of Vermilionville.
>
> I was left at this place, under an order from Gen'l Franklin as a cover for the town and the general hospital at this place. I took the cotton for defensive purposes, and will hold it in good order (effects of the weather excepted) until I am relieved.

Incredible as it seems, the Indiana lawyer-turned-warrior, who had very carefully tried to conceal his presence, strength and intentions, then turned the teamsters loose, sending them back toward the Rebel line with their receipt and possible intelligence information.

In the meantime the citizens of Vermilionville were either deserting their town en masse for the second time or were making preparations to protect themselves in the event of a battle. At Homer Bailey's school, just across the street from the courthouse, twenty-five-year-old Zelia Mouton, the wife of General Mouton, moved into the basement with her four young children; on the west side of town, plainly visible, were thousands of Confederates lined up and ready to attack; to the east, an even larger number of bluecoats were in battle formation. It appeared for all the world as though a battle would soon be joined virtually in downtown "Lafayette."

On the church steeple of St. John's, Captain Frank Swigart raised his glass for a better look:

> All were evidently ready for business. Now at sunset, the clearest hour of the day, the heavy dark lines of infantry, each regiment distinguished by its flag, was distinctly seen, while the heavy batteries, with their bright guns in line, and the squadrons of cavalry moving about, added life and meaning to the scene.

When darkness fell, the Texans advanced to a point only two hundred yards away from Bringhurst, but still they did not attack. Perhaps in realization of his gaffe, the colonel ordered his men to roll the cotton to another position, some distance away from the original site. There, under cover of darkness, they dug trenches behind the cotton, a task completed by midnight. Bringhurst then forwarded a note to General Franklin. In the morning, he wrote, you will find us safe or you "will find our bones and boot heels on the prairie."

General Franklin's reply came shortly after 1 o'clock A. M. The hospital and stores, he wrote, had been safely evacuated and the 46th should fall back to the Vermilion as quickly as possible.

Saturday, November 7, 1863

William Brandt, the courthouse recorder, notary public, and later mayor of Lafayette, looked out his window and discovered that west Vermilionville was once more in Confederate hands. For two days Brandt, age fifty, had stood at this window watching Bringhurst and his soldiers at work. He had seen them take the cotton and noticed that Broussard's men, Felix Malapart and Simon Mathieu, did not go very far away. Indeed, they had stood watching and waiting until daylight faded from the scene. Now, this morning, the cotton was gone. Apparently, thought Brandt, the Yankees took it with them, but they had not, a fact confirmed by Bringhurst many years later. Bringhurst and his regiment possessed only one wagon, and it was loaded with ammunition. Besides, they were in too much of a hurry to concern themselves with a few bales of muddy Rebel cotton. And as for Broussard's teamsters, they claimed the cotton was gone when they reached the spot. Of course the Yankees had taken it, they argued. The great cotton caper mystery was never solved, but almost anyone who knew or had ever heard of Zenon Broussard could suggest a theory, all of which led to the same conclusion.[8]

At Basil Crow's plantation, Major General William Franklin was as uncertain as ever. Union newspapers, he noticed, were propagandizing Banks' successful landing on Brazos Santiago Island, just off the coast of Corpus Christi. The amphibious operation was conducted on the same day as the disgraceful Bourbeux affair and palliated to a large degree Franklin's own failure. "We have raised our flag in Texas again," Banks proudly cabled, but Franklin knew that Banks had acquired, at the most, a very tenuous foothold on an ill-defended and insignificant piece of real estate.On the other hand, the Union had demonstrated to Napoleon, and to Maximilian in Mexico, that the Monroe Doctrine was alive and well and that the United States, if necessary, would fight to prevent foreign powers from gaining a foothold in the Western Hemisphere.

From Franklin's point of view, the worst part of the Brazos Santiago invasion was that Banks desired still more troops from his Louisiana command. "Let them be put in preparaton," Banks cabled, "but do not withdraw the force so as to notify the enemy of our purpose." Banks was well aware that his success, if it could be called that, was in large part attributable to "the recent movements in Louisiana" and subsequent deployment of Confederate forces on the Sabine. For that reason he instructed Franklin to continue to "threaten the Sabine" from Vermilionville. "This is important," he emphasized. Besides it might still be necessary to launch a major attack from western Louisiana.

So on the one hand Banks proposed to weaken Franklin's command while on the other, he (Franklin) was expected to appear aggressive. To begin with, the cigar smoking West Pointer was expected to drive the Rebels from Vermilionville, a task which might prove dangerous. Moreover, he was ordered to send out daily reconnaissance missions on the western roads toward the Mermentau, further weakening his position. At the very least he could be thankful that the wounded were out of the way. Surgeon James Hunter had seen to that. During the night he had slipped away to New Iberia heading a caravan numbering more than thirty ambulances.[9]

Even as Franklin pondered his options, including the possibility of fortifying the Vermilion position with earthworks, his attention was diverted south toward the Cote Gelee area, where the evening sky was aglow from a series of deliberately set fires. Earlier in the day General Burbridge's decimated brigade of Bourbeux survivors, en route for New Iberia, had camped for the night on the property of several planters, including Samuel Schmulen, Alcide Melancon, Joseph Bernard and Valsin Broussard. No sooner had they settled in than the usual plunder began.

Perhaps the hardest hit was Schmulen, a thirty-nine-year-old merchant from Fenetrange, Department de la Meuth, France. First they had looted his barn, then his store and then the house. "I was screaming," recalled Schmulen, "don't take everything! I got nothing to do with the war! I am a French subject!" The only reply from the embittered veterans was that "We can't guess who are French or Confederate." Then, even as Schmulen's wife lay ill in bed, all the buildings were set afire, including his house. Schmulen, aided by his children, managed to get his wife safely outside and onto a mattress he had retrieved from the burning house. He then appealed to a group of soldiers sitting around a campfire. "Please help me to put out the fire," he begged, "for it is all I have left for my wife and children."

The only person who bothered to help was Benjamin George, a fifty-year-old slave on the neighboring plantation of Onezime Melancon. After a fruitless attempt to put out the fire in the store, George was surrounded by several gun-waving, inebriated Yankees manifesting the usual Northern ignorance about black-white relations in the South. Why, they demanded, was he, a black, helping a white Southerner? Someone suggested that he had done so only to get money in the store. "They told me to give them the (money) I had taken," recalled George. "I told them that if they shot me they would not get it, because I had not taken any." Then, as if to oblige the good Samaritan, a drunken soldier took aim and fired, striking George in the right upper thigh. Benjamin George lived, but he would remain a one-legged cripple for the rest of his life.[10]

Sunday, November 8, 1863

Sunday morning was as cool and pleasant a day in southwest Louisiana as any Yankee could remember. Normally it might be a day of leisure, during which the soldiers could bathe and wash clothes, attend religious services, write letters, or forage, but the entire camp was just as restless and nervous as if they were still back on Buzzards' Prairie. According to camp rumors, General Taylor's army had been reinforced by the arrival of Confederate Generals Bankhead Magruder and Sterling Price and could be expected to attack at any moment.

The most appropriate time for a Confederate assault would be first light, or so reasoned the Union generals. For this reason the entire Vermilion force was routed out of bed by 4 o'clock A.M. and placed in line of battle until well after sunrise. They had done so the day before and the day before that. This Sunday morning would be different, however, because the Rebels had moved into Vermilionville and were plainly visible a short distance away. Even the steeple of St. John's Cathedral, which the Yankees had so successfully employed as a signal station, was occupied by Confederate signal officers. They would have to be driven off.

The long blue lines began the assault before sunrise. As they had done so many times before, they advanced with colors flying, drums beating and troops singing. The cavalry commanders—Lee, Fonda, Robinson and a newcomer, Colonel Thomas J. Lucas—led the way. Some of the newly mounted infantry regiments were anticipating their first conflict from the saddle, but if they were hoping for a big fight, they were sorely disappointed. The small Confederate force in Vermilionville merely faded away without so much as a shot being fired by either side. Once more the Stars and Stripes flew over Vermilionville.[11]

Farther north there was another battle, but it was verbal and among Confederates. General Richard Taylor, still smarting from Kirby Smith's "Fabian policy" directive, had openly criticized his superior in the presence of subordinates. His views were picked up, repeated, and invariably found their way into the newspapers, especially those printed in Alexandria where Taylor maintained his headquarters. On November 4, for example, the day following the Bourbeux engagement, the Alexandria *Louisiana Democrat* had run a vicious editorial highly critical of Kirby Smith's conduct during the Teche-Texas campaign and demanded Smith's immediate resignation. Fed up with this incessant sniping, Kirby Smith, then in Shreveport, fired off yet another salvo at Taylor:[12]

> MY DEAR GENERAL: I inclose you an article cut from the *Louisiana Democrat* of the 4th (November, 1863). I feel convinced that it will only be necessary to call your attention to these attacks to have them controlled; being made at your headquarters, they go abroad with the impression of your sanction or as being the re-echo of your views.
>
> I know not why it is that the people of that section for whom I have exerted myself most, and for the defense of whose country I have made most sacrifices, are the only people in the (Trans-Mississippi) department who misappreciate my motives and falsify my acts.
>
> I have always accused myself of an undue partiality for the District of Louisiana. I have incurred the ill-will of the district commanders of both Texas and Arkansas in my efforts to sustain you, to increase your command, and to insure the success of your military operations...
>
> I should not notice this attack, but that it comes from a paper printed at your headquarters. I shall not let it influence my feelings or affect the cordial relations existing between us, but I consider it due to both of us that it should be brought to your attention.

Monday, November 9, 1863

As usual, daylight on the Vermilion found several thousand shivering bluecoats formed in a line of battle roughly paralleling Pinhook road. For the second time during this moribund Texas expedition they had awakened to a heavy white frost. Even the mudholes were frozen solid. This morning, at least, they would not have to wait for very long. The Signal Corps team atop St. John's reported the all-clear signal shortly after first light and all returned to camp.

If they were going to remain here, reasoned Franklin, they would have to fortify this position. Each day, it seemed, he lost one or two regiments to General Banks. Only two days before, the recently-mounted 75th New York, together with the 130th Illinois, was ordered to New Iberia to fill a vacuum created at that location by Banks' demands. It was also getting quite chilly at night and the men did not have overcoats. Many, in fact, still did not have tents but were forced to rely on their ingenuity in constructing a plank lean-to. Today he would approve foraging expeditions to bring in more building materials.

Among those hit hardest by Franklin's decision was Jean Vigneaud, alias "*Gros Jean*," who owned a livery stable at the corner of North Main and Madison (currently Buchanan) just across from the city jail. Vigneaud, age thirty-five, had come to Louisiana from the Department of Haute Garonne, France, at an early age and had built up a sizeable business in downtown Vermilionville. During the spring invasion he had lost horses to the notorious Yankee "pilot," or guide, known as Drexel (or Drexler). Worse still, the Yankees had occupied his stable as a military barracks from early October until the pullback from Buzzards' Prairie. During that period, they had taken saddles, bridles and blankets, carriage harnesses, a dozen or so iron spindled Studebacker carriages, several hundred bushels of corn and ten tons of hay.

Now, they were back again. Like so many demolition experts they proceeded to dismantle his stable, plank by plank. Wagonload after wagonload of weatherboarding, roof boards and floor boards disappeared in the direction of Vermilion Bayou until by nightfall nothing remained of his building except the frame.

A short distance away, also on Madison Street, lived Antoine Lacoste, a fifty-two-year-old blacksmith, wheelwright, and carriage maker from Paysac, Arrondisement de Cahors, France. Lacoste, like his friend Vigneaud, had built up a lucrative trade in the Attakapas country, and he was also a craftsman, an artisan *par-excellence*. Few people anywhere could build a finer wagon, buggy or cart than could Lacoste and his sons, Leopold and Louis.

In the springtime, he and another blacksmith, Romulus McBride, had lost more than most residents. Some of the Union regimental blacksmiths had taken valuable implements and supplies, including saws, chisels, forges, anvils, vices, stocks and dies, hammers, tongs and files. They had also taken buggy springs, guns, sugar, Pittsburg coal, iron and turpentine, mules, horses and trappings. In addition they had arrested McBride for some trifling offense, an act which so disturbed his wife that she soon became an invalid.

Lacoste had heard that the Yankees were "building little huts" down by the Vermilion, so he was not surprised when they called on him once more. This time they were after the large piles of wheelwright and carpenters' lumber, running into the thousands of board feet, which he kept in storage. The Federals immediately proceeded to load it onto "a strong four-horse wagon, with tires three inches wide," which he had just constructed for Sosthene Mouton and was in the process of painting.

Well, he wasn't going to quarrel with them over lumber or a wagon; nor did he open his mouth when they bored into his barrel of green rum and commenced drinking it, but when they started to haul off his screw-plate, that was just too much. Both he and his German-born helper, Auguste Falan, grabbed hold of one end while the Yankees were on the other and a general tug-of-war commenced.

"You can take anything else," shouted Lacoste in French, "but leave that!"

The soldiers, uncomprehending, began shouting in English, "Let go! Let go!"

Lacoste would not.

The scuffle was finally settled when a drunken soldier picked up a bar of iron and struck the obstinate old man on the leg. Fortunately, it was but a glancing blow and did no serious injury, but his efforts had been futile. The Yankees took the screw-plate and left.[13]

Former Governor Alexandre Mouton was also having troubles. His rebellious seventeen-year-old daughter, Anne Eliza, or "Pussy" as she was called, was shamelessly carrying on with a Union officer. "Pussy," a graduate of a Washington, D. C. school of music, was an excellent pianist, organist and harpist, and on occasion, was seen entertaining her friend at the keyboard with soft music and songs of love. At other times they could be seen strolling the grounds together or sitting and conversing in the whispered tones of lovers. When reproached and reprimanded for her "disgraceful behavior" she very promptly announced to her horrified family that she was hopelessly enamored of the handsome young stranger in blue, and had accepted his proposal of matrimony—pending, of course, her father's approval.

Even worse than "Pussy's" behavior was the food problem at Ile Copal. For almost three weeks, ever since the old governor returned from Opelousas to find that young Cecilia had passed away, it had been a desperate struggle for survival. Mouton, tall, portly and dignified in appearance, sat upon his veranda each day puffing on an unlit pipe while surveying the desolate scenes around him:

> His broad fields, lately covered with crops, were trodden down by soldiers; his extensive outbuildings were torn down; his negro cabins were deserted; and himself and family confined to his house by a guard.

He had only to ask and it would be given, but he would neither beg nor accept the charity of these despised and contemptible officers of the United States. Besides, with so many grandsons and nephews at the place, some food could be secured from hunting, fishing and gathering.

GOVERNOR ALEXANDRE MOUTON (Courtesy Lafayette History Museum)

Not that Mouton wasn't doing his share. Late each afternoon, just as the teamsters were feeding the mules, he would stroll across the grounds, stopping from time to time to engage some private soldier or Negro in conversation. Strangely enough he did not mind begging from them the little corn which their mules wasted. Once dried in the attic or before the fireplace and then pounded into a coarse meal, such corn was both edible and palatable, especially when made into corn bread.

At other times, "in the dead of night," the governor would slip past the guards "to gather up the ears of corn from under the noses of the cavalry horses." Though he was almost always observed, virtually all the guards chose to ignore his actions, frequently looking the other way. "His spirit was unbroken," wrote a New Yorker. "He never would submit to northern rule, but was glad to beg from the feed boxes of our teams."[14]

Tuesday, November 10, 1863

The tiny village of Vermilionville, or what was left of it, began taking on a ludicrous appearance. A great many once substantial buildings, mainly barns, stables, cotton gins, sugar houses, slave cabins and unoccupied dwellings had been reduced to little more than skeletal frames. In some cases private homes had been stripped of weather-board siding even as the occupants cowered inside. Almost overnight an army numbering in the thousands had practically denuded and dispossessed this little town of only a few hundred.

While the good people of "Lafayette" were fretting over their losses, the Yankees on Vermilion Bayou were indulging their fantasies. Little huts of all descriptions and shapes began to appear. A few were constructed with arched doorways over which were draped Spanish moss or a camouflage of leaves, limbs and vines; others were graced with large front porches, or joined to a neighbor's hut by a covered walkway; still others were nothing more than crude lean-tos. The excess lumber—and there was plenty of it—was used as sleeping boards, firewood and walkways along company streets. It appeared as though these thoughtless and destructive intruders were digging in for a long occupation.[15]

In the camp of the 24th Indiana, where the terrible "Fzs" and Harry Watts were quartered, someone passed the word to prepare for a food foraging expedition. For almost a week they had "blessed" the quartermaster "for the inexpressible privilege of looking into empty haversacks." Heretofore the generals had deemed it best not to permit foraging because of the proximity of the Rebels. Today, however, was a beautiful fall afternoon one week after the disgraceful affair that everyone would rather forget and a company of the 24th Indiana soon set off in search of food.

Crossing over to the south bank of the Vermilion, the Hoosiers soon came across a company of foragers from the 24th Iowa who were engaged at the time in a strange ritual with a "rebel calf." The latter, "refusing to take the Oath of Allegiance, was duly executed without trial" and the Iowans had something to eat other than camp rations.

Farther along near the plantation home of Eugene Meaux, the Hoosiers broke into even smaller details and began the search for forage in earnest. German "Fzs," in quest of a pumpkin, looked in every "nook and corner," and was about to give up when suddenly he was startled by the appearance of a huge masculine porker "fleeing from the wrath of another party." Harry Watts looked on as the curious soldier instantly "fixed bayonets and awaited the terrible onslaught." Down the narrow lane came the bewildered porker "snorting at every jump." As he came opposite "Fzs," the latter made a "furious charge, running his bayonet clear through the hog and into the rail fence."

Unfortunately the animal was traveling at such a "fearful rate" that the bayonet snapped neatly in two and the hog kept going. Determined to gain his prize, "Fzs" then started after the wounded porker with his musket, clubbing it all the while with the butt. In the process, however, the stock splintered to pieces leaving the frustrated soldier no alternative but to "schwear und gott dam" the hog to death. Finally, with his prize laying at his feet, "Fzs" started off in search of hauling assistance, but only to find the wagons already loaded and ready to leave.

"Fzs" left the "defunct porker with regret," recalled Private Harry Watts, "but managed to secure a 'punkin' which he carried in triumph to camp."[16]

A hundred miles or more north in Pineville, Louisiana, there was another triumphant occasion of sorts. That very day Corporal Joseph Powers, a member of James Garfield's 42nd Ohio, borrowed a trick from his bluecoated 2nd Louisiana (Confederate) captors. Reversing the situation, Powers somehow managed to acquire a Confederate officer's uniform. Approaching the gate, the gray-coated Yankee returned the guard's salute and walked out into freedom. He would pass himself off as a Rebel courier all the way to safety in New Orleans.

There had been other attempts, some successful and some not, but insofar as the tormented Confederate guards were concerned, they were not always unhappy to see a breakout succeed, especially if it included members of the ill-behaved 60th or 67th Indiana regiments. That very day, for example, a number of twice or thrice-captured escapees, some of them from as far away as the Tyler, Texas, prison compound, were being paraded back into camp. Among the newcomers was a ventriloquist who decided to practice his art that night upon the unsuspecting guards. After notifying the others of his intentions, the soldier caught the guard's attention by looking up toward the empty and dilapidated loft of his quarters and feigning surprise at seeing a non-existent "Sam." He then inquired in a loud voice: "Sam! What are you doing up there?"

"I'm getting out," cried the fictitious Sam, and indeed his labored voice seemed to indicate he was squeezing through a crack. Boards were creaking and separating at the seams and soon there was a loud "thump!" as he jumped to the ground.

Several Rebel guards set off in hot pursuit, but only to find that Sam was gone. Then it was Jim's turn and then John and so on throughout much of the night.

The following morning some very confused guards counted and recounted until they discovered that only one soldier, Joseph Powers of Ohio, had made good his escape. Much to their regret, all the Hoosiers were present and accounted for.[17]

Wednesday, November 11, 1863

General William Franklin was growing more nervous by the hour. That very morning, long before daybreak, he had sent out General Lee's cavalry division to reconnoiter the dangerous area around Carencro Bayou. Apparently Rebel reinforcements were arriving from beyond the Sabine and, according to reports from his spies and informers, were massing up near Buzzards' Prairie for an attack.

If that should prove to be the case, reasoned Franklin, his position was most precarious. Not only could the Texans flank the Vermilion camp, coming in from the south, but the Rebel guerillas near St. Martinville were acting up again. Only yesterday they had captured a signal officer, the second such capture in less than a month. It would be best, he thought, to retreat to New Iberia as soon as possible. There he could join Burbridge in a more defensible position, but if he delayed much longer the guerillas and their Texas friends just might be able to block his avenues of retreat. "If the enemy get between me and New Iberia," he wired his superiors, "it will embarrass me much to fight them."

If the regimental commanders did not share Franklin's anxieties, they at least felt the impact. The evening before they had been instructed to remain with their commands in camp and in a state of battle readiness. Such a simple order would have been nothing for a well disciplined and thoroughly trained army, but to keep the soldiers of the XIII Corps in camp, especially at this location, required a great deal more than just a command.

Much to the embarrassment of "Fzs," the pumpkin eater, the 24th Indiana chose to resolve the issue by holding a dress parade, to be followed by company drill and inspection. Not only was the big German the butt of jokes for losing his porker the day before, but he had been unable to replace his broken weapons. There he stood, in full battle regalia, with "his mutilated three inch bayonet," and busted musket. "At the command of 'Charge Bayonets!'," recalled Harry Watts "The scene of a big six-footer charging with so short a bayonet was so ludicrous that the boys in the ranks quivered with pent up risibilities which after parade broke forth in loud guffaws of laughter."[18]

Several miles north out near Carencro settlement, the situation was anything but funny. Captain Arthur W. Marsh, Colonel John Fonda and some five-hundred mounted Yankees were riding hard. On their tail, shooting and yelling like so many wild Indians, were more than three thousand Texas Rangers. Dogs were barking, chickens fled in panic, and the frightened residents flew to windows and doors to see what the commotion was all about.

Captain Marsh, a twenty-five-year-old Hamilton, Illinois, farmer, was barely able to take to the saddle, much less fight Texans. Though debilitated by diarrhea and recovering from a bout with typhoid-malarial fever, he had nonetheless been selected to head up the 118th Illinois Mounted Infantry, a position once held by John Fonda. It was this regiment under Marsh, which had plundered and confiscated its way from Opelousas to Plaissance and beyond to Ville Platte. It was he who had taken Minister James Earl Bradley into custody. Now, it was he who was fleeing for dear life.

For Fonda and Marsh and the others, the scene must have conjured up a chilling sense of *deja vu*, a feeling that they had witnessed this same predicament before. And indeed they had. The reconnaissance mission to the Carencro was almost identical in nature to those up near Buzzards' Prairie. First Fonda's horse, the 2nd and 3rd Illinois Cavalry regiments and the 118th Illinois Mounted Infantry, took the lead. Then they drove the Confederate pickets from their positions in a wooded coulee behind Antoine Emile Mouton's plantation. As the Texans raced back to camp, Fonda's horse entered the densely settled prairie and passed on through Carencro settlement.

The mission—to estimate the strength of the Confederates on the Carencro—turned out to be quite simple. Green's entire cavalry division, 3500 strong, was neatly lined up in battle formation to greet the boys from Illinois. So were 4000 infantrymen from Walker's Texas division as well as the Cornay, Semmes and Valverde artillery batteries. Fonda and Marsh had tangled with this same bunch too many times already and had always come out on the short end. Now, as they had done so many times before, they turned tail and ran, with Green's division in hot pursuit.

Thundering over the prairie, the Yankees ran back through the lines of Colonel Thomas Lucas and his newly formed cavalry brigade, some of whom were plundering houses in Carencro. The latter, composed of newly mounted infantry, was "as little at home on horseback as a lands-man upon a yardarm. They could not manage their horses and were greatly handicapped with their long guns." The situation would have been funny, noted an Illinois cavalryman "had the occasion been less grave." As it was, the mounted soldiers joined the rout and the chase continued on down the road.

Nearing the plantation home of Confederate General Alfred Mouton, Captain Marsh was much relieved to note that the grounds were almost surrounded by a high hedge and the remains of a rail fence. By then it had become evident that they were not going to outhorse the real horsemen so the mounted infantry was ordered to dismount and fight like the foot soldiers they were.

"It was a hot place," recalled Samuel Fletcher of the 2nd Illinois Cavalry. "The bullets zipped past our ears like a flight of hornets," but the Texans "smelt a rat" and the stampede was temporarily arrested.

Fletcher, a private from Lane, Illinois, was astonished to note that the Confederate muskets were superior to those of the Illinois soldiers. The Texans stood off at about three-quarters of a mile and "would throw a ball with great force and accuracy which would go over our lines, while ours served to kick up dust a quarter of a mile ahead." Occasionally, recalled Fletcher, a Texan would yell: "A little more powder."

Fonda reasoned that the best way to get out of this predicament was to fall back alternately, leaving Marsh and the 118th to cover the first movement. Mounting up, he had just given the command "Four's Right!" when the famed Valverde Battery dropped a devastating barrage on the retiring Yankees, creating momentary pandemonium.

Captain Marsh, still on his horse, galloped back to the hedge and shouted to his men to make a run for it. What happened then was recorded by Surgeon Madison Reece in his medical journal:

> He had given the order, and had just turned around when he was struck, and fell from his horse dead. The ball entered the right scapulae and escaped from the left breast...A column of blood was projected three feet from his body showing that a large vessel had been severed...

So near was the enemy that many of the dead and wounded, numbering about two dozen, were abandoned on the field. Then, as had happened so many times before, Colonel Fonda was saved from complete humiliation by the arrival of Nims' 2nd Massachusetts Battery and a brigade of New York infantrymen. The skirmish finally ended just north of Vermilionville, at the current location of Four Corners, after a prolonged artillery duel between Nims' and the Valverde Batteries.

Even as the Federals beat a hasty retreat toward the Vermilion, a hoary-headed old Negro, back on Alfred Mouton's plantation, stood gazing upon three nude corpses. He had watched the entire affair from behind the doors of a slave cabin. Within moments after the Yankees rushed off, a group of ragged Confederates had dismounted at the late scene of action and proceeded to strip the dead right down to and including their drawers, but they had also looked after the Yankee wounded and loaded them onto wagons.

The old man picked up a spade and began digging. He had been born a slave and would have died a slave if it had not been for these "Linkum Sojers." He had wanted to run off with the Yankees, enlisting with Van Alstyne as had many of the others, but was unable to do so because of advanced age. At the very least he would see to it that the dead Yankees were not left for the Carrion Crow vultures.[19]

"PEELING" UNION DEAD after skirmish near Carencro. ***(Leslie's Illustrated Weekly)***

At Carencro settlement several miles north of General Mouton's plantation, Oswald Patte resolved to take some long delayed action. The scion of a celebrated European violinist and himself an accomplished musician, he had come to Louisiana from his home in Amiens, Department de la Somme, with the Charles Boudousquee Opera Troupe. Although he "was not looked upon as an Ole Bull or Paganini," he nonetheless was reputed to be among the best violinists in the South. In more recent years he had married a local Spanish girl, Andrea Ynojosa, and was employed as a professor of music at both Madame Murr's Female Academy in Vermilionville and at St. Charles College in Grand Coteau.

One week before, when the Yankees retreated from the Carencro, they had raided his house. Not only had they taken six of his finest linen shirts and other goods but they had stooped so low as to steal Andrea's embroidered underwear. On the present morning, while the slaves had been milking the cows, a group of Illinois cavalrymen had surrounded the place. At first it had seemed as though they were just being mischevious, drinking up all the fresh milk from the pails and squirting milk at one another from the cows' teats, but when they left, they had taken with them all the cattle, sheep and horses.

Patte had immediately began to think of a way to save his valuable instruments in Vermilionville, among which was a rare Stradivarius violin. The latter, a gift to his father from the Portuguese royal family, was at Madame Murr's Academy. Surely the instruments would not be safe there, he thought, and must be removed to a place of safekeeping, but where and how? The problem was partially resolved by his mother-in-law, Mrs. Antonio Ynojosa (nee Celeste Arseneaux) who, in spite of the military activities of the day, was planning a trip to Vermilionville. Patte quickly penned a note and asked her to deliver it to his good friend, Dr. B. J. Salles, M. D.

According to the note, Patte's instruments, then valued at about $5,000, were located at the home of Pierre Bemalle, who lived next door to the Academy. As a deep personal favor to Patte, would Dr. Salles "go at said Academy, take out from there all his instruments and bring and deposit them at his (Dr. Salles') residence?" It was thought that Salles, "being a French subject and an eminent physician," would not be troubled by the Yankees.

Honoring the request to his good friend, Dr. Salles set off afoot toward the Academy. He was accompanied by a neighbor, Alfred Joseph Godard and an unidentified female servant. To their great relief they found the instruments intact and unharmed. Returning by the same route, boxes over their shoulders, they had almost reached home when a Captain Packinpaw rode up. Alfred Godard recalled:

> When about a few yards from Dr. Salles' residence, and just at the corner of the last square, we were suddenly all three surrounded by a body of U. S. soldiers, numbering about fifteen. A captain asked the doctor what he was carrying on his shoulders. Salles told him, and the captain replied: 'Well we need just such things. We have some musicians in our camp, but no instruments'. Dr. Salle's servant wanted to resist the captain, but a revolver shown to her by one of the soldiers made us give up the boxes.

Ironically it appears that neither Pierre Bemalle's residence nor Mrs. Murr's Academy was plundered by the bluecoats. In fact Mrs. Murr, whose Confederate husband, Auguste (a prominent member of the pre-war *Comites de Vigilance)* was killed at Shiloh, took up with a Yankee. By contrast, Dr. Salles, Joseph Godard and the *domestique* were all taken into custody. Oswald Patte, for all his concerns, never saw his Stradivarious again.[20]

For some reason Basil Crow's cotton gin, or what was left of it, caught fire that night, making a "great light" on the Vermilion. It was an appropriate ending to a terrible day, or as an Iowan put it: "The day closed with a blaze..." And in the distance nervous pickets fired away at shadows and barking dogs thoughout the night.[21]

OSWALD PATTE, accomplished violinist posing with his rare Stradivarius (courtesy Mrs. Fernand Gouaux, Lafayette).

Thursday, November 12, 1863

Colonel George Robinson's 3rd Engineer Regiment, *Corps d'Afrique* , inured as it was to grimy, dirty work, had already staked off the area for rifle pits and abatis. The camp itself, situated between Pinhook road and the Vermilion, extended from Ile Copal in the north to a point just downstream from Pinhook Bridge. To the west and north, there was nothing but open defenseless fields and prairies, sometimes broken by a coulee or *marais* . In order to protect this exposed position, a long crescent-shaped rifle pit would have to be dug along the entire front, a distance of more than two miles.

And so the work began. "A pile of fresh earth was soon thrown up near the residence of the old Governor," recalled Surgeon Harris Beecher. "Fields, roads, pleasure grounds and gardens suffered alike from the pick and spade." Though most of the work was performed by the *Corps d'Afrique* engineers, they were ably assisted by "punishment details" of illegal foragers, shirkers, goldbrickers and others who were guilty of some minor infraction. When completed, this irregular line would roughly parallel the bayou, extending from a bend in the Vermilion just above the governor's mansion to a fork in Coulee Mine, several hundred yards upstream from its mouth. A secondary set of pits would be constructed to the rear, roughly in the area now called Bendel Gardens.

DIGGING TRENCHES IN LAFAYETTE. A small section of these works are still visible in Girard Park. The artist, C.E.H. Bonwill, did not identify the plantation in the background. *(Leslie's Illustrated Weekly).*

Directly in front of the earthworks, along the entire two-mile or so length, the hardworking engineers felled trees and with mules dragged them into place with their tops outward. These "slashes," as they were called, were fronted by yet another crude barrier, an "abatis," or rows of sharpened limbs pointed toward the area of approach. So formidable were these obstacles that it would be all but impossible for cavalry or infantry to pass without paying dearly. So confident was General Franklin that he would soon signal his Chief-of-Staff in New Orleans: "My position here is good against double my number."[22]

It was also a day for white flags. Early that morning, a group of Texans had come in offering to return the Union wounded for some of their own. Someone, seeing the truce team, started a rumor to the effect that the Rebels were demanding an immediate and unconditional surrender of the entire Union force on the Vermilion. At other times and places the prospect might have been ridiculed, but when coupled with the recent skirmishes and the feverish activity in the trenches, the rumor seemed at least plausible and served to further undermine confidence and morale. Not since that fateful night before the battle of November 3rd had the men been so edgy and nervous.

Then it was the Yankee's turn for a white flag. Major Benjamin P. Marsh, the twenty-eight-year-old adjutant of the 2nd Illinois Cavalry went to inquire about the remains of his deceased brother. He had participated in the reconnaissance mission the day before, but had been spared the agony of witnessing those last moments. Escorted to the scene by several Texans, Marsh was soon joined by a white-headed old black man.

Through an interpreter the old fellow apologized for not being able to place the bodies in a coffin, or even to wrap them in blankets. The sad major, tears streaking his face, thanked him for his thoughtfulness and proceeded to exhume the three bodies. Two would be given a military burial on the Vermilion. As for his little brother Arthur, Major Marsh planned to escort him all the way back to Hamilton, Illinois, for a decent burial at home.[23]

Back in Vermilionville near the point where Colonel Bringhurst had piled up the missing cotton, a Yankee picket spotted two mounted Texans coming in under the universal white flag of truce. The sentry was quickly joined by the corporal and sergeant of the guard, as well as the officer of the day.

As the Texans drew near, someone noticed that a third person, apparently a prisoner, was leading the way. It was an unusual sight, not so much because their captive was afoot but because he was gagged with a cloth, his hands and arms bound with a rope, and he was wearing a noose about his neck which was attached to a saddle horn. Surely the prisoner must be a real troublemaker, commented a bystander.

Indeed he was. He was none other than redoubtable Michael Fox, the notorious New Hampshire private who had narrowly escaped an appointment with destiny before the firing squad. The unshorn Texans, growling and complaining about the unprincipled character of their charge, turned him over, spat a wad of exhausted tobacco on the ground, and departed without so much as demanding a *quid pro quo* arrangement. An observer was heard to comment: "The rebs don't like'em any better'n we do."[24]

Friday, November 13, 1863

Friday-the-thirteenth was shaping up as a rotten day for ten-year-old Alexandre Mouton and his mischevious brothers and cousins at Ile Copal. Returning from the mouth of Coulee Mine with a long string of river perch, a Yankee, apparently the captain of the kitchen, confiscated their catch. Stepping to the door with his prize, the Yankee addressed old Edith, the one time family cook: "Say Auntie, you know how to cook these things, don't you? Now, you prepare them the best way!" Old Edith took the fish "with her usual bow for the white folks" and disappeared into the kitchen. It was the last the disappointed little boys ever saw of their fish.

All was not lost. For weeks these innovative little barefoot boys had brought home all the food the Mouton family could eat. The menu wasn't always varied, nor was it usually desirable, but it was wholesome, abundant, and best of all, it spared them the ignominious last resort of accepting the proffered charity of these despicable Yankees.

Crossing the trench where the black engineers were throwing up earthworks, a half dozen or more little boys, clad in dresses as was the custom of the day, set off across the field. So well did the Yankees know them and what they were up to that no one troubled them about passes or permits. Finally, on reaching a spot where they had sequestered the tools of their avocation, the miniature foragers halted. All around them, always plentiful at this time of year, were thousands of blackbirds. If they couldn't have fish for dinner, they would at least have blackbirds.

Catching the birds was not difficult. They possessed neither cages nor guns but they had devised something even better, a trap called a *bois malin.* Young Alexandre recalled:

> With a very large barn door laying flat on the ground, one end is raised to an angle of 45 degrees, under which we would lay scraps of food gotten from the officer' kitchen (our kitchen). Once elevated to that height, the blackbirds had not to be coaxed, for in a very short time the ground under this door was covered. The skillfull act consisted of pulling (jerking) a rope that was fastened to the stick that held the barn door from the ground.

The first time they had tried this contraption, the falling door merely "blew all the birds out from under on both sides." That problem was soon solved by borrowing an auger from a Yankee and drilling the door full of holes. After that the trap came crashing down with a deadly impact.

"The dead birds were very plentiful," recalled Alexandre, "and well the old expression could be repeated: 'as thick as black birds'."

Once back at Ile Copal, little Caesar Mouton, Alexandre's even younger cousin, began chafing over the stolen fish. As darkness began to settle over the mansion, he called Alex aside and "with a look of great interest" enlisted the latter in a plot to steal a sack of dried apples from the kitchen.

"The thing to do," argued Caesar, "is to figure how to have Edith leave the kitchen."

There was also the problem of getting the hot merchandise out of the freestanding building and into the house, a distance of several yards. A guard was posted near the entrance, meaning that a window would have to be used. Then again, little Caesar was neither tall enough nor strong enough to lift the heavy sack to the window. Alex would have to do the inside job while Caesar would be the under-the-window man.

Their plans formulated, Little Alex strolled casually into the kitchen, trying his best to look inconspicuous.

"Hello Honey," said old Edith, at the same time asking why the boy made himself so scarce.

After a few minutes of small talk, Alex noticed "two tubs of meal water" which Edith had forgotten to feed the general's horse.

"Edith," said the concerned Alex, "do you know what is going to happen to you? Night is almost here and you have not taken the white water to the horses trough."

Edith gasped and began to thank the little boy for the reminder. "I always said you was a smart boy," she said, "I will have to repay you for this." Without another word she picked up the pails and hurried off.

Alex worked rapidly. "I took the sack and put it on a white-legged stool used for milking cows," he recalled. The heavy load was then transferred several inches higher to a hutch, then higher still to a table and, finally, to the window sill.

Looking out into the darkness Alex whispered: "Caesar, Caesar, you there?"

"I'm here," answered the little boy, whereupon Alex shoved the heavy sack out the window, almost crushing his fellow conspirator.

Alex strolled as nonchalantly from the kitchen as when he had entered. Passing the uninterested guard, he quickly darted to the back and helped Caesar out from under the sack. The two little boys then struggled through the *parterre*, or flower garden and up a back stairway to the attic.

Later that night, after a supper of blackbird fricassee and cornbread, everyone except little Alicia Mouton was delighted by the mysterious appearance of dried apple dessert. The three-year-old tot, Alexandre's younger sister, wasn't sure she wanted any because they looked like ears—human ears.

Well, if they were ears, she was told, they were *les oreilles des Yankees* so she should eat them. The name stuck, and from that day forward the cache in the attic went by the code name "Yankee ears."[25]

Friday-the-thirteenth had not been such a rotten day after all.

CHAPTER EIGHTEEN

BACK TO THE ATTAKAPAS

Wednesday, November 11, 1863

AT JUDGE JOHN MOORE'S plantation home in New Iberia on the west bank of Bayou Teche, Brigadier General Stephen Gano Burbridge was also having troubles. Unlike Generals Franklin and Washburn, whose military reputations had been badly tarnished on Bayou Bourbeux, the tall Kentuckian came out of the disgraceful affair unscathed. His reward, if it could be called that, was command of a relatively safe and desirable behind-the-lines position.

Not that there was all that much to command. Banks, the Major General Commanding, was still toying with a precarious foothold in Texas and was daily siphoning off troops. Thus on the one hand Burbridge was expected to defend New Iberia, an important supply and communications link, while on the other he was constantly weakened by Banks' incessant demands for more troops. Already Generals Lawler and Washburn had departed, taking with them the entire 1st Division of the XIII Corps. General Franklin and the main body of the Army of the Gulf was still dug in on Bayou Vermilion, twenty-five miles north, and "Pap" McGinnis, with his 1st Brigade of the 3rd Division was camped six miles away on Spanish Lake. That left Burbridge with only two brigades of infantry—one of which was his decimated brigade from the Bourbeux disaster—and the newly organized 3rd Cavalry Brigade.[1]

Even Burbridge's presence at the Moore mansion was creating problems. When he first moved into the large and imposing structure he had "flaunted his brigade flag over the entrance gate" but only to have it insulted and snubbed by two fair-skinned young Southern ladies. Unfortunately for all, that particular flag was the same which had been brought off the bloody Bourbeux battlefield and, as a result, was zealously defended by the hot-blooded young officers on Burbridge's staff. In one emotion-charged confrontation, the offending ladies, Leila and Mary Robertson, were placed under house arrest for disobeying a command to salute the flag.[2]

Such disrespect and obstinancy probably made it easier for Burbridge to commandeer all the outbuildings, the family kitchen, and the lower floor of the dwelling. As was common under such circumstances, the inhabitants, including Mrs. Moore (nee Mary Clare Conrad Weeks), several children and grandchildren, were strictly confined to the upper apartments. It was there that the elderly mistress fell mortally ill. Some claimed her illness resulted from a refusal to eat so long as the Yankees occupied her home; others attributed it to heartbreak; a Confederate account claimed that she was "deprived of the comforts she would have bestowed upon the humblest of her servants." At any rate Mrs. Moore would not survive the winter.[3]

SHADOWS ON THE TECHE, the plantation home of Judge John Moore (Contemporary photograph)

Burbridge was also concerned about the boat landing on Madame Eugene Olivier's plantation three miles below the town. It was the only supply link between Federal forces operating in western Louisiana and the quartermaster's stores in Brashear City, but an indeterminate number of Confederate guerillas were daily threatening this vital route. So far these roving bands of Rebels, led by Major St. Leon Duperier, had inflicted only minor damage on the invaders. They were far more successful, however, in tying down large numbers of Union troops who might be more usefully employed elsewhere.

Worse still, the black contrabands coming in from the west were daily reporting that large numbers of Texans under Generals Price and Magruder were crossing the Vermilion near Abbeville. Should these forces succeed in linking up with the guerillas who were then camped near St. Martinville, the Union troops up in Lafayette Parish would be effectively cut off from their overland base of supplies.[4]

In the meantime, the produce of St. Martin, St. Mary, St. Landry, Lafayette and Vermilion parishes was attracting speculators like so many greedy vultures. Even the soldiers were complaining:

> When General Burbridge arrived, he found New Iberia filled with gamblers, speculators, sutlers, camp followers and rebel citizens from all parts of the country. Each one of the motley mass had all sorts of passes, permits, and protections; oaths, obligations and orders, signed, countersigned and indorsed, approved, recommended and respectfully forwarded. Some with hoop skirts and buckshot; some with baby shoes and gun caps; some looking for cotton they had abandoned years ago and some in the patriotic duty of buying cotton at the very reasonable price of 20 cents per pound and selling it in New Orleans at 70 and 80 cents, all, however, vehemently acting for the good of the Union.

In spite of two Union invasions in less than a year, there were still enormous quantities of sugar, cotton, rum, molasses, grain and livestock safely hidden from the prying eyes of Yankee foragers and confiscating teams. The owners of these goods were only too happy to settle with a speculator for a fraction of the pecuniary gain that could be acquired in the New Orleans market. So lucrative, disorderly and widespread was the practice that it soon spilled over to officers in the Union army.[5]

If Burbridge was unsuccessful in commanding the loyalties of the females or curbing the speculators, he could at least fortify New Iberia in the event that Price and Magruder were on the march. For days, since November 9th, the all-black 25th Regiment (Union) *Corps d'Afrique* had been throwing up earthworks, abatis and slashes on the outskirts of town. Though some details are lacking, it appears that the earthworks were started on the north side of New Iberia and stretched several hundred yards from a point on Bayou Teche to the west eventually crossing the uncompleted bed of the New Orleans, Opelousas and Great Western Railroad. From the latter place the line paralleled the western side of the track as far south as Nelson's Canal.

Burbridge, like most of the other Yankees, was favorably impressed by the red hatted, hard-working, French-speaking Louisiana blacks who were constructing the works. Recruited locally, they had been in Yankee blue for less than two weeks. "Their officers strut around in all the dignity of their new and elevated position," commented a soldier from Ohio. "Their new swords glisten with bright store polish yet and their blacked boots make them feel as they have not felt for many a day."

NEW IBERIA during the war ***(Harper's Weekly)***

In spite of all the hard work, the project was progressing at a pace far too slow for Burbridge. Concerned that the Confederates might appear at any moment, the balding Kentuckian hit upon a novel idea. Why not put the speculators and idle population to work? Accordingly, he ordered the 23rd Wisconsin regiment, or what was left of it, to round up and bring to the rifle pits every able-bodied male in New Iberia.

The decision made Burbridge an instant hero, at least in the eyes of the soldiers. Typical was the reaction of a war correspondent for the *Cincinnatti Gazette*:

> Such a mess I dare say was never before seen. Nice young gentlemen in fancy kids and patent leathers, heavy operator with pocket crammed with 'legal tenders', greedy shylock vending his various wares, and sooty citizens of African descent, in one heterogeneous mass, quietly delving in mother earth side by side.
>
> Of course they thought it a great outrage that citizens should have to work on Yankee fortifications. Fair damsel with witching eye protested, elderly maiden with pious face complained, corpulent squire with stentorian voice remonstrated, thrifty speculator with patronizing air implored, and crafty shylock with tender mercies appealed, but all to no purpose. Fortifications had to be built, and citizens, speculators 'rounders', shylocks, and negroes did the

work, while soldiers stood firm at the picket post, ready to shoot down those who attempted to escape.

Of course this was justifiable. Why should not those who follow the armies, reaping golden harvests from our national calamities be made to lend a helping hand? As for impressing the citizens the general's argument was that 'an idle brain is the devil's work shop' and while they were in the ditches, he was quite sure they were not guerillaing nor carrying information to the enemy.

Putting the disreputable speculators to work was one thing, but for the innocent civilians of New Iberia it was a humiliating experience. Indeed, paroled Confederate prisoners, planters, merchants, clergymen, and alien neutrals worked side by side with former slaves, speculators and camp followers. "This was hard for the gallant Southerners to swallow," wrote an Ohio soldier to his girl friend. "As you go along the works, you can hear them talking away in their mixed French lingo, the subject being no doubt their degradation."

At one point in the ditch-digging, a certain elderly citizen, apparently exempt from work, decided to enjoy himself by taunting the Yankees. Blind in one eye, his bewhiskered face smeared with tobacco juice and hobbling along on homemade crutches, the old veteran directed some pointed barbs at several Wisconsin privates.

"If you Yanks love them darkies so much," he asked in broken English, "then why ain't you down in the trenches with them?"

"Why don't you go back to whittling wood, old man?" answered an irritated soldier.

"I'd like to go back to whittling d--- Yankees," replied the old fellow.

The insults continued, passing back and forth until two big strapping soldiers, mumbling angrily and accusing their antagonist of "cowering behind his handicap," decided to bodily remove him from the scene, but the old fellow stood his ground. Swinging his crutches wildly and cursing in French, he soon attracted the attention, the admiration and the encouragement of all the fair damsels whose husbands, brothers, sons, and boy friends were working in the trenches. A few even joined in, shouting and shoving until it appeared that a general riot was about to ensue. But alas, a gallant Union colonel, a true gentleman, stepped in and broke up the altercation. Apologizing to the ladies, he then launched a blistering verbal assault on the young privates, accusing them of unduly harassing old men and women.

Red-faced and breathing heavily, the old troublemaker hobbled away. Without a doubt he was whistling "Dixie."[6]

Thursday, November 12, 1863

On the east bank of Bayou Teche, about five miles south of New Iberia, a thirty-two-year-old Confederate major named St. Leon

Duperier watched cautiously as a Union transport steamed into sight. Ever since the Federals marched up from Brashear City, Duperier's little battalion of mounted Zouaves had harassed and evaded the enemy. Recruited from deserters in St. Martin Parish, especially from the discredited Yellow Jacket (Fournet's) Battalion, they regularly cut telegraph wires, ambushed and captured Signal Corps outposts, burned cotton to keep it from falling into Union hands and, most dangerously, shot up Yankee steamers on the Teche. It was they who had sniped at the boat carrying General Banks. Only a few days earlier they had fired upon and severely damaged the *Red Chief* and *A. G. Brown*. Today it was the *Southerner's* turn.

But the *Southerner* had come prepared. Not only was she barricaded with cotton bales about the pilot house, but an all-black company of the 22nd Infantry (Union) *Corps d'Afrique* was on board and waiting for such an ambush. Steaming upstream toward Olivier's Landing, the Union ship had just maneuvered past the burned-out bridge at Devezin Olivier's place when Duperier's guerillas, clad mainly in civilian clothing, opened fire. Almost instantly the French-speaking Louisiana blacks, dressed in Yankee blue, returned their fire. So emboldened were the "boat burners" by their recent successes, however, that they continued the ineffectual running assault up the Teche for almost three hours. The shooting finally stopped when a Union regiment, the newly mounted 75th New York, drew up on the opposite bank.

Major St. Leon Duperier had badly underestimated his adversary. Normally the east bank of Bayou Teche, bordered as it was by the mysterious Great Cypress Swamp, was strickly avoided by the invaders, but within minutes after Duperier's withdrawal, his rear guard reported that the Yankee horsemen had apparently crossed over on the steamer and were in hot pursuit. Untested in the saddle, the 75th New York dragoons were spoiling for their first mounted fight.

There then occurred a spectacle all too reminiscent of Fonda's many unsuccessful brushes with the Texans, but this time the numerically superior Yankees were on the offensive. Up on the east bank of Bayou Teche they went, shooting and yelling all the way to Fausse Pointe and into the mysterious Grand Bois "gobbling" up all who lagged behind.

Once into the forest and familiar surroundings, the outnumbered and tired Confederates regained the upper hand. Roads, as such, were non-existent. Narrow water-covered trails, in some places wide enough to accommodate only a single horse, meandered through the dark woods. Light was shut out from above by giant sweet gums, ash, moss-draped live oaks and bell-bottomed cypress trees. Enormous vines, many with the appearance of a giant serpent, twisted their way upward, through and around the heavy foliage. So forbidding was the

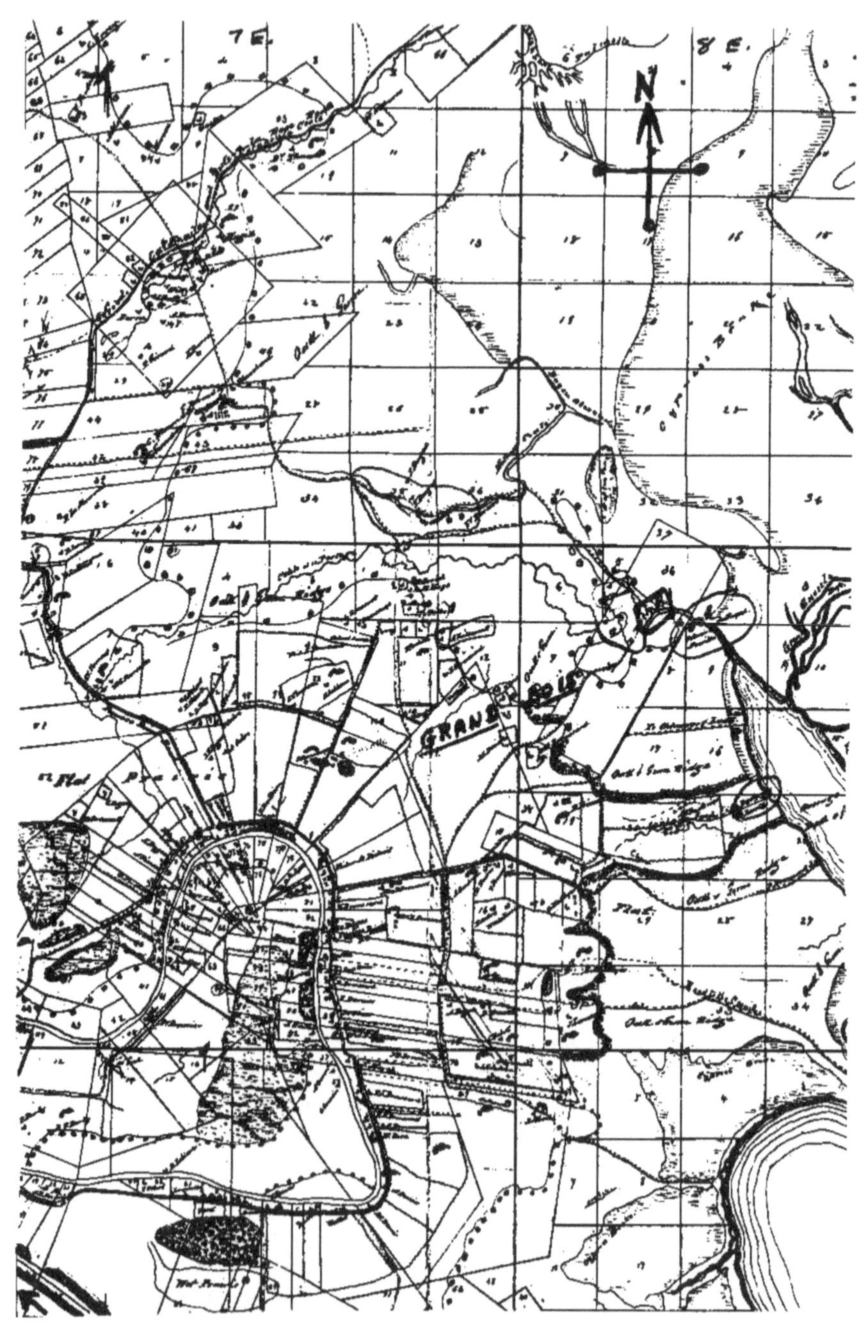

GRAND BOIS AND FAUSSE POINT east of Bayou Teche from 1863 Confederate map of St. Martin Parish. (National Archives)

area that planters along the Teche had transported and sequestered cotton, sugar, molasses and rum in out-of-the-way places along the endless trails and coulees. Some of the higher places along the Coteau Holmes harbored guarded camps of cattle, horses, sheep and even slaves. The Yankees, it was believed, would not dare enter the Grand Bois, and, even if they did, would probably not come out alive.

With the approach of darkness many of the Louisiana Cajuns, most of whom had lived in the area since birth, merely turned onto some familiar watery side trail and melded into the forest. The pursuit finally ended at the point where the main trail terminated abruptly on Bayou Portage about two miles above Grand Lake. Though the Confederates could still he heard thrashing through the woods beyond the Portage, the 75th New York dared not penetrate deeper.[7]

CONFEDERATE GUERILLAS attack an unidentified Union steamer. ***(Harper's Weekly)***

In Abbeville, Louisiana, some twenty miles west of the New Iberia camp, Francois D. Lege could not remember when he had been more frightened. Though only twenty-three-years-old he was both deputy sheriff and parish constable and, along with his father, Sheriff Alexandre Lege, was responsible for enforcing the laws of Vermilion Parish. But what should he do about these Yankees—Fonda's entire horse brigade—then dismounted between his father's and uncle's place? They were helping themselves to hogs, chickens and other produce but, so far, had done nothing really destructive.

Abbeville, located in Vermilion Parish, lay on the open prairies to the west of the Teche and was somewhat off the beaten tracks of the opposing armies. For this reason its population was swollen with refugees, conscript evaders, deserters from both sides and dependents of Confederate servicemen. On the one hand the war had brought a shortage of food, housing and medical provisions, whereas on the other it had brought an abundance of violence, illness, grief, death and hate.

Indeed the entire town was divided into two opposing camps of opinion: those who supported the Confederacy and those "abolitionists" who did not. Rare was the day that some shooting, knifing or beating did not occur. Funeral processions were common sights as were the noisy visits by "Texicans" who frequented the establishments catering to *femmes de joie,* but who seemed to derive their greatest pleasure from fighting one another, shooting their pistols in the air and stealing food. Even the parish priest, Father Jean Arthur Poyet, was an occasional participant in some fist-swinging altercation. "The people here are scarcely civilized," wrote the transient wife of a Confederate officer after she witnessed a wife beating incident.

Even more sinister were the frequent raids into town by William Vincent's jayhawk-hunting 2nd Louisiana Cavalry. Not only would they round up and arrest deserters and conscript evaders, but they harassed and frequently arrested innocent civilians suspected of harboring Union sympathizers. On two occasions they arrested Mayor Belden, whose family had come to Louisiana from Massachusetts, on trumped-up charges of espionage. Belden was tried, acquitted and eventually released, but there were many others who rode out of town with Vincent only to never be seen or heard from again.

And then the Yankees came to Abbeville. The first visit of these unwelcome bluecoats had occurred on October 7, just as the main body of invaders was approaching New Iberia. At that time they, like Vincent, had raided private homes, hotels, business establishments and coffeehouses, in the latter case "frightening the gamblers from their favorite game (poker)." On Sunday, October 18th, they had returned to arrest "Confederate sympathizers," among whom were Eugene Guignon, editor of the Abbeville *Meridional*, and a Mr. Frank. Now, they were back again and Sheriff Lege was just as helpless as before.

The only other law enforcement organzation around was the so-called Vermilion Parish "Home Guards," composed mainly of foreigners (e.g. Pierre Gueydan) and a few conscript evaders. Their objectives, according to L. M.Bernard of Abbeville, were to "guard the parish . . . against the insurrection of negroes, to keep the peace, and help the parish officers, and also to keep out of the rebel army." About the only duty they had performed so far—aside from an occasional drill and running from Confederate authorities—was to hang two blacks who had murdered Cesaire LeBlanc, one of their own. Now, with the Yankees in town, they conveniently managed to stay out of sight.

HOME GUARD in Louisiana examining Negro passes. ***(Harper's Weekly)***

Fortunately for the Leges, Fonda's horse was not in a destructive mood. They had left Vermilionville early that morning to check out the persistent rumors that Price and Magruder were crossing the Vermilion near Abbeville. Some of the officers took dinner with the sheriff and, after asking a few questions about the presence of Rebels, moved on through Abbeville.

Avoiding the home of Lasti Richard, whose wife Carmesille (nee Abshire) was then delivering a child (Lastie) the Yankees rode past the little Catholic church, which had been blown away by the same hurricane that demolished Ile Derniere in 1856, and stopped finally at the dwelling of August Olle. A baker by profession, the thirty-year-old "Gascon" Frenchman lived in downtown Abbeville in the home of Victor Boite, with a "griffone," or brown mulattress, and their three young children. Olle also owned a few head of cattle which, to the Yankees, looked about as savory as any for supper that night. Just for good measure they arrested Olle's mistress for resisting their efforts, then took a few mules and moved on.[8]

Friday, November 13, 1863

Daylight on Bayou Portage found the officers of Duperier's Battalion taking a head count. The attack on the *Southerner* had resulted in only light casualties, but the humiliating chase up the Teche was another matter. All night long, even during a cold drizzling rain, the men continued straggling in. Duperier's worst suspicion was confirmed when his adjutant, Lieutenant Martin Voorhies, reported more than two dozen men as missing, captured by the New Yorkers. This was a major blow. Rare was the occasion when Duperier's Battalion, numbering about two hundred on the rolls, could muster more than one hundred for duty because of their lackadaisical attitudes about the war.

And there was more bad news. During their withdrawal from the Grand Bois, the Yankees had passed through the little town of St. Martinville where they not only burned the bridge over the Teche and badly frightened the inhabitants, but also arrested Colonel Valsin Fournet, the ailing former commander of the Yellow Jacket Battalion. Worst of all, the enemy now knew the approximate location of the guerilla camp. Virtually everyone in the Battalion, including Duperier himself, reckoned they would be back.

Duperier was no doubt disgusted with himself, and he now would have to make some tough decisions. The Grand Bois was a hiding place for the products of the Teche country, but according to an act of the Confederate Congress, he, as the senior officer, was obligated to destroy all produce which might otherwise fall into the enemy's hands. This he was loathe to do. After all, Duperier himself was from Grand Point, and most of the planters and settlers in the Grand Bois and Fausse Pointe area were acquaintances, if not close family friends. Even the men of his command were locally recruited and could not be called upon to destroy their own or their neighbor's property. Besides, the planters could still sell to speculators and at least receive something for their labors. And even if the goods fell into Union hands, it was common knowledge that the Yankees sometimes gave receipts along with a promise that a settlement would be made after the war.

Still, some of the more conspicious caches could not be ignored. Not more than a quarter mile from Duperier's camp, at the plantation home of Terrance Boutte, at least seventy bales of cotton were stashed on skids out in the open. Farther on, at Valsin Bernard's and Emile DeCuir's, there was even more. These large piles were protected from the elements by nothing more than a few cypress boards and tree bark thrown over the top. When the Yankees came, which they surely would, the cotton would lead them right to the edge of Duperier's camp.

After making a few inquiries, Duperier learned that most of the stashed cotton belonged to planters along the Teche, including Widow Leufroy Provost of Jeanerette, a Mr. Bergerie of New Iberia and others, none of whom were old family friends. Without another thought, he detailed his second-in-command, Captain J. R. Ducros and a squad of men to torch several piles. The deed done, Duperier sat back and waited for the inevitable visit.

He would not have long to wait. Even as the Confederates went about their duties of destroying cotton, Union General Burbridge was making preparations to rid himself of these pesky guerillas. First he needed more information about their strength, their location and the nature of the countryside. It would be best, he reasoned, to send a large overnight scouting party to St. Martinville. From the latter place they could move on Duperier's territory in the Grand Bois.[9]

Saturday, November 14, 1863

St. Martinville, Louisiana, one of the original homes of the Acadians and the site of the old *Poste des Attakapas*, lies on the west bank of Bayou Teche. The little town was widely known as *Le petit Paris de la Louisianne* because of the refinement of its people, their politeness and their sociability. It was here that the tragic Emmeline Labiche, believed to be Longfellow's immortal Evangeline, discovered her long lost lover, but only to learn that he belonged to another:

> On the Banks of the Teche, are the towns of St. Maur and St. Martin.
> There the long-wandering bride shall be given again to her bridegroom.

In wartime the attractive little town served as neutral territory between the belligerents. The pickets of both sides frequently entered the town, but as though by tacit consent, they usually observed it's neutrality. In the spring, Union soldiers had even joined forces with the beleaguered citizenry to brutally suppress an incipient Negro uprising. But lately, thanks to Major St. Leon Duperier and his roving guerillas, the Yankees had turned hostile. Not only had they burned the famous bridge where the upstart blacks had been hung in the spring, but they also imprisoned some of the town's leading citizens, including Supreme Court Justice Albert Voorhies.[10] Thus it came as no surprise when Union Major Bacon Montgomery, accompanied by portions of the newly organized 3rd Cavalry Brigade, rode into town late at night. A hero of the Bourbeux affair, the twenty-three-year-old Georgetown, Missouri, farmer was looking for "French guerillas." Riding past the famous Evangeline oak where God's little angel found her lover, Montgomery and company drew up in front of the ancient St. Martin of Tours Catholic Church.

Not that they were interested in attending late Saturday services. On the contrary, their attention was centered on a small stable beside the church where six fine blooded horses—Gem, Orga, Gazell, Mazurka, Puss and Mary—were quartered.[11]

Inside the rectory was Father Ange-Marie Jan, the sixty-one-year-old priest from Pontery, Department of the Morbihan, France. Father Jan was an almost saintly figure in St. Martinville. During the 1855 outbreak of yellow fever, when practically everyone had abandoned the town and its sick, Father Jan remained "at his post of honor like a soldier." Alexandre Barde, author of the classic work on the Vigilante Committees of the Attakapas, wrote that "his ministry chained him to the bed of the dying, to show them heaven and God through the anguish of agony. He went wherever there was suffering, wherever life was ebbing."

Father Jan was no less courageous when this new plague descended on St. Martinville. "At about ten o'clock of the evening," he recalled, "my Sacristan told me that someone was taking my horses, and that the Federals were in the yard."

It was not the first time that Father Jan and the church had been visited. During the spring invasion, troops of the 114th New York, under the command of Colonel Elishu B. Smith (later killed at Port Hudson) had taken horses, hogs, cattle and corn. A few had entered the church premises where they stole some of the sacred vessels, desecrated the altar and even paraded around in sacerdotal robes.

Determined that such outrages would not occur again, Father Jan rushed out into the cold night air to find not only Yankee cavalrymen, but his slaves and household servants as well. In fact two of his servants, Amanda and her small daughter, and Oscar Ellis, a slave belonging to Alexandre Bienvenu, had hitched up his carriage and were about to drive off:

> I asked them what they were going to do with my carriage; that I had received no call to go out; the soldiers told me it belonged to them; I attempted to unharness my horses but the soldiers pushed me aside.

Growing angry, Father Jan displayed his *Sauf Conduit* signed by General Washburn, but he did not know that Washburn was in Texas and could no longer enforce the order. "I told them that I was a French subject," recalled Jan, "but they laughed at me; I had two French flags unfurled and attached to my balconies but those flags were dragged down by the soldiers."

In one last desperate attempt to save his beloved horses, the old father garnered his courage and lunged toward a Federal officer. He was going to show this pack of thieves that he would not be pushed around. Though somewhat overweight and stooped with age he nonetheless managed to wrestle the reins away even as the church beadle, Laurent Alexandre, shouted words of encouragement. Several soldiers joined the altercation and within moments had pinned both the belligerent priest and the beadle to the ground. The offended officer, red-faced and breathing heavily, then proceeded to administer a severe beating to Father Jan's backside with the flat of his saber.

ST. MARTIN OF TOURS CATHOLIC CHURCH, St. Martinville, Louisiana, where Father Ange-Marie Jan was accosted by Federal troops. (Contemporary photograph—courtesy of John Stephan, Lafayette)

Father Jan thus learned the hard way to turn the other cheek. With bruised dignity and scorched robes he stalked into the rectory, but only to be followed by four officers demanding that they be wined and dined.

In the meantime, the Missouri cavalry broke into the crib and commenced feeding the stored grain to their hungry horses. They were ably assisted by most of Jan's slaves, including Jean Baptiste Comeaux, Charles Fontenette and Eulalie John, all of whom planned to leave with the soldiers.

Not far away from the church, at the home of St. Denis DeBlanc, a young slave known only as "Lijah" decided to make his move. For weeks, ever since the Yankees had come up the Teche, he had planned to run away and go into Union lines, but more than his freedom, he wanted that magnificent stallion, "Gem." There was no finer horse in St. Martinville.

Crossing the street where the Yankees were feeding their horses, "Lijah" quietly took "Gem" by the reins, mounted up and rode out of sight. It was the last anyone ever heard of "Lijah" and "Gem."[12]

Sunday, November 15, 1863

Daylight on the Teche found Bacon Montgomery and his band of several hundred mounted plunderers crossing over onto the east bank of the bayou four miles north of St. Martinville. Proceeding south along the Teche back toward St. Martinville, they soon turned east onto the Fausse Pointe road and entered the Grand Bois. This time they were not to be outwitted by unfamiliar trails. Employing a dozen or more local blacks as guides, including Celestin Cass (a former slave of William Darden) and Charles Collins, they stopped at house after house, where they found even more guides—and prisoners. Among the latter was a Confederate Captain in Duperier's Battalion, A. Fenelon Dugas, who never stood a chance as he was captured at home in bed with his wife.

Farther along the Yankees crossed the Portage on a hastily constructed bridge of *pieux* and drew up at the edge of the guerilla camp. If they had expected to catch Duperier's force napping they were sorely surprised. Within moments they were driven off by a withering barrage of small arms fire from concealed positions.

Deprived of their main target, the Union cavalrymen continued their reconnaissance mission along the Coteau Holmes, stopping at each house along the way. At the residence of Jean Cecile Moulis, they not only asked questions regarding the Confederates, but also looted the premises. Similar deeds were perpertrated at the homes of Bernard Dauterive, Joseph Breaux and Francis Mestayer.

Approaching the Oak and Pine Alley home of Charles Durand, they entered a long drive shaded by a magnificent overhang of moss-enshrouded trees. According to legend these had once been covered with the webs of imported silk worms and sprinkled with gold dust for the wedding of Durand's daughter. Unconcerned with such matters Montgomery's men soon came upon and torched a pile of cotton which Duperier had spared. Farther along they passed within a few yards of a slave camp belonging to Louis Elvi Dugas, but without discovering it.

Perhaps the greatest outrages of the day were inflicted upon the family of Pierre Alexandre Vuillemot, a fifty-two-year-old sugar planter from Venire, Department of Haute-Saone, France. Vuillemot was at home with wife Olivanie (nee Dugas) and his daughter, Anne Louise, the wife of A. A. Flory. Many years later Madame Vuillemot explained what happened that day:

They broke down the fences; they entered the sugar-house on their horses and drove away the laborers; they capsized the coolers and the hogsheads of sugar. I closed the house and wished to prevent them from coming in (but) they fired into the house, forced their way in and commenced to search everywhere; they asked me for the keys of my armoire; I refused them whereupon they fired twice into it, breaking the doors and opening them.

Inside the armoire in a blue wooden box was a small treasure, including twelve thousand dollars in Confederate currency, seven hundred French Francs, several gold watches, some jewelry and other valuable family heirlooms.

Madame Vuillemot became quite hysterical when she realized that the Yankees were in fact going to take the contents. Screaming and crying she grabbed the box. A slave on the place, Casimir Jean Louis, recalled that "my mistress had one end and the Yankee had one end, and the Yankee bit my mistress's finger." One soldier wrenched a ring from the bitten finger while another snatched her ear pendants, "tearing away the end of one ear." Madame Vuillemot recalled that "they also twisted my neck in such a way that it remained stiff for several weeks."

Her husband, Pierre Alexandre, rushed to her assistance, "whereupon one of the Federals fired upon him with his musket, the ball passing through the rim of his hat."

Vuillemot's daughter, Anne Louise, screamed, "Be quiet, or else they will kill you." Vuillemot cooled off but, because of his attempted assault on a Union officer, he was taken into custody still grumbling and cursing in French.

With their confiscated carts, wagons, animals loaded with produce, and their pockets crammed with loot, the Yankees returned to camp in New Iberia.They had not taken Duperier, but they knew the exact location of his camp as well as the layout and treasures of the land. They would be back.[13]

Even as Montgomery's men were threatening and plundering in the Grand Bois, Harai Robinson's 1st Louisiana (Union) was perpertrating similar deeds in the little divided town of Abbeville. Early that morning they had been ordered to Vermilion Parish to burn Perry's Bridge, where it was erroneously reported that large numbers of Texans were making their way across the Vermilion.

Once more they bullied their way into homes, businesses and churches, plundering and demanding to know where the Rebels were hiding. One cavalryman galloped up to "Mandy," an old *domestique* at Mr. Kearney's and asked "if there were any rebbles (sic) in town."

"Oh yes," she facetiously replied, "plenty in every house."

"How sweet are these unbleached citizens," responded the Yankee with a grin.

Among those interrogated and badly frightened were Sophia and Susan Robertson, Mrs. A. Spaulding, a Mr. Fontelieu, "Gus" Perry, Priscilla Bond and Mrs. Albert G. Maxwell (nee Martha Nixon). So angered was Mrs. Maxwell by their abrupt entry, subsequent plunder and rude behavior that she shouted after them to go "as far in hell as a pigeon could fly."

As a parting gesture, one of Robinson's Yankees took a shot at old Dr. H. Abadie who had stuck his head out the window to render some gratuitous insult. The bullet splintered the shutters but fortunately missed its target. So intense was the hatred generated by such visits that Priscilla Bond, the ailing wife of a Confederate officer, wrote in her diary that Louisiana should change the name of Bayou Carrion Crow "to Yankee Carion since we killed so many Yankees there."[14]

Monday, November 16, 1863

Major General William Franklin, still at Ile Copal near Vermilionville, was a much relieved man. For days he had been fighting a semantic battle with his superiors in New Orleans. On the 13th, for example, he had received an ambiguous message directing him to "make such arrangements as you think will best secure the occupation of as much of the Teche country as your present force can hold."

What did that mean, wondered Franklin? An overland invasion of Texas via southwestern Louisiana had not yet been written off. For the time being, Franklin's objective was to keep the Confederates east of the Sabine while Banks secured his foothold in the Lone Star State. That, however, could be done from New Iberia just as well as Vermilionville. There the Teche was navigable at all seasons, while to furnish the army on Vermilion Bayou would mean wagoning supplies over defenseless prairies for some twenty-five miles; and if the rumors about Price and Magruder were true, the Vermilion position could be flanked, thereby cutting off his supply base. With these thoughts in mind, the commanding general wired New Orleans:

> With the large force of cavalry of the enemy, he can make it very uncomfortable for us between here and New Iberia, and, besides, he can get to New Iberia...before I can. I think it will be well to make that point (New Iberia) our extreme one. What do you think of this, or does your dispatch mean the Teche proper? That is, do you consider Vermilion a part of the Teche country?

Receiving no reply, Franklin fired off another message detailing the consequences of remaining on the Vermilion. When that too was ignored, the general decided to take the initiative. With or without permission from Banks he was withdrawing to New Iberia.[15]

GENERAL FRANKLIN'S ARMY retreating from Vermilionville.
(Leslie's Illustrated Weekly)

Thus at 7 o'clock A. M., much to the delight of Vermilionville's civilian population, the Army of the Gulf, or what was left of it, began its retrograde march. In spite of strict orders to the contrary, the wooden shanties on the Vermilion were soon ablaze and "immense fires lit up the sky." Moving across the newly constructed wooden bridge over the Vermilion—the India rubber pontoons had long since been replaced—the troops reached the southeast bank where the bloodless battle of Pinhook Bridge had occurred more than a month before. "It was a splendid sight to see the army form," wrote a Bostonian, "and move off over the prairie with bands playing."

No sooner had the last Union soldier crossed the Vermilion than a team of black engineers, protected by a rear guard section of Nims' Battery, proceeded to drench the structure with coal oil. Despite some frantic last ditch efforts by a group of Texas horsemen to drive them off, the bridge was "soon enveloped in smoke and flames, black clouds of the former rolling above the trees." It was the third time in less than a year that Pinhook Bridge had burned.[16]

Never had the Texans been more welcome in Vermilionville. There was a time when they had been cursed and insulted. Citizens had openly stated their preference for Yankees over Texas rule. Now, after almost six weeks of the former, it was clear where their preferences lay. Crowds thronged the streets to cheer on the hirsute horsemen of Green's cavalry who, like so many conquering heroes, waved and blew kisses to the onlookers while showering the streets with tobacco juice. From virtually every rooftop and window there fluttered the Confederate Stars and Bars. Much to the delight of all, a brigade band struck up the "Texas Rangers":

> Come all you Texas Rangers, wherever you may be,
> I hope you'll pay attention and listen unto me,
> My name is nothing extry, the truth to you I'll tell,
> I am a roving Ranger and I'm sure I wish you well.

Then it turned to the stirring strains of "Dixie" and back to the "Texas Rangers" again. An old Texas veteran, reading Kipling's *Tommy* many years later, was reminded of that paradoxical occasion:

> Oh it's Tommy this, an' Tommy that, an' Tommy go away,
> But it's 'Thank You Mr. Atkins', when the bands begin to play.
> It's Tommy this, an' Tommy that, an' 'Chuck him out, the brute!'
> But its 'Saviour of 'is country' when the guns begin to shoot.

Aside from the fact that the Yankees were gone, there was not much to cheer about. A Texas Confederate, Private John R. Cox, wrote his parents:

> If you were ondley hear to look round and see the distruction. All of the fences burnt up, corn riunt, house burnt, cattle shot down. Ther air plenty of family hear that has not got a ear of corn. No pin can discribe it.

Another Confederate, Colonel Gustave Breaux, a native of Vermilionville, was equally appalled:

> Desolation as usual mark their steps. Fences and buildings are torn to pieces and burned. Crops are stolen away and destroyed, even when not used. Hogs and cattle and sheep and chickens are all taken away. That they should take what they need is perhaps only what could be expected, but that they should have killed only for mischevious purposes...shows what an infamous people we have to deal with. Robbery and plunder seem to be their only end.

Although the physical losses were great, the subsequent recriminations would be even worse. Many of Vermilionville's citizens had committed the cardinal sin of openly siding with the invaders. Others, perhaps a majority, had signed the infamous loyalty oath. Before the invasion and occupation neighbors and friends had conversed openly and freely, frequently disagreeing without being disagreeable, but no more. An ugly tone of hate, ostracism and hostilities would soon set neighbor against neighbor, relative against relative, white against black, and friend against friend. The occupation would leave such scars for generations.

The conquering Texans, however, were unconcerned with such local matters. Still singing the "Texas Rangers" they quickly moved into the abandoned campground between Pinhook road and the Vermilion. Before nightfall their "sappers and miners were put to work," and by daylight on the following morning, there was yet another Pinhook Bridge. The Texans were anxious to go Yankee hunting:[17]

> Twas at the age of sixteen I joined this jolly band.
> We marched from San Antonio unto the Rio Grande,
> Our Captain, he informed us, perhaps he thought it right,
> Before you reach the station boys, I'm sure you'll have to fight.

Tuesday, November 17, 1863

By 10 A. M., the first of Franklin's long blue columns began marching into New Iberia. They had spent a cold, but otherwise dry and clear, night at the old Rebel camp of instruction on Spanish Lake (or Lake Tasse) and had been on the march since 5 o'clock. Some of the regiments continued on down the Teche to Nelson's Canal and beyond as far as Olivier's Landing. Others sought campsites a mile or more upstream from New Iberia. By noontime the last regiment, Colonel Thomas Bringhurst's 46th Indiana, went into camp on the north side. The Union camp now stretched from New Iberia downstream along the west bank of Bayou Teche for more than six miles.

Although most of the troops were exhausted from the march, they were also hungry for fresh rations. For more than two weeks they had lived on army rations while skirmishing daily with the Rebels. Now that they were in a relatively safe location, or so they believed, many reverted back to their old habits of illegal foraging and began drifting in and out of camp by the dozens. A few of the less fortunate ones walked right into the arms of the waiting Texans. In fact by late afternoon more than two dozen stragglers, nine foraging wagons and a half dozen or more pickets had fallen captive to the 5th Texas Cavalry.

Then, as though to warn the Yankees against foraging, a large portion of Green's Confederate cavalry drew up in one long ragged gray line fronting the uncompleted railroad bed. Lieutenant A. A. Rigby of the 24th Iowa thought it amusing as the remaining stragglers came rushing in "under full sail." Colonel John Slack, who at the time was dictating orders in a letter to his wife, thought the Rebels were the most "impudent" bunch he had ever confronted. At any rate Nims' Battery and the heavy Parrotts of the 17th Ohio soon sent them "skedadaling."[18]

The Texans had made their point. The camp in New Iberia was not going to be any more comfortable than the one just vacated on the Vermilion.

As night fell over the gloomy Union camp, another event of some significance occurred. Private Michael Fox, the condemned prisoner of the 8th New Hampshire regiment, then camped near Nelson's bridge, plotted another daring breakout. Though handcuffed and under the watchful eye of an armed guard, Fox enlisted the assistance of Privates John Cane and Ned McCabe. Sometime during the night, after the others had gone to sleep, McCabe jumped the guard "catching his gun with both hands while Cane struck him in the jaw and knocked him senseless." Cane and McCabe, who related this story more than forty years later, then helped Fox outside the lines and pointed him in the direction of Opelousas. The last notation in Fox's service record states simply: "Deserted from New Iberia, La. under sentence of death."[19]

Wednesday-Thursday, November 18-19, 1863

Captain George Wilhelm, a thirty-three-year-old redheaded, blue-eyed native of Scioto County, Ohio, decided to amuse himself by playing on the ignorance of some of his unsuspecting comrades in the 56th Ohio. An unrepentant prankster, Wilhelm had once been badly wounded and captured at Champion's Hill near Vicksburg. Applying his talents to the situation then, the wounded officer managed to trick his captors and escape, an act which earned him and his practical jokes a place of everlasting respect in the regiment. Addressing himself now to a group of fellow officers in the cold morning air, Wilhelm inquired "if they felt like taking a horn before breakfast?"

In the parlance of the time "taking a horn" meant a drink of liquor, and there were plenty of takers. Within moments a large group of officers and enlisted men, with Wilhelm at the head, could be seen "wending their way up the levee of the bayou" and downstream toward Olivier's Landing.

Finally, about a mile south of camp, the thirsty group came upon the tannery of Francois Lanet and Jules Poirson. Captain Wilhelm, pointing to a large pile of cowhorns beside the Teche, "invited each one present to help himself to a choice horn, a long or a short one."[20]

Back in camp the men received some incredible news. For the time being, it was announced, the Great Texas Overland Expedition was suspended. In the meantime each regiment was ordered to prepare for remaining stationary for at least thirty days. This, of course, meant foraging for food and lumber, but General Franklin added some words of warning. Pickets from Green's cavalry division, he had heard, were now camped around Spanish Lake. As a precautionary measure foragers should avoid the areas to the immediate north and west. In addition, each regiment was to strictly adhere to regulations. In other words, there would be no excessive destruction or looting, no individual foraging and, when goods were taken, a receipt would be furnished.

As usual, such regulations were a joke to the officers and men of the XIII Army Corps. The 77th Illinois, under the command of a Major Hotchkiss, was lectured by General Burbridge before departing on a foraging expedition: "Now Major," said the Kentuckian, "I hope you will observe these orders very strictly, and tell your men for me, that if they should unfortunately catch any chickens or geese, or anything else, they must be very careful and not get bitten."

Three very "emphatic cheers" went up for Burbridge.

With so much disrespect for army regulations, and indifference to the suffering of the innocent civilians, it was inevitable that the desire to plunder would soon spread to the better disciplined soldiers of the XIX Army Corps. In the 8th Vermont, Colonel Stephen Thomas made it a practice to lecture his men whenever the sight of sleek cattle or sheep attracted their attention: "Now don't let me see you touch one of those animals!" he would warn, emphasizing the word *see*. And it was presumed that he never did *see* his soldiers engaged in such acts.

Aside from geese, chickens, cattle, sheep, yams, and sugar, the products in highest demand were building materials. If they were going to remain in camp for a month they might as well be comfortable. "We had made it a practice during the past year to never lie on the ground," wrote Private Augustus George Sinks of the 46th Indiana:

> After taking all the loose boards and board fences, we went for a number of unoccupied houses and appropriated them for making bunks. Samuel Johnson and myself built us a house high enough to stand in, covering it with our ponchos. We built a small brick chimney by the side of the door. The brick we obtained by tearing up the culvert on the uncompleted railroad near us. The men would go several miles up the bayou and tear down sugar houses, corn cribs, etc. and make a raft of the lumber, float it downstream to camp and build their huts.

Sinks failed to mention that in many instances private homes were dismantled, board by board, whether they were occupied or not. In the case of Jean Pierre Senac, a thirty-one-year-old butcher from Bernadette, Department of the Haute-Pyreness, France, the Yankees took the entire dwelling house, several outhouses, a barn and all the fencing. Another Frenchman, thirty-seven-year-old Jean Cazes, also of the Haute-Pyrenees, lost his dwelling house, a slaughterhouse and a chicken house as well as fences, livestock, grain, wagons, guns, sugar and even the bed which he shared with his New Orleans mistress, Marianne Courtois.

UNION CAMP IN NEW IBERIA alongside Bayou Teche. A corduroyed road in the foreground was also made of confiscated lumber. *(Leslie's Illustrated Weekly)*

For at least three full days, November 18-20, the plunder and destruction continued unabated. In St. Mary Parish at the present location of Patoutville, the rather extensive plantation of Madame Appoline Fournier was a favorite target. The administrator of her estate, Hypolite Patout, recalled some of the visits:

> ...during three consecutive days, bands of soldiers belonging to the infantry entered her plantation and came into her house and into her and her daughter's bed-rooms, in fact everywhere...And after the above acts were done by whites, the negroes of the 19th Army Corps appeared on the scene. These colored troops stayed some hours upon the place, invading her home, entering into the rooms by battering in the doors when closed against them...They said they had a right to the property, and also a right to burn up the place.

In New Iberia, lumber was stolen from Bernard Laplene, whose coffee house still served as the Union communications center. Livestock, furniture and even the kitchen sink disappeared from the residence of Raymond Deffez. The mayor of New Iberia, Alexis Derouen, then living on Weeks Street, was also visited; so was Dr. Alfred

Duperier, a loyal Unionist, as well as Elie Montague, Louis and Etienne Frilot, Joseph Robin, J. D. Swain, Moses Adler, Ester Levy, Jacques Foucade, and many, many others.

Before long, citizens were filing into New Iberia by the dozens, angrily demanding to see the Union commander. General Franklin, then quartered with Burbridge at the Moore mansion, became quite concerned, especially on hearing reports that the XIX Army Corps was also involved in the thoughtless plunder.

Summoning Weitzel for a showdown, the commanding general soon became embroiled in a heated exchange regarding the behavior of the Easterners. At one point, even as Franklin was shaking an accusatory finger in Weitzel's face, two privates, members of the 8th Vermont Infantry, walked past carrying a load of geese over their shoulders. Their commander, Colonel Stephen Thomas, had once been a renegade Democratic politician, stoutly opposed to all coercion of the South, and it appeared as though his men were about as defiant.

"Here is a clear case," shouted the commanding general, while throwing his exhausted cigar to the ground and gesticulating toward the Vermonters.

"I think not," replied Weitzel in an equally loud voice. Then, addressing himself to the culprits, Weitzel added: "You bought the geese, didn't you!" Of course they had, not being so stupid as to reply in the negative.

As the frightened soldiers scurried off to their mess tents, Franklin, outwitted and disgusted, must have wondered if anyone could control the foraging. He apparently threw up his arms in resignation because from that day forward he refused to grant an audience to the endless stream of complaining citizens. Instead, he appointed Major Wickham Hoffman, his adjutant, to explain to the plundered planters "that it was preferable that whatever was on the plantation should be taken by and for the use of the United States army than to fall into the clutches of the Confederate army."[21]

CHAPTER NINETEEN

SKIRMISHES IN EVANGELINE COUNTRY

Friday, November 20, 1863

WHILE HIS men were out foraging, illegal or otherwise, General William Franklin toyed with a proposal which might both divert the men's attention and salvage his own tarnished military reputation. He had been disgraced on the fields of battle from Fredericksburg to Sabine Pass and the Bourbeux and must have doubted his own ability to command. And he, along with Banks, was the subject of considerable political grumblings among the Radicals in Washington and just might have to endure a congressional investigation into his military conduct.

Thus it was with a great deal of reservation that he entertained another suggestion to pit his superior forces against the Confederates. According to his spies and scouts, as well as the generally unreliable accounts of contrabands, there was a large body of Rebels, estimated at between five and six hundred, occupying the old Confederate Camp Pratt, a camp of instruction on Lake Tasse or Spanish Lake. Brigadier General Alfred Lee, Franklin's cavalry commander, was spoiling for a surprise attack. Why not do to the Confederates, argued Lee, what they had done to the Yankees on the Bourbeux? But non-fighter Franklin, battle-shy and cautious as always, decided to check with New Orleans before risking another engagement.

The reply was swift and to the point. Brigadier General and Chief of Staff Charles P. Stone, Banks' voice in New Orleans, instructed the reluctant commander to make a "strong demonstration so as to ascertain whether he (the enemy) has a mere shell or a solid face in front."[1]

Although Stone did not explain what he meant by the word "strong," Franklin was taking no chances. Early on the morning of November 20th, in fact by 1 A. M., General Alfred Lee set off with three brigades of cavalry—the entire horse division—one brigade of infantry and two artillery batteries, altogether about five thousand troops. The Yankees were going mouse hunting with an elephant.

From a point about three miles west of New Iberia on the Abbeville road, the 1st and 2nd Cavalry Brigades, commanded respectively by Colonels Thomas Lucas and John Fonda, were to strike across the northern prairie to a position on the west side of Spanish Lake. The other forces, including Colonel Charles Paine's 3rd Cavalry Brigade,

General Robert Cameron's 1st Infantry Brigade (3rd Division, XIII Corps) and two artillery batteries (viz., the 2nd Massachusetts and 1st Missouri) were to take the Vermilionville stagecoach road. They would attack the Rebel camp from the front, or south side, with the intent of driving the Texans into the arms of the waiting cavalry.

From the very beginning, everything went wrong. Owing to the necessity for complete secrecy, no one had bothered to awaken the camp cooks and as a consequence the entire expedition went off without coffee or breakfast. Once out on the Abbeville road, the cavalry missed the predetermined cutoff point at Darby's plantation. Incredibly, someone had also forgotten to awaken and bring along the black guides. And if that wasn't bad enough, it soon began to rain. For days the weather had been cool, clear and beautiful, but now another cold front was passing through and the skies opened up.

On the other hand, the cold rain may have been a decisive factor favoring the Union side. The gusty winds and pelting water served to deaden the hoofbeat of the horses as they clamored over the wet prairie soil of Segura's plantation. Through the darkness and rain, long rows of horses could be dimly seen dragging the light guns of Nims' Battery. The artillery wagons trundled noiselessly over the rock-free damp turf. Only the occasional clinking of sabers and the low gruff commands of the officers suggested a military movement. Still, for all the silence, a nervous Indiana cavalryman, who also served as a correspondent for the Indianapolis *Daily Journal*, recalled that "the sound of fifteen hundred cavalry and the roar of artillery wheels seemed like a tornado sweeping across the prairie."

At Camp Pratt on the southwest side of Spanish Lake, Confederate Major Gustav Hoffman, a forty-four-year-old German from New Braunfels, Texas, was roused from a deep sleep by one of his pickets. He had been ordered to this spot along with a detail of the 7th Texas Cavalry only hours before.

"Herr Hoffman," said the Teutonic Texan in German, "something is wrong!" Off to the right, or west side of camp, explained the picket, he had distinctly heard something which "might be the Feds coming."

Major Hoffman "yawned, rubbed his eyes and mumbled that it was probably a storm coming." He then went back to bed, "little dreaming that he had spoken the truth."

As the first morning light spread over the Rebel camp, Union artillery Captain William Marland, the Medal of Honor hero from the Bourbeux affair, raised his right arm. Marland, together with the infantry and cavalry brigade, had moved to a position within one hundred yards of the Confederate pickets on the south side without being observed. Looking toward General Cameron, who then gave the affirmative nod, Marland dropped his arm, thereby signaling the 2nd Massachusetts and 1st Missouri Batteries to open fire.

The artillery barrage, unexpected as it was, created momentary pandemonium in the Rebel camp. Swearing and cursing, the Texans tumbled from their shelters, all one hundred and fifty of them. Some were pulling on boots or pants while others were rushing toward the corral. No one seemed to know which direction to run until Colonel Charles Paine's cavalrymen, led by Bacon Montgomery's 6th Missouri, commenced the assault from the south.

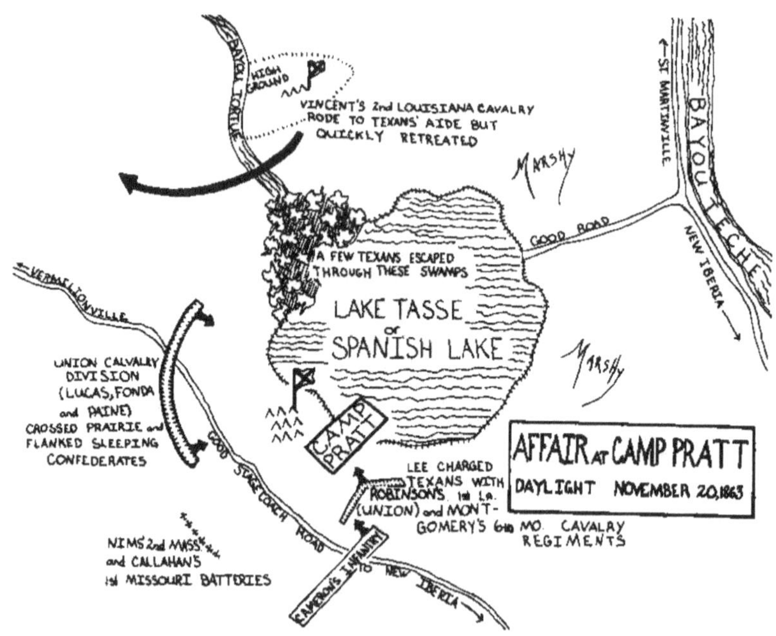

The attack bore all the characteristics of an African tribal hunt. Drums were beating, banners were waving and the horsemen from Indiana, Illinois, New York and Missouri were yelling and shooting in the air like so many wild savages trying to frighten their prey into the bag.

Within moments the object of the hunt was scattering over the prairies on the first horse available. No one bothered about saddles or blankets. Unknown to the fleeing Rebels, however, the two other Union cavalry brigades had advanced in a half cartwheel formation and were closing in from the west (roughly from the present location of the Acadiana Regional Airport). One can imagine the gratification experienced by Colonel John G. Fonda as he watched his old nemesis, the Texas cavalrymen, riding directly into the trap, most of them looking back over their shoulders at the noisy Yankee horsemen. How many times and how many miles had these same cowboys chased Fonda all over south Louisiana?

When the Texans finally realized what was happening it was too late. "They were utterly bewildered at seeing a long line of cavalry a mile long cutting off their retreat," wrote a Hoosier horseman. Most of them surrendered on the spot. Others, desperately seeking a breakout, turned back and headed north along the swampy banks of Spanish Lake but only to find still more Yankees. Closing in rapidly, the excited horsemen of Lee's cavalry began bagging their game:

> Here were horses stuck fast in the mud, and their riders floundering to get out of the mire; here a rebel horse stumbled, pitching the rider a rod over his head. Some Rebs, lying flat on their faces pretending to be dead, were awakened to consciousness by the prod of a bayonet, the whole forming as ludicrous a picture as one often sees in a drizzling November dawn.

All were not captured. Confederate Major Hoffman, mounted on a gorgeous white Arabian stallion, galloped straight into the long blue lines. So sudden and unexpected was his charge that he was through and beyond before anyone realized what was happening. Instead of pursuing, which would have been futile, many of the bluecoated cavalrymen applauded his courageous act. Another Texan, Corporal William Miller, who served as one of Green's chief cavalry scouts, escaped under similar circumstances. A few Texans even hid among the tall reeds and swamps lining the edge of the lake. At least a dozen remained thus concealed with only their heads above the chilly water.

The adjutant of the 7th Texas, twenty-eight-year-old Thomas C. Howard, was less fortunate. Though he spotted an opening in the Union lines, he declined to make a run without first pointing out the flaw to others. Dressed in a gray frock coat, which was richly embroidered with gold lace, he rode back and forth collecting stragglers and sending them safely though the hole. Finally, just as he was about to make the attempt himself, he spotted still more bluecoated horsemen whom he presumed to be confused Texans. Galloping over to their assistance Howard discovered to his horror that they were in fact the real bluecoats. Howard's subsequent capture, wrote *New York Herald* correspondent Charles Farrell, "was more provoking to him since in his pocket he had a written leave of absence."

After the smoke had cleared and the last Texan was rounded up, the jubilant Yankees counted their prize. Out of the original one hundred and fifty Rebels, only three dozen had escaped. One, a picket, had been killed and less than a half dozen were wounded. In addition the Union attackers had captured enough chewing tobacco to supply the entire XIII Corps for the remainder of the year. The Yankees, by contrast, suffered only two casualties. One young cavalryman, it seems, had fallen from his horse and broken a wrist, whereas another was accidentally shot by a careless comrade. It was a far less impressive feat than that of the Texans at Bourbeux, especially in consideration of the fact that the Rebels were outnumbered by about thirty to one, but for General Franklin and the victory-starved soldiers of the defunct Great Texas Overland Expedition, it was a laudatory accomplishment.

And for the Indian fighting Texans it was a humiliating experience. They were the ones who made swift, bold and unexpected moves, not the Yankees. It was they who believed themselves invincible, if not immortal, and it was they who could ride circles around these novice horsemen. But now it was they who found themselves mounted on pack mules and jackasses—two per animal—for the short trek to a Yankee prison in New Iberia. "So much for want of discipline and overconfidence," wrote Confederate General Taylor of the affair after "cussing like our army in Flanders."

On reaching the Union held city, the Texans were dismounted and ordered into marching formation. Then, like a Roman homecoming, the defeated were paraded through the streets to the strains of two brigade bands, one in front and one in back, and both playing "Yankee Doodle" and "Hail Columbia." The long procession was led by the conquering cavalry division of Brigadier General Albert L. Lee, the latest hero of the Texas expedition. Bringing up his rear were the big bad Texans. "They were the dirtiest, most ragged, wretched specimens of humanity that I ever saw," wrote a soldier from Wisconsin. Some were dressed in muddy Yankee blue, captured during the successful raid on Brashear City back in June. Others wore butternut or Confederate gray, if not just plain rags. Dirty and ragged under the best of circumstances they appeared especially pathetic when contrasted with their guards, a regiment of New York Zouave's (Duryee's) then dressed in their colorful baggy trousers, gaiters, short and open jackets, turbans and fez. "Such a dashing of horsemen to and fro, you never saw the like," wrote an Ohio soldier.

Finally, following closely on the heels of the prisoners were the victorious and happy soldiers of Robert Cameron's infantry brigade. All were waving and laughing and obviously enjoying the spectacle.

Even the Texans warmed to the occasion. Whereas hours before they had been disheartened, they now appeared to be enjoying their predicament. Some waved to the sullen citizens of New Iberia, while others blew kisses toward smiling ladies who had gathered upon sidewalks, balconies and verandas. For the applauding, taunting bluecoats along the route, however, the Texans were as defiant as ever, frequently making obscene gestures and nasty comments if not spitting tobacco juice toward their feet.

Many of the Union observers mistakenly attributed the Texans' blue uniforms to the Bourbeux disaster. That belief, when combined with their gratuitous comments, gestures and tobacco juice, came very close to getting them mobbed. "It made our blood boil," wrote a Wisconsin soldier who had barely escaped with his life back on the Bourbeux.

MEMBERS OF DURYEE'S ZOUAVES. These colorful soldiers stood guard over New Iberia in November 1863. ***(History of the 2nd Battalion, Duryee: Zouaves)***

The victory procession finally ended at the Odd Fellows Hall on the Petit Anse road (the current location of Iberia and Main Streets). There the prisoners were incarcerated to await transportation down the Teche and eventually to a Union compound in New Orleans.[2]

General Alfred Lee, the Kansas judge-turned-warrior, decided to retire to his quarters and write a report on the latest affair. Riding the short distance out of town, the jaded general was totally astounded when he reached his quarters—an adjunct to the main dwelling on Evert B. Smedes plantation—only to find that it had been dismantled overnight and taken as fire wood and building materials by foragers along with several other outbuildings and the fences around the house.

He was soon joined by the indignant proprietress, Sarah Cade Smedes, who was quick to point out the circumstances under which he had originally been housed there. Several weeks earlier he and Colonel Charles Paine, the commander of the 3rd Cavalry Brigade, had actually requested permission to occupy her vacant rooms. Madame Smedes, alone and cognizant of the lawlessness prevailing in the Army of the

Gulf, had gladly acceded to the request, especially after they argued that their presence would deter stragglers and criminals. Now, choking back tears, she asked Judge Lee if this was the protection he had promised. Lee, by all accounts a decent and honest man, "recoiled in shame and humbly confessed his inability to protect her."[3]

Madame Smedes was not the only one complaining that rainy November morning. Up on Bayou Vermilion near Pinhook Bridge, Confederate Major Gustav Hoffman was furious. He had followed orders, he told General Green, and had camped on the west bank of Spanish Lake believing that Vincent's 2nd Louisiana Cavalry was in his front. But Vincent, according to the Texan, "had dragged on five or six miles behind," leaving his front exposed.

Vincent told a different story. No one, he said, had ordered him to Hoffman's front, and as a result he had camped his command on a hilly spot overlooking the north side of the Lake (currently the University of Southwestern Louisiana farm). On hearing the commotion, he and his forces had rushed to the scene of action, but only to withdraw after finding themselves hopelessly outnumbered.

Still, in view of the Texans, the Camp Pratt disaster was entirely the fault of the Louisianians. Even back on Bayou "Carn Crow," as some of the cowboys spelled it, the footsoldiers of Walker's Infantry Division would soon be complaining about the "negligence" and fault of their "Kajun" comrades. In the future, they vowed, they would rely on no one except Texans.[4]

While the Texans and Louisianians were at each others throats near Vermilionville, many of the Yankees in New Iberia were listening to some emotional farewell speeches. Among the speakers was Colonel Richard Owen, a victim of circumstances. It was his brigade that had been so thoroughly trounced during the Bourbeux engagement. Though he had behaved courageously, diligently following the commands of superiors, the fact remains that he had lost a brigade. Recognizing that his military career had come to an end, he told the survivors of his old command that he was reluctantly resigning to accept a standing offer as Professor of Natural Sciences at Indiana State University in Bloomington. Walking among his men, tears in his eyes, he shook every hand.

A few paces away, Colonel James R. Slack, detailed for recruiting duty in Indianapolis, was going through similar motions. Week after week he had waxed enthusiastic over the Texas campaign, but his greatest disappointment was that his dear wife Ann was unable to join him. As a result he had seemed to take it out on her in his letters. One hopes that he left his incessant nitpicking complaints behind when he left New Iberia. At any rate, he would soon join her in Indianapolis.[5]

Sunday and Monday, November 22-23, 1863

Union newspapers circulating in the New Iberia camp contained few items of interest. News coverage had shifted from the Teche-Texas campaign to the amphibious operations on the Texas coast. Banks "successful campaign," if indeed it could be called that, was getting more attention than it deserved. There were also headline articles dated Gettysburg, November 19, 1863, describing a fiery two-hour oration given by Edward Everett at the dedication of the Gettysburg National Cemetery. A few papers also dutifully noted that President Lincoln was politely applauded for a bland five-minute address in which he had stated: "The world will little note, nor long remember, what we say here, but can never forget what they did here."[6]

Major General William Franklin, still at the Moore mansion, had other thoughts. Flushed with the excitement and success of the Camp Pratt affair, he wondered if his troops could repeat the performance at other locations. Since early October, when the Texas expedition got underway, he had lost heavily in terms of prisoners. Though he crowed to high heaven over his recent success, he well knew that the prisoner count was so lopsided in favor of the Rebels that he was embarrassed to negotiate a prisoner of war exchange. Without even including the Sabine disaster, the Confederates were ahead by a ratio of about twenty to one.

Still there was a remote chance that he could close the gap. His spies and informers from the Grand Bois had just come in with reports that Major St. Leon Duperier and his irregular battalion of Confederate guerillas—the "boat-burners" as they were now called—were back on Bayou Portage. According to Franklin's inaccurate intelligence, their numbers were placed at from two to three hundred. Here was both opportunity and peril, with the potential gains seeming to outweigh the risk.

Summoning his cavalry commanders, including Lee, Lucas, Fonda, Paine, Montgomery and Mudd, West Pointer Franklin outlined his plans for a surprise assault on the Confederate camp. Because of the hostile nature of the terrain, he explained between puffs on his cigar, there would be no artillery or infantry support. Nor could they take along the full cavalry division. There was always a danger that Green, if not Price or Magruder, might suddenly march on New Iberia from the west. As a result Fonda and Lee would have to remain behind.

Colonel Thomas J. Lucas, a horologist from Indiana and the son of a Napoleonic veteran, would lead the expedition. He was to take with him only two hundred of his best cavalrymen. Colonel Charles J. Paine, commander of the 3rd Brigade, would also go, but with only two hundred and fifty men from his command. Finally Colonel John J. Mudd, who had recently lost a brigade command because of illness, would follow along with two-hundred horsemen from his 2nd Illinois Cavalry. They were to move separately and under cover of darkness, eventually linking up in the Grand Bois for a combined assault on the Louisiana camp at daybreak.

At precisely 10 P. M. on the night of the 22nd, Lucas crossed the India-rubber pontoon at New Iberia and started up the road paralleling the east bank of Bayou Teche. At the same time Mudd's command took the St. Martinville road (present day Highway 31) from New Iberia and crossed the Teche on another pontoon near the J. F. Wyche plantation. He would follow the east bank downstream toward Fausse Pointe (or Loureauville). One hour later at 11 P. M., Paine's command was to set off on the same route as Lucas. All three were supposed to join forces at the crossroads on the trail leading east toward Dauterive's Landing.[7]

With the possible exception of Bacon Montgomery, who had previously reconnoittered the area, it was new and unfamiliar territory for most. As a result guides would have to be impressed along the way. The most logical place for procuring such services was at the Fausse Pointe plantation home of Dr. Augustus Shaw, a sometime speculator and self-professed friend of the invaders. There, near the intersection of the road leading toward Dauterive's Landing, they "recruited" Vincent and Charlot Casimer along with several other former slaves.

Shaw's next door neighbor, thirty-one-year-old John Dorville Broussard, soon got wind of the expedition. Broussard was the tax assessor for St. Martin Parish, captain of a home guard regiment and former steamboat captain. Moreover, he counted Duperier among his friends. Mounting his horse, he took a back trail leading from his Marie Louise plantation toward the Grand Bois and Bayou Portage.

The weather, noticed Broussard, could not have been more suitable for a clandestine operation. The cold front, which had brought rain and success to the Camp Pratt affair, had passed through. It was replaced by the flow of warm southerly breezes bringing in moisture and occasional light rain from the gulf. These conditions, when combined with the swampy lowlands of the Great Cypress Swamp, resulted in a heavy layer of pea soup fog which not only restricted visibility to a few feet but lent a ghostly aura of mystery to the forest.

Not that it wasn't eerie enough already. Even the flora and fauna seemed to conspire with the elements to bring the forest alive. Broussard, riding alone, must have mumbled under his breath as he heard the nocturnal music of the swamps. The chirping of crickets, the croaking of frogs and the roar of bull alligators, when combined with the cacophany of hoots, coos, screeches, whistles, cackles and wails from above, filled the primeval forest with a discordant and meaningless mixture of frightening sounds.

Surely Broussard must have recalled the many tales of nocturnal *sabbats*, when devils and demons, hook-nosed wrinkled old women and individuals of ill repute would fly overhead; dogs would bark, trees would overturn and there would be screams, laughing and the playing of musical instruments. This was the devil's sabbath passing by and carrying away by magic whirlwinds those people who dared venture into the forest at night. Then there was the *feu-follet*, a mysterious dancing light (presumably marsh gases) believed to be an evil spirit frightening horses, pursuing its victims and causing them to lose their way in marshy places. Bad luck, no matter where it occurred in southwestern Louisiana, was usually blamed on the *feu-follet*.

JOHN DORVILLE BROUSSARD (Courtesy of George Broussard, New Iberia)

Without encountering *sabbats* or *follets*, Broussard finally reached Bayou Portage and the camp of the Confederate guerillas whereupon he was escorted into the commander's tent by Lieutenant Martin Voorhies. But Duperier, instead of preparing his troops, merely "laughed at Mr. Broussard's statement." It was one thing for them to come in broad daylight and during dry weather, argued Duperier, but at night and in the rain? Towering over the blond headed Broussard in the dimly lighted tent, the tall handsome guerilla commander made the same mistake as had Texas Major Hoffman back on Camp Pratt. "It's impossible for the Federal cavalry to come to our camp," he scoffed. Duperier added that the Federals were probably just on a scouting mission along the left bank of the Teche. Thanking Broussard for the warning, but without so much as passing on the information to his pickets, the commander went back to bed. He apparently had not heard of the imaginative and successful raid on Camp Pratt.[8]

At that very moment the scouts of Mudd's command were approaching the rendevous point. The lead horsemen, carrying turpentine-fueled lanterns, moved cautiously over the fog enshrouded trail while straining their eyes in search of the crossroads. So thick was the fog and so spooked were the guides, that they failed to find the crossroads and proceeded on toward Dauterive's Landing.

Paine and Lucas were more fortunate. By midnight they had joined forces at the crossroads and settled down for a few hours rest before moving toward the Portage and their inevitable clash with St. Leon Duperier.

About five miles south of Duperier's camp near Dauterive's Landing on the shores of Grand Lake, Colonel John Mudd finally realized his mistake. Well he might as well make the most of the occasion. Storming the large Dauterive home in the wee hours of the morning, he awoke and captured Captain B. D. Dauterive, a company commander in Fournet's Yellow Jacket Battalion.

A short distance away at the landing itself, there was a Confederate gun emplacement—two small pieces—manned by less than a dozen Rebels. This pathetic "stronghold," which dignified itself by the name "fortress," was taken from behind in a bloodless skirmish. Mudd's cavalrymen merely walked in and roused eight sleeping Confederates with the prod of a bayonet.

COLONEL THOMAS LUCAS
(Library of Congress)

COLONEL CHARLES PAINE
(Library of Congress)

At 3:30 A M. Lucas and Paine turned north at the crossroads and moved cautiously toward the Portage "carefully beating the fields on both sides with flankers." Along the way they raided and "thoroughly searched all the dwellings, outhouses and buildings" on several adjoining plantations, including those of W. D. Broussard, Moise Bonin, D.

Prince, and Euzebe Neuville. At the latter place, inside an old sawmill, they impressed a former slave who had recently adopted the name of Alfred Lee, the same as the Union cavalry commander. "They caught me...and made myself and another man named Jack Paul show them the way to the old Portage," recalled Lee. "We went part of the way with them, showed them the road, then left."

Colonel Charles J. Paine, a wealthy Harvard educated Massachusetts attorney, skilled yachtsman, and a grandson of a signatory to the Declaration of Independence, led his men across the Portage on a submerged bridge of *pieux*. It was the same spot where the 75th New York had turned back after chasing Duperier up the Teche a week or more before. In the meantime Lucas moved downstream about a mile and crossed on another submerged bridge near Neuville's plantation. Lucas moved up the Portage toward the Rebel camp whereas Paine proceeded downstream.

As they closed in on Duperier from either side, both forces found themselves muddling along without benefit of roads or trails. Occasionally someone would be knocked from their mount by a low hanging limb or become entangled in vines; others would catch the limb in time but only to carry it forward to be released upon some unfortunate rider to the rear. At the very minimum such accidents would shower the horseman with water, scatter noxious leaflets of poison ivy and not infrequently dump a huge glob of soggy Spanish moss into the lap of some unsuspecting soul. It was the most frightening expedition that most had ever participated in.

Paine's command, closing from above, moved with precision. The advance guard, under Major Bacon Montgomery, ran up on Duperier's pickets at 6:00 A.M. even before it became light enough to see. Since Paine was afraid his units would lose touch in the murky gray, he had previously passed the word that when Montgomery spotted the Rebels his bugler was to sound the charge and all the other buglers would pick up the call and repeat it. So, moments after the first sleepy picket was swept up, the solemn stillness of the early morning was broken by the sound of so many blaring bugles echoing through the swamps that Duperier's men must have thought the Second Coming was upon them. Under it the Yankee cavalry rushed toward the Rebel camp in a thundering, galloping charge, "gobbling" up sleepy guerillas from left to right, swinging sabers wildly from side to side and shouting with all the jubilant confidence of an army that now believed itself invincible.

There then occurred a spectacle similar to that at Camp Pratt three days earlier. The Louisianians, about seventy-five altogether, scattered in every direction, many of them jumping into and swimming the bayou or running right into the lines of the Union cavalrymen in the confusion. Duperier could thank his lucky stars that Colonel Lucas' command, still entangled in briars, underbrush and vines, was unable to cut off their retreat from the other direction. As a result most of the Rebels got away, including Duperier, Voorhies and Ducros, who swam to the safety of an Indian mound on the opposite shore.

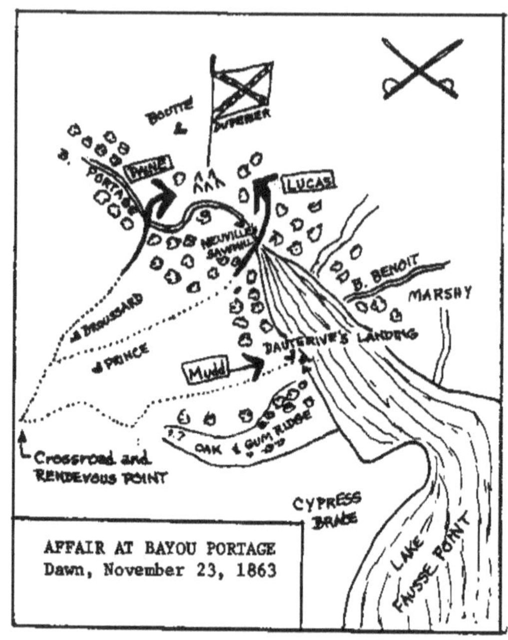

AFFAIR AT BAYOU PORTAGE
Dawn, November 23, 1863

Still, it was a disaster for Duperier's guerillas. Four officers were captured, including Lieutenants Sully Berard and Pierre Manual, and thirty-one enlisted men; two others were killed. The Yankees also took twenty-five horses, about fifty stand of arms and the battalion colors. These losses, when combined with those of a week or so earlier at the hands of the 75th New York, spelled doom for the little battalion. Demoralized and sick of war, most of the survivors simply went home.

Major St. Leon Duperier, alone and discredited, would soon ride up to Confederate headquarters on Pinhook Bridge and officially disband the organization. But for all practical purposes, the 2nd Louisiana Mounted Zouaves, C.S.A., ceased to exist as of daylight on the morning of November 23, 1863.

The victorious Yankees, suffering nothing more serious than a few cases of poison ivy and bramble scratches, seemed unable to withdraw from the Grand Bois without inflicting still more damage on the innocent civilians. Though jaded, hungry and wet, many of them headed toward Terrance Boutte's for breakfast. After a lavish meal consisting of most of the barnyard animals, they arrested their host for complicity.

Farther along, they came across a large pile of cotton belonging to Joseph Chourreau, a thirty-six-year-old Frenchman from Latone, Canton d'Aurignac. Having no means for transporting the cotton, they proceeded to burn it. They also torched the cotton of J. R. Bagary, Casse Bertrand Castex and Eugene Walet. Another planter, Louis Bernard, was arrested for complaining about the plunder in his home and barnyard; cotton and produce was also stolen or destroyed at the homes of Alexandre Edward Broussard, Camille Hebert, Zepherin Broussard and Dosite Breaux.

All things considered it was a lucrative day for the Yankees. Now that the Confederates were cleared from the Grand Bois and Coteau Holmes, the foraging parties could soon move in.[9]

Wednesday, November 25, 1863

Shaken by the Camp Pratt disaster, as well as the news from the Grand Bois, the Texans decided to make several changes in their picket arrangements. No longer would they run their outposts right up to Union lines; nor would they concentrate their pickets in one area, preferring instead a more elastic arrangement with one group in front and one or more reserve units to the rear. They would be more vigilant in the future and, most importantly, it would be an all-Texas affair. In other words there would be no Louisianians to foul up their operations.

It was just such an arrangement that brought Joseph C. Roberts, a twenty-eight-year-old lieutenant from Guadalupe County, Texas, to a point about two miles north of Spanish Lake near the present location of Cade. For twenty-four hours he had stood watch at this, the most advanced outpost with only one company of Rangers from the 4th Texas Cavalry. He was expecting the relief guard, under Captain William L. Alexander, to replace him at daylight, but the noise he heard was too early for the relief, and it was coming from the wrong direction. Straining his eyes in the early morning light, Robert's worst suspicions were soon confirmed. There, coming over the horizon and lined up in battle formation, was General Alfred Lee's entire cavalry division.

Mounting up rapidly, the Texans dashed toward the secondary picket line, some of them firing their revolvers in the air to give advance warning, but they were too slow. Looking around, they were horrified to see the bluecoated horsemen, led by Colonel John J. Mudd, "come like demons, not in one column but in three, each of which were twice our number." Surely the Texans were reminded of a refrain from the "Texas Rangers":

> I saw the Injuns coming, I heard them give a yell,
> My feelings of this moment, no human tongue can tell,
> I saw their glittering lances and their arrows round me flew,
> And all my strength, it left me, and all my courage too.

Just as it seemed that all was lost, the fleeing Rebels were joined by Alexander and his relief guard of two-hundred cavalrymen. But two-hundred Rebels, even Texans, were no match for more than 3500 charging, fired up Yankees. By then the entire Union division, including, Lee, Lucas, Fonda, Paine, Mudd, Montgomery, Robinson, and the others were not only charging directly upon them, but some had gained the advance and were flanking them from both sides. "In a few moments," wrote a Texan, "they were in and amongst us, with glittering blades and hellish yells."

Apparently they were fired up with more than the prospect of victory. In fact a little gunpowder mixed with whiskey was a not uncommon stimulant resorted to by both sides. It would "make men fight like demons," wrote a Yankee. "It fairly crazes them." Indeed, one of the fleeing Texans noted that the Union charge, "was made with a desperation known only to those who have been under under the influence of whiskey or gunpowder, or both."

Putting spurs to their animals, a veritable horserace was made to Pinhook Bridge, "the like of which has but seldom been seen in war." Most of the Texas Rangers, mounted on superior horses, won the race, but not before some seventy-eight of them were rounded up and captured:

> Now all of us were wounded, our noble captain slain,
> The sun was shining sadly across the bloody plain,
> Sixteen brave Rangers as ever roamed the West,
> Were buried by their comrades, with arrows in their breast.

At any rate Colonel William Vincent, whose 2nd Louisiana helped to drive the Yankees away, must have smugly wondered who the cowboys would blame this one on.

No one was more delighted than Union Colonel John G. Fonda. Among the Texas prisoners, noted Fonda, was an officer riding the very horse which had been shot from under him on November 3rd. The same wound which had lost him the horse and trappings had slowed the animal, making his rider easy prey. Looking inside the saddlebag marked J. G. F., the Illinois Colonel found not only his personal correspondence, but a revolver which he carried since the beginning of the war.[10]

Even as the Texans lamented their losses in Vermilionville, General William Franklin in New Iberia made preparations for the following day, November 26, which had been set aside for the observance of Thanksgiving. And there were a few things to be thankful for, at least among the Yankees. They had not taken the Lone Star State, as originally intended, but were successful in keeping the Texans pinned down east of the Sabine. In the last few days, it seemed the tide had even turned in favor of the invaders. Success, reasoned Franklin, should be rewarded, and with that he issued a paradoxical order which, when viewed in the context of the occasion, was unique for its boldness, if not sheer audacity:

> Hdqtrs. XIX Corps
> New Iberia, La.
>
> I. To-morrow having been designated by the President as a day for national thanksgiving and prayer, it will be observed accordingly by divine service in each regiment and battery.
>
> II. A ration of whiskey will be issued to each enlisted man of the command.

"The General's idea of theology," wrote one bemused New Yorker, "was so badly confused that the Chaplains were horror-struck." There were even some serious arguments as to whether the men should have their whiskey before or after service. In the case of the 114th New York, then without a chaplain, some of the troops protested that "in lieu of a sermon, they were entitled to an extra quantity of whiskey." Though reluctant to do so, Franklin also ordered out the forage wagons. In fact, by midmorning an unusually long mule train, drawn by more than two-hundred and fifty teams, was underway. Escorted by portion of the 48th Ohio and 24th Iowa Infantry regiments, the long cumbersome train broke into two sections, one of which headed southwest on the Petit Anse, or Avery Island road, and the other north on the Vermilionville road toward the now secure communities near Spanish Lake.

The northernmost wagon train concentrated their efforts on the area just west of Camp Pratt in the tiny community known as Le Coteau. It was not the first time that Yankees had been in Coteau. In the previous spring, soldiers of the XIX Army Corps had cleaned out Paul Gary, Antoine Viator, Jules Hulin, Emilien Melancon, Victorin Hollier, Elizabe LeBlanc, Ferdinand Romero, Villemont Romero, Dupre Romero, Prosper Romero and Francois-Marie Entremont.

Entremont, a forty-six-year-old Frenchman from d'Annecy, Department of the Haute-Savoie, had come to Louisiana via Sardinia in 1860. Though not particularly well educated, he nonetheless had secured a position as school master in Thibodauxville (and later Franklin), eventually working his way from cart peddler to his very own country store in Coteau. Now, for the second time in his short career as a merchant he stood by helplessly watching as soldiers of the United States made "perquisitions on his domicile," taking tobacco, eggs, demijohns of rum, horse blankets, carpet bags, napkins and the equivalent of $90.00 in fifty-cent pieces.

In the meantime, out on the Avery Island road south of New Iberia, another detail stopped at the small *boucherie de campagne* of Simon

Courrege, an "ignorant" thirty-four-year-old Frenchman. Like Entremont, Courrege had come up the hard way, acquiring a partnership in a lucrative meat trade with Jean Pierre Senac. Long before daylight he and his wife had slaughtered several animals, cut up the meat and distributed it to their customers in order that they might get home for breakfast. Thus when the Yankees came they found Courrege resting in his shed, near the chopping block and scales.

Although he and Madame Courrege "treated them very kindly" the Federals immediately set about confiscating everything. The little pen where several unfortunate animals had spent their last night was disassembled plank by plank. Even the raised crossbar on which animals were hoisted for dressing was torn down and carted off. They then began rounding up the farm produce, including geese, chickens, cattle, horses, mules, and sheep as well as hay, corn and other goods. When it seemed as though nothing else remained they turned destructive, knocking over the kitchen window *tablette*, breaking windows and smashing furniture. Madame Courrege cooked some eggs at their request and gave them milk but, according the the frightened lady "*les soldats ne se trouvaient pas satisfaits; qu'ils entraient dans toutes les chambres de la maison, ouvraient les armoires, le garde-manger et furretaient partout.*" ("The soldiers were not satisfied; as they entered all the rooms of the house, opened the armoires, the food pantry and searched everywhere.")

Simon Courrege was beside himself with rage. Rushing up to a French-speaking officer, who at the time was dutifully noting the quantities of confiscated produce in a little pad, the butcher commenced cursing, complaining and threatening.

Ignoring his antagonist, the officer tore a receipt from his pad, handed it to Courrege and mounted his horse. Riding away he turned and shouted to the cursing Frenchman: "*Vous devez-vous estimer heureux que je vous donne un recu!*" ("You ought to be happy that I gave you a receipt!")

In the meantime the long train lumbered on, stopping along the way to clean out the neighboring plantation of Henry Jacobs, where they set up a slaughter pen. They then called on Leyssan Pierre, Abadie Mathieu, Joseph Segura, Jacques Destouet, Jean Pierre Senac and Cesair DeBlanc as well as the Riggs, Wagoners, Domingues, Romeros and Derouens. Returning via the Abbeville road, the foragers also visited the Leleus, Migues, Viators, Johnsons and Darbys.

The Yankees would have a Thanksgiving dinner to be remembered a long, long time, not only by those who ate it, but also by those who provided it.[11]

Thursday, November 26, 1863

For the first time in weeks the soldiers of the occupying army felt relatively secure in their otherwise hostile surroundings. No longer need they be concerned about Rebels on Spanish Lake or guerillas in the Great Cypress Swamp. Even the rumors about Price and Magruder seemed to be subsiding. For once they could reflect on the beauty of the Teche country, on the cooperative nature of the warm autumn weather and on such trivia as the usefulness of Spanish moss. "The soldiers sleep as soundly on it as the denizens of those fine mansions can in their fine upholstery," wrote one soldier.

Indeed there was a great deal to be thankful for and General Franklin had spared no efforts to make this Thanksgiving a most memorable occasion. Not only were the men treated to one of the most lavish meals of the campaign, but horse racing was still in vogue, and thousands of soldiers congregated on the open plain to witness this, their favorite sport. Enormous hospital tents had been pitched in the vicinity of each brigade. These would be used for patriotic speeches, as well as for religious services.

For once during this campaign, reasoned General Franklin, American soldiers were going to behave in a manner befitting the Old Flag. Toward this end he invited the citizens of New Town to the observance, and some, including New Iberia's leading Unionist, Dr. Alfred Duperier, broke bread with the Yankees. Food and medicine was distributed to the needy, and special arrangements for transporting civilians to and fro were set up.

The speeches, singing and sermons were also noteworthy. A large wooden platform had previously been constructed near the headquarters of General McGinnis and, at the appointed hour, regiment after regiment marched in amid the flying of colors and music of brigade bands playing patriotic tunes. Before long practically every Union soldier in the Attakapas country, rifle in hand, was formed in a hollow square around the platform to hear patriotic speeches, prayers, sermons, choral singing and discourses on patriotism from some twenty-odd different speakers ranging from private to general.

Chaplain John T. Simmons of the 28th Iowa mesmerized the audience by delivering a soul stirring sermon on the significance of the parable of the mustard seed. Chaplain Lyman Chittenden of the 46th Indiana rendered a resounding interpretation of the 43rd Psalm. General Weitzel spoke about the patriotism of Davy Crockett (claiming that if Crockett were alive he would be fighting for the Union); and Colonel Thomas Bringhurst delivered the "veteran" speech, urging the men to re-enlist in the volunteer army. Generals Franklin, McGinnis and Burbridge, each in turn, told the men that they should be thankful for the seemingly "good times and prosperity of our country amid a great rebellion." Next Thanksgiving, said Burbridge, they would probably be home with the family enjoying the occasion, as in years past, "in the good old fashioned way, with turkey, chicken and fixins."

But it was Brigadier General Robert Alexander Cameron, a thirty-five-year-old former newspaper editor and Republican legislator from New York, who captured the hearts and imagination of all. A handsome giant of a man with full beard and open genial manner, Cameron was noted for his deep stentorian voice, witty manner and singing talents. Mounting the platform he commenced his address.

GENERAL ROBERT CAMERON
(Library of Congress)

"I know what a great many of you are thinking this moment," he intoned, "thinking what it is that you have to be thankful for—rusty bacon, inhabited hard tack, a queer mixture of beans, peas and barley which the quartermaster calls coffee, no tents and harrassing marches. But look at the other side," continued Cameron, "the rebs get nary a sniff."

After several other thought-provoking witticisms—punctuated by roaring applause—Cameron concluded by directing the choir in several patriotic tunes. Finally, turning back to his audience, the handsome general asked the men to join the chorus in singing the Doxology. By that time the patriotic fervor was at its highest pitch and the very grounds seemed to rumble and tremble with the soul stirring strains:

> Praise God from whom all blessing flow.
> Praise Him, all creatures here below.
> Praise Him above, Ye heavenly host,
> Praise Father, Son, and Holy Ghost.

"Every head in that vast assemblage was uncovered," wrote a soldier from Illinois, "as in the presence of Him who rules among the nations."[12]

Monday, November 30, 1863

New Iberia, like Opelousas and Vermilionville before it, began taking on the appearance of a disaster zone. All the vacant houses, buildings and fences had long since disappeared; the weatherboard siding, flooring and sometimes the roofing was stripped, even from occupied dwellings; for miles around the plantations had been searched and the produce confiscated; most of the Negroes, except for the "decrepit and lame" had run away or had been conscripted into the Union army; Confederate money was selling for ten percent of face value; and the citizens were "suffering to a great extent for the very necessaries of life." Still, they appeared before the provost marshal taking the Oath of Allegiance, not so much in the futile hope that their property would be protected, but as a safeguard against starvation. A Union officer, Lieutenant Henry Warren Howe of Lowell, Massachusetts, wrote home that "I can't pity them for they are all Secesh."

So impoverished was the vicinity around the Union camp that foraging parties were forced out farther and farther. Some went to the Grand Bois, others to St. Martinville and still others to Prairie Carlin, west of New Iberia.[13]

Heading in the latter direction was Colonel John J. Mudd, the ailing forty-year-old Chicago businessman and his 2nd Illinois Cavalry. Only three days before, during a reconnaissance mission to Abbeville, he had sighted an enormous herd of cattle grazing on the rich open pasture lands. The mission had been so long and tiresome, however, that he had been unable or unwilling at the time to drive them in. But today, just to be certain that Mudd's mission would succeed, General Franklin had ordered Lee's entire cavalry division to make a show of force near Pinhook Bridge while Mudd drove in the cattle.

On reaching Bayou Petit Anse out on the Abbeville road, the Illinois cavalrymen were disappointed to find that Confederates had recently burned the bridge. The day was also bitterly cold, but at least the sun was shining and R. J. Broussard's barn stood nearby. Within a very short period of time a portion of what had once been the barn was connected to the remaining stringers and the horsemen crossed over in single file.

Leaving a small party to guard the bridge, the Illinois horsemen moved on, soon passing to the south of Lake Peigneur, or Lake Simonette as it was sometimes called. Once in Vermilion Parish, near the vicinity of present-day Delcambre, Mudd spotted a large herd of cattle grazing *au large* near the Vacherie of Jean Reau. Galloping over to the ranch house, the Illinois colonel was told by Reau that most of the cattle belonged to a certain Dr. Smith of New Iberia as well as to Francis Foucade, Faustin Dupuy, the Delcambres (Louis, Charles and Theodule) and several other local ranchers. Reau, formerly a captain of the pre-war *comites de vigilance*, was merely guarding them from outlaws and jayhawkers, but he was no match for the confiscatory agents of the United States. Mudd quickly wrote out a receipt for the animals and, through an interpretor, explained that the owners could ask for compensation after the war.

A poor rancher by any standard, Reau now watched helplessly as the large bleating and lowing herd disappeared over the horizon in the direction of New Iberia. Strangely enough, they had not taken his personal mount; nor had they plundered his house. In fact, except for taking some two dozen of his cattle they had treated him quite courteously. Reau quickly strapped on his coveted belt of the vigilantes which he always wore when on an important expedition and rode furiously toward the retreating cloud of dust. Perhaps thought Reau, he could still save his livestock.

Approaching the astonished Colonel, Reau shouted: "You are taking all the cattle I have!"

"And how many is that?" asked Mudd.

On learning that it was only two dozen, the Union colonel permitted Reau to separate out his livestock from the rest. So grateful was the old cattleman that he followed along for several miles chatting amiably with Mudd. Many years later he recalled that occasion:

> While we were traveling together I was followed by a fine pointer dog which I was raising for my own use; the Colonel manifested a desire to buy that dog as a present to his daughter who, he said, had lost her pet dog. I first refused...Subsequently, on reflection that the colonel had done me a favor, I concluded to make him a gift of that dog.

Such instances of mutual compassion were rare. Even as Mudd's horsemen drove the cattle toward New Iberia, his guards, at Petit Anse Bayou, were relieving the Cesair Deblanc family of a "sumptuous dinner of sweet potatoes, roast pork and corn bread" as well as most of their household valuables.

Just as they were completing their meal a picket dashed up and reported that a small party of bluecoated riders, possibly Rebel pickets, were approaching along the bayou near the home of Pierre Landry. The commander of the guard detail, Lieutenant James S. McHenry of Lane, Illinois, mounted up and rode off to meet them with a dozen of his own men.

Halting within shouting distance, McHenry asked the strange riders to identify themselves by naming their command. When there was no reply, one of the Yankees, Waldo Aulis, remarked, "I will speak to them gently and see if they will answer." With that, he leveled his carbine, fired, and dropped a Rebel horse.

The unfortunate Confederates, thinking themselves confronted by a much larger force, turned tail and ran—right into a tall cypress fence corner. After another brief exchange of fire, the only casualty being another horse, eighteen disgusted, cursing and disgraced Texas Rangers surrendered to only thirteen elated Yankees.[14] Thus the month of November, which had started on such a sour note for the Union side, ended with yet another humiliating experience for the overconfident Texans.

CHAPTER TWENTY

THE FINAL DAYS

Wednesday, December 2, 1863

IN ST. MARTINVILLE, Louisiana, about seven miles upstream from New Iberia, the citizens seemed ready to wage their own private war against the Yankees. Fiercely independent and embittered by the occasional raids on their little town, the menfolk gathered at an unidentified location to discuss their plight. There was nothing at all unusual about such a meeting. Before the war they had frequently gathered as members of the vigilante committees to act on some perceived travesty of justice. Among those present were members of the defunct Duperier Battalion, deserters from Fournet's Yellow Jacket Battalion, soldiers on furlough from other regiments, home guard militiamen led by Captain John D. Broussard, and a sprinkling of planters, merchants, clergymen and other civilians.

The crowd grew bigger as the day wore on and also grew angrier with the mention of each abuse. It was a sacrilege, someone argued, what they had done to poor old Father Jan. The arrest of citizens Voorhies, Fournet and the others was a crime; so were the raids on the planters' and merchants' homes. The burned out bridge over the Teche was a terrible inconvenience and it dare not be reconstructed for fear that it would only be torched again.

Speaker after speaker reminded the assembled conspirators of St. Martinville's proud heritage. Settled principally by a class of intelligent French immigrants, among whom were the Deblancs, Declouets, Delahoussayes, Pellerins, Darbys, Dauterives, Gonsoulins and others, they had overcome adversity, including floods, incendiarism, yellow fever and bandits. In the latter case they had initiated a committee of vigilantes and had expelled the culprits from the country.

"*Les Federaux son des bandits !*" shouted an old man, setting off head noddings and mumbled approvals.

There then occurred an ugly phenomenon which has both plagued and puzzled mankind since the beginning of time. What had once been a peaceful gathering of intelligent, concerned citizens soon became an angry, shouting mob demanding retribution.

Whether they had come to the meeting armed and ready for action or had gone home to procure weapons is uncertain. What is known is that the disorderly mob, numbering about 100, began plodding toward the Union pickets located some two miles south of St. Martinville. Some rode on horses; others were in wagons and caleches, while still others walked. Armed with shot guns, Bowie knives, and even ancient flintlocks, they more closely resembled Antonio O. Conselheiro's Brazilian rebels of *Os Sertaos* than a fighting unit. God-fearing and self-righteous, they were going to show these barbarian "Americans" what they had shown the pre-war bandits: not to mess around with St. Martinville.

One can imagine the astonished look that came over the face of the first Union picket who sighted this motley crew. Did he laugh or did he shake his head in pity, wondering if this is what the Confederacy had come to? At any rate the pickets mounted up, all two dozen of them, and debated whether they should turn tail and run or stay and fight. When it became apparent that the mob mentality was fast evaporating in the presence of armed adversaries, the Yankees grew bolder, lined up in battle formation and charged. The incipient rebellion was thus nipped in the bud, and the disorganized mob scurried back toward the relative safety of St. Martinville. Incredibly, no one was killed, but a dozen or more of the reluctant Rebels was captured and the attractive little town of St. Martinville lost whatever remained of its questionable claim to neutrality.[1]

Thursday, December 3, 1863

Jean Baptiste Eugene Duchamp de Chastaigne, a fifty-year-old St. Martinville druggist, had just opened his store at the corner of Main and Port street when he noticed a body of several hundred Union cavalrymen accompanied by a section of artillery filing into town. A graduate of the *Universite de France* and a former captain of the St. Martinville Vigilante Committee, Duchamp stood in front of his store and watched curiously as a French-speaking artillery officer galloped up. "He told me to close up," recalled the druggist, "as I did not know with whom I had to deal."

Though a French citizen and a native of Martinique, Duchamp had some good reasons to be concerned. Three sons served the Confederacy. One, Captain Charles L. Duchamp, had been badly wounded at Gettysburg and was home recuperating with his wife and newborn son, Joseph Arthur. Surely he would be arrested if they found him. Across the street, at the famous store of Broussard and Tetrou, a Confederate flag fluttered from a mast. Another flew a block away over the store of Auguste Maraist.

Only yesterday Duchamp had stood in front and "hurrahed" for those flags. He had also watched as the chief of police, Adolphe Bienvenu, confiscated and destroyed Don Louis Broussard's rum. Fearful of a Union occupation, Bienvenu had been ordered by Confederate authorities "to destroy all the rum in town and burn the cotton to prevent the (Union) soldiers and negroes from getting it and becoming intoxicated and causing trouble." Though Broussard protested, he had finally given in and even helped "by breaking in the heads of the barrels and letting the rum run into Bayou Teche."

The rum was gone now but Eugene Duchamp was horrified to notice that the Confederate flags were still flying. Normally such outward manifestations of Confederate sympathies would have been removed well in advance of a Union visit, but, because of the excitement of the previous day's activities and the rapidity with which the Yankees entered town, there simply wasn't time.

Before the war the store of Broussard and Tetrou had been the scene of one of the worst tragedies in the Attakapas. Eleven people had lost their lives in a fiery holocaust that was deliberately set by bandits. So impassioned were the residents over this incident that they had initiated the *comites de vigilance.* Now, there was the real danger that the Federals would burn the store again as retaliation for flying the Stars and Bars. At any rate there would be hell to pay for those Rebel flags, thought Duchamp.

Bolting his front door, Duchamp had just stepped back when someone began pounding away. If he didn't open up shouted an unseen figure in English, the door would be broken in. Moving quickly, Duchamp released the latch, but only to be overrun by the thirty or forty soldiers. Smashing and pillaging they took or broke everything in the store, including chewing and smoking tobacco, quinine, morphine, opium, paragoric, castor oil, laudanum and other patented medicines, as well as several hundred dollars worth of surgical and dental instruments.

Over on Port Street, an eleven-year-old Negro named Louis Gagne watched as a line of wagons more than a block long drew up and stopped in front of Duchamp's warehouse. After breaking in the doors they took out some "heavy planks and by placing one end of them on the wagons and the other on the sidewalk, they rolled the sugar of Mr. Duchamp into their wagons," thirty-five hogsheads in all.

Unknown to the foragers, Private Baptiste Malagarie, a Confederate soldier from Cote Gelee (present-day Broussard) huddled in Duchamp's warehouse attic where he had taken refuge. Looking through a crack in the attic's side, Malagarie watched as several hogsheads of brown sugar was broken open at the request of the "colored people who stood around." A big redheaded sergeant, standing on back of a wagon, then began to yell: "There niggers, you want some sugar? Come help yourself!"

Several of the young blacks, including Louis Gagne, Hilaire Valmont and Louis Condeley, began scooping the sugar into wooden buckets and small barrels taken from Duchamp's warehouse. Laughing and joking they headed down the street where they ran head-on into the angry druggist. "He remonstrated to us about our taking his sugar," recalled Gagne, but the youngsters were defiant, especially since the Yankees were in town, and began taunting him.

"If you play the fool," Gagne answered smartly, "we will have these soldiers to beat you with the flat of their sabers."

Duchamp, on the urgings of two friends, Gustave Voorhies and Sebastian Hitter, soon cooled off, but only long enough to notice that his warehouse was being ransacked by the intruders. Rushing up to a Union officer, the angry Frenchman demanded to know why they were taking his sugar.

"Because we have use for it," replied the officer, at the same time proffering a receipt.

"Will that receipt pay my northern creditors?" Duchamp snapped facitiously.[2]

After emptying Duchamp's store and warehouse they started on Jules Oger's coffeehouse then located on Main Street between Port and Church in the Sandoz Building. Oger, like Duchamp, had an interesting background. A citizen of Etempes, Department of Seine and Oire, France, he had come to St. Martinville in 1852 and worked himself up from street peddler to drinking stand attendant and eventually to proprietor of "the finest coffee-house in St. Martinville." Like many other Frenchmen he successfully evaded the conscription laws of Louisiana, sometimes risking his life to elude the long legal arm of Captain George H. Brown, St. Martinville's much despised enrolling officer and his enforcement authority, Captain Alcide Fuselier.

So Oger was all the more perplexed when the invading Yankees burst through a locked back window and accused him of "entertaining a nest of rebels in his coffeehouse." Pierre Juste Moity, a frequent customer at the establishment, watched curiously as they slashed and ripped apart billiard tables, smashed bottles of Madeira and Cognac and threw glasses and sugar dishes against the wall.

In the street outside was Misin Olivier, a thirty-five-year-old free man of color, who watched as the Federals "entered in considerable numbers," soon emerging with billiard balls, bottles of liquor, demijohns, cigar-boxes and other goods. "From the noise that I heard," he recalled, "I judge that they broke a large quantity of glass-ware."

Pierre Wiltz, a Confederate prisoner, just happened to be passing by about that time in the company of an armed guard. "The soldiers and officers were all drunk," he complained, "and poured a demijohn of Anisette over me."

One of the officers inside the coffeehouse, on examining a drawer, found a collection of papers ridiculing the Confederate government. Considering this as evidence that Oger was in fact opposed to the Confederacy, the Yankee commenced shouting: "Stop! Stop! He is a good Union Man," but, recalled Oger, "the soldiers had already cleaned me out."[3]

Then it was Sebastian Hitter's and Auguste Maraist's turn, as well as Charles Landry, the village blacksmith and butcher, and Valmont Richard and Charles Gauthier. Incredibly they emptied the store of Broussard and Tertrou without noticing the Confederate flag. Finally, someone, somehow, even dared steal another horse from old Father Jan.[4]

While the foragers went about their business of cleaning out St. Martinville, even nastier deeds were being carried out by the cavalrymen. From their prisoners of the day before, they had extracted a long list of names of those who had participated or led the mob which attacked the pickets. Stopping at house after house, Harai Robinson's 1st Louisiana Cavalry questioned, insulted, abused and occasionally arrested the inhabitants. They were ably assisted in their efforts by the 118th Illinois, now headed by Colonel Thomas Logan.

A short distance outside of town at the plantation home of Darcourt Landry, they questioned his children, Alexandre, Leontine and Numa. Breaking into the sugar house they proceeded to open several hogsheads of sugar "and told our slaves to help themselves," but, recalled Darcourt Landry Jr., "the slaves (among whom was Bob and Ben Taylor) refused to take any." Similar scenes occurred at the homes of Dr. David de Laureal, a native of the Island of Guadeloupe, Edouard Detiege and Ursin Olivier.[5]

They came at last upon the ancient plantation home of Charles Olivier Duclosel and his wife, Marie Emerante, nee Latiolais. Duclosel, aged, obese and gouty, was among the biggest landholders and sheep raisers anywhere in the Attakapas. His old "raised cellar" cottage style house, with its *boussilage* walls of mud and *barbe espagnole* and exposed cypress beams, had been built for the widow of Chevalier Paul Augustin Le Pelletier de la Houssaye almost three quarters of a century before. Though it bore no particular marks of distinction at the time, it stands today as the "Acadian" House, the center of attraction in the Evangeline-Longfellow State Park.

Whether or not Duclosel was implicated in the previous day's activities is uncertain. At any rate the cavalrymen stormed the house, soon arresting and carrying away the ailing old man, his son, Pierre, and a daughter. According to an inflammatory Confederate account of the intrusion, the cavalrymen then proceeded to behave in a characteristic manner. Questioning Madame Duclosel, who was sixty-years of age and afflicted with aneurism, they forced her to kneel before them whereupon they

> ...gratified their fiendish rage in abusive and indecent epithets, and disregarding the blood that flowed profusely from her dilated arteries, they rocked her backward and forward, pushed her to the

right and left, and threw her down and raised her up, until exhausted nature could bear no more, and she sank in a swoon.

Duclosel's eldest son, Pierre, was beaten and then thrown into a turkey cage atop a Yankee wagon for attempting to stop the abuse. Meanwhile, the old man, who had not been known to walk more than a short distance for years, was pushed over a mile of muddy road toward St. Martinville.

THE ACADIAN HOUSE, St. Martinville, home of Charles Olivier Duclosel during the Union occupation. (Contemporary photograph—Courtesy of John Stephan, Lafayette)

The procession of drunken soldiers, prisoners and booty soon came upon the house of Ann Pradand, a poor sixty-six-year-old seamstress and widow (of Claude Grosbois) from Grandbourg Canton, Department of Breux. Rushing into her residence amid a chorus of Indian war whoops they proceeded to "burst open the bureau drawers with their bayonets," soon departing with silver, pillow cases, napkins and all her meager savings.

Not to be outdone by this band of thugs, Madame Pradand followed the procession into St. Martinville and observed along the way as they broke into the homes of Olive Leontine Billeaud (Joseph Locker's widow) and John Herd. Once in town, she confronted a Federal captain standing before the turkey cage of Pierre Duclosel near the Evangeline Oak. The elder Duclosel, she noted, was seated in a chair (although a Confederate account would subsequently accuse his captors of forcing him to "stand the remainder of the day in one of the streets.")

Addressing the captain in French, widow Pradand tearfully related the shameful events which brought her to St. Martinville, but the officer, whoever he was, did not speak the local language. He therefore prevailed upon the younger Duclosel to translate her heated admonitions into English. Thus the pathetic little lady, clad in black vestments and wearing the customery *garde-soleil*, was forced into the ludicrous situation of directing her complaints, which seemed trivial by comparison, toward the cramped occupant of a turkey cage.

"It was a shame and an outrage," she shrieked, "to rob an old woman."

Replied the officer: "If you can point out the men who robbed you I will make them return the property."

Looking around, widow Prandand immediately realized the hopelessness of her situation. There she stood, amid a sea of bluecoats, all of whom "looked the same."

"How do you expect me to recognize them among the band of thieves that you have here?" she tearfully asked.

Offended now, the Union Captain looked her straight in the eye and loudly proclaimed: "God damn St. Martinville! God damn St. Martinville!"

For all their house searching and abuse the Yankees turned up only five bonafide Confederates—Major R. A. Howard, an unidentified captain and three privates, but at least, reasoned the intruders, the citizens of the plundered little town would think long and hard before threatening another Federal outpost.[6]

Sunday-Monday, December 6-7, 1863

Among the geomorphological wonders of southwestern Louisiana are the massive "salt islands" which rise like lush oases from a flat countryside of marsh or prairie surroundings. One of these, Jefferson Island, then known as Miller's Island (also called Dupuy's or Orange Island) is located on a straight north-south line with Petit Anse, Grand Cote and Cote Blanch Islands. Like the others it is separated from its geological neighbor by a distance of about six miles. But unlike the others, which rise above salt marsh and gulf, Jefferson Island is inland where it overlooks beautiful Lake Peigneur (or Simonette) and the surrounding prairie. About twelve hundred acres in size, it was then characterized, as it is today, by hills, valleys, plains, bluffs and forests.

It was also an excellent location for observation posts. A sentry or picket, when situated on the highest spot on the island, could survey military operations for miles around. Thus it came as no surprise when General Franklin's spies and scouts informed him that seventy or eighty Rebel pickets were posted there. Here, reasoned the Union general, was yet another golden opportunity to run up the prisoner scoreboard. Without another thought he resolved to send out an invasion force under cover of darkness.

Among those getting the nod for the nocturnal expedition were Harai Robinson's 1st Louisiana Cavalry and Captain Benjamin Thurber's recently mounted 75th New York dragoons. At one time the 75th New York had been the laughing stock of the cavalry, armed as they were with long infantry Enfields, mounted on whatever was available and using a crude variety of odd shaped and multi-colored civilian trappings. But no more. As they took the Abbeville road from New Iberia at dusk, sabers at their sides, they were decked out in the latest, including new cavalry-blue uniforms, regulation bridles, shiny high boots and fine McClellan saddles. In fact everything was new except the horses, the men and the Enfields.

Crossing Bayou Petit Anse on the same bridge constructed by Mudd's cavalryman a few days before, the New Yorkers soon reached their destination. About midnight the party crossed a marshy approach on a "miserable apology for a bridge" and began to deploy in a circle around the loftiest point of the island. The men were then ordered to lie down beside their horses and rest until daybreak, at which time they would advance concentrically toward a house where it was believed the Confederates were concealed.

The New Yorkers were far too excited to sleep. For weeks they had awaited their first mounted battle. They had chased Duperier up the Teche and captured a few stragglers, but by no stretch of the imagination could that be considered a battle. They had also participated in the Camp Pratt affair, and in the chase of the Texans up to Vermilion Bayou, but battles they were not. Even though they were now accompanied by the battle-hardened veterans of the 1st Louisiana, it was they who were appointed to lead the attack.

At the appointed hour, even before the sun burst over the crystal clear waters of Lake Peigneur, the New Yorkers mounted up and commenced the advance. Approaching cautiously at first, they soon moved to a position within only fifty yards or so of the dwelling without setting off a Rebel alarm. Thinking to take them totally by surprise, Captain Thurber raised his saber and ordered a charge on the plantation house.

And it was a most noble charge, a thundering, galloping ascent from all directions amid the crackling of bugles and shouts of men going into combat. Leaning forward and standing on their stirrups, shaggy hair flying beneath broad brimmed cavalry hats, glittering sabers thrust before them, several hundred men reached their objective without drawing Rebel fire. Dismounting rapidly, their spirits undiminished, they trampled down flowers, shrubbery, a little white picket fence and each other in a frantic headlong rush toward the front door, back door, side doors and windows. Battering and breaking they rushed into the house amid broken glass and splinters, shrieking and yelling in a manner that would do honor to an Apache, if not the satirical creations of Don Miguel de Cervantes.

But alas, instead of Confederates, for whom they were looking, the windmill tilting New Yorkers awoke and nearly scared the wits out of fifty-seven-year-old Faustin Dupuy, his wife Mary Honorine, and their teenage sons, Adam and Alcee.

And the Rebels? Why, none of them had come around for weeks, confessed the ruffled proprietor.

Dupuy, though badly shaken, soon regained his composure and reluctantly invited the redfaced officers to take breakfast with him. He was a Union man, or so he claimed, and had been victimized by the marauding Texans on numerous occasions for refusing them oranges and other supplies. Before long, recalled a visitor

> ...he was cussing the Confederacy in general and everything related to it, saying that they had neither the forces nor the brains to carry on the war and, if he had his way, he would hang them all...

In the meantime "the troops admired the splendid mansion and the beauties of a fine orange grove just lighted up by the rising sun." Without a doubt, they gazed upon one of the loveliest scenes in Louisiana. Alexis Carlin,of St. Mary Parish, had been its first owner. Then it had passed to a Scotsman named Randolph, and more recently to John Fitz Miller, a wealthy New Orleans businessman. And each had left his mark. Randolph, for example, had planted more than six thousand orange trees, two thousand bearing pecan trees and vast orchards of figs, peaches, quinçe, lemons and palms. Set amid a backdrop of ancient moss draped live oaks and stately magnolias, and overlooking the surrounding countryside and lake, it was a veritable tropical paradise.

Though the New Yorkers could and did appreciate the "loveliness of the scene" their less aesthetic qualities predominated when they discovered that a vast herd of fine fat cattle were grazing in an adjacent pasture; that Dupuy's barns were overflowing with corn and oats; that huge bins on the plantation contained thousands of bushels of oranges; and that hundreds of fat chickens strolled unmolested in the barnyard.

Collecting a generous sample of each, including several thousand cigars gratuitously bestowed upon them by the "captured" proprietor, the troops returned to New Iberia to become the envy of all. Unfortunately for Dupuy, the sight of the golden fruit, the fragrance of the burning cigars and the savory aroma of roasting chicken was just too much for the others. Before the day was over, plans were being made to send out the foraging trains, legal or otherwise. So Faustin Dupuy, who had irately protested when the Confederate helped themselves to a few oranges, now found himself entertaining Union foragers almost everyday for a three-week period.

I hereby certify that in accordance with Order of War Department, dated July 22. '62. I have taken for Military purposes from [illegible] Dupuy of St. Martins Parish [illegible] the following property to wit:

1863
Dec 19th | 24 loads of corn | 600 [illegible]

And that the purchases were necessary for the public service and have been accounted for on my Property return for the month ending 1863

E. V. Hitch 1st Lieut
A. A. Q. M. 1st Brigade
Cavalry Division

COPY OF RECEIPT for confiscated goods taken from Faustin Dupuy's Plantation in December 1863. (National Archives and Records Service)

In the meantime some rather incredible news was drifting in from St. Martinville. The defiant citizens of that little town, still smarting over their rough treatment at the hands of the Federals, had made yet another attack on the pickets; and this time some of the Yankees had been injured.[7]

Sunday, December 13, 1863

Though peace was not exactly at hand, the prospects for the prisoners of war never seemed brighter. For days messages had been passing back and forth on the subject of a prisoner exchange. Only one day before both sides had even entered into negotiations at the halfway station, or the stagecoach stop, at a Mr. Boutte's plantation not far north of Spanish Lake. The prisoners, it was agreed, would be exchanged on a one for one basis with the only exceptions being those Yankees captured while illegally foraging. The latter, as far as General Franklin was concerned, were nothing more than common criminals and should be treated as such. As for the excess Union prisoners (the count was still lopsided in favor of the Confederates) they too would be included in the exchange but would remain in a Union parole detention center in New Orleans until the Federals could parole an equal number of Confederates.

There was, however, one vexing problem. For weeks the eccentric proprietor of the *New York Herald*, James Gordon Bennett, had been pressing General Banks' staff to seek the release of his correspondent, William Gatchell. The Confederates, he argued, were making war on noncombatants.

But so were the Yankees, argued Confederate General Taylor, erroneously arguing that John G. Pratt, though once a Confederate militia general, was a civilian when captured near his home in Grand Coteau. The same was true of Judge Alfred Voorhies of St. Martinville, Daniel O'Bryan of Vermilion Parish and Romulus McBride of Lafayette. The Confederates would exchange Gatchell, said Taylor, for Pratt, Voorhies, O'Bryan and McBride, a deal the Yankees refused to make. As a result all would remain incarcerated for several more months.[8]

On the one hand, the sometimes bitter and very personal war between the Texans and Yankees seemed to be cooling off, but on the other the invaders and the citizens of St. Martinville were on another collision course. Since the affair of December 7, when two pickets were wounded, there had been several other sniping incidents. Although it was uncertain whether the acts were carried out by civilians or soldiers, one fact was clear—St. Martinville was harboring the guilty parties.

Thus it came as no surprise when Colonel John Mudd's 2nd Illinois Cavalry entered St. Martinville from the south and set about searching houses. In the process they uncovered and captured thirty-three-year-old Simeon Belden, a Massachusetts-born attorney and a captain in Fournet's Yellow Jacket Battalion, as well as a certain Sergeant Delahoussaye. At the home of Joseph Sullice, a fifty-three-year-old French planter from the Department of Haute-Savoie, they turned up and "captured" saddles, horse collars, tobacco, pecans, a hat and four shirts.

On entering the home of Felix Voorhies, Confederate soldier (and, later, judge and author of *Acadian Reminiscenses)* a Union search party came upon a midwife attending Modeste Potier Voorhies, then in an advanced stage of labor. Before the day was out she would present Voorhies with yet another son, Charles Felix Voorhies.

In the meantime Colonel Harai Robinson and a portion of the 1st Cavalry Brigade of Lee's Division drew up on the east bank of Bayou Teche directly across from the Evangeline Oak. At the same time the citizens of St. Martinville were leaving Sunday services and, in the European tradition, began gathering to bask and chat in the warm sunshine of the open square. So accustomed were they to the presence of bluecoats that hardly a soul noticed the soldiers. Suddenly, without warning or provocation of any sort, Robinson's 1st Louisiana Cavalry raised their pieces, took aim and enfiladed the crowded square with a volley of musketry.

Just why this malicious act was carried out remains a genuine mystery. Some of the Yankee-haters claimed it was done by express orders from General Franklin, which was highly unlikely, whereas Union authorities subsequently argued that it was the deed of "skulkers and stragglers," which seems an appropriate enough description for Robinson's "Louisianians." At any rate it occurred, scattering the frightened citizens in all directions and creating havoc in the square. Families became separated, mothers shrieked for their lost children and people were trampled in a headlong rush for safety. Incredibly, only one person was killed, an old man "of hoary head and tottery step" (probably Alexandre Wiltz) who had been struck by a Yankee bullet even as he was "receiving the kindly greeting of a passing friend."

When Confederate General Green, then in Vermilionville, was informed of the St. Martinville incident, he immediately fired off an irate communication to General Franklin:

> (It) is impossible for the Confederate Army to protect those of our citizens who are within or near the lines of the Federal Army...the firing was, as I have been informed, upon men, women and children promisciously as they were returning from church...I call your attention to this matter for the reason that I do not believe such barbarity to be sanctioned by the officers of the Federal Army.

Franklin's reply was instant and to the point:

> On the occasion referred to in your letter, several of your men were in town, were driven from it by our people, and found on the prairie in rear. It was unfortunate and greatly to be deplored that many peaceable people were in the streets at the time, but it is still more unfortunate that the inhabitants encourage a small force to remain in or about their town if they expect to undergo none of the horrors accompanying a state of war.

EVANGELINE OAK on the right bank of Bayou Teche in St. Martinville, where the legendary Evangeline found her lover, was also the scene of the Sunday shooting incident. (Contemporary photograph—courtesy of John Stephan, Lafayette)

So this is what it had come to. The Great Texas Overland Expedition had begun with unstained flags and brigade bands and weeping ladies waving handkerchiefs to the departing soldiers. They were going to rout the Rebs from Texas and Louisiana and take on Napoleon and Maximilian as well. But now it had come down to burning and destroying barns, houses and cotton, stealing money, beating priests, frightening and arresting innocent civilians, ripping the ear lobes of old women and enfilading crowds of Sunday worshipers.

Whatever the circumstances, it was a disgraceful and cowardly act, unworthy of those who fought under the Old Flag, but it also had a positive effect. The citizens of St. Martinville stopped sniping at Union pickets. The Yankees, for their part, prudently avoided the independent little town.[9]

Wednesday, December 16, 1863

Up in Lafayette Parish, just north of Pinhook Bridge on the Vermilion, Confederate General "Tom" Green was bidding farewell to Colonel

William Vincent and his Louisiana cavalrymen. He had come to Louisiana to fight Yankees, he said, but now the action was in Texas where Banks was threatening Galveston and Houston. Half of his horse division—Sibley's old brigade—had already departed (much to the delight of the Louisianians). Wearing a wide brimmed hat and dirty gray overcoat as protection against the unusually cold weather, Green mounted up and rode to the front of the column of Texans then forming on Pinhook road. Turning toward Vincent, the bold little Texas general, his nose turned bright red by the biting cold wind, rendered a quick informal military salute with his gloved hand. Then, spurring his horse forward he motioned to the bugler to start the command. "*Allons!*" he shouted in deference to the long weary campaign in French-speaking Louisiana, "*Allons au Texas!*"[10] As usual someone struck up a tune and the cowboys rode west to the stirring strains of the "Texas Rangers":

> I have seen the fruit of rambling, I know its hardships well,
> I have crossed the Rocky Mountains, rode down the streets of Hell,
> I have been in the great Southwest, where wild Apaches roam,
> And I tell you from experience, you'd better stay at home.

EPILOGUE

ON JANUARY 6, 1864, following an outbreak of smallpox in New Iberia, the remaining forces of the United States began falling back toward Franklin during a driving ice storm. For most it was a nightmarish three-day trek through snow, ice and mud, and many were the diaries, letters and narratives comparing the march to the little Corsican's retreat from Moscow. Others, however, slipped from the ranks and lazily floated themselves and their confiscated goods down the Teche in cauldron kettles, skiffs, sugarroolers, massive wooden plantation doors, and even armoires supported on rails.

For the next two months the citizens of Franklin, already reduced to penury by the movement of the opposing armies, were to endure the indignities and hardships which had long since befallen New Iberia, Opelousas, St. Martinville, Grand Coteau, Vermilionville, Brashear City, Abbeville, Patterson and Centerville. Though the main camp was established on the Carlin plantation, northeast of town on the banks of the Teche, their foraging parties were soon scouring the area, frequently going out as far as Patoutville, Irish Bend, Cypremort Point, Avery Island and Centerville. Among those hardest hit were Martial Sorrel and Mary Porter, who claimed to be loyal Unionists, as well as Independence Alpha, Henry Colligan, William Saxon, Hiram Anderson, Thomas Rice, Serazin Broussard (of vigilante committee fame), Charles Landry, Jean Begnaud, Edward Provost, a Mrs. Sterling (of Franklin) and a Mr. Kempe (of Cypremort Point) and dozens of others.

As for the Great Texas Overland Expedition it had simply run out of steam, as had Banks' other invasion at Brazos Santiago. But neither General Banks nor his superiors in Washington were willing to write off the Lone Star State. Thus in the early spring of 1864 yet another invasion was set in motion to restore Texas to the Union, the fifth in two years. Up the Teche once more marched the very same men in blue, through New Iberia and across to Vermilionville (where they found Pinhook Bridge in flames again) and on to Grand Coteau, Opelousas and Washington, this time encountering only minor Confederate resistance.

The expedition, called the Red River Campaign, ended in yet another disaster—for both sides. Although the defending Confederates were eventually victorious, driving the invaders from north and central Louisiana and keeping them out of Texas for the remainder of the war, it was a Pyrrhic victory. Colonel William Vincent's entire 2nd Louisiana Cavalry was captured early in the fighting, as was Edgar's Battery; General Alfred Mouton, who led his Cajuns in a courageous charge, salvaged his men's reputation as fighters, but lost his own life; the mainly Cajun 18th Louisiana Infantry lost every single officer to the killed, wounded or captured category as well as a large portion of its men. Few regiments on either side, at any time during the Civil War, suffered such frightful losses.

General "Tom" Green, tanked up on Louisiana rum, led a foolhardy cavalry charge on a Union gunboat and was decapitated by a Union shell. A Confederate scribe, Theophilus Noel, bitterly lamented that Green subsequently became a bigger-than-life legend in hero worshiping Texas, with statues, speeches and even a county renamed in his honor, but Texas simply ignored the fact that "three hundred riderless horses ran off the field, three hundred Texans lay on the field to answer roll call no more—rum, rum, rum, green Louisiana rum, rum, rum."

As might be expected, another flare-up soon occurred between General Richard Taylor, who wanted to press his advantage, and the more cautious Kirby Smith. So bitter was the enmity and so heated the words that Taylor, by his own request, was relieved of command in the District of Western Louisiana. Wrote Taylor to Smith: "After the desire to serve my country, I have none more ardent than to be relieved from longer service under your command."

If the Confederates suffered heavily during the ill-fated Red River Campaign, it was an unparalleled disaster for the army of General Banks. Nims' entire 2nd Massachusetts Battery of Light Artillery, the best in the Army of the Gulf, fell into Confederate hands intact, as did most of Colonel Bringhurst's foraging Hoosiers of the 46th Indiana. All 72 of those magnificent Vermont horses in Nims' Battery were shot to death on the field; Colonel John J. Mudd, who had only recently recovered from a wound, was killed as was Colonel Lewis Benedict of the 162nd New York and Private Henry Heffelfinger, who had attempted to assasinate General Lawler at Opelousas; Colonel Harai Robinson was badly wounded and barely escaped capture; similar circumstances befell General William Franklin who subsequently resigned in disgust, the victim of one too many military disasters.

General Nathaniel P. Banks had fought his last military battle. During the retreat his men hooted, cursed him, and shouted derisive epithets whenever he came near; Radical Republicans once more began to clamor for his scalp; and General Grant, who had repeatedly urged Lincoln to replace Banks, stepped up his efforts to oust the political general. Finally, on May 18, 1864, Banks was succeeded as military commander in the Department of the Gulf by Major General E.R.S. Canby. Banks, disgraced and shorn of military command, eventually had to endure a Congressional investigation into his conduct during the war. It was one of the great ironies of the times that this honorable man of vision, competent administrator and able politician (if not military tactician) would never regain the political prestige he held before the war, whereas the military heroes, who possessed little political or administrative skills, would dominate the Washington scene for years. Banks nonetheless returned to Congress, off and on, until he was forced into retirement in 1890 "owing to an increasing mental disorder." He died at his home three years later.

General William Franklin, likewise disgraced, left the military to serve as vice-president and general manager of the Colt Fire Arms Manufacturing Company. He died in 1903.

General C. C. Washburn, commander of the XIII Corps, returned to an active political life in Wisconsin and served as congressman and governor.

General E.O.C. Ord, one of the few competent general officers in the Department of the Gulf, remained in the regular army, maintaining his rank as general until his retirement in 1881. While on a ship to Vera Cruz he was striken with yellow fever and died in Havana in 1883.

General Cuvier Grover also remained in the regular army, despite the loss of an arm at Cedar Creek, until his death on active duty in 1885.

General Godfrey Weitzel, the "boy general," likewise remained in the regular army as a Colonel of Engineers. On numerous occasions he testified before commissions investigating claims for damages filed by Louisiana residents against the United States. He always claimed that the troops under his command had not pillaged or robbed while in Louisiana, arguing that such depredations were committed by Negroes and Confederates.

General Stephen Gano Burbridge, one of the few untarnished commanders in the disgraceful Bourbeux affair, was unable to return to his Kentucky plantation after the war because of the strong Confederate sympathies in that area. "My services to my country," he lamented, "have caused me to be exiled from my home." He subsequently moved to Georgetown (Washington, D. C.) and became a relatively successful businessman until his death in Brooklyn in 1894.

General George Francis McGinnis held several minor public offices after the war, the highest of which was postmaster of the city of Indianapolis, where he served until his death in 1910.

General Michael K. Lawler, the big irascible Irishman, left the military in 1866 as a brevet major general and spent several years as a horse trader in the occupied South. He lived uneventfully on his farm near Equality, Illinois, until his death in 1882.

General Albert Lindley Lee, the cavalry commander, resigned in 1865 following a series of disagreements with his superiors, mainly E.R.S. Canby, and spent the next few years in Europe. He lived in New York City as a businessman until his death in 1907.

General Robert Cameron moved to Colorado after the war where he organized Union Colony, which became Greeley, and Fountain Colony, which became Colorado Springs. He died in 1894.

Colonel Harai Robinson, commander of the 1st Louisiana Cavalry (Union) was on the verge of being promoted to the rank of brigadier until he became implicated in a scandal and was accused of selling and misusing military property in New Orleans. Arrested, he was brought before a military commission by order of General Canby, was tried and discharged under other than honorable circumstances, and then was turned over to the civil authorities of New Orleans for trial. Both Franklin and Burbridge wrote to President Johnson on his behalf, but apparently to no avail. After many years of unsuccessful appeal Robinson was finally granted an honorable discharge in March, 1875.

Colonel Richard Slack was finally promoted to brigadier general in November, 1864. On his release from the army in 1866 he was breveted major general.

Colonel Theodore Buehler, the unfortunate commander of the 67th Indiana, was released by Confederate authorities in late December 1863, but only to be brought before a military commission on trumped-up charges of incompetency and cowardice before the enemy. Apparently Buehler was the scapegoat for the Bourbeux disaster. Stripped of his commission and released from the service, Buehler appealed his case for reinstatement through Governor Morton of Indiana all the way to President Lincoln. Though numerous letters were written on Buehler's behalf, arguing persuasively that his surrender was the "only alternative to death," Lincoln nonetheless decided the case in favor of Banks, Washburn and Ord, who demanded Buehler's dismissal.

Colonel Edmund Jackson Davis, the fiesty little commander of the 1st Texas Cavalry (Union) left the military as a general in 1865 and returned to Texas where he declined an offer, tendered by General Sheridan, to serve as chief justice of the Texas Supreme Court. Aligning himself with the Radical Republicans, he sponsored a series of constitutional conventions advocating harsh and vindictive measures of punishment for those who had worn the gray. Elected to the governorship in rigged balloting in 1869 he distinguished himself as an incompetent, corrupt, carpetbag governor, one of the worst in the Reconstruction states. Defeated in the next election he refused to yield his office, barricading himself, the carpetbag legislature and a company of Negro troops in the state capital. Besieged there by Texas Rangers, former Confederates and Democrats who were converging on Austin from all across the state, he finally surrendered the office when Grant refused his request for military assistance. Until his death in 1883 Davis remained one of the most despised men in Texas. Not until 1979 would another Republican sit in the Texas state house.

Colonel Charles J. Paine left the military in 1866 as brevet major general. Until his death in Weston, Massachusetts, in 1916 he was prominent in yachting circles, taking part on several occasions in defending the coveted "America's Cup."

Colonel Thomas J. Lucas likewise left the military with the rank of brevet major general. Returning to his home in Laurenceburg, Indiana, he ran unsuccessfully for a congressional seat. He served as postmaster in his hometown until his death in 1908.

General Edmund Kirby Smith, commander of the Trans-Mississippi Confederacy, was the last to surrender. Hearing of General Robert E. Lee's arrest he fled to Mexico and thence to Cuba, fearful of being tried as a war criminal. Returning to the United States in late 1865 he established an unsuccessful insurance and telegraph business. He subsequently served as president of the University of Nashville and as mathematics professor at the University of the South at Sewanee until his death in 1893.

General Richard Taylor, commander of the Army of Western Louisiana, surrendered his forces to E.R.S. Canby in Alabama on May 4, 1865. Returning to his home in Louisiana he found that his estate had been confiscated and sold. So impoverished was he that he was forced to sell his personal mount for money. Remarked Taylor: "The man of Uz admitted that naked he came into the world and naked must leave it; but to find himself naked in the midst of it tried even his patience." Nonetheless Taylor survived by taking advantage of his background and pre-war friendships with Presidents Grant and Johnson, and spent much time in European court circles where he was known by the sobriquet "Prince Dick." His book, *Destruction and Reconstruction,* was published the year of his death in 1879 and was characterized as "among the most facinating of military memoirs." In the book, Taylor recounts that while he was attending a convention in Philadelphia, he found himself the target of a vicious editorial attack. Just as it seemed he was to be run out of town, or arrested, he was rescued by a former Union colonel who came limping to his defense. The Union officer was none other than Joshua J. Guppey of the 23rd Wisconsin, the prisoner whom Taylor had befriended and given a lift to Alexandria after the Union disaster on Bayou Bourbeux.

Colonel Oran Roberts, commander of the Texas infantry brigade in Walker's Division and former president of the Texas Secession Convention, returned home to find himself the object of carpetbag persecutions. Elected to the U. S. Senate he was denied his seat. Nonetheless, Judge Roberts, one of the most respected men in Texas, became chief justice of the Texas Supreme Court and eventually governor in 1879. He subsequently established the Department of Law at the University of Texas which he headed until his death in 1898. Roberts also wrote a comprehensive volume on Texas in the Civil War.

Captain Joseph Sayers, commander of the famed Valverde Battery, likewise returned to Texas politics, serving as United States congressman and governor of Texas.

Colonel William Vincent, commander of the jayhawk-exterminating 2nd Louisiana Cavalry, returned to his mercantile pursuits in New Orleans. He served as state commander of the United Confederate Veterans; was director of the extensive Charity Hospital in

New Orleans, as well as several banks and insurance firms; and helped to found a number of specialized health clinics and hospitals.

Major St. Leon Duperier, commander of the Confederate Zouave Battalion, apparently remained in the Fausse Pointe area after the war. His frequent appearances and depositions before the U. S. Court of Claims, the French and American Claims Commission and the Mixed Commission on British and American Claims, all of which were investigating claims for reparations on the part of Louisiana residents, constituted an important source of information for this work.

James Earl Bradley, the Methodist Episcopal Minister of Opelousas, crossed the Great Cypress Swamp, hailed a Yankee steamer to New Orleans and marched his dear Annie to the altar. They resided in Opelousas for many years after the war.

Ozeme Carriere, Ursin Carriere, Carmelite Saunier (nee Carriere), Don Louis Saunier and Martin Guillory, f.m.c. and a dozen or so other jayhawkers of the Mallet Woods met violent deaths in late 1865 at the hands of the Confederate conscripts returning home. In some cases entire households were firebombed and murdered, children as well as grownups and innocents and as well as guilty. The violence and terror on all sides left a residual of hate, family division and bitterness that lasted for generations.

Desire Arnaud, the little Frenchman on Buzzards' Prairie, did not survive the winter of 1863. In fact, shortly after Union forces evacuated, his emaciated body was pulled from the water well behind his house. Some attributed his death to suicide, others to Ozeme Carriere, and still others to Yankee stragglers or runaway slaves. Whatever the circumstances his demise remains a mystery to this day. His blind wife, Sarah, lived with her brother on Burleigh Lane near Grand Coteau until her death at age eighty-four in 1891. For all her great personal loss, destruction and suffering she was eventually awarded the paltry sum of $2,450 after filing a claim with the French and American Claims Commission.

Thelismar Guidry, the owner of Ile Carencro, died in 1871 at the age of forty-one, the victim of war wounds from Shiloh and too much drink. His wife Constance lost the plantation and lived in penury until her subsequent remarriage. She died in 1906 at age seventy-two. Their home, which served as Union headquarters for Camp Carrion Crow and a makeshift hospital after the Bourbeux disaster, inspired this work and currently is the home of the writer.

Governor Alexandre Mouton, former president of the Louisiana Secession Convention, died at Ile Copal in 1885, a venerable and respected elder statesman. His daughter Mathilde, the wife of Confederate General Frank Gardner, was widowed shortly after the war. Almost all her children died at an early age. When her last surviving son, Alfred Frank Gardner, Jr., died, she had his tomb cast in broken marble as indicative of her own broken life. Mathilde died about 1906.

Governor Mouton's older daughter, "Pussy," was not permitted to marry her Yankee friend. In grief she turned to music and religion, dressing in black vestments until her death. On the other hand a brother of "Pussy,"one of the miniature foragers who helped sustain the family during that tragic autumn of 1863, incurred the wrath of the family by marrying a *femme de coleur libre.* Little Alexandre Mouton, whose exploits kept the family going, became a successful businessman. His memoirs constituted an important source of information for this book.

And whatever happened to that "merry devil," Michael Fox?For more than a half century after the war, veterans of the 8th New Hampshire Regiment debated his whereabouts. A different story, ranging from the ridiculous to the sublime, surfaced at each annual meeting of the Regimental Association. Some said that he was returned to the regiment a second time by the same two growling Texans who brought him in near Vermilionville; others claimed that he defected to the Rebels, eventually becoming an aide to Confederate General Richard Taylor; still others argued that Fox died in a Rebel prison in Tyler, Texas, or was hung for cattle rustling in Mexico alongside some deserters from Billy Wilson's Zouave Regiment.

According to his service record Fox never returned to his regiment. Characteristically no one thought to cancel the bureaucratic process which had been set in motion by General Franklin's recommendation to Banks that the death sentence be carried out. On February 24, 1864, several months after Private Fox had deserted for the last time, General Banks approved the death sentence, but "respectfully forwarded" the entire matter "for the action of the President." On August 22, 1865, President Andrew Johnson finally got around to reviewing Fox's case. He then signed an executive decree which "ordered that (Fox) be dishonorably discharged the service with the loss of all pay, allowances and bounty and be imprisoned at hard labor for one year."

Big Mike Fox never went to that prison. Nor did he ever return to his home in Manchester, New Hampshire. According to one of the old New Hampshire veterans, Fox made his way back to the friendly family in Opelousas where he eventually married his Cajun girl and settled down to the sedentary life of a Louisiana planter. Whether true or not, this romantic version is the only one with a happy ending to the strange saga of Michael Fox.

- - - -

In the years following the war hundreds of Louisiana residents filed claims against the United States for damages resulting from invasion, occupation and confiscation. Especially heavy were the demands of the French and British government on behalf of their citizens living in Louisiana or in other parts of the South. There was also political pressure from Southerners claiming to have remained "loyal" to the Old Flag during the hostilities.

Some of these claims were contrived, most were exaggerated and many were filed under false pretenses. Though each claim was thoroughly investigated—and many rejected—many millions of dollars were subsequently awarded. Ironically, the vast majority of claimants were either former speculators, who had subsisted off the misery and losses of others during the war, or slaveholders (among whom were numerous *gens de coleur libre)* whose wealth and income had been generated by that "peculiar institution." For the most part these people did not assist the Confederacy, but claimed exemption from military duty as plantation masters, administrators or foreigners and sent their sons to Europe to evade conscription.

On the other hand the poor Cajuns, who owned relatively few slaves, who could not afford to purchase a substitute for military service or send their sons to Europe, and who were no less French than more recent immigrants, could claim nothing because they had worn the gray, albeit reluctantly. They had received no protection papers, no guards at their front doors, and even though many—if not most—were opposed to secession, they could make no claim against the government for their losses at the hands of Union soldiers. It was just another chapter in the long continuing saga of the tragedy of the Acadians.

Former slaves fared little better. Their labor had generated the income and wealth on the plantation, but their lot, like that of the Cajuns, was to subsist on their own meager resources. The alternative, which most chose, was to serve their liberators. It was only natural that they had become "wild with joy" when the Yankees came marching through. They had plundered alongside, and sometimes at the urging of, the white soldiers; they had served as scouts and soldiers, frequently leading the way to Confederate hideouts and to hiding places of produce. White Southerners died or were wounded because of this assistance; others imprisoned and fortunes lost. What was especially galling as far as whites were concerned was that many blacks served the oppressive and corrupt carpetbaggers faithfully during the Reconstruction, thus sowing the seed for a century or more of class and racial conflict.

\- - - - - -

There are precious few physical reminders in present day Acadiana of that fateful autumn of 1863. Unlike other states, Louisiana has a poor record of marking and preserving historical locations. Most of the fortifications and trenches and trees and houses and battle sites and campgrounds described in this work have long since fallen to the pitiless demands of "progress." Until very recently the location of the battle of Bayou Bourbeux was an overgrown field collecting the usual amount of discarded washing machines, beer cans and other garbage. It is now rapidly becoming a sort of rural subdivision of modern houses on small plots. A lone marker, erroneously placed several miles away from the actual scene of fighting, is the only testiment to the men who struggled and died there. The Yankees who were buried at the site have long since been disinterred and moved to Chalmette National Cemetary near New Orleans. The Texans remain, their actual location unmarked and only recently ascertained by the writer.

Desire Arnaud's ditch remains, as does Chretien Point which, after generations of neglect and vacancy—once serving as a cowstall and haybarn—has been tastefully restored to its former elegance by Jeanne and Louis Cornay. The only reminders of that tragic autumn is a neat bullet hole in the front door and a slightly crooked balcony where a cannon explosion partially destroyed a column. The stairway incident in *Gone with the Wind*, when Scarlett ended the life of a Yankee straggler, was inspired by the real life experience of Madame Chretien, who shot a bandit to death on the spiraling staircase before the war. The staircase at Chretien Point was faithfully reproduced for Tara in the movie.

General John Pratt's house disappeared years ago as did Urbaigne Lavergne's, John Gardiner's and Desire Arnaud's. Charles Lavergne's house still stands on the old road between Opelousas and Sunset and there are still vestiges of the old *bois d'arc* hedge, but the Rogers' home, used as a Confederate hospital following the Bourbeux affair, was being dismantled for its valuable cypress lumber even as this book was going to press. A new house was only recently constructed nearby, the slab of which was poured virtually over the burial site of those who expired under the knives of Confederate surgeons.

The Academy of Sacred Heart at Grand Coteau and the St. Charles College stands much as it did in 1863. Petitin's store and home have long since disappeared, as have Dunbar's pharmacy, and the St. Charles Hotel, but a number of other homes dating back to that period remain, including the Duffy home and McPherson's Plantation house.Until recently, little had been done to preserve or protect Grand Coteau's unique historical buildings and architectural lines with the result that ranch style houses, mobile homes and even a junk yard are rapidly replacing the graceful old homes that once dotted the landscape.

In Opelousas, the old Prudhomme plantation—Ringrose—which served as General Grover's quarters, was only recently rescued from being razed and turned into a hospital parking lot, thanks to the civic-minded efforts of people like Kenneth Deshotels. The present day St. Landry Catholic Church and Opelousas Courthouse occupy the same sites as those mentioned in this work but are not the same buildings.

A few of the older houses around Port Barre (Barre's Landing) Notleyville and Leonville date back to the year 1863 and were the scenes of the plunder described in this work. The XIII Corps camp was located in what is today downtown Port Barre, but the XIX Corps campsite (Camp Barri-Croquant) is still unspoiled (and unmarked) farmland.

Neither will the casual visitor find markers of any sort to indicate the events that occurred at Ville Platte, Plaissance, Church Point (Plaquemine Brule) or Lawtell near the Mallet Woods. The only reminder of the clash between Judge Roberts and Judge Lee north of Washington is a solitary headstone over the grave of an unidentified Confederate soldier at Homeplace. On the other hand the entire town of Washington, whose graceful old homes stand much as they did in 1863, was very recently placed on the National Register of Historic Places.

In Lafayette (Vermilionville) there is a lone historic marker at Pinhook Bridge. A very small segment of the trenches dug by the *Corps d'Afrique* is still visible in Girard Park. Henri Monnier's old house still stands, but Ile Copal, Governor Mouton's mansion, has long since disappeared as have the homes of Basil Crow, Emile Mouton (only recently burned) and General Alfred Mouton. The trees on Jefferson Street (Emma K. Lane) fell to the bulldozers years ago as did the trenches and fortifications on the south bank of Bayou Vermilion. Present day St. John's Cathedral is not the same building as the one mentioned in this work, but is on the same site.

There is nothing at Spanish Lake, Jefferson Island (Orange Island), Bayou Petit Anse, Bayou Portage, Olivier's Landing, or Nelson's Canal to indicate the significant events which occurred there. In fact the scene of Duperier's last stand on Bayou Portage seems to be nothing more than a convenient garbage dump; and the Bayous Vermilion, Teche, Courtableau, Carencro and Bourbeux are badly polluted. On the other hand the Weeks home at New Iberia (The Shadows), the St. Martin of Tours Catholic Church, the Evangeline Oak and the Duclosel home in St. Martinville (The Acadian House) have been magnificently preserved, as has Madame Porter's home in Irish Bend (Oak Lawn Manor).

In closing this narrative, the writer is reminded of an anecdote related to him several years ago by an old Cajun. It seems that a certain Madame Guilbeau, a widow living near the site of Camp Carrion Crow during and after the war, was much disturbed by the train noise when the Opelousas, New Orleans and Great Western Railroad line was finally completed across her property. In her feeble protests she frequently greased the rails with hog fat, sought out the advice of *gris gris* shamons and, on one occasion, even attempted to burn the wooden tressle over the Carencro.

When all her efforts proved futile, she settled down and accepted the noise and inconvenience. A few years before her death she was asked by a friend why she had finally acquiesed. "*Mais cher,*" replied the old woman in the unique patois of southern Louisiana, "whenever I hear that train coming, what with all the dogs barking and everything, I just close my eyes, sit back and pretend that the roaring noise is the hoofbeats of the Texicans chasing them damn Yankees right out of Louisiana."

APPENDIX A

ARMY OF THE GULF IN SOUTHWESTERN LOUISIANA
AUTUMN 1863

Major General Nathaniel P. Banks, Department Commander
Major General William B. Franklin, Field Commander

XIII Army Corps
Major General Cadwalader C. Washburn

1st Division—Brigadier General Michael K. Lawler

1st Brigade—Colonel David Shunk
- 33rd Illinois Infantry, Colonel Charles Lippincott
- 99th Illinois Infantry, Colonel George Bailey
- 8th Indiana Infantry, Colonel Charles Parish
- 18th Indiana Infantry, Colonel William Charles

2nd Brigade—Colonel Charles Harris
- 21st Iowa Infantry, Colonel Salue Van Anda
- 22nd Iowa Infantry, Major Ephraim White
- 23rd Iowa Infantry, Colonel Samuel Glasgow
- 11th Wisconsin Infantry, Major Jesse Miller

3rd Brigade—Colonel Lionel Sheldon
- 49th Indiana Infantry, Colonel James Keigwin
- 69th Indiana Infantry, Colonel Oran Perry
- 7th Kentucky Infantry, Colonel John Lucas
- 22nd Kentucky Infantry, Colonel George Monroe
- 16th Ohio Infantry, Major Milton Mills
- 42nd Ohio Infantry, Major William Williams
- 120th Ohio Infantry, Major Willard Slocum

Artillery Support
- 2nd Illinois, Battery A, Lieutenant Herman Borris
- 1st Indiana Battery, Lieutenant Lawrence Jacoby
- 7th Michigan Battery, Lieutenant George Stillman
- 1st Wisconsin Battery, Lieutenant Daniel Webster

3rd Division—Brigadier General George F. McGinnis

1st Brigade—Brigadier General Robert A. Cameron
- 11th Indiana Infantry, Colonel Daniel Macauley
- 24th Indiana Infantry, Colonel William Spicely
- 34th Indiana Infantry, Lt. Colonel Robert Jones
- 46th Indiana Infantry, Colonel Thomas Bringhurst
- 29th Wisconsin Infantry, Lt. Colonel William Greene

2nd Brigade—Colonel James R. Slack
47th Indiana Infantry, Lt. Colonel John McLaughlin
24th Iowa Infantry, Lt. Colonel John Wilds
28th Iowa Infantry, Colonel John Connell
56th Ohio Infantry, Colonel William Rayner

Artillery Support
2nd Illinois, Battery E, Lieutenant Emil Steger
1st Missouri, Battery A, Lieutenant Charles Callahan
2nd Ohio Battery, Lieutenant William Harper
16th Ohio Battery, Captain Russell Twist

4th Division—Brigadier General Stephen G. Burbridge

1st Brigade—Colonel Richard Owen
60th Indiana Infantry, Captain Augustus Goelzer
67th Indiana Infantry, Lt. Colonel Theodore Buehler
83rd Ohio Infantry, Colonel Frederick Moore
96th Ohio Infantry, Lt. Colonerl Albert Brown
23rd Wisconsin Infantry, Colonel Joshua Guppey

2nd Brigade—Colonel William J. Landrum
77th Illinois Infantry, Colonel David Grier
97th Illinois Infantry, Lt. Colonel Lewis Martin
130th Illinois Infantry, Major John Reid
19th Kentucky Infantry, Lt. Colonel John Cowan
48th Ohio Infantry, Captain Joseph Lindsey

Artillery Support
Chicago Mercantile Battery, Captain P.H. White
17th Ohio Battery, Captain Charles Rice

XIX Army Corps
Major General William B. Franklin

1st Division—Brigadier General Godfrey Weitzel

1st Brigade—Colonel George M. Love
30th Massachusetts Infantry, Lt. Colonel William Bullock
116th New York Infantry, Major John Sizer
161st New York Infantry, Lt. Colonel William Kinsey
174th New York Infantry, Lt. William Watkins

3rd Brigade—Colonel Robert M. Merrritt
12th Connecticut Infantry, Lt. Colonel Frank Peck
75th New York Infantry, Captain Henry Fitch
114th New York Infantry, Colonel Samuel Per Lee
160th New York Infantry, Lt. Colonel John Van Petten
8th Vermont Infantry, Colonel Stephen Thomas

Artillery Support
1st Maine Battery, Captain Albert Bradbury
6th Massachusets Battery, Lieutenant Edwin Russell

3rd Division—Brigadier General Cuvier Grover

1st Brigade—Colonel Lewis Benedict
- 110th New York Infantry, Colonel Clinton Sage
- 162nd New York Infantry, Colonel Lewis Benedict
- 165th New York Infantry, Lt. Colonel Gouverneur Carr
- 173rd New York Infantry, Colonel Lewis Peck

2nd Brigade—Brigadier General James McMillan
- 14th Maine Infantry, Colonel Thomas Porter
- 26th Massachusetts Infantry, Colonel Alpha Farr
- 8th New Hampshire Infantry, Lt. Colonel George Flanders
- 133rd New York Infantry, Colonel Leonard Currie

Artillery Support
- 4th Massachusetts Battery, Captain George Trull
- 1st United States, Battery F, Lieutenant Hardman Norris
- 25th New York Battery, Captain John Grow
- 1st United States, Battery L, Captain Henry Closson

Cavalry Division—Brigadier General Albert L. Lee

1st Brigade—Colonel Edmund Davis
- 1st Texas Cavalry, Colonel Edmund Davis
- 1st Louisiana Cavalry, Colonel Harai Robinson
- 118th Illinois Mounted Infantry, Colonel John Fonda
- 6th Missouri Cavalry, Major Bacon Montgomery
- 14th New York Cavalry, Lt. Colonel John Cropsey

2nd Brigade—Colonel John J. Mudd
- 2nd Illinois Cavalry, Lt. Colonel Daniel Bush
- 3rd Illinois Cavalry, Captain Robert Carnahan
- 15th Illinois Cavalry, Captain Joseph Adams
- 36th Illinois Cavalry, Captain George Willis
- 1st Indiana Cavalry, Captain James Carey
- 4th Indiana Cavalry, Captain Andrew Gallagher

Not Brigaded
- 87th Illinois Mounted Infantry, Colonel John Crebs
- 16th Indiana Mounted Infantry, Colonel Thomas Lucas
- 2nd Louisiana Mounted Infantry, Colonel Charles Paine
- 2nd Massachusetts Battery, Captain Ormand Nims

Engineers and Unattached Units
Major David C. Houston

- 3rd Engineers, Corps d'Afrique
- 15th Infantry, Corps d'Afrique
- 22nd Infantry, Corps d'Afrique
- 25th Engineers, Corps d'Afrique
- Independent Kentucky Infantry

APPENDIX B

ARMY OF WESTERN LOUISIANA, CSA

AUTUMN 1863

Major General Richard Taylor, Field Commander

Walker's Texas Division—Major General John G. Walker

1st Brigade—Colonel Overton Young

8th Texas Volunteer Infantry, Colonel B. A. Phillpot
13th Texas Dismounted Cavalry, Colonel J. H. Burnett
18th Texas Volunteer Infantry, Colonel William H. King
22nd Texas Volunteer Infantry, Colonel R. B. Hubbard
Halderman's Battery, Captain Horace Halderman

2nd Brigade—Colonel Horace Randall

28th Texas Dismounted Cavalry, Colonel E. H. Baxter
11th Texas Volunteer Infantry, Colonel O. M. Roberts
14th Texas Volunteer Infantry, Colonel Ed. Clarke
Gould's Battalion, Major E. S. Gould
Daniel's Battery of Light Artillery, Captain J. M. Daniel

3rd Brigade—Colonel George Flournoy and T. J. Scurry

15th Texas Volunteer Infantry (Speight's Regiment), Colonel Harrison
16th Texas Volunteer Infantry, Colonel J. Shepard
16th Texas Dismounted Cavalry, Colonel William Fitzhugh
17th Texas Volunteer Infantry, Colonel R. T. P. Allen
19th Texas Volunteer Infantry, Colonel R. Waterhouse
Edgar's Battery of Light Artillery, Captain William Edgar

Louisiana Infantry Brigade
Brigadier General Alfred Mouton

18th Louisiana Infantry, Colonel Leopold Armant, 1180 men
24th Louisiana Infantry (Crescent Regiment), Colonel A. W. Bosworth
26th Louisiana Infantry, Colonel Henry Gray, 798 men
10th Battalion (Yellow Jacket), Colonel Valsin A. Fournet, 5 companies
11th Battalion, Colonel J. H. Beard
12th Battalion (Confederate Guards Response), Colonel Franklin H. Clack
1st Louisiana Artillery (St. Mary's Cannoneers), Captain F. O. Cornay
5th Louisiana Artillery (Pelican Battery), Captain Thomas A. Faries

Green's Cavalry Division
Brigadier-General Thomas Green C.S.A.

1st Cavalry Brigade—Colonel Arthur P. Bagby

4th Texas Cavalry—Colonel William P. Hardeman
5th Texas Cavalry—Colonel Henry McNeill
7th Texas Cavalry—Colonel William Steele
2nd Cavalry Regiment (Arizona Brigade)—
Colonel George W. Baylor
13th Texas "Horse" Battalion—
Lieutenant Colonel Edwin Waller Jr.

2nd Louisiana Cavalry—Colonel William Vincent
Valverde Battery—Captain Joseph Sayers

2nd Cavalry Brigade—Colonel James P. Major
1st Regiment Partisan Rangers—Colonel Walter P. Lane
3rd Regiment (Arizona Brigade) Partisan Rangers—
Colonel George T. Madison
6th Regiment Partisan Rangers—Colonel B. W. Stone
1st Confederate Battery—Captain Oliver Semmes.

APPENDIX C

LIST OF OATHTAKERS* IN SOUTHWESTERN LOUISIANA

NAME	DATE	LOCATION
Andre, Jean	November 3, 1863	Vermilionville
Andres, T.	October 7, 1863	Olivier's Landing
Armeda, G.	October 7, 1863	Olivier's Landing
Armeda, L.	October 7, 1863	Olivier's Landing
Arnaud, J. F. Desire	October 17, 1863	Carrion Crow B.
Arnou, Adolfe	October 28, 1863	Barre's Landing
Baxter, I. H.	July 22, 1865	Franklin
Beaudreu, J. Rousseau	October 19, 1863	Bourbeux B.
Belfona, Emiel	October 28, 1863	Barre's Landing
Beraud, Camille	December 3, 1863	New Iberia
Bertrand, Vincent	November 5, 1863	Vermilionville
Bonin, Achilde	October 8, 1863	Olivier's Landing
Bonnag, Aristerel	December 22, 1863	New Iberia
Boudreau, Marseille	December 30, 1863	New Iberia
Bourg, John E.	October 27, 1863	Barre's Landing
Boute, Voltair	October 8, 1863	Olivier's Landing
Bouteaux, Massell	November 19, 1863	New Iberia
Breaux, Hervien	November 24, 1863	New Iberia
Broussard, Camille	December 22, 1863	New Iberia
Burnett, L. T.	November 21, 1863	New Iberia
Butaud, Philogene	October 5, 1863	Cypremort
Carlin, Belfort	September 30, 1863	Bayou Salle
Chretien, J. F.	December 18, 1863	New Iberia
Cobleur, William	November 9, 1863	Vermilionville
Colder, J. H.	December 30, 1863	New Iberia
Colder, P. C.	December 30, 1863	New Iberia
Cormier, Emile	November 20, 1863	New Iberia
Cory, Henry	November 20, 1863	New Iberia
Devilliers, Charles C.	October 28, 1863	Barre's Landing
Duncan, James	December 31, 1863	New Iberia
Ega, Charles	November 3, 1863	Vermilionville
Eifer, Frank	December 15, 1863	New Iberia
Falgourt, C.	October 7, 1863	Olivier's Landing
Falgourt, Victor	October 7, 1863	Olivier's Landing
Frederick, Francis	November 3, 1863	Vermilionville
Fredericks, Charles W.	November 20, 1863	New Iberia
Frilot, Alcide	October 5, 1863	St. Mary Parish
Frilot, Jules	October 27, 1863	Barre's Landing
Gall, Jaspar	January 4, 1864	New Iberia
Garlington, W. M.	November 10, 1863	Vermilionville

Garry, J. P.	October 8, 1863	Olivier's Plantation
Gates, Alfred	July 27, 1863	Franklin
Goulas, A.	October 8, 1863	Olivier's Landing
Grady, James	December 2, 1863	New Iberia
Hargrave, Harrison	December 30, 1863	New Iberia
Hawkins, W. H.	November 11, 1863	Vermilionville
Hebert, Alex	December 17, 1863	New Iberia
Hebert, Philibert	August 25, 1865	Franklin
Henriques, J.	October 28, 1863	Barre's Landing
Herbert, Lucian	November 20, 1863	New Iberia
Hornsby, W. R.	October 8, 1863	Olivier's Landing
Jacobs, Alex	December 2, 1863	New Iberia
Jean, Lastie	November 10, 1863	Vermilionville
Johnson, J. J.	October 6, 1863	Olivier's Landing
Kory, A.	October 28, 1863	Barre's Landing
Landry, Robert	December 26, 1863	New Iberia
Lege, Joisin	October 27, 1863	Barre's Landing
Legnon, Darius	October 5, 1863	Cypremort
Lele, Edward	December 4, 1863	New Iberia
Lemelle, Alexandre	October 27, 1863	Barre's Landing
Louvier, Tederique	October 8, 1863	Olivier's Landing
Lusfe, Casper	November 26, 1863	New Iberia
Lyons, Thomas	November 28, 1863	New Iberia
McCarthy, E.	November 28, 1863	Barre's Landing
McKerall, Wilson	July 27, 1865	Franklin
Magie, T.	December 28, 1863	New Iberia
Marguet, F.	October 10, 1863	Carrion Crow B.
Marsh, Jonas	December 28, 1863	New Iberia
Meullion, Alphonse	October 27, 1863	Barre's Landing
Miller, Joseph C.	October 18, 1863	Carrion Crow B.
Moise, J. W.	January 11, 1864	Franklin
Morrow, William W.	November 10, 1863	Vermilionville
Norwood, R. H.	December 19, 1863	New Iberia
Oquan, Louis	November 4, 1863	Vermilionville
Oubre, P.	December 27, 1863	New Iberia
Ozeme, Philogene	November 18, 1863	New Iberia
Patout, Celestin	October 8, 1863	Olivier's Landing
Paultron, Joseph	November 9, 1863	Vermilionville
Perne, L.	January 2, 1864	New Iberia
Rather, Edward	January 4, 1864	New Iberia
Riggs, L. W.	November 28, 1863	New Iberia
Robinson, Adolphe	December 30, 1863	New Iberia
Roy, Aimi	October 30, 1863	Barre's Landing
Sanders, John T.	December 15, 1863	New Iberia
Sandoz, Ami	October 10, 1863	Carrion Crow B.
Savoie, D'Ojean	October 18, 1863	Carrion Crow B.
Savoie, Joseph J.	October 18, 1863	Carrion Crow B.
Savoie, Don Louis	October 19, 1863	Bourbeux B.
Savoie, John R.	October 19, 1863	Bourbeux B.

Sharp, John	November 20, 1863	New Iberia
Tarkington, I.	September 9, 1865	Franklin
Tassitt, C. R.	July 24, 1865	Franklin
Theriot, Joseph	December 28, 1863	New Iberia
Verret, Valgran	October 10, 1863	Carrion Crow B.
Vigneaud, N.	December 24, 1863	New Iberia
Vincent, Emille	November 9, 1863	Vermilionville
Walker, J. M.	December 26, 1863	New Iberia
Washington, G. M.	September 26, 1865	Franklin
Watch, Ege	December 24, 1863	New Iberia
Wilberding, J. H.	October 29, 1863	Barre's Landing
Wirlop, George W.	December 15, 1863	New Iberia

Source: Records of District and Parish Provost Marshals, Department of the Gulf, Old Book 1255-1257, Oaths of Allegiance, Record Group 393, National Archives, Washington, D. C.

*Most of the oathtakers appeared before Provost Marshals Edwin Molineaux or Henry Inwood. The names are reproduced here as they appeared on the oaths. Since many names were barely legible there are bound to be numerous errors in spelling. Regrettably the list is incomplete and includes only a few of those appearing in the XIX Corps camps. No extant lists could be located for those who took the oath in XIII Corps camps.

APPENDIX D

ROLL OF HONOR
THE GREAT TEXAS OVERLAND EXPEDITION
OCTOBER-DECEMBER 1863

(Incomplete)

Union

Name and Rank	Unit	Date and Nature of Death
Albert, V. G. Pvt.	60th Indiana	Nov. 3 Gunshot Head
Akeman, Frank	97th Illinois	Nov. 1 R. R. Accident
Ballard, William M.	23rd Wisconsin	Nov. 3 Bourbeux
Blanchard, G. Cpt.	96th Ohio	Nov. 3 Gunshot Lungs
Bowman, H. M. Pvt.	60th Indiana	Nov. 3 Gunshot Knee
Campbell, John C. Pvt.	96th Ohio	Nov. 4 Gunshot Lungs
Chandler, Henry Pvt.	118th Ill. Mtd. Inf.	Oct. 24 Gunshot Lungs
Cobb, Abram Sgt.	96th Ohio	Nov. 3 Gunshot Lungs
Coffelt, Perry Cpl.	60th Indiana	Nov. 3 Gunshot, Bowels
Cooper, Isaac J.Pvt.	96th Ohio	Nov. 3 Gunshot Head
Corbitt, John	97th Illinois	Nov. 1 R. R. Accident
Cox, Joseph Pvt.	60th Indiana	Nov. 3 Gunshot Lungs
Crosby, George Pvt.	2nd Illinois Cav.	Nov. 11 Gunshot Lungs
Draper, George	97th Illinois	Nov. 1 R. R. Accident
Elliot, Patrick M.Pvt.	96th Ohio	Nov. 28 Gunshot
Endicott, H. C. Sgt.	60th Indiana	Nov. 2 Gunshot, Bowels
Feerer, Henry Pvt.	96th Ohio	Nov. 17 Gunshot (Nov. 3)
Franks, Henry W. Pvt.	96th Ohio	Nov. 4 Gunshot Abdomen
Gue, Jeremiah Capt.	24th Iowa	Nov. 1 Gunshot Lungs
Hendricks, Thomas Lt.	67th Indiana	Nov. 4 Gunshot
Hilliard, James Sgt.	23rd Wisconsin	Nov. 3 Gunshot Lungs
Jack, Alonzo Pvt.	23rd Wisconsin	Nov. 3 Gunshot, Bowels
Kelly, J. R. Pvt.	60th Indiana	Nov. 3 Gunshot Thigh
McGarvey, George Cpt.	60th Indiana	Nov. 3 Gunshot Hand
McKeever, James Pvt.	23rd Wisconsin	Nov. 3 Gunshot Face
Manlief, R. Pvt.	16th Indiana Mtd. Inf.	Oct. 5 Gunshot
Marsh, Arthur Capt.	118th Ill. Mtd. Inf.	Nov. 11 Gunshot Lungs
Martin Lt.	97th Illinois	Nov. 1 R. R. Accident
Mecay, Alexander Pvt.	96th Ohio	Nov. 3 Gunshot Lungs
Miller, John	97th Illinois	Nov. 1 R. R. Accident
Oleson, Ole J.	23rd Wisconsin	Nov. 3 Bourbeux
Osborn, C. W.	97th Illinois	Nov. 1 R. R. Accident
Polk, George, Drummer	97th Illinois	Nov. 1 R. R. Accident

Powers, Clarence Pvt.	118th Ill. Mtd. Inf.	Oct. 24 Brain Concussion
Reed, William	97th Illinois	Nov. 1 R. R. Accident
Reid, David W. Pvt.	96th Ohio	Nov. 4 Gunshot Groin
Rodgers, John Pvt.	1st La. Cav.	Nov. 3 Gunshot
Rogers, Peter, Pvt.	60th Indiana	Dec. 24 Exposure
Sherman, Clarence Pvt.	1st La. Cav.	Nov. 20 Gunshot (Oct.12)
Smith, Richard	97th Illinois	Nov. 1 R. R. Accident
Smith, T. B.	97th Illinois	Nov. 1 R. R. Accident
Stanfield, Jesse, Pvt.	96th Ohio	Nov. 3 Gunshot Head
Walker, Joseph Pvt.	60th Indiana	Nov. 3 Gunshot, Bowels
White, Isaac K. Cpt.	96th Ohio	Nov. 3 Gunshot Lungs
Williams, Charles Pvt.	24th Iowa	Nov. 1 Illness
Williams, Jabez Pvt.	23rd Wisconsin	Nov. 3 Gunshot, Bowels
Williams, Joseph Pvt.	60th Indiana	Nov. 3 Gunshot Lungs
Wheeler, William H. Pvt.	96th Ohio	Nov. 3 Bourbeux
Woods, Martin	97th Illinois	Nov. 1 R. R. Accident
Young, Jacob Sgt.	96th Ohio	Nov. 3 Gunshot Head
Young, Joseph Cpl.	118th Ill. Mtd. Inf.	Sept. 26 Dysentery

Confederate

Name and Rank	Unit	Date and Nature of Death
Bowman, J. J. Pvt.	28th Tex. Cavalry	Nov. 2 Shot for Desertion
Bisons, D. Pvt.	11th Texas Inf.	Nov. 3 Bourbeux
Brantly,————Pvt.	Baylor's Texas Cav.	Nov. 3 Bourbeux
Clark, A. L. Pvt.	Waller's Texas Btn.	Nov. 3 Fractured Thigh
Cook, C. Pvt.	11th Texas Inf.	Nov. 3 Bourbeux
Duncan, N. D. "Greens"	11th Texas Inf.	Nov. 9 Gunshot (Nov.3)
Duncan, W. H. Pvt.	18th Texas Inf.	Nov. 3 Bourbeux
Edwards, Samuel Pvt.	15th Texas Inf.	Nov. 3 Bourbeux
Evetts, Samuel Pvt.	15th Texas Inf.	Nov. 3 Bourbeux
Field, H. S. Pvt.	15th Texas Inf.	Nov. 3 Bourbeux
Fleming, T. J. Pvt.	11th Texas Inf.	Nog. 3 Bourbeux
George, D. M. Pvt.	18th Texas Inf.	Nov. 3 Bourbeux
Green, R. C. Pvt.	18th Texas Inf.	Nov. 3 Bourbeux
Green, J. F. Pvt.	18th Texas Inf.	Nov. 6 Thigh (Nov. 3)
Humphrey, David Pvt.	15th Texas Inf.	Nov. 3 Bourbeux
Johnson, L. R.Pvt.	18th Texas Inf.	Nov. 3 Bourbeux
King, John Pvt.	15th Texas Inf.	Nov. 3 Bourbeux
Lallier, V. A. Pvt.	5th Texas Cav.	Oct. 21 Gunshot Side
Litton, D. Pvt.	15th Texas Inf.	Nov. 3 Bourbeux
Long, J. M. Pvt.	15th Texas Inf.	Nov. 3 Bourbeux

McDonald, Barney Pvt.	4th Texas Cav.	Oct. 13 Gunshot Head
Morgan, Wm. H. Pvt.	4th Texas Cav.	Oct. 13 Gunshot Breast
Moulder, Joseph Pvt.	4th Texas Cav.	Oct. 13 Gunshot Thigh
Odom, John Pvt.	18th Texas Inf.	Nov. 3 Bourbeux
Pribble, W. F. Pvt.	15th Texas Inf.	Nov. 3 Bourbeux
Ramsey, J. C. Sgt.	18th Texas Inf.	Nov. 3 Bourbeux
Reddy,———————Pvt.	18th Texas Inf.	Nov. 3 Bourbeux
Russell, W. O. Pvt.	18th Texas Inf.	Nov. 3 Bourbeux
Robinson, J. A.	7th Texas Cav.	Nov. 3 Bourbeux
Setton, J.D. Pvt.	15th Texas Cav.	Nov. 3 Bourbeux
Spegies, G. J. Sgt.	15th Texas Inf.	Nov. 3 Bourbeux
Stillwell, J. L. H. Capt.	11th Texas Inf.	Nov. 7 Gunshot (Nov. 3)
Terry, J. R. Cpl.	18th Texas Inf.	Nov. 6 Gunshot (Nov. 3)
Thompson, W. A. Pvt.	11th Texas Inf.	Nov. 3 Bourbeux
Wair, W. H.	5th Texas Cav.	Oct. 13 Carrion Crow
Welch, William Pvt.	Madison's 3rd Tex. Cav.	Nov. 3 Bourbeux
Whitesides, Johnson Pvt.	5th Texas Cav.	Oct. 21 Gunshot Head
Wilkins, Rutherford Pvt.	Stone's 6th Tex. Cav.	Nov. 3 Bourbeux
Wimberely, L. Pvt.	11th Texas Inf.	Nov. 6 Gunshot (Nov. 3)
Wright, W. C.	Waller's Tex. Btn.	Oct. 21 Opelousas
Zimmerman, W.	4th Tex. Cav.	Oct. Disease

Sources: Houston *Tri-Weekly Telegraph*, November 16, 20, 1863; Theophilus Noel, *A Campaign from Santa Fe to the Mississippi*, Houston, 1961, pp. 160-63; John M. Bronough Papers, The Texas Collection, Baylor University; Records of the Adjutant Generals Office 1780's-1917, "List of Killed, Wounded or Missing for the Battle of Grand Coteau" and "List of Killed, Wounded or Missing in 60th Regiment Indiana Infantry," Record Group 94, National Archives, Washington, D. C.; Indianapolis *Daily Journal*, December 1; Madison Reese Collection, Illinois State Historical Library; Madison *Wisconsin State Journal*, December 7, 1863.

APPENDIX E

REINTERMENTS IN CHALMETTE NATIONAL HISTORICAL PARK, NEAR NEW ORLEANS, LOUISIANA (1868)

ORIGINAL LOCATION OF GRAVE	NO. OF BODIES	DATE REMOVED (1868)
Near Berwick, Louisiana		
Dr. Rhodes Plantation, 3 miles N.	4	April
Mr. Smith's Plantation, 5 miles N.	2	April
Near Franklin, Louisiana		
P. C. Bethel's Plantation, Left bank, 3½ miles S.	1	April
L. Hardings Plantation, 3 miles N.	1	April
Orphans Home Association, 4 miles N.	1	April
Near Pattersonville, Louisiana		
P. C. Bethel's Plantation, 5 miles N. W.	1	April
Mr. Cornay's Plantation, 4 miles N. W.	1	April
Mrs. Knight's Plantation, 3½ miles N. W.	25	March
Madame Meade's Plantation, 3 miles N. W.	1	April
Madame Meade's Upper Plantation, 6 miles N. W.	1	April
Sarah Robin's Plantation, Pattersonville	1	April
Major Weightman's, Left bank, 4½ miles N. W.	3	May
Near New Iberia, Louisiana		
Episcopal Church Yard, New Iberia	3	April

Leon Frilou's Plantation, 5½ miles S. E.	1	April
Mrs. Hopkins' Place, New Iberia	20	April
Mrs. Lewis's Plantation, New Iberia	3	April
Mr. Nelson's Plantation, 3 miles S. E.	5	April
D. Olivier's Plantation, 3 miles S. E.	1	April
Chas. Olivier's Plantation, 3½ miles S.E.	1	April
Mrs. Weeks's Place, ½ mile S. E.	12	April
Or. Bayard's Plantation, 2½ miles S. E.	1	April
T. J. Bronson's Plantation, 8 miles S.	1	April
Catholic Grave Yard, New Iberia	73	April
Near Vermilionville, Louisiana		
Perry Moses Plantation, 2 miles South	2	May
L. Riggs's Plantation, Vermilionville	3	May
Madame Whitington's Plantation, 2 miles South	2	May
Near Grand Coteau, Louisiana		
J. Woodruff's Plantation, Near Grand Coteau	2	June
J. D. Guidry's Plantation, Bayou Carencro	4	May
Madame Guilbeaux's Plantation, Bayou Carencro	3	May
Guidry's Plantation, Bayou Carencro	16	May
McDowell's Plantation Near Grand Coteau	4	May
Mouton's Plantation, Lafayette Parish, Bayou Carencro	14	May
Mrs. Guidry's Garden, Bayou Carencro	1	June

Near Barre's Landing, Louisiana		
Capt. Little's Plantation, 3 miles S. W.	1	May
R. Deshotels' Plantation ½ mile W.	4	May
Madame DeJean's Plantation, ½ mile E.	3	May
Littles' Plantation, 2½ miles W.	1	June
Near Opelousas, Louisiana		
Methodist Grave Yard, Opelousas	4	May
Frezer's Plantation, Near Opelousas	1	June
J. R. Richard's Plantation, Near Opelousas	1	June
St. Claire's Plantation, St. Landry Parish	1	June
Richard's Plantation, Bayou Bourbeux	2	June
Prejean's Plantation, Near Opelousas	1	June
Near Washington, Louisiana, St. Landry Parish		
Prescott's Plantation, Near Washington	2	May
Catholic Burial-Ground, Washington	6	May

Source: Quartermaster General's Office, Roll of Honor, August 1868, Index, pp. 13-14, Provided by Veterans Administration, National Cemetery System, Washington, D.C.

FOOTNOTES

CHAPTER ONE

FROM NEW ORLEANS TO BERWICK BAY

1. Most of the background information relating to this campaign is contained in the following sources: U. S. Congress, *Report of the Joint Committee on the Conduct of the War*, 2nd Session, 38th Congress (Washington, 1865) II, 98-130; Ludwell H. Johnson, *Red River Campaign, Politics and Cotton in the Civil War* (Baltimore, 1958), 5-48; *The War of the Rebellion: A Compilation of the Official Records of the Union and Confederate Armies* (Washington: 1880-1901), Series I, Vol. XXVI, Part I, 332-395, cited hereinafter as *Official Records; Springfield Daily Republican*, September 7, 1863; J. A. Padgett, "Some Letters of George Stanton Denison," *Louisiana Historical Quarterly*, XXIII, 1205-1206.
2. The French presence in Mexico was occasioned by the failure of the Mexican government, under Benito Juarez, to repay a large outstanding loan. British and Spanish forces originally joined the expedition but quickly settled their claims and withdrew. French Emperor Napoleon III, however, declared that France "had no interest in the United States becoming the sole mistress of the Gulf of Mexico and the sole dispenser of the products of the new world." His forces subsequently captured Mexico City in mid-1863, and Mexico was informed that she would soon have a European prince as ruler. Bertita Harding, *The Phantom Crown* (Indianapolis, 1934), 1-52. See also "The French Emperor's Policy in America," *Harper's Weekly*, V, VII,no. 320 (February 14, 1863), 98.
3. Elias P. Pellet, *History of the 114th Regiment, New York State Volunteers* (Norwich, N.Y. 1866), 154-56; Harris H. Beecher, *Record of the 114th Regiment N.Y.S.V.* (Norwich, N.Y., 1866), 253-54; Hovey Papers, IndianaUniversity, Bloomington, 68; Sylvester Bishop Letters, September 10 and 25, 1863, Indiana Historical Society Library, Indianapolis; *Chicago Tribune* September 1, 10 and October 1, 1863; John William DeForest, *A Volunteer's Adventures. A Union Captain's Record of the Civil War* (New Haven, 1946), 153-55; J. W. DeForest, *Miss Ravenel's Conversion from Secession to Loyalty* (New York, 1939), 203-04. Fiction based on his war-time experiences in Louisiana; James K. Hosmer, *The Thinking Bayonet* (Boston, 1865), another ficticious work based on actual war-time experience.
4. Grant's "death" was widely reported at the time. A few sources include *The Era* of New Orleans, September 5, 1863; Julius V. Wood Letters, Western Reserve Historical Society, Cleveland, letters of September 2 and 9, 1863; and Nannie M.Tilley (ed.) *Federals on the Frontier.The Diary of Benjamin F. McIntyre, 1862-1864* (Austin), 218-19.
5. Banks was outranked by only three Union generals at the time (Winfield Scott, John Fremont and George McClellan), Fred Harvey Harrington, *Fighting Politician, Major General N. P. Banks* (Philadelphia, 1948), 54-55.
6. *Ibid.*,1-55; Nathaniel P. Banks' Papers, microfilms in University of Texas Archives, Austin; John Esten Cooke (ed.) *Surrey of Eagle's Nest or The Memoirs of a Staff-Officer Serving in Virginia* (New York, 1866), 195.

7. *Official Records*, vol. XXXIV, pt. 3, 332-33. See also pp. 252-53, 293, 316 and 409-10; T. H. Williams, "General Banks and the Radical Republicans in the Civil War," *New England Quarterly* XII, 268-80.
8. T. E. Dabney, "The Butler Regime in Louisiana," *Louisiana Historical Quarterly*, Vol. XXVII, 487-526.
9. President James Monroe, in his message to Congress on December 2, 1823, contended that Europe and the Americas constitute two separate and distinct spheres of political activity. Specifically, he reiterated the principle accepted by U. S. presidents since George Washington that "the American continents, by the free and independent condition which they have assumed and maintain, are henceforth not to be considered as subject for future colonization by any European Power." Secretary of State Seward was a zealous adherent of the doctrine. Dexter Perkins, *Hands Off* (Boston, 1941), 1-15; *Official Records*, vol. XXVI, pt. 1, 673; *Senate Executive Document*, 38th Congress, 2nd Session, no. 11, pp. 459-60, 470; and "The Mexican Empire", *Harper's Weekly* (September 12, 1863), 578, and "France in Mexico", *Harper's Weekly* (September 19, 1863), 594.
10. *Official Records, XXVI, pt. I, 285-312, 683, 766-67;* Clement A. Evans (ed.), *Confederate Military History* (Atlanta, 1899, vol. XI (Texas), 111; Frank X. Tolbert, *Dick Dowling at Sabine Pass* (New York, 1962); and "The Disaster at Sabine Pass," *Harper's Weekly* (October 10, 1863), 646.
11. T. B. Marshall, *History of the Eighty-Third Ohio Volunteer Infantry* (Cincinnati, 1912), 108-09; See also William Bentley, *History of the 77th Illinois Volunteer Infantry* (Peoria, 1883), 205-06.
12. Beecher, *Record of the 114th Regiment*, 253-54.
13. So abusive were the women of New Orleans toward the Union officers and soldiers that General Butler on May 15, 1862 issued General Orders No. 28 stating "that hereafter, when any female shall, by word, gesture, or movement, insult or show contempt for any officer or soldier of the United States, she shall be regarded and held liable to be treated as a woman of the town plying her avocation." The order not only infuriated Southerners but was denounced in the North and abroad, especially in England.
14. Some interesting wartime descriptions of New Orleans and surrounding areas are contained in Thomas W. Knox, *Camp-Fire and Cotton-Field: Southern Adventures in the Time of War* (New York, 1865), 391-400; *State Journal*, Madison, Wisconsin, October 30, 1863; Isaac Jackson Papers, William L. Clements Library, Ann Arbor, August-September 1863 letters. Most of this correspondence has been edited and published by a grandson, Joseph Orville Jackson, *Some of the Boys, the Civil War Letters of Isaac Jackson* (Carbondale, Illinois), 122-33; Carl Hatch (ed.) *Dearest Susie, A Civil War Infantryman's Letters to His Sweetheart* (New York, 1971), 68-77; Julius Wood Letters, September 2 and 9, 1863; Thomas B. Marshall Papers, Ohio Historical Society, Columbus, diary entries for August and September 1863; Tilly, *Federals on the Frontier*, 206-18; E. E. Blake, *A Succinct History of the 28th Iowa Volunteer Infantry* (Belle Plains, Iowa, 1896), 23.
15. Harai Robinson Papers, Department of Archives and Manuscripts, Louisiana State University, Baton Rouge, Louisiana; Records of the Adjutant General's Office, Record of Events Cards for the 2nd Rhode Island and 1st Louisiana Cavalry Regiments, National Archives; Service record Harai Robinson in National

Archives; Records of the Judge Advocate General, "Mutiny at Thibodaux, La.," National Archives; *Official Records*, Series 1, vol. XXVI, pt.1, 262-73; French and American Claims Commission, "Theodore Valade against the United States," no. 214, especially depositions and/or letters of General W. H. Emory and Captain A. W. Corliss, National Archives; Service record and court-martial proceedings of William H. Smith (2nd Rhode Island Cavalry), National Archives.

16. John M. Stanyon, *A History of the Eighth Regiment of New Hampshire Volunteers* (Concord, N. H., 1892), 210; Blake, *A Succinct History of the 28th Iowa*, 23; Other sources describing the track or the train ride from Algiers to Brashear include James Hall, *Cayuga in the Field. A Record of the 75th N. Y. Volunteers* (Auburn, 1873), 146; Lawrence Van Alstyne, *Diary of an Enlisted Man* (New Haven, 1910), 186-87; H. W. Howe, *Passages from the Life of Henry Warren Howe* (Lowell, Mass., 1899), 53, 143-44; Thomas H. Bringhurst, *History of the Forty-Six Regiment, Indiana Volunteer Infantry* (1888), 72; *A History of the Trials and Hardships of the Twenty-Fourth Indiana Volunteer Infantry* (Indianapolis, 1913), 86-87; Augustus George Sinks Collection, Indiana State Library, Indianapolis, p. 51; A. A. Rigby Diary, Iowa State Department of History and Archives, Des Moines, entry September 14, 1863, 23; *State Journal*, Madison, Wisconsin, November 25, 1863, p. 2; and Theophilus Noel, *Autobiography and Reminiscences of Theophilus Noel* (Chicago, 1904), 257-58.
17. *Official Records*, vol. XXVI, pt. II, 230-31; Richard Taylor, *Destruction and Reconstruction* (New York, 1879), 145.
18. Stanyon, *A History of the Eighth Regiment of New Hampshire Volunteers*, 210
19. *State Journal*, Madison, Wisconsin, November 25 by war correspondent H. A. Fenney; A. A. Rigby Diary, entry September 14, 1863. The name was changed from Brashear to Morgan City, February 8, 1876; Emerson Bentley, *Morgan City, The Commercial Entrepot of Attakapas* (New Orleans, 1876); The 8th U. S. Census (1860) for St. Mary Parish identifies most of the proprietors, officials and others who lived there at the time; see also The Morgan City Historical Society, *A History of Morgan City*, (Morgan City, 1960), 15-16.
20. *Official Records* Vol. XXVI, pt. II, 232-33, 245-47, 251-53, 255-62.
21. Beecher, *Record of the 114th Regiment, 251; Official Records*, vol. XXXVIII, Pt. II, 374, 408; U. S. Congress, *Report of the Joint Committee on the Conduct of the War*, 2nd Session, 38th Congress (Washington, 1865), vol. 1, Ezra J. Warner, *Generals in Blue* (Baton Rouge, 1964), William B. Franklin Papers, Manuscripts Division, Library of Congress, Washington, D. C.
22. *Official Records*, vol. XXVI, pt. II, 246-47, 581.
23. Beecher, *Record of the 114th Regiment*, 131; Albert Stearns, *Reminiscences of the Late War* (Brooklyn, 1881), 21-28.
24. Sylvester Bishop Letters, correspondence of September 25, 1863; Ross Kidwell Papers, Indiana Historical Society Library, Indianapolis, correspondence of October 2, 1863.
25. Calvin P. Alling Reminiscences. The State Historical Society of Wisconsin, 12; Other descriptions of Berwick are contained in the Daniel Webster correspondence, State Historical Society of Wisconsin, letters of November 4, 13 and 18, 1863; Lloyd Nauscawen Letters, State Historical Society of Wisconsin, letter September 20, 1863; Augustus George Sinks Collection, 51; Beecher, *Record of the 114th Regiment*, 255, Hovey Papers, 68, Blake, *A Succinct History of the*

28th Iowa, 23; French and American Claims Commission, "Jean Dupre against the United States," No. 540, June 17, 1881. National Archives, Washington, D.C.; Frank Moore (ed.) *The Rebellion Record, A Diary of American Events*, vol. 7, Document 19, pp. 75-76. The latter two sources contain excellent descriptions of the burning of Berwick.

26. *Official Records*, XXVI, pt. I, 335, 783.
27. Howe, *Passages from the Life of Henry Warren Howe*, 144; *A History of the Trials and Hardships of the Twenty-Fourth Indiana*, 87; Bringhurst, *History of the Forty-Sixth Regiment*, 72,73; *History of the Sixteenth Battery of Ohio Volunteers Light Artillary, USA*, (1906), 96; E. Dane Letters, correspondence September 21, 1863 in L.S.U. Library Archives, Baton Rouge.
28. F. H. Mason, *The Forty-Second Ohio Infantry*, (Cleveland, 1876), 241-42; B. F. Stevenson, *Letters from the Army* (Cincinnati, 1884), 256-61.
29. Ira B. Gardner, *Recollections of a Boy Member of Co. I, Fourteenth Maine Volunteers* (Lewiston, Me. 1902), 24.
30. Rueben B. Scott, *The History of the 67th Regiment, Indiana Infantry Volunteers* (Bedford, Indiana 1892), 48; Isaac Jackson Papers, letters October 6, 1863; also George Crooke, *The Twenty-First Regiment of Iowa, Volunteer Infantry* (Milwaukee, 1891), 116.
31. Beecher, *Record of the 114th Regiment*, 256-57; other accounts of this rivalry are found in Hall, *Cayuga in the Field*, 146; Howe, *Passages in the Life of Henry Warren Howe*, 114; Crooke, *The Twenty-First Regiment of Iowa*, 117; Hartford, Wisconsin, *Home League*, October 17; Nauscawen Letters, correspondence dated September 11, 1863; and Harry P. Whipple, *The Diary of a Private Soldier* (Waterloo, Wisconsin,1906), 27.
32. *A History of the Trials and Hardships of the 24th Indiana*, 88; Hovey Papers, 68-69.
33. This incident is described by Bringhurst, *History of the Forth-Sixth Regiment*, 73-74; The identity of the unfortunate proprietress remains uncertain. Among those maintaining hotels or boarding establishments at the time were Mrs. H. Mayo,Mrs. O'Donnell, Joseph Vallie and a certain Cavanaugh, Mr. Costello, Mrs. Lynch and Maria Louisia Israel. The latter, who owned a hotel jointly with Joseph Vignes, filed a claim after the war for damages resulting to the hotel from occupation and carelessness. French and American Claims Commission, "Maria Louisia Israel against the United States," No. 462, filed June 6, 1881, National Archives, Washington, D. C.; see also *8th U. S. Census* (1860), St. Mary Parish; and Emerson Bentley, *Morgan City*, advertisements in back.
34. Most of these individuals subsequently filed claims against the United States under the auspices of the French and American Claims Commission. "Jean Maurice Villien against the United States," no. 171; "Ambroise Narcisse Lucas against the United States," No. 300; "Maria Landry (daughter of Louis LaForest) against the United States," no. 274; "Pierre Loustaunau against the United States," no. 301; "Charles Forgues against the United States," no. 138 (depositions of Pierre Lahitte, John R ggio, Benjamin Leroy, Valentin Aucoin, John Burk, Mary Church and Stephen Thomas); and "Stephanie Trone against the United States," no. 417: All are filed in the National Archives, Washington, D. C.
35. Records of the Judge Advocate General, Court-martial Case File of Private Richard Hughes, National Archives, Washington, D. C.; A. A. Rigby Diary, entry September 24, 1863; William Titus Rigby Diary, University of Iowa Library

Archives, Iowa City, entry September 24, 1863; Levi L. Hoag Diary in the Katherine Gue Leonard Collection, Iowa State Department of History and Archives, Des Mones, September 24, 1863 entry; *A History of the Trials and Hardships of the Twenty-Fourth Indiana* 87; Thomas D. Williams, *An Historical Sketch of the 56th Ohio Volunteer Infantry*, 58; and Whipple, *Diary of a Private Soldier*, 27-28.

CHAPTER TWO

UP THE TECHE

1. *Official Records*, Vol. XXVI, pt. I, 752.
2. Records of the Judge Advocate General, Court-martial proceedings of Surgeon A. C. Livingston, Exhibit B, National Archives, Washington, D. C.
3. See, for example, the report of Brigadier General William Dwight dated Washington, La. April 27, 1863, *Official Records*, Vol. XV, Series I, p. 373; Harris H. Beecher, *Record of the 114th Regiment, N.Y.S.V.* (Norwich, NY., 1866), 148-49; J. F. Moors, *History of the Fifty-Second Regiment Massachusetts Volunteers* (Boston, 1893), 133-34; George W. Powers, *The Story of the Thirty-Eighth Regiment of Massachusetts Volunteers* (Boston, 1866), 74-79; and James K. Hosmer, *The Color Guard* (Boston, 1864), 155-56.
4. Surgeon A. C. Livingston of the 110th New York Infantry, for example, was arrested, court-martialed and subsequently sentenced to be cashiered for lagging behind to care for ill soldiers. Court-martial proceedings, A. C. Livingston.
5. Beecher, *Record of the 114th Regiment*, 258.
6. These are shown on a detailed Confederate map of St. Mary Parish, maps Z-33-113 and 114, record group 77, National Archives, Washington, D. C.; also Department of the Gulf, map no. 8, *Atchafalaya Basin*, record group 77, National Archives; some of these are also mentioned in the report by John G. Pratt, *Official Report Relative to the Conduct of Federal Troops in Western Louisiana during the Invasion of 1863 and 1864*, compiled from sworn testimony under direction of Governor Henry W. Allen (Shreveport, 1865), 15, 31-32, 36-37, 39, 46; *A History of the Trials and Hardships of the 24th Indiana Volunteer Infantry* (Indianapolis, 1913), 89; Thomas Brainard Marshall Papers, diary entry for October 5, 1863, Ohio Historical Society, Columbus; A. A. Rigby Diary, entries for October 2-4, 1863,Iowa State Department of History and Archives, Des Moines.
7. *Official Records*, vol. XXVI, pt. I, 698; *Chicago Tribune*, September 10, 1863.
8. For an excellent account of the Confederate participation in the Fordoche affair see George W. O'Brien's diary entries for September 28-29, 1863 at University of Texas Library Archives, Austin; also *Official Records* vol. XXVI, pt. I,, 320-32.
9. George Crooke, *The Twenty-First Regiment of Iowa Volunteers Infantry* (Milwaukee, 1891), 117; Beecher, *Record of the 114th Regiment*, 239.
10. "Diary of an Unidentified Assistant Surgeon of the 60th Indiana" (actually surgeon James B. Hunter), Manuscripts Department, Lilly Library, Indiana University, Bloomington, entry October 7, 1863; William Titus Rigby Papers, correspondence dated Franklin, October 4, 1863, University of Iowa Libraries, Iowa City.
11. *Official Records*, series 1, vol. XV, 234-35; John M. Stanyan, *A History of the Eighth Regiment of New Hampshire Volunteers* (Concord, 1892) 162-64, 335; James Hall, *Cayuga in the Field, A Record of the 75th NewYork Volunteers* (Auburn, N. Y., 1873), 147; Augustus George Sinks Collection, 52, Indiana State

Library, Indianapolis; Henry P. Whipple, *The Diary of a Private Soldier* (Waterloo, Wisconsin, 1906), 28.

12. Harry Watts Diary, 94-95, Indiana State Library, Indianapolis; *An Historical Sketch of the 162nd Regiment, N.Y. Vol. Infantry* (Albany, 1867) 21-22; Miss Mamie Yeary (compiler)' *Reminiscences of the Boys in Gray 1861-1865* (Dallas, 1912), 626.
13. Ellen Betts erroneously identified Palfrey as Parson in B. A. Botkin's (ed.), *Lay my Burden Down, A Folk History of Slavery* (Chicago, 1945), 125-30; Charles P. Roland, *Louisiana Sugar Plantations During the American Civil War (Leiden, 1957), 24-25;* Donald Hebert, *Southwestern Louisiana Records*, vol. 4 (Eunice, La. 1975), 384; 8th U. S. Census (1860) for St. Mary Parish; William Palfrey Papers, "Plantation Journal" entries for September-October 1863, and correspondence dated Bayou Cypremort, June 29, 1865, L.S.U. Library Archives, Baton Rouge; Surgeon A. C. Livingston Court-martial proceedings; conversations with Mrs. Paola Palfrey of Lafayette and David Stiel, Franklin, Louisiana.
14. For a Confederate account of the Battle of Bisland see "Reminiscences of C. C. Cox," *Southwestern Historical Quarterly*, vol. 6, no. 3, (January 1903), 224-25; an excellent Union source is George N. Carpenter, *History of the Eighth Regiment, Vermont Volunteers* (Boston, 1886), 82-105.
15. Harry Watts Diary, 96.
16. Pratt, *Official Report Relative to the Conduct of Federal Troops in Western Louisiana*, 14-15; 8th U. S. Census (1860) for St.Mary Parish, 73; Orton Clark, *The Military History of the One Hundred and Sixty-First New York Volunteers, Infantry* (Bath, N.Y., 1865), 130; French and American Claims Commission, "Ester Levy against the United States," No. 579 (deposition of William Nelson); William Perrin, *Southwest Louisiana, Biographical and Historical*, (Baton Rouge, 1971), 374 in pt. 2.
17. *Leslie's Illustrated Weekly*, vol. XVI, September 10, 1864, 385; Hall, *Cayuga in the Field*, 148; Pratt, *Official Report Relative to the Conduct of Federal Troops in Western Louisiana*, 14-15, 38; 8th U. S. Census (1860) for St. Mary Parish, 41; Godfrey Weitzel's deposition in French and American Claims Commission, "Aruns Sorrel against the United States," Case No. 594; National Archives, Washington, D. C.
18. Elfa Lavonia Fontenot, "Social and Economic Life in Louisiana 1860-1865 as Recorded by Contemporaries," 1933; unpublished Master's Thesis at Louisiana State University, Baton Rouge, 20-22; Roland, *Louisiana Sugar Plantations*, 4-5; Harry Watts Diary, 96-97; Richmond, Indiana *Palladium*, October 20, 1863; "Diary of an Unidentified Surgeon," entries October 7-8, 1863; Marshall Papers, diary entry October 7, 1863; Thomas B. Marshall, *History of the Eighty-Third Ohio Volunteer Infantry* (Cincinnati, 1912), 110; E. B. Blake, *A Succinct History of the 28th Iowa Volunteer Infantry* (Belle Plains, Iowa, 1896), 25; *Wisconsin State Journal*, November 25, 1863; Whipple, *Diary of a Private Soldier*, 28; Calvin P. Alling Reminiscences, 12, State Historical Society of Wisconsin, Madison; Lacon, *Illinois Gazette*, November 11, 1863; William Titus Rigby Papers, correspondence dated Franklin, La., October 4, 1863.
19. Crooke, *The Twenty-First Regiment of Iowa Volunteer Infantry*, 117; Henry Warren Howe, *Passages from the Life of Henry Warren Howe* (Lowell, Mass., 1899), 145; Homer Sprague, *History of the 13th Infantry Regiment of Connecticut Volunteers* (Hartford, 1867), 122; John William DeForest, *A Volunteer's Adventures, A Union Captain's Record of the Civil War* (New Haven,1946), 157; Richmond, Indiana *Palladium*, October 20, 1863.
20. Levi Hoag Diary in the Katherine Gue Leonard Collection, Iowa State Department of History and Archives, Des Moines, entry October 4, 1863; Harry Watts Diary, 96; "Diary of an Unidentified Surgeon," entry October 8, 1863; Howe, *Passages from the Life of Henry Warren Howe*, 54; *A History of the Trials and Hardships of the 24th Indiana*, 89.

21. Lawrence Van Alstyne, *Diary of an Enlisted Man* (New Haven, 1910), 205.
22. William Riggs' depositions in French and American Claims Commission, "Ester Levy against the United States," No. 579; "Joseph Decourt against the United States," No. 33; "Raymond Deffez against the United States," No. 113; and "Aruns Sorrel against the United States," No. 594; all of these are filed in the National Archives, Washington, D. C.
23. H. A. Fenney letter of November 12, 1863 in the *Wisconsin State Journal*, November 25, 1863; R. B. Scott, *The History of the 67th Regiment Indiana Infantry Volunteers* (Bedford, Indiana, 1892), 48.
24. Unsigned letters dated Scare Crow (actually Carencro) Bayou, October 17, 1863 in the Lacon, *Illinois Gazette* November 11, 1863; Ezra J. Warner, *Generals in Blue, Lives of the Union Commanders* (Baton Rouge, 1964), 54-55; Charles A. Dana, *Recollections of the Civil War* (New York, 1898), 65; and Mixed British and American Claims Commission, "Lucie Garrett and Charles Fleming vs. the United States," Claim No. 309, National Archives, Washington, D. C.
25. Florence Blackburn and Fay G. Brown, *Franklin Through the Years*, 1972; Clark, *The 116th Regiment of New York Volunteers*, 130; *The Military History of the One-Hundred and Sixty-First New York*, 20; Beecher, *Record of the 114th Regiment*, 151; Hall, *Cayuga in the Field*, 148; Harry Watts Diary, 96-97; Scott, *History of the 67th Regiment Indiana Infantry*, 48; Richmond, Indiana *Palladium*, October 22, 1863; "Diary of an Unidentified Surgeon," October 8, 1863 entry; John Bering and Thomas Montgomery, *History of the Forty-Eighth Ohio Veteran Volunteer Infantry* (Hillsboro, Ohio, 1880), 108; Thomas J. Williams, *An Historical Sketch of the 56th Ohio Volunteer Infantry*, 58; T. B. Marshall Diary, October 8, 1863 entry; William Titus Rigby Diary (October 4, 1863 entry) and correspondence (October 4, 1863); Levi Hoag Diary, October 4, 1863; A. A. Rigby Diary, October 4, 1863 entry; Jacob T. Foster Memoirs, The State Historical Society of Wisconsin, Madison.
26. "Aruns Sorrel against the United States," depositions of George O. Foote, Captain Allen Hayes, Sampson Pecantel, Joseph and Theogene Lognan, Francois L. Grappe, A. J. Simmons, Jules Pecot, Pierre Larrey, Phillip Jean, Telephorus Lockett, Alexis Louis, Nicolas Cerf, H. B. Carlin, Jesse Baldwin, Simon Jones, Edward Harrington and others; also U. S. Court of Claims (Southern Claims Commission), "Euphrasy Carlin vs the United States,"Case No. 18408, "Celestin Carlin vs the United States," No. 8875, and "Dr. John Rhodes vs. the United States," No. 12324, National Archives.
27. Howe, *Passages from the Life of Henry Warren Howe*, 54; Harry Watts Diary, entry October 5, 1863; Augustus George Sinks Collection, 52; A. A. Rigby Diary, entry October 4, 1863; Charles A. Lucas "A Soldier's Letters from the Field" *Iowa Historical Record* Vol. XVI (1900) 219-20; Whipple, *Diary of a Private Soldier*, 28; William Bentley, *History of the 77th Illinois Volunteer Infantry* (Peoria, 1883), 206-207.
28. B. F. Stevenson, *Letters from the Army* (Cincinnati, 1884), 261, 263; Lew Wallace, *An Autobiography* (New York, 1906), 340-50; Warner, *Generals in Blue*, 276-77; Dana, *Recollections of the Civil War*, 65; A. A. Rigby Diary, entry October 4, 1863.
29. *Official Records*, vol. XXVI, pt. II, 291; *The Era*, New Orleans, November 21, 1863; Caroline Whitcomb, *History of the Second Massachusetts Battery of Light Artillery* (Concord, N. H.), 55; Van Alystyne, *Diary of an Enlisted Man*, 202; *Trials and Hardships of the 24th Indiana*, 89; Clement Evans (ed.), *Confederate Military History*, (Atlanta, 1899), vol. X (Louisiana) 606-09; Gustave A. Breaux Diaries, Tulane University Archives, New Orleans, entry March 9, 1864; W. R. Howell Papers, University of Texas Archives, Austin, entries August 9-14, 1863; Miss Mamie Yeary (compiler), *Reminiscences of the Boys in Gray 1861-1865* (Dallas, 1912), 576.

CHAPTER THREE

FROM FRANKLIN TO NEW IBERIA

1. *Official Records*, vol. XXVI, pt. I, 738; Harris H. Beecher, *Record of the 114th Regiment N.Y.S.V.* (Norwich, N.Y., 1866), 258; Charles Andrew Emerson Diary, entries for October 4-5, 1863, New Hampshire Historical Society, Concord; J. W. DeForest, "Forced Marches," *Galaxy*, vol. 5 (1868), 708-18; Harry Watts Diary, 97, Indiana State Library Archives, Indianapolis; Augustus George Sinks Collection, 52, Indiana State Library Archives, Indianapolis; Madison, *Wisconsin State Journal*, November 2, 1863; Daniel Webster and Don Cameron, *History of the First Wisconsin Battery Light Artillery* (Washington, D. C., 1907).
2. R. B. Scott, *The History of the 67th Regiment Indiana Infantry Volunteers* (Bedford, Indiana, 1892), 49.
3. Homer B. Sprague, *History of the 13th Infantry Regiment of Connecticut Volunteers* (Hartford, 1867), 122; A similar incident is recorded by Elden B. Maddocks, *History of the Twenty-Sixth Maine Regiment* (Bangor, 1899), 35.
4. John G. Pratt (Commissioner) *Official Report Relative to the Conduct of Federal Troops in Western Louisiana* (Shreveport, 1865), 18; A. L. Fusilier deposition in French and American Claims Commission, "Aruns Sorrel against the United States," No. 594, National Archives, Washington, D. C.
5. Cecil D. Eby, Jr. (ed.), *A Virginia Yankee in the Civil War: The Diaries of David Hunter Strother* (Chapel Hill, N. C.), 169; A. L. Fusilier's depositions in "Aruns Sorrel against the United States." Fusilier's wife, Louise Marie Corine Perret, also filed a claim against the United States in the U. S. Court of Claims (Southern Claims Commission), "Corinne Perret against the United States," claim no. 6321. National Archives, Washington, D. C.; Edwin Bearss (ed.) *A Louisiana Confederate; Diary of Felix Pierre Poche* Nachitoches, La., 1972), 7, 39, 43, 61.
6. James R.Slack Correspondence, letter dated Franklin, October 5, 1863 in Indiana State Library Archives, Indianapolis; Harry Watts Diary, 97; Charles A. Dana, *Recollections of the Civil War* (New York, 1898), 64; Ezra J. Warner, *Generals in Blue* (Baton Rouge, 1964), 449-50; John R. Slack service record, National Archives, Washington, D. C.
7. Pratt, *Federal Troops in Western Louisiana*, 22.
8. French and American Claims Commission "Widow Pierre Stouff against the United States," No. 397, National Archives; also deposition of Widow Stouff in "Sorrel against the United States," 85.
9. "Sorrel against the United States," depositions of Paul Corner, Horatio Guenard, Dr. Anibal Maguire, Jean Deyris, Louis Pimorin and Edouard Sillan.
10. *Ibid.* Depositions of General Cuvier Grover, Alexander Mason, William Riggs, Simeon Belden, Louis Ranson, D. C. Paul, James C. Murphy and Augustus Bergerie.
11. French and American Claims Commission, "Estate of Theodore Fay against the United States," No. 525, pp. 1-31, National Archives, Washington, D. C.: Eby, *A Virginia Yankee in the Civil War*, 169.
12. Lew Wallace, *An Autobiography* (New York, 1906), 324-25; Dana, *Recollections of the Civil War*, 64; Warner, *Generals in Blue*, 299-300.
13. Thomas H. Bringhurst and Frank Swigart, *History of the Forty-Sixth Regiment Indiana Volunteer Infantry* (Regimental Association, 1888), 74-75; Henry P. Whipple, *The Diary of a Private Soldier* (Waterloo, Wisconsin, 1906), 28; William Titus Rigby Diary, entry October 5-6, 1863, University of Iowa Libraries, Iowa City.
14. "Sorrel against the United States," depositions of Hyacinthe Balthazar, Julien Etienne and Dorlice Garrett, 793-98; "Widow Stouff against the United States," Memorial.

15. French and American Claims Commission. "Desire and Coralie Guiberteau against the United States," No. 441, deposition of Adam Nathan, National Archives, Washington, D. C., and Mixed British and American Claims Commission, "Annibal Maguire vs. the United States," No. 33, National Archives, Washington, D. C.
16. Harry Watts Diary, 98-99; Hovey Manuscript, 71-72, Lilly Library, Indiana University, Bloomington.
17. "Sorrel against the United States," depositions of Cuvier Grover, Nathaniel P. Banks, Aristide Legnon, John Trimble, Marius Sennett, Watt Lockett, Thomas Jordan, Henry Johnson, Terrence Pellerin, Alphonse Beaudeaux and Toussaint Richards.
18. R. B. Scott, *The History of the 67th Regiment*, 49.
19. Beecher, *Record of the 114th Regiment*, 155-56; Weeks Papers, letters of John Leigh to Judge Moore dated Houston, October 12, 1863 and John Moore to W. F. Weeks dated Mansfield, La. October 2, 1863. L.S.U. Library Archives, Baton Rouge.
20. C. Peter Ripley, *Slaves and Freedmen in Civil War Louisiana* (Baton Rouge, 1976), 25-68; Albert Stearns, *Reminiscences of the Late War* (Brooklyn, 1881), 16, 22-28; Henry Murray Calvert, *Reminiscences of a Boy in Blue* (New York, 1920; Lawrence Van Alstyne, *Diary of an Enlisted Man* (New Haven, 1910), 223; Edgar Richmond, Civil War Letters, and James E. Karn Papers and Correspondence at the State Historical Society of Wisconsin; Weeks Papers, letter to Judge Moore from daughter Lilly dated New Iberia, September 10, 1863, and John Ransdell to Thomas Moore dated Elmwood, May 24, 1863 and Emfield, May 31, 1863; Pratt, *Federal Troops in Western Louisiana*, 52-53; Weitzel deposition in "Sorrel against the United States," 377-85.
21. Napier Bartlett, *Military Record of Louisiana* (Baton Rouge, 1964), 57-58; and Eby, *A Virginia Yankee in the Civil War*, 170-71.
22. U.S. Court of Claims (Southern Claims Commission), "Dubriel Olivier against the United States," No. 19763. National Archives, Washington, D.C.; also Sprague, *History of the 13th Infantry Regiment*, 122.
23. John William DeForest, *A Volunteer's Adventures; A Union Captains' Record of the Civil War* (New Haven, 1946), 579.
24. R. B. Scott, *History of the Forty-Sixth Regiment*, 76; Harry Watts Diary, 99-101, Hovey Manuscript, 73-74.
25. French and American Claims Commission, "Jules Poirson against the United States," No. 476; Van Alstyne, *Diary of an Enlisted Man*, 201-02; Augustus George Sinks Collection, 52; and Mixed British and American Claims Commission, "Ellen Burke vs. the United States," No. 130, National Archives, Washington, D. C.

CHAPTER FOUR

AND OVER THE PRAIRIES

1. Lew Wallace, *The Prince of India* (New York, 1893), 78; Orton Clark, *The 116th Regiment of New York Volunteers* (Buffalo, 1868), 130; Harris Beecher, *Record of the 114th Regiment N.Y.S.V.* (Norwich, 1866), 156; Thomas B. Marshall Papers, diary entry for October 10, 1863. Ohio Historical Society, Columbus; Arthur W. Bergeron, Jr. (ed.), "Prison Life at Camp Pratt," *Louisiana History*, vol. 14 (Fall, 1973), 387; Hartford, Wisconsin *Home League*, November 7, and December 19

and December 26, 1863; James Hall, *Cayuga in the Field, A Record of the 75th N.Y. Volunteers* (Auburn, 1873), 148; "A Soldier's Letters from the Field," *Iowa Historical Record*, vol. XVIII (1902), 220, 226.

2. Duperier had been very active in St. Martin Parish politics. In 1855, for example, he was elected to the state legislature on the Know Nothing Ticket. *Opelousas Courier*, November 16, 1855; following the war both he and Fontelieu became powerful Republicans. Miscellaneous issues of *Louisiana Sugar Bowl*, and Alfred Duperier "A Narrative of Events connected with the Early Settlement of New Iberia" (edited by Glenn R. Conrad), *Attakapas Gazette*, vol. VII (September, 1972), 111-23; see also U. S. Court of Claims (Southern Claims Commission) "Alfred Duperier vs. the United States," claim no. 9436; and "Faustin Dupuy vs. the United States", claim no. 13723, National Archives, Washington, D. C.; also depositions of Duperier in French and American Claims Commission, "Raymond Deffez against the United States," no. 113, "Aime Hervien against the United States," no. 237, and "Bernard Suberbielle against the United States," no. 234.
3. French and American Claims Commission, "Joseph Decourt against the United States," no. 33 (depositions of Judge Soloman, Henry Taylor, Jean Saintes, Joseph Bertrand, Dr. Mestayer, Homer Etienne, Victor Codden, J. D. Swayne, Alfred Duperier, Philip Rozier) and "Bernard LaPlane against the United States, no. 245, National Archives, Washington, D. C.; John G. Mudge, "A Night on Picket," *The Boston Journal*, November 19, 1892; Mixed Commission on American and British Claims, "David Robert vs. the United States," no. 47 (depositions of Dr. Henry Stubenger, Louis C. Champeau, Joseph D. Boutte, Patrick Burke and Martin Bryant), National Archives; George Crooke, *The Twenty-First Regiment of Iowa* (Milwaukee, 1891), 117; Hall, *Cayuga in the Field*, 148.
4. *Official Records*, XXVI, pt. I, 380, 755, 759, 767-68; Beecher, *Record of the 114th Regiment*, 259; Hall, *Cayuga in the Field*, 148-49.
5. Camp Pratt was also a subject of derision for many Louisiana families who, when confronted by some Confederate veteran boasting of "dubious claims to brilliant military service, would express a belief that the braggart never went farther than Camp Pratt." See "Glimpses of Iberia in the Civil War" (probably written by Mrs. Edward Weeks), 9-10, in Weeks Family Papers, U.S.L. Library Archives, Lafayette; and "Prison Life at Camp Pratt," *Louisiana History* (Fall 1973), 387; An excellent description of camp life, commanders and recruits is to be found in Mixed Commission on British and American Claims, "Martha A. Rayne vs. the United States," no. 74. Portions of this claim were adjudicated before the U. S. Court of Claims, "Robert Parker Rayne vs. the United States." Both are filed in the National Archives.
6. Contrary to prevailing opinions the Acadians were not entirely without slaves. See the U. S. Bureau of the Census, "Slaves Schedules of the Seventh Census of the United States" (1850) especially for the Parishes of St. Martin, Lafayette, Vermilion and St. Landry; also Vaughan Baker, "Patterns of Acadian Slave Ownership in Lafayette Parish, 1860," *Attakapas Gazette*, IX (September 1974), 144-48.
7. Richard Taylor, *Destruction and Reconstruction* (New York 1879), 105-109.
8. See, for example, U. S. Court of Claims, "Jules Perrodin vs. the United States," no. 3546, National Archives, Washington, D. C. Perrodin and other French citizens were conscripted into a Louisiana Confederate regiment but were discharged by virtue of their alienage status.
9. Some of the information concerning the behavior and sentiments of Acadians during the Civil War survives only as oral tradition and was derived from personal interviews with elderly citizens, especially Raoul Sibille of Bristol, Mrs. Willis Courville, Will Richard and Hypolite Miller of Sunset, Oge Guilbeau of Carencro and others who requested anonymity; other sources include The Weeks Family Papers in L.S.U. Library Archives, correspondence from Judge Moore to W. F.

Weeks dated New Iberia, May 20, 1863, and letter from Lilly to Father, New Iberia, September 10, 1863; "The Terror at the South," *Harper's Weekly*, VII (December 19, 1863), 802; The New Orleans *Era*, November 21, 1863; "Faustin Dupuy vs. the United States," deposition of Faustin Dupuy, Alfred Duperier and Louis Delcambre; "Martha Rayne against the United States," French and American Claims Commission, "Jules Oger against the United States," National Archives, Washington, D. C.; Gustave A. Breaux Diaries, Tulane University Archives, New Orleans. Entries for November-December 1863 and January-March 1864; Richard Taylor, *Destruction and Reconstruction* (New York, 1879), 105-07, 162; Arthur W. Hyatt Collection, Diary vol. V, L.S.U. Library Archives, Baton Rouge. Entries for September-December 1863; W. Randolph Howell Papers, University of Texas Library Archives, Austin. Diaries entries for August-September 1863; John C. Brightman Letters, University of Texas Archives, Austin, Letters dated Washington, La. June 1, 1863; F. L. Olmsted, *A Journey Through Texas, or a Saddle-trip on the Southwestern Frontier* (New York, 1857), 402-05; A. Rhodes "The Louisiana Creoles" *The Galaxy* XVI, 252-59; *Opelousas Patriot* October 5, 1861; Roger W. Shugg, *Origins of Class Struggle in Louisiana* (Baton Rouge, 1939), 45-50, 177-81; Timothy F. Reilly, "Early Acadiana Through Anglo-American Eyes," *Attakapas Gazette*, XII (Spring 1977), 3-20; "Prison Life at Camp Pratt, *Louisiana History* (Fall 1973), 388-89; *Official Records* XXXIV, p. II, (962-67, 977) XXVI, Pt. I, 778; Richmond, *Indiana Paladium*, letter dated Vermilion River, La. October 22, 1863 in the Walter Burke Papers at USL Library Archives, Lafayette; John William DeForest "Forced Marches," *Galaxy*, vol. V, 712.

10. Beecher, *Record of the 114th Regiment*, 171; H. A. Fenney in letter to the *Wisconsin State Journal*, November 25, 1863; A. R. Waud, "Acadians of Louisiana," *Harper's Weekly*, X (October 20, 1866), 670; and B. F. Stevenson, *Letters from the Army* (Cincinnati, 1884), 265-66; See also E. E. Blake, *A Succinct History of the 28th Iowa Volunteer Infantry* (Belle Plains, Iowa, 1896), 24-25; and John T. Simmons, *History of the 28th Iowa Volunteer Infantry* (Washington, 1865).
11. According to local tradition, the earliest settlers were troubled by the lack of timber on the hills. Thus when the cold "northers" came through they suffered a great deal. For this reason it was called "Cote Gelee," or frozen hills. William H. Perrin, *Southwest Louisiana, Biographical and Historical* (Baton Rouge, 1971 reprint), 184.
12. John G. Pratt, *Official Report Relative to the Conduct of Federal Troops in Western Louisiana* (Shreveport, 1865), 29; see also Beecher, *Record of the 114th Regiment*, 159-60.
13. Beecher, *Record of the 114th Regiment*, 259; Clark, *The 116th Regiment of New York Volunteers*, 130.
14. Henry Thompson's dispatch dated Vermilion Bayou October 13, 1863 in *New York Herald*, October 31, 1863, p. 3; H. A. Fenney dispatch dated New Orleans, November 22, 1863 in *Wisconsin State Journal*, November 25,1863, p. 2; *Official Records*, XXVI, pt. I, 755.
15. *Ibid;* also Perrin, *Southwest Louisiana*, 13; B. F. Stevenson, *Letters From the Army* 266; *Wisconsin State Journal*, November 7, 1863; Beecher, *Record of the 114th Regiment*, 257; Clark, *A History of the Eighth Regiment of New Hampshire Volunteers* (Concord, 1892), 210-11.
16. William Blake Eager Papers, L.S.U. Library Archives, Baton Rouge, especially letter dated Franklin, January 3, 1864; *New York Herald*, October 31, 1863; French and American Claims Commission, "Aruns Sorrel against the United States," no. 594 (depositions of Cuvier Grover, Godfrey Weitzel and Charles F. Benjamin), National Archives; U. S. Court of Claims (Southern Claims Commission), "Anna and Mary Porter vs. the United States," no. 11731, National Arc-

hives, Washington, D. C.; Homer Sprague, *History of the 13th Infantry Regiment of Connecticut Volunteers* (Hartford, 1867), 109-10; James K. Hosmer, *The Color Guard* (Boston, 186), 130-31.

17. *Official Records*, XXVI, pt. 1, 380, 734, 756; *Leslie's Illustrated Weekly*, XVII (November 21, 1863), 132; "Decourt against the United States," consul's brief, p. 7.
18. Pratt, *Federal Troops in Western Louisiana*, 17-19, 35.
19. Alexandre Mouton Memoirs in the U.S.L. Library Archives, Lafayette, p. 4; some alternative explanations for the name "Pinhook" are given in Harry Griffin, *The Attakapas Country* (Gretna, La., 1974); Pratt, *Federal Troops in Western Louisiana*, 28-29, 39; Gouverneur Morris, *The History of a Volunteer Regiment, Sixth Regiment New York Volunteers* (New York, 1891), 103-07.
20. *Official Records*, XXVI, pt. 1, 381, 386; Howell Papers, diary entry October 9, 1863; James A. Hamilton Diary, University of Texas Archives, Austin, entry October 9, 1863; Julius Giesecke Papers, University of Texas Archives, Austin, diary entry October 9, 1863.
21. Walter Lord (ed.) *The Fremantle Diary* (Boston, n.d.), 18; Ezra Warner, *Generals in Blue* (Baton Rouge, 1964), 114-115.
22. *Boston Journal* August 8, 1861 and February 22, 1903; Caroline Whitcomb, *History of the Second Massachusetts Battery of Light Artillery* (Concord, N.H.), 16-17, 55; J. F. Moors, *History of the Fifty-Second Regiment Massachusetts Volunteers* (Boston, 1893), 59; Service record and court-martial proceedings of Ormand Nims, National Archives, Washington, D. C.
23. Frank Moore (ed.), *The Rebellion Record: A Diary of American Events*, vol. 7 (New York, 1869), 539-40.
24. J. W. Merwin, *Roster and Monograph 161st Reg't. N.Y.S. Volunteer Infantry*, 119; William E. Jones, *The Military History of the One Hundred and Sixty-First New York Volunteers, Infantry* (Bath, N.Y., 1865), 16; Clark, *The 116th Regiment of New York Volunteers*, 130-31.
25. *History of the Second Battalion Duryee Zouaves* (1905), 22; Hall, *Cayuga in the Field*, 149; Beecher, *Record of the 114th Regiment*, 259-60; Charles Andrews Emerson Diary, New Hampshire Historical Society, Concord, entry for October 9, 1863; Stanyon, *A History of the Eighth Regiment of New Hampshire Volunteers*, 268.
26. Depositions of Jefferson Caffery and Euphemie Chreighton in French and American Claims Commission, "Jean Pierre Gueydan against the United States," no. 226, National Archives; also Alexandre Mouton Memoirs; Howell Diary; Giesecke Papers; Hamilton Diary.
27. Among the sources consulted on ammunition, weapons and tactics were Francis T. Miller (ed.), *The Photographic History of the Civil War* (New York, 1911), vol. 5; William J. Hardee, *Rifle and Light Infantry Tactics* (Philadelphia, 1855); William Gilham, *Manual of Instruction for the Volunteer and Militia of the United States* (Philadelphia, 1861); Daniel Butterfield, *Camp and Outpost Duty for Infantry* (New York, 1862); Bell I. Wiley, *The Life of Billy Yank* (Indianapolis, 1952).
28. Confederate losses, if there were any, were so negligible as to not merit mention in General Taylor's report of the affair. *Official Records* XXVI, pt. I, 386-88; on the other hand the correspondents for the *Richmond Palladium* (October 30, 1863) and the *New York Herald* reported finding a number of freshly dug Confederate graves; see also Frank Moore, *The Rebellion Record*, 539-40; and Emerson Diary, entry for October 9, 1863.
29. *Official Records*, XXVI, pt. I, 16, 78, 83, 380, 721, 734, 756-57; Moore, *Rebellion Record*, 539-40; Stevenson, *Letters from the Army*, 262; Beecher, *Record of the 114th Regiment*, 260; Henry Thompson's dispatch, *New York Herald*, October 31, 1863; Alexandre Mouton Memoirs.

CHAPTER FIVE

PAUSE ON THE VERMILION

1. Henriette Odeide Mouton was married to her cousin Joseph Sosthene Mouton, a major in a Louisiana Confederate regiment. Their six children were Alexandre, Bordat, Olivier, Fred, Frank and Alida. They subsequently raised six more children: Alice, Alfred, Disney, Coralie, Aimee and Rousseau. Harry Lewis Griffin, *The Attakapas Country, A History of Lafayette Parish, Louisiana* (Gretna, La., 1974), 191-92.
2. Alexandre Mouton's extensive, though sometimes rambling, memoirs are stored with the Lucille Meredith Mouton Griffin Papers at the University of Southwestern Louisiana's Dupre Library Archives in Lafayette. Portions are cited in Griffin's book, *The Attakapas Country*, 142-46; See also William E. Jones, *The Military History of the One-Hundred and Sixty-First New York Volunteer Infantry* (Bath, N.Y., 1865), 16; *The Palladium*, Richmond, Indiana, October 30, 1863; and, *The New York Herald*, October 1863.
3. According to oral tradition, Sosthene Dugas, the grandfather of Leon Dugas, was so fascinated by the illumination that he climbed a nearby tree and witnessed the entire bridge-building operation; O. E. Hunt, "Engineer Corps of the Federal Army" in *The Photographic History of the Civil War*, edited by Francis T. Miller, vol. 5 (New York, 1911), 222-26; "Diary of an Unidentified Assistant Surgeon of the 60th Indiana," entry October 13, 1863. Manuscripts Department, Indiana University's Lilly Library, Bloomington; *Official Records*, XXVI, pt. I, 381, 758; Jones, *The Military History of the One Hundred and Sixty-First New York*, 16.
4. Beecher, *Record of the 114th Regiment*, 260; Depositions of Chreighton family members in French and American Claims Commission, "Jean Pierre Gueydan against the United States," no. 226, National Archives; and James Hall, *Cayuga in the Field* (Auburn, 1873), 149.
5. *Official Records*, XXVI, pt. I, 381.
6. Perhaps the best war-time description of Ile Copal is in Harris Beecher, *Record of the 114th Regiment, N.Y.S.V.* (Norwich, N.Y., 1866), 170-71; Also Leslie's Illustrated Weekly, vol. XVII (May 14, 1864), 113, 116; B. F. Stevenson, *Letters from the Army* (Cincinnati, 1884), 268-69; *The Vermilion*, U.S.L. student newspaper, November 20, 1920 (also cited in Griffin's *The Attakapas Country*, 53-54); Elizabeth M. Schumacher, "The Political Career of Alexandre Mouton," unpublished master's thesis, Louisiana State University, Baton Rouge, 1935, p. 17.
7. Banks considered Mouton "a man of large influence and intelligence, and has wielded with an iron hand his power over the masses of the people in this part of the country..." *Official Records*, Series I, vol. XV, 311; A slave on the Mouton plantation, Benjamin Stewart, explained what happened during the first invasion of Ile Copal in "Gueydan against the United States;" See also Elias P. Pellet, *History of the 114th Regiment, New York State Volunteers* (Norwich, NY., 1866), 155-56; Alexandre Mouton Memoirs; Beecher, *Record of the 114th Regiment*, 271-72; William Gatchell's dispatch in the *New York Herald* October 31, 1863, p. 3; Alexandre Barde, *Histoire des Comites de Vigilance aux Attakapas* (St. Jean Baptiste, 1861), 320-23; Conversations with Miss Alida Martin and Miss Eva Mouton, descendants of Governor Mouton.
8. *Official Records*, XXVI, pt. I, 381; Caroline Whitcomb, *History of the Second Massachusetts Battery of Light Artillery* (Concord, N.H.), 55; *Boston Journal*, February 22, 1903.
9. Alexandre Mouton Memoirs.
10. *Ibid.* The background information on General Grover was derived from *Leslie's Illustrated Weekly*, XV (January 17, 1863), 263; Ezra Warner, *Generals in Blue*,

Lives of the Union Commanders (Baton Rouge, 1964), 193-94; *Harper's Weekly*, VIII (November 12, 1864), 733-34; and Cuvier Grover's service record in the National Archives, Washington, D. C.

11. Stevenson, *Letters from the Army*, 262.
12. U. S. Congress, "Red River Expedition" in *Report of the Joint Committee on the Conduct of the War*, 2nd Session, 38th Congress, vol. 2, (Washington, 1865), 117-20; These letters are also published in *Official Records*, vol. XXVI, pt. I, 767-68, 889.
13. This fact is readily evident in the October-December, 1863 correspondence of his brigade commanders, Colonels James R. Slack (2nd Brigade, 3rd Division, XIII Corps) and Richard Owen (1st Brigade, 4th Division, XIII Corps), Indiana State Library Archives, Indianapolis, and Slack and Owen service records, National Archives, Washington, D. C.
14. *Official Records*, XXVI, pt. 1, 381-82, 759, 761-62.
15. *Ibid.* 381; Court-martial transcript of Surgeon A. C. Livingston, National Archives, Washington, D. C., John Deforest, *A Volunteer's Adventures: A Union Captain's Record of the Civil War* (New Haven, 1946), 156; Beecher, *Record of the 114th Regiment*, 260-61; "Gueydan against the United States."
16. Emma K. Lane, currently Jefferson Street, was named for Governor Mouton's second wife, Emma Kitchell Gardner (the sister of Confederate General Frank Gardner) whom he met in Washington while a senator. Griffin, *The Attakapas Country*, 42-43; William Titus Rigby Papers, correspondence dated October 17, 1863, University of Iowa Libraries, Iowa City.
17. Hall, *Cayuga in the Field* 99; Beecher, *Record of the 114th Regiment*, 117; William Titus Rigby Papers, correspondence dated October 22, 1863; Harry Watts Papers, 113; Indiana State Library, Indianapolis; Griffin, *The Attakapas Country*, 52-53.
18. Regimental newspaper of the 16th Indiana, dated Vermilionville, La. November 7, 1863.
19. A Louisiana Confederate officer, Felix Pierre Poche, also made some negative comments about the females of Vermilionville. Edwin Bearrs (ed.) *A Louisiana Confederate, Diary of Felix Pierre Poche* (Natchitoches, La., 1972), 13.
20. Thomas Brainard Marshall Papers, diary entry October 10, 1863, Ohio Historical Society, Columbus; C. W. Gerard, *A Diary of the Eighty-Third Ohio Vol. Inf.* (n.p., n.d.), 55-56; Alonzo Gilbert Jack Correspondence, letter dated Vermilion, La., October 13, 1863, State Historical Society of Wisconsin, Madison; Letter from soldier dated Vermilionville, October 17, 1863 in Madison, *Wisconsin State Journal*, November 7, 1863.
21. *Official Records*, XXVI, pt. II, 233, 235, 243, 260-63, 282-83; 291 and 335; Robert L. Kerby, *Kirby Smith's Confederacy, The Trans-Mississippi South* (New York, 1972), 243-46; Richard Taylor, *Destruction and Reconstruction* (New York, 1879), 108-09; Clement Evans (ed.), *Confederate Military History* vol. X (Louisiana) by John Dimitry (Atlanta, 1899), 105-06; W. Randolph Howell Papers, diary entry October 9-11, 1863, University of Texas Archives, Austin; Julius Giesecke Papers, diary entry for October 9-11, 1863, University of Texas Archives, Austin.
22. John G. Pratt's report in *Official Report Relative to the Conduct of Federal Troops in Western Louisiana* (Shreveport, 1865), 28-29, 39.
23. H. A. Fenney's report in the *Wisconsin State Journal*, November 25, 1863, p.2; Beecher, *Record of the 114th Regiment*, 171; Louisiana Acadian houses are described in Lauren C. Post's *Cajun Sketches From the Prairies of Southwest Louisiana* (Baton Rouge, 1962) 83-91; and Jay Ditchy (ed.) *Early Louisiana French Life and Folklore* (New Orleans, 1966, 24-26.
24. Dr. Thomas Arceneaux, former U.S.L. Dean of the College of Agriculture, authority on Acadian history and folklore, and owner of the old Arceneaux homestead, assures me that the correct spelling is Beaubassin (of Nova Scotia origin) not Beau Bassin as written by most people.

25. H. A. Fenny's letter to the *Wisconsin State Journal*, November 25, 1863.
26. The quote is from J. W. Merwin, *Roster and Monograph, 161st Reg't, N.Y.S. Volunteer Infantry* (n.p., n.d.), 109, 119; Jones, *The Military History of the One-Hundred and Sixty First New York Volunteers* (Buffalo, 1808), 131-32; *Official Records*, XXVI, pt. I, 337, 367, 369; *New York Herald*, October 31, 1863.
27. James Earl Bradley Collection, diary entry for October 10, 1863, L. S. U. Library Archives, Baton Rouge; Opelousas *Courier*, miscellaneous issues for early October 1863; J. F. Moors, *History of the Fifty-Second Regiment Massachusetts Volunteers* (Boston, 1893), 127-41; James K. Ewer, *The Third Massachusetts Cavalry in the War for the Union* (Boston, 1903), 77-86; Thomas E. Chickering, *Diary of the Forty-First Regiment Infantry, Massachusetts Volunteers* (Boston, 1863), 9-11; French and American Claims Commission, "Jules Perrodin against the United States," no. 90, National Archives, Washington, D. C.
28. David M. Ray Papers, correspondence dated St. Landry Parish, October 11, 1863 and Mary J. Minor Letters, correspondence dated October 11, 1863 from W. B. Hunter in the University of Texas Library Archives, Austin; Arthur W. Hyatt Collection, vol. V, 45-46, L.S.U. Library Archives, Baton Rouge.

CHAPTER SIX

YANKEES ON THE CARRION CROW

1. The most popular and widely accepted version for the name Carencro is from an Indian legend mentioned in the Duralde letters in the Bureau of American Ethnology. Duralde's letter states only that "a beast of enormous size had perished" somewhere along the banks of the "bayou called Carencro." This has been distorted by more recent writers into the unlikely story that it took the Carrion Crow vultures so long to devour the beast that the Indians—who could not possibly have known the English name for these vultures—commenced calling the surrounding country Carencro. Duralde's letter is also printed in John R. Swanton, *Indian Tribes of the Lower Mississipi Valley and the Adjacent Coast of the Gulf of Mexico* (Washington, 1911), 366; quotations in the narrative are from James Hall, *Cayuga in the Field* (Auburn, 1873), 149; Harris H. Beecher, *Record of the 114th Regiment N.Y.S.V.* (Norwich, N.Y., 1866), 261; Orton S. Clark, *The 116th Regiment of New York Volunteers* (Buffalo, 1868), 131; John M. Stanyon, *A History of the Eighth Regiment of New Hampshire Volunteers* (Concord, N.H., 1892), 336; Wickham Hoffman, *Camp Court and Siege* (New York, 1877), 81; and George N. Carpenter, *History of the Eighth Regiment Vermont Volunteers* (Boston, 1886), 141.
2. Succession Records of David Guidry (No. 257), Modeste Borda (No. 2001), Onezime Guidry (No. 1501) and Julie Pothier (No. 2148) and marriage license Thelismar and Constance Guidry (No. 816), in St. Landry Parish Courthouse, Opelousas.
3. *Official Records*, Series 1, vol. XV, 325, 345, 373-74, 379 and 383; The New Orleans *Era*, April 1863.
4. Constance Guidry was born September 5, 1833 to Onesime and Julie (nee Potier) Guidry. She entered the Academy of Sacred Heart in 1845 and was characterized by one of her exasperated teachers as "*insignificante.*" She married Thelismar in October 1850. The Academy of Sacred Heart, *School Register of Sacred Heart Academy*, Grand Coteau, 1827-1887; Donald J. Hebert, *Southwest Louisiana Records*, vol. 3 (Eunice, Louisiana); depositions of Constance and Thelismar Guidry in French and American Claims Commission "Jules Perrodin against the United States," no. 90, National Archives; and conversations with descendants of Constance Guidry.

5. Thelismar Guidry was born May 22, 1830 to Joseph D. Guidry and Celeste Mouton (sister of Governor Mouton). He entered St. Charles College along with Alfred Mouton in 1840. Guidry entered the 18th Louisiana Infantry, in Captain H. L. Garland's Company, October 5, 1861. According to the *8th United States Census* (1860) for St. Landry Parish Guidry's holdings were valued at about $27,800 (or about $195,700 in terms of 1978 currency). His father, Joseph D. Guidry, owned holdings valued at $143,000 (or about $1 million in 1978 currency) p. 165. St. Charles College, *Liber Continens Onania quae in Collegio Publice Exhibentur, A.M.D.G.* St. Charles College School Register 1838-1919, Grand Coteau; Service record Thelismar Guidry in National Archives; *Official Records*, series 1, vol. X, pt. 521; Depositions of Thelismar Guidry and Jean Pierre Rubin in "Perrodin against the United States."
6. John and William Campbell were the sons of William Campbell (then a Confederate soldier) and Alida Guidry, a sister of Constance, who died of yellow fever in 1857. Hebert, *Southwest Louisiana Records* vol. 6, 260.
7. Deposition of Constance Guidry, Victoria Green and Augustin Domingue in "Jules Perrodin against the United States," Conversations with descendants of Constance Guidry.
8. *Official Records*, XXVI, pt. I, 337.
9. *Ibid.*, 761.
10. St. Charles College *School Register* in College Archives, Grand Coteau, p. 41; Conversations with Raoul Sibille, a son of Louis Sibille, Sunset, Louisiana; *8th United States Census* (1860) for St. Landry Parish.
11. According to oral tradition, McBride, a heavy-drinking trouble-making, French-speaking Irishman, had ambushed and killed several Yankees in one of Colonel Chickering's foraging parties during the spring campaign. In order to avoid detection he and a brother interred the corpses under the front gallery of Walter McBride's house.
12. Conversations with Mrs. Willis Courville, Sunset, Louisiana; Arthur W. Hyatt Collection, company records of October, 1863, in L.S.U. Library Archives, Baton Rouge; and Records of District and Parish Provost Marshalls, Army of the Gulf, "Oath of Allegiance," old Book 1255-1257. Record Group 393. National Archives.
13. *New York Herald*, November 8, 1863; Clement Evans (ed.), *Confederate Military History*, vol. XI, on Texas by O.M. Roberts (Atlanta, 1899), 138-39.
14. Letters from John R. Cox to wife and parents, especially correspondence dated Sheco, La. October 29, 1863 in William M. Oden Papers; letters from W. B. Hunter to Sister Mary, October 11, 1863 in Mary J. Minor Letters; Edwin Pinckney Becton Collection, correspondence October 3, 1863; and William P. Head Papers, correspondence of October 12, 1863. All the foregoing are located in the University of Texas Library Archives, Austin.
15. Samuel H. Fletcher, *The History of Company A, Second Illinois Cavalry* (n.p., 1912), 122; Hall, *Cayuga in the Field*, 151-55.
16. *Official Records*, XXVI, pt. I, 762.
17. Hall, *Cayuga in the Field*, 151-52.
18. French and American Claims Commission, "Romain Joseph Francez against the United States," no. 164, National Archives; Harry L. Griffin, *The Attakapas Country* (Gretna, La., 1974), 125; Jay K. Ditchy (ed.), *Early Louisiana French Life and Folklore from the Anonymous Breaux Manuscript*, vol. II, no. 3 (New Orleans, 1966), 56-58.
19. French and American Claims Commission, "Simon Mathieu against the United States, no. 159 (depositions of Hypolite Francis, Joseph Dupre, P. L. Rice, Laurent Arceneaux, Jean Broussard, Louis Girod and Alcee Broussard), National Archives.

20. Several weeks later Etiene Mouton had occasion to see one of these stallions in the possession of Colonel John B. Van Petten of the 160th New York. French and American Claims Commission, "Joseph Baque against the United States," no. 135 (also depositions of A. C. Melchoir and Noel Guidry), National Archives.
21. French and American Claims Commission, "Jacques Crouchet against the United States," no.165 (depositions of Henri Crouchet, John Carmouche, Jean Breaux, Felicien Domingue, R. L. McBride, F. Martin and W. N. Rogers), National Archives.
22. Thomas B. Marshall Papers, diary entries for October 1863, Ohio Historical Society, Columbus; Madison, *Wisconsin State Journal,* November 25, 1863; Richard Taylor, *Destruction and Reconstruction* (New York, 1879), 105-07; French and American Claims Commission, "J. H. Wilberding against the United States," no. 588; "Catherine Grimmer against the United States," no. 88; "Caroline Follain against the United States," no. 252, (depositions of Joseph Boudreaux, Charles Eaglin and Thomas Linton); "Theophile Sanvald against the United States," no. 892, (depositions of Oscar Dardean, Mozart Guidry, Thomas Williams and John Schrewe) and "Isaac Levy against the United States," no. 253, National Archives; U. S. Court of Claims, "Eugene Petetin vs. the United States," no. 1999, and Jean B. Pollingue vs. the United States," no. 17105 and 1212, National Archives; also Mixed Commission on British and American Claims, "Alice and Ellen Duffy vs.the United States," no. 160, National Archives.
23. Edwin Bearrs (ed.), *A Louisiana Confederate; Diary of Felix Pierre Poche* (Natchitoches, La., 1972), 15, 114, 137, 144, 299.
24. On one occasion Father Francis Abadie, S. J., was arrested as a possible Union spy when crossing Confederate lines near Baton Rouge. Hardly had he been brought into camp, however, than a dozen or more soldiers recognized him and vouched for his identity. St. Charles College Archives Microfilm P-20, 137-45.
25. Perhaps the most prominent was Father Darrius Hubert, S. J.; Other wartime members of the staff were P. Felix Benausse (Rector), P. Franciscus Lespes (Minister), F. Anthony Free (Dean), P. Anthony Vialleton (Parish Pastor), P. Joseph Anthonioz (Treasurer), P. Joseph Rodiut (Pastor) and P. Francis Abadie. Among the faculty were Peter Bouige (Humanities), Henry Begley (Grammar), James Lonergan (Grammar), P. Conrad Widman (Counselor), P. Joseph Delahays (Prefect) and P. Nicolas Simon (Prefect). Unpublished manuscript by Michael Kenny, S. J. "Jesuits in our Southland 1566-1946. Origin and Growth of New Orleans Province," St. Charles College Archives, Grand Coteau, 72-73; *Catalogus Provinciae Lugdunensis et Missionis Neo-Aurelianensis,* vol. IV, 1862-1871 (Lyon, France) 67-68; and A.M.D.G. *St. Charles College, Grand Coteau, La. 1912-1913,* Diamond Jubilee 1838-1913 (Grand Coteau, 1912), 7-16 in St. Charles College Archives.
26. *Diarium Ministri 1858-1882,* entries for October 12, 1863, 60-61, and *Historia Domus 1837-1942,* 22-23, St. Charles College Archives, Grand Coteau; Henry Thompson's dispatch in *New York Herald,* October, 1863.
27. John G. Pratt's report in *Official Report Relative to the Conduct of Federal Troops in Western Louisiana* (Shreveport, 1863), 33; Undated newspaper clipping from the *Richmond Palladium* (Indiana) in the Burke Papers, U.S.L. Dupre Library Archives, Lafayette; *New York Herald,* October 31, 1863; *Official Records,* XXVI, Pt. I, 383; and *8th United States Census* (1860) for St. Landry Parish which places the value of Pratt's property near Opelousas at $110,000 (about $780,000 in 1978 currency); *The Connecticut Courant,* Hartford, Nov. 7, 1863.
28. Conversations with Mrs. Willis Courville, Sunset, Louisiana; Hall, *Cayuga in the Field,* 151-55; and Records of the Adjutant-Generals Office 1780's-1917, "Regimental Returns of the 75th New York Infantry," October-November 1863, Record Group 94, National Archives, Washington, D. C.

29. *Diarium Ministri* 1858-1882, 60-61; St. Charles College Microfilm P-20, 137-45; *Liber Continens Ordinationes, Responsa, Declarationes, Decisiones, Pertinentia,* ad. coll. Sti. Carli, 99, St. Charles College Archives, Grand Coteau.
30. Henry W. Howe, *Passages from the Life of Henry Warren Howe* (Lowell, Mass., 1899), 55; W. R. Howell Papers, diary entries for October 12-13, 1863, University of Texas Archives, Austin; Theopilus Noel, *A Campaign from Santa Fe to the Mississippi* (Houston, 1961), 103; Beecher, *Records of the 114th Regiment*, 261.

CHAPTER SEVEN

WESTERNERS IN VERMILIONVILLE

1. B. F. Stevenson, *Letters from the Army* (Cincinnati, 1884), 263; Service record Michael K. Lawler, National Archives; Charles A. Dana, *Recollections of the Civil War* (New York, 1898), 65; and Ezra Warner, *Generals in Blue* (Baton Rouge, 1964), 276-77.
2. Jay K. Ditchy (ed.), *Early Louisiana French Life and Folklore from the Anonymous Breaux Manuscript* (New Orleans, 1966), 45-46.
3. Cecilia's headstone, placed many years after the war, erroneously notes the date of her death as September 12, 1863; Alexandre Mouton memoirs in Lucille Meredith Griffin Collection, U.S.L. Library Archives, Lafayette; interviews with Miss Alida Martin and Eva Mouton, descendants of Governor Mouton; William Titus Rigby Papers, correspondence dated Vermilionville, October 22, 1863, University of Iowa Library Archives, Iowa City; William Gatchell's dispatch in *New York Herald*, October 31, 1863; Benjamin Steward's deposition in French and American Claims Commission, "Jean Pierre Gueydan against the United States," no. 226, National Archives; *Leslie's Illustrated Weekly*, vol. XVII (November 28, 1863), 156; Harry L. Griffin, *The Attakapas Country* (Gretna, La., 1974), 76-77; and F. L. R. Santis and Charles L. Souvay, C. M., "An Historical Sketch of the Church of Lafayette, Louisiana, 1821-1921," unpublished manuscript, 47-48.
4. Gaillard Hunt, *Israel, Elihu and Cadwallader Washburn, A Chapter in American Biography* (New York, 1925), 297-343; Dana, *Recollections of the Civil War*, 71-72; Warner, *Generals in Blue*, 542-43.
5. Gustave A. Breaux Diaries, entry for December 23, 1863, Tulane University Archives, New Orleans; undated copy of *Richmond Palladium* from the Burke Papers, U.S.L. Library Archives, Lafayette; *Official Records* XXVI, pt. I, 382, 778; John G. Pratt, *Official Report Relative to the Conduct of Federal Troops in Western Louisiana* (Shreveport, 1865), 33-39; Records of District and Parish Provost Marshalls, Department of the Gulf, Old Books 1255-1257, "Oaths of Allegiance," Record Group 393 in National Archives.
6. Also arrested were a number of paroled prisoners of war from the Vicksburg campaign, including Sergeant A. D. Landry, Corporal Alfred Peck, Privates Jules Duhon, A. Guidry, V. Comeau, Marshall Faber and a certain Zeringue. *Official Records*, Series II, Vol. VI, 696-720; *Wisconsin State Journal*, November 7, 1863; "Gueydan against the United States," 35, 310-311; Pratt, *Federal Troops in Western Louisiana*, 31-34; *Richmond Palladium* in Burke Papers.
7. Depositions of Jefferson Caffery, Valsin Broussard, Marcel Melancon, Theodore Fontelieu, Hermina Dugat, Jules Weber, Francois Francis, Norbert Landry, Alexandre B. Guidry, Uranie Louis, Jules Guidry, Ursin Grange, Marcel Boutte, Joseph Breaux, Armand Breaux, Emile Chreighton, Sylvege Broussard, Venance

Trahan, Evariste Trahan, Jacques Bonnemaison, Edward Fabre, N. R. Norwood, Alfred Duperier, Joseph O. Segura and Andre Victor in "Gueydan against the United States;" Pratt, *Federal Troops in Western Louisiana*, 41; Alexandre Barde, *Histoire des Comites de Vigilance aux Attakapas*, (Saint Jean Baptiste, 1861).

8. William Barney Letters, correspondence dated Vermilion Bayou, October 11, 1863. State Historical Society of Wisconsin, Madison; L.Carrol Root, ed. "The Experiences of a Federal Soldier in Louisiana," *Louisiana Historical Quarterly*, vol. 19 (July, 1936), 646; Julius V. Wood Papers, correspondence dated Camp Vermilion, October 11, 1863. Western Reserve Historical Society, Cleveland; "France in Mexico," *Harpers Weekly*, VII,(September 19, 1863), 594.
9. A. A. Rigby Diary, entries for October 11-12, 1863, Iowa State Department of History and Archives, Des Moines; William Titus Rigby Diary and Correspondence October 11-12, 1863; Levi Hoag Diary, entries for October 11-12, 1863 in Katherine Gue Leonard Papers, Iowa State Department of History and Archives, Des Moines; E. E. Blake, *A Succinct History of the 28th Iowa Volunteer Infantry* (Belle Plains, Iowa, 1896), 24; T. B. Marshall Notes and Diary, entries for October 11-12, 1863, Ohio Historical Society, Columbus; Henry P. Whipple, *The Diary of a Private Soldier* (Waterloo, Wisconsin, 1906), 29; Robert Steele Letters, correspondence dated October 11, 1863, State Historical Society of Wisconsin, Madison; and Alexandre Mouton Memoirs.
10. Harry Watts Papers, entries for October, 1863, Indiana State Library, Indianapolis; Hovey Manuscript, entries for October 1863, Indiana University, Bloomington; Daniel Webster Papers, correspondence dated Brashear City, November 13, 1863, State Historical Society of Wisconsin, Madison; Madison Reece Collection, medical reports for October-December 1863, Illinois State Historical Library, Springfield; *Official Records* XV, Series I, 373; *Wisconsin State Journal*, November 25, 1863.
11. Warner, *Generals in Blue*, 349-50; *Harper's Weekly*, VIII (October 15, 1864) 661; Service record E. O. C. Ord, National Archives.
12. Albert O. Marshall, *Army Life, from a Soldier's Journal* (Joliet, Illinois, 1884), 289-93; Levi Hoag Diary, entry October 12, 1863; A. A. Rigby Diary, October 12, 1863; William Titus Rigby Papers, letter October 17, 1863; T. B. Marshall Diary, October 12, 1863; T. B. Marshall, *History of the Eighty-Third Ohio Volunteer Infantry* (Cincinnati, 1912), 111; Whipple, *Diary of a Private Soldier*, 29; Hartford, *Wisconsin Home League*, December 26, 1863; Alonzo Gilbert Jack Papers, correspondence October 13, 1863, State Historical Society of Wisconsin, Madison; *Wisconsin State Journal*, November 7, 1863; *Milwaukee Sentinel*, November 2, 1863; Harry Watts Diary, October 1863; *A History of the Trials and Hardships of the Twenty-Fourth Indiana Volunteer Infantry* (Indianapolis, 1913), 90; Augustus George Sinks Collection, 53, Indiana State Library Archives, Indianapolis; *Official Records*, XXVI, pt. I, 763; David Shunk service record, National Archives.
13. Harris Beecher, *Record of the 114th Regiment N.Y.S.V.* (Norwich, 1866), 270-72; Elias Pellet, *History of the 114th Regiment New York State Volunteers* (Norwich, 1866), 155-56; William Titus Rigby Letters, correspondence October 22, 1863; Stevenson, *Letters from the Army*, 268; Service records Frank Gardner, Nathan Dudley and Alfred Mouton, National Archives; and Alexandre Mouton Memoirs.
14. F. L. Klement, *Copperheads in the Middle West* (Chicago, 1960), 103-33; H. S. Merrill, *Bourbon Democracy of the Middle West* (Baton Rouge, 1953), 8-9, 53-54; Clement Vallandigham, *Harper's Weekly*, VII, 338, 362, 365, 828; John W. Headley, *Confederate Operations in Canada and New York* (New York and Washington, 1906), 222-30; J. L. Vallandigham, *Life of Clement L. Vallandigham* (Baltimore, 1872); H. Van Fossan, "Clement L. Vallandigham," *Ohio Archaeological and Historical Quarterly*, XXIII (1914), 256-67.

15. Levi Hoag Diary, October 15, 1863; "A Soldier's Letters from the Field," *Iowa Historical Record*, XVI, XVII and XVIII (1900-02), 220-21; William Titus Rigby Papers, October 12-13, 1863; T. B. Marshall Notes and Diary, October 13-14, 1863; Julius V. Wood Papers, October 17, 1863; Isaac Jackson Papers, correspondence October 13, 1863 in William Clements Library, University of Michigan, Ann Arbor; Nannie Tilley (ed.), *Federals on the Frontier,.The Diary of Benjamin F. McIntyre* (Austin, Texas), 234.
16. "A Yankee in Louisiana: Selections from the Diary and Correspondence of Henry R. Gardner 1862-1866," *Louisiana History*, V,(Summer 1964), 276; Thomas L. Livermore, *Numbers and Losses in the Civil War in America 1861-65* (Boston, 1901), 50;*Official Records* XXVI, pt. I, 737; Albert Stearns, *Reminiscences of the Late War* (Brooklyn 1881), 13-25; "Our Colored Troops in Louisiana," *Harper's Weekly*, VIII, (February 28, 1863), 143; Rossiter Johnson, *Campfires and Battlefields* (New York, 1958), 139; and C. Peter Ripley, *Slaves and Freedman in Civil War Louisiana* (Baton Rouge, 1976), 25-68.
17. Lawrence Van Alstyne, *Diary of an Enlisted Man* (New Haven, 1910), 173-95.
18. Robert Phelps Papers, correspondence of October 15, 1863 in the Earl Hess Collection, Military History Institute, Carlisle Barracks, Pa.

CHAPTER EIGHT

THE RESISTANCE STIFFENS

1. Ezra Warner, *Generals in Gray* (Baton Rouge, 1959); Clement Evans (ed.) *Confederate Military History*, vol. XI, (Atlanta, 1899), 224, 245-46.
2. Richard Taylor, *Destruction and Reconstruction* (New York, 1879), 125-26, 141-42 and 178-79; Frank Moore (ed.), *The Rebellion Record*, vol. 7 (New York, 1865), 78; and Walter Lord (ed.), *The Fremantle Diary* (Boston), 45-47; see also Stephen B. Oates, *Confederate Cavalry West of the River* (Austin, 1961); Stephen Oates, "Supply for the Confederate Cavalry in the Trans-Mississipi," *Military Affairs*, XXV (1961), 94-99; and Martin Hardwick Hall, *Sibley's New Mexico Campaign* (Austin, 1960), 37-39; and Theophilus Noel, *Autobiography and Reminiscences of Theophilus Noel* (Chicago, 1904), 90.
3. Taylor, *Destruction and Reconstruction*, 162; *Official Records* XXVI, pt. I, 374; Moore, *The Rebellion Record*, vol. 7, 78-79, 84; Noel, *Autobiography and Reminiscences*, 39; Edwin Bearrs, (ed.), *A Louisiana Confederate; Diary of Felix Pierre Poche* (Natchitoches, La., 1972), 68, 155-56; Weeks Family Papers, correspondence dated New Iberia, September 10, 1863 in L.S.U. Library Archives, Baton Rouge; *New York Herald*, November 9, 1863; and *Milwaukee Sentinel*, November 2, 1863.
4. W. T. Wroe, "New Mexico Campaign in 1861-62," unpublished, undated manuscript in Confederate Museum, Austin, Texas; Odie Faulk, *General Tom Green, Fightin' Texan* (Waco, 1963); Walter P. Lane, *The Adventures and Recollections of General Walter P. Lane* (Marshall, Texas, N.D.); Noel, *Autobiography and Reminiscenses*, 143; Taylor, *Destruction and Reconstruction*, 178; Dudley Wooten, *A Comprehensive History of Texas*, Vol. II, (Dallas, 1898), section on Green; Evans, *Confederate Military History, 231-38;* Charles Spurlin (ed.), *West of the Mississippi with Waller's 13th Texas Cavalry Battalion* (Waco, 1971).
5. *Official Records* XXVI, pt. I,, 384-95 and pt. II, 291, 294-95, 327, 340-41.

6. W. R. Howell Papers, diary entry October 13, 1863, University of Texas Archives; In the St. Charles College Archives: *Historia Domus 1837-1942*, 22-23; Michael Kenny, S. J., "Jesuits in the Southland 1566-1946," 72-73, unpublished manuscript; Microfilm P-20, 137-45; and *Diarium Ministri*, 1858-1882, entries for October 1863.
7. Samuel H. Fletcher, *The History of Company A, Second Illinois Cavalry* (1912), 119, 189-94; Service record, John J. Mudd, National Archives; *Official Records* XXVI, pt. I, 383.
8. Clement Evans, (ed.), *Confederate Military History, Louisiana* vol. X, by John Dimitry (Atlanta, 1899), 607; Service record J. L. Hallet, National Archives; *Official Records*, XXVI, Pt. I, 353, 389; "Returns of 2nd Louisiana Cavalry," microfilm copy at U.S.L. Library Archives, Lafayette.
9. Conversations with Oge Guilbeau, Carencro, Louisiana, a grandson of Oge Guilbeau.
10. James Hall, *Cayuga in the Field* (Auburn, 1873), 149-50.
11. *Register of Births*, Church of Grand Coteau, St. Charles Catholic Church Archives; George Reinecke (ed.), *Early Louisiana French Life and Folklore from the Anonymous Breaux Manuscript* (New Orleans, 1966), 29, 37.
12. Harris H. Beecher, *Record of the 114th Regiment, N.Y.S. V.* (Norwich, N. Y., 1866), 262.
13. Houston *Tri-Weekly Telegraph*, October 28, 1863, November 11, 1863; W. B. Hunter correspondence of October 11, 1863 in Mary J. Minor Letters, University of Texas Archives; Austin, *State Gazette*, October 28, 1863.
14. Hall, *Cayuga in the Field*, 151-55.
15. Theophilus Noel, *A Campaign From Santa Fe to the Mississippi* (Houston, 1961), 103; Howell Papers, diary entry October 14, 1863; Julius Giesecke Papers, diary entry October 14, 1863; Beecher, *Record of the 114th Regiment*, 262; *Official Records*, XXVI, pt. I, 338; and Henry Howe, *Passages from the Life of Henry Warren Howe* (Lowell, Mass., 1899) 55.
16. Henry P. Whipple, *The Diary of a Private Soldier* (Waterloo, Wisconsin, 1906), 31; Hartford, Wisconsin *Home League*, November 28, 1863.
17. Service records Michael Fox, Charles Annis and John Stokes, National Archives; John M. Stanyon, *A History of the Eighth Regiment of New Hampshire Volunteers* (Concord, N. H., 1892), 338-42; Charles Andrews Emerson Narrative, 49, in the New Hampshire Historical Society, Concord; other background information on the 8th New Hampshire is available in the Daniel Veasy Durgin letters of the Cram Papers and the Clark Carr Letters in the New Hampshire Historical Society.
18. Service records of William Gannon and Ezra Bell and the Court-Martial proceedings of William Gannon in the National Archives, Washington, D. C.
19. W. R. Howell Papers.
20. The six-gun Valverde Battery consisted of three six-pounders, two twelve-pound field howitzers and one twelve-pound mountain howitzer. Hall, *Sibley's New Mexico Campaign*, 83-100, 213.
21. W. R. Howell Papers, diary entry October 15, 1863; Giesecke Papers, diary entry October 15, 1863; Noel, *A Campaign From Santa Fe to the Mississippi*, 103; *New York Herald*, October 31, 1863; Houston, *Tri-Weekly Telegraph*, November 16 and December 16, 1863; Caroline Whitcomb, *History of the Second Massachusetts Battery of Light Artillery*, (Concord, N.H.), 55-56; *Boston Journal*, February 22, 1903; Howe, *Passages from the Life of Henry Warren Howe*, 55, Surgeon John M. Bronough Papers, list of wounded and dead for 1863, Baylor University Archives, Waco; *Official Records*, Pt. I, 338-39.
22. Conversations with Raoul Sibille, Sunset, Louisiana, a grandson of Joseph Sibille; and *Opelousas Courier*, October 10, 1863.

23. Alonzo Gilbert Jack Correspondence, letter dated October 16, 1863, State Historical Society of Wisconsin, Madison; Beecher, *Record of the 114th Regiment*, 262; J. T. Woods, *Services of the Ninety-Sixth Ohio Volunteers* (Toledo, Ohio, 1874), 39; Thomas B. Marshall Papers, diary entry October 15, 1863, Ohio Historical Society, Columbus.
24. W. R. Howell Papers; Giesecke Papers; Houston, *Tri-Weekly Telegraph*, December 16, 1863; Noel, *Autobiography and Reminicences*, 57; Evans, *Confederate Military History*, 236-37.
25. The extant correspondence between General N. P. Banks, Colonel Thomas Chickering and the Mother Superior of Sacred Heart, now in the possession of the Archives of the Academy of Sacred Heart, make it clear that Federal forces did in fact protect and even provide assistance in the form of food and provisions for the Academy. In a final note written in April 1863, Banks wrote the Mother Superior that "My small service to you is the only real pleasure I have had in Opelousas"; also in the Sacred Heart Archives are the *Lettres Annuelles* 1859-1862, pp. 367-69 and 1863-1866, p. 160 relating the quality of wartime life at the Academy and surrounding areas; *School Register of Sacred Heart Academy*, Grand Coteau, 1827-1887; and *Historia Domus*, 1837-1942, pp. 62-69, St. Charles College Archives, Grand Coteau; see also Roger Baudier, *The Church of Our Lady of the Sacred Heart* (Church Point, 1954) for general background.
26. Wickham Hoffman, *Camp Court and Siege* (New York, 1877), 81-82; *New York Herald*, October 31, 1863; Theodore Devalcourt deposition in French and American Claims Commission, "Jules Perrodin against the United States," no. 90, National Archives, Washington, D. C. Devalcourt was the captain referred to by David Hunter Strother in Cecil B. Eby, Jr. (ed.), *A Virginia Yankee in the Civil War* (Chapel Hill, N.C.), 173.
27. *New York Herald*, October 31, 1863; T. B. Marshall Papers, diary entries October 15-16, 1863; and Julius V. Wood Papers, correspondence dated October 17, 1863

CHAPTER NINE

WESTERNERS ON THE BOURDEUX

1. Few homes have generated so much oral tradition as Chretien Point. Much of it is obviously contradictory, erroneous and misleading. Some of these oral sources have been duly noted and acknowledged in the many pictorial and descriptive works on Louisiana plantations, including *inter alia*, Harnet Kane, *Plantation Parade* (New York, 1941), 217-18; and Herman Seebold, *Old Louisiana Plantation Homes*, vol.I, 342-47; perhaps the most authoritative source relating the Civil War events at Chretien Point are the voluminous reparation claims for damages estimated at $55,521.90 made by family members to the U.S. Court of Claims, now filed in the National Archives, specifically "Hypolite Chretien vs. the United States," Congressional Claim no. 9572, "Atheais Chretien LeMore vs. the United States," no. 11253 and "Felicite Neda Chretien vs. the United States," no. 14812. These claims, as in the case of other claims cited in this work, contain detailed depositions of family members, friends, Union and Confederate soldiers, former slaves, and many others as well as relevant documentation; according to the *8th U.S.Census* (1860) p. 164, for St. Landry Parish the 2,300 acre Chretien plantation was valued at $216,000 (about $1,520,000 in 1978 currency); other wartime sources mentioning Chretien Point include the Gustave A. Breaux Diaries, entry

for December 27,1863 and January 12,1864 Tulane University Archieves; Edwin Bearrs (ed.), *A Louisiana Confederate; Diary of Felix Pierre Poche* (Natchitoches, 1972), 145; and *Leslie's Illustrated Weekly*, vol. XVI (November 28,1863), 156; Joseph Karl Menn, *The Large Slaveholders of Lousisiana, 1860* (New Orleans, 1964), 365-70; Jeanne and Louis Cornay, the current owners of Chretien Point provided much valuable information as did Ronnie and Carmen Daigle of Sunset, "Buck" Hebert of Opelousas, Mrs. Willis Courville of Sunset, Mrs. Alcues Leger of Sunset and Mrs. Fernand Gouaux of Lafayette

2. James Earl Bradley papers, diary entry Octobei 16, 1863 and Arthur W. Hyatt Collection, diary entries for October 15-16, 1863 in L.S.U. Library Archives, Baton Rouge; Service record J. J. Bowman, National Archives; and Houston *Tri-Weekly Telegraph*, November 13, 1863.
3. Henry Howe, *Passages from the Life of Henry Warren Howe* (Lowell, Mass., 1899), 55; Augustus George Sinks Collection, p. 53, Indiana State Library, Indianapolis; Harry Watts Diary, p. 103, Indiana State Library, Indianapolis; Thomas H. Bringhurst, *History of the Forty-Sixth Regiment Indiana Volunteer Infantry*, (1888), 76; Hartford, Wisconsin *Home League*, October 17, 1863; and *Official Records* XXVI, pt. I, 338, 765.
4. Harry Watts Papers, 103-04; *A History of the Trials and Hardships of the Twenty-Fourth Indiana Volunteer Infantry* (Indianapolis, 1913), 90; Bringhurst, *History of the Forty-Sixth Regiment*, 76; Isaac Jackson Papers, correspondence October 18, 1863, in William Clements Library, University of Michigan, Ann Arbor; Thomas B. Marshall Papers, diary entry October 16, 1863, Ohio Historical Society, Columbus; Julius V. Wood Papers, correspondence dated October 19, 1863, Western Reserve Historical Society, Cleveland; Henry Whipple, *The Diary of a Private Soldier* (Waterloo, Wisconsin, 1906), 29; Samuel Gordon Collection, correspondence dated November 16, 1863, New Iberia to wife in Illinois State Historical Library, Springfield; William Gatchell's dispatches in *New York Herald*, November 1, 1863; W. R. Howell Papers, diary entry October 16, 1863, University of Texas Archives, Austin; French and American Claims Commission, "Joseph Bloch against the United States" no. 275, National Archives; *Official Records* XXVI, pt. I, 338, 768; Theophilus Noel, *A Campaign from Santa Fe to the Mississippi* (Houston, 1961), 103; and "Diary of an Unidentified Surgeon of the 60th Indiana," October 16, 1863 entry, Lilly Library, Indiana University, Bloomington.
5. *Bohemian Life; or Autobiography of a Tramp* (San Francisco, 1884); T. B. Marshall Collection, entries for October 16, 1863; Theophilus Noel, *Autobiography and Reminiscences of Theophilus Noel* (Chicago, 1904), 85-86. Because of conflicting sources there seems to be some question as to whether this exchange actually occurred at the time and place indicated or at Vicksburg several months earlier.
6. The tragic story of Desire and Sarah Arnaud is related in detail in French and American Commission, "Augustus Burleigh against the United States," no. 251, National Archives; according to the *8th U. S. Census* (1860) for St. Landry Parish, p. 235, the Arnaud's holdings were valued at $15,500 (or about $110,000 in terms of 1978 currency); see also David C. Edmonds, "Tragedy on Buzzards' Prairie," *Attakapas Gazette*, X (Winter 1975), 181-91; Desire Arnaud Succession Record, no. 2726, 1865, St. Landry Parish Courthouse, Opelousas, Louisiana; and the Lacon, *Illinois Gazette* November 11, 1863.
7. James Hall, *Cayuga in the Field* (Auburn, 1873), 152; Harris Beecher, *Record of the 114th Regiment N.Y.S.V.* (Norwich, NY, 1866), 262; Orton Clark, *The 116th Regiment of New York Volunteers* (Buffalo, 1868), 132; and Howe, *Passages from the Life of Henry Warren Howe*, 55.
8. *Official Records* BXVI, pt. I, 339, 771.

9. Marshall Papers, diary entry October 17, 1863, Whipple, *Diary of a Private Soldier*, 29; "Diary of an Unidentified Surgeon," October 17, 1863 entry; Bringhurst, *History of the Forty-Sixth Regiment*, 77; *New York Herald*, November 1, 1863; Lacon, *Illinois Gazette*, November 11, 1863; W. R. Howell Papers, diary entry October 17, 1863; and Noel, *A Campaign from Santa Fe to the Mississippi*, 103.
10. This story was related in a letter dated October 17, 1863 by Julius V. Wood of the 96th Ohio Infantry. I have checked funeral and other records all over St. Landry Parish in an unsuccessful effort to identify the family. Apparently she was buried on the spot without ceremony.
11. Lawrence Van Alstyne, *Diary of an Enlisted Man* (New Haven, 1910), 194-97; Jay K. Ditchy, *Early Louisiana French Life and Folklore from the Anonymous Breaux Manuscript* (New Orleans, 1966), 48-58; the carrier pigeons are mentioned in "Letters from Lawson Jefferson Keener," unpublished correspondence dated August 4, 1864 in the possession of Mrs. Lawson Keener Lacy, Longview, Texas; Alexandre Barde, *Histoire des Comites de Vigilance aux Attakapas* (Saint-Jean Baptiste, 1861), various sections on Coco.
12. *Official Records*, XXVI, pt. I, 772-73.
13. Service Record, John G. Fonda, National Archives; Madison, *Wisconsin State Journal*, December 7, 1863; *Report to the Adjutant General, State of Illinois*, vol. VI, "History of the One Hundred and Eighteenth Infantry" (Springfield, 1900), 316; *Trials and Hardships of the Twenty-Fourth Indiana*, 90-91; Bringhurst, *History of the Forty-Sixth Regiment*, 77; W. R. Howell Papers, diary entry for October 19, 1863; Julius Giesecke Papers, October 19, 1863 diary entry; and *Official Records* LIII, Series 1, 474.
14. Bradley Papers, diary entry October 19, 1863; Hyatt Diaries, entry for October 19, 1863; and John M. Bronough Papers, medical notes and correspondence October 19-20, 1863 in the Texas Collection, Baylor University, Waco, Texas.
15. *Official Records*, LIII, Series I, 474.
16. Fortunately for Gannon, the court was not vindictive. Along with its decision went a recommendation to the Review Board for clemency. In the meantime he was returned to his regiment for duty. Service records and court-martial proceedings of William Gannon and A. C. Livingston, National Archives; and John M. Stanyon, *A History of the Eighth Regiment of New Hampshire Volunteers* (Concord, 1892), 339-42.

CHAPTER TEN

THE ROAD TO OPELOUSAS

1. Robert L. Kirby, *Kirby Smith's Confederacy* (New York, 1972), 114, 244-48; Joseph Howard Parks, *General Edmund Kirby Smith C.S.A.* (Baton Rouge, 1962; Ezra Warner, *General's in Gray* (Baton Rouge, 1959); Arthur W. Hyatt Diary, entry October 8, 1863, L.S.U. Library Archives, Baton Rouge.
2. Richard Taylor, *Destruction and Reconstruction* (New York, 1879), 189-90; Warner, *Generals in Gray;* Jackson Beauregard Davis, "Life of Richard Taylor" *Louisiana Historical Quarterly*, XXIV (January, 1941), 50-67; Theophilus Noel, *Autobiography and Reminiscences* (Chicago, 1904), 94-95; Hyatt Diary, entry October 8, 1863; *Official Records*, XXVI, pt. I, 386-91.
3. *Official Records*, XXVI, pt. II, 341-42.

4. One of the most candid expositions of the famous Smith-Taylor feud is contained in a letter written by an unidentified Confederate officer which fell into Union hands during the disastrous Red River Campaign and was subsequently published in Frank Moore, *The Rebellion Record,* Vol. 9 (New York, 1871), 751-57; Kirby, *Kirby Smith's Confederacy* 114, 244-48; Hyatt Diary, entry October 8, 1863; Ludwell Johnson, *Red River Campaign* (Baltimore, 1958), 88-89, 181-83, 281-83.
5. *Official Records*, XXVI, pt. I, 773.
6. Thomas B. Marshall Diary, entry October 20, 1863 in Ohio Historical Society, Columbus; Isaac Jackson Papers, correspondence October 20, 1863, William Clements Library, University of Michigan in Ann Arbor; William Barney Letters, October 20, 1863, State Historical Society of Wisconsin in Madison.
7. Lawrence Van Alstyne, *Diary of an Enlisted Man* (New Haven, 1910), 197-201.
8. Barney Letters, October 20, 1863; Jackson Papers, October 20, 1863; Henry Whipple, *Diary of a Private Soldier* (Waterloo, Wisconsin, 1906), 20; *A History of the Trials and Hardships of the Twenty-Fourth Indiana Volunteer Infantry* (Indianapolis, 1913), 91; Noel, *Autobiography and Reminiscences,* 85-86; "Diary of an Unidentified Surgeon," October 20, 1863 entry, Lilly Library, Indiana University, Bloomington.
9. Thomas Bringhurst, *History of the Forty-Sixth Regiment Indiana Volunteer Infantry* (n. p., 1888), 79 (Bringhurst erroneuosly cites the date of this event as November 5, 1863); Augustus George Sinks Collection, 53, Indiana Library, Indianapolis; Service record Charles Baum, National Archives; and conversations with descendants of Constance Guidry.
10. *Official Records*, XXVI, pt. I, 339-40, 388-89; Samuel Gordon Papers, correspondence November 16, 1863, Illinois State Historical Library, Springfield; Julius Giesecke and W. R. Howell Diaries, entries October 21, 1863 in University of Texas Library Archives, Austin; *8th U. S. Census* (1860) for St. Landry Parish, 239-40.
11. Harris Beecher, *Record of the 114th Regiment N.Y.S.V.* (Norwich, NY, 1866), 262-64.
12. James Hall, *Cayuga in the Field* (Auburn, 1873), 152.
13. W. R. Howell Diary, October 21, 1863; John Bronough Collection, medical notes on casualties for October 1863, Baylor University Archives, Waco, Texas; William Barney Letters, correspondence October 22, 1863; Marshall Papers 46-47; T. B. Marshall, *History of the 83rd Ohio Volunteer Infantry* (Cincinnati, 1912), 111-112; Isaac Jackson Papers, correspondence October 26, 1863; Samuel Gordon Papers, correspondence November 16, 1863; Bringhurst, *History of the Forty-Sixth Regiment,* 76; Sinks Collection, 53; Harry Watts Diary, 104-05, Indiana State Library, Indianapolis; Henry Thompson's dispatch in *New York Herald,* November 1, 1863; Orton Clark, *The 116th Regiment of New York Volunteers* (Buffalo, 1868), 132; and William E. Jones, *The Military History of the One-Hundred and Sixty-First New York Volunteers, Infantry* (Bath, N.Y., 1865), 16; "Diary of an Unidentified Surgeon," entry October 21, 1863; and Julius V. Wood Papers, correspondence dated October 27, 1863, Western Reserve Historical Society, Cleveland, Ohio.
14. French and American Claims Commission, "Augustus Burleigh against the United States," no. 251 (depositions of Joseph Boudreaux, William and James Burleigh and Sarah Arnaud), National Archives.

CHAPTER ELEVEN

FROM OPELOUSAS TO BARRE'S LANDING

1. According to Dr. John M.Bronough, senior surgeon of the old Sibley Brigade, medical facilities were set up in the Payne, Hebrard and Donatte homes as well as at other locations. Bronough Papers, medical notes for October-December 1863, Baylor University, Waco, Texas.
2. Unpublished manuscript by F. L. R. Santis and Charles L. Souvay, C. M. "Rummaging through Old Parish Records, Historical Sketch of the Parish of Opelousas, Louisiana," 1921 in the possession of U.S.L. Dupre Library Archives, Lafayette, Louisiana; Background information on Fathers Gilbert and Francois Raymond, St. Landry Catholic Church Archives, Opelousas, Louisiana; *8th U.S. Census* (1860) for St. Landry Parish, 286; *Official Records*, XXVI, pt. II, 294-95.
3. James Earl Bradley Papers, diary entry October 21, 1863, L.S.U. Library Archives, Baton Rouge, Louisiana.
4. Donald J. Hebert, *Southwest Louisiana Records, 1860-65*, vol. 7 (Cecilia, Louisiana), 216.
5. Arthur W. Hyatt Diaries, entry October 21, 1863, L.S.U. Archives, Baton Rouge; George W.O'Brian Diary, entry October 21, 1863, University of Texas Archives, Austin; W. R. Howell Papers, diary entry October 21, 1863, University of Texas Archives; and Julian Giesecke Diary, entry October 21, 1863, University of Texas Archives.
6. Samuel Gordon Papers, correspondence November 6, 1863, Illinois State Historical Library, Springfield, Illinois; conversations with Dr. Edward Boagni of Baton Rouge, Louisiana.
7. Harry Watts Diary, 106, Indiana State Library, Indianapolis; Augustus George Sinks Collection, 54-55; Indiana State Library, Indianapolis; Thomas H. Bringhurst, *History of the Forty-Sixth Regiment Indiana Volunteer Infantry* (n. p., 1888), 77; Gordon Papers, correspondence November 6, 1863; James R. Slack Papers, correspondence October 31, 1863, Indiana State Library, Indianapolis; Isasc Jackson Papers, correspondence October 26, 1863, University of Michigan, Ann Arbor; Thomas B. Marshall Papers, diary entry October 21, 1863, Ohio Historical Society; Julius V. Wood Papers, correspondence October 27, 1863, Western Reserve Historical Society Columbus; Lacon, *Illinois Gazette* November 25, 1863; Harris Beecher, *Record of the 114th Regiment N.Y.S.V.* (Norwich, N.Y., 1866), 172; John C. Brightman Papers, correspondence June 1, 1863, University of Texas Library Archives; Edwin Bearrs (ed.), *A Louisiana Confederate, Diary of Felix Pierre Poche* (Natchitoches, 1972), 15; *Official Records* XXVI, pt. I, 339-40; and Albert O. Marshall, *Army Life from a Soldier's Journal 1861-64* (Joliet, Illinois, 1883), 204.
8. Beecher, *Record of the 114th Regiment*, 264-65; Harry Watts Diary 106; Hovey manuscript, 77-78, Indiana University, Lilly Library, Bloomington; Isaac Jackson Papers, correspondence October 26, 1863.
9. Among the first settlers was Jacques-Guillaume Courtableau who secured a land grant of about three thousand acres at the source of Bayou Teche and the waterway which bears his name. His small trading post, consisting of a store and warehouse, eventually passed on to Charles Barre, who gave his name to the landing. The same site, when the Federals came in 1863, belonged to the Honore Dejean Family. Claude Oubre, "Port Barre; A Crossroads in the Opelousas Country," *Attakapas Gazette*, XI(Spring, 1976), 43.
10. Depositions of Eugene Riquet, Joseph Melancon, Valsin Dupre and Charles Andre, French and American Claims Commission, "Dominique Lalanne against the United States," no. 134, National Archives, Washington, D.C.; also "E. C.

Drouet (Estate of Louis Eugene Riquet) against the United States," no. 617, National Archives; and U. S. Court of Claims (Southern Claims Commission), "Jules A. Dejean (Admin. of Honore Dejean) vs. the United States," no. 19026, National Archives.

11. French and American Claims Commission, "Catherine Grimmer against the United States," no. 88 (depositions of Samuel Holabird, Theophile Sanvald, Benjamin Dejean and AugustinLemoine) and "Jules Perrodin against the United States," no. 90 (depositions of Thomas Chickering and Samuel Holabird), National Archives.
12. Deposition of Charles Andre in "Lalanne against the United States,"; U.S. Court of Claims (Southern Claims Commission), "Raimondi Deshotels vs. the United States," no.2728, National Archives; T. B. Marshall Papers, diary entry October 22, 1863; T. B. Marshall, *History of the Eighty-Third Ohio Volunteer Infantry* (Cincinnati, 1912), 112; *A History of the Trials and Hardships of the Twenty-Fourth Indiana Volunteer Infantry* (Indianapolis, 1913), 91.
13. Julius V. Wood Papers, correspondence October 27, 1863; Harry Watts Diary, 106; Augustus George Sinks Collection, 54-55; Isaac Jackson Papers, correspondence October 26, 1863; "Diary of an unidentified surgeon of the 60th Indiana," entry October 21, 1863, Lilly Library, Indiana University, Bloomington.
14. See for example, *Official Records*, XXVI, pt. 1,340.
15. Beecher, *Record of the 114th Regiment*, 264.
16. Depositions of Pierre Arnault, widow Adolphe Arnault, Joseph Melancon and Charles Andre in "Dominique Lalanne against the United States"; "Raimondi Deshotels vs the United States," "Jules Perrodin against the United States"; also deposition of Ludger Lastrapes in French and American Claims Commission, "Pierre Gustave Gibert against the United States," no. 609, National Archives.
17. Depositions of John Roy, Leon Mistric, Philogene Auzenne, Geraud Donatte, Alcide Dekerlegard, Evariste Wright and Jacob Hirsch in French and American Claims Commission "Joseph Camy against the United States, no. 60, and "Victoire Tessa Prevot against the United States," no. 172 (especially depositions of Jacque Thompson, Benjamin and Balthazar Bob and Jules Perrodin), National Archives; also *8th U. S. Census* (1860) for St. Landry Parish, 193.
18. Depositions of Manuel Anderson, Jean B. Hebert, Edmond Hamilton, Faustin Lalonde, Emil Hauguel and Pierre G. Gibert in French and American Claims Commission "Emil Eugene Hauguel against the United States," no. 233; "Romain Dupre against the United States," no. 67 (especially depositions of Joseph Ward and Charles Ranton) National Archives; also *8th U. S. Census* (1860) for St. Landry Parish, 193.
19. *Milwaukee Sentinel*, November 13, 1863; Bell Irvin Wiley (ed.), *This Infernal War, The Confederate Letters of Sgt. Edwin H. Fay* (Austin, Texas, 439.
20. Court-martial proceedings and service record of Private Michael Fox, National Archives; also Charles A. Emerson diary, November 17, 1863 entry, New Hampshire Historical Society; and John M. Stanyon, *A History of the Eighth Regiment of New Hampshire Volunteers* (Concord N. H., 1892), 339-42.
21. The two officers, Lieutenants R. H. Ryall of the 6th Missouri Cavalry and George W. Naylor of the 2nd Illinois Cavalry, were subsequently thanked by General Franklin for their "unusual courage, caution, intelligence,...daring and energy." The author was unable to learn more about the mission. *Official Records* XXVI, pt. 1, 774-75; and service records of Ryall and Naylor in National Archives.
22. There is a great deal of information about the foraging activities in and around Barre's Landing (Port Barre) during the spring occupation in U. S. Court of Claims, December term, 1880 "Henry Peychaud, Syndic of Bellocque, Noblum & Co. vs the United States," no. 3497, National Archives, especially depositions of Pierre Laborie, Theodore Valade, Fennimore Poiret, Captain David Bunker,

Captain F. G. Pope, Jules Noblom and others; also French and American Claims Commission, "Augustin Guidry against the United States," no. 90, National Archives.

23. *Official Records* XXVI, pt. 1, 340.
24. Charles A. Dana, *Recollections of the Civil War* (New York, 1898), 65; B. F. Stevenson, *Letters from the Army* (Cincinnati, 1884), 267)69; William Titus Rigby Papers, correspondence October 22-24, 1863 and diary entries October 22-23, 1863, University of Iowa Libraries, Iowa City; James R. Slack papers, correspondence for October 1863; Levi L. Hoag Diary, entry October 23, 1863 in Katherine Gue Leonard Collection, Iowa State Department of History and Archives, Des Moines.
25. According to the *8th U. S. Census* (1860) for St. Landry Parish, Hollier's holdings were valued at only $2000.00; he occasionally advertised his services as glazier in the *Opelousas Courier* and the *Opelousas Patriot;* also Joseph Hollier Succession Record No. 5623, dated January 17, 1900 in the St. Landry Parish Courthouse, Opelousas.
26. Alfred A. Rigby Diary, entry October 23, 1863, Iowa State Department of History and Archives, Des Moines; William T. Rigby Papers, diary entry October 23, 1863 and correspondence started October 22 and completed October 24, 1863.
27. Henry Hefflefinger service record, National Archives; William Rigby Papers, diary entry October 24, 1863.
28. A. A. Rigby Diary, October 24, 1863; William Rigby Diary October 24, 1863.
29. F. H. Mason, *The Forty-Second Ohio Infantry* (Cleveland, 1876), 243-44; Hoag Diary, entry October 24, 1863; *The Era,* New Orleans, November 12, 1863; *Official Records,* XXVI, pt. II, 390; depositions of Joseph Jenison, Hypolite Guidry and others in "Jules Perrodin against the United States," no. 90; and French and American Claims Commission," Eugene Giroud against the United States," no. 477 (depositions of Alcinder Daigle, Joseph and Hypolite Guidry, Antoine Fontenot and Elbert Gantt), National Archives.
30. *Official Records,* XXVI, Pt.II, 232, 390; *History of the Second Battalion Duryee: Zouaves* (New York, 1904), 22; Houston *Tri-Weekly Telegraph,* November 13, 1863; J. P. Blessington, *The Campaigns of Walker's Texas Division* (Austin, 1968), 137; John C. Brightman Letters, correspondence June 1, 1863 in University of Texas Library Archives, Austin.
31. French and American Claims Commission "Philibert Rogay against the United States," no. 545, National Archives; *Official Records* XV, 393, 919; Arthur W. Bergeron, Jr. (ed.), "Prison Life at Camp Pratt," *Louisiana History,* vol. 14 (Fall 1973), 389; Theophilus Noel, *Autobiography and Reminiscences* (Chicago, 1904), 39; Artrhur W. Hyatt Diaries, entries August 29, September 22, October 8, 22-24, 1863; Napier Bartlett, *Military Record of Louisiana* (Baton Rouge, 1964), 17-62.
32. Alfred Mouton's wife was Zelia Mouton, a second cousin when he married her in 1854. As of 1863 they had four children. Harry L. Griffin, *The Attakapas Country* (Gretna, La., 1974), 43-44, 124, 133, 135, 143; William Arceneaux, *Acadian General Alfred Mouton and the Civil War* (Lafayette, 1972), 24-25; Alexandre Barde, *Histoire des Comites de Vigilance aux Attakapas* (St. Jean-Baptiste, 1861), 330-31, 383; *Official Records,* X, pt. 1, 522 and XV, 176-180, 390; Clement Evans, (ed.), *Confederate Military History,* vol. 10 on Louisiana (Atlanta, 1899), 811-13; Richard Taylor, *Destruction and Reconstruction* (New York, 1879), 108-109, 165; Ezra Warner, *Generals in Gray* (Baton Rouge, 1959); *The Era,* New Orleans, November 21, 1863; Hyatt Diary, entry October 8 and 24, 1863; and conversations with Miss Alida Martin, a grand-daughter of General Mouton.

CHAPTER TWELVE

IN OPELOUSAS COUNTRY

1. Charles Emerson Diary, entry October 24, 1863, New Hampshire Historical Society, Concord; U. S. Court of Claims, "Cornelius Donato vs. the United States," no. 19763, National Archives; William Perrin, *Southwest Louisiana, Biographical and Historical* (Baton Rouge, 1971), pt. 1, 56; Harris Beecher, *Record of the 114th Regiment N.Y.S.V.* (Norwich, N.Y., 1866), 172-73; French and American Claims Commission, "Dominique Lalanne against the United States," no. 134 (especially depositions of Leopold and Onezime Marks, Bleze Motte, Francois Trainor, Josephine and Willis Eves, Pierre Casse, Francois Vinsonneau, Charles Gauthier, Abraham Millspaugh and Jacob Ehrhard) and "Francois Vinsonneau against the United States," no. 82, National Archives; *Official Records*, XXVI, pt. I, 355; Records of District and Parish Provost Marshals, Army of the Gulf, Old Book 1255-1257, Oaths of Allegiance, Record Group 393, National Archives; John C. Brightman Letters, correspondence June 1, 1863 in University of Texas Library Archives, Austin.
2. Ezra Warner, *Generals in Blue* (Baton Rouge, 1964), 278-79; *Official Records*, XXVI, pt. I, 340, 377-78, and pt. II, 390; Samuel Farrow Papers, correspondence October 28, 1863 and James M. Campbell Diary in University of Texas Library Archives, Austin; J. P. Blessington, *The Campaigns of Walker's Texas Division* (Austin, 1968), 135-36; Clement Evans (ed.), *Confederate Military History*, vol. XI (Texas) by O. M. Roberts (Atlanta, 1899), 27-37; Samuel Gordon Papers, correspondence November 19, 1863; and Madison Reece Collection, medical notes for October 1863 in Illinois State Historical Library, Springfield; Miss Mamie Yeary (compiler), *Reminiscences of the Boys in Gray 1861-1865* (Dallas, 1912), 626.
3. Gordon Papers, correspondence November 19, 1863; Reece Collection, medical notes,October 1863.
4. According to the *8th U. S. Census* for St. Landry Parish (1860) Auguste Donatte, f.m.c., owned 60 slaves and possessed property valued at $68,600. A. D. Meuillon's property was valued at $56,100 and Alphonse Meuillon's at $43,460, pp. 182-83, 226; U. S. Court of Claims, "Felix Auzenne vs.the United States," no. 14680, National Archives; U. S. Congress, *House Miscellaneous Document* 254, 52nd Congress, 1st Session (re. A. D. Meuillon), *House Miscellaneous Document III*, 53rd Congress, 2nd Session (re. Alphonse Meuillon) and *Senate Document* No. 27, 58th Congress, 2nd Session (re. Cornelius Donato); see also H. E. Sterkx, *The Free Negro in Ante-Bellum Louisiana* (Cranbury, N. J., 1972), 91-159, 297-305; Alexandre Barde, *Histoire des Comites de Vigilance aux Attakapas* (Saint-Jean Baptiste, 1861), 10, 16, 26, 337-38; *Opelousas Patriot*, August 6, 1859; *Opelousas Courier*, January 14, 1859, March 3, 1860 and September 8, 1860; George Reinecke (ed.), *Early Louisiana French Life and Folklore from the Anonymous Breaux Manuscript* (New Orleans, 1966), 29-37; Hartford, *Wisconsin Home League*, November 7 and 28, 1863; Henry Whipple, *The Diary of a Private Soldier* (Waterloo, Wisconsin, 1906), 30; Thomas B. Marshall Papers, diary November 25, 1863, Ohio Historical Society, Columbus; and *Milwaukee Sentinel*, November 13, 1863.
5. French and American Claims Commission, "Romain Dupre against the United States," no. 67 (depositions of Joseph Ward, Joseph Richard, and Charles Ranton); "Victoire Tessa Prevot against the United States," no. 172 (deposition of Jacques Thompson, Benjamin and Balhazar Bob, Jules Perrodin and Nicholas Joe) National Archives; James Hall, *Cayuga in the Field* (Auburn, 1873), 151-55.

6. *Official Records* XXVI, pt. 1, 341-42, 778 and XXXIV, Series 1, pt. II, 962-66, 976-77, 1025; Bell Irvin Wiley (ed.), *This Infernal War* (Austin), 419; John G. Pratt's report in *Official Report Relative to the Conduct of Federal Troops in Western Louisiana* (Shreveport, 1865), 26-27; Napier Bartlett, *Military Record of Louisiana* (Baton Rouge, 1964), 36; Succession record Hilaire Carriere 2773 and Ozeme Carriere in St. Landry Parish Courthouse, Opelousas; *The Era*, New Orleans, November 21, 1863; Gustave A. Breaux Diary, entries December 27, 1863, March 9, 1864 and May 29, 1864, Tulane University Library Archives, New Orleans; Jacqueline Voorhies, "The Jayhawker Massacre," *Attakapas Gazette*, XI (Spring 1976), 34-36; *Opelousas Courier*, November 5, 1865; and conversations with Edvin Matte of Lawtell, Louisiana.
7. *Official Records*, XXVI, pt. 1, 337, 776-77, 780; Beecher, *Record of the 114th Regiment N.Y.S.V.*, 264-65; C. Peter Ripley, *Slaves and Freedmen in Civil War Louisiana* (Baton Rouge, 1976), 25-39, 40-68; H.W. Howe, *Passages from the Life of Henry Warren Howe* (Lowell, Mass. 1899), 56; John M. Stanyon, *A History of the Eighth Regiment of New Hampshire Volunteers* (Concord, N. H., 1892), 337.
8. James Early Bradley Papers, diary entries October 26, 28 and November 2, 1863, and correspondence dated October 28, 1863 in L.S.U. Library Archives, Baton Rouge; French and American Claims Commission, "Theodore Valade against the United States," no. 214 (especially depositions of Collin George Adams and Adolphe and Sebastian Malveau, g.c.l.), National Archives; *8th U. S. Census* (1860) for St. Landry Parish; Service record Arthur W. Marsh, National Archives; deposition Collin Adams in U.S. Court of Claims "Henry Peychaud, Syndic of Bellocque, Noblom & Co. vs. the United States," no. 3497, National Archives.

CHAPTER THIRTEEN

YANKEE JUSTICE IN ST. LANDRY PARISH

1. Isaac Jackson Papers, correspondence October 26, 31, 1863, in William Clements Library, University of Michigan, Ann Arbor; Julius V. Wood Papers, correspondence October 27, 1863, Western Reserve Historical Society, Cleveland; *Official Records*, XXVI, pt. I, 776, 781.
2. Harry Watts Diary, 106-07, Augustus George Sinks Collection, 54, and James R. Slack Papers, correspondence October 31, 1863 in Indiana State Library Archives, Indianapolis; *A History of the Trials and Hardships of the Twenty-Fourth Indiana Volunteer Infantry* (Indianapolis, 1913), 91; T. B. Marshall Papers, diary entry October 29, 1863, Ohio Historical Society; Henry Whipple, *Diary of a Private Soldier* (Waterloo, 1906), 31; George Crooke, *The Twenty-First Regiment of Iowa Volunteer Infantry* (Milwaukee, 1891), 118.
3. Bleze Motte, who came to Louisiana from the Department of Haute Garonne, France, was sometimes farmer, sometimes storekeeper and always a peddler. He was never married but lived with a colored woman, Celeste Rideau, whom he had purchased at the successional sale of Joseph Lastrapes. She subsequently bore him six children. French and American Claims Commission "Bleze Motte against the United States," no. 131 (especially depositions of Celeste Rideau), "Theodore Valade against the United States," no. 214 (deposition of Esprit Bonnet), and "Jules Perrodin against the United States," no. 90 (especially depositions of the Malveaux family), National Archives.

4. Madison Reece Collection, medical notes for October 1863, and Samuel Gordon Papers, letter dated November 19, 1863, Illinois State Historical Society, Springfield; James Earl Bradley Papers, diary entry November 2, 1863, L.S.U. Library Archives; *A History of the Trials and Hardships of the Twenty-Fourth Indiana*, 91; Slack Papers, correspondence October 31, 1863; Whipple, *Diary of a Private Soldier;* Levi Hoag Diary, entry October 30, 1863; *History of the Second Battalion Duryee Zouaves* (New York), 1904), 22; Caroline Whitcomb, *History of the Second Massachusetts Battery of Light Artillery* (Concord, n.d.), 56; *Official Records*, XXVI, pt. 1, 378.
5. William Perrin, *Southwest Louisiana*, pt. 2, (Baton Rouge, 1971), 73; Bradley Papers, diary entry November 2, 1863; *Official Records*, XXVI, pt. II, 294-95.
6. Records of the Provost Marshal-General's Office, court-martial proceedings of Michael Fox, Record Group 110, and service record of Michael Fox in National Archives; John Stanyon, *A History of the Eighth Regiment of New Hampshire Volunteers* (Concord, 1892), 338-42; Charles Emerson Diary, entries October-November 1863, New Hampshire Historical Society, Concord; Records of the Adjutant-General's Office, Record Group 74, Regimental Returns of the 8th New Hampshire Regiment, National Archives.
7. *Ibid,;* Calvin P. Alling Reminiscenses, 12, State Historical Society of Wisconsin, Madison; William Titus Rigby Diary, entry October 31, 1863; Dana King, "In the Southwest," *Stories of our Soldiers* (Boston, 1893), 206-14.
8. In fairness to General Franklin it should be pointed out that he may have planned to commute the death sentence all along. In fact the original copy of the execution order contains a note to that effect: "The order was issued when today (October 30, 1863—the day before the execution) I learned what, of course, I ought to have known before, that the commander of an Army in the field has no legal power to carry out a death sentence. The whole matter is forwarded (to General Banks) with the recommendation that the sentence be carried out." My guess is that he planned to announce his decision before the assembled group. On the other hand he may have postdated the above comments in order to save himself from further embarrassment. Service record and court-martial proceedings Michael Fox; Stanyon, *A History of the Eighth Regiment of New Hampshire Volunteers*, 338-42; Regimental Returns of the 8th New Hampshire Regiment, Record Group 74, National Archives; Emerson Diary, October-November 1863 entries.
9. *Official Records*, XXVI, pt. 1, 341, 354, 779, and pt. II, 392; *New York Herald*, November 1, 16, 17, 23, 1863; Hall, *Cayuga in the Field*, 156-57; Harris Beecher, *Record of the 114th Regiment*, 267; Harry Watts Diary, 107, Sinks Collection, 54; Reuben B. Scott, *The History of the 67th Regiment Indiana Infantry Volunteers* (Bedford, Indiana, 1892), 50; Slack Papers, correspondence November 1, 1863; Gordon Papers, correspondence November 20, 1863; Marshall Papers, diary entry November 1, 1863; *An Historical Sketch of the 162nd Regiment N. Y. Vol. Infantry* (Albany, 1867), 22.
10. There was so much trouble in Opelousas following the Union occupation that the military authorities closed all coffeehouses while outlawing the sale of liquor to soldiers or civilians. *Opelousas Courier*, November 21, December 5 and December 26, 1863; see also Bradley Papers, diary entry November 2, 1863.

CHAPTER FOURTEEN

DOUBLE TRAGEDY ON BUZZARDS' PRAIRIE

1. William Titus Rigby Papers, diary entries October 28 and November 1, 1863, University of Iowa Library Archives, Iowa City; A. A. Rigby Diary, entry November 1, 1863, Iowa State Department of History and Archives, Des Moines; Service record of Charles Williams and Records of the Adjutant-general's office, Regimental Returns of the 24th Iowa Infantry, Record Group 94, National Archives; S. H. M. Byers, *Iowa in War Times* (Des Moines, 1888), section on 24th Iowa.
2. Jay K. Ditchy (ed.), *Early Louisiana French Life and Folklore from the Anonymous Breaux Manuscript* (New Orleans, 1966), 45-51; *Diarium Ministri , 1858-1882* , 60-65 and *Historia Domus , 1837-1942* , St. Charles College Archives, Grand Coteau.
3. The funeral records of the St. Landry Catholic Church in Opelousas, the Church of St. Charles in Grand Coteau, St. John's Cathedral in Lafayette and St. Martin of Tours Church in St. Martinville indicate that an inordinate number of civilian deaths occurred, especially among the elderly and very young, during and following the spring and fall campaigns of 1863; see also the work of Rev. Donald J. Hebert, Southwest Louisiana Records vol. 7, 1861-65 (Cecilia, 1976), which surveys the area more extensively.
4. James R. Slack Papers, correspondence dated November 1, 1863, Carrion Crow Bayou in Indiana State Library Archives, Indianapolis.
5. Harry Watts Diary, 107-08, Indiana State Library, Indianapolis; Hovey Manuscript, 78-79, Lilly Library, Indiana University, Bloomington.
6. The Confederate assassin was never identified by the Yankees. The writer discovered his identity in the Priscilla Bond Diary, 163, Louisiana State University Library Archives, Baton Rouge; see also Regimental Returns of the 2nd Louisiana Cavalry, November 1863, National Archives.
7. *Official Records* , XXVI, pt. I, 356; Levi Hoag Diary, entry November 2, 1863 in the Katherine Gue Leonard Collection, Iowa State Department of History and Archives, Des Moines; A. A. Rigby Diary, November 2, 1863 entry; William Titus Rigby Papers, diary November 2, 1863; Regimental Returns of the 24th Iowa for October-November 1863; Charles A. Lucas, "A Soldier's Letters from the Field," *Iowa Historical Record* , XVI, XVII and XVIII (1900-02), 221-222; Thomas H. Bringhurst, *History of the Forty-Sixth Regiment Indiana Volunteer Infantry* (n. p., 1888), 77; service record Jeremiah Gue in the National Archives.
8. Bringhurst, *History of the Forty-Sixth Regiment* , 77-78; August George Sinks Collection, 54, Indiana State Library, Indianapolis; Henry Whipple, *The Diary of a Private Soldier* (Waterloo, Wisconsin, 1906), 31; A. A. Rigby Diary, November 2 entry; and French and American Claims Commission, "Augustus Burleigh against the United States," no. 251, especially deposition of Joseph Boudreaux, National Archives.
9. William Titus Rigby Diary; A. A. Rigby Diary; Levi Hoag Diary; and John T. Simmons, *History of the 28th Iowa Volunteer Infantry* (Washington, 1865); service record Elias Skinner, National Archives.

CHAPTER FIFTEEN

DISASTER ON THE BOURBEUX

1. *Official Records*,XXVI, pt. 1, 354-57, 364; H. A. Fenney's dispatch in *Wisconsin State Journal*, November 25, 1863; James B. Hunter Diary, entry November 2, 1863, Indiana University, Bloomington; Lacon, *Illinois Gazette*, November 25, 1863; Augustus Sinks Collection, 54, Indiana State Library, Indianapolis; Thomas H. Bringhurst, *History of the Forty-Sixth Regiment Indiana Volunteer Infantry* (n.p., 1888), 77; Rueben B. Scott, *The History of the 67th Regiment Indiana, Infantry Volunteers* (Bedford, 1892), 50-51; Samuel Gordon Papers, correspondence November 17, 1863, Illinois State Historical Society, Springfield; Thomas B. Marshall Papers, diary entry November 2, 1863, Ohio Historical Society, Columbus; Isaac Jackson Papers, correspondence November 6, 1863. William Clements Library, University of Michigan, Ann Arbor; Caroline Whitcomb, *History of the Second Massachusetts Battery of Light Artillery* (Concord, 1912), 59; *Milwaukee Sentinel*, November 25, 28, 1863.
2. Charles A.Dana, *Recollections of the Civil War* (New York, 1898), 65; J. T. Woods, *Services of the Ninety-Sixth Ohio Volunteers* (Toledo, 1874), 41; Scott, *The History of the 67th Regiment, 50-51; Wisconsin State Journal*, November 25, 1863.
3. Regimental returns of the 1st Louisiana Cavalry (Union), National Archives; Woods, *Services of the Ninety-Sixth Ohio*, 39-40; H. W. Howe *Passages from the Life of Henry Warren Howe* (Lowell, Mass., 1899), 145-46; *Wisconsin State Journal*, November 25, 1863; Hartford, *Wisconsin Home League*, November 28, 1863.
4. Oran Roberts' Papers, University of Texas Archives, Austin.
5. *Milwaukee Sentinel*, November 28, 1863; *Wisconsin State Journal*, November 25, 1863; Hartford, *Wisconsin Home League*, November 28, 1863; Henry P. Whipple, *The Diary of a Private Soldier* (Waterloo, Wisconsin, 1906), 31; Robert Steele Letters, correspondence November 6, 1863, State Historical Society of Wisconsin, Madison; Ella Lonn, *Foreigners in the Union Army and Navy* (Baton Rouge, 1951), 91; Milo M. Quaife, *Wisconsin, Its History and Its People* (Chicago, 1924); Frederick Merk, *Economic History of Wisconsin During the Civil War Decade* (Madison, 1916); and Larry Gara, *A Short History of Wisconsin* (Madison, 1962).
6. Depositions of Sarah Burleigh Arnaud in French and American Claims Commission, "Augustus Burleigh against the United States," no. 251, National Archives; conversations with Mrs. Willis Courville, Sunset, Louisiana.
7. *Official Records* XXVI, pt. 1, 356-59; Bringhurst, *History of the Forty-Sixth Regiment*, 78; James R. Slack Papers, correspondence dated November 6, 1863 in Indiana State Library Archives, Indianapolis; Charles A. Lucas "A Soldier's Letters from the Field," *Iowa Historical Record*, XVI, XVII and XVIII (1900-02), 221-22.
8. George F. Reinecke (ed.), *Early Louisiana French Life and Folklore from the Anomymous Breaux Manuscript* (New Orleans, 1966), 38-44; marriage records in the St. Landry Catholic Church Archives, Opelousas.
9. Roberts' Papers, report dated November 6, 1863; J. P. Blessington, *The Campaigns of Walker's Texas Division* (Austin, 1968), 130; Houston *Tri-Weekly Telegraph*, November 16, 1863; G. L. Robertson Papers, University of Texas Archives, Austin.
10. Roberts' Papers, November 6, 1863 report; Blessington, *The Campaigns of Walker's Texas Division, 138-41; Houston Tri-Weekly Telegraph*, November 16, 1863; *Official Records*, XXVI, pt. 1, 393-95.
11. Hunter Papers, diary entry November 3, 1863.

12. Steele Letters, correspondence November 6, 1863; Major Brigdon quoted Burbridge as saying "and its a damn hot place," *Milwaukee Sentinel*, November 28, 1863; *Wisconsin State Journal*, November 25, 1863.
13. Houston *Tri-Weekly Telegraph*, November 20, 1863.
14. Theophilus Noel, *A Campaign from Santa Fe to the Mississippi* (Houston, 1961), 107-08; Richard B. Harwell (ed.), *Songs of the Confederacy*, (New York, 1951), 92-94.
15. Charles' brother, Alexandre, was a member of the 8th Louisiana Infantry at the time. Conversations with Lucius Lavergne; *8th U. S. Census* (1860), for St. Landry Parish; *New York Herald*, November 20, 1863; Andrew B. Booth, *Records of Louisiana Confederate Soldiers*, v. 3 (New Orleans, 1920), 675.
16. The 67th Indiana was also captured at Mumfordsville, Kentucky, September 17, 1862; Scott, *History of the 67th Regiment, 51-52; Official Records*, XXVI, pt. 1, 355-56, 360, 363-66; Proceedings of a Military Board in the case of Theodore E. Buehler, and service Record of Theodore E. Buehler, National Archives; David C. Edmonds, "Surrender on the Bourbeux, Honorable Defeat or Incompetency under Fire," *Louisiana History* XVIII (Winter 1977), 63-86; *Chicago Tribune*, November 23, 1863; Lacon *Illinois Gazette*, November 25, 1863.
17. Woods, *Services of the 96th Ohio Volunteers*, 43-44; Scott, *The History of the 67th Regiment*, 51-52; "List of Killed, Wounded or Missing, 4th Division 13th Army Corps in the Battle of Grand Coteau, Louisiana, November 3, 1863," Records of the Adjutant-General's Office, 1780's-1917, National Archives.
18. Houston *Tri-Weekly Telegraph*, November 16, 20, 1863; Blessington, *The Campaigns of Walker's Texas Division*, 138-45; Roberts' Papers, report of November 6, 1863; Miss Mamie Yeary (compiler), *Reminiscences of the Boys in Gray 1861-1865*, (Dallas, 1912), 304.
19. *Wisconsin State Journal* November 21, 25, 1863; Hartford, *Wisconsin Home League*, November 28 and December 5, 1863; *Milwaukee Sentinel*, November 25, 1863; *Illinois Gazette*, November 11, 1863; *Official Records*, XXVI, pt. 1, 363-66; Steele Letters, correspondence dated November 6, 1863. Alonzo Gilbert Jack Correspondence, State Historical Society of Wisconsin, Madison.
20. Records of the Adjutant-General's Office, "List of Killed, Wounded or Missing in the 60th Indiana Infantry," National Archives; *Indianapolis Daily Journal*, December 1, 1863.
21. Woods, *Services of the Ninety-Sixth Ohio*, 46; Robert Bartlett, *Roster of the Ninety-Sixth Regiment, Ohio Volunteer Infantry* (Columbus, 1895); Julius V. Wood Papers, correspondence dated November 15, 19, 1863, Western Reserve Historical Society, Cleveland.
22. *Wisconsin State Journal*, November 25, 1863; Frank Moore (ed.), *The Rebellion Record*, vol. 8, (New York, 1865), 151-53; Woods, *Services of the Ninety-Sixth Ohio*, 43-44.
23. Charles Farrell's dispatch, *New York Herald*, November 20 1863; *Official Records*, series II, vol. VI, 698, 737; John G. Pratt's Report in *Official Report Relative to the Conduct of Federal Troops in Western Louisiana* (Shreveport, 1865), 34.
24. Jacksons' Papers, correspondence dated November 6, 1863. Jackson's experiences are also published in Joseph Jackson (ed.), *Some of the Boys* (Carbondale, Illinois), 144-48; Marshall Papers, diary entry November 3, 1863; Thomas B. Marshall, *History of the Eighty-Third Ohio Volunteer Infantry* (Cincinnati, 1912), 112-15; *Cincinnati Enquirer*, November 22, 1863; C. W. Gerard, *A Diary of the Eighty-Third Ohio Vol. Inf.* (n.p., n.d.), 56.
25. Woods, *Sevices of the Ninety-Sixth Ohio*, 47; Bartlett, *Roster of the Ninety-Sixth Regiment*, 173-79; Service record Albert H. Brown, National Archives.
26. *Illinois Gazette*, November 11, 1863; *Wisconsin State Journal*, November 25, 1863; *New York Herald*, November 20, 1863; *Cincinnati Enquirer*, November 22, 1863;

A History of the Trials and Hardships of the Twenty-Fourth Indiana Volunteer Infantry (Indianapolis, 1913), 92; Gordon Papers, correspondence dated November 19, 1863.

27. Woods, *Services of the Ninety-Sixth Ohio*, 45-46; *Illinois Gazette*, November 11, 1863; *Chicago Tribune*, November 23, 1863.
28. John Griffin Jones Papers, correspondence dated November 6, 1863, Manuscript Division of the Library of Congress, Washington, D. C.; Service Record John Griffin Jones, National Archives.
29. *Official Records*, XXVI, pt. 1, 358, 361, 371; Service Record William Marland, National Archives; Whitcomb, *History of the Second Massachusetts*, 57-59; *New York Herald*, November 20, 1863.
30. Sarah Burleigh Arnaud deposition in "Augustus Burleigh against the United States," conversations with Mrs. Willis Courville, Sunset, Louisiana.
31. Harry Watts Diary, 109-10, Indiana State Library, Indianapolis; Hovey Manuscript, 80, Lilly Library, Indiana University, Bloomington.
32. *Wisconsin State Journal*, November 25, 1863; *Milwaukee Sentinel*, November 28, 1863; Moore, *The Rebellion Record*, vol. 8, 151-53; Bringhurst, *History of the Forty-Sixth Regiment*, 78-79; *A History of the Trials and Hardships of the Twenty-Fourth Indiana*, 92-93; Slack Papers, correspondence of November 6, 1863; Jackson Papers, correspondence of November 6, 1863, *Illinois Gazette*, November 11, 1863; John A. Bering and Thomas Montgomery, *History of the Forty-Eighth Ohio Veteran Volunteer Infantry*, (Hillsboro, Ohio, 1880), 110; Whipple, *The Diary of a Private Soldier*, 31; Sinks' Collection, 54.
33. Houston *Tri-Weekly Telegraph*, November 20, 1863; *A History of the Trials and Hardships of the Twenty-Fourth Indiana*, 93.
34. Depositions of William Burleigh and Sarah Burleigh Arnaud in "Augustus Burleigh against the United States;" conversations with Mrs. Willis Courville, Sunset, Louisiana; Charles Spurlin (ed.), *West of the Mississippi with Waller's Battalion* (Hillsboro, Texas, 1971), Appendix IV.
35. Birth records in the Church of St. Charles Archives, Grand Coteau, Louisiana.
36. *Official Records*, XXVI, pt. 1, 358; William Titus Rigby Papers, diary entry November 3, 1863, University of Iowa Libraries, Iowa City; A. A. Rigby Diary, entry November 3, 1863; and Levi Hoag Diary, entry November 3, 1863 in the Katherine Gue Leonard Collection, Iowa State Department of History and Archives, Des Moines; Thomas J. Williams, *An Historical Sketch of the 56th Ohio Volunteer Infanry* (n.p., n.d.), 59-62; Sylvester C. Bishop Letters, correspondence dated November 6, 1863, Indiana Society Library, Indianapolis.
37. Blessington, *The Campaign's of Walker's Texas Division*, 143; Houston *Tri-Weekly Telegraph*, November 16, 1863; Roberts' Papers, report dated November 6, 1863; Regimental returns of the 1st Louisiana Cavalry (Union), National Archives; Letters of Stephen G. Burbridge (June 12, 1866) and William Franklin (May 14, 1866), in Harai Robinson Papers, Department of Archives and Manuscripts, Louisiana State University, Baton Rouge; Yeary, *Reminiscences of the Boys in Gray*, 304.
38. Gordon Papers, correspondence November 19, 1863; *Official Records*, XXVI, pt. 1, 359-61.
39. Hartford, *Wisconsin Home League*, November 28, 1863.
40. *Official Records*, XXVI, pt. 1, 394.

CHAPTER SIXTEEN

HOSPITALS AND PRISON CAMPS

1. James R. Slack Papers, correspondence dated November 6, 1863, Indiana State Library Archives, Indianapolis; *Cincinnati Enquirer*, November 22, 1863; J. T. Woods, *Services of the 96th Ohio Volunteers* (Toledo, 1874), 48; Thomas B Marshall Papers, diary entry November 3, 1863, Ohio Historical Society, Columbus.
2. *Official Records*, XXVI, pt. I, 359-59; Records of the Adjutant General's Office, 1780-1917, "List of Killed, Wounded and Missing in the Battle of Grand Coteau, La.," National Archives; Indianapolis *Daily Journal*, December 1, 1863.
3. John Griffin Jones Papers, correspondence dated November 6, 12, 21, 1863, Library of Congress.
4. *New York Herald*, November 20 1863; Lacon *Illinois Gazette*, November 26, 1863; Houston *Tri-Weekly Telegraph*, November 16 and 20, 1863; J. P. Blessington, *The Campaigns of Walker's Texas Division* (Austin, 1968), 145; *Official Records*, XXVI, pt. I, 394-95; conversations with Lucius Lavergne (Urbaine Lavergne's grandson) Sunset, Louisiana, and Henry Kempt and Seth Lewis, Opelousas, Louisiana.
5. Woods, *Services of the 96th Ohio*, 48; Deposition of Marella Chevis (a servant at Chretien Point) in U. S. Court of Claims, "Hypolite Chretien vs. the United States," no. 9572, National Archives.
6. Frank McGregor Papers, correspondence November 6 and 12, 1863, Military History Institute, Carlisle Barracks, Pennsylvania. Most of McGregor's letters have been edited and published by Carl E. Hatch, *Dearest Susie, A Civil War Infantryman's Letters to his Sweetheart* (New York, 1971), 77-81. McGregor's letters are also available at the York County Historical Society (Pennsylvania) and the Ohio Historical Society, Columbus.
7. "Diary of an Unidentified Surgeon of the 60th Indiana" (actually James B. Hunter) entries November 3, 5, 1863, Lilly Library, Indiana University, Bloomington; Service record James B. Hunter, National Archives; Depositions of Constance and Thelismar Guidry, Augustin Domingue, Achille Babineaux and Victoria Green in French and American Claims Commission, "Jules Perrodin against the United States," no. 90, National Archives; Conversations with Marie Sibille and Lucille Sibille Landry, Cankton, Louisiana. Julius V. Wood Papers, correspondence October-December, 1863 in Western Reserve Historical Society, Cleveland, Ohio; "List of Killed, Wounded and Missing in the Battle of Grand Coteau, La."; H. W. Howe, *Passages from the Life of Henry Warren Howe* (Lowell, Mass., 1899), 145-46; George Worthington Adams, *Doctors in Blue* (New York, 1952), 66-68, 112-20.
8. Dr. John M. Bronough Papers, medical notes for November 1863 in the Texas Collection, Baylor University, Waco, Texas; Blessington, *The Campaigns of Walker's Texas Division*, 145; Theophilus Noel, *A Campaign from Santa Fe to the Mississippi* (Houston, 1961), 103-06; Houston *Tri-Weekly Telegraph*, November 20, 1863; John Q. Anderson (ed.), *A Texas Surgeon in the C.S.A.* (Tuscaloosa, 1957), preface; *Official Records*, XXVI, pt. I, 374-75, 394-95; conversations with Robert Daly, Opelousas, Louisiana; Adams, *Doctors in Blue*, 129; James Earl Bradley Papers, diary entry November 4, 6, 1863 in Louisiana State University Library Archives, Baton Rouge; Miss Mamie Yeary (compiler), *Reminiscences of the Boys in Gray* (Dallas, 1912), 613.
9. Harris H. Beecher, *Record of the 114th Regiment, N.Y.S.V.* (Norwich, N.Y., 1886), 267-68; *An Historical Sketch of the 162nd Regiment, N. Y., Vol. Infantry (Albany,*

1867), 22; *History of the Second Battalion, Duryee Zouaves* (New York, 1904), 23; William E. Jones, *The Military History of the One Hundred & Sixty-First New York Volunteers, Infantry* (Bath, N. Y,. n. d.), 17.

10. *Official Records*, XXVI, pt. I, 344, 374; "Diary of an Unidentified Surgeon," entry November 4, 1863.
11. Beecher, *Record of the 114th Regiment*, 68; Orton Clark, *The 116th Regiment of New York Volunteers* (Buffalo, 1868), 133-34; A. A. Rigby Diary, entry November 4, 1863 in Iowa State Department of History and Archives, Des Moines; Hartford, *Wisconsin Home League*, December 5, 1863.
12. Robert Steele Letters, correspondence dated November 20, 1863, State Historical Society of Wisconsin, Madison; Robert S. Weddle (ed.), *Plow-Horse Cavalry* (Austin, 1974), 95.
13. Reuben B. Scott, *The History of the 67th Regiment Indiana Infantry Volunteers* (Bedford, Indiana, 1892), 53-55; Richard Taylor, *Destruction and Reconstruction* (New York, 1879), 108; Bradley Papers, diary entries November 4 and 6, 1863; *Official Records* XXVI, pt. I, 375; W. R. Howell Papers, diary entry November 6, 1863, University of Texas Library Archives, Austin; Samuel Farrow Papers, correspondence dated November 14, 1863, University of Texas Library Archives, Austin.
14. Oran M. Roberts Papers, University of Texas Library Archives, Austin.
15. Deposition of Constance Guidry in "Jules Perrodin against the United States"; George N. Carpenter, *History of the Eighth Regiment Vermont Volunteers* (Boston, 1886), 260, 266.
16. "Diary of an Unidentified Surgeon," entry November 5, 1863; depositions of Constance Guidry in "Jules Perrodin against the United States."
17. Depositions of Celestine Cantrelle Chretien in U. S. Court of Claims, "Hypolite Chretien vs. the United States," no. 9572, "Felicite Neda Chretien vs. the United States," no. 14812, and "Athenais Chretien Le More vs. the United States," no. 11253, National Archives; Blessington, *The Campaigns of Walker's Texas Division*, 145; Julius Giesecke Papers, diary entry November 4, 5, 1863 in University of Texas Library Archives, Austin; and conversations with Mrs. Alcues Leger, Sunset, Louisiana.
18. Depositions of William, James and Augustus Burleigh, Sarah Burleigh Arnaud and Joseph Boudreaux in French and American Claims Commission, "Augustus Burleigh against the United States," no. 251, National Archives.

CHAPTER SEVENTEEN

RECRIMINATIONS AND RETREAT

1. Sylvester C. Bishop Letters, correspondence dated November 6, 1863, Indiana Historical Society, Indianapolis; Harry Watts Diary, 110-111, Indiana State Library, Indianapolis; T. B. Marshall Diary, entry November 5-6, 1863, Ohio Historical Society, Columbus.
2. John A. Bering, *History of the Forty-Eighth Ohio Vet. Vol. Inf.* (Hillsboro, Ohio, 1880), 111.
3. French and American Claims Commission, "Benoit Cazaudebat against the United States," no. 712, and "Andrea Ynojosa against the United States", no. 641 (depositions of Joseph and Alfred Godard, Clarisse Prince, Pierre Bemelle, Andrea Brown, Evariste Guidroz, Charles Clerc, Edward Foreman, R. L.

McBride and Jean B. Clement) National Archives; conversations with Dean Thomas J. Arceneaux, Carencro, Louisiana.

4. French and American Claims Commission, "Caroline Joseph against the United States," no. 709 (depositions of Jacob Bloch, Abraham Hass and Gottchalk Fietel, National Archives.
5. *Chicago Tribune*, November 23, 1863; Lacon *Illinois Gazette*, November 11, 1863; Hartford, Wisconsin *Home League* November 28 and December 5, 1863; Milwaukee *Daily Sentinel*, November 28, 1863; Alexandria *Louisiana Democrat*, November 11, 1863, Houston *Tri-Weekly Telegraph*, November 11, 1863; *Opelousas Courier*, November, 1863; *Shreveport News*, November 24, 1863; *New York Herald*, November 20, 1863; *Cincinnati Enquirer*, November 22, 1863; Isaac Jackson Papers, correspondence of November 6, 1863 in the University of Michigan Library Archives, Ann Arbor; Priscilla Bond Diary, L.S.U. Archives, Baton Rouge.
6. *Official Records*, XXVI, pt. 1, 354, 358, 360-1; service record and transcript of "Hearings in the Case of Theodore Buehler," National Archives; David C. Edmonds, "Surrender on the Bourbeux, Honorable Defeat or Incompetency under Fire," *Louisiana History* XVIII (Winter, 1977), 63-86.
7. There was also a standing joke on Broussard, related as the "gospel truth" in oral tradition. Broussard, it seems, had received a note from Hypolite Chretien, neither of whom knew the other, requesting a meeting at some exclusive coffee house in Opelousas. The wealthy Chretien, his resources exhausted by the spring occupation of St. Landry Parish, needed a short-term loan to tide him over to the spring planting. Chretien arrived at the rendevous point dressed in his finest gentlemens' attire. Helped out of his vehicle by a servant, the paralyzed Chretien called upon several men standing nearby. "Here," he asked, "who will watch my horse and buggy for a quarter?" A grimy bystander, unshorn and dressed in rags, immediately acceded to this generous offer. Chretien then entered the club and began looking inquisitively for Broussard among the well-groomed guests, but could not find him. Just as he was about to leave, thinking he had been stood up by the money-lender, he was approached by the proprietor. "Monsieur," said he, "that gentleman holding your horse is Zenon Broussard."
8. Depositions of Thomas Bringhurst, James Watts, Francois Abadie and Antoine Guchereau in French and American Claims Commission, "Francois Abadie against the United States," no. 507; Thomas Bringhurst and Frank Swigart, *History of the Forty-Sixth Regiment Indiana Volunteer Infantry* (1888), 79-81; Augustus George Sinks Collection, 54-55, Indiana State Library, Indianapolis; *Official Records*, XXVI, pt. 1, 353; conversations with Miss Alida Mouton and Mrs. Fernand Gouaux, Lafayette, Louisiana.
9. Hunter and the wounded spent one night quartered in the Planters' Hotel in New Iberia. The following day they caught the steamer *Red Chief* at Olivier's Landing for the trip down the Teche. From Brashear they were transported via boxcar to the University Hospital in New Orleans. James B. Hunter Diary, Indiana University Library, Bloomington; *Official Records*, XXVI, pt. 1, 787.
10. Depositions of Benjamin George and Samuel Schmulen in French and American Claims Commission, "Samuel Schmulen against the United States," no. 371 National Archives.
11. *Official Records* , XXVI, pt. 1, 346, 379; Bringhurst, *History of the Forty-Sixth Regiment* , 81; Levi Hoag Diary, entry November 8, 1863, Iowa State Department of History and Archives, Des Moines; William T. Rigby Papers, diary entry November 8, 1863, University of Iowa Library, Iowa City.
12. *Official Records* , XXVI, Pt. II, 394-95.
13. French and American Claims Commission, "Jean Vigneaud against the United States," no. 116 (depositions of Isaac Butcher, Jean B. Broussard, A. M. Martin,

Leland Rigues, Auguste Monnier and Jean Gerac) and "Antoine Lacoste against the United States," no. 232 (depositions of Jeanne Salvant, William Caldwell, Alfred Chargois and Eliza Glaude), National Archives; *Official Records* , XXVI, pt. I, 345, and Series II, vol. VI, 710.

14. Harris Beecher, *Record of the 114th Regiment, N.Y.S.V.* (Norwich, N.Y., 1866), 270-71; Elias Pellet, *History of the 114th Regiment, New York State Volunteers* (Norwich, N.Y., 1866), 155-56; portrait and undated newspaper clipping in the possession of the Lafayette History Museum (formerly Governor Mouton's townhouse) Lafayette, Louisiana; conversations with Miss Eva Mouton, Franklin Mouton and Paola Palfrey, Lafayette, Louisiana.
15. "Antoine Lacoste against the United States," no. 232; J. W. Merwin, *Roster and Monograph, 161st Reg't, N.Y.S. Volunteer Infantry* (n,p., n.d.), 119-20.
16. A. A. Rigby Diary, entry November 10, 1863, Iowa State Department of History and Archives, Des Moines; Harry Watts Diary, 111-12; Hovey Manuscript, 81-82, Indiana University Library, Bloomington; French and American Claims Commission, "Victor Ruotte against the United States," no. 307, National Archives.
17. New Orleans *Era*, November 12, 1863; Reuben Scott, *The History of the 67th Regiment, Indiana Infantry Volunteers* (Bedford, Indiana, 1892), 58-59.
18. *Official Records* , XXVI, Pt. I, 346; Harry Watts Diary, 112-13; Hovey Manuscript, 82-83.
19. Arthur Marsh service record, National Archives; *Official Records* , XXVI, pt. 1, 344-45, 368, 373; Madison Reece Collection, medical notes for November 1863, and Samuel Gordon Papers, correspondence November 19, 1863 in the Illinois State Historical Library, Springfield; *Report of the Adjutant General of the State of Illinois* , vol. VI, "History of one Hundred and Eighteenth Infantry," (Springfield, 1900), 316-17; Samuel H. Fletcher, *The History of Company A, Second Illinois Cavalry* (1912), 122-25; Henry Whipple, *The Diary of a Private Soldier* (Waterloo, Wisconsin, 1906), 32; Joseph L. Brent Collection, correspondence November 12, 1863, Tulane University Archives, New Orleans; Houston *Tri-Weekly Telegraph* , November 25, 1863; Julius Giesecke Papers, diary entry November 11, 1863; W. R. Howell Papers, diary entry November 11, 1863, and foreword of James M. Campbell Diary in University of Texas Library Archives, Austin; Merwin, *Roster and Monograph* , 119; *History of the Second Battalion Duryee Zouaves* (New York, 1904), 23; *An Historical Sketch of the 162nd Regiment N.Y. Vol. Infantry* (Albany, 1867), 23; Orton Clark, *The 116th Regiment of New York Volunteers* (Buffalo, 1868), 134; Caroline Whitcomb, *History of the Second Massachusetts Battery* (Concord, N.H.), 59-60; H. W. Howe, *Passages from the Life of Henry Warren Howe* (Lowell, Mass., 1899), 56.
20. "Andrea Ynojosa against the United States," no. 641; conversations with Mrs. Fernand Gouaux, Lafayette, Louisiana. Mrs. Gouaux is a descendant of Oswald Patte.
21. William T. Rigby Diary, entry November 11, 1863.
22. Regimental returns of the 3rd Engineer Regiment, month of November, National Archives; Beecher, *Record of the 114th Regiment* , 270; Clark, *The 116th Regiment of New York Volunteers* , 134; A. A. Rigby Diary, entry November 13, 1863; Levi Hoag Diary, entry November 12, 1863; William T. Rigby Papers, correspondence November 13, 1863 and diary entry November 13-14, 1863; *Official Records* , XXVI, pt. I, 346, 799; *A History of the Trials and Hardships of the Twenty-Fourth Indiana Volunteer Infantry* (Indianapolis, 1913), 94.
23. Madison Reece Collection, notes for November 1863; Samuel Gordon Papers, correspondence November 19, 1863; Levi Hoag Diary, November 12, 1863.
24. John M. Stanyon, *A History of the Eighth Regiment of New Hampshire Volunteers* (Concord, H. H., 1892), 341-42; service record of Michael Fox, National Archives.

25. Recalling the incident many years later Mouton wrote: "I am frank to say, I am a Catholic and have never confessed this to any priest. It surely must not have bothered me, and I am willing to vouch for Caesar likewise." Alexandre Mouton Memoirs in the Lucille Meredith Mouton Griffin papers, University of Southwestern Louisiana Library Archives, Lafayette.

CHAPTER EIGHTEEN

BACK TO THE ATTAKAPAS

1. The 3rd Cavalry Brigade, organized November 7, 1863 and commanded by Colonel Charles Paine, was made up of the 15th Illinois Cavalry (Company F), 4th Indiana Cavalry (Company C), 2nd Louisiana (Mounted) Infantry, 6th Missouri Cavalry and the 14th New York Cavalry. *Official Records* , XXVI, pt. 1, 376; the other infantry brigade commanded by Burbridge was the 2nd Brigade, 4th Division which moved from Franklin to New Iberia November 11,1863. John Bering, *History of the Forty-Eighth Ohio Vet. Vol. Inf.* (Hillsboro, Ohio, 1880), 110; William H. Bentley, *History of the 77th Illinois Volunteer Infantry* (Peoria, 1883), 214.
2. John Pratt's report in *Official Report Relative to the Conduct of Federal Troops in Western Louisiana* (Shreveport, 1865), 30, 35-36; "Glimpses of Iberia in the Civil War," 9-10 in Weeks Family Papers, University of Southwestern Louisiana Archives, Lafayette (also edited and annotated by Vaughn Baker under the same title in *Attakapas Gazette* , VI, no. 3, 73-94); the two ladies were identified by Maurine Bergerie, *They Tasted Bayou Water* (New Orleans, 1962), 21, as Elizabeth Devalcourt and Liza Robertson.
3. *Ibid* ., Mrs. Moore died December 29, 1863, one week before Union forces evacuated New Iberia. She was the widow of David Weeks, builder and original owner of Shadows on the Teche, whom she married in 1818. She married Judge John Moore in 1841.
4. *Official Records*, XXVI, pt. 1, 362-63.
5. *Ibid* ., 362; Among the local speculators and middlemen were Jean Pierre Gueydan of Abbeville, Dr. Augustus Shaw of Loreauville, Ester, Mathias and Michael Levy of New Iberia, Zenon Broussard of Carencro and David Roos and Joseph Bloch of Opelousas. French and American Claims Commission, "Joseph Chourreau against the United States," case no. 43, "Annie Louise Flory against the United States," no. 604, "Jean Pierre Gueydan against the United States," no. 226, National Archives; *Cincinnati Gazette* letter published in the *Milwaukee Sentinel* , December 8, 1863.
6. *Cincinnati Gazette* and *Milwaukee Sentinel*, December 8, 1863; Records of the Adjutant-General's Office, Returns of the 25th Regiment (Union) *Corps d'Afrique*, National Archives; Thomas B. Marshall Papers, diary entry November 10, 1863, Ohio Historical Society, Columbus; Bering, *History of the Forty-Eighth Ohio*, 110; J. T. Woods, *Services of the 96th Ohio Volunteers* (Toledo, Ohio, 1874), 49; T. B. Marshall, *History of the 83rd Ohio Volunteer Infantry* (Cincinnati, 1912), 115; Frank McGregor Papers, correspondence dated New Iberia, November 12, 1863 in Carlisle Barracks; Isaac Jackson Papers, correspondence dated November 11, New Iberia, University of Michigan Library Archives, Ann Arbor; Samuel Gordon Papers, correspondence of November 20, 1863, Illinois State Historical Library, Springfield; George Peva Diary, entry November 9,1863, Indiana Historical Society Library, Indianapolis; Hartford, Wisconsin *Home*

League, December 19, 1863; Conversations with Dr. George Broussard, New Iberia, Louisiana.

7. *Official Records*, XXVI, pt. 1, 362, 801; Depositions of St. Leon Duperier and others in "Joseph Chourreau against the United States," no. 43 and "Ester Levy against the United States," no. 579, National Archives; Clement Evans (ed.), *Confederate Military History*, vol. X (Atlanta, 1899), 322; Lawrence Van Alstyne, *Diary of an Enlisted Man*, (New Haven, 1910), 225-27; James Hall, *Cayuga in the Field, A Record of the 75th N. Y. Volunteers* (Auburn, 1873), 159.
8. French and American Claims Commission, "Jean Pierre Gueydan against the United States," no. 226 (depositions of Laurent Bazus, L. M. Bernard and Jean Abadie) and "August Olle against the United States," no. 582 and 644, National Archives; *Official Records*, XXVI, pt. I, 362-63,799; Priscilla Bond Diary, entries October 7 and 18, 1863.
9. Depositions of St. Leon Duperier, Martin Voorhies, J. R. Ducros and others in "Chourreau against the United States" and "Levy against the United States"; *Official Records*, XXVI, pt. 1, 362.
10. Mixed British and American Claims Commission, "Martha A. Rayne vs. the United States," case no. 74, National Archives; Pratt, *Federal Troops in Western Louisiana*, 27-28; William Henry Perrin, *Southwest Louisiana Biographical and Historical* (Baton Rouge, 1971 reprint), 71; *Official Records* XXVI, pt. 1, 382, 765, 773; J. F. Moors, *History of the Fifty-Second Regiment Massachusetts Volunteers* (Boston, 1893), 158; Deposition of Albert Voorhies in U. S. Court of Claims, "Celestine Chretien vs. the United States," no. 14812, National Archives.
11. The horses were purchased by Father Jan from Pierre Delacroix and trained by his stable keeper, Monroe Baker.
12. French and American Claims Commission, "Ange-Marie Jan against the United States," no. 543 (depositions of Alfred Hitter, Thomas Walker, Edgar Woodley, Monroe Baker and Jean B. Comeaux) and "Annie Louise Flory against the United States," no. 604 (depositions of Dr. Augustus Shaw, Louis Bernard, Evariste Broussard, Leonard Ranconnet, Martin Voorhies and St. Leon Duperier), National Archives; Harris Beecher, *Record of the 114th Regiment NYSV* (Norwich, 1866), 162; Pratt, *Federal Troops in Western Louisiana, 28; Official Records*, XXVI, pt. 1, 363; Alexandre Barde, *Histoire des Comites de Vigilance aux Attakapas*, St. Jean Baptiste, 1861.
13. U. S. Court of Claims, "Francis Mestayer vs. the United States" no. 21144, National Archives; French and American Claims Commission, "Chourreau against the United States," no. 43, "Levy against the United States," no. 579 and "Flory against the United States," no. 604; Pratt, *Federal Troops in Western Louisiana*, 23-24.
14. Priscilla Bond Diary, entries November 15-22, 1863. L.S.U. Archives, Baton Rouge.
15. *Official Records*, XXVI, pt. 1, 346, 799; *Milwaukee Sentinel*, December 8, 1863; *New York Herald*, December 6, 1863.
16. William E. Jones, *The Military History of the One Hundred & Sixty-First New York Volunteers* (Bath, N.Y., 1865), 17; Caroline Whitcomb, *History of the Second Massachusetts Battery of Light Artillery* (Concord, N.H., 1912), 60; *New York Herald*, December 6, 1863; H. W. Howe, *Passages from the Life of Henry Warren Howe* (Lowell, Mass., 1899), 57.
17. In the University of Texas Library Archives the Julius Giesecke Papers, diary entry November 16, 1863, W.R. Howell Papers, diary entry November 16, 1863, and John R. Cox correspondence dated Camp Carn Crow (sic), November 21, 1863 in the William Oden Papers; Gustave Breaux Diaries, entry November 23, 1863, Tulane University Library Archives, New Orleans; Theophilus Noel, *A Cam-*

paign from Santa Fe to the Mississippi (Houston, 1961 reprint), 108; Edwin Bearrs (ed.), *A Louisiana Confederate; Diary of Felix Pierre Poche* (Natchitoches, 1972), 85.

18. Rufus Dawes Papers, notes dated November 17, 1863, Military History Institute, Carlisle Barracks; Cyrus Stockwell Papers, diary entry November 17, 1863 in the Western Reserve Historical Society, Cleveland, Ohio; Charles A. Lucas, "A Soldier's Letters from the Field," *Iowa Historical Record*, vols. XVI, XVII and XVIII, p. 225; William Titus Rigby Papers, diary entry November 17, 1863, University of Iowa Libraries, Iowa City; A. A. Rigby Diary, November 17, 1863 and Levi Hoag Diary, November 17, 1863, Iowa State Department of History and Archives, Des Moines; James R. Slack Papers, correspondence dated New Iberia, November 17, 1863 and Harry Watts Diary, 113, in the Indiana State Library Archives, Indianapolis; George Peva Diary, entry November 17, 1863, Indiana Historical Society Library, Indianapolis; Thomas Bringhurst, *History of the Forty-Sixth Regiment, Indiana Volunteer Infantry* (n.p., 1888), 81.
19. John M. Stanyon, *A History of the Eighth Regiment of New Hampshire Volunteers* (Concord, N.H., 1892), 340-41; Charles Emerson Diary, entry November 17, 1863, New Hampshire Historical Society, Concord; Michael Fox service record and court-martial proceedings, National Archives.
20. Thomas J. Williams, *An Historical Sketch of the 56th Ohio Volunteer Infantry* (n.p., n. d.), 17, 62; George Wilhelm service record, National Archives; French and American Claims Commission, "Jules Poirson against the United States," no. 476.
21. Gordon Correspondence, November 20, 1863; Sylvester Bishop Letters, correspondence of November 25, 1863, Indiana Historical Society Library, Indianapolis; Augustus George Sinks Collection, 57, Indiana State Library Archives, Indianapolis; Bentley, *History of the 77th Illinois*, 214; George Carpenter, *History of the Eighth Regiment Vermont Volunteers* (Boston, 1886), 142-43; Among those filing lengthy claims in the French and American Claims Commission not already noted were Bernard Laplene (case no. 245) Hypolite Patout and Appoline Fournier (no. 239) Jean Cazes (no. 58) Raymond Deffez (no. 113) Eugene Vidale and Jean Pierre Senac (no. 645) and Jacques Foucade (no. 418), National Archives.

CHAPTER 19

SKIRMISHES IN EVANGELINE COUNTRY

1. *Official Records*, XXVI, pt. 1, 810.
2. *Ibid.* 346-47, 369; Richard Taylor, *Destruction and Reconstruction*, (New York, 1879), 150-51; Samuel Gordon Papers, correspondence, November 11, 1863, and Madison Reece Collection, medical notes for November in Illinois State Historical Library, Springfield; Harry Watts Diary, 113, and Augustus George Sinks Collection, 57, in the Indiana State Library, Indianapolis; *A History of the Trials and Hardships of the Twenty-Fourth Indiana Volunteer Infantry* (Indianapolis, 1913), 94-95; Thomas Bringhurst, *History of the Forty-Sixth Regiment* (n.p., 1888), 81-82; Indianapolis *Daily Journal*, December 9, 1863; James Stevenson, *History of the Sixteenth Indiana Mounted Infantry* (New Orleans, 1864), preface; William Titus Rigby Diary, entry November 20, 1863 in University of Iowa Libraries, Iowa City; A. A. Rigby Diary, November 20, 1863 and Levi Hoag Diary, November 20, 1863, in Iowa State Department of History and

Archives, Des Moines; Charles Lucas, "A Soldier's Letters from the Field," *Iowa Historical Record,* XVI, XVII, and XVIII, 225; John Griffin Jones Papers, correspondence November 2, 1863, Library of Congress; Robert Steel Papers, correspondence November 20, 1863, State Historical Society of Wisconsin, Madison; Henry Whipple, *The Diary of a Private Soldier* (Waterloo,1906), 32-33; *New York Herald,* November 29 and December 6, 1863; James Hall, *Cayuga in the Field,* (Auburn, 1873), 159; Caroline Whitcomb, *History of the Second Massachusetts Battery* (Concord, N.H.), 60; William Oden Papers, correspondence November 21, 1863, W.R. Howell Diary, November 20, 1863 and Julius Giesecke Diary, November 20, 1863 in the University of Texas Library Archives, Austin; Frank McGregor Papers, correspondence November 24, 1863, Carlisle Barracks; Mamie Yeary (compiler), *Reminiscences of the Boys in Gray* (Dallas, 1912), 360, 667.

3. John Pratt, *Official Report Relative to the Conduct of Federal Troops in Western Louisiana* (Shreveport, 1865), 38; Sinks Collection, 57.
4. Theophilus Noel, *A Compaign from Santa Fe to the Mississippi* (Houston, 1961 reprint), 109; William Oden Papers, letter of John R. Cox, November 21, 1863.
5. Service records of Richard Owen and James Slack, National Archives; James Slack Papers, correspondence November 17, 1863, Indiana State Library Archives, Indianapolis; George Peva Diary, November 20-21, 1863, Indiana Historical Society Library, Indianapolis.
6. Indianapolis *Daily Journal,* November 6, 1863; *New York Herald,* November 17, 1863; New Orleans *Era,* November 21, 1863; *Chicago Tribune,* November 17, 1863; Lacon *Illinois Gazette,* November 11, 1863; Cincinnati *Enquirer* November 22, 1863.
7. The expeditionary force consisted of the 2nd Illinois (John Mudd), 1st Indiana (Elihu Rose), 2nd Louisiana (Alfred Hodson) and the 6th Missouri (Bacon Montgomery); *Official Records,* XXVI, pt. 1, 347-48, 370-71, 375-77, 801; Ezra Warner, *Generals in Blue* (Baton Rouge, 1964), 285-86; Service record of Thomas J. Lucas, National Archives.
8. *The Weekly Messenger,* St. Martinville, October 21, 1905; New Iberia *Enterprise,* October 21, 1905; William H. Perrin, *Southwest Louisiana Biographical and Historical* (Baton Rouge, 1971 reprint), pt. 2, 93; French and American Claims Commission, "Joseph Chourreau against the United States, no. 43 (depositions of Martin Voorhies, St. Leon Duperier, J. R. Ducros, Edmond LeBlanc, Ernest and Desire Judice, Joseph Breaux, John D. Broussard, Charles Dugas and Alfred Lee) National Archives; George Reinecke (ed.), *Early Louisiana French Life and Folklore from the Anonymous Breaux Manuscript* (New Orleans, 1966), 48-50; conversations with George Broussard, a grandson of John Dorville Broussard, New Iberia.
9. Depositions of Martin Voorhies, St. Leon Duperier, J. R. Ducros and others in French and American Claims Commission" Ester Levy against the United States," no. 579, "Joseph Chourreau against the United States," no. 43, "Casse Castex against the United States," no. 228, (especially deposition of A. Fenelon Dugas), "Adelaide Moulis against the United States," no. 611, National Archives; *Official Records* XXVI, pt. 1,347-48, 370-71, 375-77; *A History of the Trials and Hardships of the Twenty-Fourth Indiana* , 94-95; Ezra Warner, *Generals in Blue* , 354-55; Service record of Charles J. Paine, National Archives.
10. *Official Records* , XXVI, pt. 1, 349, 892; Noel, *A Campaign from Santa Fe to the Mississippi* , 109-10; John M. Stanyon, *A History of the Eighth Regiment of New Hampshire Volunteers* (Concord, H. H., 1892), 201-02; Reece Collection, medical notes November, 1863; Correspondence of J. W. Stevens dated November 26, 1863 in possession of his grandson, Chester B. Stevens, Independence, Iowa; Giesecke Diary, November 25, 1863; Howell Diary, November 25, 1863; George Carpenter, *History of the Eighth Regiment Vermont Volunteers* (Boston, 1886), 141-42.

11. The current roads do not follow the same trails used by the foragers. Most of the foraging occurred near the present day communities of Davids and Migues. John A. Bering, *History of the Forty-Eighth Ohio Vet. Vol Inf.* (Hillsboro, Ohio, 1880), 25; French and American Claims Commission, "Jean Cazes against the United States," no. 58, (depositions of Louis Narcisse, Marcel Boutte, and Martin Bryant), "Jean Pierre Senac against the United States," no. 645 (depositions of Jacques Destouet and Marie Decuir), "Simon Courrege against the United States," no. 143 (depositions of Joseph Segura, Charles Clerc, Eugene Simon, Leyssan Pierre and Abadie Mathieu), "Francois Marie Entremont against the United States," no. 95, "Eugene Vidale against the United States," no. 645, National Archives; U. S. Court of Claims, Joseph O. Segura vs. the United States," no. 9930, National Archives; Lucas, "Soldiers Letters from the Field," 225, A. A. Rigby Diary, November 25, 1863; Levi Hoag Diary, November 25, 1863; James F. Fitts, "Facetiae of the War," *Galaxy* , vol. 6, 1868, 326.
12. William Bentley, *History of the 77th Illinois Volunteer Infantry* (Peoria, 1883), 215-16; Sinks Collection, 58; Bringhurst, *History of the Forty-Sixth Regiment* , 82; R. B. Scott, *The History of the 67th Regiment, Indiana, Infantry, Volunteers* (Bedford, Indiana, 1892), 66; Lucas, "Soldiers Letters from the Field," 225-26; Diaries of Levi Hoag, A. A. Rigby and William Titus Rigby, November 26, 1863; Steele Correspondence, November 26, 1863; Harris Beecher, *Record of the 114th Regiment N.Y.S.V.* (Norwich, 1866), 273-74; McGregor Letters, December 2, 1863.
13. H. W. Howe, *Passages from the Life of Henry Warren Howe* (Lowell, Mass.,1899), 146-47; Harry Watts Diary, 113; Sinks Collection, 57; Sylvester Bishop Letters, correspondence November 25, 1863, Indiana Historical Society Library, Indianapolis; Elias Pellet, *History of the 114th Regiment, New York State Volunteers* (Norwich, NY., 1886), 157; Beecher, *Record of the 114th Regiment,*, 273; J. W. Merwin, *Roster and Monograph 161st Reg't. N.Y.S. Volunteer Infantry* (n.p.,n.d.), 120; William E. Jones, *The Military History of the One Hundred & Sixty-First New York Volunteers, Infantry* (Bath, N.Y., 1865), 17; Cyrus Stockwell Papers, diary entries November 1863 in The Western Reserve Historical Society, Cleveland.
14. The Petit Anse affair is erroneously referred to as the "Affair at St. Martinville" in *Official Records* XXVI, pt. 1, 455. See also p. 352; Pratt, *Federal Troops in Western Louisiana*, 24; Samuel H. Fletcher, *The History of Company A, Second Illinois Cavalry* (n.p., 1912), 126-30; depositions of Jean Reau and others in French and American Claims Commission, "Jacques Foucade against the United States," no. 418 (depositions of Antoine and Jean Reaux and G. W. Kendall, commander of the gunboat *Diana*) National Archives.

CHAPTER TWENTY

THE FINAL DAYS

1. Cecil D. Eby (ed.), *A Virginia Yankee in the Civil War* (Chapel Hill) 172; *Official Records* , XXVI, pt. 1, 831; Dr. Alfred Duperier, "A Narrative of Events Connected with the Early Settlement of New Iberia," *The Enterprise* , New Iberia, March 25 and April 1, 1899; Burke Collection, undated newspaper clipping from the *Richmond Paladium* in the University of Southwestern Louisiana Library Archives, Lafayette; *A History of the Trials and Hardships of the Twenty-Fourth Indiana Volunteer Infantry* (Indianapolis, 1913), 95; French and American Claims Commission, "Ange Marie Jan against the United

States," no. 543, and "Joseph Chourreau against the United States," no. 43, National Archives; D. Leon Delelis Scrapbook. Undated, unidentified newspaper clippings in French at the L.S.U. Library Archives, Baton Rouge.

2. U. S. Bureau of the Census, *8th U. S. Census* (1860) for St. Martin Parish, 87; William H. Perrin, *Southwest Louisiana Biographical and Historical* (Baton Rouge, 1971 reprint), pt. 2, 320-23; Clement Evans (ed.), *Confederate Military History* , vol. X (Atlanta, 1899), 396; French and American Claims Commission, "Eugene Duchamp against the United States," no. 114 (depositions of Baptiste Malagary, Sebastian Hitter, Alexandre Lede, Jules Oger, Alphonse Tertrou, Hanson Kelly, Thomas Walker, Emile Landry and Auguste Maraist) and "Ester Levy against the United States," no. 579, National Archives; Perrin, *Southwest Louisiana* , 336; John G. Pratt, *Official Report Relative to the Conduct of Federal Troops in Western Louisiana* (Shreveport, 1865), 42.

3. French and American Claims Commission, "Jules Oger against the United States," no. 99 (especially depositions of Alcide Fusilier, Pierre Juste Moity, Pierre S. Wiltz and Misin Olivier), National Archives.

4. French and American Claims Commission, "Charles Amedee Gauthier against the United States," no. 96 (depositions of Casimir and Henry Bonhomme, Edgar Moore, Valmont Richard, Charles Landry, and Ursin Olivier) National Archives.

5. *Ibid* .; also French and American Claims Commission, "David de Laureal against the United States," no. 97 (depositions of Eugene Duchamp, Evelina de Laureal, Edouard Detiege, Augustin Ambroise and Charles Landry) and Ester Levy against the United States," no. 579 (depositions of Numa and Darcourt Landry, Adolphe Bienvenu and Antoine Narcisse) National Archives.

6. French and American Claims Commission, "Anne Pradand against the United States," no. 98 (deposition of Anne Pradand, Jules Oger, Olive Leontine Billeaud, Phillippe Marquette and Olivia Frederick), National Archives; "History of the Longfellow-Evangeline State Park," undated, University of Southwestern Louisiana Library Archives, Lafayette; Pratt, *Federal Troops in Western Louisiana* , 32-33; John Griffin Jones Papers, correspondence dated December 3, 1863 in Library of Congress, Washington, D. C.; *Official Records* , XXVI, pt. 1, 831 and vol. VI, series 2, 715-16; Delelis Scrapbook, undated newspaper clippings.

7. James Hall, *Cayuga in the Field, A Record of the 75th N.Y. Volunteers* (Auburn, 1873), 160-61; *Official Records* , XXVI, pt. 1, 835; U. S. Court of Claims, "Faustin Dupuy vs. the United States," no. 13723 and 9132 (depositions of Theodule and Louis Delcambre, Drs. Alfred and Frederick Duperier, Jean Pierre Landry, William Robertson, Charles Mestayer and Michael Hebert), National Archives; Bureau of the Census, *Eighth U.S. Census* (1860) for St. Martin Parish, 73; Alan Downer (ed.), *The Autobiography of Joseph Jefferson* (Cambridge, 1964), 343-51; Diamond Crystal Salt Co., *Milestones in Salt* , 12; Succession records of Rosemund Broussard and Dennis Carlin, and transaction books 8 (p. 185) and 13 (p. 249) in St. Martin Parish Courthouse, St. Martinville, La.

8. *Official Records* , Series 2, vol. VI, 697-701, 710,.720, 737-38, 813-19, 989.

9. Mixed British and American Claims Commission "Martha Ann and Robert Parker Rayne vs. the United States," no. 74 (depositions of James R. Belden, Thomas Anderson and Fergus and Charles Fuselier), National Archives; French and American Claims Commission, "Joseph Sullice against the United States," no. 277 (depositions of Sullice and Jean Martin) National Archives; *Official Records*, series 2, vol. VI, 710, 713-14, 720; Pratt, *Federal Troops in Western Louisiana*, 27-28; Delelis Scrapbook, undated newspaper clippings.

10. *Official Records*, vol. XXVI, pt. II, 498, 508, 512; Theophilus Noel, *A Campaign from Santa Fe to the Mississippi* (Houston, 1961 reprint), 111; Julius Giesecke Papers, diary entries December 15-16, 1863; W. R. Howell Papers, diary entries December 15-16, 1863, and John S. Ford memoirs, funeral oration, University of Texas Library Archives, Austin; Odie Faulk, *General Tom Green, Fightin' Texan* (Waco, 1963), 58; John M. Bronough Papers, Medical notes for December 1863 in the Texas Collection, Baylor University, Waco.

BIBLIOGRAPHY

MANUSCRIPT COLLECTIONS

Academy of the Sacred Heart, Archives
Grand Coteau, Louisiana

Banks, Nathaniel P. Correspondence
Chickering, Thomas E. Correspondence
Lettres Annuelles, 1859-1866
School Register of Sacred Heart Academy, Grand Coteau, La. 1827-1887.

College of St. Charles, Archives Division
Grand Coteau, Louisiana

Banks, Nathaniel P. Correspondence
Catalogus Provincial Lugdunensis et Missionis Neo-Aurelianensis, IV, 1862-1871.
Diarium Ministri 1858-1882.
Franklin, William P. Correspondence.
Historia Domus, 1837-1942.
Hoffman, Wickham Correspondence.
Liber Continens onania quae in Collegio Publice Exhibentur A.M.D.G. St. Charles College School Register 1838-1919.
Liber continens ordinationes, responsa, declarationes, decisiones, pestinentia, ad coll. Sti. Carli.
Untitled Microfilm P. 20 containing notes and correspondence with Major-General William Franklin.

Illinois State Historical Library
Springfield, Illinois

Augur, C. C. Collection.
Gordon, Samuel Papers (118th Illinois Mounted Infantry)
Reece, Madison Collection (118th Illinois Mounted Infantry)

Indiana Historical Society Library
Indianapolis, Indiana

Bishop, Sylvester C. Letters. (11th Indiana Infantry)
Bowlus, Ezra Letters. (60th Indiana)
Himes, Timothy L. Letters
Kidwell, Ross Papers. (11th Indiana Infantry)
Morse, Justus Letters. (47th Indiana Infantry)
Peva, George Diary. (60th Indiana Infantry)

Indiana State Library
Indianapolis, Indiana

Sinks, Augustus George Collection. (46th Indiana Infantry)
Slack, James R. Correspondence. (46th Indiana Infantry)
Watts, Harry Diary. (24th Indiana Infantry)

Indiana University, Manuscripts Division, Lilly Library
Bloomington, Indiana

Hovey Manuscript. (24th Indiana Infantry)
Hunter, James B. Diary. (Listed as "Diary of an unidentified assistant surgeon of the 60th Indiana Infantry")

Iowa State Department of History and Archives
Des Moines, Iowa

Haverly, Charles E. Collection. (28th Iowa Infantry)
Hoag, Levi L. in Katherine Gue Leonard Collection. (24th Iowa Infantry)
Rigby, Alfred A. Diary. (24th Iowa Regiment)

Library of Congress, Division of Manuscripts
Washington, D. C.

Franklin, William B. Papers.
Jones, John Griffin Papers. (23rd Wisconsin Infantry)

Louisiana State University
Department of Archives and Manuscripts
Baton Rouge, Louisiana

Bond, Priscilla Diary. (Wife of a Confederate officer at Abbeville, Louisiana)
Bradley, James Earl Diary. (Methodist Minister, Opelousas, Louisiana)
Chickering, Thomas E. "Diary of Forty-First Infantry, Massachusetts Volunteers." (also 3rd Mass. Cavalry)
Dane, E. Letters. (Union soldier)
Delelis, O. Leon Scrapbook. (Schoolmaster and editor, St. Martinville and Breaux Bridge)
Eager, William Blake Papers. (162nd New York Infantry)
Guess, George W. Letters. (31st Texas Cavalry)
Hinckley, Orahmel Papers. (Steamboat Captain, Washington, Louisiana)
Hyatt, Arthur W. Collection. (18th Louisiana Infantry)
Moore, Thomas O. Papers. (Louisiana politician and planter)
Palfrey, William T. Papers. (Louisiana planter)
Robinson, Harai Papers. (1st Louisiana Cavalry-Union)
Weeks, David and Family Papers. (Louisiana planters)

Military History Institute, Carlisle Barracks, Pennsylvania

Dawes, Francis Diary. (24th Iowa Infantry)
Gordon, George Diary. (18th Indiana Infantry)
McGregor, Frank Letters. (83rd Ohio Infantry)
Phelps, Robert Letters in Earl Hess Collection. (87th Illinois Infantry)

New Hampshire Historical Society
Concord, New Hampshire

Carr, Clark. (8th N. H. Infantry)
Durgin, Daniel Veasy. (8th N. H. Infantry)

The State Historical Society of Wisconsin Archives and Manuscripts Madison, Wisconsin

Alling, Calvin P. Reminiscenses. (11th Wisconsin Infantry)
Barney. William Letters. (29th Wisconsin Infantry)
Foster, Jacob T. Memoirs. (1st Wisconsin Battery Light Artillery)
Jack, Alonzo Gilbert Correspondence. (23rd Wisconsin Infantry)
Karn, James E. Papers and Correspondence. (23rd Wisconsin Infantry)
Nauscawen, Lloyd Letters. (29th Wisconsin Infantry)
Richmond, Edgar Letters. (23rd Wisconsin Infantry)
Steele, Robert Letters. (23rd Wisconsin Infantry)
Webster, Daniel Correspondence. (1st Wisconsin Battery Light Artillery)

Tulane University, Howard Tilton Memorial Library Archives New Orleans, Louisiana

Breaux, Gustave A. Diaries. (30th Louisiana Volunteer Infantry)
Brent, J. L. Collection. (Chief of Ordnance and Artillery, District of Western Louisiana, C.S.A.)

University of Southwestern Louisiana Archives and Manuscripts Collection and Jefferson Caffery Louisiana Room Dupre Library, Lafayette, Louisiana

Brand Book for Opelousas and Attakapas Districts, 1739-1888.
Burke, Walter Papers. Newspaper Clipping. (67th Indiana Infantry)
Debaillon Family Papers. (Information on early Lafayette settlers)
Griffin, Harry Lewis Papers. (Photographs)
Mouton, Alexandre Memoirs in the Lucille Meredith Mouton Griffin Papers.
Mouton, Governor Alexandre Papers. (Louisiana politician and planter)
Pintado, Vincent Papers. (Microfilm from original in Louisiana State Land Office.)
Weeks Family Papers. (New Iberia history)

University of Texas, Library Archives Austin, Texas

Banks, Nathaniel P. Papers. (on Microfilm)
Becton, Edwin Pinckney Collection. (Walker's Texas Division)
Brightman, John C. Letters. (18th Texas Volunteer Infantry)
Campbell, James M. Diary. (118th Illinois Mounted Infantry)
Cox, John R. in William Oden Papers. (Gould's Texas Batallion)
Farrow, Samuel Papers. (Walker's Texas Division)
Giesecke, Julius Papers. (4th Texas Cavalry)
Guess, George W. Letters. (31st Texas Cavalry)
Hamilton, James A. Diary. (15th Texas Volunteer Infantry)
Head, William P. Papers. (16th Texas Dismounted Cavalry)
Howell, W. Randolph Papers. (5th Texas Cavalry)
Hunter, W. B. Letters in Mary Minor Papers. (Walker's Texas Division)
O'Brian, George W. Diary. (Spaight's Texas Battalion)
Ray, David M. Papers. (16th Texas Dismounted Cavalry)
Roberts, Oran M. Papers. (11th Texas Volunteer Infantry)
Sayers, Joseph Papers. (Valverde Battery)
Spaight, Ashley Wood Papers. (Spaight's Texas Regiment)

Western Reserve Historical Society
Cleveland, Ohio

Stockwell, Cyrus H. Papers. (77th Illinois Infantry)

Wood, Julius V. Papers. (96th Ohio Infantry)

Other Manuscripts

Bronough, John M. Papers. Baylor University, Library Archives. Waco, Texas. (5th Texas Cavalry)

Jackson, Isaac Papers, William L. Clements Library Archives, University of Michigan, Ann Arbor, Michigan. (83rd Ohio Infantry)

Keener, Lawson Jefferson Letters. Possession of Mrs. Rogers Lacy, Longview, Texas. (Morgan's Texas Battalion)

Marshall, Thomas Brainard Papers. Ohio Historical Society, Columbus, Ohio. (83rd Ohio Infantry)

Norton, Sylvester H. Papers. Minnesota Historical Society, Columbus Ohio. (83rd Ohio Infantry)

Rigby, William Titus Papers, University of Iowa Libraries, Iowa City, Iowa. (24th Iowa Infantry)

Stevens, J. W. Correspondence. Possession of Chester Stevens, Independence, Iowa. (118th Illinois Mounted Infantry)

Taylor, Richard Papers. A. G. O. Military Archives, Jackson Barracks, New Orleans, Louisiana.

Wroe, W. T. Papers. Confederate Museum, Austin, Texas. (Sibley's Brigade)

WAR CLAIMS AND ADJUDICATIONS NATIONAL ARCHIVES, WASHINGTON, D. C.

French and American Claims Commission, Record Group 76. Memorials, depositions and other documentation in connection with 726 claims filed by French citizens residing in the United States. More than 500 of these relate and document the treatment of civilians in Louisiana by Union military forces. Many of these run into the hundreds of pages of sworn testimony. Among the more relevant claims consulted for this work were the following:

Abbadie, Francois, no. 543
Arnaud, Desire, no. 251
Baque, Joseph, no. 135
Bloch, Joseph, no. 275
Bonnemaison, Jacques, no. 21
Burleigh, Sarah, no. 251
Camy, Joseph, no. 60
Castex, C. Bertrand, no. 228
Cazaudebat, Benoit, no. 712
Cazes, Jean, no. 58
Chourreau, Joseph, no. 43
Courrege, Simon, no. 143
Crouchet, Jean, no. 165
Decourt, Joseph, no. 33
Deffez, Raymond, no.113
DeLaureal, David, no. 97
Drouet, E. C., no. 617
Duchamp, Eugene, no. 114

Dupre, Jean, no. 540
Dupre, Romain, no. 67
Entremont, Francois, no. 95
Fay, Theodore, no. 525
Flory, Anne Louise, no. 604
Follain, Caroline, no. 252
Forgues, Charles, no. 138
Foucade, Jacques, no. 418
Francez, Romain J., no. 164 and 508
Gauthier, Charles A., no. 96
Gibert, Pierre G., no. 609
Giraud, Eugenie, no. 477
Grimmer, Catherine A., no. 88
Guchereau, Pierre, no. 546
Gueydan, Jean P., no. 229
Guiberteau, Desire, no. 441
Guidry, Augustin, no. 583
Hauguel, Emil E., no 233
Hervien, Aime, no. 237
Huguet, August S., no. 536
Israel, Joseph and Maria, no. 462
Jan, Ange-Marie, no. 543
Joseph, Caroline, no. 709
LaCoste, Antoine, no. 232
Lalanne, Dominique, no. 134
Landry, Marie A., no. 274
LaPlene, Bernard, no. 245
Levy, Ester, no. 579
Levy, Henriette, no. 253
Loustaunau, Pierre, no. 301
Lucas, Ambroise N. no. 300
Mathieu, Simon, no. 159
Mote, Bleze, no. 131
Moulis, Adelaide, no. 611
Mouret, Pierre R., no. 42
Oger, Jules, no. 99
Olle, Adolphe, no. 582
Patout, Hypolite, no. 239
Perrodin, Jules, no. 90
Poirson, Jules, no. 476
Pradand, Anne, no. 98
Prevot, Victoire T., no. 172
Rizan, Omer, no. 167
Rogay, Philobert, no. 545
Ruote, Victor, no. 307
St. Laurent, Roume, no. 483
Sanvald, Theophile, no. 89
Schmulen, Samuel, no. 371
Sorrel, Aruns, no. 594
Stouff, Widow Pierre, no. 397
Suberbielle, Bernard, no. 234
Sullice, Joseph, no. 277
Thevenet, Philippe, no. 22
Trone, Stephanie, no. 417
Valade, Theodore, no. 214
Vidale, Eugene, no. 645
Vigneaud, Jean, no. 116
Villien, Jean M. no. 171
Vinsonneau, Francois, no. 82
Ynogosa, Andrea, no. 641

Mixed Commission on British and American Claims, Record Group 76. Memorials, depositions and other documentation in connection with 478 claims on the part of British citizens damaged by Union operations during the Civil War. Only a few of these relate to Louisiana. Among the more relevant adjudications examined for this work were:

Burke, Ellen, no. 130
Duffy, Alice and Ellen, no. 160
Fleming, Charles, no. 309
Garrett, Lucie, no. 309
Garry, Michael, no. 60
Maguire, Annibal, no. 38
Rayne, Martha Ann and Robert Parker, no. 74
Robert, David, no. 47

U. S. Court of Claims, Southern Claims Commission. Record Group 123. Memorials, depositions and other documentation filed by "loyal" Louisiana residents against the United States for damages by Union forces operating in Louisiana. The exact number of such claims could not be established as they were filed over a period of many years, in some cases later than 1900. Nonetheless there are at least one thousand such claims, many of which contain hundreds of pages of sworn documentation. The following is a select list of those used in this work:

Auzenne, Felix, no. 14680
Carlin Celestin, no. 8875
Carlin, Euphrazee, no. 18408
Chretien, Hypolite, no. 14812
Courrege, Simon, no. 3694
Donato, Cornelius, no. 19763
DeJean, Jules and Honore, no. 19026
Deshotels, Raimondi, no. 2738
Duperier, Alfred, no. 9436
Dupuy, Faustin, no. 13723
Gantt, Elbert, no. 5014 and 8950
Gardiner, John J. no. 14396
Grevenberg, Euphemie, no. 17
Lastrapes, Alfred, no. 16413
Lemore, Athenais Chretien, no. 11253
McBride, Romulus L., no. 16956
McPherson, Virginia
Meuillion, Alphonse and A. D.
Olivier, Dubriel, no. 19763
Perrodin, Jules, no. 3546
Petetin, Eugene, no. 1999
Peychaud, Henry, Syndic of Bellocque, Noblon & Co., no. 3497
Rhodes, John & Parmeda, no. 12324
Riggs, William A., no. 244
Saizan, Pierre, no. 7009
Segura, Joseph O., no. 9930

DOCUMENTS IN THE NATIONAL ARCHIVES AND RECORDS SERVICE

Office of the Judge Advocate General. Court-martial Case Files of: Buehler, Theodore; Fox, Michael; Gannon, William; Hughs, Richard; Livingston, A.C.; Nims, Ormand. Record Group 94.

Records of District and Parish Provost Marshalls, Army of the Gulf, Old Book 1255-1257, Oaths of Allegiance, Record Group 393.

Records of the Adjutant General's Office, Letters Received, Volunteer Service Division. Record Group 94.

Records of the Adjutant General's Office, 1780's-1917. Compiled Military Service Records, Civil War: Bringhurst, Thomas; Brown, Albert; Buehler, Theodore; Fonda, John G.; Fox, Michael; Gannon, William; Goelzer, Augustus; Gue, Jeremiah; Guidry, Thelismar; Guppey, Joshua; Heffelfinger, Henry; Hunter, James B.; Livingston, A. C.; Marland, William; Marsh, Arthur W.; Montgomery, Bacon; Naylor, George W.; Nims, Ormand; Owen, Richard; Robinson, Harai; Ryall, Richard; Shunk, David; Slack, James R.; Steele, Robert; Vincent, William; Wilhelm, George; Williams, Charles.

Records of the Adjutant General's Office, 1780's-1917. "List of Wounded Sent from New Iberia to New Orleans," "List of Killed, Wounded or Missing in the Battle of Grand Coteau" and "List of Killed, Wounded or Missing in the 60th Regiment Indiana Infantry, Battle of Grand Coteau, La., November 3, 1863."

Records of the Adjutant General's Office, 1780's-1917. Record Group 94. Record of Events Cards for 75th New York Mounted Infantry, 1st Louisiana Cavalry, 2nd Rhode Island Cavalry, 8th New Hampshire Infantry, and 3rd Engineers, *Corps d'Afrique*.
Records of the Provost Marshal General, State of Louisiana, Letters Sent, Letters Received, Property Confiscated, Seizures, January 1863 to December 1865. Record Group 110.
Quartermaster-General's Office, Roll of Honor, August 1868.

CHURCH AND COURTHOUSE RECORDS

Lafayette Parish Courthouse. Conveyance, succession and marriage records. Lafayette, Louisiana.
St. Charles Church Archives. Grand Coteau, Louisiana. Birth, marriage, baptismal and funeral records.
St. John's Cathedral Archives, Lafayette, Louisiana. Marriage, baptismal and funeral records.
St. Landry Catholic Church Archives, Opelousas, Louisiana. Birth, marriage and funeral records.
St. Landry Parish Courthouse, Opelousas, Louisiana. Conveyance, succession and marriage records and police jury minutes.
St. Martin of Tours Catholic Church, St. Martinville, Louisiana. Marriage, baptismal, birth and funeral records.
St. Martin Parish Courthouse. St. Martinville, Louisiana. Conveyance, succession and marriage records.
St. Mary Parish Courthouse. Franklin, Louisiana. Conveyance, succession and marriage records.

OFFICIAL PUBLICATIONS

French and American Claims Commission, *Record of Claims*. 78 vols. Washington, D. C.: Gibson Bros., 1884. These are the printed works of the 726 claims of the French and American Claims Commission. (See War Claims and Adjudications).
Pratt, John G., Compiler. *Official Report Relative to the Conduct of Federal Troops in Western Louisiana During the Invasions of 1863 and 1864.* Shreveport: News Printing Establishment, 1865.
Report of the Adjutant General of the State of Illinois, vol. VI. Springfield, 1900.
Secretary of War. *The War of the Rebellion: A Compilation of the Official Records of the Union and Confederate Armies*. 128 Vols. Washington, 1880-1901.

U. S. Bureau of the Census. *Population Schedules of the Eighth Census of the United States, 1860.* Vol. 15 for the parishes of St. Mary, St. Martin, St. Landry, Lafayette and Vermilion, Louisiana.

U. S. Congress. *House Miscellaneous Document 254, 52nd Congress,* 1st Session. Washington, D. C.

U. S. Congress. *House Miscellaneous Document 111, 53rd Congress,* 2nd Session. Washington, D. C.

U. S. Congress. Joint Committee on the Conduct of the War. *Report of the Joint Committee on the Conduct of the War at the Second Session, Thirty-Eighth Congress.* 3 vols. Washington, 1865.

U. S. Medical Department. *Medical and Surgical History of the War of the Rebellion (1861-1865).* Washington, D. C.: 1875-1888. Six volumes.

U. S. Senate. *Senate Document No. 27,* 58th Congress, 2nd Session. Washington, D. C.

U. S. War Department. *Atlas to Accompany the Official Records of the Union and Confederate Armies.* Washington: Government Printing Office, 1891-95.

BOOKS—PRIMARY

Anderson, John Q. *A Texas Surgeon in the C.S.A.* Tuscaloosa: Confederate Publishing Company, 1957. (Walker's Texas Division)

Bartlett, Robert F. *Roster of the Ninety-Sixth Regiment, Ohio Volunteer Infantry.* Columbus: Press of Hann and Adair, 1895.

Bearrs, Edwin, ed. *A Louisiana Confederate; Diary of Felix Pierre Poche.* Natchitoches: Louisiana Studies Institute, Northwestern State University, 1972.

Beecher, Harris H. *Record of the 114th Regiment, NYSV.* Norwich, N.Y.: I.F. Hubbard, 1866.

Bentley, William H. *History of the 77th Illinois Volunteer Infantry,* Peoria: Edward Hine, 1883.

Bering, John and Montgomery, Thomas. *History of the Forty-Eighth Ohio Veteran Volunteer Infantry.* Hillsboro: Highland News Office, 1880.

Bigelow, James K. *Abridged History of the Eighth Indiana Volunteer Infantry.* Indianapolis: Ellis Barnes, Book and Job Printer, 1864.

Blake, E. E. *A Succinct History of the 28th Iowa Volunteer Infantry.* Belle Plains: Union Press, 1896.

Blessington, J. P. *The Campaigns of Walker's Texas Division.* Austin: Penberton Press, 1968.

Botkin, B. A., ed. *Lay my Burden Down, A Folk History of Slavery.* Chicago: University of Chicago Press, 1945.

Bringhurst, Thomas H. and Swigart, Frank. *History of the Forty-Sixth Regiment Indiana Volunteer Infantry,* 1888.

Calvert, Henry Murray. *Reminiscences of A Boy in Blue.* New York: G. P. Putnam's Sons, 1920. (11th N. Y. Infantry)

Carpenter, George N. *History of the Eighth Vermont Volunteers 1861-1865.* Boston: Press of Deland and Barta, 1886.

Chickering, Thomas E. *Diary of Forty-First Regiment Infantry Massachusetts Volunteers*. Boston: J. E. Farwell Printers, 1863.

Chittenden, Newton H. *History and Catalogue of the 4th Regiment Wisconsin Volunteers from June 1861-March 1864*. Baton Rouge: Gazette and Comet Book and Job Office, 1864.

Clark, Orton S. *The 116th Regiment of New York Volunteers*. Buffalo: Printing House of Mathews and Warren, 1868.

Crooke, George. *The Twenty-First Regiment of Iowa Volunteer Infantry*. Milwaukee: King, Fowle and Co., 1891.

Dana, Charles A. *Recollections of the Civil War*. New York: D. Appleton and Co., 1898.

Deforest, John William. *A Volunteer's Adventures: A Union Captain's Record of the Civil War*. New Haven: Yale University Press, 1946, (12th Conn. Infantry)

Eby, Cecil D. Jr., ed. *A Virginia Yankee in the Civil War, The Diaries of David Hunter Strother*. Chapel Hill: University of North Carolina Press, 1961.

Ewer, James K. *The Third Massachusetts Cavalry in the War for the Union*. Boston: Historical Committee of the Regimental Association, 1903.

Fletcher, Samuel H. *The History of Company A, Second Illinois Cavalry*, 1912.

Flinn, Frank M. *Campaigning with Banks in Louisiana, '63 and '64, and with Sheridan in the Shenandoah Valley in '64 and '65*. Lynn, Mass.: 1887.

Ford, Orrin B. *Biography of O. B. Ford, Written by Himself*. Yale, Oklahoma: Yale Record Print. (24th Iowa Infantry)

French, Frank F. *The Lost Detachment*. Humboldt, Iowa: 1907. (29th Wisconsin Infantry)

Gardner, Ira B. *Recollections of A Boy Member of Co. I, Fourteenth Maine Volunteers*. Lewiston: Lewiston Journal Co., 1902.

Gerard, C. W. *A Diary: The Eighty-Third Ohio Vol. Inf. In the War*. n. p., n. d.

Hatch, Carl E. ed. *Dearest Susie, A Civil War Infantryman's Letters to his Sweetheart*. New York: Exposition Press, 1971. (83rd Ohio Infantry)

Hall, James. *Cayuga in the Field. A Record of the 75th N. Y. Volunteers*. Auburn 1873.

History of the Second Battalion, Duryee: Zouaves. New York: Peter de Baun and Co., 1904. (165th N. Y. Infantry)

History of the Sixteenth Battery of Ohio Volunteers Light Artillery. n. p. 1905.

A History of the Trials and Hardships of the Twenty-Fourth Indiana Volunteer Infantry. Indianapolis: Indianapolis Printing Co., 1913.

An Historical Sketch of the 162nd Regiment N. Y. Vol. Infantry. Albany: Weed, Parsons and Company, 1867.

Hoffman, Wickham. *Camp, Court and Siege; A Narrative of Personal Adventure and Observation During Two Wars*. New York: Harper and Brothers, 1877.

Hosmer, James K. *The Color-Guard*. Boston: Walker, Wise and Co., 1864. (52nd Massachusetts Infantry)

Howe, Henry Warren. *Passages from the Life of Henry Warren Howe*. Lowell, Massachusetts 1899. (30th Massachusetts Infantry)

In The Southwest, Stories of Our Soldiers. Boston: The Boston Journal Newspaper Co., 1893.

Irwin, Richard B. *History of the Nineteeth Army Corps*. New York: G. P. Putnam's Sons, 1893.

Jackson, Joseph Orville. "*Some of the Boys...*" *The Civil War Letters of Isaac Jackson*. Carbondale: Southern Illinois University Press, 1960. (83rd Ohio Infantry)

Jones, William E. *The Military History of the One-Hundred and Sixty-First New York Volunteers, Infantry*. Bath, N. Y.: Hull and Barnes Printers, 1865.

Knox, Thomas W. *Camp-Fire and Cotton-Field, Southern Adventure in Time of War*. New York: Blelock and Co., 1865.

Lane, Walter P. *The Adventures and Recollections of General Walter P. Lane*. Marshall, Texas: News Messenger Pub. Co., n.d. (Major's Texas Brigade)

Lord, Walter (ed.). *The Fremantle Diary*. Boston: Little, Brown and Company, n. d.

McManus, Thomas. *Battle Fields of Louisiana Revisited a Second Time*. Hartford: Fowler and Miller Co., 1898. (25th Connecticut Infantry)

Maddocks, Elden B. *History of the Twenty-Sixth Maine Regiment*. Bangor: Charles H. Glass and Co., 1899.

Marshall, Albert O. *Army Life; From a Soldier's Journal, 1861-64*. Joliet, Illinois: Chicago Legal News Co., 1883. (33rd Illinois Infantry)

Marshall, T. B. *History of the Eighty-Third Ohio Volunteer Infantry*. Cincinnati, 1912.

Mason, F. H. *The Forty-Second Ohio Infantry*. Cleveland: Cobb, Andrews and Co., 1876.

Merwin, John W. *Roster and Monograph 161st Reg't, N.Y.S. Volunteer Infantry*. Elmira: Gazette Print, 1902.

Moore, Frank, ed. *The Rebellion Record, A Diary of American Events*. New York: D. Van Norstrand, 1865.

Moors, J. F. *History of the Fifty-Second Regiment Massachusetts Volunteers*. Boston: George Ellis Press, 1893.

Noel, Theophilus. *A Campaign from Santa Fe to the Mississippi*. Houston: Stagecoach Press, 1961. (4th Cavalry)

Olmsted, F. L. *A Journey Through Texas; or, a Saddle-trip on the Southwestern Frontier*. New York, 1857.

Pellet, Elias P. *History of the 114th Regiment, New York State Volunteers*. Norwich, N.Y.: Telegraph and Chronicle Power Press, 1866.

Perry, Oran. *Recollections of the Civil War*. Indiana Library, 1928.

Powers, George W. *The Story of the Thirty-Eighth Regiment of Massachusetts Volunteers*. Cambridge Press, 1866.

Scott, R. B. *The History of the 67th Regiment Indiana Infantry Volunteers*. Bedford: Herald Book and Job Print, 1892.

Scott, Robert G. *Memoirs and Poetic Sketches*. Camden, Missouri: Reveille Print. (24th Iowa Infantry)

Simmons, John T. *History of the 28th Iowa Volunteer Infantry*. Washington: William H. Moore, 1865.

Smith, George G. *Leaves from a Soldier's Diary*. Putnam, Conn.: G. G. Smith, 1906. (1st Louisiana Infantry—Union)

Sprague, Homer B. *History of the 13th Infantry Regiment of Connecticut Volunteers*. Hartford: Case, Lockwood and Co., 1867.

Spurlin, Charles, ed. *West of the Mississippi with Waller's 13th Texas Cavalry Battalion*. Hillsboro, Texas: Hill Junior College, 1971.
Stanyon, John M. *A History of the Eighth Regiment of New Hampshire Volunteers*. Concord: Ira C. Evans Printer, 1892.
Stearns, Albert. *Reminiscences of the Late War*. Brooklyn, 1881. (131st N.Y. Infantry)
Stevenson, B. F. *Letters from the Army*. Cincinnati: W. E. Dibble and Co., 1884. (22nd Kentucky Infantry—Union)
Stevenson, James. *History of the Sixteenth Indiana Mounted Infantry*. New Orleans, 1864.
Taylor, Richard. *Destruction and Reconstruction, Personal Experiences of the Late War*. New York: D. Appleton and Co., 1879.
Tilley, Nannie M. ed. *Federals on the Frontier, the Diary of Benjamin F. McIntyre*. Austin: University of Texas Press, 1963. (34th Iowa Infantry)
Van Alstyne, Lawrence. *Diary of an Enlisted Man*. New Haven: Tuttle, Morehouse and Taylor Company, 1910. (128th New York Infantry)
Wallace, Lew. *Lew Wallace, An Autobiography*. New York: Harper and Brothers, 1906. (11th Indiana Infantry)
Whipple, Henry P. *The Diary of a Private Soldier*. Waterloo, 1906. (29th Wisconsin Infantry)
Wiley, Bill Irvin ed. *This Infernal War, the Confederate Letters of Sgt. Edwin H. Fay*. Austin: University of Texas Press, 1959.
————. *Fourteen Hundred and 91 days in the Confederate Army*. Jackson, Tennessee: McCowat-Mercer Press, 1954. (W. P. Lane Rangers)
Williams, Thos. J. *An Historical Sketch of the 56th Ohio Volunteer Infantry*, n.p., n.d.
Yeary, Mamie ed. *Reminiscences of the Boys in Gray 1861-1865*. Dallas: Smith & Lamar Publishing House, 1912.

BOOKS—SECONDARY

Adams, George Washington. *Doctors in Blue*. New York: Henry Schuman, 1952.
Alcott, Louisa May. *Hospital Sketches*. Boston: Roberts Brothers, 1895.
Arceneaux, William. *Acadian General Alfred Mouton and the Civil War*. Lafayette: University of Southwestern Louisiana, 1972.
Barde, Alexandre. *Histoire des Comites de Vigilance aux Attakapas*. Saint-Jean Baptiste, 1861.
Bartlett, Napier. *Military Record of Louisiana*. Baton Rouge: L.S.U. Press, 1964.
Baudier, Roger. *The Church of our Lady of the Sacred Heart*. Church Point, La., 1954.
Bentley, Emerson. *Morgan City, the Commercial Entrepot of Attakapas*. New Orleans, 1876.
Billings, John D. *Hardtack and Coffee*. Boston: 1887.
Blackburn, Florence and Brown, Fay G. *Franklin through the Years*. Franklin, La., 1972.
Boatner, Mark Mayo. *The Civil War Dictionary*. New York: David McKay Co., Inc. 1962.

Booth, Andrew B., Compiler. *Records of Louisiana Confederate Soldiers and Louisiana Commands.* New Orleans: 1920.
Byers, S.H.M. *Iowa in War Times.* Des Moines: W. D. Condit & Co., 1888.
Cable, George Washington. *Creoles and Cajuns; Stories of Old Louisiana.* Gloucester: Peter Smith, 1965.
Culver, Newton. *Brevet Major Isaac N. Earl: A Noted Scout of the Department of the Gulf.* Madison: State Historical Society of Wisconsin, 1916. (4th Wisconsin Infantry)
DeForest, John William. *Miss Ravenel's Conversions from Secession to Loyalty.* New York: Harper & Brothers, 1939. (Fiction based on author's experiences with 12th Connecticut Infantry in Louisiana)
Ditchy, Jay K. ed. *Early Louisiana French Life and Folklore from the Anonymous Breaux Manuscript.* New Orleans: Louisiana Folklore Society, 1966.
Downer, Alan, ed. *The Autobiography of Joseph Jefferson.* Cambridge: Belknap Press, 1964.
Dyer, Frederick. *A Compendium of the War of the Rebellion.* New York: Thomas Yoseloff Publishers, 1959.
Eddy, Thomas M. *The Patriotism of Illinois.* Chicago: Clark & Co. Publishers, 1866.
Evans, Clement, ed. *Confederate Military History.* Atlanta: Confederate Publishing Company, 1899.
Faulk, Odie. *General Tom Green, Fightin' Texan.* Waco: Texian Press, 1963.
Gara, Larry. *A Short History of Wisconsin.* Madison: State Historical Society of Wisconsin, 1962.
Griffin, Harry L. *The Attakapas Country: A History of Lafayette Parish.* Gretna: Pelican Press, 1959.
Hall, Martin Hardwick. *Sibley's New Mexico Campaign.* Austin: University of Texas Press, 1960.
Harrington, Fred Harvey. *Fighting Politician, Major-General N. P. Banks.* Philadelphia: University of Pennsylvania Press, 1948.
Harris, Gertrude. *A Tale of Men Who Knew Not Fear.* San Antonio: Alamo Printing Co., 1935.
Headley, John W. *Confederate Operations in Canada and New York.* New York: Neale Publishing Co. 1906.
Hebert, Rev. Donald J. *Southwest Louisiana Records.* Eunice and Cecilia, Louisiana: 1974-77, vols. 1-10.
Higginson, Thomas Wentworth, Compiler. *Massachusetts in the Army and Navy During the War of 1861-65.* Boston: Wright & Potter Printing Co.,1896.
Hosmer, James K. *The Thinking Bayonet.* Boston: Walker, Fuller and Co. 1865. (Ficticious work based on experiences in Louisiana campaign with the 52nd Massachusetts Infantry.)
Hunt, Gaillard, *Israel, Elihu and Cadwallader Washburn.* New York: The MacMillan Co., 1925.
Johnson, Ludwell H. *Red River Campaign.* Baltimore: John Hopkins Press, 1958.
Johnson, Rossiter. *Campfires and Battlefields.* New York: The Blue and the Grey Press, 1958.
Kane, Harnett. *Plantation Parade.* New York: Bonanza Press, 1945.

Kerby, Robert L. *Kirby Smith's Confederacy, The Trans-Mississippi South 1863-1865*. New York: Columbia University Press, 1972.
Klement, F. L. *Copperheads in the Middle West*. Chicago: University of Chicago Press, 1960.
La Bree, Benjamin, ed. *The Pictorial Battles of the Civil War*. New York: Sherman Publishing Co.,1885.
Livermore, Thomas L. *Numbers and Losses in the Civil War in America, 1861-65*. Boston: Houghton Mifflin and Co., 1901.
Lonn, Ella. *Foreigners in the Union Army and Navy*. Baton Rouge: L.S.U. Press, 1951.
Lossing, Benson J. *Pictorial History of the Civil War*. Hartford: Thomas Belknap, Publisher, 1877-80.
Menn, Joseph Karl. *The Large Slaveholders of Louisiana, 1860*. New Orleans: Pelican Publishing Co., 1964.
Merk, Frederick. *Economic History of Wisconsin During the Civil War Decade*. Madison: State Historical Society of Wisconsin, 1916.
Merrill, H. S. *Bourbon Democracy of the Middle West*. Baton Rouge: L.S.U. Press, 1953.
Miller, Francis T. *The Photographic History of the Civil War*. New York: Review of Reviews Co., 1911.
Morgan City Historical Society. *A History of Morgan City, Louisiana*. Morgan City, 1960.
Noel, Theophilus. *Autobiography and Reminiscences of Theophilus Noel*. Chicago: Theo. Noel Co. Print, 1904. (4th Texas Cavalry)
Olivier, Jane. *The Church of St. Charles. A Short History*. Grand Coteau, La., 1975.
Parks, Joseph Howard. *General Edmund Kirby Smith, C.S.A.* Baton Rouge: L.S.U. Press, 1962.
Perrin, William Henry. *Southwest Louisiana Biographical and Historical*. Baton Rouge: Claitor's, 1971 reprint of 1891 edition.
Quaife, Milo Milton. *Wisconsin, Its History and Its People*. Chicago: S. J. Clark Publishing Co., 1924.
Raphael, Morris. *The Battle in the Bayou Country*. Detroit: Harlo Press, 1975.
Ripley, C. Peter. *Slaves and Freedmen in Civil War Louisiana*. Baton Rouge: L.S.U. Press, 1976.
Roland, Charles P. *Louisiana Sugar Plantations During the American Civil War*. Leiden: E. J. Brell, 1957.
Seebold, Herman Boehm de Bachelle, *Old Louisiana Plantation Homes and Family Trees*. New Orleans: Pelican Press, Inc., 1941.
Shugg, Roger W. *Origins of Class Struggle in Louisiana*. Baton Rouge: L.S.U. Press, 1939.
Smith, J. Frazer. *White Pillars: Architecture of the South*. New York: Bramhall House, 1941.
Squier, Ephraim G., ed. *Frank Leslie's Pictorial History of the Civil War*. New York: F. Leslie.
Sterky, H. E. *The Free Negro in Ante-Bellum Louisiana*. Cranbury, N. J.: Fairleigh Dickinson University Press, 1972.
Swanton, John R. *Indian Tribes of the Lower Mississippi Valley*. Washington: Government Printing Office, 1911.

Tolbert, Frank X. *Dick Dowling at Sabine Pass.* New York: McGraw-Hill, 1962.
Vallandigham, J. L. *Life of Clement L. Vallandigham.* Baltimore, 1872.
Wallace, Lewis. *The Prince of India; or, Why Constantinople Fell.* New York: Harper and Brothers, 1893.
Warner, Ezra J. *Generals in Blue, Lives of the Union Commanders.* Baton Rouge: L.S.U. Press, 1964.
————. *Generals in Gray, Lives of the Confederate Commanders.* Baton Rouge: L.S.U. Press, 1959.
Weddle, Robert S. *Plow Horse Cavalry, The Caney Creek Boys of the Thirty-Fourth Texas.* Austin: Madrona Press, 1974.
Whitcomb, Caroline E. *History of the Second Massachusetts Battery (Nims' Battery) of Light Artillery, 1861-1865.* Concord, N. H.: The Rumford Press, 1912.
Whitman, William and Charles True. *Maine in the War for the Union.* Lewiston: Nelson Dingley & Co., 1865.
Wiley, Bell Irvin. *The Life of Johnny Reb.* Indianapolis: Bobbs-Merrill Co., 1943.
Winters, John D. *The Civil War in Louisiana.* Baton Rouge: L.S.U. Press, 1963.
Wooten, Dudley G. *A Comprehensive History of Texas.* Dallas: Scarff, 1898.

PERIODICALS

Baker, Vaughn. "Patterns of Acadian Slave Ownership in Lafayette Parish." *Attakapas Gazette,* X (September 1974), 144-48.
Barde, Alexandre. "The Vigilante Committees of Vermilion." *Attakapas Gazette,* X (Summer 1975), 84-97.
Bergeron, Arthur W. ed. "Prison Life at Camp Pratt," *Louisiana History,* XVI (Fall, 1973), 386-91.
Conrad, Glenn R., ed. "Reminiscences of the 60's and 70's by Louis Paul Bryant." *Attakapas Gazette,* X (Spring, 1975), 2-11.
Dabney, Thomas Ewing. "The Butler Regime in Louisiana." *Louisiana Historical Quarterly,* XXVII (April 1944) 487-526.
DeForest, John William. "Forced Marches." *The Galaxy,* V (1868) 708-18. (12th Connecticut Infantry)
Edmonds, David C. "Surrender on the Bourbeux, Honorable Defeat or Incompetency Under Fire." *Louisiana History,* Vol. XVIII (Winter 1977), 63-86.
————. "Tragedy on Buzzards' Prairie." *Attakapas Gazette,* X (Winter 1975), 181-91.
Fitts, James F. "Facetiae of the War." *The Galaxy,* XI (1868), 320-27. (114th New York Infantry)
Griffin, Harry Lewis. "Early Louisiana Justice," *Proceedings of the Mississippi Valley Historical Association,* Vol. VIII (1914-1915) 146-59.
Harper's Weekly, Vols. VII-X. 1863-1866.
Leslie's Illustrated Weekly, Vols. XV, XVI, 1863.

Lucas, Charles A. "A Soldier's Letters from the Field," *Iowa Historical Record*, XVI, XVII (1900-1901-1902).
Maury, Dabney H. "Sketch of General Richard Taylor." *Southern Historical Society Papers*, Vol. VII, (1879).
Mouton, Sister Odeide, "The Academy of the Sacred Heart; Grand Coteau." *Attakapas Gazette*, IX (December 1974), 190-95.
Oates, Stephen B."Supply for the Confederate Cavalry in the Trans-Mississippi." *Military Affairs*. XXV (1961).
Oubre, Claude. "Port Barre: A Crossroads in the Opelousas Country." *Attakapas Gazette*, XI (Spring 1976), 43-44.
Padgett, J. A. "Some Letters of George Stanton Denison, 1854-1866." *Louisiana Historical Quarterly*, XXIII, 1132-1240.
"Remembrances." *The Bivouac*, III (1865), 209-211.
"Reminiscences of C. C. Cox."*Southwestern Historical Quarterly*. Vol. 6, no. 3. 1903.
Rhodes, A. "The Louisiana Creoles." *The Galaxy*, XVI.
Root, L. Carroll, ed. "The Experiences of a Federal Soldier in Louisiana." *Louisiana Historical Quarterly*. Vol. 19 (July 1936), 635-67.
Shannon, Fred A. "The Life of the Common Soldier in the Union Army, 1861-1865." *The Mississipi Valley Historical Review*, XIII (March 1927), 465-82.
Van Fossan, H. "Clement L. Vallandigham," *Ohio Archaeological and Historical Quarterly*, XXIII (1914), 256-67.
Warner, Charles Dudley. "The Acadian Land." *Harper's Magazine*, Vol. LXXIV (February, 1887), 345.
Williams, T. H. "General Banks and the Radical Republicans in the Civil War." *New England Quarterly*, XI, 268-80.
"A Yankee in Louisiana: Selections from the Diary and Correspondence of Henry R. Gardner 1862-1866." *Louisiana History*, V (Summer 1964), 276.

NEWSPAPERS

Attakapas Register, Franklin, Louisiana.
Boston Journal, Boston, Massachusetts.
Caddo Journal, Shreveport, Louisiana
Chicago Tribune, Chicago, Illinois.
Cincinnati Enquirer, Cincinnati, Ohio.
Connecticut Courant, Hartford, Connecticut.
Daily Republican, Springfield, Illinois.
Des Moines Register, Des Moines, Iowa.
Home League, Hartford, Wisconsin.
Illinois Gazette, Lacon, Illinois.
Indianapolis Daily Journal, Indianapolis, Indiana.
Indianapolis Journal, Indianapolis, Indiana.
Indianapolis Sentinel, Indianapolis, Indiana.
Iowa City Republican, Iowa City, Iowa.
Logansport Journal, Logansport, Indiana.
Louisiana Democrat, Alexandria, Louisiana.

Louisville Journal, Louisville, Kentucky.
Milwaukee Sentinel, Milwaukee, Wisconsin.
New Iberia Enterprise, New Iberia, Louisiana.
New Orleans Bee, New Orleans, Louisiana.
New Orleans Era, New Orleans, Louisiana.
New Orleans Picayune, New Orleans, Louisiana.
New York Herald, New York, New York.
Northampton Gazette, Northampton, Massachusetts.
Opelousas Courier, Opelousas, Louisiana.
Opelousas Journal, Opelousas, Louisiana.
Opelousas Patriot, Opelousas, Louisiana.
Planters' Banner, Franklin, Louisiana.
Richmond Palladium, Richmond, Indiana.
Shreveport News, Shreveport, Louisiana.
Springfield Republican, Springfield, Illinois.
State Gazette, Austin, Texas.
Sugar Bowl, New Iberia, Louisiana.
Tri-Weekly Telegraph, Houston, Texas.
Weekly Messenger, St. Martinville, Louisiana.
Wisconsin State Journal, Madison, Wisconsin.

UNPUBLISHED WORKS

Fontenot, Elfa Lavonia. "Social and Economic Life in Louisiana 1860-1865 as Recorded by Contemporaries." Unpublished Master's Thesis, Louisiana State University, 1933.

Garland, Albert Nutter. "E. Kirby Smith and the Trans-Mississipi Confederacy," Unpublished Master's Thesis, Louisiana State University, 1947.

"History of the Longfellow-Evangeline State Park." Undated Manuscript in the University of Southwestern Louisiana Library Archives, Lafayette.

Kenney, Michael, S. J. "Jesuits in our Southland, 1566-1946; Origins and Growth of New Orleans Province." Unpublished Manuscript in College of St. Charles. Grand Coteau, Louisiana.

Leland, Edwin Albert. "Organization and Administration of the Louisiana Army during the Civil War." Unpublished Master's Thesis, Louisiana State University, 1938.

Pecot, Marguerite A."The Cajun." Unpublished Master's Thesis, Louisiana State University, 1932.

Rogers, Henrietta Guilbeau. "History of the Committees of Vigilance in the Attakapas Country." Unpublished Master's Thesis, Louisiana State University, 1936.

Santis, FLR and Souvay, C. M. "An Historical Sketch of the Church of Lafayette, La. 1821-1921." Copy in University of Southwestern Louisiana Center for Louisiana Studies, Lafayette.

————. "Rummaging through Old Parish Records, Historical Sketch of the Parish of Opelousas, La." Copy in University of Southwestern Louisiana Center for Louisiana Studies, Lafayette. (This work and the above work have since appeared in Hebert, Donald J. *A Guide to Church Records in Louisiana, 1720-1975.* Eunice, La., Donald Hebert, 1975.)

Schumacher, Elizabeth M."The Political Career of Alexandre Mouton." Unpublished Master's Thesis, Louisiana State University, 1935.

ORAL SOURCES

Arceneaux, Dr. Thomas J. Lafayette
Barry, Dr. Robert. Sunset
Bentley, Dr. Doris. Lafayette
Boagni, Dr. Edward. Baton Rouge
Brasseaux, Carl. Lafayette
Brinkhaus, Senator Armand. Sunset
Broussard, Dr. George. (deceased) New Iberia
Carroll, Father James, S. J. Grand Coteau
Conrad, Professor Glenn R. New Iberia
Cornay, Jeanne. Chretien Point
Courville, Mrs. Willis. Sunset
Daigle, Carmen and Ronnie. Sunset
Daly, Robert. (deceased) Opelousas
Davy, Sylvan. Sunset
Deshotels, Kenneth. Washington
Dimmick, J. C. Shuteson
Fontenot, Mary Alice. Lafayette
Fontenot, Ruth. Opelousas and New Orleans
Gouaux, Mrs. Fernand. Lafayette
Guilbeau, Oge. Carencro
Hebert, Buck. Opelousas
Kempt, Henry. (deceased) Opelousas
Landry, Mrs. Lloyd. Cankton
Lavergne, Lucius. Sunset
Leger, Mrs. Alcues. Sunset
Lewis, Seth. (deceased) Opelousas
McBride, Professor James Patrick. Lafayette
Martin, Miss Alida. Lafayette
Matte, Edvin. Lawtell
Mouton, Miss Eva. Lafayette
Mouton, Dr. Franklin. Lafayette
Mouton, Sister Odeide. Grand Coteau
Miller, Hypolite. (deceased) Sunset
Palfrey, Paola. Lafayette
Raphael, Morris. New Iberia
Richard, Willie. Sunset
Sibille, Jules Leroy and Louise Theresa. Bristol
Sibille, Lowell. Sunset
Sibille, Marie. Cankton
Sibille, Raoul. Bristol
Stiel, David. Franklin

INDEX

www.ingramcontent.com/pod-product-compliance
Lightning Source LLC
Jackson TN
JSHW030712120126
96731JS00009B/11

* 9 7 8 1 9 5 9 5 6 9 1 4 5 *